THE PSYCHOPATHIC GOD

ADOLF HITLER

75

Accurate scholarship can
Unearth the whole offence
From Luther until now
That has driven a culture mad,
Find what occurred at Linz,
What huge imago made
A psychopathic god:
I and the public know
What all schoolchildren learn,
Those to whom evil is done
Do evil in return.

—W. H. Auden,
"September 1, 1939"

The circumstances in which the cover portrait was painted were remarkable. Richter had been invited in 1941 to do a portrait of Reich Marshal Hermann Göring. When he learned that a visit from Hitler was expected, it was arranged for him to sketch the Führer, with the proviso that he do so from a well-concealed hiding place. Richter was unimpressed with Hitler's face until someone mentioned the word "Jew." When Hitler heard that word, Richter later recalled, his face was immediately transformed into something at once demonic and defensive, a haunting look which Richter quickly sketched and later that night, put down in oils. He labeled it "A German Worker" and hung it in a shed where it survived the war. Richter had also painted Field Marshal von Schlieffen, Chancellor Stresemann and President of the Reichstag Löbe, but he considered the Hitler portrait to be his masterpiece. The art critic of *Die Zeit* called it "the only really authentic portrait of Hitler . . . perhaps the most important historical portrait that any German artist has ever had the opportunity to paint."

THE
PSYCHOPATHIC GOD
ADOLF
HITLER

ROBERT G. L. WAITE

DA CAPO PRESS • NEW YORK

Library of Congress Cataloging in Publication Data

Waite, Robert George Leeson, 1919-
    The psychopathic god: Adolf Hitler / Robert G. L. Waite.
        p.   cm.
    Originally published: New York: Basic Books, c1977. With new introd.
    Includes bibliographical references and index.
    ISBN 0-306-80514-6
    1. Hitler, Adolf, 1889-1945 — Psychology. 2. Heads of state — Germany —
Biography. I. Title.
DD247.H5W23   1993
943.86'092 — dc20   92-36790
[B]   CIP

First Da Capo Press edition 1993

This Da Capo Press paperback edition of *The Psychopathic God* is an unabridged
republication of the edition first published in New York in 1977, with the
addition of a new foreword by the author and some emendations. It is reprinted
by arrangement with Basic Books.

Published by Da Capo Press, Inc.
A Subsidiary of Plenum Publishing Corporation
233 Spring Street, New York, N.Y. 10013

FOR ANNE

And for Geoffrey and Peter

FOREWORD
To the Da Capo Edition

DURING THE YEARS since *The Psychopathic God* was first published in 1977, historians of the Third Reich have raised a challenging question about the importance of its Führer. "Structuralist" historians have argued that Hitler really didn't run the Nazi show—that major decisions were made and executed, not by a so-called "Führer," but by the internal dynamics of impersonal party, governmental, and military structures. Indeed one influential German historian has concluded that Hitler was actually a "weak dictator" who acquiesced to forces he could not control.

This recent research in institutional history has made valuable contributions to our knowledge of how the Nazi government actually functioned. Yet, in my view, it does not displace Adolf Hitler as the dominating force of the Third Reich.

Nor can it respond adequately to some of the most intriguing questions of all history: How could this peculiar person, at once so terrible and banal, evoke such enthusiastic support from the German people? What was he really like, this little man with the Charlie Chaplin moustache, who bestrode Europe like a colossus and established one of the most vicious and certainly the most popular tyrannies the world has ever known?

This book was written in an effort to respond to these questions, to discover the warped person within the murderous dictator, and to suggest ways in which Hitler's psychopathology contributed to his rise to power, affected his public policy, and propelled his downfall.

The text has not been substantially altered and the pagination remains the same as in the original edition. Any modifications that I have made in my conclusions about Hitler in the fifteen years since this book was first published will be incorporated in the work I am now completing, *Kaiser and Führer: A Comparative Study of Personality and Politics*.

R.G.L.W.
Williamstown and Temagami
July 1992

CONTENTS

CHAPTER 3

Contents

CHAPTER 4

The Past As Prologue: Hitler and History

PREFACE:
The Search for Hitler

Adolf always remained a psychological puzzle to me.
—unpublished letter of August Kubizek,
Hitler's boyhood friend

Do I then know this person at all, at whose side I spent so many years?
—Alfred Jodl, letter to his wife

You will never learn what I am thinking. And those who boast most loudly that they know my thought, to such people I lie even more.
—Hitler to Franz Halder

IT SEEMS LIKELY that more will be written about Adolf Hitler than about anyone else in history with the exception of Jesus Christ.

A British journalist, noting the number of books, articles, novels, television, cinema, and stage dramas about Hitler on display in London in 1972, commented wryly that it was the best year the *Führer* ever had in England. But he did even better in Germany the following year, when no less than fourteen major books about him appeared, including a massive biography which reviewers hailed as definitive and predicted would finally halt "The Hitler Wave." * They were mistaken. By 1975, the thirtieth anniversary of his death, there were already 50,000 serious works about him and his Reich.[1] In 1976 there appeared yet another 1000-page volume which was proclaimed "the definitive biography for generations to come." ** And so it goes.

Hitler's personality will continue to challenge those who seek to answer one of the most intriguing questions of all history: how it was possible for this strange little man, at once so banal and so terrible, to hold a great nation enthralled in cruel yet popular tyranny and to conquer a continent.

One must sympathize with Lord Bullock, the distinguished author of an early and still indispensable biography, when he looked back on his subject's boyhood and confessed, "For my part, the more I learn about Adolf Hitler, the harder I find it to explain and accept what followed. Somehow the causes are inadequate to account for the size of

---

* Joachim C. Fest, *Hitler: Eine Biographie,* 1190 pages, (Frankfurt, Berlin, Vienna, 1973)

** Advertisement in *The New York Times Book Review,* 19 September 1976 of John Toland's *Adolf Hitler,* 1057 pages, (New York, 1976)

the effects. It is offensive to our reason and to our experience to be asked to believe that the [youthful Hitler] was the stuff of which . . . the Caesars and Bonapartes were made. Yet the record is there to prove us wrong. It is here, in the gap between the explanation and the event, that the fascination of Hitler's career remains." [2]

There is indeed a gap between explanation and event. Did Adolf Hitler undergo some remarkable transformation of character as he grew from feckless youth to masterful dictator? If so, what brought about the metamorphosis? Or did his personality, formed decisively in early childhood, remain essentially unchanged? Did he therefore succeed because of a shift in external circumstances? What were the conditions of Germany in 1933 which found in him the leader appropriate to its needs? Is it possible that in the dying years of the Weimar Republic his very psychopathology became a political asset?

Apart from the intellectual challenge, there may be another reason for Hitler's appeal to biographer, novelist, historian, and dramatist: the profound, almost magnetic, horror associated with his name. When in *Heart of Darkness* Joseph Conrad probed deeply into man's capacity for evil, he found there "the fascination of the abomination." As long as people are fascinated by the range and depth of evil, Hitler will find readers, for he was the Moloch who devoured human beings in a regime that was "the negation of God erected into a system of government." [3]

It is to be expected that biographers will differ in their interpretations of Hitler. They will do so in part because he was notably successful in his efforts to deceive both himself and anyone seeking to know him. His private letters and memoirs are designed more to camouflage than to reveal; both consciously and unconsciously he lied about himself and his family. He prided himself on being "the best actor in Europe" and hid behind many masks. He could appear gentle, considerate, and charming, or vicious and vindictive; at times he seemed the soul of reasonableness, at times a crazed fanatic; to some people he was a just and enlightened ruler, a Messiah, to others a blindly destructive tyrant. Biographers are dependent on the sources they use; and because Hitler's contemporaries saw him in different ways, their memoirs, letters, and diaries offer wildly conflicting testimony.

Spurious memoirs have also provided false leads in the search for Hitler. Responsible historians, for example, have accepted one Josef Greiner as a reliable source for Hitler's years in Vienna, yet Greiner in all probability never knew Hitler—his "memoirs" are not to be trusted. Psychological studies have been based on a totally fraudulent account written by someone posing as Hitler's "psychiatrist." A popular biography, relying on the remarkably inventive memoirs of Hitler's sister-in-law, concluded that Hitler's visit to Britain as a youth was important in determining his foreign policy; yet Hitler had never been in England.*

---

* For a discussion of these books, see Appendix, "A Note on Spurious Sources."

Preface

Not only the quality of the sources used but the special interests of the author will influence the kind of history written. The historian of traditional bent is likely to ignore psychological evidence and may regard as trivial the facts that are most revealing to the historian who has some knowledge of psychoanalytic method. In dealing with such complex phenomena as Hitler and Nazi Germany, we need many different approaches. No one method, taken by itself, is fully satisfying, and no historian has a monopoly on historical truth. As Carl Becker once prayed with puckish piety, "Oh, History, how many truths are committed in thy name!" [4]

I have written this book as "psychohistory" because, quite simply, I believe that the career of Adolf Hitler raises questions that can be answered neither by psychology nor by history working alone. My emphasis is on the personality of the man. But my training as a historian reminds me that important as his personality was to the Third Reich —and the Nazi dictatorship is unimaginable without him—he is not the whole story. We will not understand his career without knowledge of the broader historical setting. But neither will we understand it without knowing more about him as a person. Hitler's behavior often appeared so irrational and otherwise inexplicable to me that it seemed prudent to consult specialists who have devoted their training and talents to understanding pathological personalities.

Admittedly, there are dangers and embarrassments in seeking this kind of professional help. A historian who begins a foray into psychology with the high purpose of demonstrating the complexity of historical causation may then come to believe—mistakenly—that the same Oedipal key fits every private lock,[5] that all biographical problems are reducible to Freudian or neo-Freudian symptomatology. That the results can be deplorable is shown clearly enough in Sigmund Freud and William Bullitt's study of Woodrow Wilson. In books such as this, careers of distinguished men become textbook cases of abnormal psychology; complex personalities are reduced to a diagnosis.

The facile use of psychological terminology is neither convincing nor helpful. To label Hitler a "paranoid schizophrenic" explains little. There are many such pathetic, disoriented people in the mental institutions of the world, each convinced that he really is Hitler (or Napoleon) and that he could take over the world if given half a chance. A label in itself provides little understanding. But careful examination of individuals who exhibit the behavioral patterns designated by a label may yield useful results. When investigation demonstrates that Hitler acted very much like certain kinds of neurotic monorchids or borderline personalities, consultation with professional analysts and the study of clinical literature can provide clues to Hitler's behavior that escape a more conventional biographer.

Psychohistorians (regrettable word!) are frequently accused of making too much of psychological causation, to the neglect of other historical forces. The charge is sometimes justified. And it is no defense to point out that specialists in intellectual, military, or economic history sometimes yield to analogous temptations, exaggerating the importance of one specially favored approach to the complexities of the past. We need to keep a sense of proportion. If psychology can be useful in getting at some problems, let us use it; if other kinds of analysis are more appropriate, let us use them. In the search for Hitler, we are not constrained to choose between clinical psychology on the one hand and, say, political history on the other. Our task is rather to join hands in a cooperative effort to find the most satisfying explanation of the man and his times. Thus psychology should be seen as a supplement to other legitimate modes of historical inquiry, not as a substitute for them. Psychology can be helpful to the historian. More claim than that should not be made—nor any less.

The facts about any person's life pose problems. Seldom are they as "hard" or as "cold" as we first imagine. Sometimes they are downright slippery; and always there is a qualitative difference among them. The most readily verifiable may not be the most revealing. Thus, we have many accurate accounts of *what* Hitler did. But to explain *why* he did some of these things may require us to go beyond narrative history and to examine a different and more elusive species of fact. At this point, once again, the biographer's most helpful guide can be the trained psychologist. For whenever the question "Why?" is raised, the biographer will find himself, willy-nilly, adopting a psychological point of view. Even when he assures us that he will have absolutely no truck with psychology, that he will rely instead on "basic human insight" or on something called "common sense," he cannot avoid making psychological assumptions. Erik Erikson's comment on this issue must be taken very seriously:

> Biographers categorically opposed to systematic psychological interpretation permit themselves the most extensive psychologizing —which they can afford to believe is common sense only because they disclaim a defined psychological viewpoint. Yet *there is always an implicit psychology behind the explicit anti-psychology.*[6]

A poignant illustration of Erikson's observation is provided in the work of a brilliant English historian who has written extensively on the career of Adolf Hitler. A. J. P. Taylor disdains the use of abnormal psychology in treating his subject because, in his view, Hitler can be understood as a normal person. He was "the ordinary German writ large." He was not really an aggressive man. If, upon occasion, he may have sounded rather belligerent, we must realize that he did not mean what he said; he was not the kind of person whose words should be taken seriously.* Actually, Mr. Taylor assures us, Hitler harbored no aggressive schemes whatever: "He did not make plans for world conquest or for anything else." Like Winston Churchill and Franklin Roosevelt, the patriotic Hitler simply wanted to make his country strong. Once we recognize that one essential fact, Taylor has written, "*all* his actions were rational." [7]

Having thus disposed of the unconscious and the irrational—as well as the life-work of analysts from Freud through Erikson—Taylor feels free to give his own psychological analysis of Hitler's personality: the Führer can be understood as an eminently sensible, fair-minded, and passive person whose most striking trait was patience, whose ambitions were limited, whose motivations and ideas were "commonplace," and whose actions were consistently rational. Ironically, on the same page in which Taylor expresses confidence that he personally has escaped "from the mystic regions of psychology" he tries to explain Hitler's "willful ignorance" of the United States by suggesting that he hated America because he associated it—in some undisclosed way—with the Austria he held in contempt. In the very assertion that Hitler did not mean what he said, the British historian has made an important psychological judgment about the way Hitler's mind worked.

The question, it must be repeated, is not *whether* historians will use psychology, for assuredly we will; the question is whether we will seek the help of professionals, or as amateurs try to do it all by ourselves. We will use psychology because our job is to interpret the past and to explain why events took place, and that involves human motivation—which immediately involves us with the workings of the mind. Barbara Tuchman has put the matter succinctly: "Every thoughtful historian is a psychohistorian because the psyche, as an inseparable component of the human record, is obviously part of our material. We all know that." [8]

My approach relies heavily on formal psychology, and so differs from Taylor's and from other traditional historians of Hitler. I disagree completely with Alan Bullock, for example, when he writes that Hitler's "personal life . . . throws little if any light on his place in history." [9] I differ from these historians because I proceed from a fundamentally different premise: namely, that Hitler was a pathological personality whose career cannot be understood without a careful examination of his personal life. Unaided, the traditional methods of historical analysis and common sense are inadequate to that task.

---

* Among the many words of Hitler's which Taylor does not take seriously may be listed the following: his statement to his military commanders on 30 May 1933 that his objective was to conquer *Lebensraum* in the East; his directive of 30 May 1938, marked "Top Secret," in which he wrote, "It is my unalterable decision to smash Czechoslovakia through military action in the near future"; and his orders to his generals on the eve of the Polish campaign to "close your hearts to pity . . . act brutally."

Common sense tends to assume that people act rationally, that they behave, by and large, as they intend to behave, and that they are consciously aware of their motivations. But when, as with Hitler, the subject refuses to be sensible and behaves strangely, irrationally, perversely, the historian relying on common sense finds himself in difficulties. His inclination will be to skirt such issues. But are not irrational, apparently nonsensical acts also a part of the biographer's data? Is it really enough to label them "strange" or pronounce them "unimportant"? Is it not the responsibility of the historian to try to explain such behavior, particularly when the consequences are great, both for the subject and for others? Are we not obliged to recognize the power of the irrational to motivate human beings? To conclude that a person's conduct—for example, Hitler's orders to kill all the Jews of Europe or his decision to invade the Soviet Union—was "irrational" should not terminate a discussion; it should rather initiate the most serious inquiry into the irrational bases for such historic decisions.

It seems to me that Hitler must be seen at the same time as both a mentally deranged human being and a consummately skillful political leader of high intelligence. To treat him solely as a rational statesman, as Taylor does, or as an ambitious tyrant, as Bullock does, is to misjudge the complexity of his personality and to misunderstand a great deal of his historical behavior. On the other hand, Hitler could analyze a political or diplomatic problem brilliantly and respond with shattering effectiveness. To ignore that fact and to become preoccupied with his abnormalities or to reduce him to textbook patterns of abnormal behavior—explaining his political career in terms of sexual perversion or unresolved Oedipal feelings—is to caricature both Hitler and history.

Some students of Hitler have been quite ready to conclude that he was mentally ill, but they are unwilling to investigate the nature of his illness or to discuss its effect on his career. For example, one popular biographer is content simply to repeat that Hitler was psychotic: "there was madness in him almost from the beginning . . . he was insane." A noted British historian writes that Hitler "had always been . . . a violent megalomaniac . . . in the end he lost all touch with reality." An American diplomatic historian, in the preface to his detailed study of Hitler's war aims, asserts that his subject was a "pathological egoist" who suffered from megalomania. But there is no indication in the rest of his book that the author takes his own descriptions seriously; he makes no effort to show the relationship between Hitler's psychopathology and his foreign policy, and treats the Führer's policy as if it were that of a psychologically healthy person. Recently, even A. J. P. Taylor has come to the conclusion that Hitler was "a crazy neurotic," but Taylor is not interested in pursuing a diagnosis which would require extensive revision of his thesis that Hitler was a sensible and circumspect statesman. The leading German biographer calls Hitler "a neurotic character" who was imprisoned by "an overpowering psychosis." He then reaches the remarkable conclusion that Hitler was some sort of "Unperson." None of these historians has listed in his bibliography a single work of theoretical or clinical psychology dealing with the mental disorder he has assigned to Hitler.[10]

Other historians who dismiss psychology as a tool in understanding Hitler have turned instead to a kind of demonology. Arguing that he was so completely inhuman that he is inaccessible to any type of rational analysis, they have called him Demon, Evil, and Fiend and consigned him to outer darkness. Evil he no doubt was by any measure of morality; but to remove him completely from human experience can have serious consequences. One of them is set forth by a thoughtful writer in the *Frankfurter Allgemeine Zeitung* (11 October 1972) who warned his countrymen against "demonizing Hitler" and setting him apart from humanity, for to do so would be to diminish their own responsibility. The German journalist concluded that the terrifying thing about Hitler was not his uniqueness but his banality: "He was one of us. We knew that from the beginning. We should not forget it now."

Another consequence of demonization is that it sets unacceptable limits to the range of inquiry into problems of history and human personality. Thus, for example, a traditional historian who has written a useful book on the Gestapo has given up on his efforts to understand the man who directed Hitler's secret police. The author concludes that because such a strange person cannot be understood by traditional biographical methods, he cannot be understood at all: "All attempts to analyze the character of Himmler have failed, as I think all must fail . . . because they entail the understanding of a madman in terms of human experience. . . . He was one of those terrifying beings foreign to normal human behavior." [11] To dismiss Hitler or Himmler as madmen or fiends, incomprehensible to "normal" people, is to say that critical judgment about them is not possible. Such an attitude is not only obscurantist, it is antihistorical. Hitler happened. He was a human phenomenon which the historian must seek to understand.

I must concede at once that if conventional historians tend to dismiss the irrational and to forget that man is not only a creature of flesh and blood but of compulsions and neuroses, those of us interested in the psychological aberrations of our subjects may be tempted to overemphasize pathological behavior.

That is one of the problems of this book. The stress here falls on aspects of Hitler's life and career which have been neglected by previous historians. My intention has not been to write a complete life and times of Hitler; this book is designed not to replace but to complement several fine biographies. I have also neglected many aspects of Hitler's government which have been treated in excellent monographic studies. Instead, I have emphasized those peculiarities of Hitler's personal life and public career which may be understood more fully through psychology, and I have stressed the response of the culture to that personality.

Readers will find a good deal of conjecture in this book, particularly in the discussion of the vitally important first years of Hitler's life and in the effort to show how Hitler's psychopathology may have influenced his political actions. Conjecture is of course increased when the evidence is fragmentary. But all the evidence in the world never can obviate speculation about personalities and events.

At the turn of the 20th century, it became fashionable to imagine that history was a "Science." It was seriously believed that the historian, working in the archives dispassionately and examining primary materials "objectively," could reach incontrovertible conclusions with the confidence of the physical scientist in his laboratory. J. B. Bury gave classic expression to this conviction in his inaugural lecture as the Regius Professor of History at Cambridge University in 1902. With majestic confidence he asserted that "History is a science, no less and no more." Bury's contemporary, the humanist historian George M. Trevelyan, disagreed. He shocked many colleagues by concluding that "in the most important part of its business, history is not scientific deduction but an imaginative guess. . . ." [12]

It should go without saying that historians owe it to their craft and their conscience to examine all the evidence they can find and use all their ingenuity and honesty in interpreting it. And when they guess, they are certainly obliged to do so carefully and conscientiously. But in the end, any historian's efforts to reconstruct past events and dead personalities will involve guesswork. As an act of imaginative reconstruction, his work will remain fallible, flawed, and incomplete. Since it is not given to historians to know the full truth about the past, some of us may find solace in St. Paul's confession as it comes to us in modern translation: "Now we see only puzzling reflections in a mirror. . . ." [13] Certainly no biographer can ignore the warning of Henry James: "Never say you know the last word about the human heart." [14]

Acknowledgments

IT IS A PLEASURE to express my thanks to people and institutions who, through the years, have helped in the preparation of this book. For fellowships and grants-in-aid, I am indebted to the John Simon Guggenheim Foundation, the American Council of Learned Societies, the Fulbright Commission, the Social Science Research Council, and Williams College. The staffs of several archives and libraries have given me generous and imaginative assistance: The Oberöesterreichisches Landesarchiv of Linz, the Oesterreichische Nationalbibliothek in Vienna; the Bundesarchiv in Coblenz; the Bayerische Staatsbibliothek, Bayerisches Hauptstaatsarchiv, and the Institut für Zeitgeschichte, Munich; the United States Document Center, Berlin; the Institute for Contemporary History and the Wiener Library, London; the National Archives and the Library of Congress Manuscript Division, Washington, D.C.; the Hoover Institution, Stanford, Calif.; and the Williams College Library. Before his death, the Linz archivist, Dr. Franz Jetzinger, graciously permitted me to examine valuable documents in his personal collection, as did the late Dr. Ernst Hanfstaengl of Munich, who also shared with me his vivid memories of his former Führer.

The artwork following pages 68 and 160 is from the following sources: *von Stuck paintings: Stuck,* Otto Julius Bierbaum, Bielefeld and Leipzig, 1901. *Photographs:* (as a baby; father; Geli Raubal; Eva Braun; in 1932; with von Hindenberg; at Obersalzberg; as Wagnerian hero; in Paris) *Hitler wie ihn Keiner Kennt,* Heinrich Hoffmann. (Sketch by schoolmate) *Aus Hitlers Jugendzeit,* Hugo Rabitsch, Munich, 1938. (Mother) *Aus Adolf Hitlers Heimat,* Albert Reich, Munich, 1933. (Stefanie) *The Young Hitler I Knew,* August Kubizek, Boston, 1955.

Since my purpose has been to combine insights of psychology and of history in an effort to reach a fuller understanding of Hitler, I am particularly grateful for advice from distinguished members of both professions. I have profited enormously from extensive discussions with Erik H. Erikson and with Norbert Bromberg, professor of clinical psychiatry at the Albert Einstein College of Medicine, who contributed the title of the book by first calling my attention to Auden's poem. Richard O. Rouse, the Mary A. and William Wirt Warren Professor of Psychology at Williams College, and Lawrence H. Climo, staff psychiatrist of the Austen Riggs Center, also made generous contributions of time and knowledge to the chapters on Hitler's psychological development.

The historians William L. Langer and James MacGregor Burns gave me acute criticism, wise counsel, and friendly encouragement. They both undertook the chore of reading a much longer version of the manuscript and assisted in making painful but necessary excisions to remove extraneous material. Three specialists in German history who have reservations about a psychological approach to historical problems and who possess a lively and laudable concern for factual detail have helped correct my mistakes. Hans W. Gatzke of Yale kindly pointed out errors in earlier essays; Reginald H. Phelps of Harvard and Richard W. Reichard of Queens College checked the entire manuscript with meticulous care. These gentlemen, of course, must not be blamed for inaccuracies which, despite their vigilance, in all probability survived.

Special thanks are due Fred Stocking of Williams and Edwin Barrett of Hamilton, both of whom labored mightily to smooth my uneven prose. The book has also gained greatly from Martin Kessler's perceptive and demanding editorial supervision and Geoffrey Horn's expert copyediting. Friends and colleagues who have read and criticized parts of the manuscript include Dudley Bahlman, John Hyde, Manly Johnson, Peter Loewenberg, Roger Louis, Thomas McGann, Neill Megaw, Irwin Shainman, and Lauren Stevens. Barbara Stoddard and the Faculty Secretarial Staff went beyond the call of secretarial duty to type and retype many drafts of the same paragraphs. To all these people I am deeply grateful

My warmest thanks, however, are reserved for my wife, closest friend, and collaborator, Anne Barnett Waite. She listened to most of it many times, lent her humor, and prepared the index. She sustained me throughout the venture and, in troubled waters, helped to keep the project afloat.

R. G. L. W.

Williamstown
Fall 1976

CHAPTER 1

The Image and the Man

> . . . he is like a child, kind, good, merciful. Like a cat: cunning, clever, agile. Like a lion: roaring, great and gigantic. A great guy, a man! [*ein Kerl, ein Mann!*]
> —Joseph Goebbels, diary entry of July 1926

> . . . he was a character out of the pages of Dostoyevsky, a man "possessed."
> —André François-Poncet, French Ambassador to Germany, 1931–1938

> How is it possible that he captivated me so, and for more than a decade?
> —Albert Speer, diary entry for 20 November 1952

AS FÜHRER of the Germans, Adolf Hitler probably exerted more direct personal power than any ruler in history. He created both his own political theory and a government that could not exist without him. It was he who set the standards for art, music, medicine, and poetry. His whim became national law. He dictated statutes which set forth the religion of household servants, the colors artists could use in paintings, the way lobsters were to be cooked in restaurants, and how physics would be taught in the universities. He decided whom Germans might marry, what they could name their children, where they could be buried. At his command thousands of young soldiers died in hopeless battle, many with his name on their lips. On his orders millions of people were tortured, maimed, murdered. He was the arbiter of the fate of nations. Few dictators have enjoyed so much genuine support from so great a number of people.

The magic of his appeal is best remembered by an American journalist who saw him enter Nuremberg one September day in 1934:

> Like a Roman emperor Hitler rode into this medieval town at sundown today past solid phalanxes of wildly cheering Nazis who packed the narrow streets that once saw Hans Sachs and the *Meistersinger*. Tens of thousands of Swastika flags blot out the Gothic beauties of the place, the facades of the old houses, the gabled roofs. . . . About ten o'clock tonight I got caught in a mob of ten thousand hysterics who jammed the moat in front of Hitler's hotel shouting: "We want our Führer." I was a little shocked at the faces, especially those of the women. . . . They reminded me of the crazed expressions I saw once in the back country of Louisiana on the faces of some Holy Rollers who were about to hit the trail. They looked up at him as if he were a Messiah, their faces transformed. . . .[1]

As Sir Alan Bullock has noted in his superb biography, no statesman ever showed greater understanding of the irrational and emotional factors in politics or exploited them more masterfully. Few have had clearer insights into the weaknesses of opponents or greater ability to turn them to personal advantage. Hitler was adroit in the manipulation of his own charisma and used personal appeal with consummate artistry. As the occasion or audience demanded, he could be charming or brutal, generous or vicious. He was adored by housewives and artists, peasants and architects, professors and plumbers, children and generals. He was a ruthless opportunist with an almost perfect sense of timing, knowing instinctively the precise moment to strike.

Hitler was also a man with a faith that moved mountains. Like all really great political leaders, he combined political realism with unshakable belief in his historic destiny. Above all else, he had the capacity to make men want to follow him. David Lloyd George, himself a notable practitioner of the political arts, stood in awe of Hitler and, after an extensive visit in Germany, proclaimed him to be one of the truly great men of the ages:

> The old trust him; the young idolize him. It is not the admiration accorded to a popular Leader. It is the worship of a national hero who has saved his country from utter despondency and degradation. . . . He is as immune from criticism as a king in a monarchical country. He is something more. He is the George Washington of Germany—the man who won for his country independence from all her oppressors. To those who have not actually seen and sensed the way Hitler reigns over the heart and mind of Germany, this description may appear extravagant. All the same, it is the bare truth.[2]

Winston Churchill was also impressed. In 1937 he looked at Hitler's accomplishments and called them "among the most remarkable in the whole history of the world." [3]

Hitler's rise had indeed been one of history's great political success stories. The unknown and uneducated common soldier of World War I, who had been a failure in all his undertakings, had come to power in 1933 in a country that despaired of solving its social and political problems. Within five years he had given his nation stability and hope. A grateful people hailed him as the leader and savior who had eliminated unemployment, stabilized their currency, provided them with effective social legislation, and given millions of workers attractive vacations. He had sent the youth of the land singing and marching down sunlit roads; he had forged a new community of the German people; he had built magnificent freeways and promised automobiles to every laboring man; he had humbled the victors of Versailles and wiped out their treaty, which all Germans called the Treaty of Shame. In a series of brilliant and bloodless coups, he had created a triumphant Greater Germany, proud and strong, remilitarized the Rhineland, and annexed Austria and Czechoslovakia.

If only he had died before World War II, mused one perceptive German historian. Hitler might well have been remembered by his countrymen as "Adolf the Great, one of the outstanding figures in German history." [4]

PHYSICAL CHARACTERISTICS

Any attempt simply to describe Adolf Hitler—his physical appearance and personal interests—immediately confronts the complexities of the man. We look at his unimpressive, even ludicrous figure and wonder how it was possible for a great nation to hail him as their leader and savior; we are perplexed by his preoccupation with the length of his fingers, the width of his nostrils, the shape of his skull, and the color of his eyes. His personal habits also seem odd. In this chapter we simply note some of his most striking characteristics and patterns of behavior, along with the themes which keep recurring in his written and spoken words. Later on, we must respond to questions that are as obvious as they are difficult: Why was he so concerned about these specific things—why so disturbed by such trivialities? What do his preoccupations and idiosyncrasies reveal about him? How did they affect his personal life and public career?

Physically, Hitler did not seem well cast for his role as national hero and historic force. He looked rather like an apprentice waiter in a second-class Viennese cafe. Barely five feet, nine inches tall, he weighed, during his better days, about 150 pounds. But he had a tendency to put on flabby weight, and his posture deteriorated through the years. His shoulders were narrow, his chest somewhat sunken with skin white, shiny, and hairless. Deficiencies of his torso gave rise to unfounded rumors that he wore special padding in his uniform. His legs were unusually short, his knees slightly knocked and quite chubby, his feet very large. He did not appear to his best advantage in the baggy riding britches and huge jackboots he often wore. His walk was rather mincing; he tended to drag his left foot. He wore a Charlie Chaplin mustache.

He was fascinated by his hands, which were finely structured with long, graceful fingers. He also took special interest in the hands of others. In his library there was a well-thumbed book containing pictures and drawings of hands belonging to famous people throughout history. He liked particularly to show his guests how closely his own hands resembled those of Frederick the Great, one of his heroes. He was convinced that he could judge people's character and loyalty on the basis of their hands. On meeting someone for the first time, he would not only stare carefully into the stranger's eyes but also closely examine his hands. Men would gain favor or disfavor on the basis of the shape and nature of these extremities. Those of Professor Ludwig Troost, his architect of modest talent, were very strongly formed. Hitler admired them greatly.

When his Eagle's Nest in the Kehlstein was being built, a piece of rock shaped like a hand was found. Hitler was intrigued with it. He called it the "Hand of Wotan" and had it mounted in a special case, almost as if it were a holy relic.[5]

Hitler's hair was very dark brown, almost black. He parted it on the right side, his famous forelock falling over the left temple. His nose was large and coarse. His bushy mustache was cut just wide enough to help conceal the offending feature. His teeth were brownish-yellow and covered with fillings and bridges. He shielded his mouth with his hand when he laughed.

The most impressive feature of his otherwise coarse and rather undistinguished face was his eyes. They were extraordinarily light blue in color, with a faint touch of greenish-gray. Almost everyone who met him mentioned his strangely compelling eyes. This includes Robert Coulondre, the French ambassador, and the German dramatist Gerhart Hauptmann who, when first introduced to Hitler, stared into his famous eyes and later told friends, "It was the greatest moment of my life!" Martha Dodd, daughter of the American ambassador, was not disappointed in the famous eyes, finding them "startling and unforgettable. . . ."[6]

Hitler himself often observed that his eyes were very like those of his mother. Her eyes, in turn, reminded him of the Medusa—whose glance, it will be recalled, turned men to stone or impotence. Hitler was absolutely enthralled with Franz von Stuck's striking portrait of a Medusa of terrifying eye. On seeing it for the first time in Hanfstaengl's home, he exclaimed, "Those eyes, Hanfstaengl! Those eyes! They are the eyes of my mother!"

He knew the power of his own slightly protruding, shining eyes, whose lashless eyelids added to their curiously hypnotic effect. He practiced piercing glances in front of a mirror and used them whenever he met strangers. At dinner or at the tea table he would attempt to stare down a guest. His architect, Albert Speer, apparently liked to play the game too: "Once when we were seated at the round table in the tea house, Hitler began staring at me. Instead of dropping my eyes I took it as a challenge. Who knows what primitive instincts were involved in such staring duels? I had had others and always used to win them, but this time I had to muster almost inhuman strength, seemingly forever, not to yield to the ever mounting urge to look away—until Hitler suddenly closed his eyes, and turned to the woman at his side." [7]

His eyes had always been impressive. A boyhood friend recalled that in Adolf's countenance

> the eyes were so outstanding that one didn't notice anything else. Never in my life have I seen any other person whose appearance —how shall I put it—was so completely dominated by the eyes. They were the light eyes of his mother but her somewhat staring, penetrating gaze was even more marked in the son and had even more force and expressiveness. It was uncanny how those eyes could change their expression, especially when Adolf was speaking. . . . In fact, Adolf spoke with his eyes, and even when his lips were silent one knew what he wanted to say. When he first came to our house and I introduced him to my mother she said to me in the evening, "What eyes your friend has!" And I remember quite distinctly that there was more fear than admiration in her words. If I am asked where one could perceive, in his youth, this man's exceptional qualities, I can only answer, "In the eyes." [8]

Women in particular continued to be impressed and frightened by his eyes. Nietzsche's sister, typically, was fascinated and disturbed by them: "They . . . searched me through and through." The penetrating quality remained to the end. A young military adjutant who saw his Führer just before Hitler killed himself in 1945 was deeply shocked by the appearance of "a sick, almost senile old man." But the eyes were still effective: "Only in his eyes was there an indescribable flickering brightness . . . and the glance he gave me was strangely penetrating." [9]

Hitler's library shows that he was very much interested in the study of heads. Many of his books were devoted to the pseudo-sciences of phrenology and craniology. His own head, understandably enough, held particular fascination for him. An American correspondent reports that Hitler summoned a group of medical specialists to his

Munich apartment one winter day in 1937 to examine and measure his head. The leader of the group, who must have been acutely embarrassed by the whole affair, was Professor Ferdinand Sauerbruch, a surgeon of international reputation. He was obliged to watch as phrenologists and craniologists, armed with all manner of calipers and tapes, took meticulous measurements of every conceivable part of the Führer's skull. They measured from ear to ear; from forehead to vertebrae; from eye socket to eye socket; from eye to ear; from ear to chin. . . . All measurements were annotated and compared with those computed from the death masks or portraits of famous people. Hitler was as delighted as a child to hear his experts proclaim that he had certain measurements remarkably like those of Frederick the Great or Bismarck or Napoleon. He nodded benignly and said, "Yes, yes, record it all." Posterity seems to have been deprived of the annotated drawings that were made on that day.[10]

What was there about Hitler's past that made him so concerned about his head, eyes, hands, and nostrils? Why did he play that staring game with dinner guests?

PERSONAL QUALITIES

Childishness

One of the striking personal characteristics of this political giant who bestrode Europe for a decade was his infantilism. There was in him little capacity for mental, emotional, artistic, or sexual growth. The tastes, opinions, and life-style of the chancellor were those of the child and adolescent of Leonding, Linz, and Vienna.

He sought to cling to his childhood by remembering it in dozens of sentimental soliloquies about his boyhood escapades; he was convinced that a magic elixir of youth really did exist, and he thought seriously of sending an expedition to India to find it. He became a vegetarian partly because he believed that a diet which (he reminded his secretaries) prolonged the lives of elephants would also add to his own.

Like a child, he sought oral gratification by sucking inordinate amounts of sweets and chocolates. The granddaughter of Richard Wagner remembered that as a little girl she and her sisters were fascinated by the amount of sugar and chocolates Hitler consumed while visiting their mother. He told them that he ate two pounds of chocolates every day. They waited expectantly for him to miscount the number of teaspoonfuls of sugar he invariably put in his tea, but he never miscalculated. Always there were seven—it was his favorite number. His valet recalls that his master was particularly drawn to chocolates in moments of tension. During a "Führer conference" he would leave the room, down several chocolates, then return to the meeting. In moments of agitation, the leader of the Thousand Year Reich had the habit of sucking his little finger.[11]

The child of Leonding liked to go on expeditions and picnics: the adult enjoyed doing the same things. Diary entries of a close associate record the Führer's enthusiasm. In April 1926, on a motor trip to Württemberg, Hitler "was like a youth, exuberant, singing, laughing, whistling." On a picnic to the Königssee he was "like a beloved, spontaneous child—enthusiastic and rapturous." [12]

Hitler took boyish delight in circuses and became very excited when female performers were endangered by wild animals. But his favorite diversion was movies. A director of the German UFA Studios recalled that Hitler had given a standing order "to have every new film, German and all foreign films shown at the Chancellery." His regular routine was to see at least one film a night. His idea of sacrificing for the war effort was to give up his beloved movies. After the start of the war he saw only newsreels; after Stalingrad, no newsreels. Of the hundreds of films he saw, two were particular favorites: Disney's *Snow White and the Seven Dwarfs*, which was shown many times, and *King Kong*. He was absolutely enthralled by the story of the great ape who loved a little blond girl no bigger than his finger. He talked about the film for days. His favorite movie actress was Shirley Temple.[13]

The Führer liked to play games. One of them, called *Biberspiel* (Beaver Game), was played sedulously by the entourage on his personal train. Anyone who saw a man with a beard called out "Beaver!" and counted up his triumphs. There was great excitement, his secretary assures us, when the Führer won—which he usually did. He also invented a game of bowling played at the Berghof. He would take three balls and if he knocked down all the pins, someone else could have a turn; if he failed, the game was over. He also liked to see how fast he could undress and dress himself. His valet—who was not allowed in Hitler's bedroom—would stand by the door with a stop watch and call "*Los!*" When Hitler had finished dressing, he would cry "*Schluss!*" and rush out of the room to see if he had broken his record.[14]

He enjoyed games that hurt or embarrassed other people. An effective actor and an excellent mimic, he worked up routines which poked fun at the one-armed publisher, Max Amann, and an assistant press director who was deaf. He liked to frighten and confuse his subordinates by having someone call them on the telephone with imperious "Führer orders" while he whispered instructions that were designed to intimidate the victim.[15]

There was nothing childish about Hitler's prewar diplomatic coups: they were executed with a mature and masterful sense of timing and a remarkable ability to exploit the weaknesses of his victims. But his instinctive reaction to his triumphs was a childlike pleasure in the "surprises" he had played on an unsuspecting world. A member of his intimate circle recalled that during the military reoccupation of the Rhineland in March 1936, which crushed the treaties of Versailles and Locarno under the jarring cadence of the Wehrmacht's boots, "Hitler's face assumed that expression which [we] knew so well meant that he was enjoying a little joke of his own." During the occupation of Austria in March 1938, he led his unsuspecting entourage to the middle of a bridge over the Inn River. They were astonished when Austrian children greeted Hitler as their Führer and presented him with flowers. Hitler "turned round and laughed joyously at our surprised faces. Another surprise packet had come off!" When he forced President Hacha of Czechoslovakia to sign his country over to him in March 1939, Hitler ran up joyously to his secretaries and exclaimed, "Children, I am so happy, I'd really like to stand on my head!" Informed that the Soviet-Nazi Pact had been signed in August 1939, he turned to his court and exclaimed, " 'Won't that just make the world sit up again!' And in a mood of complete abandon . . . he slapped himself delightedly on the knee and exclaimed, 'That will really land them [the Western Powers] in the soup!' " [16]

A newsreel camera recorded for history the reaction of the man who, after the fall and humiliation of France, had just been proclaimed "The Greatest Military Commander of All Time": he giggled and slapped his thigh with delight.

Hitler characteristically dealt with disappointment and opposition in much the same way he had as a pampered mother's boy in Leonding and Linz: he sulked, ran away and hid, or staged a temper tantrum. A British diplomat recalls that when a dinner conversation did not go according to the Führer's liking, "He behaved throughout like a spoiled, sulky child."

His famous rages were seldom caused by important political or military defeats. When thwarted in his bid for the presidency in 1932, defeated at Stalingrad or the Battle of the Bulge, or confronted by assassination attempts, he took it all calmly and with great self-control. At the end, when defeat was obvious and the decision had been made to die in Berlin, many in his entourage were in a state of hysteria. But not Hitler. His stenographer recalled that at the last military conference he was "generally composed" and the one who "kept his nerves best under control." [17] His rages tended to be occasioned by little things. When someone disagreed with him, a valet forgot his favorite mineral water, or it was suggested that he had whistled a tune incorrectly, he would scream or beat his fists upon the table or the walls, sometimes spreading himself out as if crucified. No reliable witness, however, ever saw him lying on the floor chewing a rug. The sobriquet *Teppichfresser* (carpet eater) was not justified.

It has sometimes been suggested that Hitler's fury was carefully staged for effect, that it was a weapon in his armory used to frighten opponents into submission. Certainly he enjoyed his success in reducing the old and ill President Hacha of Czechoslovakia into trembling submission by screaming threats to obliterate Prague. But one of the more detailed and graphic pictures given by an eyewitness to an outburst suggests neither premeditation nor command over his own actions. A Swedish visitor in August 1939 had just predicted that England would resist Nazi aggression against Poland:

> Hitler jumped up and became very agitated. He nervously paced up and down and declared, as if he were talking to himself, that Germany was invincible. . . . Suddenly he stopped in the middle of the room and stared straight ahead. His speech became more and more garbled, his whole behavior gave the impression of a person who was not at all himself. Sentences tumbled after one another. . . . "If there is a war," he said, "I'll build U-Boats, U-Boats, U-Boats, U-Boats!" His voice became increasingly indistinct and gradually one could no longer understand him. Suddenly he collected himself, raised his voice as if addressing a vast assembly and screamed, "I'll build airplanes, airplanes, airplanes, airplanes and I'll annihilate my enemies!" At this moment he acted more like a demon in bad fiction than a human being. I looked at him in amazement. . . .[18]

On other occasions he deliberately used his dramatic talents to good effect. In any case, whether calculated or not, his temper tantrums were the weapons of a child, the means little Adolf had used to frighten his doting mother into compliance with his demands.

Hitler went to the Western Front during World War II as commander in chief of all German military forces in much the same way he had gone on picnics as a boy. One of his secretaries, Fräulein Schroeder, recalled that Hitler liked to take sudden trips and not tell his friends where they were going. He would make them guess. One day early in 1940 he told his entourage that they were going on "a little trip"—but would not say where. A guessing game started which was diverted into false channels by Hitler and by those who were in on the game: maybe you should take bathing suits along . . . perhaps you can bring back a sealskin trophy. To make the game more fun, the Führer had ordered the nameplates removed from the towns through which the official train was passing. Not until the entourage arrived at headquarters and heard artillery fire did Hitler announce proudly that he had fooled them all. He proclaimed in boyish triumph: "This morning the offensive against the Western powers has begun!" [19]

Both as boy and man, Hitler liked to read about Germanic gods and American cowboys and Indians. He was particularly taken with the adventure stories of Karl May, a German who wrote about the American frontier without visiting the locale and who concocted a strange "Western" language which his heroes spoke in a type of Teutonized Texan drawl. The hero, Old Shatterhand—he used expletives like "Hang it all, fellows!" [*Zum Henker, Kerle!*], "Well, I shall be *bounced*," and "Pshaw and damnation, sir!"—was an incredible marksman who knocked out the eyes of Indians or broke a hangman's rope at 50 yards with his 48-shot rifle. Always victorious in the face of staggering odds, he defeated his enemies through the power of his will, bravery, and treachery.

Hitler of course was not alone in his admiration for May's intrepid hero. The books sold by the thousands, and a generation of German boys were enthralled by Old Shatterhand's exploits. Few, however, could match Hitler in the intensity of his loyalty or the longevity of his infatuation. As chancellor, he had a special shelf built in his library to hold, in a place of honor, the results of May's prolific pen, specially bound in vellum. He read and reread the stories and commended them highly in his *Tischgespräche*. They served—along with the movie version of *Grapes of Wrath*—as a main source of his knowledge about America. He also had the idea that Karl May knew best how to fight the Soviet Army, telling his valet, "I have ordered every officer to carry with him . . . Karl May's books about fighting Indians. That's the way the Russians fight—hidden like Indians behind trees and bridges, they jump out for the kill!" [20]

Hitler's passion for building and rebuilding on an enormous scale will be discussed later. But here, too, one notes a childlike quality: the master of Germany playing with building blocks. A former minister of finance recalled with amazement the scene he encountered when he was summoned to Hitler's office to discuss a loan from the Reichsbank to finance one of the Führer's building projects:

> When the door was opened, there was Hitler lying on the floor with a number of toy buildings carefully arranged in front of him. . . . Hitler did not arise when his guest was announced, but invited his guest to join him on the floor. His first remark was "Isn't this beautiful? We must make Berlin the most beautiful city in the world." The official agreed that it was, but maintained that its realization at the moment was impossible. . . .
>
> But Hitler was not defeated. He lay flat on his stomach staring at the models for a considerable period of time in silence. Suddenly he turned to his visitor and said like a little child with tears in his voice, "But you can't take this away from me. I will be so unhappy. You must let me have it!" . . .[21]

The Führer liked to build things; he also liked to knock them down. In the basement of the Reichschancellery there was a miniature cannon with a barrel about 30 inches long and a special silencer built into the chamber. Hitler delighted in loading, aiming, and firing the little piece himself. His targets were wooden buildings and figures of "enemy" soldiers: Polish, English, French, and Russian—the Russians were painted with ugly, leering faces. As a very special favor to his friend Mussolini, Hitler let him play with his toy, loading and shooting it himself.[22]

Ever since he was a little boy, Adolf had been afraid to be left alone at night. As an adult he insisted that his entourage or guests stay up with him and talk—or rather hear him talk—often until dawn. He told Eva Braun, quite frankly, "I really shudder at the thought of being alone at night." After his guests had left, he often rang for his dull-witted adjutant, Schaub, and had him sit with him until daybreak.[23]

Hitler's personal immaturity found expression in the government he established for Germany. The Third Reich was in many ways the historic actualization of a perverse child's fantasies—William Golding's *Lord of the Flies* further brutalized and made real. The social orders created by both adolescents (Adolf and Jack) demanded contempt for the weak, mindless destruction, murder of the innocent, gratuitous cruelty, forced happiness decreed by the leader, total commitment to primitive symbols, and incessant marching and song. The meaning of song was much the same; only the words were different. The Nazi version, "The blood of the Jew will squirt from our knives," parallelled the children's chant of "Kill the pig! Spill his blood! Do him in!"

The solutions Hitler found to complex political and moral problems were often childishly and cruelly simple. He startled British diplomatists by saying that the best way to deal with passive resistance in India was to kill the leaders of the Congress Party. "Shoot Gandhi," he said, "and if that does not suffice to reduce them to submission, shoot a dozen leading members of Congress; if that does not suffice, shoot two hundred more and so on until order is established." [24]

Humorlessness and Rigidity

Neither the boy nor the man had a sense of humor. The only close friend of his youth said that Hitler was totally lacking in a spirit of self-irony and that "one thing he could not do was to pass over something with a smile." Many years later a high official of the Foreign Office recalled: "I never experienced a normal bantering conversation at his table . . . Concerning people, Hitler's judgments were usually bitter and derogatory. Qualities such as forbearance, humor and self-irony were completely foreign to him." A private secretary who was with him at the end of his life noted that Hitler liked to play tricks on people and sometimes gave a "sort of barking gurgle when he read of some *Schadenfreude* . . . [but] I must say that I never once heard him laugh heartily." And a valet who had served him a dozen years reported, "He never laughed out loud. At least I never once heard him break out in a hearty laughter." Speer disagrees about the laughter, but not about his humor or the source of his merriment: "Hitler had no humor . . . although he could laugh loudly . . . sometimes literally writhing with laughter. Often he would wipe tears from his eyes during such spasms.

He liked laughing, but it was always laughter at the expense of others." He never told off-color stories nor permitted them to be told in his presence. Moreover, he had a horror of being laughed at. Before wearing a new suit or hat in public he would have himself photographed privately and consult with his photographer over the suitability of his new wardrobe.

He is said to have laughed uproariously at one joke which he liked to have repeated: "Question: 'Why is a swan's neck so long?' Answer: 'So that the swan doesn't get drownded [sic].'" [25]

Hitler was as inflexible as he was humorless. Time and time again he spoke of flexibility as weakness and of obstinacy as strength. He was proud of his rigidity and thought of it as the key to his success. "I have attained success," he remarked, "because I would never allow myself to be deterred through weakness from a perception once it was given me." [26]

During his nightly wartime monologues, he looked back longingly —and interminably—on his youth to emphasize the same point he had made in his memoirs: how little he had changed. He insisted, for example, that his early years in Vienna were absolutely crucial to his career because "at that time I formed an image of the world and a view of life which became the foundation for my actions . . . I have had to change nothing." Even the thought of changing his ideas was "very embarrassing" to him. He reminisced by the hour about past political decisions and victories which he attributed to inflexible stubbornness. He was fond, for example, of reminding his entourage of the successful gamble he had taken in marching into the Rhineland in 1936, and concluded, "What saved us was my *unshakable obstinacy* and my amazing aplomb." [27]

Four thoughtful people who observed four different periods of his life all stressed the same characteristic. His boyhood friend wrote that Hitler's single most evident trait was "the unparalleled constancy in everything that he said and did. There was in his nature something firm, inflexible, immovable, obstinately rigid. . . . Adolf simply could not change his mind or nature. . . . How often did I experience this!" Forty years later a physician who knew Hitler well agreed: "It was impossible for anyone to induce Hitler to change his views. . . . Anyone who [tried to do so] produced only a stronger fixation of his prejudices." A Swiss diplomat also affirmed that it was counterproductive to try to dissuade Hitler from a line of action. While serving as the League of Nations' high commissioner in Danzig, Professor Carl Burckhardt, a distinguished relative of the great historian, was incensed by the persecution of Polish Jews and tried to intercede on their behalf. He discovered that his efforts only led to further persecution, noting sadly, "Every protest only had the result of goading Hitler on to the most brutal attack." Finally, Albert Speer, who knew Hitler best during World War II, was convinced that the Führer's intellectual development stopped with the world as he had known it in Vienna in 1910. The

Ringstrasse remained for him absolute perfection in city planning; the rifle he had used in World War I was quite good enough for German soldiers three decades later.[28]

Inability or refusal to change was also manifest in the details of his life-style and personal habits. The letters he wrote as an adult contained the same grammatical mistakes and spelling errors as the postcards sent from Vienna and from the Front during World War I. His vocabulary in private conversation showed a surprising number of words he had learned as a boy in rural Austria. In the so-called *Tischgespräche* we find him speaking of *Dirndln, Tschapperln,* and *Bazis,* of *Gigerln* and *Lackln*; he also uses such expressions as *krampfig* and *Wortgegloedel.* In more formal writings and speeches he had a penchant for repeating favorite words and phrases. Thus, in his memoirs dictated in 1924, in his second book (written in 1928), and in conversations recorded in 1934 and 1943 he spoke repeatedly of "The Holy Grail of the German Blood" and referred to the Jews as the "Ferment of Decomposition."[29]

As a youth in Vienna, he promised himself that one day he would write a great political work and designed the cover for it. It was adorned with a swastika, with the author's name given as it would appear so often in the future: "A. Hitler." The actual book, written years later, went through many editions, but Hitler could not bring himself to change it. A careful analysis of all the German editions of *Mein Kampf* shows that Hitler permitted his publishers to make only minor changes to correct grammatical mistakes.[30]

Intimates all agreed that Hitler's daily routine was followed to the smallest detail. As chancellor, when taking his dog for a walk, Hitler went through the same field every time, and each time he threw a piece of wood from exactly the same spot in exactly the same direction. Any attempt to persuade him to deviate from the pattern would result in considerable agitation and anger on his part. A boyhood friend from Linz remembers similar behavior. Adolf had the habit of returning always to the same lonely spot outside town where "every bush and tree was familiar to him."

His personal hygiene was highly routinized: he washed his hands many times every day; he brushed his atrocious teeth after every meal. He kept the same suits, raincoats, shoes, and hat year after year; he wore a necktie until it disintegrated. He listened to the same records so often that he knew the serial numbers in his vast collection by heart.

At Berchtesgaden and in the Chancellery, the noon and evening meals had a fixed seating order made out according to his written instructions. The slightest deviation from his chart would draw down his fury. The topics discussed at meals remained constant, the same subjects coming up over and over and over again. After dinner every evening before the war there were one or two movies, some of them repeated many times. At midnight there was the nightly gathering around the blazing fire, where Hitler would talk on and on about the same events from his past in a monologue which was virtually pro-grammed. His press chief of a decade described the paralyzing repeti-tion: "He remained perpetually in the same company, among the same faces, in the same atmosphere and, I may also say, in the same state of monotony and boredom, producing eternally the same speeches and declarations."

Hitler's last will and testament of April 1945 contains not one new idea. Line for line, and virtually word for word, his last official state-ment is a repetition of the program he had set forth in *Mein Kampf* and in any one of his earlier speeches. And at the end, with his Reich crashing down upon him, when an aide suggested that perhaps some things might possibly have been done differently, Adolf Hitler cried out in baffled anguish, "But don't you see, I can not change!" [31]

Feelings of Unworthiness

One of history's most ruthless rulers was beset by feelings of guilt and unworthiness. His written and spoken words reveal a preoccupation with his problem—and manage to convey at the same time that he was the special object of the Almighty's concern. He sought, for example, to quiet any doubts about his worthiness as the chosen one of God or of History by insisting that he really *was* worthy. In a speech in Munich on 22 April 1927: "The Lord gave us His blessing because we *deserved* it. . . ." Or again at Nuremberg on 16 September 1935: "God continues to bestow His Grace only on him who continues to *merit* it." And years later in the New Year's Proclamation of 1 January 1944: "The great Judge of all time . . . will always give victory to those who are the most *worthy*." And the proclamation of the next year: "I carry my heavy burdens with dutiful thanks to Providence which has deemed me *worthy*." [32]

He was often disturbed by qualms of conscience and sought to dull its demands. The only possible way "to find internal peace," he said, was to "rid the race of the *consciousness of its own guilt*." He concluded on another occasion that "*conscience* is a Jewish invention. It is a blem-ish like circumcision." His task was "freeing men from . . . the *dirty and degrading* [ideas of] *conscience* and *morality*." He insisted that Germans must learn to "distrust the intelligence and the *conscience*." His preoccupation with conscience was not limited to human beings, he was convinced that dogs too suffer from a "bad conscience." [33]

Hitler prided himself on being a hard and utterly ruthless man. Yet he worried about sin and guilt, and found that "the feeling of being *guilty* . . . paralyzes every sincere and firm decision." He fretted over "a little sinner, conscious of his *guilt*." In this respect, his memory of his trial for treason following his abortive attempt to seize power in Germany during the Beer Hall Putsch of 1923 is revealing. This politi-cal revolutionary who had sought to overthrow the Weimar Republic did not, as might be expected, recall castigating the government and his enemies or summoning his countrymen to a new social and political order. His mind was on something else: "History, as the Goddess of a higher truth and better law, will nevertheless some day laughingly tear up this verdict and *acquit us all of guilt and sin.*" [34]

Personal worries about unworthiness, guilt, and punishment were projected onto the nation. Thus, Hitler concluded that the real reason for Germany's defeat in 1918 was neither political nor military: "Germany was defeated because of her *unworthiness.*" And again, "The military defeat of the German people is not an *undeserved* catastrophe but rather a *deserved punishment* by *eternal retribution.* We more than *deserved* this defeat." [35]

The concerns that bothered him at the beginning of his political career were with him at the end. In his last New Year's proclamation to the German soldiers, on 1 January 1945, he said: "I bear this my lot with humble thanks to Providence which has considered me *worthy enough* to take on. . . . this decisive work in the history of the German people."[36]

FEARS AND OBSESSIONS

Time As an Enemy

Hitler distrusted time and tried to avoid its demands. Because he did not want to know about its passage, he sought to confuse night and day. With lights ablaze, he would stay up all night; and in the daytime, even on lovely days of brilliant sunshine, while traveling far behind the lines in his special train during the war, he insisted on drawing the curtains and turning on the lights.[37]

There was one clock in his office, an antique musical timepiece which had apparently belonged to his family; but he would never allow it to be wound up. Hitler never wore a wristwatch. Sometimes he put an old-fashioned gold watch in his jacket pocket. It had a spring-cover which concealed the face. He always seemed to forget to wind it, so that when he needed to know the time he asked others to tell him what it was.[38]

Time was an enemy he often sought to conquer by saying that an idea of his or a building he designed or anything else he approved of was the greatest "of all time." While he did not personally invent the famous sobriquet "The Greatest Field Commander of all time" [*Der grösste Feldherr aller Zeiten*], he loved the sound of the phrase and grinned like a schoolboy when he heard it applied to himself. As the

meticulous and indefatigable German editor of his speeches and proclamations has noted, the phrase "of all time" is repeated in speech
after speech.

The compulsive and deadly serious games that he played about
time—such as how fast he could dress—involved "defeating" time. Yet
Hitler never really won these games. Time was constantly coming back
to taunt him. Thus he would tell his intimates over and over, "I have
no time." He had "no time to be ill"; he had no time to tie his own tie, so
he wore pretied cravats or had one tied for him by his valet.[39]

At the end of his career, he blamed time for his defeat. "The
war came too soon," he said in one of his last soliloquies. "I did not have
the time to form people according to my politics. . . . we never have
enough time. Always conditions press down upon us and we . . . lack
time. Time always . . . works against us." [40]

Hitler never had enough time. Yet no ruler in all history wasted
more of it in pointless little trips and excursions, in being driven about
in his cars, in hours of interminable talk and twaddle. Perhaps he felt
that if he was filling up the hours with words, he was in some way
dominating or "killing" time. Certainly he was destroying it for other
people.

Constantly he tried to deceive time. Had there been any important way that time had deceived him? We should try to find out.

Death and Decapitation Motifs

Throughout his life, Hitler was infatuated with death. Even in
moments of victory, death was on his mind. At the close of the tremendous Nuremberg Party Rally of 1934, which he had billed as "The
Triumph of the Will," his thoughts turned less to triumph than to his
own death: "When my eyes are closed in death, I do not know, but the
Party will live on." And in the midst of World War II, he kept talking to
his entourage about the imminence of his own death.[41]

Hitler was captivated by the depiction of putrefaction and death in
Makart's huge canvas *Plague in Florence*, which he wanted desperately
for the museum he was planning for his hometown of Linz. When he
finally acquired the painting in 1940, a secretary reports that he
was as overjoyed as a schoolboy and clapped his hands as he exulted
over the piles of greenish yellow corpses. He had filmstrips made of
the execution of criminals and enjoyed watching them die. He also tried
to quiet fears of his own death by asserting that he had the power to
determine the death of others, saying, "I do not play at war, I command
in war. . . . I insist that *I have the right* to send the youth to their
death." [42]

Hitler hated the moon because he considered it to be dead. On a
lovely, star-filled autumnal night in 1924 while he was a prisoner at
Landsberg am Lech, he turned to his fellow inmate Rudolf Hess and

remarked: "You know, Rudi, it's only the moon I hate. For it is something dead, and terrible, and inhuman. And human beings are afraid of it. . . . It is as if in the moon a part of the terror still lives which the moon once sent down over the earth. . . . I hate it! That pale and ghostly fellow." [43]

During the 1920s, Hitler was very much interested in a young woman named Mimi Reiter—of whom more later. On his third date with her, he took her to the graveyard where her mother was buried. He stood staring down at the grave for some time and then muttered something that Miss Reiter never quite understood: "I'm not like that yet" [*Ich bin noch nicht so weit*]. Once, in a restaurant, Miss Reiter ordered her favorite food, *Wienerschnitzel*. When Hitler looked disgusted, she asked if she had done something wrong. Hitler replied: "No, go ahead and have it, but I don't understand why you want it. I didn't think you wanted to devour a corpse . . . the flesh of dead animals. Cadavers!" Many years later, Hitler still made fun of people who ate meat. He called their meat broth "corpse tea," and he told what he considered an amusing story about crayfish: A deceased grandmother had relatives who threw her body into a brook to lure the crayfish; the crayfish ate her body, and the relatives then caught and ate the crayfish. On another occasion, while a guest was dining on smoked eel, he remarked that eels were best fattened when fed with dead cats.[44]

All his life, Hitler showed unusual interest in crayfish, lobsters, and crabs, partly because *Krebs* (crabs) is the German word for cancer. He was particularly concerned about dying from cancer, the disease which had killed his mother. He talked to intimates about his fear, and was morbidly preoccupied with the disease and its cure. He was also deathly afraid of water. During a boat ride on the Tegern Lake, for example, he panicked and "seemed absolutely convinced that the boat would capsize." Typically, he insisted it was not he but the ladies who were so badly frightened they ought to return to shore.[45]

Hitler's concern about death was manifested publicly during the Third Reich. The Nazis were much more effective in staging death celebrations than they were in fêting life. Memorable ceremonies were staged at the tombs of Prussian kings, at Hindenburg's monument at Tannenburg, at memorial services for Horst Wessel, and at the annual November commemoration of the martyrs of the Beer Hall Putsch. The leitmotif of death sounded impressively at every Party rally.[46]

Major political and military decisions were determined by the Führer's fear of imminent death and concern over the passage of time. He expressed his sense of urgency when giving his reasons for running for president in 1932: "I don't have time to wait. . . . I can't lose a single year. I've got to get to power shortly to solve the gigantic problems during the time remaining for me. I have *got* to. I have *got* to." And on another occasion: "I need ten years of lawmaking. The time is short. I have not long enough to live. . . ." [47]

Hitler's decision to go to war in September 1939 was associated with his fear of getting old. He wanted to have the war while he was young enough to enjoy it. In a major speech to the commanders of his armed forces on 22 August 1939, he spoke of the need for war and the reasons why it should not be delayed: "Essentially all depends on me, on my existence, because of my political talents. . . . My existence is therefore a factor of great value. But I can be eliminated at any time by a criminal or a lunatic. No one knows how much longer I shall live. Therefore, better a conflict now." And to one of the Party leaders he confided, "You see I'm getting old and need glasses. Therefore I prefer to have this war now that I am fifty rather than at sixty." [48]

He sought to defeat death by leaving imperishable memories and monuments to his greatness. He also wished to raise a generation of young Germans who would be immune from the fear that beset their Führer: "A brutal youth. . . . They shall learn *to overcome the fear of death*. . . ." But it was really not he, Hitler insisted, who was afraid of death. "The Jews," he said, "fear death above everything else." [49]

Hitler believed that his own death would bring a continuation of fame. He was convinced, for example, that he would live on longer in memory than Napoleon: "I know how to keep my hold on people after I have passed on. I shall be the Führer they look up at and go home to talk of and remember. My life shall not end in the mere form of death. It will, on the contrary, begin then." On another occasion, he told his doctor: "I shall become the greatest man in history. I have to gain immortality even if the whole German nation perishes in the process." [50]

The idea of suicide was persistent throughout his life. As a boy, when he thought a girl had not reciprocated his love, he plotted a dual suicide with her. In 1923, during the Munich Putsch, he drew three hostages aside and said, "You must be victorious with me or die with me. If things go wrong I have four bullets in my pistol: three for my fellow workers if they desert me, and the last bullet is for me." And again when he returned to the Beer Hall: "Morning will either find a German national government in Germany or us dead." After the Party's defeats in the election of 1932, Hitler said despondently to Goebbels that "if the Party disintegrates, I'll make an end of it all within three minutes." Years later he thought back on this period of dejection and recalled, "Yes, I thought of shooting myself because there was no longer any way out for me." Another acquaintance confirmed that Hitler was terribly depressed at the beginning of 1933. "He said that he could never succeed, that everything was against him and that 'I'll put an end to my life with a bullet.' " [51]

A fragment from Hitler's conference with Wehrmacht leaders on 1 February 1943 shows Hitler's continuing concern with his own suicide, as well as the suicides of others. In the midst of an oration about cowardice among the German generals he shouted, "When one's nerves break down, there is nothing to do but say 'I can't go on' and shoot oneself." He then went back again and again to the story he had so often told of a lovely woman, "a really beautiful woman," who was insulted by her husband and told to leave. "So the woman goes off, writes a letter of farewell, and shoots herself." A few minutes later he told the story of yet another beautiful woman whose husband had died: "She said she couldn't go on living, in spite of her children. Then she shot herself. That's what a woman can do. She's got the strength and soldiers haven't." Hitler's comments about suicidal women may have reflected his experience with Eva Braun, who understood him better than most people. He had first met her in 1930 but had paid her scant attention until first in 1932 and again in 1935 she attempted to kill herself. Hitler was so impressed that he invited her to move into the Berghof. In 1938, when he became momentarily infatuated with Miss Unity Mitford, Fräulein Braun again threatened suicide and Hitler immediately restored her to favor. As we shall see, five of the six women with whom Hitler had intimate relations committed suicide—or came perilously close to doing so.[52]

Among the many childish games Adolf Hitler played was a form of substitute suicide. He disliked tying his own necktie and had his valet do it for him. Hitler made a game of it—but one that he took very seriously. He would hold his breath and count slowly to ten. If Linge could finish the knot before Hitler had finished counting, the Führer was greatly relieved.[53]

Decapitation was the form of death which particularly fascinated Hitler. He spoke often of severed heads. Not only did he make his famous promise that when he came to power "heads will roll in the sand," but a statement years before to an intimate suggests that he sometimes thought of the possibility of his own decapitation. On 24 July 1926 he confided, "My head will not roll in the sand until I have completed my mission." [54]

When Hitler flipped a coin to determine whether he should go on a picnic, heads did not win. Heads invariably lost.

When he was asked what he would do upon first landing in England, he replied without hesitation that he wanted most to see the place where Henry VIII chopped off the heads of his wives.

When Hitler designed a sort of promissory note for the Party in the mid-1920s—redeemable when he became ruler of Germany—he showed an idealized German warrior holding in his right hand a sword dripping blood, and in his left hand the severed head of a woman suspended by her blond hair. Under the picture in heavy Gothic type was printed "Warrior of the Truth, Behead the Lie." It is noteworthy that the Warrior is enjoined not to fight, not to pierce, but to decapitate the young lady.[55]

Hitler's definition of politics was one that does not seem to have occurred to Aristotle, Jefferson, Gladstone, or Lincoln: "Politics is like a harlot; if you love her unsuccessfully she bites your head off."[56]

The historic figures he particularly admired were associated in his mind with decapitation. He saw in Cromwell the foe of parliamentarianism, Communism, and Catholicism, but he particularly admired him because he had the courage to have a king beheaded. "Ah, Cromwell," he said, "that's my man. He and Henry VIII are the only two positive figures in English history." He was also greatly impressed with Frederick William I and the decapitations he ordered. He saw a film in 1923 entitled *The Life of Frederick the Great* and talked repeatedly about the scene that pictured young Prince Frederick as he was forced to watch the executioner chop off the head of his closest friend. Hitler commented "That is the way German justice should be handled: either acquittal or beheading." [57]

As soon as he became chancellor, he restored the use of the headman's ax, but his preferred method of execution seems to have been the rope. A special decree of 29 March 1933 saw to it that hanging by the neck was introduced for an exceptionally large number of cases. His own fear of strangulation was further projected onto others in the grisly orders he gave for the execution of generals who had conspired against him in the plot of 20 July 1944. He ordered that each man be "hung on a meathook and slowly strangled to death with piano wire, the pressure being periodically released to intensify his death agonies." Hitler had a color film made of the scene. He "loved the film and had it shown over and over again; it became one of his favorite entertainments." [58]

Hitler was infatuated with the Medusa. He once expressed great enthusiasm for the mosaic Medusa head in the rotunda of the University of Munich, and one of his favorite paintings was by Franz von Stuck, a sinister, flashing-eyed Medusa which he had first seen in a book in Hanfstaengl's house. When he designed his gigantic desk for the Chancellery, three heads adorned the front panels. One was of the Medusa, with writhing snakes emerging from her hair.[59]

Freud believed that men who are fascinated with decapitation and the legend of the Medusa's head are expressing castration anxiety in a disguised form. As we shall see, Hitler showed his own concern about loss of testicles in many other indirect ways. But he also talked explicitly about it. He told the French ambassador, for example, that the Poles were castrating German citizens. And he tried to persuade the League of Nations' representative in Danzig that the Nazi press was attempting to tone down stories of Polish atrocities: "No one believes me about this, but I have ordered that the sensational cases, such as *castration*, should not be mentioned in the press. They excite public opinion too much." [60]

Blood

Just as primitive tribes attribute magical significance to blood, so did Hitler. He was sure, for example, that all of human history was explicable in its terms and, in one of his messier metaphors, observed that "blood is the cement of civilization." His theory greatly simplified the historical problem of explaining the rise and fall of cultural life on earth. Everything depended upon one factor alone: the purity or impurity of blood.

He used the word often in describing his rise to power. He promised that his opponents would "drown in a bloodbath"; he spoke of the sacred "Blood Flag" of 9 November 1923; he established a special "Blood Order" for those who had marched on that day. He also introduced the idea of *Blutkitt* (blood cement) in training his elite guard, the SS. He seems to have come across the idea in reading a book about Genghis Khan while a prisoner in Landsberg in 1924—though he may have heard that it was also practiced in Egypt and in Renaissance murder societies. (Similar techniques have been employed by the Mau Mau and the Manson cultists.) The idea, briefly, is this: in order to enforce absolute loyalty and obedience, organizers of terror societies force a prospective member, as part of his initiation rite, to commit an act which directly and flagrantly violates his most important personal taboos. Such an atrocity, by cutting the initiate off from society and from his previous value system, ties him irrevocably to the new organization because it is the only group which sponsors and approves the outrage he has perpetrated. In psychological terms, the traumatic act he has been obliged to commit reinforces his newly acquired superego, his value system, his new conscience.

In Hitler's Germany, medical doctors of the SS were required to perform, or to watch, "medical experiments" such as skin grafts and abdominal surgery on the unanesthetized bodies of Jewish or Polish "patients." Other initiates of the SS were forced to kill Jewish babies before the eyes of their mothers. Hitler's theory was that after members of his SS had participated in such activity, they would feel drawn together by the bonds of a common experience. The technique seems to have worked rather well.*

---

* The process of acquiescing to atrocity through participation in it is well illustrated in the experience of Professor Doctor Hans Hermann Kramer, who had a distinquished medical career and was chairman of the medical faculty at the University of Münster before joining the SS. One of his first assignments as an SS doctor at Auschwitz was to observe what was euphemistically called a *Sonderaktion* (a "Special Action"), a method of mass execution. Prisoners, especially mothers and their babies, were customarily thrown alive into pits measuring 20 by 40 meters on piles of wood soaked in gasoline. The piles were then ignited. When Dr. Kramer experienced his first *Sonderaktion* he found the experience shattering: "Awful. . . . Dante's Inferno. . . . I cannot stand it." But his diary indicates that after repeated performances he was able to take them in stride and indeed could discuss them with equanimity. "*September 6, 1942:* Today, Sunday, excellent lunch: tomato soup, half a hen with potatoes and red cabbage . . . sweets and marvelous vanilla ice. . . . In the evening at 8 o'clock outside for a *Sonderaktion*. . . . *September 23, 1942:* Sixth and seventh *Sonderaktion*. . . . In the evening at 20:00 hours . . . a real banquet. We had pike . . . good coffee, excellent beer and rolls" (Elie A. Cohen, *Human Behavior in the Concentration Camp* (New York, 1953), 236 and *passim*.)

Blood also played a very important role in Hitler's private life. Apparently he thought a great deal about drinking and sucking blood. He wondered, for example, what the blood soup of the ancient Frisians tasted like; in commenting on the history of the world as the chronic warfare of one people against another, he said, "One creature *drinks the blood* of another. The death of one nourishes the other." And he wrote that the Jew was a spider which "*sucked the people's blood* out of its pores."

He liked to have his own blood drawn from his body, and enjoyed telling his secretaries what fun it was to watch leaches as they sucked it out. When one of them shuddered and said she didn't like the looks of the horrible animals, he stopped her by saying, "Don't say that. They're sweet little, dear little animals who have done me a great deal of good." He also had his doctor, Morrell, draw his blood and save it in test tubes so that he could gaze at it. Was he afraid that there was something wrong with his own blood?

He liked to taunt members of his intimate circle when he saw them eating meat. Referring to Morell's collection of the Führer's own blood, he said, "I will have blood sausage made from my excess blood as a special culinary treat for you. Why not? You like meat so much." He repeated the offer.[61a]

Hitler's great concern about infected blood was manifested in dozens of political speeches and was the underlying reason for the Nuremberg Racial Laws, which he called "The Laws for the Protection of German Blood and German Honor." He personally supervised the wording of the text. His private and public speeches are redolent with metaphors of disease, blood poisoning, illness, tuberciles, spirochetes, and microbes. Toward the end of February 1942, just after the Wannsee Conference which organized the "final solution" to the Jewish problem, Hitler listed himself among the great benefactors of mankind who had isolated dangerous disease germs: "The discovery of the Jewish virus is one of the greatest revolutions that has ever taken place. The fight we are carrying on is of the same nature as that waged by Pasteur and Koch during the last century. How many diseases have their origin in Jewish virus! . . . We shall only retain our health when we eliminate the Jew." [62]

Of all the infections to which mortal flesh is prone, Hitler most feared—and was most fascinated by—syphilis. As a young man he talked about the disease by the hour.[63] Years later, when he wrote his memoirs, he devoted page after passionate page to the evil power of the disease, insisting that it was the true reason for Germany's defeat in 1918 and proclaiming that the struggle against syphilis was the most important single task confronting statesmen. In reaching for the worst epithet he could hurl at the Weimar Republic, he accused it of surrendering the German nation "to syphilization" by Jews and Negroes.[64]

Cleanliness and Purity

Hitler often talked about dirt. People he disliked were usually described as being filthy. Thus the schoolteachers who gave him unsatisfactory grades had "*filthy* necks and uncared for beards"; modern artists sat on "the *dung-heap* of literary Dadaism"; and liberals were "*dirty* and false." To democrats he would say, "Out with you, cowardly wretch! Step back, you are *soiling* the steps." The Jews were particularly filthy: "The smell of these caftan wearers often made me ill. Added to this were their *dirty* clothes . . . and physical *uncleanliness.* . . . Was there any form of *filth* . . . in which at least one Jew did not participate? When carefully cutting open such a growth one could find a little Jew, blinded by the sudden light, like a *maggot* in a rotting corpse. . . . If the Jews were alone in this world they would suffocate . . . in *dirt* and *filth.*" Hitler used the same kind of word in speaking of the Jewish people, *Entjudung* (de-Jewing), as one would use in speaking of delousing or fumigation.[65]

Hitler was a scrupulously, indeed compulsively, clean person. His boyhood friend recalls that during their Vienna days "even more than from hunger, he suffered from a lack of cleanliness, as he was almost pathologically sensitive about anything concerning the body. At all costs, he would keep his linen and clothing clean." As Führer and chancellor, he washed his hair every day, scrubbed his hands very often, brushed his teeth and rinsed his mouth after every meal. He shaved twice a day and never used after-shave lotion or scent. He told a British journalist that when he was poor in Vienna he had resolved that someday he would be rich enough to have two luxuries: an open fireplace in every room and to change his shirt twice a day. His well-tailored shirts were generally made of white silk.[66]

Food and Drink

Throughout his life, Hitler seemed inordinately concerned about food. His speeches on foreign policy repeatedly demanded new sources of food supply; private conversations were often devoted to lengthy homilies on healthy foods; his library contained a dozen books on special diets. He told his dentist that a particular kind of noxious bacteria infected his colon and hoped that a regimen of special food would destroy it.[67]

He may have become a vegetarian to clean up a chronic stomach disorder, but he gave a whole variety of other reasons for avoiding meat. He told one doctor that he had been a vegetarian since early youth, but to others he said that prior to 1931 he had eaten large quantities of meat, particularly fat pork. His secretary also gives the year 1931 as the beginning of his vegetarian diet, saying that after the suicide of his beloved niece, Geli, he found meat repulsive. He confided to others, however, that all his life he had been plagued by excessive perspiration and had discovered as a young man that when he ate no meat there was a great improvement: he did not sweat so much, and there were fewer stains on his underwear. He was also convinced that eating vegetables improved the odors of his flatulence —a condition which bothered him a great deal.

Hitler also believed that a vegetable diet would prolong his life and increase his stamina. Elephants, he observed, lived longer than lions; horses outrun dogs, who get tired, pant, and drool. Then, too, Wagner had been a vegetarian, and Hitler announced: "I don't touch meat largely because of what Wagner says on the subject." [68]

Only rarely did he drink wine or beer, and never stronger spirits. As he testified at his trial in 1924, "I am almost a complete teetotaler and only take a swallow of water or beer because of the dryness of my throat." After he became prominent, he had a special dark beer of less than 2 percent alcohol content especially brewed for him in the Holzkirchen Brewery of rural Bavaria. [69]

Wolves

Among his other obsessions, Hitler was fascinated with wolves. As a boy he was well pleased with his first name, noting that it came from the old German "Athalwolf"—a compound of Athal ("noble") and Wolfa ("wolf"). And "noble wolf" he sought to remain. At the start of his political career he chose "Herr Wolf" as his pseudonym. His favorite dogs were Alsatians—in German *Wolfshunde*. One of Blondi's pups, born towards the end of the war, he called "Wolf" and would allow no one else to touch or feed it. He named his headquarters in France *Wolfsschlucht* (Wolf's Gulch). In the Ukraine his headquarters were *Werwolf* (Man Wolf), and in East Prussia *Wolfsschanze* (Wolf's Lair)—as he explained to a servant, "I am the Wolf and this is my den." He called his SS "My pack of wolves." Later he would recall with exaltation how in the early days of the movement his Storm Troopers pounced upon the opposition "like wolves" and were soon "covered with blood."

In an article in his party newspaper written in 1922, Hitler used an unusual metaphor to describe how the crowds began to react to him: they began to realize, he said, "that now *a wolf has been born*, destined to burst in upon the herd of seducers and deceivers of the people." He had his sister Paula change her name to Frau Wolf. The special agent he chose to supervise purchases for his Linz Library and Museum was a Dr. Wolfhardt (literally, "hard wolf"). He approved of naming the Volkswagen factory "Wolfsburg."

When he telephoned Winifred Wagner, he would say, "Conductor Wolf calling!" The secretary he kept longer than any other (more than

20 years) was Johanna Wolf. She recalled that while Hitler addressed all other secretaries formally as "Frau" or "Fräulein," he invariably called her "Wölfin" (She-Wolf). One of his favorite tunes came from a Walt Disney movie. Often and absent-mindedly he whistled "Who's Afraid of the Big Bad Wolf?"—an animal, it will be recalled, who wanted to eat people up and blow their houses down.[70]

Why this infatuation with wolves? Was Hitler trying to submerge feelings of inadequacy and dependence by creating a counterimage of himself as the lone wolf—tough, independent, resourceful, cunning, remorseless, and strong? Were there other reasons why, throughout his life, he was so attracted to wolves? We shall return to the question in later chapters.

HITLER AS RELIGIOUS LEADER

Since Hitler saw himself as a Messiah with a divine mission to save Germany from the incarnate evil of "International Jewry," it is not surprising that he likened himself to Jesus. On one occasion during the 1920s, as he lashed about him with the whip he habitually carried, he said that "in driving out the Jews I remind myself of Jesus in the temple." At another time he said, "Just like Christ, I have a duty to my own people. . . ."

At a Christmas celebration in 1926 he thought it appropriate to compare his own historical importance favorably with that of Jesus. Christ had changed the dating of history; so would Hitler, for his final victory over the Jews would mark the beginning of a new age in the history of the world. "What Christ began," he observed, he, Hitler, "would complete." And in a speech on 10 February 1933 he parodied the Lord's Prayer in promising that under him a new kingdom would come on earth, and that his would be "the power and the glory, Amen." He added that if he did not fulfill his mission, "you should then crucify me."[71]

He liked to remind his followers that a turning point in his life came in 1919, when he undertook his mission. He told an aide that during the preceding autumn, as he lay wounded in a military hospital, he had received a supernatural vision which commanded him to save Germany. And through the years he came back repeatedly to stress the importance of the year 1919. In a speech to the commanding generals of the Wehrmacht on 23 November 1939, he began two paragraphs with the same idea:

When I began my political work in 1919 I based it. . . .

27

The first resolution was made in 1919 when, after long internal struggles, I became a politician and took up the battle against my enemy.

Manifestly the date was important to Hitler. He was at that time 30 years old—the same age another Messiah is reported to have begun his mission to save mankind.

That he saw himself as the special agent of God and identified with Him was made manifest on many occasions:

> I go the way that Providence dictates for me with all the assurance of a sleepwalker.
>
> —Speech of 14 March 1936, Munich

> God has created this people and it has grown according to His will. And according to *our* will [*nach unserem Willen*] it shall remain and never shall it pass away.
>
> —Speech of 31 July 1937, Breslau

> I believe that it was God's will that from here [Austria] a boy was sent into the Reich and that he grew up to become the leader of the nation.
>
> —Speech of 9 April 1938, Vienna [72]

Hitler did not like to be told that the ways of God were not always revealed to him. On one occasion an aide noted that "God does not let people look at the cards He holds" [*Der liebe Gott lässt sich nicht in seine Karten sehen*]. Hitler immediately broke forth into such a paroxysm of fury that he himself feared a heart attack. He gave orders that the aide never repeat the offensive phrase.[73]

The feeling that he was being specially guided from on high grew more intense through the years. On 16 September 1935 he said, "What was denied to millions of men was given to us by Providence, and our work will be still remembered by the last members of posterity." In a speech in his hometown of Linz, 12 March 1938: "When I once departed from this city, I carried with me the very same confession of faith that fills me today. . . . If Providence once then called me from out of this city . . . then Providence must thereby have given me a mission. . . ."[74]

His convictions were reinforced by miraculous escapes from assassination. After the failure of the bomb plot of 20 July 1944 he told a naval aide, "Now the Almighty has stayed their [assassins'] hands once more. Don't you agree that I should consider it as a nod of Fate that it intends to preserve me for my assigned task." His valet remembers that Hitler was very calm, saying, "That is new proof that I have been selected from among other men by Providence to lead greater Germany to victory." And again, "Because I have been saved while others had to die, it is clearer than ever that the fate of Germany lies in my hands." [75]

His version of human history was essentially one of religious mythology. He believed that a pure German people had lived in an early Garden of Eden. But this pure race had been attacked by the Devil, made incarnate in the form of the Jew. Indeed, he said explicitly that "the Jew is the personification of the Devil and of all evil." And thus he reached his conclusion that in fighting the Devil he was doing the work of Almighty God. In Hitler's theology, a different original sin replaced the one committed in the biblical Garden of Eden. "The mixture of the races is the original sin [*Erbsünde*] of this world," he claimed. "The sins against blood and race are the original sins of this world." He thought of World War II in eschatological terms, and saw himself as the commander of the forces of good standing at Armageddon and battling the forces of Satan. "Often it seems to me as if we are all being tested by the Devil and Satan, and we must pass through Hell together until we finally obtain ultimate victory."

He did not view the Party and the Reich merely as secular organizations. "I consider those who establish or destroy a religion much greater than those who establish a State, to say nothing of founding a Party," he had written in *Mein Kampf*. And years later he told his followers, "We are not a movement, rather we are a religion." [76]

The institutional pattern he used for creating his New Order was the Roman Catholic Church, which had so greatly impressed him. As a boy he had dreamed of being an abbot. When he became Führer, however, he raised his sights and saw himself as a political Pope with an apostolic succession. He announced to a closed meeting of the faithful in the Brown House during 1930: "I hereby set forth for myself and my successors in the leadership of the Party the claim of political infallibility. I hope the world will grow as accustomed to that claim as it has to the claim of the Holy Father."

He also fancied himself as a religious leader of the non-Christian world he planned to conquer. "I'm going to become a religious figure. Soon I'll be the great chief of the Tartars. Already Arabs and Moroccans are mingling my name with their prayers." [77]

Hitler saw striking parallels between his Ministry of Propaganda and Enlightenment and the Church's Congregation for the Propaganda of the Faith (*Congregatio de Propaganda Fide*). He remarked that his task was not to communicate knowledge "but holy conviction and unconditional faith." He viewed the 25 articles of his Party as "the dogma of our faith" and the "rock" upon which the Party was built. [78] Hitler's proclamation of the "Thousand Year Reich" has religious resonance. He was also fond of speaking of the "inseparable Trinity" of State, Movement, and *Volk*. As the sign and symbol of his movement Hitler chose a special type of cross, and personally modified the design of this *Hakenkreuz*.

The colossal Assembly Hall planned for his new capital of Germania should be seen as a secular cathedral rather than a civic building. The dome was to be large enough to encompass the Dome of St. Peter's seven times—a favorite number. As Albert Speer has noted, "It was basically a hall of worship. . . . without such cult significance the motivation for Hitler's main structure would have been senseless and unintelligible." [79]

In reminiscing about the institutions and ideas that had influenced him, Hitler said that he had learned a great deal from Marxist terrorism, from the Protocols of the Elders of Zion, and from the Freemasons. But, he concluded, "Above all, I have learned from the Jesuit order." Certainly the oath of direct obedience to the Führer was strikingly reminiscent of the special oath that Jesuits swear to the Pope. Moreover, Hitler spoke of his elite SS, who wore the sacred symbol and dressed in black, as his Society of Jesus. He also ordered SS officers to study the *Spiritual Exercises* of Ignatius of Loyola for training in the rigid discipline of the faith. [80]

The close parallel between commitment to God and the sacred oath of allegiance to Hitler is seen in a description of public oath-taking recorded in the Nazi newspaper *Westdeutscher Beobachter*:

> Yesterday witnessed the profession of the religion of the blood in all its imposing reality . . . whoever has sworn his oath of allegiance to Hitler has pledged himself unto death to this sublime idea. [81]

The bolts of excommunication and anathema which Hitler hurled against nonbelievers and heretics were not unlike those of a Gregory VII:

> Woe to them who do not believe. These people have sinned . . . *sinned* against all of life . . . it is a miracle of faith that Germany has been saved. Today more than ever it is the duty of the Party to remember this National Socialist confession of faith [*Glaubensbekenntnis*] and to bear it forward as our holy [*heiliges*] sign of our battle and our victory. [82]

The Nazis, like the Catholics, had their prophets, saints, and martyrs. The Führer sanctified his disciples who fell during the Beer Hall Putsch when he said, in dedicating their memorial, that their death would bring forth "a true belief in the resurrection of their people . . . the blood that they shed becomes the baptismal water of the Third Reich." [83]

Hitler's holy reliquary was the Brown House, containing the sacred Blood Flag which had been borne by the martyrs of 9 November 1923. It was Hitler and Hitler alone who could perform the priestly ritual of touching the Blood Flag to the standards of the Brown Shirts.

The Image and the Man

Hitler substituted Nazi high holy days for traditional religious holidays. The Nazi holidays included 30 January, the day he came to power in the year he referred to as "the holy year of our Lord 1933," and 20 April, his own birthday and the day when the Hitler Youth were confirmed in their faith. The holiest day, and the one which served as a kind of Nazi Good Friday, was 9 November, celebrated as the Blood Witness [*Blutzeuge*] of the movement.

Hitler also provided the holy scriptures for his new religion, and *Mein 'Kampf*, instead of the Bible, took the place of honor in the homes of thousands of German families. With a lack of humor typical of the regime, the Nazis chose this title to replace the prayer book as the appropriate wedding gift for young couples.

The parallel between Hitler and the Messiah was made explicit in German schools. On 16 March 1934 children wrote out the following dictation approved by Hitler's Ministry of Enlightenment and Propaganda:

> Jesus and Hitler. As Jesus freed men from sin and Hell, so Hitler freed the German people from destruction. Jesus and Hitler were persecuted, but while Jesus was crucified Hitler was raised to the Chancellorship. . . . Jesus strove for Heaven, Hitler for the German earth.

The League of German Girls developed a new version of the Lord's Prayer which was a supplication not only *for* the Führer but *to* him as a deity:

> Adolf Hitler, you are our great Leader. Thy name makes the enemy tremble. Thy Third Reich comes, thy will alone is law upon earth. Let us hear daily thy voice and order us by thy leadership, for we will obey to the end even with our lives. We praise thee! Heil Hitler! [84]

And smaller children were taught to use this grace before meals:

> Führer, my Führer, sent to me from God, protect and maintain me throughout my life. Thou who hast saved Germany from deepest need, I thank thee today for my daily bread. Remain at my side and never leave me, Führer, my Führer, my faith, my light. Heil my Führer! [85]

Hitler's disciples seem to have been less successful in their efforts to popularize these new words for the favorite Christmas hymn of the German people:

> Silent night! Holy night!
> All is calm. All is bright.

Only the Chancellor steadfast in fight
Watches o'er Germany by day and by night
Always caring for us.

Silent night! Holy night!
All is calm. All is bright.
Adolf Hitler is Germany's wealth,
Brings us greatness, favor and health.
Oh, give us Germans all power! [86]

In public speech and private soliloquy, and in ways in which he may not have been aware, Hitler himself spoke the very words of Christ and the scriptures. In talking to his Brown Shirts on 30 January 1936 he echoed the words of Jesus to his disciples as recorded in St. John's Gospel, saying, "I have come to know thee. Who thou art, thou art through me and all I am I am through thee." He reminded one of his disciples that "I have come to Germany not to bring peace but a sword." In a public speech in Graz in 1938 he used the words of Jesus as recorded by Matthew when he announced that Almighty God had created the Nation, "and what the Lord has joined together let not Man set asunder." [87]

He was particularly prone to Biblical quotations when talking to his Hitler Youth. On 5 September 1934 he told them, "You are flesh of our flesh and blood of our blood." In 1932 he advised them either to be "hot or cold, but lukewarm should be damned and spewed from your mouth." [88] The phrasing is too close to the New Testament to be coincidental. The Book of Revelation (3:15–16) reads:

I know thy works. Thou art neither cold nor hot; I would thou wert cold or hot. So then because thou art lukewarm, and neither cold nor hot, I will spew thee out of my mouth.

He was fond of calling for a faith that could move mountains, saying on 31 January 1935, "If you had not had faith, who could have led thee? Faith can remove mountains, can free also nations." And in May of the same year, speaking about faith, he reminded the faithful, "It is the strength which in the end can remove the mountains of resistance!" *

During one of his last suppers with his followers when he invited them to partake of their Leader's body by eating blood sausage made from his own blood, was he not saying, "Take, eat: this is my body which is broken for you . . ."?

---

* He apparently had never learned the second part of the quotation from Paul's letter to the Christians at Corinth: "And though I have the gift of prophecy and understand all mysteries and all knowledge; and though I have all faith to remove mountains, and have not love, I am nothing" (1 Corinthians 13:2).

A MAN OF CONTRASTS

Hitler was a person of contrasts, a man of dualities who thought and spoke in disjunctives. Anybody accused of crime should either be acquitted or beheaded; "the only choice," he said, "is between life and death, victory or destruction, glory or ignominy. . . . We shall be conquering heroes or sacrificial lambs." The battle against the Jews, he predicted, could end "either with the victory of the Aryan side or its annihilation and victory of the Jews." Or again, "One is either a hammer or an anvil." A person either followed him blindly or was a traitor. A leader could be either brutal and hard as steel or as soft and weak as a woman. There was absolutely no other alternative.[89]

The urbane and perceptive French ambassador André François-Poncet was fascinated by the dual nature of the person he visited so often: "The same man, good-natured in appearance and sensitive to the beauties of nature, who, across a tea table, expressed reasonable opinions on European politics, was capable of the wildest frenzies, the most savage exaltation and the most delirious ambition." [90]

Creation and Destruction

The constant battle within him between the opposing forces of destruction and creativity was brought into particularly sharp focus during a conversation prior to the war with Professor Burckhardt, the League of Nations representative for Danzig. Burckhardt had asked for an interview in an effort to achieve a peaceful settlement of the Polish problem. At one moment Hitler shook with rage, crashed his fists against table and walls, and screamed in a voice cracking with fury, "If the slightest incident occurs I will smash the Poles without warning, so that not a trace of Poland will ever be found. I'll smash them like lightning with the full power of a mechanized army. . . ." Then he suddenly stopped, turned to look pensively out the window at the glorious Alps, and observed quietly, "How fortunate I am when I am here. I have worked hard enough. Now I need a rest. . . . Oh, how gladly would I stay here and work as an artist. I am an artist, you know." Years later, in the midst of war, he mused, "Wars come and go. What remains is only the values bestowed by culture. Hence my love of art, music, and architecture—are they not the powers which point the way for future humanity?" [91]

Albert Speer has described the constant conflict between destruction and creation, observing in his memoirs that he concentrated on Hitler's architecture "not only because it was my field but because I believe at least one pregnant clue to this strange man lies there. It was not his avocation; it was his obsession. And long before the end I knew that Hitler was not destroying to build, he was building to destroy." [92]

Thoughts of death and destruction kept intruding on plans for creation. In setting forth grandiose plans for magnificent stone buildings greater than the pyramids, and while proclaiming that he was "building for all eternity," he felt compelled to add a note of finality and death: "We are the last Germany. If we should ever go down, then there will no longer be a Germany." In planning the colossal Assembly Hall in Nuremberg, he included in his sketches one showing what the building would look like as a ruin.[93]

The life-long interplay between destruction and creativity is seen vividly during the last days. He spent his 56th and last birthday, 20 April 1945, working until 3 o'clock in the morning on plans for the "greater Linz" which he had fussed over for many years. But during this same period he also called forth an orgy of destruction. Farms and woodlands were to be burned, cattle slaughtered. Works of art, monuments, palaces, castles, churches, theatres—all were to be obliterated. The idea is conveyed clearly in an editorial which, at Hitler's express command, appeared in the Party organ *Völkischer Beobachter* on 7 September 1944: "Not a German stock of wheat is to feed the enemy, not a German mouth to give him information, not a German hand to offer him help. He is to find . . . nothing but death, annihilation and hatred." [94]

Psychologists have noted that fire is an expressive symbol of destruction, "admirably suited to the venting of aggressive, destructive tendencies." Hitler was fascinated by fire. He said that he would like to have a fireplace in every room of his house. The nightly conversations at the Berghof were held, summer and winter, in front of a gigantic fire which Hitler tended himself. He "delighted in throwing fresh logs on the roaring flames."

He worked himself into a frenzy of delight over the pictures of great capitals of Europe in flames. In 1939 he reveled in a newsreel of the bombing and burning of Warsaw, crying ecstatically to an intimate, "That is how we will annihilate them!" In 1940 he was delighted with pictures of the burning of London and the prospects of destroying it totally. "Have you ever looked at a map of London?" he gloated. "It's so closely built up that one source of fire alone would suffice to destroy the whole city, as happened once before, 200 years ago. Göring wants to use innumerable incendiary bombs of an altogether new type to create sources of fire in all parts of London. Fires everywhere. Thousands of them. Then they'll unite in one gigantic area of conflagration. Explosive bombs don't work, but it can be done with incendiary bombs—total destruction of London. What use will their fire department be once that really starts!" He was, it will be recalled, furious with the commandant of Paris for not setting that city afire; he kept sending the famous interrogatory telegram, "Is Paris burning?" Hitler also associated death with fire, once remarking that the best way to die would be to be burned in one's own home, which would make, he said, "a magnificent funeral pyre." As we shall see, however, his efforts to have his own body consumed by fire were notably less than magnificent.[95]

Honesty and Duplicity

Hitler had a double image of his own integrity. He considered himself an honest and straightforward man who would, for example, abide by treaties "blindly and faithfully"; but he also saw himself as a clever dissimulator who could "fool people" into believing anything and who was, he said, "the greatest actor in Europe." Playing this role, he confided that "Treaties will be honored only as long as they are useful. . . . Treaties exist for the purpose of being broken at the most convenient moment." [96]

In August 1939, when it was suggested to him by a Swedish emissary that the British, after their long experience with his broken word, might not believe his promises with regard to Poland, Hitler was horrified at the thought. He stopped his pacing, turned in hurt surprise and cried, "Idiots! Have I ever in my entire life ever told a lie?" [97]

The question must be answered affirmatively. During the Blood Purge of June 1934, he had ordered the murder of hundreds of people he suspected of opposing him. But two years later in a public speech he said:

> I must make here the solemn declaration: On the road of our movement there lies not one single opponent whom we have murdered!

Repeatedly he gave his "sacred word" to Germany and the world: he had "no intention of threatening anyone"; he had "no territorial demands to make in Europe"; he had no intention whatever of "interfering in the internal affairs of Austria or of annexing Austria"; he swore that "peace will never be broken by us"; he would personally guarantee "the inviolability" of all his neighbors' territory. "That is not a phrase," he said, "that is our sacred will." [98]

One reason he felt obliged to insist so stridently that he was an honest man may have been that he was aware of his own propensity to prevaricate. He admitted as much in a revealing comment at the beginning of a speech he gave in Berlin on 10 September 1943. He broke a long silence after the catastrophe of Stalingrad by saying:

> Freed from the heavy burden of expectation weighing on us for a long time, I now consider that the moment has come again to address myself to the German people *without having to resort to lies, either to myself or to the public.*[99]

He lied for tactical reasons, but he also lied, gratuitously, over matters of little apparent importance. He gave, for example, many different versions of the time and occasion when he stopped smoking. He told his secretaries that as a young boy he smoked "a long porcelain pipe ... like a chimney ... even in bed," but had given it up at an early age. To others, however, he confided that he had not quit smoking until years later when, in Vienna as a young man, it occurred to him that money spent on tobacco might be better invested in food. But he also said on another occasion that he quit smoking in 1922 because he was afraid that it would impair the quality of his speaking voice.[100]

His entourage knew how much he delighted in reading Karl May and other novelists he recommended, but he said, "I never read a novel. That kind of reading annoys me." [101]

Hitler's memory was incredibly precise. But curiously he forgot —or failed to tell the truth about—generally known facts of his personal life. A long letter of 29 November 1921 contains patent inaccuracies about his family, describing his father, for example, as a "postal official" when actually he had been a career customs inspector. Years later, in the *Tischgespräche*, Hitler's father was made out to be a local judge.

Hitler's father and mother—and their ancestors, as far as we can tell—were born in Austria and were citizens of the Austrian or Austro-Hungarian Empire. Hitler, on at least two occasions, tried to give a different impression. In a public speech on 22 February 1933 in Forscheim, Bavaria, he told his audience, "I myself by my descent, my birth, and family am a Bavarian ... for the first time since the founding of the Reich the inheritance of Bismarck is in the hands of a Bavarian [*eines Bayern*]." In front of leading English and German diplomats who knew better, on 23 September 1938 in Bad Godesberg, he attempted to persuade Neville Chamberlain that he too was Anglo-Saxon, saying that since his own ancestors "came from Lower Saxony [*Nieder sachsen*]" he and the British prime minister could perhaps "claim common ancestry." [102]

Why did Hitler feel it necessary to dissimulate about his family ancestry?

Realism and Fantasy

Hitler was a hard-headed pragmatist with a remarkable capacity to deal effectively with the realities of political life; he was also a person who lived in a fantastic dream world. When as a boy he dreamed of rebuilding his hometown, his plans became reality for him. As his only friend and confidant of those years recalled, "Hitler lived so much in his vision of the future Linz that he adapted his day-to-day habits to it; for instance he would visit the 'Hall of Fame,' the 'Memorial Temple' or our 'medieval open-air museum.'" As a teenager he fell in love with a girl named Stefanie. Although she never knew that he existed, he built a villa for her—in his fantasy—and furnished it with infinite care. He was particularly concerned about the placement of the piano in the music room and the shape of the vases in the halls.

Years later, he had other building fantasies, even beyond those described by Speer. Another admirer recalled that shortly after the invasion of Norway in 1940 he made plans to convert the fjords into a colossal resort with mile upon mile of public baths and playgrounds. The swimming pools of the fjords, he said, must be "the high point in the bath life of the future of Europe." There the most beautiful women on the continent would swim, sunbathe, dance, and play. Power coming from hydroelectric sources in Norway would light the huge resort area during the short Northern days and warm the glass-enclosed swimming pools. Although his architect, Dr. Fritz Todt, was then in the midst of important war plans, Hitler insisted that he stop to draw up detailed plans for the entire area. He was also told to build huge bridges to connect the resort with the *Reichsautobahn*.[103]

Hitler's extraordinary capacity for self-deception is illustrated in his fantasy about one of the greatest turning points of his political career. In his memoirs, and in a dozen midnight reveries, he lingered lovingly over what he believed to be the triumphant reception of his first important political speech in the Munich Hofbräuhaus on 24 February 1920. He recalled vividly his anxiety before that important event, asserting that he personally planned the whole affair with great care and that he converted and captivated a hostile audience. It was this night that proved him an orator and mover of men. A great personal victory, it was also the most important meeting in the history of the struggling little German Workers' Party. Hitler chose this event as a fitting close for the first volume of his memoirs: "I was confronted by . . . people united by a new conviction, a new faith, a new will. . . . A fire had been lighted, and out of its flames there was bound to come some day the sword which was to regain the freedom of the Germanic Siegfried and the life of the German nation. And side by side with the coming rise, I sensed that there walked the Goddess of Inexorable Revenge. . . . Thus the hall became slowly empty. The movement took its course." [104]

That Hitler's fantasy does not at all jibe with historical fact has been carefully documented. The main speaker that night was not Hitler at all, but a Dr. Dingfelder; Hitler's name was not even mentioned in Party advertisements announcing the meeting. The *Völkischer Beobachter* was less than enthusiastic about the future Führer's efforts: only one sentence on an inside page was given to his speech. Moreover, it was the hated Marxists who prevailed that night. As the jubilant, singing crowd left the meeting, the Platzl reverberated to the sound of the *Internationale*.[105]

Such is the "historical truth" of the matter—yet it might be noted that a more important historical truth is the reality of Hitler's fantasies about himself. He believed in them, and his beliefs altered the course of history.

After he became chancellor, the worlds of fantasy and reality continued to interconnect in his life and in the life of the Third Reich. He himself sometimes became confused by his own fantasies and experienced difficulty in separating them from reality. In a highly revealing statement he confided to his doctors: "I suffer from tormenting self-deception." [106]

Toward the end, the images he had created of himself grew stronger than reality and destroyed him. The self-proclaimed worker of miracles was required to produce the miracles. And with frantic intensity he applied his mind and his will to the problem. Thus he convinced himself that Roosevelt's death in April 1945 meant the salvation of Germany; or that British war prisoners would volunteer to fight with the Nazis against the Russians in an "Anti-Bolshevik Legion." It became an article of his faith that the Russians in April 1945 were on the verge of collapse, and that Churchill and Roosevelt would join him against the U.S.S.R.[107]

As we shall later see, when the military miracles he conjured up failed to appear, he summoned forth one final illusion of supernatural omnipotence and ended his terrestrial life.

Courage and Cowardice

Hitler was both a brave man and a coward. As a private first-class (*Gefreiter*) during World War I, he had won, and deserved to win, the Iron Cross, both first and second class. Yet fear was one of the driving emotions of this man who spoke so often of courage. The world to Hitler was devil-filled and threatened at any moment to undo him. Anyone with the stamina to read the entire *Tischgespräche* can list a whole catalog of people who evoked fear and apprehension in the Führer. They included priests, hunters, Jews, liberals, journalists, Communists, Freemasons, judges, Jehovah's Witnesses, academics, Poles, meat eaters, Frenchmen, poets, Englishmen, cigarette smokers, Americans, and skiers. There was, finally, innate peril rooted in man himself: human beings could never be trusted.

Thus, everywhere he looked there was cause for apprehension:

Nothing is anchored anymore, nothing is rooted in our spiritual life anymore. Everything is superficial, fleeing past us. Restlessness and haste mark the thinking of our people. The whole of life is being torn completely apart. . . .

As one German writer has observed, "It is legitimate to ask whether any practical politician of stature has ever expressed convictions of this kind as frequently and as emphatically." [108]

In addition to all the threats that encompassed Germany, there were others that beset him personally. He was frightened by all manner of germs, by water, by moonlight, and by horses—although he loved to look at pictures and statues of stallions. He was afraid that his body odors were offensive and was so disturbed by his flatulence that he took huge quantities of "Dr. Köster's Anti-Gas Pills,"—which contained strychnine and atropin. He was convinced that microbes "pounced" on him personally.[109]

Since his fears were so many, so great, and so unbearable, he felt a great need to consolidate them all into one single fear that he could recognize, one that would explain all others, and one upon which he could release all his pent-up anger and hatred. He found it, as we shall see, in the Jewish people.

Other Personal Dualities

Hitler could be a delightful and considerate dinner companion. He was also a boor, offensively gauche, insufferably rude. He did not like women guests to wear lipstick and often told them that lipstick was manufactured—variously—from sewage, human fat, or kitchen garbage. Once, when ladies at the table were served suckling pig, Hitler announced loudly, "That looks exactly like a roast baby to me." [110]

At social gatherings he was often timid, vulnerable, ill-at-ease. He nervously checked and rechecked preparations for his teas and worried whether his guests would have a good time. He fretted over which tie he should wear. Anxiously he would seek reassurance that everything was fine. He would mutter while planning the event, "I'll show them that I know as much as they do about such matters." [111]

Hitler was both frugal and profligate. His eating habits—with the exception of chocolates, cake, and other sweets—were austere. At one time he developed a liking for caviar but gave it up because it was "sinfully expensive." His spartan field headquarters during the war reminded his generals of a combination of "a monastery and a concentration camp."

Yet Hitler was a very rich man. The revenue he received from having his portrait on German stamps added to royalties from *Mein Kampf* came to over a million dollars. He had owed over half a million Reichsmarks in back taxes when he became chancellor, but he ordered these obligations canceled, and he paid no taxes after 1934. As his architect reminds us, he threw away billions of marks on unnecessary and unused buildings. "I have forgotten how many secret headquarters I ordered built for him—nine, I think, seven of which he seldom or never used." [112]

Hitler swung between the two poles of rigidity and movement. He wanted many things to remain the same—political ideas, personal habits, wearing apparel, members of his entourage, military strategy. And he prided himself on being a rigid person. Yet there was always a desire to change things and to move about a great deal—to redesign and rebuild, to take sudden trips and excursions. He did not like to think of his political organization as a party. He called it his movement (*meine Bewegung*) and insisted on that usage.

He was vicious and vindictive, capriciously and unpredictably cruel. He was also kindly and considerate. Sometimes he liked to think of himself as a very humane person, but on other occasions he saw himself as barbarous. "Yes," he said, "we are barbarians! We want to be barbarians! It is an honorable title." Indeed, his self-image kept oscillating between the two extremes of kindliness and barbarity. Late in the night of 28–29 September 1941 he mused, "Thank God I always avoided persecuting my enemies." But any inclination to "softness" and charity was immediately countered by assertions of hardness and brutality. One day at lunch, for example, he reflected, "When I think about it, I realize that I'm extraordinarily humane." But a few moments later, he announced: "I see no other solution but the extermination [of the Jews]."

He sometimes expressed conflict over his self-image in adjacent sentences. On the night of 25–26 September 1941, for example, he said, "I would prefer not to see anyone suffer, not to do harm to anyone. But then I realize that the species is in danger and . . . sentiment gives way to the coldest reason." And on the night of 1–2 February 1942: "I was pitiless. . . . But in a general way I can say that I am full of moderation. I am certainly not a brutal man by nature." [113]

He not only talked about being kind and considerate, but many of his actions really did show genuine concern for other people. He sent flowers to his secretaries on their birthdays; on long motor trips he insisted that his chauffeurs be fed before he himself ate; he sent at least two hand-painted thank-you postcards to the kindly Jewish doctor who had treated his mother and himself; he remembered his family and servants in his will; he remembered the 40th anniversary of a general's military service. He once reminisced about an old woman who had been kind to him many years before he came to power when she had rented him a room in Munich. He told an aide to find out if she were still alive and to arrange an allowance for her. When another of his former landladies became senile and deranged, Hitler was invariably gentle and considerate, spending hours in quiet talk to soothe her. He had also lived in rooms belonging to a tailor in Munich named Josef Popp. When Popp died in 1935 his family received from Hitler a monthly stipend of 150 marks with the understanding that they would not divulge the source of the income. Nor did he forget his boyhood friend's mother. In 1944 he sent Frau Kubizek a food package on her 80th birthday. His friend commented, "I never discovered how he came to know about it."

He was particularly kind to children, and showed his thoughtfulness on many occasions. One day in 1928 he stood with several bereaved children at the grave of their mother, holding their hands and praying with them. Men who knew him well have said that their children "simply adored him," and that Hitler was never so completely relaxed and genuinely friendly as when he was in the company of little children. "It was one of the few moments," a close associate recalls, "when a warm human feeling broke through." [114]

He also had tender feelings about animals. During his Vienna days he always saved a bit of dried bread to feed the birds and squirrels in the Schönbrunn where he went to read on summer evenings. Hitler was very fond of birds and felt particularly drawn to ravens, a bird which in German literature often appears as the omen of misfortune and death. He gave special orders that ravens must never be molested.

During the first months after he attained power, Hitler signed three separate laws on the protection and treatment of animals, and the official *Reichsgesetzblatt* dutifully records in great detail definitions and penalties for cruel treatment, mishandling, and misfeeding. One regulation, dated 14 January 1936, shows particular solicitude about the suffering of lobsters and crabs. Hitler's decree sets forth new regulations for their preparation in all German restaurants:

> Crabs, lobsters, and other crustaceans are to be killed by throwing them in rapidly boiling water. When feasible, this should be done individually.

High officials in Hitler's government had apparently debated the question of the most humane death for lobsters before this decree was passed, and two officials of the Ministry of Interior had prepared a scholarly disquisition on whether it was kinder to kill lobsters by placing them in cold water which was slowly brought to a boil or by pushing them headfirst into boiling water. The final decision, obviously, was that abrupt immersion in rapidly boiling water was the more humane. As jurists noted in the official introductory comments on the Law for the Protection of Animals, the purpose of the law, as approved by Adolf Hitler, was "to awaken and strengthen compassion [*Mitgefühl*] as one of the highest moral values of the German people." [115]

Hitler's kindness to crustaceans did not always extend to human beings. During the same period that he fretted over lobsters, he is reported to have said to an associate, "Do I intend to eradicate whole races? . . . Of course I do. . . . Cruelty is impressive. Cruelty and brutal strength. . . . The masses want it. They need the thrill of terror to make them shudderingly submissive. I do not want concentration camps to become old age pensioners homes. Terror is the most effective way of politics." [116]

The man who was constantly surrounded by people, and whose charisma appealed to millions of people, was a lonely person with no capacity for friendship. He abused and deserted August Kubizek, the only friend of his youth. He ordered the death of Ernst Röhm, a *"du"* friend of the early battle years. Rudolf Hess, whom he had once endearingly called "my Rudi . . . my Hesserl" and whose loyalty to Hitler was canine, was openly ridiculed as "the greatest mistake of my life." Albert Speer, an admirer who wanted desperately to be close to Hitler and who had said of him, "If Hitler could have had a friend, I would have been that friend," also said that Hitler's attitude toward his intimates was one of contempt: "He seemed to enjoy destroying the reputation and self-respect of even his close associates and faithful comrades." [117]

Hitler was a lethargic person who frittered away thousands of working hours in idle self-indulgence. Day after day and in all-night sessions he forced his associates to listen to interminable and empty dissertations on trivia. Yet he was also a man of remarkable energy and capacity for hard work. In the electoral campaign of 1932, for example, he traveled tirelessly by airplane—though he was frightened by air travel—and in one day spoke to several hundred thousand people. On his first campaign swing across Germany he visited 21 towns in seven days; on the second, 25 towns in eight days; on the third, 50 towns in 16 days; on the fourth, another 50 towns in 24 days.[118]

He had a taste for erotic art and pornography; he was also a prude with unctuous concern for proper conduct. He did not permit swearing or off-color jokes; gentlemen never removed their coats no matter how warm the weather. He was shocked at Stalin for having his picture taken while smoking a cigarette and furious with Mussolini for being seen in public in bathing trunks. Great statesmen, he observed in one of his more perishable political pronouncements, do not run around bare-chested. He was terribly afraid that "some skillful forger would set my head on a body in bathing trunks!" [119]

To limit the number of times a tailor touched him, he would have many shirts and suits made at one fitting; these were expected to last for years. He was embarrassed to disrobe before doctors and never allowed an X ray of his chronically ailing stomach. He rejected out-of-hand Himmler's suggestion that some of his ailments might be alleviated by a masseur. He liked to have his body carefully covered at all times, and even in the hottest weather he wore long white underwear—as was observed for the first time in public on that sultry, hot day of 20 July 1944, when the bomb explosion tore off part of his trousers.[120]

He was careful to say that he was not in the least embarrassed by nudity—it was others who were: "The idea of nakedness torments only the priests, for the education they undergo makes them perverts." [121]

Hitler was both a pathetic little man filled with self-pity and an awesomely effective dictator. In childish bids for sympathy, he sniffled about the loneliness of his life and how he would be neglected and forgotten when he grew old:

Perhaps one of my former associates will visit me occasionally, but I can't count on it. Aside from Fräulein Braun, I'll take no one with me. Fräulein Braun and my dog. I'll be lonely, for why should anyone voluntarily stay with me for any length of time? Nobody will take notice of me anymore. They'll all go running after my successor. Perhaps once a year they'll show up for my birthday.[122]

One day during the electoral campaign of 1932, according to an intimate, Hitler was feeling sorry for himself as he slurped vegetable soup and asked plaintively for assurance that the vegetable diet would cure his stomach cramps, excessive sweating, and melancholy. But then he started talking about his determination to come to power. He jumped up, strode around the room, and convinced himself once again of his greatness. Before one's eyes, the whining hypochondriac was transformed into the great demagogue who could electrify skeptics and force them to become true believers in his destiny.[123]

The Führer flatly denied that he was ever bothered by fears of weakness. Max Planck remembered a remarkable interview with Hitler in which he shouted that it was "libelous" for anyone ever to accuse him of having weak nerves. "I tell you," he screamed, "I have nerves of steel!" When he said that, Planck recalled, "He pounded his knee, spoke ever faster, and worked himself into such a fury that there was nothing for me to do but . . . to excuse myself." A military aide who observed his Führer closely concluded, "The strong nerves which he so often praised, he himself did not possess." [124]

Hitler felt it necessary to protest often that he never had any feelings of inferiority. "Only an insane person," he once said, "could say that I have an inferiority complex. . . . They are absolutely crazy. *I have never had an inferiority complex!*" And again, a few weeks later: "Do the English really imagine that with respect to England I could have an inferiority complex?" [125]

One evening during the war, Hitler was whistling a classical air. When a secretary had the temerity to suggest that he had made a mistake in the melody, the Führer was furious. He showed his vulnerability—and his lack of humor—by shouting angrily, "I don't have it wrong. It is the composer who made a mistake in this passage." His press chief, who followed him closely for ten years, recalled that if an associate corrected him on any point of fact, in any field of knowledge, "no matter how valid the correction, Hitler could not admit his mistake." His personal interpreter insisted that "throughout the time I interpreted for Hitler [1935–1945] I never once heard him make . . . an admission of error even to his closest friends." [126]

Such statements need some qualification. On rare occasions Hitler could, in fact, admit a mistake. But when he did so, he invariably hedged his admission in a number of ways. He would proclaim something a colossal blunder when he and his entourage knew it was trivial;

or he would seem to admit an error and then immediately conclude that someone else was to blame. Thus, he called collaboration with Vichy France "our greatest political blunder . . . that too was the work of our great minds in the Wilhelmstrasse!" Or else a mistake was the result of some errant human virtue. He had been too kind or too tolerant: he had once been guilty of discussing politics with a woman; he had been "too soft" about Freemasonry; he had underestimated the "pernicious influence of the Jews on Churchill's Englishmen"; he had been too lenient in failing to throw a Danish statesman into jail; too tolerant of the Italians; much too kind to the Jews. . . .

Throughout his life he insisted that other people were to blame for his own failures. As a youth, when he was rejected by the Viennese Academy of Art, his roommate recalled how "he cursed the old-fashioned, fossilized bureaucracy of the Academy where there was no understanding of true artistry. He spoke of the trip-wires which were cunningly laid—I remember his very words!—for the sole purpose of ruining his career." [127]

Years later, at the end of his career, he blamed his military failures on a number of different people. "He talks constantly of betrayal," an intimate reported on 23 April 1945, "in the Party leadership and in the Army. The SS also lies to him now." Soon he would add "the betrayal of my Allies" to the list of those responsible for his defeat.[128]

He could not abide the thought of his own mistakes; nor could he tolerate others being superior to him in any way. Thus he ridiculed "so-called military experts" or "effeminate intellectuals," or suddenly quit playing a game of bowls or "Beavers" when anyone else was winning. His attitude about personal superiority expanded to include the nation. Germans, he insisted, were superior in all human endeavors from food preparation to music, architecture to dog training, poetry to weight lifting. Since he was absolutely sure that Germany would win the Olympic Games in 1936, he simply could not comprehend the success of the decadent and racially defiled Americans. When shown pictures of the Golden Gate Bridge he said that Germany must build a bigger bridge in Hamburg. Told that a span there would not be as long as the one in San Francisco, he sulked for a time and then said brightly, "Well, we'll build ours wider." Informed that the widest avenue in the world was in Buenos Aires, he said that his new capital, "Germania," would have a street wider than any other street in the world.[129]

Hitler surrounded himself with people to whom he could feel superior. With the exception of Albert Speer, they were either men of intelligence inferior to his own or men with physical or emotional deficiencies he could ridicule. His personal adjutants, Brückner and Burgdorff, were notably deficient in mental endowment, as were the three SS aides who were also with him almost daily: Fegelein, Günsche, and Rattenhuber. Among 30 candidates who applied for the position of personal chauffeur to the Führer, Hitler selected the shortest man in the group and kept him as his personal driver for the rest of his life, even though it was necessary to put special blocks under the seat so that he could see over the steering wheel. Rudolf Hess, for many years the deputy Führer, was mentally disturbed; Joseph Goebbels, the brilliant minister of enlightenment and propaganda, had a club foot; Heinrich Hoffmann, the court photographer, was an alcoholic with a deformed back; both his first treasurer, a man named Meier, and Max Amann, his press business manager, were one-armed, and Amann was dwarflike in stature; Dietrich Eckart, Hitler's closest intellectual collaborator, was addicted to drugs and died of alcoholism; an assistant press chief was stone deaf; his adjutant Julius Schaub had a bad limp; the leader of his Brown Shirts, the homosexual Ernst Röhm, was replaced by the one-eyed Victor Lutze; Heinrich Himmler, dread *Reichsführer* of the SS, was a neurotic hypochondriac; Julius Streicher, *Gauleiter* and editor of *Der Stürmer*, was a sexual pervert; Robert Ley, head of the Labor Front, was a garrulous dullard and drunkard who had a speech defect; Martin Bormann, the immensely influential Party secretary, was an alcoholic. Hermann Göring, head of the Luftwaffe, was a man of high intelligence who was addicted to morphine. During most of World War II he was "in a near-comotose state of narcotic stupor." But to Hitler, he was "the greatest genius in aviation history." Joachim von Ribbentrop, a stupid, shallow, servile, and vindictive man, remained one of Hitler's favorites and was hailed by him as "the greatest foreign minister since Bismarck." [130]

He constantly pleaded with his subordinates to reassure him of his own ability. A minor official of the German Embassy in Paris, for example, recalled that on the eve of the Nazi invasion of the Rhineland in 1936 he was summoned to a conference attended by the political and military power structure of the Third Reich. The young and inexperienced official was amazed when his Führer kept asking him for assurance that the invasion of the Rhineland would be successful and that the French would not resist: "Repeatedly he asked me the curious question whether I could 'guarantee' him success." [131]

His valet recalled that before an important speech Hitler was nervous and unsure of himself. He would rehearse important passages in front of a mirror and interrupt himself by turning to ask his servant apprehensively, "Does that sound all right? . . . Do you think I am ready to go before the audience? . . . Do I look like the Führer? Do I really look like the Führer?"

A servant of many years recalled, "It was surprising how often Hitler drew parallels between himself and Napoleon," and noted that Hitler liked to "outdo" Napoleon in many different things. It bothered him, for example, when he learned that the French emperor could keep more secretaries busy than he. To compensate, Hitler started to dictate in a much louder voice. He also found solace in being able to excel Napoleon in something else: "Napoleon could dictate to several secretaries at the same time. To make up for that, I can read with one glance an entire page of a book." [132]

Fretful worries about his own image alternated with glowing assertions of indispensability, historic greatness, and immortality. Thus, to the same valet, Linge: "My life is worth more than one or two divisions. Without me the army and Germany would collapse." He told the Austrian chancellor, "I have made the greatest achievement in the history of Germany, greater than any other German." Ever since his youth, Hitler was convinced that he alone understood the real meaning of world history. Thus, when an intimate asked him the most revealing statement he had made about himself in his memoirs, Hitler replied at once: "A short sentence at the very beginning of the book [actually it appears on p. 11] in which I say that as a youth I learned the meaning of history." His feeling that he had mastered all history led him, in 1919, to set forth detailed plans for a book he planned to entitle *Die Monumentalgeschichte der Menschheit* (Monumental History of Humanity).[133]

In a speech to the commanding generals of the Wehrmacht on 23 November 1939, he laid particular stress on the special importance of his own person: "I must in all modesty say that my own person is indispensable. Neither a military nor a civilian personality could replace me. . . . I am convinced of the strength of my brain and my resolution. . . . The fate of the Reich is dependent entirely upon me." As the war progressed, Hitler saw himself as the personification of Germany, and the single focus for all the attacks of the enemy. That he believed the entire world was personally against him was made clear in a speech of 15 February 1942:

> Today I have the honor of being this enemy because I have created a world power out of the German Reich. I am boundlessly proud that I was blessed by Providence with the permission to lead this battle. . . .[134]

And at the very end—with his world crashing about him as he cowered in the air raid shelter and planned his own suicide—he still saw himself as a genius with nerves of steel. In his last political testament, he observed that during his lifetime he had made "the most difficult decisions that ever confronted mortal man." And when a secretary, Traudl Junge, asked him as she was typing up this last testament on 29 April 1945 if National Socialism would survive after his death, Hitler answered emphatically in the negative: "The German people have shown that they are not worthy of my movement. Perhaps in a hundred years another genius will take up my ideas and National Socialism like a phoenix will arise again from the ashes." He assured himself that a special place was reserved for him and the other immortals, saying, "I shall feel I am in my proper place if after my death I find myself, together with people like me, on some sort of Olympus. I shall be in the company of the most enlightened spirits of all times."[135]

But the pendulum kept swinging back. After making assertions of omnipotence and infallibility, he worried about failure and defeat. His memoirs recall how many times during the early days of the Party "I had forebodings and was filled with a depressing fear." Fear followed him after he attained power. Constantly he was "obsessed by frightful nervous apprehension" that he was going to fail. He tried to reassure himself by insisting that he had absolutely no such fears, feeling it necessary to say, for example. "I have no fear of annihilation. . . . Cities will become heaps of ruins. Noble monuments . . . will disappear forever. . . . *But I am not afraid of this.*" He compressed his thinking into a familiar disjunctive which included the alternative of disaster. "There are two possibilities:" he said in 1936, "to win through with all my plans or to fail. If I win I shall be one of the greatest men in history. *If I fail* I shall be condemned, despised, and damned." [136]

At the very height of prewar success, failure was on his mind. On 10 November 1938, for example, he addressed the German press in what should have been a moment of triumph. His first big pogrom against the Jews in the *Kristallnacht* had just been completed with the acquiescence of the German people. Preceding months had marked a series of other victories: reintroduction of universal military training; occupation of the Rhineland; a highly successful plebiscite approving his withdrawal from the League of Nations; *Anschluss* with Austria; and most recently, the triumph of the Munich agreement. And yet this speech of 10 November is studded with foreboding. The words *Angst, Rückschlag, Niederlage,* and *Misserfolg* keep reappearing:

> I must tell you that I often have one single *misgiving.* . . . I become almost *anxious.* . . . I have had nothing but successes but what would happen if I were to suffer a *failure*? Yes, gentlemen, even that can happen. . . . How would [the masses] act if we had a *failure*? Formerly, gentlemen, it was my greatest pride that I built up a Party that even in time of defeat stood behind me. . . .[137]

Even in the Declaration of War speech of 1 September 1939 he was thinking of the defeat of 1918 and insisting that he never knew the word "capitulation." He also felt the need of naming successors:

> Once again I have put on that tunic which to me is the holiest and dearest of all. I will only remove it after the victory or I will not survive the end. If anything should happen to me in this battle my successor will be [Field Marshal] Göring. If anything should happen to [him] his successor will be Hess. . . . One word I have never learned and that word is capitulation. . . . A November 1918 will never be repeated. We recognize again only one basic fundamental goal; it is completely unimportant if we live, but it is necessary that our people, that Germany, lives.[138]

Not even the triumphant smashing of Poland could quiet his fears. In a speech of 23 November 1939, thoughts of victory were again shrouded in concern about failure and capitulation. As his propaganda machine was thundering out proclamations of triumph, Joseph Goebbels was recording wistfully in his diary, "It is touching to hear the Führer express his wish that he may be privileged to live to see the day of victory." [139]

Thus we deal with a man who was so deeply divided that he often appeared torn between opposing qualities: omnipotent and vulnerable, sophisticated and savage, creative and destructive, pragmatic and fanatical, brave and cowardly, lethargic and industrious, rigid and malleable, pathetic and masterful, cruel and kind.

In our attempt to understand Hitler, we shall return to the problem of his dualities.

HITLER AND WOMEN

Women of all ages were attracted to Adolf Hitler. Motherly types such as Frau Bruckmann, wife of the publisher, and Frau Bechstein, widow of the piano manufacturer, and another woman in her 60s, a retired schoolteacher named Carola Hoffmann, would feed him his favorite tortes, cluck approval, stroke his head, and call him "My little wolf" as he sat at their knee. Once, when Hitler found himself alone with Hélène Hanfstaengl, he ran to her, hid his head in her lap and murmured, "If only I had someone to take care of me!" When Hitler made an important speech in Düsseldorf in January 1932, the wives of industrialists paid a cloakroom attendant a mark each for the privilege of holding the bouquet that had been presented to him upon entering the hall—they were thrilled by the thought that they could actually smell the same flowers the Führer had sniffed.

The magnetism he exerted on women was also observable in his youth. As he walked the streets of Vienna in 1908, women stopped to look at him. One evening at the opera, as he and his friend took their places in the promenade, a liveried attendant handed Adolf a note. He was not at all surprised and simply said, "Another one." Years later, when he was chancellor, an American coed found him "quietly charming, tender in speech and glance, modest with this strange tenderness and appealing helplessness." And the Princess Olga, on a state visit to Berlin, reported that Hitler "has a remarkable charm despite all the reports of his ruthlessness. . . . He gives the impression of being softhearted, particularly when children are mentioned . . . tears would come to his eyes." [140]

Hitler was aware of his capacity to attract women and enjoyed doing so. He was particularly anxious to convince women that he was a man of overpowering virility. On one occasion, he had invited a young woman, Pauline Kohler, to the Obersalzberg to see his books. She recalled that during the course of a dull perusal in which she was losing interest, her host sought to gain her attention by suddenly stretching out his hand in the Nazi salute. He affected a deep voice and roared, "I can hold my arm like that for two solid hours. I never feel tired when my storm troopers and soldiers march past me and I stand at this salute. I never move. My arm is like granite—rigid and unbending. But Göring can't stand it. He has to drop his hand after half an hour of this salute. He's flabby. But I am hard. For two hours I can keep my arm stretched out in the salute. That is four times as long as Göring. That means I'm four times stronger than Göring. It's an amazing feat. I marvel at my own power." [141]

Hitler's dualities are particularly apparent in his attitude toward women. He revered and idealized them; he also treated them with contempt and sought to degrade them. As Erik Erikson was first to notice, Hitler showed his ambivalence in the way he talked about abstract forces that controlled his life. He made these forces into contradictory female images who were sometimes generous and kind but also capriciously cruel and treacherous. All his life he seemed surrounded by unpredictable supernatural female beings: Dame Sorrow, the Goddess of Fate, Lady Care, the Goddess of Misery. Thus, in the opening sentence of *Mein Kampf* we are told that the hero was born in Braunau because a kindly Fate designated that town to be the place of his birth. But it was "an unmerited, mean trick of Fate" that he was "born in a period of peace between two wars." This was the same "inexorable hand of the Goddess of Fate" which decides the destiny of nations. Here Hitler reveals his concern about the power of women by changing the neuter German noun *das Schicksal* to the feminine, *die Göttin*. In a letter of 1914 he makes another special grammatical point in order to feminize a noun. In lamenting his life spent with "Friend Care and Want," he chooses the feminine form and writes that he had *keine andere Freundin als Sorge und Not*.

And in a speech of 13 August 1920 in the Hofbräuhaus in Munich, he speaks of "the greatest goddess on earth, who oppresses man the most: the goddess called Misery" [*Die Göttin der Not*]. Years later, in a May Day speech in Berlin in 1927, this goddess was still preying on his mind:

> In spite of all Party dogmas and Party principles, the Goddess of Misery will come and beat on the door of a people which feel more and more the pain of want. A people slowly perishes if this want is not satisfied.

And again—we are back to his memoirs—when he was poor, "Poverty clasped me in *her* arms." When he felt depressed: "Dame Sorrow was my foster mother." To Hitler, misery was a female. In hearing about these statements, Karl Menninger asked, "What had Hitler's mother done to him to make him distrust and hate women so?" [142] It is a question we shall pursue in a later chapter.

Of course, the hero of Hitler's memoirs learned to bear up under all the travail and anguish—"All this cruelty of Fate"—and even learned to accept his sufferings as "the wisdom of Providence" because she hardened him for the service of Nature, "that cruel Queen of all Wisdom," until she had guided him to another turning point in his life, when during World War I "Fate graciously permitted" him to become a soldier. The war was lost because, as he said in a Berlin speech on 30 January 1940, "Providence turned *her* face from the German people." When he decided to become a politician in order to save the "Motherland," it will be recalled that as he left the Hofbräuhaus during the night that he imagined to be so crucial to his political career, Hitler walked side by side with "the Goddess of Inexorable Revenge." At his trial in 1924, he was sure that the "Goddess of History's eternal judgment will smilingly tear up" the jury's verdict. [143]

Hitler idealized women as wives and mothers and rhapsodized about the institution of marriage. As a boy he had talked to Kubizek about "pure marriage," which alone could keep alive "the Flame of Life." Indeed a main reason he had planned, as an adolescent, to establish one day a new "Reich" was to make sure that he could accomplish two main objectives: eradicate prostitution, "the Sin of Iniquity," and preserve "the Flame of Life." In the new Germany of his boyhood dreams—and years later in legislative reality—early marriage would be encouraged by state loans to young couples, attractive and inexpensive housing, and special bonuses for children. When he became chancellor, Hitler set aside a special day to pay homage to motherhood: on 12 August (the birthday of his own mother) fecund German mothers were awarded the Honor Cross of the German Mother. There were three classes: bronze for more than four children, silver for more than six, and gold for more than eight. Regulations printed in Hitler's newspapers required all members of Nazi youth organizations to treat mothers with the respect due to war heroes and to salute the wearers of the Mother's Honor Cross. [144]

Typically, Hitler never defined "the Flame of Life," but his boyhood friend Kubizek understood that he meant it to be a "symbol of sacred love which is awakened between men and women who have kept themselves pure in body and soul and are worthy of a union which would produce healthy children for the nation." Decades later, Hitler continued to sentimentalize marriage. In one of his nightly reveries he asked rhetorically, "Is there a more lovely consecration of love, pray, than the birth of a handsome babe glowing with health? . . . Nature blesses the love of two beings by giving them a child. . . . To my way of thinking the real ideal is that two beings should unite for life and that their love should be magnified by the presence of children." He eulogized the institution of marriage, but he also approved Himmler's idea of establishing SS stud farms and passed legislation legitimizing the results of their eugenic labors.[145]

Hitler was absolutely furious at the suggestion that women should be emancipated from their traditional place in the kitchen, the church, and the nursery, asserting that "the term 'female emancipation' is a term invented by the Jewish intellect and its meaning is of the same spirit." At the first general membership meeting of the Nazi Party in January 1921, Hitler had the following regulation passed: "A woman can never be admitted into the Leadership of the Party or into the Executive Committee." In the Third Reich women were declared ineligible for jury service because, the Führer said, "they cannot think logically or reason objectively since they are ruled only by emotion." [146]

He expressed his own ideal of womanhood to the wife of the early SA leader, Franz von Pfeffer:

> A woman must be a cute, cuddly, naïve little thing—tender, sweet, and stupid.
>
> *Eine Frau muss ein niedliches, molliges, Tschapperl sein: weich, süss und dumm.*[147]

On another occasion he noted to an aide that while he thoroughly enjoyed having beautiful women near him it was not necessary for them to be intelligent or original. "I have enough ideas for both," he said.[148]

Apart from the studied air of superiority he affected in their presence, there are other indications that Hitler really was frightened by females. His sister recalled that Adolf, as a very small boy, was terrified at the thought that a girl might kiss him. "When mother wanted him to get up in the morning she had only to say to me, 'Go and give him a kiss.' She said it not very loud but enough for him to hear; as soon as he heard the word 'kiss,' and that he was to get one from me, he was out of bed in a flash because he just couldn't stand that." Many years later, at a New Year's Eve party in 1924, a young and attractive woman maneuvered Hitler under the mistletoe and gave him a good-natured kiss. A witness recalled the consequences: "I shall never forget the look of astonishment and horror on Hitler's face! . . . Bewildered and helpless as a child, Hitler stood there biting his lips in an effort to master his anger. The atmosphere which after his arrival had shown a tendency to become more formal now became almost glacial." [149]

Hitler continued to be intimidated by the thought of physical contact with women, and compared sexual intercourse to the trauma a soldier faces in battle. In making the comparison he quite typically projected his own fears: it was not he who was afraid of women, but women were afraid of men. In his awkward prose:

The revelation that her encounter with her first man is for a young woman can be compared with the revelation that a soldier knows when he faces war for the first time.[150]

After he came to power he was anxious about displeasing his motherly patron, Frau Bechstein. On one occasion when he felt that he had done something wrong, the Führer was so fearful of a tongue-lashing that he sought out the Wagner children to run interference for him. Friedelind Wagner—the granddaughter of the Meister—recalled that "throughout luncheon he tried to persuade us children to make the call for him to soften Frau Bechstein's blows, but we were so amused at the thought of [Hitler] trembling before her that we refused to go." [151]

One of the reasons Hitler never ordered total economic mobilization during the war was that he was afraid of how women would react if they were deprived of beauty parlors and cosmetics. Dr. Goebbels, who urged total mobilization, recorded his disappointment at Hitler's refusal either to send women into the factories or to cut down on their beauty aids. In an entry in his diary of 10 May 1943—well after the catastrophic German defeat at Stalingrad—Goebbels records Hitler arguing that "women after all constitute a tremendous power and as soon as you dare to touch their beauty parlors they are your enemies." [152]

He could not trust women. Like the Goddess of Fate, they were by nature hypocritical, fickle, and false. "Women have the quality," he said, "which we men do not have: they kiss a friend at the same time that they are sticking them in the back with a stiletto." He convinced himself of their inferiority to men and showed his contempt by insulting them publicly. This was true of even the women closest to him. Eva Braun, for example, had given him full measure of loyalty and love. But Hitler would say loudly in her presence that "a highly intelligent man should take a primitive and stupid woman." He recalled on another occasion that he had made the mistake of discussing politics with women and some actually had the temerity to disagree with him. He commented on the incident: "But I shut their mouths by saying, 'you will not claim that you know men as I know women.'" He then concluded: "In short, gallantry [sic] forbids one to give women an opportunity of putting themselves in situations that do not suit them."

Hitler was intrigued by the spectacle of women in danger of their lives. He was particularly fond of watching pretty women in a circus on the high trapeze and tightropes. In 1933, for instance, he sent flowers and chocolates worth several hundred marks to the girls who had performed especially dangerous feats for him during a command performance. He could remember all their names. He was not particularly impressed with wild animal acts unless pretty women were involved. Then he watched avidly, his face flushed, and his breath came quickly in little whistling sounds as his lips worked violently.[153]

The Image and the Man

He was intrigued by women's deaths. As we have noted, he approved when they committed suicide; he also approved of their murder. He did not often show clemency in capital cases—for which he had reinstituted death by decapitation—but during the single year 1935 he pardoned six condemned murderers. Five of the six had been found guilty of killing their wives. Subsequent statistics on his pardons are are not available because as the German press announced in the fall of 1935, henceforth "mercy acts" of the Führer would not be publicized.[154]

In a favorite metaphor, Hitler compared women to the masses, both of whom were to be dominated by the audacious man of passion and power. In lines notable for sadistic overtones and exaltation of brutality, he said:

> Like a woman whose psychic feeling is influenced less by abstract reasoning than by undefinable sentimental longing for complementary strength, who will submit to the strong man rather than dominate the weakling, thus the masses love the ruler rather than the suppliant. . . . They neither realize the impudence with which they are spiritually terrorized nor the outrageous curtailment of their human liberties, for in no way does the delusion of this doctrine dawn on them. Thus they see only the inconsiderate force, the brutality and the aim of its manifestations to which they finally always submit.[155]

At another time, Hitler compared the masses to wild horses; he was the stallion who could control them. He also thought of women as a circus audience: juvenile, naïve, and susceptible to thrills. He concluded that "Someone who does not understand the intrinsically feminine character of the masses will never be an effective speaker."[156]

He often said that he was never so happy or fulfilled as after giving a successful speech. On these occasions he would leave the stage soaked with perspiration, physically and emotionally spent. The written text of his speeches cannot possibly convey the intimacy he felt between himself and his audience. His speeches began as he stood very erect, rocking back and forth slowly on his heels, his voice carefully modulated and deliberately low. After a period of gentle introductory foreplay, he would move with mounting excitement toward the climax. The last five minutes have best been described as an "orgasm of words." He once told an intimate of the very great importance he attached to the delicate matter of sensing the precise climactic moment, which, he said, must be mutually shared between himself and his audience. "By feeling the reaction of the audience, one must know exactly when the moment has come to throw the last flaming javelin which sets the crowd afire."[157]

That the masses were for him a sexual substitute to be conquered through oral aggression is shown in a passage that throbs with passion and sexual symbolism:

> Only a storm of burning *passion* [*Leidenschaft*] can turn people's destiny, but only he who harbors *passion* in himself can arouse *passion*.

> *Passion* alone will give to him who is chosen by her the words that, like beats of a hammer, are able to open the doors to the heart of the people.

> He to whom *passion* is denied and whose mouth remains closed is not chosen by Heaven as the prophet of his will.[158]

A distinguished German female historian recalled attending a Nazi Party rally in 1933 and hearing Hitler's spontaneous exclamation to his audience after he had reached his rhetorical climax: "Aren't you as *enthralled* by me as I am by you? [*Bin ich nicht Euch so verfallen wie Ihr mir?*]" The author adds, "The erotic character, not only of the words but also of the accompanying gestures, was unmistakeable." [159]

Hitler was fond of quoting one of the few lines he knew from Nietzsche: "Thou goest to women? Do not forget thy whip!" Whips, of course, are the traditional symbol and sign of sadomasochistic impulses. During the decade before he became chancellor, Hitler habitually carried heavy riding whips with which, in moments of excitement, he lashed about him, beat against his thighs, or whipped his hand as if he were a little boy being punished. The three whips he treasured most had been given to him by three motherly old ladies.[160]

His sexual gratification—when not achieved through the sublimation of passionate demagogic triumphs—may have been attained by a massively masochistic practice, degrading alike to himself and to his sexual partner. He is reported to have ordered young women to squat over him and to urinate or defecate on his head while he watched (see below, Chapter 3).

Here, then, was the man called Führer and Messiah of the Germans. His image was that of awesome power; but as a person he was infantile and vulnerable, beset by childish fears and neurotic compulsions, torn by contradictions. He was an infallible dictator who anxiously sucked his little finger; who longed to create and lusted to destroy; who ordered the massacre of the innocents and fretted over the death of ravens and lobsters; who exalted women and debased them; who spoke the words of Jesus and hated all mankind.

This peculiar man was one of the most compelling personalities of history, and one of its greatest enigmas. What follows is an attempt to understand him and the forces that brought him power and victory, humiliation, and defeat.

CHAPTER 2

The Intellectual World of Adolf Hitler

Bear in mind that my brain works in about the same way as a calculating machine.

—Adolf Hitler

As a human figure, lamentable; as a political mind, one of the most tremendous phenomena in all history.

—Konrad Heiden

INSIGHT INTO Hitler's personality, his appeal to the German people, and his career as dictator must begin with an inquiry into the nature of his remarkable mind, his peculiar artistic and literary tastes, and his ideas about life and politics. This discussion takes on importance when one realizes how often Hitler's private fantasies became historical reality.

Everyone who knew Hitler was struck by his incredibly retentive memory and the extraordinary range of his factual knowledge. He could remember the trademark and serial number of the bicycle he had used in 1915; the names of the inns where he had stayed overnight 20 years previously; the streets down which he had driven during past political campaigns; the age, displacement, speed, strength of armor, and other data of every capital ship in the British and German navies; the names of the singers and their roles in the operas he had seen in Vienna as a youth; the names of his commanders and their precise armaments down to the battalion. He had a note-perfect knowledge of the prelude to *Die Meistersinger* and whistled it in his curious, penetrating vibrato; he memorized the entire libretto of *Lohengrin*; he knew the production figures per man-day of work in England, France, America and Italy.

He played games with his knowledge, betting that a specific item in his vast store of information was correct. Almost invariably it was, and Hitler was happy as a schoolboy to be told he had the right answer. "I often asked myself," a secretary recalls, "how one human brain could preserve so many facts." [1]

Hitler used his phenomenal memory as a weapon in his system of personality defense. It helped him in his efforts to convince himself and others that he really was a person of great intellectual ability, in no way inferior to those who were better educated or better trained. After impressing a naval aide with an incredible recitation of statistics on naval ordnance, he said, "Bear in mind that my brain works in about the same way as a calculating machine." [2] It was a fairly accurate description. Medical doctors were equally impressed. A German physician who was in Hitler's entourage for many years said that the Führer's knowledge of medicine and biology was technical and detailed and "went far beyond that of the average intelligent layman." And another doctor concluded, "In ten years I was not able to catch him in a single factual error." [3]

Hitler also used his data bank as a defensive weapon to ward off displeasing arguments. When field commanders on the Eastern Front pointed out the strength of the enemy, Hitler would either dismiss their argument as irrelevant—his steel-like will would overcome all problems—or overwhelm the doubter with production statistics and precise weaknesses in the armament of the enemy. Or he would undercut and embarrass commanders by demanding from them information that they simply could not remember. If, for example, they raised objections to a tactical plan, he would bombard them with questions such as the name and rank of each of their subordinate commanders or the military decorations each was entitled to wear. When a field commander admitted ignorance of these matters, Hitler would provide the answers triumphantly and announce that he had more knowledge of their sector than they had.[4]

He had little interest in coming to grips with difficult intellectual problems, and had the habit of repeating the same question about a complex historical event without making an effort to investigate the answer. In January 1942 he observed, "I often wonder why the ancient world collapsed." Months later, in September, he asked the same question in exactly the same words: "I often wonder why the ancient world collapsed." It apparently did not occur to him to study the problem in the available historical literature, or to invite historians to discuss the question with him.[5]

Although he lacked all formal training in history, Hitler planned in 1919 to write a huge work dealing with the origins and development of mankind. He entitled it, with habitual modesty, *Die Monumentalgeschichte der Menschheit* (Monumental History of Humanity). The book was never completed, but the Federal Archives in Coblenz contain records of Hitler's original notations for it, as well as page after page of notes for speeches in 1919–1920. They show the tenacity of the author's basic ideas, and his confidence that someday he would put them into practice. The central ideas of 1919 remained at the core of his later political thinking: all human history must be written in terms of conflict between Aryans and Jews. The undergirding law of civilization is this: "Racial purity is the highest principle." He proclaimed the coming of a "new Reich whose slogan will be *Germany Awaken!*"; expressed the need for "unmerciful thinking about truth and reality," and insisted that salvation can come only through a "dictator of genius." [6]

Hitler shows here a characteristic which proved to be an enormous political asset. He was what Jacob Burckhardt called a "terrible simplifier." Neither innovative nor disciplined, his mind had a remarkable capacity to simplify ideas and reduce them to effective political slogans and programs while, at the same time, creating the illusion that he was thereby achieving a higher wisdom.[7]

That Hitler's mind worked with simple and sometimes startling logic is illustrated in a rare interview he granted an American journalist just before coming to power in 1933. When H. V. Kaltenborn pointed out that Hitler had no electoral mandate from the German people, the Nazi leader set forth his reasons for claiming the right to dominate the government. By his reckoning, 37 percent of the total vote entitled him to 75 percent of the political power:

> Under the rules of democracy, a majority of 51% governs. I have 37% of the total vote which means that I have 75% of the power necessary to govern. That means I am entitled to three-quarters of the power and my opponent to one-quarter. . . . We bring into the business of government 75% of the capital investment . . . and this takes no account of the plain truth that every unit of my investment is worth twice that of the others. My 15 million voters are in reality worth 30 million.[8]

His capacity to simplify and push through one clear policy amid the confusions of complex economic and social issues was brilliantly demonstrated as soon as he got into office. John Kenneth Galbraith has noted that Hitler had the insight to perceive the right economic policy at the right time. Immediately in 1933 he instituted a concerted and coordinated policy of deficit spending and public works. Like Franklin Roosevelt he "sensed that reputable economists were poor guides to policy," but he went well beyond FDR in the energy and clarity of his actions. To those who object that Hitler did not know enough about economics to understand what he was doing, Galbraith comments with tongue only partly in cheek, "This may be so. But in economics it is a great thing not to understand what causes you to insist on the right stand." A careful student of Hitler's economic policy agrees and concludes that he was one of the most underestimated statesmen of the twentieth century, a man who "succeeded spectacularly in the area of economic recovery." [9]

One is less impressed with the quality of Hitler's mind as it ranged over a vast number of subjects in the so-called *Tischgespräche*—the nightly disquisitions he gave to captive audiences at field headquarters during the war. Notes were dutifully taken by members of his entourage who had been told to preserve the pronouncements of their leader for posterity. While only a small fraction of the total *pensée* has been preserved, and only a few samples can be given here, they are enough to show Hitler's confidence in his ability to speak authoritatively on almost any topic.

He felt particularly knowledgeable about American history and social life: "In the single year, 1641, fifty thousand Irish left for North America.* . . . Transplant a German to Kiev, and he remains a German. But transplant him to Miami, and you make a degenerate of him—in other words, an American. . . . Everything about the behavior of American society reveals that it's half-Judaized and the other half Negrified. . . . You can't imagine anything as miserable or degenerate as [American] farmers. . . ."

Although he had never mastered his own language and knew no other, he considered himself an expert on linguistics and literary criticism. "The English language," he said, "is incapable of expressing a poetic or philosophic idea. . . . One hour of instruction in French once a week is quite enough. . . . The three greatest books in the world are *Gulliver's Travels*, *Don Quixote*, and *Uncle Tom's Cabin*. . . . In no country is Shakespeare so badly acted as in England."

He had strong views about art: "Anyone who sees and paints a sky green and pastures blue ought to be sterilized." [10]

He often lectured his entourage on philosophy, theology, and biblical studies: "It is on the foundation of Kant's theory of knowledge that Schopenhauer built the edifice of his philosophy, and it is Schopenhauer who annihilated the pragmatism of Hegel. . . . It is certain that Jesus was not a Jew. The Jews, by the way, regarded Him as the son of a whore—of a whore and a Roman soldier. . . . When Paul preached in Athens in favor of the Jews, Athenians shook with laughter. . . . It's impossible to escape the problem of God. When I have time, I'll work out the formulae. . . ."

History and cultural anthropology were among his stronger suits: "Russia has never suffered a famine. . . . To label the Bulgarians as Slavs is pure nonsense; originally they were Turkomans. The same applies to the Czechs. It is enough for a Czech to grow a mustache for anyone to see, from the way it droops, that his origin is Mongolian.

* In point of fact, there was virtually no Irish immigration to America in 1641. The total population, including whites and blacks, in all colonies in America was about 26,600 in the year 1640. Ten years later the total population was 50,400. See *Historical Statistics of the United States: Colonial Times to the Present*, 756.

. . . The favorite soup in Greece came from Holstein. . . . Caesar's soldiers had a horror of eating meat. That is why they had magnificent teeth. . . ."

He was also proud of his command of scientific and medical knowledge: "No one in the Middle Ages suffered from high blood pressure. Their constant brawls were ample safeguard against it. . . . Now, thanks to the safety razor, the world's blood pressure is rising. . . . It has been proved that a diet of potato peelings and raw potatoes will cure beri-beri within a week. . . . Nowadays humanity depends basically on the whale for its nourishment. . . . All half-caste families —even if they have but a minute quantity of Jewish blood in their veins—produce regularly at least one pure Jew each generation. Roosevelt affords the best possible proof of the truth of this opinion."

Under the rubric of miscellaneous knowledge and automotive expertise might be included the following: Any Turkish porter "can move a piano by himself. . . . As to what gives the Mercedes-Benz its beauty . . . I can claim that fatherhood."

That humor was not one of the Führer's strong points is suggested by the observation that "national pride is a source of strength. But pride often goes before a fall." [11]

A perceptive and heroic secretary who survived thousands of hours of Hitler's verbal barrages and lived to experience the Führer's last days in the Berlin air raid shelter noted that through it all something was missing. "Even to this day I can't define it exactly. My feeling is that in this whole deluge of words, there was lacking the humane note—the magnanimity of a cultivated human being." [12]

HITLER'S READING

> His library contained no classic and no single book of humane or intellectual value.
> —Christa Schroeder,
> one of his secretaries

> I read to confirm my ideas.
> —Adolf Hitler

Presumably the books that a man reads and remembers provide insight into his intellectual interests and the nature of his mind. But in Hitler's case the clues are confusing and the extent of his reading not easily determined.

He liked to give the impression that he was a voracious reader who devoured "mountains of books." But his spoken and written words, though they show a very considerable fund of miscellaneous information, do not reveal that he had read any serious books of literature, history, philosophy, or science. The information he collected and cited seems to have come largely from newspapers, pamphlets, popular magazines, and translations of digests of the foreign press. He looked upon books as weapons useful in his battle for power, and judged them on the basis of whether they supplied him with arguments that confirmed his own prejudices. Thus, as he said, he could get all he wanted from any book in a few minutes' reading. Here, as in so many other areas of his life, his adolescent attitudes remained with him. As his friend Kubizek recalled, Adolf looked for and found in his reading what suited him. He would often end a discussion by citing an authority and saying, "You see, the man who wrote this is of exactly the same opinion." [13] Nor did Hitler's life-style encourage systematic reading. As Party leader and later as chancellor, his evenings at home were usually spent in seeing movies and talking until dawn. The mornings were given over to sleep, the afternoons to travel or conferences.

The few books which he indisputably did read, repeatedly and with enthusiasm, are not notable for their intellectual challenge. In addition to Karl May's adventure stories, he was very much taken with the adventures of a horse called Raubautz and followed him avidly as he moved from civilian life (*Raubautz Wants to Live*) to the cavalry (*Raubautz Becomes a Soldier*). He was so fond of these short and simple novels that he kept several in all his residences, and would often quote passages from them to entertain his guests. He also kept by his bedside a copy of a naval almanac, the *Flottenkalender*, which gave specifications of ships and the armaments of all navies of the world, information with which he impressed naval experts in his entourage.[14]

Hitler later looked back on two periods of his life as having been of particular importance to his education: his years in Vienna, which he hailed as "the hardest but most thorough school" in training him for the future, and his imprisonment at the fortress of Landsberg (11 November 1923–20 December 1924), of which he said, "Landsberg was my college education at state expense." [15]

His companion of the first year in Vienna left two quite different impressions of Adolf's reading interests. In his published memoir, Kubizek provided a long and predictable list of the books he claims Hitler had read, including the standard classics one would expect to find in any German reading list: Fichte, Schiller, Goethe, Schopenhauer, Hegel, Nietzsche, and so forth. But in a private letter to the Linz archivist and biographer Franz Jetzinger, Kubizek said that there were only two books that Hitler studied carefully and talked about repeatedly: one was a child's book on Nordic gods and heroes, the other a volume on archaeological digs relating to German tribes. One of these books contained a sketch of the swastika which impressed Hitler: "Adolf said at that time that the German people needed a symbol which would represent the basic concept of Germandom." [16]

Hitler himself inadvertently drops hints that he had not really done all the serious reading he often claimed. In his later memoirs and conversations it is noteworthy that he can recall the names of the newspapers he read in Vienna but does not mention the title of a single book dealing with the social problems he professed to solve. Hitler also gives us insight into the way he approached the study of important social or intellectual questions. He says that when he first became aware of the "Jewish problem," and again when he decided to study Marxism, he sought insight and understanding by purchasing "some pamphlets" on these subjects.

His own commentary on the role that his stay in prison played in his education is also revealing. Immediately after saying that the prison was for him a college education, he undercuts and deprecates formal education and systematic reading. In a long, convoluted, and fuzzy sentence he insists that his method of reading for the confirmation of his views was infinitely better than any other, since "I recognize the correctness of my views in the long run throughout the history of the world and of nature, and was convinced of the contradictory and hypocritical 'intellectualizing' of the professors and high priests of the universities. Anyway, will-power is greater than knowledge." [17]

During the "battle years" before he attained power, Hitler often borrowed books. Indeed he borrowed so many and so often from a private library belonging to a right-wing nationalist that the owner, Friedrich Krohn, is probably right in suspecting that Hitler had only skimmed through them in order to impress his patron with his industry and knowledge. At any rate, of the more than 100 books and pamphlets he borrowed during the years 1919–1921, almost two-thirds were tawdry anti-Semitic and racist pamphlets: *Goethe and the Jews, Secret Law of the Jews, Luther and the Jews, Bolshevism and Jewry, Schopenhauer and the Jews*, Henry Ford's *The International Jew: A World Problem, Wagner and the Jews, Extracts from the Talmud*, and so forth. He also borrowed histories of medieval and modern Germany, church histories and exposés of the Catholic church, and a translation of writings of Montesquieu and Rousseau.[18]

Certainly Hitler wanted to give the impression of wide reading and great erudition by amassing an impressive collection of books. An intimate who prided himself on being something of an intellectual claimed that Hitler's private library contained some 6,000 books.[19] Toward the end of World War II, American soldiers found a part of the personal library hidden in a salt mine in the neighborhood of Berchtesgaden. The books, numbering about 2,000, were shipped to Washington, where they are now housed in the Rare Books Division of the Library of Congress—standing grotesquely next to the private collections of Thomas Jefferson, Woodrow Wilson, and Oliver Wendell Holmes.

While his library gives some indication of his reading tastes, it must be approached with caution as a key to his intellectual interests. Most of the books were not chosen by Hitler himself; they were presented as gifts. The fact that Hitler accepted and preserved them, however, would seem to indicate a degree of approval of their contents—or at least a desire to have the reputation for having a lot of books. In any case, the present collection is only about one-third of the total he seems to have possessed. One would like to know what has been lost. Moreover, with the exception of the handful of books that bear his signature and notations in pencil, there is no way of knowing whether he actually read the volumes in his library. While many of the books contain the ponderous swastika-emblazoned book-plate of the Führer, only three have his personal autograph.

With these caveats duly noted, let us look at his library. As in most personal collections, one notices both what is present and what is lacking. Notably absent here are the great writings of world literature. There are a few thin anthologies and digests of some classics, but there is no edition of Goethe or Schiller or Shakespeare. Typically, there is a slim volume dedicated to him by Heinrich Himmler and ambitiously entitled *Von Tacitus bis Nietzsche: die Gedanken und Meinungen aus zwei Jahrtausenden* (From Tacitus to Nietzsche: Thoughts and Opinions from Two Millennia). There are no works on political theory—no Hegel and no Machiavelli. Nor are the great historians represented; there is no Ranke but there is also no Treitschke, and no philosopher save Fichte. The two philosophers whom Hitler sometimes quoted and thoroughly misunderstood, Schopenhauer and Nietzsche, are absent. There is virtually no trace of any work of enduring value.[20]

Certain themes which dominate the collection attract our attention because, as we shall see in later chapters, they loomed large in both Hitler's private life and his public policy. Hitler's lifelong concern about health, food, and nourishment is attested by many books on popular medicine, miraculous healing, cooking, vegetarianism, and special diets of all kinds. Stories about Wotan and the gods of German mythology and books about magic symbols and the occult also reflect the Führer's lifelong interests. Among the dozens of volumes on pseudo-science, tracts on the "science" of racism and anti-Semitism take pride of place. Representative of this *genre* is a volume by J. Lanz von Liebenfels—of whom much more later: *Das Buch der Psalmen Teutsch: das Gebetbuch der Ariosophen Rassen-mystiker und Antisemiten* (The Book of German Psalms: The Prayerbook of Arios-Racial Mystics and Anti-Semites).

One particular volume may provide insight into Hitler's political preferences as a youth and, indeed, as an adult: Berthold Otto's *Der Zukunftsstaat als Sozialistische Monarchie* (The Future State as a Socialist Monarchy). The book, which was published in 1910 and was thus available to young Hitler during his Vienna years, is heavily underlined—presumably by Hitler, though there are no marginal comments to identify the handwriting of the person who marked up the book with such enthusiasm. The author, in urging the establishment of militaristic socialism, pressed an idea which was clearly congenial to Hitler: the new military-socialist state must be headed by a strong leader (the author had in mind a reincarnation of Frederick William

I of Prussia). He also called for a "biological conception of the state," exalted a "scientific world view," and demanded the destruction of liberal attitudes and institutions. One can imagine the pale blue eyes of the young rebel of Vienna flashing as he furiously underlined this passage: "It is a simple matter to transform all justice and law." Also underlined is a passage (p. 71) attacking "the stupidity of liberal-bourgeois attitudes" and insisting that "the whole system must be changed," as well as lines calling for a "new socialism" rooted in "biological conceptions of state organization" (p. 300). There is particularly heavy underscoring of the author's conclusion that society can only be transformed by a leader of mystery and power.

Hitler's library also contained a large collection of books on military history and strategy. The edition of Clausewitz, *Vom Krieg* (On War), was especially well thumbed.

Two other books seem to have interested Hitler particularly— if, as seems likely, the blue-penciled underlining and marginal marks are his own. One is a work entitled *Auswanderungs-Möglichkeiten in Argentinien* (Emigration Possibilities in Argentina), where a passage noting that the country could provide ample space for German settlement is underscored. There are two travel guides, one to the city of Brussels and the other to Berlin, the latter written by the well-known Jewish critic, Max Osborn. The book—which is inscribed in pencil "A. Hitler, Fournés, 22 November 1915"—was apparently much read, but with no underlining or marginal comments. During the war Hitler had been stationed near Fournés, not far from Lille. It is known that he went on furlough to Berlin in 1917. The Library of Congress has facsimiles of three postcards (including one of the Kaiser Wilhelm Memorial Church) sent from the German capital to his sergeant and later press chief, Max Amann. There is no mention of the artistic riches of the city.

HITLER AND THE ARTS

Art demands fanaticism.

—Adolf Hitler

The attributes Hitler assigned to great political leaders were those that fit his own self-image. True statesmen, he said, should begin their careers as he had, at the age of 30. And they should also be musical (he considered himself "perhaps the most musical of all Germans"). In 1925 he ruled out General Ludendorff as a political leader because he had no ear for music. In 1945, when talking about possible successors, he rejected Heinrich Himmler because he was not musical enough. Only musical people, he was convinced, feel "the vibrations of the folkic soul [*Volksseele*]" they alone find "the sensitive word that can move men"; they alone can "put the correct political action into effect." [21]

Music was terribly important to Hitler. As Karl Menninger has noted, good music can help combat destructive tendencies in deeply divided personalities. It is, he writes, "a bulwark against self-destruction." [22] That it played such a role for Hitler is suggested by a description which Kubizek has given of the effect that Wagner had upon young Adolf: "When he listened to Wagner's music, he was a changed man; his violence left him, he became quiet, yielding and tractable. He no longer felt lonely and outlawed and misjudged by society. He was intoxicated and bewitched. . . . From the stale, musty prison of his back room he was transported into the blissful regions of German antiquity, that ideal world which was the lofty goal for all his endeavors." [23]

Hitler was not particularly interested in the classical music of balance and restraint. He disliked Bach, Handel, Haydn, and Mozart, preferring Grieg, Bruckner, and above all Wagner.* He wanted to make Linz a shrine for Bruckner's works, to be for him what Bayreuth was for Wagner. At the age of 19 he drew up detailed plans for the Linz Concert Hall, which he solemnly consecrated to Bruckner's memory. Years later, his enthusiasm unabated, he tried to buy the manuscript of Bruckner's Third Symphony for $7,500. [24]

Hitler was not impressed with Italian opera because he found it based upon "trickery and deception." Quite apart from that, it had one unforgivable fault: it was not German. As his friend recalls, "For him nothing counted but German ways, German feeling and German thought. He accepted none but the German masters." [25]

Hitler As "Creative Artist"

Adolf Hitler considered himself a creative artist. He said on several occasions that the main reason he had entered politics was to implement his artistic plans; again and again he expressed regret that the war had interrupted their fulfillment. In discussing the careers of other great men on the night of 5 May 1942, he observed, "If the war had not come along, I would certainly have become an architect and perhaps, yes, even probably, one of the best architects if not *the* best architect in Germany." And as he contemplated suicide a few years later, he was heard to sigh regretfully, "Ah, what an artist dies in me!" [26]

The paintings and drawings he produced as a youth were not good enough to gain him admission to the Vienna Art Academy. But they sold well enough to art dealers—or to those who wanted something pleasant to show off their elaborate picture frames—to help

* Wagner's influence is discussed below, pp. 99–113.

finance his life in Vienna. On the average, his paintings brought about $10.00–$15.00. He also did some water colors during World War I, and his careful pictures of French buildings and Bavarian churches suggest that he had modest talent.

One of Hitler's lifelong habits was to doodle at the table, on those rare occasions when he was not dominating the conversation. As a boy in Linz he drew severed heads to entertain a schoolmate who was a boarder in his mother's home on the Humboltstrasse. Forty years later Baldur von Schirach recalls that after meals the Führer would sit "drawing on one of the little cards he always had with him, mostly heads of men and women." Several sketches of the heads have been preserved in the Library of Congress Manuscript Division.[27]

Hitler's early sketches for buildings, triumphal arches, memorials, and bridges—carefully collected by Albert Speer—became the actual working diagrams for the buildings he and Speer started to erect many years later. Indeed, so closely did Hitler supervise the execution of the public buildings in the Third Reich that they must be considered a part of his own artistic creation.

Two things dominate his architectural thinking: massive size and the use of domes and columns. The meeting hall (*Kuppelhalle*) he planned for his new capital of "Germania" was to be situated on the *Prachtallee* ("Avenue of Splendor"), which was to be twice the width and three times the length of the Champs Elysées. The dome of the *Kuppelhalle* was to be 825 feet in diameter, with a volume 16 times that of St. Peter's. Some 180,000 people were to assemble under its roof. The Arch of Triumph, originally sketched by Hitler in 1925, was to stand 400 feet high. Fifty of Napoleon's paltry triumphal arches in Paris could have fitted within the Führer's gate of glory. A third gargantuan building, Hitler's personal palace, was to be erected on the new capital's "Adolf Hitler Platz." It was to include, among other features, a dining hall that could seat 2,000 guests and a reception room with a volume of over 74,000 cubic feet—designed to dwarf the White House, with its reception room of 57,600 cubic feet. In discussing these plans with Speer in 1935, Hitler remarked, "I made these drawings ten years ago. I've always saved them because I never doubted that some day I would build these edifices and this is how we will carry them out." With the beginning of the war in 1939, however, Hitler expanded his plans. Speer recalls he had first suggested to Hitler that a golden German eagle with a swastika in its talons might top the *Kuppelhalle*. Hitler now decided that the design would no longer do. It was altered so that the eagle held a globe clutched in its claws.[28]

Hitler also planned a monument to the Party in Munich, to be built about 100 yards from the traditional symbol of Munich, the *Frauenkirche*. Hitler's erection would be over twice as high. He sketched a monstrous Party Hall at the Chiemsee with a ground floor of 263 by 361 feet and a height of 391 feet. Hitler planned a stadium at Nuremberg with a seating capacity of 400,000 and a volume of 11,100,000 cubic yards, more than three times the volume of the pyramid of Cheops.[29]

His infatuation with columns was so well known among his personal entourage that they sometimes made cautious little jokes about it. On one occasion when Hitler was remodeling one of his buildings, Göring said jokingly that one of the halls should have at least 400 columns. The remark got back to Hitler, who took it seriously and said it was a fine idea but unfortunately the floor plans would not permit quite that many. One of his doctors observed that "He was particularly partial to pillars that went right up to the roof." [30]

Hitler's colossal buildings served no human purpose, but that does not mean they were nonfunctional in a deeper political and psychological sense. Functional they were, as Hitler had planned: they dominated and intimidated all who saw them. Thus the overpowering domes, the relentless columns flanking hundreds of meters of passageway which a visitor was obliged to traverse before he was finally ushered into the cavernous office of the Führer, guarded by two forbidding SS men. The whole impression was one of impersonal, cold, and terrifying power. When Hitler saw the gigantic proportions of his new Chancellery, he remarked with satisfaction, "Good, good! When the diplomats see that, they will learn to know *fear* [*werden sie das Fürchten lernen*]." Albert Speer is quite right in reflecting in his memoirs that Hitler's buildings were "the very expression of a tyranny." [31] It took Speer a very long time indeed to reach that conclusion.

Taste in Art

Hitler's taste in painting is shown both in his private collection and in the works he allowed to be exhibited in Nazi Germany, for he was arbiter of artistic taste in the Third Reich. Approved paintings were shown in the new House of German Art he dedicated in Munich in 1937 —an enormous, high-columned white mass which Müncheners still call the *Weisswurstpalast*. Over its portal in block letters of bronze was emblazoned the motto which set forth his personal theory of aesthetics: *Die Kunst ist eine erhabene und zum Fanatismus verpflichtende Mission* ("Art is an ennobling mission demanding fanaticism"). At first it was planned that a jury of art critics would select the paintings to be hung in the new museum. But when Hitler learned that examples of abstraction would be included, he was furious and shouted that no "degenerate" art would appear in his new gallery. The jury was dismissed, and Hoffmann, Hitler's personal photographer and a man who has been called by a distinguished art historian "abysmally ignorant" of art, was ordered to screen thousands of paintings. Hitler personally made the final selections.[32]

It is extraordinarily difficult to differentiate between the paintings which Hitler acquired as his private property and those he intended for Linz, where he had planned as a personal monument an enormous museum with a colonnaded facade over 150 meters in length. In either case, his taste ran heavily to 19th century romantic landscapes, insipid pastoral scenes, and erotic nudes.

The money spent on books and paintings for the Linz Art Center was particularly noteworthy when one considers that these amounts were set aside in the midst of war. During 1943 and 1944 some 3,000 paintings were purchased for Linz at a total cost of 150 million RM. With the Allies about to land in Normandy, Hitler completed negotiations for the purchase of the Mannheimer collection, one of the finest in Europe, for a total of 6 million RM. As Russia counterattacked from the East and the Allies moved in from the West, "expenditures for the year 1944 jumped another 548,766 RM. In 1945 up to the last entry on 1 March [an additional] 53,094 RM had been spent." In the salt mines at Alt-Aussee alone—the largest but not the only cache —there were 6,755 paintings and 237 cases of books for the Linz Center.[33]

When the Austrian Chancellor Schuschnigg visited Hitler for his disastrous conference on 11 February 1938 in the Obersalzberg, he admired a Madonna by Dürer. Hitler also boasted that he had "the best collection of the works of Spitzweg in the world" and that he had "paid 80,000 marks for a Defregger." [34] Defregger, a native of the Tyrol, delighted in peasant scenes such as *The Prize Horse* or *The Dance* showing peasants doing the *Schuhplattler*. All of Defregger's characters are chaste, beautiful, handsome, honest, and kind.

Hitler also admired Eduard Grützner, whose pictures of tipsy monks and inebriated butlers seem to have amused him. He was convinced that Grützner was greatly underrated. "Believe me, this Grützner will someday be worth as much as a Rembrandt. Rembrandt himself couldn't have painted that better." Hans Makart was another favorite. When Hitler acquired *Plague in Florence*, a secretary recalled, "his enthusiasm was boundless. He ordered all of us to admire it with him and stood entranced before the huge painting which was completely incomprehensible to me. I found the macabre theme and especially the yellowish-green corpses repulsive, but I didn't convey my repugnance for fear of spoiling his pleasure." [35]

But the artist who impressed him most was Franz von Stuck. Indeed, he once told Ernst Hanfstaengl that the two artists who had the greatest impact on his life were Richard Wagner and Franz von Stuck. He was "absolutely enthralled by them both." [36] On going to Hanfstaengl's spacious and art-cluttered home on the Pienzenauerstrasse in Munich he would invariably ask for a volume which contained Stuck's paintings. He pored over them as his breath escaped in little gasps. The volume that Hitler perused so passionately contained the following pictures: *Das böse Gewissen* (*The Evil Conscience*), a title that intrigued him; *Die Sinnlichkeit* (*Sensuality*), showing a voluptuous nude smiling enigmatically as a huge black snake slithers through her legs and around her neck; *Verfolgung* (*Pursuit*), in which a black centaur

—a favorite theme of Stuck's—chases a well-breasted blonde; and *Das Laster* (*Depravity*), depicting a nude lying on the floor laughing as a black snake moves slowly through her thighs.*

Four other pictures by von Stuck were particularly important to Hitler. One was the Medusa head in which von Stuck catches brilliantly the fascinating eyes which turned man to stone and impotence. Hitler was so fond of another painting, *Siren with Harp*—a wild-eyed nude with snakelike tail—that he acquired it in the fall of 1940 for his Linz collection. The theme and title of a third picture had obvious appeal for Hitler. It was called *Die Sünde* (*Sin*) and again shows a nude of flashing eyes with the apparently inevitable python undulating around her body. Hitler acquired it in the 1930s and hung it in his apartment in the Prinzregentenstrasse in Munich. It is now exhibited in the Neue Pinakothek.[37]

Hitler's intimate association with the fourth painting by von Stuck is best told as a personal memoir. One day in Munich during the summer of 1967, one of our sons burst into our apartment, asking excitedly, "Do you know that there is a portrait of Hitler in the Municipal Gallery at the Lenbach House?" I replied with paternal condescension that that was not possible. He asked if I would just come and take a look. Together we saw what indeed appeared to be a portrait of the Führer under the title *Die wilde Jagd* (*Wild Chase*). In this terrifying picture, von Stuck has caught the spirit of the Teutonic legend of Wotan the mad hunter, the personification of death and destruction, who rides forth at night leaving horror in his wake.[38] The huntsman in von Stuck's picture bears an uncanny likeness to Adolf Hitler. There is the dark brown hair with the famous forelock over the left temple, the brooding eyes, the large nose, the memorable little mustache. A blood-red cape swirls in the wind, and he brandishes a bloody sword. Hitler's favorite images are also pictured: decapitation, wolves, and death. At the tip of the sword there seems to dangle a human head; wolflike animals howl at the horse; hollow-eyed little creatures yell soundlessly; and ravished women and corpses are left in the path of the galloping horseman.

To the student of Hitler, however, the most arresting thing about this portrait of rampaging destruction is the inscription in the lower left-hand corner. It reads: "*Franz Stuck, Mein erstes Ölgemälde, 1889.*" That was the year in which Adolf Hitler was born.

How shall one interpret these historical facts? What is their meaning? It is known that the picture was acquired (inventory #G1405) in 1929 and exhibited in the Public Gallery in Munich at the old Glass

---

* The leading authority on von Stuck has catalogued the following themes; Women as the personification of sin, evil, or depravity: 23 paintings (with 10 listed under the title of "sin"). Pursuit and possession of women: 14 paintings. Men dueling over women: 25. Centaurs: 29. Women dominating men: 23. Sensuality, temptation, or women as seducers of men: 26. See Heinrich Voss, *Franz von Stuck, 1863–1928: Werkkatalog der Gemälde* . . . (Munich, n.d.), 251ff.

Paintings by his favorite artist, von Stuck, on themes that especially appealed to Hitler.

"Sinnlichkeit" (Sensuality)

"Verfolgung" (Pursuit)

"Das Laster" (Depravity)

"Das böse Gewissen" (Evil Conscience)

"Die Sünde" (Sin)

"Die Sirene" (The Siren)

Palace until the fire of 1931. It was later transferred to the Lenbach House. It is also known that Hitler was a habitué of art galleries, that he was in Munich during this period, and that he was an avid admirer of Stuck. He was also a person who took coincidence of dates as more than coincidental, seeing in them some secret meaning.

Is it not possible that Hitler, sometime in the 1920s, saw the picture and was immensely excited by it; that he pictured himself, very literally, as the Wild Huntsman, and adopted von Stuck's figure as his own self-image? It seems likely that he adjusted his personal appearance—forelock, mustache, and the red cape he affected at Nuremberg party rallies—to conform to this image of the hard-riding apotheosis of brutality, power, and destruction.

Literary Imagination

> I should like to write. . . . Wars pass by. The only things that exist are the works of human genius.
>
> —Adolf Hitler

As a youth, Hitler toyed with the idea of becoming a dramatist. Night after night in his walk-up room in the Stumpergasse of Vienna he stayed up long after midnight working over plays and operas under a smoking kerosene lamp. His grandiose projects required elaborate settings ranging from Hell to Heaven, with forests, mountains, and lakes in between. He was furious when his roommate suggested that he might begin his career with more modest productions. He never seems to have finished any of his projects, but we do have a prospectus for one of his plays:

> Holy Mountain in the background, before it the mighty sacrificial block surrounded by huge oaks; two powerful warriors hold the black bull which is to be sacrificed, firmly by the horns, and press the beast's mighty head against the hollow in the sacrificial block. Behind them, erect in light-colored robes, stands the priest. He holds the sword with which he will slaughter the bull. All around solemn, bearded men leaning on their shields, their lances ready, are watching the ceremony intently.

When his roommate asked what it was all supposed to mean, Adolf replied tersely that it was a play set in the Bavarian Mountains at the time of the coming of Christianity. The men who lived in the mountains did not accept the new faith and had bound themselves by a sacred oath to kill the Christian missionaries. The central conflict of the drama was between Bavarian Mountain men and Christianity.[39] Given Hitler's relationship with his father, it seems likely that there may have been quite another "central conflict" in this drama (see below, Chapter 3, p. 134ff).

Letters that Hitler wrote from Vienna in 1908 and Munich in 1914 show that as a young man of 20 and 25 he still merited the "unsatisfactory" mark in German that he had received as a schoolboy.* The same simple grammatical mistakes occur in letters and postcards dating from both his adolescent and his mature years. He continued to misspell such common words as theater, deaf, namely, immediately, going, destiny, corruption, injustice, Bismarck, as well as concepts that were important to his thinking: Darwinism, Bolshevism, socialism—and even anti-Semitism and pogroms.[40]

A few samples of the youthful Hitler's prose will indicate his style, his interests, and his idea of humor. His closest friend and roommate, who was visiting Linz, had written that he had developed a serious eye condition and also that he would return to Vienna with a viola. Hitler sent him a letter on black-edged mourning paper written in what he apparently considered to be a humorous vein. (Spellings and punctuation approximate as closely as possible the original.)

> Dear Gustl. . . . You write that the weather with you is so nice that I am almost sorry to hear it, however if it did not happen to be raining with us, it would be fine not only in Linz. I was also very pleased that you rightly are bringing a viola with you. On Tuesday I will buy myself two kr. worth of cotton Wool and 20 kreuzer of plaster, for my ears of course. It filled me with deep sorrow to hear that you are going blind; so now you will hit even more and more wrong notes, now misread the music you will end up blind I after a while will go deef [sic]. Lackaday! But in the meantime I can wish to you and your esteemed parents at least one more happy Easter Monday and greet Them as well as also you most heartily and humbly
>
> As your friend Adolf Hitler

Another letter of 1908 expresses his fury at the effrontery displayed by the Linz officials in planning to rebuild the municipal theatre without consulting him:

> Have you read the final decision of the Community Council with respect to the new teatre [sic]. It looks as if they're going to patch up the old shack once again. But this can't be done because They would not get official permission.—in any case all their fine phrases show that these super gentlemanly and ultra

---

* Hitler could not forgive or forget the low grade in German and insisted that it was entirely his teacher's fault. Years later he remembered that "congenital idiot" and "repellent creature." This "disgusting teacher had succeeded in giving me an intense dislike for my mother-tongue! He asserted that I would never be capable of writing a decent letter! If this blundering little twerp [dieser Stümper, dieser kleine Knirps]. . . ." (Secret Conversations, 549).

authoritative elements have as much idear [sic] of building a teatre [sic] as a hippopotamus has of playing a violin. If my handbook of architecture did not look so miserable I would like very much to pack it up and send it along to the Teater-Founding-Companies-Design-and-Construction-Execution-Committee's address as follows "To the all present high and mighty worshipful Comitoria for the eventual construction and ultimate establishment . . ." and herewith I close Greeting you and your esteemed parents many times and remain your friend Adolf Hitler.

A third letter, written in 1914 from Munich, is an attempt to explain why he had not registered in Vienna for military service at the prescribed time. It shows, in addition to his prose style, early evidence of a lifetime concern about conscience, guilt, and penance, and a self-image of suffering and penury which did not correspond with objective fact. Actually during the period he is discussing (1908–1909) he was living comfortably on an orphan's pension plus his inheritance; and at a later date he was to show that he was not in fact "too proud to accept" the life savings of a crippled aunt whom he had persuaded to finance his career as an artist. His total income in 1908–1909, for which he did not one stroke of manual labor, was about the same as that of a junior attorney or postal official. But Hitler did not see it that way:

And as far as appertains unto my sin or omission in the autumn of 1909, this was an infinitely bitter period for me. I was a young inexperienced man without any financial support and too proud to accept it from no matter whom, let alone ask for it. Without monetary help, cast on my own resources, the few *Kronen* often only *Heller* obtained through my work barely sufficed to give me somewhere to sleep. For two years I had no other friend [*Freundin*, literally female friend] but care and want, no other companion but everlasting insatiable hunger. I never learned the meaning of that beautiful word youth. Today after five years the souvenirs are still with me in the form of chilblains on fingers, hands and feet. And yet I cannot look back on those days without a certain pleasure now that the worst is over. Despite the greatest need in the midst of a more than doubtful surroundings I have always preserved my good name, been untainted in the eyes of the law and clean before my own conscience except for that one failure to report for military duty which at that time I knew nothing about. It is the only thing for which I feel responsible and for that a modest fine should surely offer up penance enough and I would certainly not refuse willingly to make payment.[41]

Since he never finished his "Monumental History of Humanity" (see p. 56), Hitler's major literary production remained *Mein Kampf*.

This two-volume work was begun in the summer of 1924 while he was enjoying special concessions as a prisoner in Landsberg am Lech. As he strode diagonally across the room, he dictated first to Emil Maurice and then to Rudolf Hess, who typed up Hitler's thoughts on an old Remington portable while a gramophone thundered Wagner. On Saturday nights Hitler would try out the effect of dictated passages by orating them to the coterie of Nazis who were imprisoned with him. The first volume was nearly completed when he left Landsberg on 20 December 1924. The second volume was dictated at the Haus Wachenfeld in Platterhof in Upper Salzberg with the collaboration of Max Amann, the financial director of the Party publications. It was gone over by Father Bernard Stempfle, a Jesuit editor of an anti-Semitic newspaper who was subsequently murdered at Hitler's orders during the Blood Purge of 30 June 1934. Others who read the proofs included the printer, Adolf Müller, the geopolitician Professor Haushofer, and Ernst Hanfstaengl. The original manuscript was sent as a memorial gift to Hitler's motherly patroness of many years, Frau Bechstein.

The original title, "Four and One Half Years of Battle Against Lies, Stupidity and Cowardice: Account Settled," was changed to *Mein Kampf* at the suggestion of Max Amann. By the 1940s, it had been translated into 16 languages and had become one of the most published books in the world.[42]*

According to the count of an indefatigable German literary critic, the work contains over 164,000 errors in German grammar and syntax. Not even the careful editing of friends or the thoughtful translation of an excellent American edition can rescue meaning from much of the prose. Here, for example, is Hitler setting forth his thinking about race —a concept of fundamental importance to his ideology:

> The conception of *völkisch* in consequence of its boundlessness, is not a possible foundation for movement and offers no measure for the membership of such a movement. The more practically undefinable this conception is, the more and freer interpretation it permits, the more increases also the possibility of having recourse to it. The insertion into the political fight of so undefinable a conception, interpretable in so many senses, leads to the diminution of every energetic fighting unity, as it is incompatible with this to leave to the individual the definition of his faith and his will.
>
> For this reason it is a disgrace to see in these days those who drift about with the word *völkisch* on their caps.[43]

---

* In 1976, Hitler's *Mein Kampf* still appeared on a publisher's list of "the best sellers of all time" in Germany. Classified grotesquely as *belles-lettres,* it easily won class honors with total sales in excess of 9,800,000 copies. (*Die Zeit,* Nr. 26. 25 June 1976)

A few more examples will suggest the difficulty of following his meaning:

> This is a proposal which is meant well by just as many people as it is usually ill understood by most, in order to cause the greatest conceivable harm one can possibly imagine.
>
> Protestantism in itself represents the considerations of Germanism better, as far as this lies based in its birth and later tradition altogether, but it fails at the moment when this defense of national interests must take place in territory which in general lines is either lacking in its conceptual world or is simply rejected for one reason or another.

Metaphors become rather mixed:

> For it is the remarkable thing of the battle of language altogether that its waves perhaps wash hardest around the school in particular, the planting ground of the coming generation. Every path that leads to this is expedient and its non-fulfillment must be characterized as a crime unmindful of duty.

Hitler had the habit of feminizing various forces that attacked him or rendered him impotent. He also had recurrent nightmares about suffocation. In the following passages he gets into stylistic trouble with "Dame Poverty," who is trying to strangle him:

> Whoever has not himself been on the tentacles of this throttling viper will never know its fangs.

An uncharitable critic has pointed out that a viper has no tentacles, that a snake which kills with its coils has no venom, that a man being throttled by a snake would not feel its fangs.[44]

Although *Mein Kampf* was a smashing success, Hitler planned a still more important literary work which would preserve his thinking for posterity. This plan seems to have been one of the reasons he approved having his thoughts taken down during the table conversations and staff conferences. "When the war's over," he mused, "I shall retire. Then I would like to devote five or ten years to clarifying my thought and setting it down on paper. Wars pass by. The only things that exist are the works of human genius."[45]

This scheme was abandoned, one suspects, because he was not really interested in putting his ideas on paper. "All enormous world revolutionary events," he said, "have not been brought about by the written, but by the spoken word."[46] His forte was indeed the spoken word, and few men in history have approached his power as a demagogue.

IDEOLOGY

> Our ideology is intolerant . . . and peremptorily demands . . . the complete transformation of public life to its ideas.
>
> —Adolf Hitler

Whether one considers Hitler's political ideas worth talking about depends, in part, on one's interpretation of his personality. Those who see him as a person of adroit calculation conclude that a discussion of his guiding ideas is both perverse and pointless. He was, it is said, an opportunist pure and simple. Driven by lust for power, he used any idea that helped him and abandoned it if it did not.

The most perceptive reply to this argument has been given in a valuable study of Hitler's *Weltanschauung*:

> . . . one may call this opportunism, but it has its goals. . . . One may call this power politics for the sake of power, but it has a clearly defined purpose beyond the pure wielding of power. One may call it lacking in principles, but it is not devoid of intelligible considerations of principles. . . . One might say with Polonius that there is method in this madness, even though madness it is.[47]

Those who minimize the importance of Hitler's ideology also point out that the whole Nazi movement showed contempt for ideas and stressed activism. Thus Göring's reply to the question of where the philosophy of National Socialism could be found: "It is written on the faces of the marching Storm Troopers." And his more famous comment: "Every time I hear the word 'culture,' I release the safety catch on my revolver." *

It has also been noted that Hitler's ideas were not original. His crude concepts of militarism, race, anti-Semitism, and will to power have run pandemically through German history. And it is emphasized that there is not one new idea, constructive or destructive, in the entire movement. Hence, according to this view, it is both naïve and irrelevant to talk seriously about his political ideas.

But one can also see Hitler quite differently—as a man of conviction. Basically he was, as Alan Bullock has noticed, "an intellectual, in a double sense, that he lived intensely in a world of his own thought and that words and ideas were the instruments of his power." [48]

While he could be an opportunist when the occasion required, he saw himself finally not as a Machiavellian but as an instrument of God. He believed in his ideas. And most important, he established

---

* Actually the comment was first put in the mouth of the *Freikorps* martyr Albert Leo Schlageter in a play by Hanns Johst produced in 1933, but it was appropriated by the Nazis.

his government on the basis of those ideas. Indeed, seldom in human history has the theory of a government been so ruthlessly consistent with its practice; never have ideas been more fully implemented in a society. His ideas on racism determined the laws, the art, the education, and the wage scales of the Third Reich. They determined that physics in the universities must be taught without Einstein, and psychology without Freud. They decided whether millions of people would live or die. A distinguished student of the Third Reich is justified in concluding that the role of ideas was of crucial importance in the development of Hitler's government, and that the history of those ideas is the history of their underestimation.[49]

Leaders of Western democracies in the 1930s—and later historians such as A. J. P. Taylor—underestimated Hitler disastrously and misunderstood him almost completely because they thought (quite rightly) that his ideas were ridiculous and beneath contempt. They failed to realize that Hitler believed in those ideas. They greatly overestimated his opportunistic and manipulative side and underestimated his commitment to ideology. It is of the utmost importance to emphasize that Hitler was a man both of contrivance *and* conviction, an opportunist *and* a fanatic. His foreign policy is not explicable without understanding that duality. Nor is his massacre of the Jews. The hard historic fact about the genocide is that it was not caused by the exigencies of war, nor was it a political maneuver to cope with internal unrest and domestic conflict. These people were killed as the result of one of Hitler's ideas: the idea of a superior race and the need to exterminate what he considered to be the vermin that were attacking it. The horror of Hitler was this: he meant what he said, he lived by his ideals, he practiced what he preached.

Upon occasion, it is true, Hitler manipulated his ideas and made exceptions to them in the name of expediency. After Pearl Harbor he hailed the Japanese as "Asian Nordics" and exempted them from the social and civil disabilities of his racial laws. A favorite Jewish vegetarian cook was surprised to discover that her ancestors had all been Aryanized by one of the Führer's decrees, and Göring was permitted to announce "I determine what constitutes being a Jew." But those were exceptions. Seen collectively, his ideas form one cohesive structure of "staggering logicality and consistency." [50]

Those who seek to understand Hitler's personality must study his political thinking, for it often gave expression, sometimes in ways that he was not aware of, to his deep-seated psychological impulses and desires. Hitler was no exception to the truth that a political theorist's ideas about society are rooted in his conception of man. Hitler considered mankind treacherous, irrational, base, and generally incapable of judgment. The people were "as stupid as they are forgetful"; they were "weak and bestial" or "lazy and cowardly." He spoke of the "granite like stupidity of humanity" and "the great stupid mutton-herd of our sheep-like people." [51]

Since he held mankind in such contempt, it is small wonder that he considered duplicity and cunning high attributes of statescraft. Consider the political leaders he admired, those he ignored, and those he despised. He was an avid reader of history, yet in the records we have of thousands of hours of commentary and many pages of his writings on human history and the great political leaders of the past, there is no mention of Pericles or Justinian, of Henry II or Elizabeth I; none of Chatham or Gladstone or Disraeli; none of Washington, Jefferson, or Lincoln. He regarded Winston Churchill and Franklin D. Roosevelt as fools and scoundrels: "Neither of the two Anglo-Saxons is any better than the other. . . . Churchill and Roosevelt, what impostors! . . . Roosevelt, who both in his handling of political issues and in his general attitudes, behaves like a tortuous petty-fogging Jew, himself boasted recently that he had 'noble' Jewish blood in his veins. The completely Negroid appearance of his wife is also a clear indication that she, too, is a half-caste." He saw Winston Churchill as "the undisciplined swine who is drunk eight hours of every twenty-four." Stafford Cripps, he said, was "a man without roots, a demagogue and a liar." [52]

His favorite examples of statesmanship came from the East. He applauded the trickery, for example, of Kings Ferdinand and Boris of Bulgaria: "Under the rod of the old fox, son Boris himself became a young fox and was able to work his way out of the complicated tangle of Balkan affairs." As for the Grand Mufti of Jerusalem, ah, there indeed was a "predominantly sly old fox . . . his quite exceptional wisdom puts him almost on equal terms with the Japanese. And what cunning diplomats the Japanese are!" To Rasputin he attributed a "power that could have contributed to the Slavic element a healthy life-affirmation." But his greatest praise was reserved for Joseph Stalin —a rival worthy of his steel. He spoke admiringly of "the cunning Caucasian" who commanded "unconditional respect," who was indeed, "in his own way, just one hell of a fellow! He knows his models Genghis Khan and the others very well." Stalin, he repeatedly said, was one of the "most extraordinary figures in world history." The reason for Hitler's feeling is revealing: "For him [Stalin], Bolshevism is only a means, a disguise designed to trick the Germanic and Latin people." [53]

Struggle: "The Father of All Things"

The essence of Hitler's political thought was distilled in one speech delivered at Chemnitz on 2 April 1928. The thousands upon thousands of words that preceded and followed are merely an elaboration of these few sentences:

The first fundamental of any rational *Weltanschauung* is the fact that on earth and in the universe force alone is decisive. Whatever goal a man has reached is due to his originality plus his brutality.

Whatever man possesses today in the field of culture is the culture of the Aryan race. The Aryan has stamped his character on the whole world. The basis for all development is the creative urge of the individual, not the vote of majorities. The genius of the individual is decisive, not the spirit of the masses. All life is bound up in three theses: struggle is the father of all things, virtue lies in blood, leadership is primary and decisive.[54]

Struggle was indeed "the father of all things." His memoirs repeat the refrain: "He who wants to live should fight, therefore, and he who does not want to battle in this world of eternal struggle does not deserve to be alive. Even if this were hard, this is the way things are . . . victory is forever contained only in attack." [55]

Public speeches of the 1920s trumpeted the same message and gave the German people a clear picture of the kind of government they would get under Hitler. Seldom has a man aspiring for public office been so explicit in his purposes and so open in his promises. In an early and important speech at Essen on 22 November 1926, he said: "Force is the first law. . . . Only through fighting have states and the world become great. If one should ask whether this struggle is gruesome, then the only answer could be: for the weak, yes, for humanity as a whole, no. . . ." Subsequent speeches emphasized and reemphasized the same points. One more example, from a speech in Munich on 21 November 1927, must suffice: "Politics is nothing else than the struggle of a people for its existence in this world; it is the eternal battle of a people, for better or for worse, for its existence on this planet. . . . Man [is] the most brutal, the most resolute creature on earth. He knows nothing but the extermination of his enemies in the world."

That the idea of "battle" was not mere metaphor was made clear on several occasions. From the beginning, Hitler promised war—as he did in Munich as early as 1928 and 1929: "There is no distinction between war and peace. . . . One is either a free lord or a slave. The final decision lies with the sword. . . . The battlefield is the final test of the foreign policy of a people. . . ."

It is not accurate to speak of the wars Hitler had in mind as mere acts of aggression. As his policy in Eastern Europe would make manifest, he wanted wars of pillage and annihilation. Such warfare was for Hitler the highest form of human endeavor, the greatest expression of life's purposes, the fate of all being: "One creature drinks the blood of another. The death of one nourishes the other. One should not dribble about humane feelings . . . the struggle goes on." [56]

Struggle and battle also dominated the domestic scene in Nazi Germany, as Hitler infused society with martial terminology and values. He spoke of the "battle for culture . . . a front-line spirit in the arts . . . the battle for population . . . the battle for the cradle." The symbol of his Reich was a line from his Party's anthem: "brown battalions marching." A Party propagandist in 1935 triumphantly announced the progress of the idea of a nation drilled like a battalion to follow their Führer's command and to ask no questions about destination:

> The German nation is on the way finally to finding its life-style.
> . . . It is the style of a marching column regardless of where and for what purpose this marching column is employed.[57]

To Adolf Hitler there was something deeply personal about conflict. Exaltation of war was not mere rhetorical bombast and it was not merely a diplomatic ploy; it was a personal necessity. Hitler needed war in a literal sense. He had always needed war. "I did not establish the *Wehrmacht* in order not to strike," he once said. "The decision to strike was always in me [*war immer in mir*]."[58]

Lebensraum

All his life, Adolf Hitler had been fascinated by space. He loved to shape and control it in colossal domed and long-columned buildings; he wanted to bind it together by superhighways and gigantic canals; he liked to travel through it in his open Mercedes. The vast spaces of Eastern Europe constantly beckoned him.

Since, with Hitler, personal feelings often became public policy, the demand for *Lebensraum* became a guiding principle of Nazi military planning. That Germany's destiny lay in the East and that its pursuit would mean war with Russia was a promise made as early as *Mein Kampf* and repeated in many public and private speeches. So clear and explicit was the promise that it seems best to quote Hitler directly and at some length on this matter:

> The demand for the reestablishment of the frontiers of the year 1914 is political nonsense of such a degree and consequence as to look like a crime. . . . The frontiers of the year 1914 signify nothing at all for the future of the German nation. . . . They would lead to an additional bleeding of our national body. . . . As opposed to this we National Socialists must cling unflinchingly to our foreign policy aims, that is, to guarantee *the German nation the soil and territory to which it is entitled on this earth.*
>
> *We terminate the endless German drive to the South and West of Europe and direct our gaze towards the land of the East. We finally terminate the colonial and trade policy of the pre-war period and proceed to the territorial policy of the future.* But if we talk about new soil and territory in Europe today we can think primarily only of *Russia* and its vassal border states.[59]

In a dozen public speeches of the 1920s and in his second, "Secret Book" of 1928 he repeated the demands and gave warning of his intent: "When nations are in need, they do not ask about legal rights. There is then only one question. Does a people have the power to acquire the soil and territory which it needs? . . . For centuries the cry of our forefathers has rung out: Give us space!" [60]

Hitler's long dreams of *Lebensraum* in the East seemed about to be fulfilled during the first months of his war against Russia. Again and again, as his Table Conversations show, he talked excitedly about "the grandeur of the open spaces" and planned how he would settle thousands of square miles of land. To those who asked if it would be sufficient to set his frontier at the Urals he replied, "For the present it is enough. . . ." He envisaged vast spaces connected by an *Autobahn* stretching to the Crimea ("our Riviera") and the Caucasus. He saw the Danube—the river of his boyhood—as "the river of the future." It would be connected by an enormous system of canals from the Moselle, Rhine, and the Main to the Dniester, Dnieper, and Don to the Black Sea. The highways and canals "will be studded along their whole length with German towns and around these towns our colonists will settle." Germans would live grandly in "marvelous buildings and palaces" and in "handsome, spacious farms." He left no doubt what would happen to local population, "the ridiculous hundred million Slavs." They would live in "pig-pens" without vaccination or "hygiene cleanliness." He might teach them enough to read German road signs, but anyone who "talks about cherishing the local inhabitant and civilizing him . . . goes straight off into a concentration camp!" [61]

The Concept of the Führer

In Nazi party headquarters in Munich, two portraits were displayed. One was of Hitler's personal hero, Frederick the Great; the other was of himself. Under his picture was a caption which caught the essence of the *Führerprinzip* and set forth a political act of faith in the Third Reich: "Nothing happens in this Movement, except what I wish." A respected historian of Nazi Germany concurs: "There was and there is no National Socialism without Hitler. The two are identical . . . everything else is simply a misunderstanding." [62]

The leadership principle was actually never articulated in any detail by Nazi writers. It was not possible to do so, for it rested on faith, not reason. Ultimately it was a mystery. Unable to discuss it rationally, the Nazis often resorted to mysticism and bad metaphysics. Alfred Rosenberg, for example, assures us that "the Führer is the ultimate essence of the dynamic and *völkisch* being"—a construct that could be as meaningfully rendered, "The Führer is the Ultimate Whichness and the Whole Works." Hitler himself tended to speak obliquely about the concept, preferring to say what he considered himself *not* to be: "I never felt myself as a dictator of my people, but only and always their Führer." And again: "I am not the Head of the State in the sense of either being dictator or monarch. I am now the Führer of the German people. I could have given to myself . . . quite other titles." The title itself, he preferred to believe, had been bestowed upon him by admiring women. Thus on the night of 3–4 January 1942 he told his entourage: "There is no finer title than that of Führer. . . . As for the expression 'My Führer' I imagine it was born in the mouth of women." [63]

It should be emphasized that Hitler's idea of the leader was not one of the many things he took from Italian Fascism. Mussolini's *Duce* was the leader of the state; the German *Führer* was a great deal more than that. Indeed, any political writer in the Third Reich who attempted to limit the *Führerprinzip* to the leadership of the state was in danger of being called a Fascist—a pejorative term in Nazi Germany. Hitler and those theorists who understood him properly advanced a theory that went far beyond what was called the "impersonal state" to emphasize the unlimited personal power of Adolf Hitler. [64]

At another, more rarefied level, the Führer was a mystical and magnetic force drawing together Volk and State. He was the *Volksgeist*. "The essential link which in the National-Socialist theory of the state unites the people with the Führer is a mystical conception. . . . He is no representative to whom the people has given a mandate; he is the incarnation of the Spirit of the People, and it is only through his interpretation that the People is led to a full realization of itself." This statement, as Alan Bullock has noted, is "a faithful summary, not of Nazi propaganda, but of sober constitutional and legal opinion as it was expressed in the standard textbooks of the Third Reich." Germany's leading judicial official of the period provided a more succinct summary: "Our constitution is the will of the Führer." [65]

An important way of connecting the people with their leader was to require that they swear direct personal oaths to him. Training for oath-taking started early. Children of preschool age learned the following song:

> We love our Führer
> We honor our Führer
> We follow our Führer
> Until we are men;
>
> We believe in our Führer
> We live for our Führer
> We die for our Führer
> Until we are heroes.

When little boys graduated into the *Jungvolk* at the age of ten the first formal oath was required:

> In the presence of the Blood flag which represents our Führer, I swear to devote all my energies, all my strength to the savior of

our country, Adolf Hitler. I am willing and ready to give up my life for him, so help me God. One *Volk*, one *Reich*, one *Führer*.

Confirmation of the oath was made upon entering the *Hitler jugend* at the age of 14. The ceremony was held on the anniversary of the Führer's birth:

> I consecrate my life to Adolf Hitler; I am ready to sacrifice my life for Hitler; I am ready to die for Hitler, my savior, the Führer.[66]

When the boy grew up, more oaths confirmed his boyhood experience. If he became an educator, he joined all other teachers in Nazi Germany in swearing to be "loyal and obedient to Adolf Hitler." Similarly, every member of the German armed forces was required to take an oath unique in the history of national armies in the modern era— an oath to one man:

> I swear by God this sacred oath, that I will render unconditional obedience to Adolf Hitler, the Führer of the German Reich and people, Supreme Commander of the Armed Forces, and will be ready as a brave soldier to risk my life at any time for this oath.[67]

Hitler insisted that the only alternative to the *Führerprinzip* was the chaos of democracy. In a public speech he put the matter without undue modesty: "It is madness to think and criminal to proclaim that a majority can suddenly replace the accomplishment of a man of genius." [68]

Hitler's concept of leadership placed his political theory on a different plane from that of any other authoritarian system, including Stalin's. Royal absolutism, for example, had been based not on the person of the ruler but on the institution of monarchy. "The King is dead, long live the King!" was a cry and a concept impossible among the Nazis. Hitler and only Hitler could be the Führer. Stalin, it is certainly true, exerted enormous personal power. But he was really not supposed to, and some Marxist theorists have decried his regime as the "cult of personality." That is a key difference: Nazism was nothing without the cult of Hitler's personality. Moreover, Stalin felt obliged to justify his dictatorship by claiming that it was consistent with an explicit, rationally accessible corpus of ideas: Marxism-Leninism. Hitler needed no such sanction. He was not the interpreter of an ideology; he was the Idea made incarnate. *He was Nazism.* He and he alone was the ultimate arbiter of all matters political, social, aesthetic, cultural, moral. His whim, quite literally, became the law of the land. The final sanction for his action lay in the myth and mystery of the rationally incomprehensible—and untranslatable—chant of the Nazis: "*Ein Volk! Ein*

Reich! Ein Führer!" [69] The operative member of this trinity was the Führer.

Let us put the matter in a slightly different way. Hitler was a psychopath who reaped great political advantage from his self-delusion that he was in fact the incarnation of a great historic myth. It was a delusion that had practical consequences. To the faithful he had become, in Dietrich Orlow's useful phrase, a "myth-person." He was both an individual and an abiding myth-principle, both changeable person and changeless absolute. In order to obey the myth-principle, members of the Nazi party, perforce, were obliged to obey the person. They could find no tenable ground in theory on which they could stand in opposition to the Führer; for the Führer, by definition, was the Party. Thus Hitler had it both ways: his authority was abstract, undefined, and changeless (the *Führerprinzip*), but at the same time it was arbitrary, specific, and unpredictable (the Führer's orders). He could apply his personal will and whim whenever he chose. He could judge subordinates, but they could never judge him without abandoning the basis of their faith, namely, "that he was the personification of the eternal myth." [70]

One can get some feeling for the Nazi leadership principle by observing the images that were created of the Führer as he was hailed as leader, father, and savior in poetry, painting, prayer, and song. One poem is several cuts above the usual dreary encomium of the "follow the leader" genre and is perhaps worth repeating:

TO THE LEADER

> Benign blue eyes and iron sword-hand
> Husky voice, thou and the children's most loyal father
> Behold across the continents banded together
> Stand man and wife in the flames of the soul
> Sacredly joined, an endless chain
> Wave-encircled before the morn
> Which your shoulders alone
> Have raised across the mountain-ridges out of the
> chasms of distress.[71]

Image-building was a reciprocal process: Hitler created his own image, but in an important sense his own propaganda machine also created him and required that the image become reality. As we have seen, Hitler saw himself as an infallible leader and as a Messiah sent from God with a special mission to save his Motherland. Special birthday editions of his own newspaper, the *Völkischer Beobachter*, substantiated and embellished that claim. On 20 April 1933 he was hailed as a person of absolutely unique greatness and of "unspeakable modesty." By 1937 he had become "the best imaginable expert in every specialized field." In 1938 he was a genius of "boundless passion . . . unshakable faith . . . concentrated strength . . . iron energy . . . bold determination."

In 1939 it was announced that "Adolf Hitler is the greatest German of all times." But that was not enough. Adulation waited until 1941 before it reached its apogee: "The Führer is the highest synthesis of his race. . . . He embodies the universalism of Goethe, the depth of Kant, the dynamism of Hegel, the patriotism of Fichte, the genius of Frederick II, the realism of Bismarck as well as the tumultuous inspiration of Wagner, the perspicacity of Spengler. He embodies the inspiration of Tannenberg . . . and the dash of *Sturm und Drang*." [72]

All this raises questions that are as obvious as they are psychologically complex: What was the insatiable need within this person that required such total approval? Why all this craving for personal power? Why did Hitler condemn himself to infallibility?

Racial Theory and *Volksgemeinschaft*

Hitler's idea of race was the bedrock upon which all else depended. Struggle and conflict were important to him, but the crucial struggle of all history was racial; the *Führerprinzip* was important, but the mission of this leader was to establish a racially pure "New Order." He felt himself to be the very embodiment of that racial idea. He was not the representative of the German people; he *was*—somehow—the *Volk*, as he himself proclaimed: *"Ich bin das deutsche Volk!"*

Hitler was so preposterous and irrational when he spoke about race that he was never fully believed by eminently sensible critics. Yet he meant precisely what he said. In dozens of impassioned and sincere statements he promised the German people that he intended to establish a society based upon racial discrimination. He fulfilled that promise.

It is a simple matter to set forth his racial theory; it is not so easy to convey its importance to him as a person or to his government, where it took on the dimension of a historic force. We must listen to Hitler on this issue and take him very seriously. "The race question," he said, "not only furnishes the key to world history, but also to human culture as a whole." Mixture of the blood was to him *the* original sin and *the* cause for the decline of civilization, or the expulsion from Paradise, in Hitler's version of the Garden of Eden story: "The Aryan gave up the purity of his blood and therefore he also lost his place in the Paradise which he had created for himself. He became submerged in the race-mixture. . . . In this way culture and empires collapsed in order to make room for new formations. . . . People do not perish by lost wars, but by the loss of that force of resistance which is contained only in the pure blood. All that is not race in this world is trash." [73]

Unlike other German political theorists who joined Hegel in exalting the power of the State as "the institutionalization of God on earth," Hitler considered political forms of secondary importance: "The State is a means to an end. Its end is the preservation and the promotion of a [racial] community of physically and psychically equal living beings. This very preservation comprises first the racial stock." Hitler was impatient with those who talked either about economic or political revolution: "There is absolutely no other revolution but a racial revolution. There is no economic, no political, no social revolution. There is only the struggle of lower races against the dominant, higher races."

Art too was racial: to those who talked about the international nature of art, or of national art, Hitler replied, "Everything you say only proves that you have no understanding of art. There is in art absolutely no such thing as modern art or ancient art. . . . Dutch art, Italian art. . . . There is absolutely only one art, namely Greco-Nordic Art." [74]

Basic to his thinking—and hence to Nazi practice—was his conception of one pure racial community [*Volksgemeinschaft*] which absorbed all individuality. This community of the *Volk*, like the idea of the *Führer*, was ultimately a mystery. When Hitler tried to talk about the mystical sense of community and the sacred union of *Führer* and *Volk* before 200,000 Party leaders at a Nuremberg rally on 7 September 1934, he was overcome with emotion. Once again he evoked his personal mandate from God and spoke of a mystery:

> And it was no earthly superior who gave us that command [to lead the *Volk*]; that was given us by the God Who created our *Volk*. . . .
>   To others it seems a riddle, a mystery—this force that ever unites these hundreds of thousands, that gives them the strength to endure distress, pain and privation. They can conceive of this only as the result of an order issued by the State. They are wrong! It is not the State which gives its order to us, but we who give orders to the State! It is not the State which has created us; but we fashion for ourselves our State. For one we may appear to be a Party; to another an organization; to a third something else. But in truth we are the German *Volk*. . . . Let us pledge ourselves at every hour, on every day, only to think of Germany, of *Volk* and *Reich*, of our great nation, our German *Volk. Sieg Heil!* [75]

The massed ranks of the faithful, eyes aflame with passion, roared back the mindless chant, *Sieg Heil! Ein Volk! Ein Reich! Ein Führer!*

Hitler's racial policies all rested on the theory that there was only one truly creative force in all human history: the Aryan race. This leitmotiv was sounded through a hundred speeches and public statements: "What we see before us of human culture today, the results of art, science and techniques, is almost exclusively the creative product of the Aryan. But just this fact admits of the not unfounded conclusion that he alone was the founder of higher humanity as a whole, thus the prototype of what we understand by the word 'man.'" Hitler's propensity to play variations on this theme was shown in a speech of 2 April 1927 in Munich:

> We see before us the Aryan race which is manifestly the bearer of all culture, the true representative of all humanity. All inventions in the field of transportation must be credited to the members of a particular race. Our entire industrial science is without exception the work of the Nordics. All great composers from Beethoven to Richard Wagner are Aryans, even though they were born in Italy or France. Do not say that art is international. The tango, the shimmy and the jazz band are international but they are not art. Man owes everything that is of any importance to the principle of struggle and to one race which has carried itself forward successfully. Take away the Nordic Germans and nothing remains but the dance of apes.[76]

As there was only one heroic, creative people, so there had to be (in Hitler's disjunctive way of looking at things) one completely decadent and destructive race: the Jewish people. It is both symbolically and actually true that his political career began and ended with a warning against the "Jewish Peril," which, he was absolutely convinced, threatened all civilization.

In a letter dated 16 September 1919, called by a German historian "the first piece of writing of Hitler's political career," Hitler stated his goal as "ruthless intervention" against the Jews and their "removal" from Europe.[77] In this important early statement, Hitler is careful to emphasize that his commitment to anti-Semitism is not based on emotion or sentiment. Rather, it is the result of a cold intellectual decision. Hatred of the Jews is a part of his ideology. He writes, "Anti-Semitism based on purely emotional grounds will always find its ultimate expression in the form of programs [sic]. A rational anti-Semitism, however, must lead to the systematic legal fight. . . . Its ultimate goal however must unalterably be the elimination of the Jews altogether." At the end of his career, when he wrote his political testament to the German people, the last word of the last sentence should be noted: "Above all else I charge the leaders of this nation . . . to a scrupulous maintenance of the racial laws and to the merciless opposition to the universal poisoner of all nations, international Jewry." [78] A man who is about to die does not dissimulate. Hitler meant what he said about the Jews; he had meant it all along.

The psychological factors which contributed to Hitler's personal anti-Semitism will be discussed later (see Chapter 3, pp. 186–191). Here we must examine the political theory which raised anti-Semitism to state policy and the *raison d'être* of a government. The theory can be briefly stated. It was Hitler's idea that the Jews were responsible for all the evils in the world. They had polluted the Aryan blood and driven the Germanic people out of their racial Paradise. They were the insidious enemy lurking behind all the dangers that assailed the Motherland: Bolshevism and rapacious capitalism, Freemasonry and democracy. They were responsible for the German defeat in World War I, the inflation of 1923, and the economic depression of the 1930s. They were the force behind prostitution and the cause of decadence that Hitler saw in the whole of modern arts and letters.

The Jew was always a parasite and had never made any contribution to culture or religion. Hitler is clear on these matters: "As now [sic] the Jew . . . was never in the possession of a culture of his own, the basis for his spiritual activity has always been furnished by others. At all times his intellect was developed through the culture that surrounded him. . . . Above all the two queens of all art, architecture and music, owe nothing original to Jewry. What he achieves in the field of art is either bowdlerization or intellectual theft. . . . No, the Jew possesses no culture-creating energy whatever, as the idealism without which there can never exist the genuine development of man towards a higher level does not and never did exist in him."

Not only has the Jew no art or culture; he also has no religion.

> The Jews were always a people with definite racial qualities and never a religion, . . . but what would have been more useful and at the same time more harmless than the 'purloining' of the appearance of being a religious community? For here, too, everything is purloined, or rather, stolen. But resulting from his own original nature the Jew cannot possess a religious institution for the very reason that he lacks all idealism in any form and that he also does not recognize any belief in the hereafter.[79]

The ultimate aim of the Jews, Hitler was convinced, was to conquer the world. In an important pamphlet he wrote with Dietrich Eckart as early as 1924, under the ambitious title *Bolshevism from Moses to Lenin*, he had already concluded: "One can only understand the Jews when one realizes their final purpose: to master the world and then destroy it . . . while they pretend to raise mankind up, actually they contrive to drive mankind to despair, insanity and destruction. If they are not stopped they will destroy us." Hitler's beliefs about the existence of a vast international Jewish conspiracy bent on enslaving mankind were so ridiculous that one must believe in their sincerity. He told a private meeting of his *Gauleiter* at the end of 1939, "The Jews may deceive the world . . . but they cannot deceive me. I know that they are guilty of starting this war—they alone and nobody else." He found Jews lurking in the most unlikely places. He was sure, for example, that a small but highly influential minority of Jews really controlled Sweden and that Franklin Delano Roosevelt and Sir Stafford Cripps were both Jews, as were most of the British nobility. Jesus, on the other hand, could not have been Jewish.[80]

Terror and Propaganda

When Hitler spoke of an ideal *Volksgemeinschaft*, with *Volk* and *Führer* merged into one union of "sacred egoism," there was no doubt in his mind about the identity of the primary force behind the merger. Both his psychological needs—as we shall see—and the requirements of the *Führerprinzip* obliged him to dominate and control other people. Indeed, the most basic single characteristic of both his personal life and his system of government can be reduced to one overriding need: to force others to do his will.

Hitler relied primarily upon terror and propaganda to gain control over others. He had a remarkably keen understanding of the psychological mechanism of terror and realized that it was politically effective when it evoked insecurity, fear, and anxiety. These politically desirable feelings could be achieved by making terror indiscriminate and irrational. Uncertainty was essential. Victims should not be able to tell whether they had done something wrong, *might* have done something wrong, or failed to do something they should have done. Hitler's stress on the uncertainty and irrationality of terror was also an effective means of intimidating people who were not directly involved: nonvictims tried to reason *why* a friend or neighbor had disappeared when, very often, there was in fact no rational explanation at all. Thus the nonvictim, the mere observer, also became a prisoner of incomprehensible anxiety. And so too did members of Hitler's own entourage. For their master's idea of a practical joke was to make an intimate sick with fear that he was in disfavor with his Führer. Thus, everyone in Hitler's Germany could be brought into Hitler's system of calculated terror, in which anxiety was institutionalized.[81]

Why did Hitler need so badly to frighten other people? Of course, it is true that terror is normal operating procedure in many dictatorships. But Hitler's preoccupation with it, his particular refinements, and his continual need to keep even his friends frightened strongly suggest that with him there was a pressing personal need to terrify others. Later we try to find out what there was about his experience as a little boy that caused him to seek this kind of revenge: to terrorize others as others had once terrified him.

Propaganda was a collateral method Hitler used to gain control over the German people. In the contemporary world, the word "propaganda" is used loosely and indiscriminately. One speaks today of "good propaganda for the Republican Party"; we are assured by an adman that the selling of cigarettes is "just a question of which agency has the best propaganda." That is not what Hitler meant by the word. For him it was another form of terror. His meaning was best expressed long ago by a French historian who, in writing of the reign of Henry VIII, noted that

Henry was successful in crushing opposition by means of *"violence fait aux âmes, c'est à dire, propagande."* Hitler's propaganda was—and was intended to be—"violence committed against the soul." An editorial in Hitler's newspaper admitted as much when it noted with remarkable candor that the Führer's purpose was to achieve "complete knowledge of and mastery over the soul and the mind, the bearing and the inner conviction of the people." [82]

The pages of *Mein Kampf* devoted to propaganda techniques are the most lucid in that turgid work. The methods he sets forth are based on his deep-seated distrust and contempt for the people. He assumes that they are, in his metaphors, animals or women who willingly submit to a man of iron will and brutality. Propaganda must recognize "the importance of physical terror"; it must be radical and violent, creating not mere supporters but fanatics—a favorite word of Hitlers; "always and ever" it must appeal to the emotions and not to reason; repetition is of the essence because the masses "will lend their memories only to the thousandfold repetition of the most simple ideas"; political leaders should understand the technique of the Big Lie. The clearest exposition of this last important principle was given by Hitler himself:

> In the size of the lie there is always contained a certain factor of credibility, since the great masses of people . . . will more easily fall victim to a great lie than to a small one, since they themselves . . . lie sometimes in little things. . . . Thus such an untruth will not at all enter their heads . . . therefore, just for this reason, some part of the most impudent lie will remain and stick.

Hitler's next sentence is revealing. Having just endorsed the principle of the Big Lie, he immediately denies responsibility for so immoral a concept and blames the Jews for the idea: "Those who know best this truth about the possibilities of the application of untruth and defamation, however, were at all times the Jews." [83]

The power of Hitler's propaganda to command popular support is shown clearly in the following three stories, each involving the death of a young Nazi. In the first case, a member of Hitler's *Jungvolk*, a boy of nine who was ill with pneumonia, was required to go on a forced march in order to fulfill his obligation to the Führer. The story of his death is best told by an educator who was the director of an American school in Germany prior to World War II. He accompanied the family doctor as he visited the dying boy:

> On a cot lay the restless form of a boy with an emaciated face. The doctor touched the boy's wrist to take his pulse. The boy tore his hand away, shot it high and shouted in a delirious, unnatural voice, "Heil Hitler."
> I looked at the mother. "If only they had not made him

march," she said hoarsely. "They knew he was not well. But they said he had to march. It took days to get down to the Leuchtenburg by Kahla, in Thuringia, where they were going to promote him to *Jungvolk*. His father is a Storm Trooper. He said the boy had to go. He did not want a weakling for a son. And now—:"

From the cot came words—shrill, penetrating. "Let me die for Hitler. I *must* die for Hitler!" Over and over, pleading, accusing, beseeching, fighting against life, fighting the doctor, fighting to die.

"They told him at the ceremony that he had to die for Hitler," the mother continued. "And he's so young. . . ."

She broke then, sobbing. I looked again at the boy. His pinched face wore the expression of a Christian martyr dying for the Savior. His right hand was straight up now, stiff and unyielding. His lips kept forming the words his burning soul prompted him to utter:

"I *must* die for Hitler!"

Dr. Schroeder bent low and gave his patient another injection. The cries became moans, and subsided.

"His father says if he dies, then he dies for Hitler," the mother said tonelessly.

"Now do you see what I mean?" asked Doktor Schroeder when we were again in the car. "He wants to die. What is this strange ideology that can even pervert instincts?" [84]

During the war, a captured and badly wounded German prisoner was told by a French doctor that he was about to get a blood transfusion. The wounded prisoner replied: "I will not have my German blood polluted with French blood. I would rather die." And so he did.

Another mortally wounded young Nazi soldier was approached by a priest who was immediately rebuffed: "The Führer is my faith. I don't want anything from your church. But if you want to be good to me, get my Führer's picture out of my breast pocket." When the priest complied, the boy kissed the picture with the beatific expression usually attributed to saints and martyrs, and murmured, "My Führer, I am happy to die for you." [85]

Such, in the main, were Hitler's political ideas: exaltation of the Führer and the degradation of democracy; militarism and war; conquest of *Lebensraum* and the enslavement of other people; anti-Semitism and racism; propaganda and terror to force a nation to do the will of one man.

In a later chapter we shall discuss how it was possible for such a person to attract millions of followers in a cultured country and to establish a society dedicated to such ideas. But first, let us seek further insight into the intellectual world of Adolf Hitler by noting the kinds of minds that attracted him and shaped his thinking.

THE GENESIS OF HITLER'S POLITICAL IDEAS

> "To Adolf Hitler, my dear brother in Armanen"
> —Anonymous book inscription, 1921,
> (Hitler's private library)

Many writers, seeking the beginnings of Nazism, have followed sedulously and humorlessly the biblical injunction: seek and ye shall find. They have sought the genesis of Hitlerism in Germany's intellectual past and, lo, they have found it in many places. Luther, Fichte, Arndt, Kleist, Hegel, Treitschke, Nietzsche, de Lagarde, Langbehn, Moeller van den Bruck, Spengler, each—individually or in various combinations —has been called Hitler's precursor. An immensely popular and influential book on the rise of Nazi Germany has concluded that its beginnings lay deep in the thought of great German writers and that the Third Reich, was a predictable continuation of German history.[86]

Clearly, Hitler profited when people believed that his movement was in tune with a long-standing tradition which included Prussian militarism and political authoritarianism, German romanticism, and Austro-German *völkisch* ideology, as well as "nonpolitical" attitudes and antidemocratic thought. Taken together, this remarkable and fateful mixture has been called by a distinguished German historian "the German condition." To this "condition," Luther, Hegel, and many other fine minds—including Friedrich Nietzsche and Thomas Mann— made notable contributions (see below, Chapter 4).

But Hitler did not get his ideas from these giants of German intellectual history. Not one of their books was found in his vast library. In hundreds of hours' worth of recorded monologue, and thousands of pages of speeches and memoirs, he did not show the least indebtedness to any of the great writers of his own or any other country. His ideas came initially from a more shallow and poisonous source: racist pamphlets and newspapers he read in Vienna in the days of his youth. It was from his experience in Vienna, he himself said, that he gained the ideas that shaped his life, ideas so important to him that he found it unnecessary ever to change them.

Mentors in Vienna: Lueger, Lanz von Liebenfels, List, and Fritsch

When young Hitler arrived in Vienna in 1907, the city's famous mayor, Dr. Karl Lueger (1844–1910), was reaching the height of his power. Hitler, who called him "the greatest mayor in history," was not attracted to him by his solid civic achievements but by his strident anti-Semitism. Typically, Lueger insisted that "the dragon of international Jewry must be slaughtered so that our dear German *Volk* can be freed from its prison." [87]

Hitler also said that he learned a great deal from the *Volksblatt*, to which he "turned more and more." This newspaper was a rancid mixture of racism, sex, and calumny which apparently appealed to his fascination with pornography and prostitution. He could indulge himself with such *Volksblatt* stories as that of a Jewish madam who lured Aryan girls and housewives into lives of debauchery or of old Jewish lechers who seduced Aryan youngsters of both sexes. Other issues thundered against the "Jewification" of the opera and the university and made demands that Hitler was later to fulfill: drive out the Jews from education, business, civil service, and the arts.[88]

The greatest contributions to Hitler's social and political ideas, however, were made by shoddy racist pamphlets. In an important passage of his memoirs, Hitler describes his first personal contact with a Jew and feels the onset of his "Copernican Theory" of anti-Semitism. He then tells us that having decided to study the problem in depth, he "bought some anti-Semitic pamphlets for a few pennies." [89] These pamphlets, which were so important to the formulation of Hitler's political thinking, were distributed by a virulently anti-Semitic society called the *List-Gesellschaft*. The tracts were written by two now forgotten pamphleteers, Georg Lanz von Liebenfels (1872–1954) and Guido von List (c. 1865–1919).

Of all the racist pamphlets available to Hitler during those years, only those written by Lanz and List set forth in explicit detail the ideas and theories that became unmistakably and characteristically Hitler's own. Only they preached the racial theory of history which proclaimed the holiness and uniqueness of the one creative race of Aryans; only they called for the creation of a racially pure state which would battle to the death the inferior races which threatened it from without and within; and only they demanded the political domination of a racial elite led by a quasi-religious military leader. Hitler's political ideas were later developed and reinforced in racist circles of Munich after the war in 1919–1923, but their genesis was in Vienna under the influence of Lanz and List.*

The mystical, pseudoscientific style of these pamphlets was exactly the kind of writing that appealed to Hitler throughout his life. The pamphlets were also easily obtainable and cheap; they were brief, and

---

* While it is an oversimplification to speak of Lanz as "the man who gave Hitler his ideas," there can be no doubt that Lanz's influence was direct, important, and abiding; see Wilfried Daim, *Der Mann, der Hitler die Ideen gab: von den religiösen Verwirrungen eines Sektieres zum Rassenwahn des Diktators* (Munich, 1958), and Joachim Besser, "Vorgeschichte des Nationalsozialismus im neuen Licht," *Die Pforte* (November 1950). An unconvincing rejection of this interpretation is given by Werner Maser, who, in lightly dismissing Daim's work as unimportant, shows that he has read neither Lanz nor Hitler with sufficient care; see Maser, *Die Frühgeschichte der NSDAP: Hitlers Weg bis 1924* (Frankfurt on Main, 1965), 83–85. In his biography of Hitler, Maser makes the curious argument that Lanz could not have influenced Hitler because the older man's ideas about society were so "primitive"; *Adolf Hitler: Legende, Mythos, Wirklichkeit* (Munich, 1971), 179, 249–250.

Adolf Hitler lacked both the intellectual attentionspan and the discipline to read long and recondite books. Moreover, as will be shown in a different connection, Hitler, in the spring of 1908 after his mother's death, had a special psychological reason to seek an ideology of anti-Semitic racism. The continuing influence of Lanz and List is suggested by a book in Adolf Hitler's private library, now in the Library of Congress. Our interest is caught by the curious dedication of the flyleaf, dated 1921. It reads: "To Adolf Hitler, my dear brother in Armanen." Armanen, as we are about to see, was List's special term for a racially elite ruling class.

GEORG LANZ VON LIEBENFELS

The man who usually styled himself J. Lanz-Liebenfels * had left the Order of the Holy Cross in 1900 to establish his own secret society, the "New Temple," which heralded the coming of a racist "New Order." His society soon boasted its own periodical and a genuine ruined castle in Upper Austria at Werfenstein. One day in 1907, Lanz hoisted his swastika flag of racial purity over his citadel and led his followers in incantations to the Teutonic spirits and the stars. Like all contemporary racists, he was much taken with sacred symbols and worked hard on the specific form his swastika should take. The flag dedication at the Werfenstein may not have been the first flag of this sort, but it was certainly one of the earliest. In editions of his publications of 1907, 1909, and 1910—copies of which Adolf Hitler almost certainly read,— Lanz had used a swastika of the type later adapted by the Nazis.[90] He then dropped this form, and followed Guido von List in preferring the "Kruckenkreuz" for his New Order because it combined two movements of the swastika, rolling both the Left and Right. Or, as he drew it:

$$\text{⊔} \quad + \quad \text{⊓} \quad = \quad \text{H}$$

Lanz's production of racist literature was prodigious. Year after year dozens of tracts spewed from his pen—including one he entitled *Theo-zoology, or Tales of the Sodom-Ape Men and the Electronic God, with 45 Illustrations.* But his chief production, and the one most important to Hitler, was the New Order's official organ, *Ostara*, called after the name of the ancient Germanic goddess of spring—since Lanz looked forward to a new and glorious season of Teutonic domination.[91]

There is direct evidence that Hitler actually met Lanz and read his pamphlets. On 11 May 1951, two Munich investigators interviewed Lanz, who told them that Adolf Hitler had called on him one day in

---

* He also affected other names and titles: Adolf Lanz, Dr. Jörg Lanz, Schurl Lanz, Georg Lancz von Liebenfels, Lancz de Liebenfels. The name on his birth certificate is given as Adolf Josef Lanz. He once confided to an intimate that he took various names because he did not wish to be looked up in horoscopes, hence these "astrological pseudonyms" (Daim, *Der Mann der Hitler die Ideen gab*, 42–43).

1909. Hitler had said that he lived on the Felberstrasse in Vienna and that he had been buying *Ostara* regularly at a tobacco shop. He needed a few back numbers to make his collection complete, and he asked Lanz for them. Hitler, Lanz continued, looked so impoverished, so anxious, and so intense that he gave him the missing numbers free of charge and also two kronen so that he could take the streetcar home.

Lanz's story of a conversation with Adolf Hitler is supported by external evidence. The police records in Vienna show that Adolf Hitler did indeed live in the Felberstrasse 22, door 16, in the XV District from 18 November 1908 to 20 August 1909. Up to this time some 33 editions of *Ostara* had already appeared. During these years, a tobacco shop did in fact exist at Felberstrasse 18, that is, two or three doors away from Adolf Hitler's room.

There are several ways in which Hitler's ideas differed from Lanz's. Lanz admired Vienna and the ruling dynasty; Hitler despised the Habsburgs and their "racial Babylon:" Lanz looked to the coming of a new Jesus ("Fraja-Christus") as the leader of his New Order; Hitler was satisfied with his own credentials as Messiah. Lanz spoke less specifically than did Hitler of the Jewish peril, lumping Jews, Slavs, and Negroes together as the "Dark Ones." There is in Hitler a mystical strain, but he never became quite as asinine about it as his mentor. And Hitler certainly would never have agreed that "the heroic man is not a good speaker." [93]

But their ideas are far too similar to permit any conclusion other than that Lanz influenced Hitler both in essentials and in details. By the time Hitler was living in Vienna (1908–1913), Lanz had already worked out his racial theory of history. According to him, the blond Aryans, who were responsible for all creativity in human history, were locked in mortal conflict with "Dark Forces" that sought to destroy civilization. His theory is made manifest in a dozen pamphlets still available in the National Bibliothek in Vienna. An issue of the *Ostara* of 1907 thundered against "racial pollution"; another of 1908 called for a "New Order" that would set forth decrees banning interracial marriages; a third demanded that the racial struggle be carried on "as far as the castration knife." *

---

* Specific references here are made to the following *Ostara* pamphlets: *Rasse und Wohlfahrtspflege* (Race and Welfare); *Das Gesetzbuch des Manu und die Rassenpflege* (The Lawbook of Manu and Racial Cultivation); *Die Gefahren des Frauenrechts und die Notwendigkeit der mannesrechtlichen Herrenmoral* (The Dangers of Women's Rights and the Necessity for a Masculine Morality of Masters); *Das Geschlechts-und Liebesleben der Blonden und Dunkeln* (The Sex and Love-Life of Blonds and Dark Ones); *Einführung in die Sexual-Physik oder die Liebe als odische Energie* (Introduction to Sexual-Physics, or Love as Odylic Energy); *Die Kunst der glücklichen Ehe: ein rassenhygienisches Brevier für Ehe-Rekruten und Ehe-Veteranen* (The Art of Happy Marriages: A Racial-Hygiene Breviary for Marriage Recruits and Veterans); *Charakterbeurteilung nach der Schädelform* (Judging Character through the Shape of Skulls). Other titles will convey adequately enough the quality of the contents: "Racial Mixture and Racial Degeneration"; "Race and Painting"; "Race and Philosophy". . . .

Hitler used many phrases which were the same as or very similar to ones used by Lanz many years earlier. In a pamphlet of 1913, Lanz spoke of "The Holy Grail of German Blood that must be defended by the new Brotherhood of the Templars." In a conversation of 1934, Adolf Hitler said, with reference to his elite order of the SS: "The problem is this: how can we arrest racial decay . . . shall we form an Order, the Brotherhood of Templars round the holy grail of the pure blood?" And again: "The eternal life granted by the grail is only for the truly pure and noble!" [94]

Lanz spoke—as Hitler later would—of the "Hyra-headed Jewish Conspiracy." Hitler said that racial mixture was "the original sin"; Lanz, in a pamphlet of 1911, had called it "the crime of crimes, the sin which must not be sinned . . . *the* sin." Lanz seems to have coined the word *Rassenschande*—Racial Outrage, a term Hitler made current in his Reich. Thirty years before Hitler's racial laws, Lanz had spoken of the *Mischlingsbrut* (mongrelized brood) of the *Rassenminderwertiger* (racially inferior) who threatened German purity. Lanz clearly foreshadowed Hitler's genocide: "Bring sacrifices to Frauja, ye sons of the Gods, arise and bring Him the *Schrättlingskinder*! . . . by rooting out the original *Untermenschen* the higher heroic race arises from out the grave of racial degeneration and ascends to the heights of humanity, immortality and divinity. . . ."

Hitler's later thinking paralleled Lanz's attitude to sex and marriage. In the number of *Ostara* he called "Happy Marriage," Lanz urged men to be brutal in a physical "as well as a psychic and ethical sense." Women, he admonished, must always be treated as what they really are, "grown-up children." One is reminded of Hitler's definition of ideal women as "cute, cuddly, naïve little things."

Hitler's fury at the thought of women's liberation and participation in politics may have been inspired by Lanz's pamphlet of 1909 entitled "The Dangers of Women's Rights and the Necessity for a Masculine Morality of Masters," in which he insisted that "every world historical mistake has been caused by liberated women" and warn that "anyone who preaches women's rights and wants to view women as the equal of men commits a crime against nature." Thus, he saw women in much the same ambivalent way as did Hitler: they were as easily dominated as children, yet they posed a dangerous threat to a masculine world. In the realm of sex, as in politics, the "Dark Forces" were at work, and Lanz saw them—as would Hitler—in control of prostitution and white slavery for the diabolical purpose of polluting and dragging down the master race.

Hitler's concern about homosexuality was shared by Lanz, who concluded in a pamphlet of 1911 that homosexuality is caused by "Odylic" influences and "over-exertion of the brain." Hitler must have been greatly relieved to learn that so many of his heroes of history were —according to Lanz—practicing homosexuals. His long list included Julius Caesar, Frederick II (Hohenstaufen), Joseph II of Austria,

Frederick the Great, William III of England, Cardinal Mazarin, Condé, Charles XII of Sweden, Ludwig II of Bavaria, and "Kleist, Beethoven, and so forth." Lanz was also concerned with other problems that haunted Hitler: castration, syphilis, and cancer.

Hitler, as we have indicated, was preoccupied with his own eyes and fascinated by the power they exerted over others. In pamphlets of 1911 which Hitler almost certainly read, Lanz noted the sexual power of the human eye, writing that "The most important and decisive erotic force for people of the higher race is the *eye*" (italics in original), and again that "heroic eroticism is a love with the eyes."

The shape of a person's cranium and the length of the thumb fascinated both Hitler and his mentor. In a pamphlet of 1910 devoted to the subject, Lanz discussed the head shapes of "over-educated race-murdering educational idiots and characterless professors." He concluded that women's skulls show a lower intelligence than men and that broad-skulled, dark-pigmented people are mentally and morally inferior to blond long-heads. Detailed diagrams of distinguished skulls were provided as evidence.

Lanz's influence on Hitler may have had one other manifestation. When Hitler settled in Munich after the war, he liked to go to a little Italian café in the Schellingstrasse of Schwabing. He went back time and again, even though he was not particularly fond of things Italian. He did not much like Italian food, or Italian people—with the glowing exception of Mussolini—or Italian music. Yet he continually returned to the Osteria-Bavaria—even after he had moved across the city in the Prinzregentenstrasse. All through the 1920s and 1930s he came back to the same café. Here, hour after hour, he sipped heavily sweetened lemonade or tea, beguiled his friends, and bowed gallantly to the many ladies who, like Unity Mitford, had come to the café to sit close to the Führer. (After the fall of Hitler, the name was changed to the Osteria Italiana, but one could still sit in the semi-private room with one's back to the wall in "Hitler's Place.")

There may, of course, have been other reasons why this particular café was such a favorite of his through the years. But it seems possible, given his compulsions and his loyalties to the past, that he was originally attracted because the sound of its name had reminded him—consciously or unconsciously—of the *Ostara* pamphlets that had been so important to him as a youth in Vienna.

GUIDO VON LIST

Lanz's racist colleague and fellow pamphleteer Guido von List also contributed to Hitler's thinking during the Vienna period. List and Lanz reinforced each other. Lanz belonged to the Guido von List Society; List reciprocated by joining Lanz's Order of the Templars.

Whereas Lanz defined the enemy of Germandom generally as "the Dark Ones," List was more specific. To him the enemy was the "hydra-headed international Jewish conspiracy." A great world war was necessary to annihilate the ubiquitous enemy, he wrote excitedly in bold-faced type: **"All military preparations must be made in the most complete detail in order to fight this inevitable war which will come because it must come."** [95] To prepare for this final Armageddon, a racial state must be built to exalt the Aryans and force inferior people into slavery. He quoted with approval his friend Lanz, who had written ominously and prophetically: "A day will come in which the whole mongrelized brood (*Mischlingsbrut*) which destroys customs, religion, and society must be wiped off the face of the earth." [96]

Having set forth the founding principles for his new state, List described its bureaucratic structure. The new Reich was to be divided into units called *Gaue*, each with a *Gauleiter*. The Reich would have a leader whom List sometimes called the Kaiser and sometimes Araharl. But whatever his name, he was to be "the visible embodiment of the divine Aryan law." This new leader was necessary because "the Aryo-German demands a self-chosen Führer to whom he willingly submits." The leader is bound to his followers by a sacred oath which is strikingly similar to those later taken to Hitler as Führer. In List's version of 1911 all loyal followers make the following declaration: "I swear to God the Almighty, to the invisible Araharl and to my Kaiser as the visible Araharl according to Armanian Reich laws of followship and my duty to my Aryo-Germanic people, unconditional German loyalty, to cover and protect him with my shield, my own life and limb, goods and blood."

The new Reich would also have special racial laws to preserve the Aryans and suppress inferiors: "Only members of the Aryo-Germanic humanity of masters (*Herrenmenschheit*) enjoy the rights of citizenship; members of inferior races . . . are excluded from all positions of influence and authority." To prevent "mongrelization" and "mixing of the races" stringent marriage laws would be necessary. Every householder was to be ordered to keep a blood chart of his and his wife's racial background which would be made available to government officials upon demand.

List was particularly concerned about secret symbols, most notably the swastika and the ⚡⚡ . He considered the Runic letters ⚡⚡ particularly potent and recommended that they become the symbol of a new racially pure Reich. [97]

The first edition of List's major work *Rita der Ario-Germanen* (Laws of the Aryan-Germans) appeared in 1908, just as Hitler began his extensive stay in Vienna. A new edition of 1920, which commemorates the death of List in 1919, is of particular interest. A saccharine preface entitled "From Our Master's Last Days" describes the "saintly death of the Master" caused by his contemplation of Germany's defeat. Not even he had realized the depths of Jewish perfidy. With deceitful cunning the

Jews had started World War I and then carried out their diabolical plans to stab Germany in the back. We are assured that the Master had planned a final book which would unlock the secrets of the universe by disclosing its secret language. Fate decreed otherwise, and the Master died on 17 May 1919. But before he did, he wrote a remarkable prophecy. A letter of 1918 addressed "To our faithful disciples" enjoined them once again to crush Jewish enemies of the *völkisch* state. Then he assured his followers that victory would surely come to the pure-souled Aryans: in 1932 a racially pure community would be established in a state that would root out democracy and Jewry. The letter was signed *"mit Armanengruss und Heil."* [98]

The prediction was one year and two words off. When Hitler came to power in 1933, Germans were obliged to salute each other with the *deutsche Gruss* and *Heil Hitler*!

THEODOR FRITSCH

Hitler's ideas of race were also confirmed in Vienna by reading other anti-Semitic tracts, notably those of the influential Theodor Fritsch (1852–1934), who has been called "the most important German anti-Semite before Hitler." [99]

His most popular and influential book was entitled *Handbuch der Judenfrage* (Handbook of the Jewish Question). By 1907, it had already gone through 26 printings. On the occasion of a new edition in 1931, Hitler paid one of his rare tributes to a precursor and once again stressed the importance of his Vienna experience by writing in a dedicatory statement, "I had already studied the *Handbuch der Judenfrage* intensively during my youth in Vienna." [100] The publishers of the *Handbuch* extolled Fritsch as a "creator of handy anti-Semitism." [101]

Certainly the book was handy for Hitler. It was a veritable storehouse of purportedly factual information of the type he loved to memorize in order to impress people with his knowledge. The book also contains a long list of anti-Semitic quotations culled from famous people of history. Dozens of such remarks are attributed to Seneca, Tacitus, Erasmus, Luther, Frederick the Great, Voltaire, Kant, Herder, Goethe, Fichte, Schopenhauer, Bismarck, Edward Gibbon, Wagner, and Treitschke, among others. Armed with such quotations as these, Hitler could give the impression that he had read seriously and in depth all the works of the world's great authors.

The general thesis of the *Handbuch* was the familiar one purveyed by the List Society: the Jews—in alliance with Freemasons, Catholics, and Jehovah's Witnesses—were seizing power throughout the world, and in Germany their domination was imminent. "We recognize from these facts that we must reach the necessary conclusion, namely, that we must break this curse if we do not wish to be overwhelmed by this rottenness to our own racial purity and the whole meaning of our history." [102]

A great deal of the *Handbuch* is devoted to documenting the extent of the "Jewish peril" which had allegedly penetrated dangerously into all walks of life. The entire German press, for example, was controlled by Jews. According to Fritsch, it was Wagner who first "pointed out the pernicious influence and the degenerate nature of the parasitic Jew." Fritsch claimed that Jews were responsible for "degenerate atonal music"; he warned about "Jewification" of symphony orchestras and theaters; and he listed names of Jewish conductors, musicians, pianists, violinists, tenors, sopranos, altos, baritones, actors, and theatrical agents. The *Handbuch* also provided a long and impressive list of Jewish artists in all areas of cultural life—a list which would seem to raise questions about his argument, drawn from Wagner, that Jews are incapable of artistic creativity. List computed, for example, that while comprising only 1 percent of the total population, Jews constituted 38 percent of all German poets.

The *Handbuch* warned that Jews were a particular menace in the field of medicine and viewed as particularly ominous the number of Jews specializing in pediatrics and thus "undermining the health of German children." Even more insidious were the Jews involved in "sexual specializations, their favorite work." (Since the Jew has a totally different sexuality from the German, "he can never understand the German's sexual morality.") Freud and all his Jewish disciples, we are told, had concocted a theory whose obvious purpose was "to destroy the German soul . . . to poison the food on which the German soul feeds in order to destroy it. . . . The goal is the destruction of the German family."

This "handy guide to anti-Semitism" methodically associated Jews with most of the major crimes committed in Germany during the preceding century. Page after page of Jewish names were listed as responsible for murder, treason, rape, forgery, embezzlement, and a dozen other crimes.[103] Hitler was personally indebted to Fritsch for providing him with what he considered to be "factual proof" of the Jewish menace. After he came to power, the *Handbuch* was officially sanctioned reading in the schools of Germany.

When the grand old man of German anti-Semitism died in 1934, leading Nazis paid him fulsome tribute. Julius Streicher, the notorious editor of the pornographic anti-Semitic periodical *Stürmer*, Hitler's favorite magazine, for example, proclaimed that when he first read the *Handbuch*, scales had fallen from his eyes, his life was changed, and he had become a devout German anti-Semite. Theodor Fritsch, he intoned, was "one of those great Germans sent from God of whom little children would say 'Theodor Fritsch has helped to redeem the German people and, through the German people, Aryan humanity.' " [104]

The racial ideas of Lanz, List, and Fritsch made a particularly deep impression on Hitler because they echoed the beliefs of his greatest hero, Richard Wagner (1813–1883).

Hitler and Wagner

> My baton will yet become the scepter of the future.
>
> —Richard Wagner (c. 1880)

> Whoever wants to understand National Socialist Germany must first know Wagner.
>
> —Adolf Hitler

It is very difficult to exaggerate the importance of Wagner in Hitler's life and thought. He himself best summarized that influence when he said that anyone who sought to understand him and his movement should first understand Richard Wagner.[105]

Adolf's boyhood swung around the pole of Wagner. "My youthful enthusiasm for the Master of Bayreuth," he recalled later, "knew no bounds." As his only friend of those years noted, "Listening to Wagner meant to him not a visit to the threatre, but the opportunity of being transported into the extraordinary state which Wagner's music produced in him, that escape into a mystical dream world which he needed in order to endure the tensions of his turbulent nature. . . . He was intoxicated and bewitched. . . ." [106]

His need for Wagner did not abate in manhood. "For me, Wagner is something Godly and his music is my religion," he told an American correspondent in the 1930s. "I go to his concerts as others go to church." [107]

There was one particular dimension of Wagner that Hitler found irresistible: the forbidden passions of incest and Oedipal sex which Wagner discussed more daringly than any dramatist of his time. As we shall soon see, Hitler was terribly concerned about his own incestuous desires. So was Wagner, as his operas testify.[108] It seems likely that only he could have gotten away with the first act of *Walküre*. The opera begins, it will be recalled, with Siegmund, a warrior in flight, taking refuge one stormy night in the house of a man whose wife, Sieglinde, arouses the hero's passion. She reciprocates even though both lovers are aware that they are twin brother and sister, the children of Wotan. Brother and sister plan to elope; they kiss passionately, and only the fast curtain prevents the audience from seeing the consummation of their love. Later, Sieglinde, made pregnant by her own brother, gives birth to Siegfried, one of Wagner's and Hitler's favorite heroes. Thus, like Hitler, Siegfried was the product of an incestuous relationship.* And he too saw himself as a wolf—actually, in his case, "Wolf-Son."

In a later chapter we shall note Hitler's extraordinarily close rela-

---

* See below, Chapter 3, p. 132. The blood relationship between Siegfried's parents was closer than Hitler's. Since Siegfried's mother was his father's sister, she was also his aunt and his father was his uncle. Thus, as Barbara Stoddard has pointed out, Siegfried was his own cousin.

tionship with his mother. Here we should note the important role that Oedipal themes play in Wagner's operas, especially in *Siegfried* and *Parsifal.*

The hero of *Siegfried* spends a great deal of his waking day thinking of his mother. When in Act III, Scene 3, for example, he comes upon the beauteous Brünnhilde sleeping in the forest, he is struck by "the wildest emotion." But his thoughts immediately turn to his mother. His first impulse is to call for his mother's help; his second is to bury his face in the breast of this mother-substitute (stage instructions are Wagner's):

> (*He stares at the slumbering form in the wildest emotion.*)
>
> Burning enchantment
> glows in my breast;
> anguish and awe
> flame through my being:
> my senses falter and swoon!
>
> (*He becomes greatly distressed.*)
>
> On whom shall I call
> that he may help me?
> Mother! Mother!
> Remember me!
>
> (*He sinks, as if fainting, with his face on Brünnhilde's bosom. He rises with a sigh.*)

He is then torn by self-doubt. Lacking the courage to awaken the sleeping beauty, he chastizes himself for being so cowardly and again identifies his "fiercest longings" with his mother. He calls to her:

> Fiercest longing
> sears all my senses;
> my heart pulses wildly,
> trembleth my hand!
> What ails thee, craven?
> Can this be fearing?
> O mother! mother!
> Thy valorous child!

When Brünnhilde finally awakens, she hails Siegfried in passionate song as her long-awaited lover. Siegfried's answer is addressed, not to her, but to his mother:

> (*Breaks forth in extremest ecstasy.*)
>
> O hail to her
> who gave me my birth!

It is an unusual response to a young lady's invitation to make love.

Parsifal, like Siegfried—and like Hitler, at least in his own self-image—is a handsome, dashing, and ingenious young man who has a tendency to be trapped by beautiful, scheming young women who invariably remind him of his mother. (As we shall see, Hitler's sexual life was devoted to young women who served as mother substitutes.) The wild and wily Kundry sees at once that the way to quicken Parsifal's sexual interests is to get him thinking about his own mother. Then, winding her arms seductively about his neck, she plays his mother in a passionate scene replete with incestuous overtones. She bestows his "mother's blessing" upon him in the form of his first sexual kiss. Parsifal responds erotically to this maternal blessing: "How all things tremble, quake and groan, possessed by sinful longing."

Hitler cherished all Wagner's operas, but both as a young man in Vienna and as chancellor, his favorite was probably *Lohengrin*. He saw it at least ten times in Vienna, and as chancellor he amazed opera buffs with the fact that he knew the entire libretto by heart.[109]

Why was Hitler so extraordinarily interested in this particular opera? The music is of course compelling, but Hitler also had a special interest in the story—sufficient to make him memorize all the words of the long text. It will be recalled that the plot involves a beautiful blonde who is falsely accused and menaced by her lecherous guardian, Frederick of Telramund. To her rescue comes the gallant, pure-souled, silver-armored knight Lohengrin, bearing the redemptive power of the Holy Grail.

There are several things about this libretto which Hitler must have found appealing. He could glory in the German nationalism: *für deutsches Land das deutsche Schwert!* (for German land a German sword!). But more specifically he could identify with the heroic knight, Lohengrin. For Hitler too had "wondrous flashing eyes," and he could respond affirmatively to the ring of the words as Lohengrin's men hail him as leader and ask his commands: *"Des Führers harren deine Mannen! O bleib' und zieh' uns nicht von dannen!"* But the knight cannot stay with them, nor tarry in the bridal chamber (no more could Hitler), for he has a higher mission than to love women, namely, to serve the Holy Grail (we are reminded that Hitler talked of the "Holy Grail of German blood"). Thus, Lohengrin sings, "Farewell my love, my wife, farewell! Henceforth the Grail commands my life!"

Let it be suggested here (and discussed in detail later) that Hitler preferred *Lohengrin* to all other operas chiefly because he saw himself as the immaculate knight who rescued his beloved young mother (both Klara Hitler and the German Motherland) from his lecherous and race-contaminating old father, who had been, in point of fact, the legal guardian of Klara before he married her. It does not seem a mere coincidence that in 1938, Hitler approved of a portrait of himself as Sir Adolf, a flashing-eyed, stern-visaged knight in shining armor and Charlie Chaplin mustache astride a mighty stallion, the bearer of a new cross and the defender of racially pure Germania. Of the dozens of portraits painted of the Führer in 1938, Hitler chose this one as the official painting which alone was to be exhibited during the year.[110] (See illustrations, following p. 160.)

Hitler shared Wagner's infatuation with the mythical universe of primitive German legend. His two favorite books, which he read again and again as a youth in Vienna, were a volume on architecture and a popular edition of heroic legends entitled *Legends of Gods and Heroes: The Treasures of Germanic Mythology*.[111] The Nordic mysteries that enthralled the boy continued to intrigue the man. On the night of 25–26 January 1942, while German soldiers froze and bled on the Russian front, Hitler mused about the rhythms of life, the beauties of Greek architecture, the training of dogs, the marvels of science, and the significance of mythology. He had come to believe, he exclaimed, that science would someday actually recapture eerie emanations coming from Wagner's legendary world—vital vibrations transmitting the secrets of the cosmos. Only he and Wagner really understood these vibrations: "When I hear Wagner it seems to me that I hear rhythms of a bygone world. I imagine to myself that one day science will discover in the waves set in motion by the *Rheingold*, secret mutual relations connected with the order of the world." [112]

Years before in Vienna he had become terribly excited when his roommate, a student at the Conservatory of Music, told him that among Wagner's posthumous notes was found a sketch for an opera based on the legend of "Wieland the Smith." Hitler knew the story well. Wieland was the half-god son of a giant who had been taken captive by a king who had crippled him and forced him to work as the royal smith. For revenge, Wieland raped the king's daughter and enticed his two sons into the smithy, where he killed them. He then fashioned beakers from the boys' skulls and drank a toast to the spirit of revenge before raising himself on wings he had forged and disappearing into the flaming sky of evening. It was a splendid story, Hitler thought, and he decided to write an opera about it as a tribute to Wagner and an expression of his own genius.

The fact that he had no conception of musical composition and was unable to play an instrument did not deter him. His genius, he said, would surmount any difficulty. "I shall compose the music," he said to his friend, "and you will write it down." Adolf's idea was to take Wagnerian themes and put them into a form that he imagined would have been meaningful to the ancient Teutons. The opera was to be performed on instruments that were used at the time of the Eddas, and Hitler searched excitedly through the volumes of the Hof-Library to discover the kinds of musical instruments known to the ancient Germans. Young Hitler seems justified in thinking that his would be the first Wagnerian opera performed on rattles, drums, bone flutes, and *Luren*—brass wind instruments some two yards long, apparently used in

German antiquity as a kind of crude bugle to communicate between villages.

Adolf worked on his opera with passionate and humorless intensity, night after night composing music, drawing detailed sets of "Wolf Lake" (where the opening scene in Iceland was to take place), plotting and replotting the story. Then suddenly he stopped work. His musical tribute to Wagner remained unfinished.[113]

Wagner's Racial and Political Ideas

Wagner's contribution to music and literature was immense. W. H. Auden called him "the greatest genius that ever lived"; his importance to T. S. Eliot is manifest throughout *The Waste Land*; D'Annunzio wrote a Wagnerian novel; D. H. Lawrence, Zola, Shaw, Renoir, Joyce, Thomas Mann, Gauguin, Degas, and—for a time—Nietzsche all prided themselves in being called Wagnerian. Bruckner was profoundly influenced by him, and Mahler said that he had two teachers, Beethoven and Wagner —"after them, nobody." A musicologist has summarized Wagner's contribution to culture by saying flatly that he had a "greater influence than any other single artist on the culture of our age." [114]

All of these people were paying homage to Wagner the musician. They might have tempered their praise if they had studied his racist and political tracts with the care Adolf Hitler devoted to them. For Wagner, the creative musical genius, helped create a political monstrosity. It was he who was the primary inspiration for German National Socialism. The creator of that system himself said that any who sought to understand it "must first know Richard Wagner," and boasted that he had read everything the master had ever written. "I have the most intimate familiarity with Wagner's mental processes," he said. "At every stage of my life I come back to him." [115]

COMPARISON WITH HITLER

It is not entirely clear when Hitler first began to read Wagner's essays on race, politics, art, and religion, but it seems probable that it was during his youth in Linz and Vienna, when the composer's prose works were available in municipal libraries, and at a time when young Hitler was filling his leisure hours by going to the opera or reading racist tracts. The young man who was so much taken by Wagner's music was delighted to learn that his hero's political and racial ideas were the same as his own. And his lifelong feeling of affinity for the great composer must have been strengthened by the discovery that he and Wagner were in many ways so much alike.

Both Hitler and Wagner, in their special fields, were innovative geniuses who captivated millions of listeners; both wrote execrable prose. Had their reputations and influence depended on their written words, both would have been lost to history as obscure racist cranks.

Hitler's memoirs and speeches are virtually unreadable. Wagner's German is so convoluted and awkward that his long-suffering translator and admirer felt repeatedly obliged to explain why his English translation sounded so infelicitous. He wrote despairingly in one footnote:

> I have thought it best to quote the German of these last two sentences, as their construction presents peculiar difficulties to the translator; a remark that applies, in fact, to almost all the remainder of this article.[116]

Like Hitler, Wagner considered himself an authority on a great number of subjects. The ten volumes of his tortuous prose set forth major pronouncements on Shakespeare and American prisons; Spanish poetry and vegetable diets; the philosophy of Leibniz, Hegel, and Schopenhauer; the habits of wolves; Chinese art; the physical training of athletes; the tactics of the Turkish army; the foreign policy of Richelieu; Greek poetry; the medieval papacy; and contemporary American theatre.

An American critic has given a graphic picture of an evening's conversation with Wagner. His account would apply equally well to a night spent listening to Hitler's monologues in the Berghof or in his "Wolf's Lair" during World War II. One needs to keep remembering that the writer is talking about Richard Wagner and not Adolf Hitler:

> He was one of the most exhausting conversationalists that ever lived. An evening with him was an evening spent in listening to a monologue. Sometimes he was brilliant; sometimes he was maddeningly tiresome. But whether he was being brilliant or dull, he had one sole topic of conversation: himself. What *he* thought and what *he* did.
>
> He had a mania for being in the right. The slightest hint of disagreement, from anyone, on the most trivial point, was enough to set him off on a harangue that might last for hours, in which he proved himself right in so many ways, and with such exhausting volubility, that in the end his hearer, stunned and deafened, would agree with him, for the sake of peace.
>
> It never occurred to him that he and his doings were not of the most intense and fascinating interest to anyone with whom he came in contact. He had theories about almost any subject under the sun . . . and in support of these theories he wrote pamphlets, letters, books . . . thousands upon thousands of words, hundreds and hundreds of pages.[117]

That Wagner's opinion of his own talents was scarcely less exalted than Hitler's is suggested in a diary entry of September 1865: "I am the most German of beings [*der deutscheste Mensch*]; I am the German spirit. Consider the incomparable magic of my works." [118]

The Intellectual World of Adolf Hitler

The favorite personal defense of both men was vigorous attack and the projection onto others of any weakness felt in themselves. Wagner, for example, was notably effeminate in his tastes. He affected Parisian perfumes, lush pink-colored silken gowns, and ermine-bedecked robes, and he did much of his composing surrounded by clouds of perfume and incense as he lounged amid soft cushions. Yet he saw himself as a tough man and exalted a crude Nordic-Spartan way of life, condemning the French and the Jews for effeminate softness and thundering against such "luxury cravers" in life and music.

As with Hitler, Wagner's much proclaimed hardness was an expression of his personal need to hide weaknesses. And like Hitler he continually addressed complaints to his friends about how badly he was treated. Also like Hitler, he repeatedly threatened to end his own life. His letters sound this leitmotiv: all my friends have deserted me, and I suffer the "bare-faced ingratitude, disloyalty and treachery of people" to whom "I have shown nothing but kindness. . . . My situation is perilous; I balance on the narrowest foothold—one push and all is over. . . . Someone will be sorry one day . . . yes—I would fain perish in the flames of Valhalla." [119]

Wagner could tolerate opposition or criticism no better than Hitler. A mistress remembered how "a mild disappointment drives him almost to despair; the slightest irritation goads him into fury." [120]

Hitler's lack of humor and inability to smile at himself was shared by the man who had the greatest influence on his life. "Whoever accuses me of insincerity," Wagner wrote, "must answer for it to God—but whosoever accuses me of arrogance is a fool!" [121]

Hitler was incapable of friendship—and quite capable of betraying the most intimate trust or of sending a friend to his death. With Wagner, friendship had one purpose: to supply him with the money his genius deserved and his tastes required. His sense of honor was as tenuous as his promises, and his greed as bottomless as his vanity. He tried to seduce the wives of men who befriended him; he had raped his own wife when she was 15. When given a huge sum of money by mad King Ludwig, he spent it lavishly on himself while his wife, alone and desperately ill, was forced to depend on the charity of friends whom Wagner ridiculed. He was unable to attend his wife's funeral because of an infected finger.[122]

Both Hitler and Wagner showed a solicitude for animals they denied to human beings. Hitler fretted about the last moments of lobsters in the cooking pots of German restaurants and issued special orders to protect ravens; Wagner's heart went out to frogs. He thundered against vivisection of frogs as "the curse of our civilization" and hurled anathemas at those—most notably the Jews—who, he said, sought to "truss and torture them." [123]

Like Hitler, Wagner remained in many respects a child and showed little capacity for emotional growth. All his life he threw temper tantrums when thwarted. He was furiously jealous and would weep and sulk when his second wife showed any affection for her father, Wagner's musical rival, Franz Liszt. Like Hitler, he enjoyed playing hide-and-seek with children. A contemporary describes Wagner's childlike reactions in listening to rehearsals for the first performance of *Tristan*:

> If a difficult passage went particularly well, he would spring up, embrace or kiss the singer warmly, or out of pure joy stand on his head on the sofa, creep under the piano, jump up onto it, run into the garden and scramble joyously up a tree. . . .[124]

He shared Hitler's enthusiasm for a vegetarian diet and was if anything more confident of its therapeutic powers. An article entitled "Religion and Art" extols the merits of eating vegetables and claims that in American prisons "the most dangerous criminals have been transformed, by a wisely planned diet of vegetables, into the mildest and most upright of men." [125]

Both Hitler and Wagner tried to impress women with their physical prowess. Hitler showed women how long he could hold his arm extended in the Nazi salute. Wagner climbed trees to prove his virility to the beautiful Judith Gautier, who had sent him perfumes in which he bathed and bolts of pale silk in which he wrapped himself.[126]

The mother-love that formed so important a part of Hitler's life was shared by Wagner. As we have noted, Oedipal sex was a theme of his operas, and his private letters to his mother suggest a degree of intimacy which seems excessive, even when one takes into account the author's penchant for emotional prose and his antipathy to understatement. As a young man in his 20s he wrote:

> It is you alone, dearest Mother, whom I think of with the most heartfelt love, the deepest emotion. . . . I want to write and speak . . . to you in the tenderest tones of a lover to his beloved. . . . Ah, when I think of these last eight days of our intercourse! It is perfect balm to me, true refreshment to recall to my soul each aspect of your loving kindness! My dear, dear Mother, what a wretch were I if I could ever grow cold towards you! [127]

The story of Wagner's birth and family background shows striking parallels to Hitler's account of his own family. As we shall see, Hitler was never sure of his father's ancestry and feared that he might have been Jewish. He insisted in his memoirs, however, that all his ancestors were of pure German peasant stock. Wagner prefaces his autobiography with the promise of "unadorned veracity"—a promise broken on the very first page, where he gives misinformation about his baptism and the wrong name for his own father. He says that he was christened two days after birth and that his father was Karl Friedrich Wagner, a clerk in the police service at Leipzig.[128] Wagner was indeed born in Leipzig on 22 May 1813, but he was not baptized until 16 August of that year—a surprising delay when one notes that Frau Wagner was a devout Catholic who saw to it that all her other children were baptized within a few days of their birth.

For a century it was assumed that Wagner's parentage was as he gave it in his memoirs. Then, quite by accident in 1933, a Swiss journalist, while checking a visitors' hotel registry in the little town of Teplitz, Bohemia, made some surprising discoveries. He learned that Johanna Rosina Wagner, "wife of police clerk Wagner," had traveled from distant Leipzig across a war zone in the summer of 1813 to seek refuge from her cuckolded husband. She had come with her infant son Richard to stay with his natural father and her lover, the actor Ludwig Geyer, who was performing in Teplitz. He too had registered at the Three Pheasants Hotel.[129]

Karl Friedrich Wagner, the legal father, died 22 November 1813, and his widow married Geyer a few months later. The boy Richard was known locally as Richard Geyer, but at the age of 14, six years after Geyer's death, he readopted the name of his legal father. The reason seems clear. It was generally believed at that time that Ludwig Geyer was a Jew. Certainly his son's schoolmates thought Richard had those physical characteristics which prejudice popularly associates with Jews, and they taunted him with being Jewish. Richard's frenetic denial took several forms. Not only did he change his name, but he also denied publicly what he had long suspected in private: that his natural father was Geyer. Like Hitler, Wagner became a violent anti-Semite in an effort to persuade himself and others that he could not possibly be Jewish because he hated the Jews so much.

All this is not lacking in irony, since intensive research has "so far failed to produce a single demonstrably Jewish ancestor on the Geyer tree." But that is not the point. The point is the one we shall emphasize with Hitler: throughout their lives both men *believed* that they themselves might be "part Jewish." Hitler suspected that his grandfather might have been a Jew; Wagner believed that his natural father, Ludwig Geyer, was Jewish. Hence the shrillness of his denials, and the public insults to Jewish friends. But despite his persistent and strident anti-Semitism, many people in his day continued to consider Wagner to be Jewish.[130]

WAGNER'S ANTI-SEMITISM

Wagner's attitude towards Jews comes through clearly in his private correspondence, where, over and over again, he shows that against the Jews he did indeed bear "a grudge as necessary to my nature as gall is to blood." [131] But the fullest and most influential statement of his anti-Semitism appears in a long article entitled *Das Judentum in der Musik* ("Judaism in Music"), which originally appeared in a musical periodical of September 1850 above the signature of one "K. Freigedank [Freethought]." Wagner revised the piece in 1869 and published it separately in a widely distributed pamphlet. It is noteworthy that there was no substantial change between the first edition and its revision 20 years later.

Like Hitler, Wagner was physically repelled by Jews and considered them freaks: "We have to explain to ourselves the *involuntary repellency* possessed for us by the nature and personality of the Jews so as to vindicate that instinctive dislike which we plainly recognize. . . . instinctively we wish to have nothing in common with a man who looks like that . . . an unpleasant freak of nature." [132] German anti-Semites before Wagner had opposed the Jews on political, religious, economic, or racial grounds. Wagner believed that his contribution was to have proved once and for all that "Jewish blood" was incapable of producing anything of creative value in thought, art, literature, or music. That was to become Hitler's thesis.

When one considers that three of the most seminal minds of the modern era have been Jews, the claim of both Wagner and Hitler that Jews cannot be culturally creative is as silly as it is pernicious. The adherents of Karl Marx now number more than one-third of the people of the earth; Albert Einstein, one of the two greatest physicists in history, revolutionized our thinking about the physical universe; and Sigmund Freud did as much as anyone to expand man's understanding of himself. Wagner's insistence that Jews could never contribute to the world of music is denied by the work of the composers Mahler and Schoenberg and many of their famous pupils; by such instrumentalists as Kreisler, Schnabel, Heifetz, Menuhin, Stern, Milstein, Serkin, Rubinstein, Richter, Solomon, Shainman, and Horowitz; and by such conductors as Klemperer, Szell, Leinsdorf, and Bernstein. In reminding us of the sheer number of creative Jewish musicians, a musicologist has written, "If anyone wants to tell me this is coincidence my reply is that this is simply not creditable. The intellectual and artistic output of Jews in this century relative to their numbers is a phenomenon for which I can think of no parallel in history since Athens five centuries before Christ." [133]

Wagner, however, simply said flatly that the Jews were incapable of artistic creativity: "Our whole European art and civilization . . . have remained to the Jew a foreign tongue; for, just as he has taken no part in the evolution of the one, so has he taken none in that of the other, but at most this unfortunate homeless wanderer has been a cold and hostile observer. In this Speech and in this Art the Jew can only parrot and fake [*nachsprechen, nachkünsteln*]; he cannot truly speak poetically or create artistically." Wagner, whose own German was atrocious, insisted that no Jew would ever be able to write or speak good German: "The first thing that strikes our ear as really outlandish and unpleasant is the Jew's production of the voice sounds as a creaking, squeaking, snarling snuffle . . . an intolerably jumbled blabber [*zischender, schrillender, sumsender und murksender Lautausdruck . . . eines unerträglich verwirrten Geplappers*]." [134]

It was clear to Wagner—as it was to Hitler—that the Jews had no religion and that Jesus was not of Jewish blood. His blood, Wagner explained, was of a peculiar sort, a mysterious blood of special potency and magical power which was to be found only in one other person: Parsifal.[135] Wagner and Hitler also agreed that Christian baptism could never wipe out the faults of Jews. Even after baptism, Wagner wrote, the Jew must remain "the most heartless of all human beings."

Like Hitler after him, Wagner insisted that the Jew was, at the same time, both a cowardly degenerate and a dangerous threat to Germany. He too spoke of the need for "fighting for emancipation from the Jew" because "the Jew in truth is already more than emancipated: he rules." Again and again he warned that the German spirit was threatened by the cunning enemy: "the utterly alien element of the Jews." [136]

What Wagner called "the Jewish problem" was on his mind almost as much as it was on Hitler's. But Wagner was not sure what the solution should be. On one occasion he thought it possible that the Jews could be assimilated. But in a later article he stressed the necessity of a "grand solution" and looked forward to the time when "there will be no longer—any more Jews." He also called for a "war of Liberation" against this "enemy of mankind." [137]

His essay "Judaism in Music" ends with a cryptic entreaty quoted often, and for obvious reasons, by Nazi writers. Having called the Jews "the evil conscience of our modern civilization" and a curse upon mankind, he concludes:

> Take ye your part ruthlessly in this regenerative and self-destructive work of redemption. Then are we one and undissevered!
>
> But bethink ye that one thing can redeem you from the curse that burdens you: the redemption of Ahasuerus: *Destruction!* [138]

What did Wagner mean in this heavy-handed passage? What was the "redemption" of Ahasuerus, and how could it come through *Untergang*—a word which may be translated as *destruction, ruin, fall,* or *annihilation*?

The reference to Ahasuerus is opaque. It seems likely, however, that Wagner did not mean the Persian king of that name *; rather he meant the legendary Wandering Jew, traditionally called Ahasuerus. According to *völkisch* legend, this Ahasuerus was an evil and insidious being who had infected the German people with cholera and syphilis.

---

* In the Old Testament, Esther adroitly outmaneuvered the Persian King Ahasuerus, who had ordered a massacre of the Jews. She cajoled him into reversing the order so that Persians, and not Jews, were murdered—a deliverance celebrated by Jews as the Feast of Purim (Book of Esther, 8, 9). Was Wagner suggesting that the German people (like King Ahasuerus) had been conned by the Jew who (like Esther) had insinuated themselves into positions of power in order to destroy the German people? Was he saying that the only way to rid Germany of the Jewish enemy was by mass murder? Such a reading of the passage seems possible, but unlikely.

Accursed through the ages, he would find rest from his wanderings only in death at the end of time.

Wagner was probably not calling for the actual annihilation of the Jewish people. He may have been speaking metaphorically and saying that the "Jewish problem" would be solved only when the Jews themselves underwent the "regenerative and self-destructive" work of annihilating their own Jewishness. Only then could they join with the Germans in a cultural "redemption." Thus would Jews and Germans "become one and undissevered." If that is what Wagner meant, *Untergang* becomes something less than literal destruction.

But that interpretation is complicated. Adolf Hitler liked his ideas to be simple and brutal. Above all, for deeply personal and psychological reasons, he wanted the Jews *destroyed*. And he read in order to confirm his own prejudices; he would have found here in Wagner confirmation of his most cherished belief that the only way the "curse that burdens" could be lifted from himself and from the German people was through the annihilation of the Jews.

PARSIFAL AND THE MYTH OF ARYAN SUPERIORITY

Wagner used his journal, the *Bayreuther Blätter*, to disseminate anti-Semitism and to call for a pure Germanic culture. In this periodical he set forth a racial theory of history which reinforced at every turn the ideas which Lanz-Liebenfels, List, and Fritsch had given to Hitler: all creative and heroic impulses of history were Aryan; the decline of civilization was due to the pollution of this noble race by Jewish and other alien blood; redemption lay in the blood and the coming of a heroic leader who would establish a racially pure society which would bring about the "total regeneration . . . of the *Volksblud*" and the "resurrection of the German *Volk* itself." [139] It was consistent with Wagner's idea of the superiority of the Aryan race that it should treat others as chattel. This attitude was, he said, "quite justified in the natural sense," for the "noblest race" should exert dominion and exploitation over the lower races. [140]

Wagner's deep concern with the racial crisis which he saw all about him was not only expressed in his essays. As a perceptive critic, Robert Gutman, has noted, *Parsifal* was the "artistic counterpart" of the message he had set forth in the ponderous prose of "Herodom" —a call for Germany's racial regeneration:

> In *Parsifal* with the help of church bells, snippets of the mass and the vocabulary and paraphernalia of the Passion, he set forth a religion of racism under the cover of Christian legend. *Parsifal* is an enactment of the Aryans' fight, a struggle, and hope for redemption. . . . the temple scenes are, in a sense, black masses perverting the symbols of the Eucharist and dedicating them to a sinister God. [141]

Parsifal is many things, but one thing it is not: it is not, as has been said, "a profound statement of the Christian message." [142] It blasphemes the Christian message; it slanders ethical values. In this opera Wagner prostitutes Christian symbolism and the Christian message to extol the virtues of racial power.[143] To do so, Wagner makes his Teutonic hero into the very Son of God. In a scene taken directly from the Gospel of St. John, a woman anoints Parsifal's feet with rare perfume and dries them with her hair. The Last Supper becomes in the opera an initiation rite for German knights who bind themselves in a blood oath not to forgive their enemies but to destroy them:

> The Knights
>
> (*First half*)
>
> Take ye the bread,
> change it again
> to body's strength and power;
> true unto death,
> toil to the end
> to work as the Savior willeth!
>
> (*Second half*)
>
> Take ye the wine,
> change it anew
> to blood within you burning;
>
> (*Both halves*)
>
> Live all in one,
> brothers so true,
> to fight with courage holy.
>
> (*The Knights have risen; they pace from both sides toward each other and solemnly embrace during the music that follows.*)

At the end of the opera, it is Parsifal who is given the power to absolve mankind of sin. As the whole company gazes at him "in highest rapture," the Knights of the Holy Grail cry out:

> Wonderous great Salvation!
> The Redeemer is redeemed!

These are the last lines of the opera, and Wagner's stage instructions for the finale make his identification of Parsifal with Jesus very clear:

> (*A ray of light falls; the Grail's glow is at its brightest. A white dove descends from the dome and hovers over* Parsifal's *head.—Kundry, with her eyes uplifted to* Parsifal, *slowly sinks*

lifeless to the ground before him. Amfortas *and* Guernemanz *kneel in homage before* Parsifal, *who waves the Grail in blessing over the worshipping Brotherhood of Knights.)*

(The curtain closes slowly.)

In the whole of the New Testament, only once does a white dove descend from heaven. It hovers above the head of only one person: Jesus.

In Wagner the Grail and the spear of Parsifal are not symbols of Christ's blood shed for the redemption of all mankind; they are signs of Aryan racism. The lush incestual sexuality, the racist symbolism, the *völkisch* fetishes of *Parsifal* have nothing whatever to do with the life and teachings of the Jewish carpenter of Nazareth.[143] Wagner himself pointed out that a main purpose for writing *Parsifal* was to deliver his racial message. In an article published in the *Bayreuther Blätter* for November-December 1882, he explained that in this opera "the Kingship of this Brotherhood" was the elite of the race, "a race chosen to protect the Grail." [144]

If later generations were confused by the message of *Parsifal*, Adolf Hitler was not. "If we strip *Parsifal* of every poetic element," he said, "we learn from it that selection and renewal are possible only amidst the continuous tension of a lasting struggle." [145]

CONTEMPT FOR PARLIAMENTARY DEMOCRACY

Hiter also confirmed his contempt for parliamentary government by reading Wagner, who abhorred the idea of constitutions and had nothing but scorn for democracy, a word he put in quotation marks or labeled pejoratively "Franco-Judaical-German democracy."

In a bitter essay entitled *Was ist Deutsch?* (What is German?), Wagner said of the liberal revolution of 1848 which sought to establish a constitutional government in Germany, "I have no hesitation about styling the . . . revolutions in Germany entirely un-German"; and he dismissed liberal democrats as the "loud-mouthed movement of 1848." [146]

After Bismarck founded the Empire, Wagner continued to denigrate and ridicule parliamentary democracy. In an article which appeared in the *Bayreuther Blätter* of May 1879, he commented, "Where our un-German barbarians sit, we know: as the victors of something called universal suffrage we find them in a parliament that knows everything except the seat of German power." [147]

One of his reasons for opposing liberal democracy was that it sought peace among nations. Wagner, like Hitler, believed that war is beneficial and that the conquest of lesser breeds is sanctioned by the laws of Darwinian nature. History, he said in words that *Mein Kampf* would echo, proves that man is "a beast of prey, developing through constant progress. The beast of prey conquers countries, founds great realms by the subjugation of other subjugators, forms states and organizes civilizations, in order to enjoy his booty in peace. . . . Attack and defense, suffering and struggle, victory and defeat, domination and servitude, all sealed with blood; this is the entire history of the human race. . . ." [148]

Wagner called for an end to "the French and English nonsense" of parliaments and constitutions and demanded the establishment of a dictatorship under a heroic leader. Thus he endorsed the *Führerprinzip* without actually using the word. He preferred to talk of a "Hero" or a "*Volk*-King" or a new "Barbarossa." He had a theory that the medieval Barbarossa was a sort of spiritual reincarnation of Siegfried or Parsifal, and he helped to popularize the ancient German hope that in times of deepest distress a magnificent hero would come to save the German people. In an effort to convey all the mystery, awe, and reverence due to this "Hero wonderously become divine," Wagner created a new word —*Wahn*. As the English translator of Wagner notes, the word is "absolutely untranslatable, I shall mostly retain it as it stands. It does not so much mean an 'illusion' or 'delusion' in general as . . . a 'symbolical aspiration.' " [149] Like Hitler's Führer concept, the idea of *Wahn* is a political principle beyond explanation and beyond reason. Wagner tried and failed to give a rational explanation: "This symbol is the King. In him the citizen honors unaware the visible representative, nay the live embodiment, of that same *Wahn* which, already bearing him beyond and above his common notions of the nature of things, inspires and ennobles him. . . ." [150] Whatever this prose might have meant to other readers, it meant to Adolf Hitler a confirmation of his faith in the *Führerprinzip*: the principle that the only form of government suitable for German society was a dictatorship under a leader with godlike powers, beyond the ken or control of men or institutions.

Chamberlain, Drexler, and Eckart

HOUSTON STEWART CHAMBERLAIN

A contributor to Hitler's racial thinking and an important bridge between Wagner and Hitler was Houston Stewart Chamberlain (1855–1927). This peculiar Englishman came to worship at the shrine in Bayreuth; there he embraced—along with Wagner's political thinking —one of the master's daughters, whom he married. Chamberlain declared that the three greatest poets of humanity were Homer, Shakespeare, and Wagner, but the greatest of these was his father-in-law. In 1899 he produced his chief work, *Grundlagen des XIX. Jahrhunderts* (Foundations of the 19th Century). This ponderous and virtually unreadable tome somehow went through ten editions in a dozen years.

The thesis of the book is familiar to readers of Lanz, List, Fritsch, Wagner, and Hitler. There are shades of difference, but basically Chamberlain too believed in the racial theory of history and extolled the creativity of the Aryans: "Physically and spiritually they stand out among all men; hence they are by right, Lords of the world." Emperor William II was immensely impressed. He hailed Chamberlain as his "companion in battle" and wrote to him, "It was God who sent your book to the German people and you personally to me." [151]

Germany's defeat in 1918 at the hands of England and its allies was a terrible blow to the expatriate. But in meeting Hitler the old man found new hope, for he recognized him as the long-awaited Führer who would establish a new racial Reich. The meeting took place in October 1923 when Hitler made the first of many pilgrimages to the shrine at Wahnfried. There he was received by Wagner's widow, Cosima Wagner, mistress of Bayreuth. Hitler delighted everyone. He told Frau Wagner that her husband was the greatest influence on his life, that "it all began" in Linz after the young Hitler listened to one of Wagner's operas. He flattered Wagner's son Siegfried; he absolutely captivated the grandchildren. And then a paralyzed man "with spent eyes in the face of a child" was wheeled in. It was Wagner's son-in-law, H. S. Chamberlain. Hitler generously thanked him for all his contributions and played to the hilt the role of flashing-eyed man of destiny and racial deliverer. The next day the invalid dictated a letter to Hitler. Like so many others, he had been taken with Hitler's eyes: ". . . that you bestowed peace upon me is largely attributable to your eyes and the gestures of your hands. It is as if your eyes were equipped with hands, for they grip a man and hold him fast. . . ." The letter ended, "My faith in the Germans has never wavered for a moment, but my hope, I must own, was sunk to a low ebb. At one stroke you have transformed the state of my soul." [152]

ANTON DREXLER

Munich as well as Vienna was important to the development of Hitler's political thinking. But his experience there during the years 1919–1923 served mainly to strengthen the political ideas which, in essence, he had already formulated. Hitler himself showed in an indirect way that his political education in Munich was effective precisely because it was not an entirely new experience for him; rather, it reinforced ideas which had come to him in Vienna before the war—ideas, he said, so important to him personally and so basic to his political thinking that they had formed a "granite foundation" and required no major changes for the rest of his life.[153]

In describing his initiation into politics at Munich in 1919, Hitler stressed the importance of a little pamphlet entitled "My Political Awakening." Typically he did not identify the author of the pamphlet —with rare exceptions he did not like to admit that he had predecessors in developing his "Copernican Theory" of racism. In fact, the author was a sickly fanatic named Anton Drexler. His shabby racist tract seemed to Hitler a providential omen. Once more the "Goddess of Fate" had intervened and thrust his destiny upon him. He read the little booklet with mounting excitement and the eerie feeling that he was reliving vividly some prior experience, an experience, he wrote, "which I had gone through personally in a similar way twelve years ago. Involuntarily I saw thus my own development come to life again before my eyes." [154] Twelve years before meant 1907–1908, when he was devouring the pamphlets issued by the List Society. It was during this period that he underwent the traumatic personal experience which made him a fanatic anti-Semite.

Drexler was an adjunct member of the Thule Society, the most influential of the many racist anti-Semitic groups spawned in Munich during the immediate postwar period. Outwardly it called itself a literary and scholarly circle, and it met at the posh Hotel Vierjahreszeiten. In addition to holding discussion meetings, the Thule Society also established secret arms depots to fight "subversion and treason" and distributed scurrilous anti-Semitic literature. By the time of the Revolution of 1918, the society numbered some 1,500 members in Bavaria and included many of Hitler's later supporters. Hitler himself, it is reported, "was often a guest of the society." [155]

In addition to pledging their lives in the battle against Jews, prospective members were obliged to pass several tests. They had to prove that their Aryan blood had not been sullied for at least three generations,* indicate in a special form the amount of hair on various parts of their body (like Lanz, the society believed that non-Aryans were excessively hairy), and submit a footprint on a separate piece of paper as proof that their feet were Aryan. [156]

As early as October 1918, however, Drexler had decided that discussion groups such as the Thule Society were insufficient to create a new Germany. So, in collaboration with a sportswriter named Karl Harrer, he established the "Political Workers' Circle," which was to serve as the nucleus for a large political organization he planned to call the German Workers' Party. The topics announced for discussion at meetings of the Workers' Circle convey sufficiently the ideas of the group. On 11 December 1918 the topic was "Germany's Greatest Enemy: the Jew"; on 16 January 1919, "Why the War Came"; on 22 January, "Could We Have Won the War?"; on 30 January, "Why the War Was Lost"; and on 5 February, "What Are the Consequences of the Lost War?" The message was clear: Jews were to blame. They had caused the war and traitorously lost it. The Jews were Germany's greatest enemy; they must be removed. [157]

The actual German Workers' Party—which was to become the mighty Nazi movement—was established by Drexler and Harrer on 5 January 1919 in the Fürstenfelder tavern. It differed very little from the discussion groups and activities of the Thule Society or the other racist groups to which all the founders belonged. The party's total membership fluctuated between ten and 40 men during the first half of 1919. Its program was to meet weekly in various taverns, to lament the loss

---

* One of the reasons Hitler never joined the society may have been that he would have been unable to provide such proof.

of the war, and to explain Germany's past defeat and present difficulties by pointing to the "Jewish peril."

It was at one of the badly attended meetings of the ineffective little party, held in a tavern in the Tal on 12 September 1919, that Adolf Hitler appeared. As a political informer attached to the Bavarian Regiment No. 4 he had come to investigate the group. That evening he heard a speech by a certain Professor Baumann who raised the question of separating Bavaria from the Reich. Hitler was furious. He jumped to his feet and denounced the professor's suggestion with a passion and invective so intense the man left the meeting. Anton Drexler was enormously impressed with the magnetic newcomer's oratory and whispered in broad Bavarian dialect to the man next to him, "Man, he's got something there, we can sure use him!" As the meeting was breaking up, Drexler handed Hitler the fateful pamphlet, *My Political Awakening.*

Later that month Hitler made what he was to call "the most fateful decision of his life" and joined the German Workers' Party. But not as number 7, as he and many subsequent historians have recorded. His membership number was 555, which is to say he was the 55th member to join the party—it began its numbering at 500 to give the illusion of a strength it did not in fact possess. Hitler's number 7 was his number in the party's Workers' Committee.[158]

DIETRICH ECKART

The member of the Thule Society who most influenced Hitler and who helped reinforce his political ideas was the racist poet Dietrich Eckart, best known in Germany for his translation of *Peer Gynt.* Hitler's eyes invariably moistened whenever he spoke of Eckart. He dedicated the second volume of *Mein Kampf* to him—a highly untypical public acknowledgment of indebtedness. And years later, in a midnight reverie, he looked back upon Eckart as an admonishing father figure in whose presence he felt like a small boy: "He shone in our eyes like a polar star. . . . When he admonished someone, it was with so much wit. At that time [1922] I was intellectually a child still on the bottle." [159]

Eckart had written scathing attacks on Jews and other non-Germans in his racist periodical, *Auf gut Deutsch* (In Plain German), a journal which shows clearly Eckart had read Lanz-Liebenfels, List, Fritsch, Wagner, and H. S. Chamberlain, and that he too was fascinated with runic mysteries and such secret signs as the SS and the swastika. His poetry—which Hitler considered "as beautiful as Goethe's"—proclaimed his belief in Germany's messianic mission:

> Father in Heaven, resolved to the death
> Kneel we before Thee, Oh answer us, then!
> Does aught other people Thine awful command
> More loyally follow than we Germans do?

Is there one such? Then Eternal One, send
Laurel and victory to it, mighty with fate.
Father, Thou smilest? Oh, joy without end!
Up! and onward, onward to the holy crusade.[160]

A little known pamphlet apparently written jointly by Hitler and Eckart and published in 1924 is an important source for Hitler's political ideas during these years. Despite its ambitious title, *Bolshevism from Moses to Lenin: Dialogue Between Adolf Hitler and Me,* * there is virtually nothing in the pamphlet about Bolshevism. Hitler's concern here, as it had been in Vienna, is with race and the alleged Jewish conspiracy. He and Eckart discuss various other matters, including Freemasonry, Christianity, pacifism—but not Communism. Hitler's invectives against the "Bolshevik peril" were to come later, and for reasons of political expediency. Actually, he was never, as his propagandists later claimed, "instinctively anti-Communist." Indeed, he had grudging admiration for their radical activist theory and openly admired the way Communist leaders used their theory to control and manipulate the masses. Stalin, he often said glowingly, was "just one helluva fellow!"

Eckart was not the primary source of Hitler's ideas, as has sometimes been suggested; rather, he served to confirm and deepen the prejudices Hitler had already picked up. There is nothing important in this pamphlet which Hitler had not already learned in the writings of Lanz, List, Fritsch, Wagner, and the *Protocols of the Elders of Zion*. And the tedious refrain would be sounded literally dozens and dozens of times in Hitler's speeches and soliloquies, up to and including the Last Testament of 1945: the Jews, with their secret plans to undermine nations, were the enemies of mankind; from the time of Moses, "Jewish Bolshevism" had been developing an insidious "international conspiracy" designed to infiltrate and traduce Western civilization; it was the historic duty and destiny of Germany to destroy the "Jewish peril." In remarks he would repeat in his wartime conversations, Hitler argued that Christianity, like Judaism, was a form of Bolshevism. The "Jew Paul," he said, was responsible for emasculating Christianity with appeals to love and brotherhood: "Brotherhood! Pacifism! Drivel! and the Jew triumphant!"

In the pamphlet, Hitler and Eckart were ambivalent about Martin Luther. They praised him for his anti-Semitism and approved of the

---

* *Der Bolschewismus von Moses bis Lenin: Zwiegespräch zwischen Adolf Hitler und Mir* (Munich, 1924) There is dispute over whether Hitler was directly involved in writing the pamphlet. Nolte believes that he was coauthor; Plewnia thinks that Eckart did all the actual writing but "incorporated Hitler's ideas." Certainly Hitler neither denied authorship of the booklet nor repudiated the ideas it contains. See Ernst Nolte, "Eine frühe Quelle zu Hitlers Antisemitismus," *Historische Zeitschrift* 192 (1961); Margarete Plewnia, *Auf dem Weg zu Hitler: Der "völkische" Publizist Dietrich Eckart* (Bremen, 1970).

synagogue burning he recommended, but they found that in splitting the Christian church Luther increased the power of the Jews. Hitler and Eckart also expressed disappointment with Luther's draconian "solution to the Jewish Problem" (see Chapter 4), which they found much too moderate. The pamphlet calls for "rooting out" the Jews.[161]

Protocols of the Elders of Zion

> Through treachery and cunning we will conquer the earth.
> —*Protocols of the Elders of Zion*

> I found these Protocols enormously instructive.
> —Adolf Hitler

The Hitler-Eckart pamphlet demonstrates that inspiration, even for the most sordid literary creations, may come from many sources. One can detect traces of Lanz, Wagner, and H. S. Chamberlain, but especially evident is the influence of a famous forgery, the *Protocols of the Elders of Zion*. This classic example of the conspiracy theory of history insists that in a conclave of 1897 the "Elders of Zion" hatched a diabolical plot to undermine society, overthrow governments, plunge mankind into war, and seize power throughout the world. One passage from the *Bolschewismus* pamphlet illustrates its dependence on the anonymous forgery:

> Every, yes, every social injustice of importance which exists in the world today goes back to the subterranean influence of the Jews. . . . One can only understand the Jews when one realizes their final purpose: to master the world and then destroy it. . . . While they pretend to raise mankind up, actually they contrive to drive mankind to despair, insanity and destruction. If they are not stopped they will destroy us.[162]

Long after the *Protocols* were dismissed as a clumsy and vicious fraud, Hitler continued to believe in their validity. In a public speech of 1923 he told his audience that the German inflation of that year was all a part of the Jewish plot. "According to the Protocols of Zion," he said, "the peoples are to be reduced to submission by hunger." And in his memoirs he argued that the best proof that the *Protocols* were genuine lay in the fact that the "Jewish" *Frankfurter Zeitung* branded them a forgery.[163]

Hitler's personal indebtedness to the document remained heavy. After first reading it, he later recalled, "I saw at once that we must copy it—in our own way of course. . . . We must beat the Jew with his own weapon. I saw that the moment I read the book." And he added, "down to the veriest detail, I found these Protocols enormously instructive." Specifically, he noted how much he had profited from their advice about "political intrigue, the technique of conspiracy, revolutionary subversion, prevarication, deception, organization." [164]

In reading of the alleged conspiracy of the Jews as set forth in the *Protocols*, one has the feeling that one is reading descriptions of Hitler's own political ideas, plans, and techniques as set forth in his memoirs, speeches, or conversations in the 1930s or during World War II. Page after page, all one needs to do is substitute the words "Hitler will . . ." whenever the *Protocols* say that "the Jews will . . ." A few examples must suffice.

The first "protocol" establishes the thesis that "in laying our plans we must recognize that . . . civilization cannot exist without absolute despotism" and demand that total political power be given to one diabolical leader. Other protocols proclaim the necessity of "weakening the public mind" and "manipulating the mob" through calculated, "all-embracing terror," control of the press and education, and establishment of a Ministry of Propaganda. Gigantic mass meetings will be held; all those who oppose the dictatorship will have their property confiscated; civil liberties will be granted only to those who support the leader. He will be worshiped as a new god, and his "power will excite mystical adoration." Having crushed all domestic opposition, the leader will foment European dissension and set out on a path of conquest and domination. . . .

The first primitive version of the *Protocols* seems to have been concocted by unknown authors about 1899 in the Okhrana, the Imperial Russian Secret Police. They were utilized by the anti-Semitic Black Hundreds to help foment and justify the pogroms at the beginning of the century. Historical scholarship has been unable to identify the plagiarist who first put a bad German novel by Hermann Gödsche together with a French political tract satirizing Louis Napoleon to form the bogus *Protocols*. But there can be no doubt about the name of the man who first published them and gave them currency. He was a remarkable Russian named Serge Alexandrovich Nilus, who died believing that the *Protocols* were the genuine extracts of minutes of the first Zionist Congress held in Basel in 1897. They were stolen, Nilus insisted, by an unnamed "benefactor of mankind" from the headquarters of the Zionist movement in France.

Nilus was obsessed with the "Jewish problem" and terrified by a conspiracy which, he was convinced, sought not only to conquer the world but also to attack him personally. In his home he kept a locked chest called "The Museum of the Anti-Christ." It contained in complete or partial form many examples of the Star of David which, he had persuaded himself, was the secret sign of the Jewish international conspiracy. Since that star is formed by the intersection of two triangles, Nilus came to believe that any triangle was suspect—it might be a part of the terrible sign. Thus in his chest he hoarded a large assortment of suspicious triangles: clippings of advertisements, the triangular seals of technological colleges, pieces of church vestments, and military and diplomatic insignias employing six-pointed stars as parts of their devices. He even collected several pairs of galoshes—presumably because a Triangle Rubber Company had emblazoned its ominous trademark on the soles of its products. The picture of Nilus apprehensively tracking down old Jews who were making subversive footprints in the snow as they sloshed about hatching nefarious schemes for world domination is—as an English investigator has noted—delightful.[165]

The results of Nilus's publication of the forgery, however, were less amusing. The *Protocols* as used by the Okhrana were instrumental in fomenting pogroms which murdered thousands of Jews. A 1905 edition prepared by Nilus was published by the Imperial State Printing Shop at Tsarskoye Selo. When the forgery left Russia in 1918 it was extraordinarily successful in promoting worldwide anti-Semitism. During the 1920s, Nilus's edition was translated into 16 languages. The bishop of Warsaw officially endorsed it; in Great Britain the penny-awfuls took it up, and even the *Times* was tempted to believe in it. On 8 May 1920 the *Times* asked some worried questions:

> What are these *Protocols*? Are they authentic? If so, what malevolent assembly concocted these plans, and gloated over their exposition? Are they a forgery? If so, whence comes the uncanny note of prophecy. . . ? Have we been struggling these tragic years to blow up and extirpate the secret organization of German world dominion only to find beneath it another, more dangerous because more secret? . . . The "Elders of Zion" as represented in their *Protocols*, are by no means kinder task masters than William II and his henchmen have been.

A year later, however, in August 1921, the *Times* published the first positive proof that the *Protocols* were in fact a forgery and, in hopes of finally burying the matter, an editorial entitled "The End of the *Protocols*." But the *Times*'s expectations were premature. Throughout the 1920s the virulent message of the *Protocols* continued to spread throughout the world.[166]

In America, Henry Ford's publishing company accepted the *Protocols* as genuine and incorporated them in a widely disseminated volume, *The International Jew: The World's Foremost Problem*, some 3 million copies of which were sold or given away as a public service to high school, municipal, and college libraries. Mr. Ford later regretted publicly that he had been duped by the forgery. But the book he sponsored "probably did more than any other work to make the *Protocols* world famous." [167]

The actual courier who brought the forgery from Moscow to Munich and Hitler after World War I seems to have been Alfred Rosenberg, the man who later had some importance in formulating Nazi ideas.

But Walter Laqueur gives him far too much credit in calling him "the chief ideologist of National Socialism." [168] That title belongs to Hitler and Hitler alone.

In 1917, Rosenberg had been studying in Moscow, bent on a career not in politics but in architecture. Given his later historic role as Reich Minister for the Occupied Eastern Territories, it is not inappropriate that the design he submitted in 1917 for a diploma in engineering was one for a tremendous crematorium with adjacent graveyard.[169] Shortly after fleeing Russia and arriving in Munich, he joined the Thule Society, and from there the *Protocols* came via Dietrich Eckart directly to Hitler. The *Protocols* served Hitler both as a primer for his politics and as documentary proof of Jewish conspiracy, perfidy, and treason. They would serve the same purpose for the schoolchildren of Germany. Two years after Hitler came to power, the *Protocols of the Elders of Zion* became required reading in all German schools.

Later, Adolf Hitler would add an irony to the story more bitter and cruel than even the author could have imagined. The setting for the *Protocols* is the Old Jewish Cemetery in Prague, where the author has the diabolical "Elders of Zion" meet at midnight to plot the conquest of the world. Some 40 years after the story was written, in 1939, Adolf Hitler occupied the city; on his orders, the tiny burying ground dating from the 15th century, with its 12 layers of graves and hundreds of anonymous tombstones, became the only place in Prague where old Jews could go for their walks and where Jewish children could play since all parks and playgrounds were denied to them. Here in the Old Cemetery they crowded in among the graves of their ancestors to await their own deaths. From time to time SS guards brought in an old Jewish scholar, Dr. Tobias Jakobovic, and ordered him to blow the shofar for the amusement of the Nazis. Next to the cemetery stands the old Pinkas Synagogue. After the Holocaust, surviving Jews inscribed on its walls with meticulous and tender care in tiny letters the names of 77,290 Jewish men, women, and children of Bohemia and Moravia killed by orders of the man who had adopted the ideas of the bogus *Protocols* as his own.

Other Influences

Other racist writers supplied arguments with which Hitler padded and embroidered the basic ideas he had picked up in Vienna as a youth. He must surely have read, for example, the thin volumes and pamphlets of Adolf Harpf, who sometimes wrote under the name of Adolf Hagen, and was a co-worker with Lanz-Liebenfels. In his pamphlets of 1905–1910, Harpf, like his colleague Lanz, extolled Aryan superiority and demanded that Germany establish a new Reich which would dominate all Europe. What was needed was one powerful Leader of the Aryan super race [*Führer des Übervolkes*] who would guide them in Teutonic battle against the forces of racial degradation. Specifically he demanded a war against Russia and the establishment of a vast Aryan empire in Eastern Europe, with the Slavs serving the Germans as slave laborers.[170]

Many of Hitler's ideas on propaganda and techniques for enforcing his will on the masses came from Gustave Le Bon's influential study on the psychology of the crowd. This little book appeared in a German translation (Leipzig, 1908) as *Psychologie der Massen* and was available to Hitler in Vienna.*

Hitler's indebtedness to Le Bon bordered on plagiarism. Time after time in his famous chapter on propaganda in *Mein Kampf* he took key ideas directly from Le Bon's earlier work. One can surmise that having remembered reading the book in Vienna, Hitler had a friend bring it to him in his pleasant room in the Landsberg prison where, during 1924, he was dictating his masterpiece which served both as memoir and dissertation on political manipulation. Long before Hitler, the Frenchman had discovered that the masses are "distinguished by feminine characteristics"; they require a master for "they are always ready to bow servilely before strong authority." The effective leader should appeal always to their emotions, never to their reason; he should stage huge "theatrical meetings," for they "always have an enormous influence on crowds." He should establish a pseudoreligion. According to Le Bon, the effectiveness of propaganda depends upon violence, the big lie technique, and constant repetition: "When we read a hundred, a thousand, times that X's chocolates are the best, . . . we end by acquiring the certitude that such is the fact." The successful leader should avoid all discussion of his power; he is one who "hits upon a new formula as devoid as possible of precise meaning." He should avoid written statements, but "in his verbal program . . . there cannot be too much exaggeration. . . ."[171]

Hitler took his ideas about propaganda and the signs, symbols, and other paraphernalia of his Party from Le Bon, German racists, and Italian Fascism. The swastika, for example, was used as a racial symbol by Lanz and many other racists in the decade prior to World War I. The Ehrhardt Free Corps Brigade painted it on their steel helmets in 1920 and sang a marching song, set to a catchy old English melody, with the following chorus:

> Swastika on helmet,
> Colors of Red, White, Black,
> The Ehrhardt Brigade
> Is marching to attack!

* John Toland is mistaken when he writes that Hitler could not have been influenced by Le Bon because his work had "not been translated into German." (*Adolf Hitler* (New York, 1976), 221.) In addition to the 1908 translation, there was a second German edition in 1912, a third enlarged edition in 1919, and a fourth in 1922. (Later editions appeared in 1932, 1935, 1938 and 1939.)

The Intellectual World of Adolf Hitler

When the men of the Ehrhardt Brigade later joined Hitler's movement, they took their song with them and simply substituted *"Sturmabteilung Hitler"* for *"Die Brigade Ehrhardt."* [172]

The runic symbols, ⚡⚡ , as we have seen, were of much interest to Guido von List as the secret sign of an elite racist group.

Hitler's indebtedness to Mussolini was particularly great. From him he acquired the use of uniform colored shirts and the arm-extended salute. One of his symbols, in addition to the lictor's bundle, was the death's head. Hitler's *Sturm-Abteilungen* (Storm Troops) had a direct predecessor in Mussolini's *Squadristi*. The personal oath was sworn to the Duce before it was sworn to the Führer. Hitler's district leaders for the Party, called *Gauleiter*, were very similar to Mussolini's *Federale*. Mussolini had preceeded Hitler in consecrating flags and preserving the names of the fallen in quasi-religious ceremonies. He had also organized women and youth into separate political organizations and had established secret police.[173]

What is true of Hitler's party organization, symbols, and practices is also true of his political thought: there is not one concept that can be called his own, not a single major idea that he did not take from someone else. Hitler's strength lay not in the originality of his thinking but in his political acumen and the overwhelming magnetism of his personality. Through the alchemy of his charisma he transmuted the shoddiest racist ideas into a powerful political program and made people believe that he was their savior.

The fact that his ideas had great historical impact would in itself be reason enough to study them. But we have had a particular reason for looking into his peculiar mental world. We seek to understand his personality, and one way of doing so is to see how his psychopathology was reflected in the distorted world of his ideas; another way is to study his personal life directly. We now turn to his development from infancy, stressing those psychological experiences which helped form his personality and shape his political career.

CHAPTER 3

The Child As Father to the Man

I and the public know
What all schoolchildren learn,
Those to whom evil is done
Do evil in return.

—W. H. Auden

Every basic conflict of childhood lives on, in some
form, in the adult.

—Erik Erikson

HITLER'S GENEALOGY, which has puzzled biographers since his death, worried him all his life. It seems likely that one of the reasons he required all citizens in his Reich to identify and prove the racial purity of their ancestors was because he harbored nagging doubts about his own.

Difficulties in tracing his lineage are increased by a tangled web of family intermarriage, incest, and illegitimacy, as well as by name changes and incomplete or altered baptismal records. A few facts, however, have emerged from provincial archives, parish church records, the oral traditions of the countryside, and the sedulous research of historians.

It can be affirmed that one spring day in 1837 a middle-aged peasant woman from the tiny farming village of Stronnes in Lower Austria journeyed to a nearby hamlet to have the parish priest baptize her baby boy. The entry in the Baptismal Registry for the Parish of Döllersheim, Tomus vii, page 7, records that the woman was Maria Anna Schickelgruber, unwed daughter of Johann Schickelgruber, a farmer in Stronnes. Her baby, who was to become the father of Adolf Hitler, was christened Aloys Schickelgruber. The blank for the father's name was not filled in that day. Many years later, in 1876, the name Johann Georg Hitler was added in a different handwriting and a fresher ink.[1]

The mother never revealed the name of her lover, and over the years doubt and controversy enveloped the identity of the man who was Hitler's paternal grandfather. But the family background of his grandmother is clear. For generations, the Schickelgrubers had been farmers or itinerant farm laborers in the lovely, rolling countryside of the Austrian *Waldviertel*. Even in a part of Europe where inbreeding and incest was not uncommon, the Schickelgrubers were noted for particularly complex family interrelationships, as well as a history of mental and physical aberration. Documents later collected in the Gestapo files show, for example, that three of the children of one Joseph Veit, a cousin of Hitler's father, were mentally retarded, and one of them committed suicide in a mental institution. Other branches of the family seem to have been similarly affected—or so it was rumored.[2]

Maria Anna Schickelgruber had escaped the backbreaking labor of contemporary farm women to go to Graz, or possibly some other provincial city, as a domestic servant. There she had become pregnant and returned to her home village, at the age of 41, to bear her son, Alois, (as he later preferred to spell his name) the future father of the Führer. When the boy was five years old she married a shiftless itinerant mill worker named Johann Georg Hiedler (the name was also spelled Hüttler, Hidler, Huetler, Hittler, and Hitler). Since he was unwilling or unable to care for the boy, his older brother, a relatively stable and hardworking farmer, Johann Nepomuk Hiedler, took the child in and raised him as his own son on his farm in the village of Spital until the boy, at the age of 13, left to make his fortune in Vienna.

In the capital, Alois became an apprentice to a boot maker and began a rise in life remarkable for a man of his background and unique in the family annals. Two years after completing his apprenticeship, at the age of 18, he was accepted by the Austrian Civil Service in the Department of Inland Revenue. Thus he was to become a member of the Royal and Imperial Officialdom, entitled to all its very considerable perogatives and privileged to wear its uniform—which he would do with palpable pride for the rest of his life.

In 1876, when he was 39, he succeeded in persuading his foster father, Johann Nepomuk Hiedler, to have his birth records altered. Thus, on an autumnal day in 1876, old Nepomuk Hiedler and three of his illiterate relatives harnessed up a horse and made the trip down the narrow, winding country road from Spital to Döllersheim to fill in the blank in Adolf Hitler's official genealogy. Nepomuk swore to the aged parish priest that his foster son, Alois, now a customs inspector, had in truth been sired by his deceased brother, Johann Georg Hiedler. The priest accepted the testimony, and the original baptismal entry of 1837 was altered in the Registry for the Parish of Döllersheim. In the space "Name of the Baptized" the last name Schickelgruber was crossed out, and the space for the father's name, previously left blank, filled in, with the last name fortuitously misspelled: "Georg Hitler, Cath. religion, resident in Spital." Nepomuk and his relatives carefully made their X's, and the deed was done. The priest, Father Josef Zahnschirm, did not sign the book; but on the basis of comparison with other examples of his handwriting it can be affirmed that he, as the parish priest from 1867 to 1886, did indeed fill out the form.[3]

We must guess at the reasons why Nepomuk Hiedler made the effort to have his foster son's last name changed. He may simply have decided to comply with the wishes of a boy who had turned out so well; he may have been glad to have him bear his own family's name rather than that of the feckless Schickelgrubers. Nepomuk himself had sired no sons to carry on the name, and the old man may have been more than willing to have the sexually robust Alois assume that pleasant task. Then, too, if Alois's natural father had really been a Jew, as some rumormongers were suggesting, both the proud old farmer and the rising government official might have been anxious to "legitimize" the name in an undeniably Christian record book. At any rate, history was not given the opportunity to turn at this quiet crossroad in rural Austria. If the name had not been changed to Hitler that autumn day, the son of Alois might not have prospered so well politically. It is a bit difficult to cry with fanatic intensity "Heil Schickelgruber!"

A JEWISH GRANDFATHER?

One day toward the end of 1930, Adolf Hitler called in his private lawyer, Hans Frank, for urgent personal consultation.* Hitler had sent for him because he was about to be blackmailed by a relative who claimed to have special information that the Führer had a Jewish grandfather. Hitler was so disturbed by the threat of such a disclosure that he ordered his lawyer to investigate. Frank did so and discovered, he said, that Hitler's father had indeed been the illegitimate son of Maria Anna Schickelgruber, who had worked as a domestic in Graz "in the home of a Jewish family by the name of Frankenberger." From the day her baby—Hitler's father, Alois—was born until the boy was 14, Frankenberger paid money for the support of the child. According to Frank, when Hitler was confronted with this evidence, he said that the story of a Graz Jew's being his own grandfather was a total and complete lie. He knew it was because his grandmother had told him so.

---

* Frank would later be given special privileges and power in the Third Reich as president of the Academy of German Law, member of the Reichstag, leader of the National Socialist Lawyer's Association, *SS Obergruppenführer*, and governorgeneral of Poland. Before he was hanged as a war criminal at Nuremberg, he told this story in his memoirs.

The Child As Father to the Man

She had accepted the money from the Jew only because she was so poor.[4]

Despite Frank's reputation as the "Butcher of Poland," there would seem to be reason for believing his story. He wrote his memoirs as a condemned man who had converted to Catholicism. He wrote, in part, to expiate his sins. He had no apparent reason to misrepresent Hitler or to invent the story. That Hitler should have lied when he said his grandmother assured him that his grandfather was not a Jew—Hitler's grandmother, Maria Anna Schickelgruber, had died more than 35 years before he was born—is not particularly unusual. What is noteworthy is that Hitler made no attempt to deny that his grandmother had received money over many years from a Jew. The evidence Hans Frank produced must have been quite impressive; it was good enough to force Hitler to admit the possibility that a Jew had been very much involved with his own grandmother. But the evidence has never surfaced. Frank said it was based on correspondence between Maria Anna Schickelgruber and Frankenberger and that these letters were "for some time" in the possession of a lady related to Adolf Hitler through marriage. But Frank did not say directly whether he had ever seen the letters, and they have never been found. Further, there is nothing to corroborate Frank's statement that Maria Anna actually worked as a servant girl in the household of a family named Frankenberger—if, indeed, such a family ever existed in Graz.*

German historians and journalists have pondered the identity of Hitler's paternal grandfather through dozens of heavily argued pages.[5] Their industry is laudable, but the question they ask is not really very important and it is almost certainly unanswerable. We do not know, and we probably never will know whether in fact Hitler had a Jewish grandfather. The more important question is a different one: did Hitler think

* The research of Nikolaus Preradovic, a historian at the University of Graz, casts further doubt on the story. Preradovic set his task at finding Hitler's mysterious Jewish grandfather—called Frankenberger by Hans Frank and Frankenreiter by Hitler's step-nephew, William Patrick Hitler—in an exposé article of *Paris Soir* in 1939. Preradovic discovered that in books of the Jewish *Kultusgemeinde* of Graz there is no record of either a Frankenberger or a Frankenreiter. It is true that the records of the Jewish congregation go back only as far as 1856 and that Adolf Hitler's father, Alois, was born 20 years before. During this time, however, not only in Graz but in the entire province there is no record of one single Jew having lived there. The Jews were driven out of the area in 1496 and were not allowed to return until after 1856. The name of Leopold Frankenreiter, mentioned by Adolf Hitler's nephew, was found. But he was the son of a Catholic cobbler. Born in 1795 in Bavaria, he had moved to Graz, where he became a meat cutter. His son, who according to one story would be the putative grandfather of Hitler, was ten years old in the year 1837, when the then 41-year-old Maria Anna Schickelgruber was delivered of a child. If he was indeed the father, Preradovic has commented laconically, he must have been "a remarkably precocious boy" (*Spiegel*, no. 24, June 12, 1957). Simon Wiesenthal, who knows as much about investigating European family backgrounds as anyone, says he has searched through all the archives of Graz and has found no trace of a Jew named Frankenberger ever having lived there (Letter to the editor, *Spiegel*, no. 23, August 7, 1967).

he might have Jewish blood? The answer to this question is yes, he did. Rightly or wrongly, throughout his life Hitler lived with the awful suspicion that his own father's father was a Jew and that he himself was "poisoned" by Jewish blood. That suspicion constituted psychic reality for Hitler. It helped to shape his personality and to determine public policy.

He expressed his apprehension in many ways. Over and over again, in public speeches and private conversation, he stressed the dangers of "blood poisoning" and thereby demonstrated that he could not get the idea out of his mind: "Alone the loss of purity of the blood destroys the inner happiness forever; it eternally lowers man, and never again can its consequence be removed from body and mind." He felt the need to atone for bad blood. Unable to bring himself to admit directly his own family's "guilt," he used the defense of universalizing the "sin" by claiming that *all* Germans were involved. Thus the poisoning of German blood became the "original sin" of all humanity. To an intimate he said, "All of us are suffering from the ailment of mixed, corrupted blood. How can we purify ourselves and make atonement?" To another associate on a different occasion he suggested that the Jewish blood of Jesus was a special curse. "In the Gospels the Jews call to Pilate when Pilate hesitated to crucify Jesus: 'His blood comes over us and over our children.' I must perhaps fulfill this curse." One of the reasons he gave for not marrying and having children was his fear of tainted blood and a family history of feeble-mindedness: "The offspring of the genius have great difficulties in life. Everyone expects that they will have the same ability as their famous parent. But that seldom happens. Besides they would all be feeble-minded." [6]

Hitler's habit from childhood of having his own blood sucked out by leeches or later by the syringes of Dr. Morell suggests that he suspected there was something the matter with his blood. He wanted to get rid of it. The Führer may have been so concerned about the precise measurements of his head because he worried about his own "Jewish characteristics." It was a common misapprehension among Nazi racists that "Jewishness" could be measured cranially. Through meticulous charting of his own head, Hitler may have been trying to prove to himself that he was not Jewish.

Then, too, he kept thinking back on the story that his own grandmother, while working as a household servant, might have been seduced by a Jew. One of his most important state papers, the Nuremberg Racial Laws of 1935—which he called *Blutschutzgesetz* (The Law for the Protection of the Blood)—documented his concern. Hitler himself personally checked the wording of these laws and gave strict orders that not one word should be changed. Paragraph 3 is especially interesting. The Führer made a special point of emphasizing the following disability: "Jews cannot employ female household servants of German or related blood who are under 45 years of age." Hitler's own grandmother had been no older than 41 when she became pregnant while working, according to Hitler's suspicions, in a Jewish household.[7]

He projected the fear that haunted him onto Matthias Erzberger, the deputy of the Center Party, whom he accused of betraying Germany by accepting the Versailles Treaty. In a revealing passage in his second book, written in 1928, Hitler wrote: "Fate had chosen a man who was one of those principally guilty for the collapse of our people. Matthias Erzberger, . . . *the illegitimate son of a servant girl and a Jewish employer. . . .*" As the editor of the book has pointed out, the rumor about Erzberger had no basis in fact. The psychologically interesting point, however, is that Hitler repeated the story in writing.[8]

The mere mention of a German girl working as a household servant or charwoman was deeply disturbing to Hitler. His press chief recorded a peculiar incident which he was unable to explain but which indicates that the very thought of a Catholic chambermaid was enough to trigger a violent emotional reaction in Hitler. On this occasion in the 1930s, Hitler was informed that the mother of the manager of the hotel he frequented in Nuremberg, the Deutscher Hof, had advertised for chambermaids in a Catholic magazine. "The Führer flew into a rage entirely disproportionate to the importance of the matter; the manager was dismissed out of hand and professionally blacklisted." [9]

In one of his nightly monologues, in February 1942, the thought was still on his mind. He told his entourage about "a country girl who had a place in Nuremberg in the household of Herr Hirsch" and had been raped by her employer.[10]

Hitler did not like to talk about his family. Nevertheless, he showed a remarkable interest in his genealogy. Indeed, he was so concerned about it that he sent his own Gestapo to investigate—presumably to prove that his grandfather could not possibly have been Jewish.* But the investigators could give him no such assurance. The

---

* In the so-called *Gestapo-Berichte* (Gestapo Reports) on Hitler, which are now in the main archives of the Nazi Party, there are records of repeated investigations into the Führer's family background. Data and documents were collected in 1932, 1935, 1938, and 1940. Two separate investigations were made in 1942 and another during the period December 1943–January 1944. Some of the documents, clearly, were collected by the Party archivist with the marvelous Teutonic name, Attila Bleibtreu, who was simply gathering materials for the official archives. But the Gestapo also took a peculiar interest in Hitler's lineage. A letter of 14 October 1942, written by an SS *Obersturmbannführer* with an undecipherable name, was addressed to the *Reichsführer SS*, Prinz Albrechtstrasse, Berlin (which is to say, to Heinrich Himmler) and stamped "Secret." The letter was enclosed in the transmission of documents on the ancestors of the Führer which had been collected by the Linz branch of the Gestapo. Part of the Gestapo file, now in the Prints and Photographs Division of the Library of Congress, contains an original letter signed by Heinrich Himmler and addressed to "Martin Bormann, Secretary to the Führer." In the letter, Himmler notes formally that he is officially transmitting all his data on Hitler and requests a receipt for the file which he has sent by special courier and marked "Geheime Reichssache!" (Library of Congress, Prints and Photographs, Hitler materials). Himmler would not have sent the file to Bormann if he had been

agents of the Gestapo were no more successful than later historians in identifying Hitler's paternal grandfather. The Führer was never relieved of his suspicions.

There is other evidence suggesting that Hitler suspected his own blood was tainted through his father. He had curiously aggressive attitudes toward the villages closely associated with his parents' lives. Albert Speer was unable to explain why Hitler reacted so violently when, after a motor trip in rural Austria in 1942, Speer mentioned to his Führer that he had noticed in the little town of Spital a sign on a farmhouse which read "The Führer Lived Here in His Youth." Speer recalled,

> He instantly flew into a rage and shouted for Bormann, who hurried in much alarmed. Hitler snarled at him, how many times had he said that this village must never be mentioned. But that idiot of a *Gauleiter* had gone out and put up a plaque there. It must be removed at once.[11]

Speer found Hitler's excitement inexplicable because he was usually very much interested in refurbishing the sites of his boyhood in Linz and Braunau. The explanation would seem to be that while Hitler had indeed spent some summers on the farm in Spital, it was associated in his mind as the boyhood home of his father when he had lived there with Nepomuk Hiedler. The mere thought of his father's home and lineage was, apparently, enough to cause an emotional outburst.

The story of what happened to another village associated with Hitler's family is even more interesting. In March 1938, almost directly after taking over Austria, Hitler had a survey made of the lovely little farming village of Döllersheim—the parish where his father had been born, his grandmother buried, and the journeys made to record the birth and name of his father. The purpose of Hitler's survey of 1938 was to ascertain the suitability of using this village as an artillery range for the Wehrmacht. General Knittersched, the commanding general of Military District 17, was given orders directly from Hitler to make the area ready "as soon as possible."[12] The inhabitants were evacuated, and the parish registers removed. Round after round of heavy artillery crashed into the village, demolishing its buildings and rendering graves in the little cemetery unrecognizable. Why was Döllersheim destroyed? There are thousands of empty acres in this part of Lower Austria that would have made excellent artillery ranges. It is

---

trying to use "the Jewish grandfather" as leverage against Hitler, as is sometimes suggested. It is unlikely that Himmler and many members of the Gestapo would have become involved in investigating so sensitive a subject as Hitler's own ancestry without his explicit approval. It seems reasonable to conclude that Hitler himself had given orders for the investigations in order to prove to himself what he desperately needed to affirm: that he was of pure Aryan stock—or at least as Aryan as his own racial laws required.

unlikely that Hitler chose this particular village at random. He seems to have had a compulsion to wipe out—quite literally—the suspicion of his own Jewish blood by obliterating the birthplace of his father and the grave of his grandmother.

Hitler's uneasiness about his ancestors is suggested in a remark he made in 1930 when reporters were trying to get information about his family. "These people," he said, "must never find out who I am. They mustn't know where I come from or my family background." [13] As we have noted, he felt it necessary to lie about his ancestors, saying, for example, that they had come from Lower Saxony.

There is other evidence that Hitler worried about his own "Jewishness." The two physical characteristics he associated with Jews—body odors and large noses—were two things that bothered him about himself. Hitler's obsessive concern with personal cleanliness and his abhorrence of perfume and aftershave lotion was so great, one suspects, because he was afraid that either the smell of body odor or the use of perfume to cover it up might make people think he was a Jew. When one of his colleagues asked why Jews "always remain strangers in the nation," Hitler had a ready answer: "The Jews [have] a different smell." He expressed his repugnance for both odor and perfume publicly in a Munich speech of 29 November 1939:

> Racial instinct protected the people; the *odor* of that race deterred Gentiles from marrying Jews. At present in these days of perfume, where any dandy can assume the same *odor* as anyone else, the feeling for these finer distinctions between peoples is being lost. The Jew counts on that.[14]

Those who have commented on Hitler's physical characteristics have all said that his least attractive feature was his grossly shaped nose and unusually large nostrils—hence the bushy little mustache grown just wide enough to help conceal them. With this in mind, it is worth noting Hitler's pointed observation about the Jewish people: they have, he said, a characteristic which is "permanently common to all Jews from the ghetto of Warsaw to the bazaars of Morocco: the offensive nose, the cruel, *vicious nostrils*. . . ." [15]

THE FATHER: ALOIS (SCHICKELGRUBER) HITLER

Alois Hitler's career in the Austrian bureaucracy had been eminently respectable. After nine years of service he had achieved the title of senior assistant customs official, and by 1892 he had been promoted to higher collector, the highest rank open to a man of only an elementary school education. After continually uprooting his family, often leaving attractive homes for no apparent reason,* Alois finally moved in retirement to a little house in the village of Leonding, just south of Linz. In that village, on 23 January 1903, while sipping his morning quarter liter of wine at the *Stammtisch* of the Gasthaus Stiefler, he died without benefit of medicine or clergy at the age of 66.

It is difficult to get a balanced picture of Alois Hitler. Contemporaries who knew him well had differing impressions of him. His sexual exploits, for example, drew mixed reviews. Some villagers were shocked by his infidelities, others indifferent, others a bit envious.

We know that during his 30's he fathered a child by a country girl named Thelka, whose last name is lost to history. A few years later, in 1873, he advanced his career by marrying Anna Glassl, the daughter of a governmental inspector. The bride was physically unattractive and 14 years older than Alois, but the dowry was generous enough to provide a maidservant named Antonia Mayr who had attracted his attention. While married to Anna, Alois also had liaisons with another teen-aged maid, Franziska Matzelberger—commonly called Fanni—and also with Klara Pölzl, his 16 year old niece who would become the mother of Adolf Hitler. Klara had left the farm to come to work in the Braunau inn where Alois and his wife were then living. Apparently Alois's overtures to Fanni were sufficiently clumsy as to arouse the suspicions of his wife; in 1880 Anna Glassl Hitler won a separation. Alois then took Fanni to live with him, but only after he had agreed to send her rival, Klara Pölzl, packing—apparently off to Vienna. Fanni gave birth to a son, also called Alois. (This Alois Hitler, Jr.—Adolf's stepbrother—later became something of a black sheep, married an Irish girl, and fathered William Patrick Hitler, the nephew who reportedly tried to blackmail his famous uncle in 1930.) Alois married Fanni on 22 May 1883, the groom was 46, the bride 22. Two months after the wedding, Fanni gave birth to a daughter, Angela, who would later play a rather important role in the life of Adolf Hitler. When Fanni became ill with pulmonary tuberculosis, Alois shifted his attention back to Klara Pölzl, who had been brought back to take care of Fanni and her two children. As soon as Fanni died and he had received a papal dispensation for the wedding, Alois married Klara early one bleak winter morning in January 1885 in the parish church at Braunau. The pregnant

---

* During his 21 years of service in Braunau, where Adolf was born, the household was changed at least 12 times; during two years at Passau, the family moved twice; while posted at Linz, Alois moved many times. He had bought attractive property in the neighboring village of Fischlham. This purchase of some nine acres of land allowed Alois to indulge his favorite pastime of beekeeping; chickens and a cow helped provide for family needs; there were also fruit trees and a lovely view. But after only two years of occupancy Alois sold the place and moved his family to the village of Lambach, where they lived first in the Leingartner Inn, and then in an old mill—two changes in one year. No financial crisis seemed responsible for all these moves. Alois's income was steady, secure, and on the rise, and these were peaceful, economically stable times in rural Austria.

bride was 25, the groom 48. Klara later recalled, "We were married at six in the morning and by seven my husband was already on duty again." After the marriage, husband and wife continued to call each other "uncle" and "niece." [16]

Everyone agreed that Alois was a conscientious bureaucrat, punctilious to a fault. He was also a frugal person who provided for his family and left them comfortably off. There is no evidence—except in his son's fantasies—that he was the village drunkard. He seems to have been respected in the villages in which he lived, and the local newspaper gave him a generous obituary which concluded: "All in all, Hitler's passing has left a great gap not only in his family . . . but also in a circle of his friends and acquaintances who will preserve pleasant memories of him." [17]

Yet there were some less favorable notices. Even those associates who were interviewed by the Gestapo—and who would not be expected to put the father of the Führer in an unfavorable light—had some hesitations about his character. Frau Hörl, who worked for Alois as a cook after his second wife died, testified that he was a very strict man with a terrible temper.[18]

Alois' colleagues in the Customs Service and his cronies at the village *Stammtisch* found him a dutiful official but also a humorless person with a temper that flared with no apparent provocation. After his promotion, he insisted upon being addressed as "Herr Senior Official Hitler" and was furious when referred to with the more usual "Herr Official." He was not a heavy drinker, but he did "smoke like a chimney," and even a friendly witness found him arbitrary and unfair about his addiction. While indulging it himself, he would not allow a subordinate to smoke while on duty.

Adolf Hitler's lifelong revulsion to smoking, indeed his visceral hatred of the habit, seems to have stemmed from memories of his father's tobacco pipes. In the family household those pipes became the symbol of paternal authority. Hitler's boyhood friend remembered that even after Alois Hitler had been dead for two years the old man's presence continued to be felt in the home. His portrait dominated the entire flat, and "on the kitchen shelves I still remember there were carefully arrayed the long pipes which he used to smoke. They were almost a symbol in the family of his absolute power. Many a time when talking of him, Frau Hitler would emphasize her words by pointing to these pipes as though they should bear witness how faithfully she carried on the father's tradition."

Hitler's efforts to disregard time, or to conquer it, also seem connected with his father. Everyone who knew the old man stressed his pedantic punctuality. Indeed, a co-worker in the customs office in Braunau recalled that among punctual officials, Alois Hitler stood out as a real "demon on time." Even when there was no need to be punctilious he would never allow his assistants to leave five seconds before quitting time on any occasion.[19]

The general agreement that Hitler's father demanded silence in his presence and absolutely forbade any back talk also had reverberations for the future. Hitler would grow up to be the greatest demagogue in history; he would talk compulsively in endless monologues, forcing other people to listen to him, often all night long. He too would tolerate no back talk.

Old Josef Mayrhofer, a farmer who was for many years mayor of Leonding, had been a close friend of Alois and, after his death, was appointed Adolf's guardian. In 1948, when he was 80 but still alert and clear-minded, he admitted that Alois Hitler had been something of a tyrant: "The boy stood in awe of him . . . he was strict with his family. No kid gloves as far as they were concerned; his wife had nothing to smile about." [20]

There was indeed little to smile about in the Hitler household, and no sense of fun. The point about fun is important. Erik Erikson has shown the contribution which spontaneity and play make to a child's development. Habitually unresponsive, cold, and negative parents such as old Alois Hitler can produce in a child deep-seated desires to negate and destroy. Erikson's comments are remarkably descriptive of young Adolf's experience with his father—and his subsequent attitude toward other people:

> Anxiety and rage mostly develop where essential needs are not satisfied, growing capacities are not given opportunities, and developing gifts are denied an instructive response. For the opposite of interplay is deadness. In the child's unconscious, the habitually unresponsive adult can assume the image of a mortal enemy, while the experience of a passionate search unrequited by the environment leads to a sense of being negated and most importantly to the aimless impulse to negate and annihilate others.[21]

Like many fathers of his place and time, Alois Hitler believed in corporal punishment. Bridget Hitler, the wife of Alois Jr., testified that her husband had often told her about his childhood and described his father as a person with "a very violent temper." He "often beat the dog until it . . . wet on the floor. He often beat the children, and on occasion . . . would beat his wife Klara." Other people who knew Alois Hitler have said that his children never dared to speak in their father's presence without being told to. They were not permitted to use the familiar "*du*," but were told to address him as "*Herr Vater.*" He was accustomed to calling his son Adolf not by name but by putting two fingers in his mouth and whistling for him as he did for his dog.[22]

Let us try to reconstruct young Adolf's perception of his father as revealed by his own memories and fantasies and, indirectly, by the testimony of others.

The Child As Father to the Man

The child must have been confused by conflicting impressions. He was required to obey and revere the old man, and there was much to admire. In the carefully brushed and burnished uniform of the Imperial Customs Service, Alois Hitler was the personification of the dedicated civil servant, a very pillar of the Empire, the most prestigious father in the village. He was a man of substance and position who provided his family with economic security, material comfort, and social status. But this arbitrary and ferocious man also lived up to a little boy's dread Oedipal fantasy of a powerful and avenging enemy who launched sudden thunderbolts of terror, pain, and punishment.

In short, Hitler's attitude toward his father was one of such ambivalence that it could serve as a textbook description of Oedipal conflict. In young Adolf, as in the little boys described by Sigmund Freud, there was conflict between two opposing attitudes: the desire to emulate and to be loved by his father vied with the desire to be different from his father and to destroy him.

The ambivalence remained throughout Hitler's life. His boyhood friend recalled that "Adolf spoke of his father with great respect. I never heard him say anything against him, in spite of their differences of opinion about his career." And in his memoirs Hitler invariably talks respectfully of his father, characterizing him as a "faithful civil servant." He dwells on the parallels between their lives (both went off to Vienna) and draws a sympathetic and sentimental picture of his father leaving home to seek his fortune in the imperial capital:

> Not yet thirteen years old, the little boy he then was buttoned up his things and ran away from his homeland, the *Waldviertel*. . . . A bitter resolve it must have been to take to the road into the unknown and with only three guilders for travelling money. But by the time the thirteen-year-old lad was seventeen he had passed his apprentice's examination . . . the long time of hardship through which he had passed, of endless poverty and misery, strengthened his resolve. . . . With all the tenacity of one who had grown "old" through want and sorrow while still half a child, the seventeen-year-old youth clung to his decision . . . and became a civil servant . . . now there has been realized the promise of the vow that the poor boy once had sworn not to return to his dear native village before he had become something.[23]

The ambivalence he felt toward his father is revealed in a garbled passage of a nocturnal monologue during World War II. In one brief outburst he manages to pay tribute to his father, apparently bestow upon him an unearned title, and roundly damn him. During a violent attack upon bureaucrats and judges he says—or seems to say— ". . . at one time, I regarded jurors as men set apart for a higher life! Indeed I looked at all such state officials that way! My old father was an honorable man. A chairman of the Assizes and *Justizrat*! I had no idea then that a *Justizrat* is a private individual who lives by defending swindlers." The passage is difficult to translate, and it may be that Hitler did not really mean to call his father by a title which he never held. But the false identification of his father given in another place is unmistakable—and peculiar. In a letter of 29 November 1921, he demotes his father, and tells a lie, by writing, "I was born on 20 April 1889 in Braunau on Inn, the son of the local postal official [*Post-offizial*], Alois Hitler." [24]

His memoirs and conversations reveal a desire to emulate his father, but one can always feel the cutting edge of rivalry and the determination to triumph over an adversary. In recalling, for example, that, as a boy, he once sang in the choir of a local monastery Adolf Hitler says, "I repeatedly had an excellent opportunity of intoxicating myself with the solemn splendor of a magnificent church festival. It was perfectly natural that the position of abbot appeared to me to be the highest idea attainable, just as that of being the village pastor had appealed to my father." He was fond of depicting his relationship with his father as a battle of conflicting wills in which his own will triumphed:

> No matter how firm and determined my father might be . . . his son was just as stubborn and obstinate. . . . My father did not give up his "never" and I strengthened my "nevertheless." . . .[25]

And so it remained throughout his life. His will must prevail: first against his father, then against his political rivals, and finally against the whole world in battle.

At the time of his father's death, when Adolf was 14, he ostentatiously rejected all identification with the old man. Usually, when a father dies, the surviving male child attempts to play a father role or at least assumes a form of masculine identity of which the father would have approved. But young Hitler immediately took on negative identities—that is, the kinds of life-style which would have infuriated his father. As we shall see, he first played the effete artist and dandy. Then he ran off to Vienna to become an art student dropout and vagabond, an image his father would have found equally abhorrent.

Later on in life, however, Adolf indirectly accepted the challenge of his father "to make something of himself." He did so in a way that would have impressed and intimidated the old man: he too became a government official—but one of unbridled power. In effect, Hitler was saying, "My father always considered me a failure. I'll show him in a way he understands. Not as an artist but as a government official—I'll become so powerful that I could make and break bureaucrats like him and conquer his beloved Austria."

The mixed feelings of respect and disdain which he felt for his father were later transferred to the awesome figure of the Field Marshal–President Paul von Hindenburg who, with his uniform, close-cropped hair, impressive mustache, and portly figure, was reminiscent of Adolf's own authoritarian father. Although he despised Hindenburg, Hitler spoke of him with respect, referring to him—as he had referred to his own father—as "The Old Gentleman" [*der alte Herr*]. Just as he had felt cowed by his father, so he dreaded a confrontation with Hindenburg. "The Old Gentleman," he said, "was totally hostile to everything we stood for. . . . The Old Gentleman had said to me, 'Herr Hitler I want to hear what kind of ideas you have.' It was horribly difficult [*wahnsinning schwer*] in such an atmosphere to set forth my thinking." And again, using an expression he must have learned as a child, he warned his followers that "we must never do anything that would annoy [*was verärgert*] the Old Gentleman." [26]

While his memoirs and conversations show respect for his father, hatred and fear also keep showing through. For whether or not he was justified in doing so, Adolf saw his father as a drunken and sadistic degenerate. He confided to an intimate that as a tender young lad he was forced to go and rescue his father from the clutches of alcohol, entering a "stinking smoke-filled tavern" in order to plead with his drunken father to come home. "Oh, that was the most shameful humiliating experience I have ever had. How well I know what a devil alcohol is. It was—because of my father—the greatest enemy of my youth!" [27]

Hitler also sought sympathy from his secretaries by describing what a cruel person his father had been and how vicious had been his whippings. A secretary recalled, "He used to say, 'I never loved my father. I therefore feared him all the more. He had a terrible temper and often whipped me.'" He liked to relate how, as a young boy, he was fond of Karl May stories about Indians who proved their courage by refusing to cry out under torture. One day, as his father beat him with his cane and his frightened mother stood outside the door, Adolf counted the blows without a murmur and proudly reported, "My father gave me 230 blows!" After that, he recalled, his father never whipped him again. [28]

How can one calculate the consequences of child beating? What psychological wounds scar the child's mind as he lies hurt in body and soul, sobbing and alone, battered by his own father and deserted by a noninterfering mother? The infant must learn to comfort himself; he can trust no one else; he is overwhelmed by terror, fear, rage, helplessness, hatred. Is it not possible that the hatred which Hitler later said was so important to his life was learned in childhood's rage—the helpless hatred that sobbed: "If I were bigger, I would kill you!" Of such experiences, a prominent psychiatrist has said, are murderers made. Hitler would have agreed completely with the American criminal Caryl Chessman, who recalled the brutal whippings of his childhood and concluded that "there is nothing that sustains you like hate; it is better to be anything than to be afraid." [29]

It is, of course, possible that Adolf Hitler's memories of a drunken and sadistic father were exaggerated in order to hide personal feelings of guilt engendered by his wish to destroy his father. He may have tried to justify to others and to himself his bitter hatred by insisting that Alois was a cruel and vicious man who deserved a son's animosity. It may be objected that even if young Hitler was beaten by his father, many other children in rural Austria were certainly whipped without, apparently, receiving the psychic scars that Hitler suffered. "Well," one might say, "all boys in Austria were beaten on their backsides, so what's the difference?" The difference, as Erik Erikson has noted in his study of Luther, is this: with Hitler, as with Luther, a sensitive man remembered those punishments and talked bitterly about them later, showing that the whippings did indeed have an effect on his development. As Erikson wrote: "The assertion that the cause was too common to have an uncommon effect on one individual is neither clinically nor biographically valid. We must try to ascertain the relationship of caner and caned and see if a unique element may have given the common event a specific meaning." In Hitler's case, as in Luther's, the fact that the whippings were remembered and resented, and that he hated his father for giving them, indicates that they had an uncommon effect upon him.

The workings of hatred and love, of pleasure and pain, are complex. Hatred may be a distortion of love: pleasure may be sought through pain. Consciously, Adolf certainly resented the beatings and hated his father for hurting him; unconsciously, he may have desired the punishment as a way of winning his father's attention and love. We are suggesting the possibility that the sadomasochism we shall observe in the adult Hitler had its beginnings here. Clinical studies have shown that often, as children, people with masochistic tendencies baited their fathers into whipping them. "The desire to be punished or humiliated," a specialist in the pathology of masochism has written, is another way of "wanting to be loved . . . being beaten and being loved are fused into one single masochistic expression." [30]

As with all little boys, Adolf's image of his father was heavily influenced by the picture he had of his father's sexual relations with his mother. For Hitler this memory was traumatic because, as we shall soon see, Adolf at the age of three had seen—or imagined that he had seen—his drunken father rape his beloved young mother.

THE MOTHER: KLARA PÖLZL HITLER

Unhappiness was the lot of Klara Pölzl, the woman who was to become Adolf Hitler's mother. All her life she was pushed about to accommodate the wishes of others.

At the age of 16 she left the family farm to become a member of

Alois's household. Then she was sent into exile for four years at the demand of her employer's consort, "Fanni" Matzelberger. When Fanni was stricken with tuberculosis, Klara was summoned to care for the small children who belonged to her rival and her employer-relative-lover. "Strangely enough," one historian has concluded, "Klara's return does not seem to have aroused any hard feelings. She frequently visited Fanni in Ranshofen and joined the ill girl's widowed mother in trying to nurse her back to health." [31]

Rather than proving that Klara had no "hard feelings," her almost saintly kindness and endurance seems more likely to have demonstrated her capacity to suppress or deny her true feelings. Rage or refusal to help her rival and her inconsiderate employer would seem to have been the more direct and appropriate response to the treatment she had received.* It is of course true that Klara was the product of a peasant culture dominated by males who expected her to accept as natural behavior what a more sophisticated woman might not have tolerated. But there is no indication that Klara was intellectually subnormal or dull. She was not a simple one-dimensional person of little sensitivity; she was a woman who was successful in her struggle to control and subdue complex feelings which may well have included not only resentment and rage but also an active sense of guilt.

Klara had been living with Alois since the spring of 1884 and had become pregnant by him in August of that year, about four months before their marriage. She was a devout and conscientious Catholic, carefully instructed in the catechism of sin and penance—and the gossips of the little community of Braunau would have given her little opportunity to forget her sins. It seems reasonable to suppose that Klara, the devoted Catholic, felt acutely guilty for her adultery and for her transgressions against both the older first wife, Anna, and the younger second wife, Fanni. And Klara had survived. While the other women had been struck down by death, she had been allowed to go on living with their husband and their dowries. A sense of guilt and the need for penance and atonement help to explain Klara's apparently docile acceptance of her lot: first defeat and exile; then service to the children and abject obedience to their father; and throughout, willingness to bear gossip and scandal that surrounded her whenever she ventured into the streets of the town.

Klara began her married life with the responsibility of caring for Fanni's children, Alois Jr., age two, and Angela, three. In a few months there was added the care of her own son, Gustav. About fifteen months after his birth, a second child, Ida, was born; then promptly a third, Otto, who died within a few days. More tragedy struck when her two surviving children contracted diptheria. Day after day Klara watched in

---

* The interpretation of Klara Hitler's personality given here draws on Norbert Bromberg, M.D., "Hitler's Childhood," *International Review of Psycho-Analysis* 1 (1974). I have also profited from many discussions with Dr. Bromberg about Hitler's childhood and family life.

helpless despair as the heavy, greenish-gray mucous membrane enveloped her childrens' throats and slowly strangled them.* Gustav died in December 1887; Ida was buried in January 1888. During that same year she became pregnant again.

At half-past six on Easter Eve, 20 April 1889, an overcast day with the temperature 67 degrees Fahrenheit and the humidity 89 percent, Klara gave birth to the future Führer of the Germans in the crowded quarters of the Gasthof zum Pommern, an inn in Braunau.

Adolf was a sickly baby and must have evoked in his mother fears that he, like all her other children, would die. Her energies, already taxed by four pregnancies in rapid succession, had been further drained by worried and fruitless efforts to save her children from death, and then by having to move the household, at her husband's orders, soon after Adolf's birth. During all this time, she bore the stress of caring for the little children of her dead rival and the grief of her own children's death. Before she finally died—after giving birth to two more children after Adolf—from the ravages of breast cancer, Klara Hitler had seen her dreams of happiness in marriage and a family of healthy children repeatedly collapse. Small wonder that she struck contemporaries as a disappointed and depressed person who did not linger in conversation with neighbors but seemed always to hurry home to care for her children and her house.

She got little comfort or companionship from her husband. Even one of his closest friends admitted that Alois was "awfully rough" (*saugrob*) with his wife and "hardly spoke a word to her at home." [32] Denied affection and understanding by her husband, Klara turned with increasing intensity to her only remaining sources of consolation: her housework and her children—particularly her one surviving boy, Adolf. In villages where cleanliness was a byword, Klara's homes were considered immaculate. It was as if she sought to scrub away all sense of guilt, shame, and failure. "My predominant impression of the simple furnished apartment," the family physician recalled, "was its cleanliness. It glistened. Not a speck of dust on the chairs or tables, not a stray fleck of mud on the scrubbed floor, not a smudge on the panes in the windows. Frau Hitler was a superb housekeeper." [33] Her children were kept scrupulously clean and not allowed to soil their clothes without punishment. It seems likely that Klara tried to imbue them at an early age with some of her own feelings of guilt, sternly reminding them of the wages of sin—of which, she seems to have felt, her own melancholy existence was a living testimonial.

Her relationship to Adolf was symbiotic: mother and son clung to each other out of psychic need. Little Adolf was dependent upon Klara, but she was in equal need of him. For he was her means of proving that she really was a virtuous, loving mother despite all her self-

---

* We do not know whether Klara ever told young Adolf the way his little brother and sister had died. If she had, it would help to account for Hitler's lifelong fear of strangulation and loss of breath.

doubts and feelings of guilt—indeed, because of them. As a German psychiatrist has noted, by loving Adolf so thoroughly, Klara could combat resentments she may have unconsciously felt toward a child who "enslaved her, sucked her dry and crippled her with never-ending demands." Through Adolf, she could numb her feelings of shame and guilt for having yielded to her "Uncle's" sexual demands at the very time his wife was living and dying in the same house. Constant expressions of love for her little boy could also assuage the fear of God's wrath she must have felt had been visited upon her by the early deaths of her first three children. "No wonder that Klara not only over-fed Adolf, but anxiously hovered over him, desperately needing him as living proof of her being a good, giving, non-destructive mother whom God still loved." [33a]

Throughout his life, Hitler proclaimed his love for his mother. Indeed, the family doctor reported that many of the neighbors believed his love for her "verged on the pathological." While the doctor personally did not believe that the relationship was abnormal, he did say that, in a long practice, "I have never witnessed a closer attachment" between mother and son.[34] All his life Hitler carried his mother's picture in his pocket. In all his bedrooms—in Munich, the Berlin Chancellery, the Obersalzberg—her portrait hung over the head of his bed.[35]

Hitler always prided himself on being as "hard as steel" and "cold as ice," a person who showed no emotion in adversity. He confessed, however, to having wept twice in his life: once when he stood at the grave of his mother in December 1907; the other time at the death of his Motherland during the defeat of 1918.[36] On the evening that his mother died, during Christmas week of 1907, a neighbor reported that Adolf sat in the twilight, staring at her dead body. He lingered in the death room a long time, carefully drawing a picture of his beloved mother as she appeared in death, ravaged by cancer.[37]

A curious poem he wrote in 1923 testifies to one aspect of his love —and to the limits of his literary talent. After he came to power in 1933 he was able to have it published in an edition of a Nazi paper largely devoted to extolling motherhood.

BE REMINDED!

1 When your mother has grown old
  And you have older grown,
  When things she once did e'er so lightly,
  Are now a burden, heavy borne,
5 When her eyes so dear and trusting
  No more, as once, look forward brightly,
  When her weary, falt'ring feet
  No longer carry her step lightly—
  Then give to her a helping hand,
10 Accompany her with gladsome smile—

The hour nears when you aweeping
Must go with her on her last mile!
And if she asks, so give her answer,
And if again, let words not cease,
15 And if once more, then stay her questions
Not harshly, but in restful Peace!
And if she can't quite understand you
Explain as if 'twere joyous task;
The hour comes, the bitter hour,
20 When her dear mouth no more can ask.*

This type of verse was certainly not uncommon on such occasions. What is remarkable is that a mature person who prided himself on his literary taste should think that his own venture into the genre warranted publication. The quality of the poem is so poor that one must be wary of reading too much into it—confusing, for example, lack of poetic ability with Freudian undertones. But it is worth risking comment because the verse does reveal some psychologically interesting attitudes toward mothers. In the last lines, for example, there are clear indications of guilt feelings over memories of attacking his mother verbally or of impatiently silencing her when she asked questions that annoyed him. There are also strong indications that he was intrigued by his mother's death—indeed, that he may even have repressed a death wish. In line 10 it is surprising to find the word *Lust* (here unhappily translated as "gladsome smile") used in a poem in-

---

* *Sonntag-Morgenpost*, 14 Mai 1933 (Library of Congress, Manuscript Division, Captured German Documents, Box 791). The German reads:

DENK' ES!

1 Wenn deine Mutter alt geworden
Und älter du geworden bist,
Wenn ihr, was früher leicht und mühelos,
Nunmehr zur Last geworden ist,
5 Wenn ihre lieben, treuen Augen
Nicht mehr, wie einst, in's Leben seh'n,
Wenn ihre müd' geword'nen Füsse
Sie nicht mehr tragen woll'n beim Geh'n—
Dann reiche ihr den Arm zur Stütze
10 Geleite sie mit froher Lust—
Die Stunde kommt, da du sie weinend
Zum letzten Gang begleiten musst!
Und fragt sie dich, so gib ihr Antwort,
Und fragt sie wieder, sprich auch du!
15 Und fragt sie nochmals, steh' ihr Rede,
Nicht ungestüm, in sanfter Ruh!
Und kann sie dich nicht recht verstehen
Erklär' ihr alles frohbewegt,
Die Stunde kommt, die bitt're Stunde,
20 Da dich ihr Mund nach nichts mehr frägt.

The Child As Father to the Man

volving a dying mother. However one translates this equivocal word, the results are Oedipally interesting. Hitler seems to be accompanying his dying mother on her "last mile" (a) *gladly* and without reservation, (b) with *pleasure*, or (c) with *desire*.

One notices, again, Hitler's recurrent fascination with time—in this instance, the four when's in the first seven lines. *Then* he answers with six commands. There is also a suggestion that the time he will appreciate his mother most is when she is dying. Throughout, the temporal progression is confused and indeterminate. The mother seems to alternate between death and life. The son gives her a helping hand (line 9); he goes with her on her last mile (line 12); but then she returns to repeat her persistent questions; (lines 13–15), which he should answer patiently until her mouth is finally closed in death. In lines 13–15, the unspecified questions that will be answered *in sanfter Ruh* explicitly convey a death image; in German usage the phrase is reserved for funeral wreaths and death announcements. Hitler is answering his mother's unknown questions not merely with gentle or soft language but with the ultimate peace of the grave: *Rest in peace.*

Hitler continually proclaimed how much he loved his mother. Yet motherlove of such intensity is never unalloyed with mistrust and hatred. It is generally recognized that a man with Oedipal problems has an ambivalent attitude toward his father; it is not so widely known that he may also harbor contradictory feelings about his mother. At any time, love for the mother may turn to bitter hatred. But the hatred is usually camouflaged by extraordinary expressions of love and devotion. As Karl Menninger has observed, this kind of feeling is not mature; it depends upon "an infantile attachment which is partly *dependence* and partly *hostility* but very little *love*." Men with such feelings are not capable of normal sexual life: "If they consort with women at all, it is women who are much older or much younger than themselves and are treated either as protecting mothers or as inconsequential childish amusements. . . . These relationships . . . are determined more by hating and fearing than by love and they only masquerade as love." [38]

Hitler's ambivalence about his mother—and, by extension, his feelings about all women—were expressed indirectly in the way he looked upon the feminine goddesses he liked to allude to. They were, as we have seen, kind but also cruel, helpful but fickle, beneficent but capricious. Erik Erikson has said that no one could have talked about women the way Hitler did who had not been deeply disappointed and disillusioned with his own mother; and Karl Menninger, writing during World War II, noted that a person trained in psychoanalysis could not look upon the intensity of Hitler's hatred and sadistic cruelty "without wondering what Hitler's mother did to him that he now repays to millions of other helpless ones." He emphasized anew the importance of the mother in the raising of a child: "We must remind ourselves again and again" that it is the mother who is "chiefly responsible for the personality of [her] sons." The experience of a son who has been "wounded by a woman is one which breeds in him an eternal distrust of that woman and all other women." [39]

How in infancy was Hitler so wounded by his beloved mother? What evil did she do to him that required such "evil in return"?

ADOLF'S INFANCY AND BOYHOOD

Adolf Hitler's central emotional experiences of childhood, it seems clear, were painful, but he sought to give a different impression in his memoirs and conversations. He blended a little fact with much invention to insist that while he had lived in very humble circumstances, never far from the clutches of "Dame Poverty," his family life was one of domestic tranquillity, security, and peace—except for all those whippings from his father. Hitler described himself as a tough little kid impervious to pain; he was always the ringleader in neighborhood battles of Boers and British, cowboys and Indians, Germans and French.

Actually, young Adolf had never known economic privation. In comparison to the families of his playmates of Braunau, Passau, and Leonding, the Hitler family was comfortably situated. His father's income, in addition to his regular salary as a customs official, included living allotments according to his place of service: in Passau, 200 extra gulden; in Linz, 250. It is virtually impossible to convert 19th- and early 20th-century Austrian currency into contemporary dollars, but the father's total income was considerably more than that earned, for example, by a country lawyer or the headmaster of an elementary school. Even after he retired in 1895, when Adolf was six years old, his annual income amounted to some 2,660 kronen. It was a guaranteed income, with payments made at the beginning of every month.

Not only did Adolf live in material conditions corresponding to those of the middle class, but as the son of an official in the Royal and Imperial Civil Service he also could have basked in the prestige and status of his father's position. Alois Hitler did not live long enough to enjoy the new regulations of August 1902, which would have further increased his allotment, but his widow's pension was calculated on the basis of the new rates. Thus, Klara received on the death of Alois a lump sum of 605 kronen, a widow's pension of half her husband's annual pension (figured at the new rate), and additional benefits for each child. Her total income was only 950 kronen less than when her husband was alive.

In June 1905, Frau Klara Hitler sold her house in Leonding to one Herr Hölzl, who had lived with his wife in the Humboldtstrasse in Linz, and moved into his flat. She received a very good price for the

Leonding property. Alois had paid only 7,700 kronen for it seven years previously, and Klara now received 10,000 kronen. The pleasant and spacious Humboldtstrasse flat was much nearer to her married step-daughter and confidante, Angela. Besides, since her loving son Adolf had recently failed in the local school, his mother now had to pay for his room and board in the nearby town of Styr. It is inaccurate to speak of Klara as "a destitute widow," and unnecessary to feel sympathy for Adolf's lamentations about his impoverished childhood.[40]

Nor are clichés about his serene and well-ordered family life to be taken seriously. As psychoanalysts have noted, no person manifesting Hitler's pathological personality traits could possibly have grown up in the idyllic home environment Hitler himself has described.[41] We must also disagree with the German historians who have written that Adolf's "childhood and youth passed uneventfully" or that living conditions in his early childhood were "nearly ideal" and that "nothing happened in the Hitler household that was in any way remarkable or, as far as Adolf was concerned, important." [42]

It seems more likely that the child grew up in a home atmosphere that was charged with tension. When his father was home, there was the constant threat that his temper would erupt at any moment. Always there was the palpable tension of his mother's struggle to control and subdue her emotions of guilt, rage, and disappointment, and of her attempts to cope with the awesome and unsympathetic uncle - husband who rarely spoke to her but who demanded that she understand and respond correctly to his unarticulated moods. Children raised in such an atmosphere cannot help but be affected by it. The number of times the family household was moved would also have had an unsettling effect on the youngster. Between the ages of six and 15, Adolf attended five different schools.

We have little direct knowledge of Hitler's early childhood, of the very important formative years up to the age of four or five. Since contemporary reports are meager and Hitler's memoirs suspect, we must look to the later behavior of the adolescent and adult to see if it reveals patterns that had their inception at a much earlier age. This backward approach to understanding early childhood has been given a now classical formulation by Erik Erikson: "We approach childhood in an untraditional manner, namely, from young adulthood backward—and this with the conviction that early development cannot be understood on its own terms alone, and that the earliest stages of childhood cannot be accounted for without a unified theory of the whole span of pre-adulthood." [43]

Oral Stage

Granting that the approach is speculative, let us make, from the behavior of the adult Hitler, some retroactive guesses about the infantile foundations upon which later personality development may have been based. Phyllis Greenacre has studied closely the role of trauma in the infancy of people who later manifested traits strikingly similar to Hitler's. She stresses the particular importance of the very early years. "The existence of any conditions which seriously impair the mother-infant relationship at this time . . . increases and prolongs primary narcissism and tends to damage the early ego. . . . such fundamental disturbances may arise either through pathological conditions in the infant . . . or they may arise through a maternal disturbance of any sort that alienates the mother from emotional and bodily contact with her baby in the first months of life." [44]

We may assume that some sort of basic psychological difficulty developed in the infant Adolf, since there is evidence both of unhealthy conditions in the child and of emotional disturbances experienced by the mother. Working together, the two conditions would have impaired the vitally important mother-infant relationship. We know that at birth, and for some time thereafter, Adolf was a "sickly baby." No further details have been given, but his ailments seem to have been sufficient to cause his mother to fear that he would die in infancy, as his brother and sister had done. Worries about Adolf's health helped produce the excessive maternal solicitude which Klara showered upon her son until she died. Hitler himself confirms this overprotectiveness and indulgence when he refers to himself in his memoirs as a "mother's darling" who lived a comfortable life in his "soft, downy bed" until his mother's death. As we have noted, Hitler's family doctor reported that several of the neighbors found the mother's love for her son verged on the pathological.

The special nature of the mother-child relationship, as well as the troubled history of the relationship between Adolf's parents, suggests strongly that Klara transferred her libidinal interest from her unresponsive uncle-husband to her little son. Anxiety about Adolf's health and survival certainly would have played a part in reinforcing the displacement. There is evidence that Klara's response to her baby's sickness was to nurse him for an excessive length of time—perhaps as long as two years. A psychoanalyst has suggested that she may have done so as a way of quieting her guilt feelings and restoring her self-esteem as a mother: "In this kind of situation, the nipple is nearly forced into the baby's mouth whenever he screams, regardless of what is troubling him." [45]

Klara may have continued to force-feed Adolf because, as a peasant daughter, she believed that good food was the best medicine for any childhood complaint. As a rigorously disciplined person herself, she might well have compelled her little boy (as she often forced herself) to do what was "good for him"—in this instance, to eat food whether he wanted it or not.

A boyhood memory of a farmer, Johann Schmidt, who was an older cousin of Adolf's, supports the hypothesis that Klara tried to improve Adolf's health by forced feeding and that she continued to do so throughout his childhood. Schmidt recalled in an interview that his Aunt Klara, after her husband's death, brought her children to spend summers on the farm in Spital. He remembers that Adolf was never obliged to work in the fields and that during the summer of 1905, when he did not feel well, his mother brought "a large cup of warm cow's milk into his room every single morning" and insisted that he drink it.[46]

Hitler's oral habits and fixations in adulthood invite the conclusion that there were serious disturbances in the infant feeding process, to which the well-meaning Klara contributed. We are reminded of the adult Hitler's inordinate craving for candy, particularly in moments of crisis; the sucking of his fingers in times of excitement; his violent rages; his poor appetite; the many books in his library on food fads; his constant comment about diet. Most significant for history was his basic mistrust of others and the oral aggression of his demagoguery.

Adolf was a compulsive and aggressive talker even as a youth. As his boyhood friend recalled, Hitler was friendly only with those whom he could dominate verbally:

> Soon I came to understand that our friendship endured largely for the reason that I was a patient listener. . . . He just HAD TO TALK and needed somebody who would listen to him. I was often startled when he would make a speech to me, accompanied by vivid gestures, for my benefit alone. . . . He was never worried by the fact that I was the sole audience. . . . These speeches, usually delivered somewhere in the open, seemed to be like a volcano erupting. . . .

A close associate of his adult years shows the continuity of this oral aggression. The Führer, in one of his famous rages, sought almost literally to destroy opposition with his mouth:

> The fury raged itself out in a hurricane [*Orkan*] of words which contradiction only lashed to a greater intensity. At such times he would crush all objection simply by raising his voice. These fury-scenes occurred over both major and minor matters.[47]

During one of his beer-hall speeches of 1920, when a heckler tried to embarrass him by asking pointedly if, during the civil war in Bavaria, he had ever joined the civil guards, Hitler retorted: "I am not a member of the *Einwohnerwehr*. . . . *You can also fight with your mouth!* [*Mit dem Maul kann man auch kämpfen!*]" [48]

In a classic account of adult patients who had suffered feeding problems during the oral stage of infancy, Karl Abraham might have been describing one of Hitler's nightly monologues when he wrote that the desire to expel words "results in an obstinate urge to talk, connected in most cases with a feeling of overflowing. Persons of this kind have the impression that the fund of thought is inexhaustible, and they ascribe a special power or some unusual value to what they say. Their principal relation to other people is effected by the way of oral discharge." [49]

Melanie Klein has shown that adults who exhibit oral sadism—the need to command, subdue, and conquer opposition—are reverting to a much earlier stage of oral hatred: "In my analysis of boys and adult men I have found that when strong oral-sucking impulses have combined with strong oral-sadistic ones, the infant has turned away from his mother's breast with hatred. . . ." Such people, she notes, have an everlasting concern with diets and food fads; they worry about potency in their heterosexual relations or become deeply concerned about homosexuality. As we shall see, Hitler had similar worries. [50]

Anal Stage

Psychoanalysts from Freud to Erikson have also emphasized the importance of the "anal stage" in human development, or, in Erikson's terms, the period in which the conflict of autonomy versus shame and doubt takes place. Failing to achieve a sense of autonomy, accomplishment, and self-control, the child may feel humiliated, frustrated, and ashamed. In adulthood his behavior will be marked by indecisiveness and a desire to humiliate others. Feelings of guilt and shame may also be present. [51]

The anal period (ages two to three) is important because this is the first opportunity the child has to show a degree of mastery and control over others, especially his mother. And to a certain extent, she becomes "dependent on the will of the child." [52] This period in Adolf's life must have put excessive strain on the mother-child relationship. For it was precisely at this time, as we shall see, that little Adolf believed that his mother had betrayed him by following his father-rival to master her sexually. Retention and control of feces could have been his childish way of showing his capacity to force her to pay attention to him. His temptation then—as in later life—was to retain his feces.

It seems likely that Klara, with the best of intentions, contributed to little Adolf's difficulties. We know that she was a fastidious and compulsively clean woman, and it may be assumed that she was particularly rigorous in the toilet training of her children. That Hitler experienced difficulties in this period which further strained the mother-infant relationship is manifested in his adult behavior. We should note first how often he used anal imagery thereby showing an unconscious fixation on feces, filth, manure and odor. Let us consider a few examples:

You don't understand: we are just passing a magnet over a *manure* heap and then we will see how much iron in the *manure* pile there is and how much will cling to the magnet.

And when he [the Jew] turns the treasures over in his hand they are transformed into *dirt and dung.*

Charity is sometimes actually comparable to the *manure* which is spread on the field, not out of love for the latter, but out of precaution for one's own benefits later on.

Hitler even used an anal imagery to describe himself. During a midnight reverie in the Wolfschanze, in January 1942, he was comparing himself, once again, to Frederick the Great. But this time he noted that Frederick was outnumbered 12 to one during the Seven Years' War while he, Hitler, actually had a numerical majority on the Eastern front. He concluded that in comparison to Frederick, he, Hitler, "looked like a shithead." It was one of his favorite words.[53]

One of his most vivid memories of childhood, which he repeated both to his secretaries and to his military entourage, illustrates Hitler's preoccupation with anality. He recalled that for the only time in his life he got drunk as a teenager on Heuriger wine and wiped himself after defecation with the school certificate that he had intended to show proudly to his mother. He was overwhelmed with embarrassment both at the time and years later, when he confessed, "I am still humiliated, even from here." That he kept on telling the humiliating story indicates anal fixation. It is also consistent with a particular form of masochism which will be discussed later.[54]

As we have noted, Hitler was chronically concerned about personal body odor and flatulence. He also worried a good deal about his feces and examined them often, as his doctors reported to U.S. intelligence officers after the war. To alleviate chronic constipation, he frequently took enemas, which he insisted upon administering himself.[55]

According to Otto Fenichel and Karl Abraham, the "anal character" shows certain distinctive traits: obstinacy and stubbornness to the point of passive aggression; constant pitting of his will against others; excessive concern about time. As Abraham has noted, "Patients often save time in small amounts and squander it in large ones." [56] One thinks of Hitler and his troubles with time—he had no time to tie his own tie, yet he could squander hours in empty soliloquies. Psychoanalysts have also found a clear connection between anality and sadism. Patients are particularly noted for rigidity, stubbornness, and refusal to yield. A tendency toward compulsive repetition is also present. All patients are meticulously and compulsively clean. And so, not surprisingly, was Adolf Hitler.

THE CASE OF THE MISSING TESTICLE

Klara Hitler was not only worried about her son's feeding and toilet training. While cajoling or forcing him to eat more food, to move his bowels regularly and on schedule, and to control his bladder, she also could have fretted about an anatomical defect she may have detected in her son: one of his testicles was missing. One can speculate that she periodically felt the little boy's scrotum, checking anxiously to see if the testis had descended. Such solicitous concern would have heightened Adolf's infantile sexual feelings and increased the difficulty of a healthy mother-son relationship.

Since the matter is of considerable importance to the psychological development of Hitler from infancy onward, let us pause here and come to grips with the problem of the Führer's testicles.

It can now be affirmed that the British Tommies were right all along in the first line of their version of the *Colonel Bogey March*—they were manifestly mistaken in the last:

> Hitler has only got one ball,
> Göring has two, but very small;
> Himmler is very sim'lar,
> And Goebbels has no balls at all.

Ribald speculation yielded to medical evidence only after World War II, when the Soviet government released the report of an autopsy performed by Red Army pathologists on Adolf Hitler's body, whose partially burned remains were found in May 1945 in a shallow grave outside the Führer's Berlin air raid shelter.* The relevant medical findings are clear:

> The left testicle could not be found either in the scrotum or on the spermatic cord inside the inguinal canal, or in the small pelvis. . . .

Before pursuing the matter any further, it would be well to establish the identity of the corpse the Russians examined. Positive identification could be made only after comparing Soviet evidence of the teeth of their cadaver with the X rays, diagrams, and pictures of Hitler's head and teeth which were found after the war by U.S. authorities in the files of Hitler's doctors and his dentist, a 1911 graduate of the University of Pennsylvania Dental School named Hugo Johannes Blaschke. Werner Maser, who is sometimes considered the world's lead-

---

* Although the autopsy was performed on 8 May 1945, the report was not released until 1968, in a book published in both German and English. See Lev Bezymenski, *The Death of Adolf Hitler: Unknown Documents from Soviet Archives* (New York, 1968).

ing authority on details of Hitler's life and who claimed to have special knowledge of the dental evidence, was confident that the Soviet autopsy was fraudulent. Hugh Trevor-Roper of Oxford joined him in ridiculing its findings.[57] But after investigating claims and counterclaims, West Germany's distinguished newspaper *Die Zeit* concluded in 1972 that Maser and Trevor-Roper were mistaken and that the Russians were correct: the teeth of their corpse were indeed the teeth of Adolf Hitler.[58]

That conclusion has been independently verified by American and Norwegian specialists in dental medicine. Writing in professional journals, they set forth the evidence, showed conclusively that Maser misrepresented the facts, and affirmed that the teeth in question belonged to Hitler. An American dentist who was formerly a captain in the U.S. Army, and who had access to evidence produced by interrogations of Dr. Blaschke in 1945–1946, concluded: "There is no reason to doubt the present Russian story that the identification of Hitler's remains was successfully made on the basis of dental records." [59]

The most authoritative and detailed examination of the evidence, however, has been made by a Norwegian-American team of specialists in odontology. With meticulous professional care they have gone over all the extant roentgenological, diagrammatic, and descriptive documents from Hitler's files now in the U.S. National Archives and compared these data "tooth by tooth" with the photographic diagrammatic, and descriptive autopsy data released by the Soviets. Their findings are clear and important:

> The individual identified by means of the Hitler files located in the U.S. National Archives . . . is the same person as that of the 1945 autopsy report [as] published in 1968 on the basis of the previously unknown documents from Soviet Archives of 1945.[60]

Two conclusions thus seem incontrovertible: the body on which the Soviet pathologists performed the autopsy was that of Adolf Hitler; and in that body the left testicle was missing.

Nevertheless, there are historians who still believe that Hitler's sexual apparatus was normal and complete. They point to the undoubted fact that Hitler's Vienna roommate, his valets, and two of his doctors, Morell and Giesing, all insisted that there was nothing at all unusual about Hitler's testicles.[61] But the opinions of all these people are of dubious value on this question. All Hitler's intimates agree that he never allowed them to see him completely disrobed. And even if they had had an opportunity for casual observation, it would scarcely have been adequate to the task of verifying their claims about the contents of his scrotum.

No doubt Doctors Morell and Giesing gave Hitler some sort of physical examination. But their assurances of genital normality are not persuasive. Morell was a quack and a sycophant who believed that his Führer and benefactor was completely normal in all respects. He asserted, for example, that Hitler had "no phobias or obsessions . . . no hallucinations, illusions or paranoiac trends." [62] As for SS Doctor Giesing, he told two quite different stories. In October 1945 he assured U.S. interrogators that when, as an ear specialist he was called in to examine Hitler's ears after the bomb explosion of June 1944, he did *not examine the Führer's rectum or genitals.*[63] Later, Giesing told Werner Maser that he had once asked his Führer to lift up his nightgown so that he could make a thorough examination. The SS doctor reported that he "could not establish that there were any abnormalities of the genitals." His inability to do so is understandable. Even if the unlikely story were true, the examination was visual. Anomalies of the scrotum cannot be determined without palpation. It is not likely that Hitler would have permitted an ear specialist—or anyone else—to squeeze his scrotum. John Toland repeats a rumour that, sometime in 1933, Hitler was examined by an anonymous Berlin physician who allegedly "paid special attention to his penis and testicles." [64] Mr. Toland is unable to find any substantiation for this improbable story.

The evidence of the Soviet autopsy still stands. We know the names of the five doctors who signed the report. They were ranking pathologists of the Red Army. There would seem to be no reason why they would all compromise their reputation by submitting a fraudulent report. And there was no discernible medical or political purpose to be served by reporting falsely that one of Adolf Hitler's testicles was missing.

What happened to it is a matter of conjecture. Although Hitler might have mutilated himself late in life, there is specific evidence against the theory. Hitler's company commander during World War I reported that at that time Hitler had only one testicle. He was positive about that fact because the army periodically conducted genital inspections for venereal disease.[65]

Hitler's childhood and adult behavior indicates very strongly that his genitalia never were normal. He probably suffered either from congenital monorchism—that is, the absence of a testicle at birth—or from cryptorchism, an undescended testicle. The complete absence of a testis in the inguinal canal or the small pelvis could be accounted for by acute atrophy, which could have rendered it undetectable to the Russian doctors, whose primary purpose, after all, was to find the cause of Hitler's death, not to investigate the contents of his scrotum. In any case, whether Hitler had monorchism or cryptorchism, only one testicle would have been present in the scrotal sack, and the psychological consequences would have been the same.

A missing or undescended testicle is not in itself pathogenic; it is only so when—as with young Hitler—it occurs "within the matrix of a disturbed parent-child relationship." When that happens, Peter Blos has concluded, the condition can produce a "profoundly detrimental influence" on the psychological development of the child.[66] Dr. Blos, the well-known American child psychoanalyst and mentor of Eric Erikson, wrote a detailed study of emotionally disturbed boys suffering from the absence of a testicle at the prepubertal age of 11 or 12. He found that the symptoms in all his patients were the same. All patients showed marked mobility disturbance and hyperactivity; even bright children suddenly developed learning difficulties and lack of concentration in schoolwork. The boys exhibited accident proneness and a form of "compulsive toying with physical danger." All patients showed feelings of social inadequacy; they suffered from chronic indecision and had a tendency to lie and fantasize. In all cases, the boys blamed the mother as the perpetrator of the bodily damage; each mother was ostentatiously loved, but also hated as the parent responsible for the patient's inadequacy. The patients were concerned about bowel movements and feces. Castration fantasies were invariably present. When confronted by criticism, the patients insisted that they were special people with an unusual mission to perform or they were "magical persons." Analysts noted a pattern of preoccupation with time and with death; characteristically, patients were preoccupied with breasts and eyeballs, as substitutes for the testicle. In all cases observed, there was either a self-image of passive feminine tendencies or a defense against the fear of those tendencies and the felt necessity, as a reaction formation, to insist upon masculinity, hardness, toughness, destructiveness, and ruthlessness.[67] At one time or another in his life, Adolf Hitler exhibited *every one of these symptoms*. In fact, in reading the clinical literature dealing with disturbed boys having genital abnormalities, the student of Adolf Hitler must keep reminding himself that the American analysts are discussing their own patients and not Klara Hitler's young son.

Another child analyst stresses particularly that patients with abnormalities of the scrotal sac and testicles are deeply concerned about the female breast: "It is the breast which often occupies the center of his [the patient's] unconscious fantasies." [68] Since Adolf identified so closely with his mother, the removal of her cancerous left breast could have been a particularly traumatic experience, for it may well have symbolized for him the removal of his one remaining testicle.

Adolf's difficulties with toilet training and his fear of paternal whippings would have been greatly increased by monorchism. Dr. Anita Bell has shown that when acute fear is experienced by a child— for example, when he associates loss of feces with loss of testicles— there is a sudden contraction of the cremaster muscle, often drawing up the testicle into the inguinal canal. Similar contractions are experienced when a boy is threatened with a beating. At such times of acute anxiety, little boys often *clutch at their genitals in a gesture of reassurance*, as if the child were saying to himself, "It isn't true that something is missing, my penis is always there. . . ." [69] How dreadful to little Adolf the paternal spankings—or even threats of spankings—

must have been! The fear they aroused would have been associated with the retraction of his one remaining testicle. This extra intensity of fear may explain why Hitler's memories of beatings were so vivid.

A childhood habit of clutching at defective genitals would explain Hitler's lifelong gesture of moving his hands down to cover his crotch, particularly in moments of tension or excitement. As an American film reviewer noticed in watching the "home movies" Eva Braun made of Hitler, the repetition of the gesture is remarkable: "I was fascinated to watch the ex-corporal's gestures whenever he finds himself confronted by other people: usually he folds his hands protectively over his crotch . . . then they flutter up to his face, covering his eyes for a moment, sweep back the famous forelock and then travel down to be folded, piously, over the Führer's pelvic region." [70] A check of only two illustrated books which the Nazis published about their Führer confirms the impression. Indeed, the number of pictures showing him in this pose is striking: in two books, more than two dozen pictures of the same gesture. And in one of his last official propaganda portraits, painted in 1943 after the catastrophic defeat at Stalingrad, the Führer is shown hiding his lower torso behind the back of a chair. The date and the pose lend irony to the heroic caption: "Adolf Hitler Is Victory!" *

Another distinguishing characteristic of disturbed monorchid boys is physical hyperactivity—a voracious appetite for active outdoor games but, at the same time, a desire to avoid physical contact. There is no reason to doubt Hitler's later contention that he was a very active boy, "the little ringleader" of all neighborhood games. Indeed, all evidence shows a degree of activity that is extraordinary. In letters and interviews, former playmates all stress Adolf's unusual passion for war games. He played them by the hour, and for many years after his contemporaries had outgrown this interest. Three of his former playmates, Baldwin Wiesmayer, Franz Winter, and Johann Weinberger, all agreed that he wanted to play war games all the time: "We Leonding kids were the Boers under Hitler's leadership, the kids from Untergaumberg were the English." Another of his childhood friends, who later became the abbot of a Cistercian monastery, recalled vividly in an interview that "We were always playing at war—war games endlessly. Most of us got sick of it, but Hitler always managed to find someone who could play with him, usually younger boys." [71]

Adolf's activity on his confirmation day, May 1904, seems curious for a boy in his teens. One of his sponsors, who had also been a pallbearer at his father's funeral in 1903, recalled that the confirmation

---

* Since the right hand is often found clasped over the left, it has been suggested that the only thing the gesture reveals is that Hitler had a weak left hand. But he could have favored it in other ways: holding it tightly against his side or behind his back, or folding both hands over his chest or at his waist. Instead, he habitually clasped both hands over his crotch. For a score of examples, see *Adolf Hitler: Bilder aus dem Leben des Führers* (Hamburg, 1936), and *Mit Hitler im Westen*, ed. Heinrich Hoffmann (Berlin, 1940). The propaganda poster is now in the Imperial War Museum, London.

ceremony took place in the Linz cathedral and that he had given Adolf a prayer book and a savings bank book with a small deposit in it. On returning to his mother's home in Leonding, Adolf paid little attention to his sponsor, was unimpressed with his gifts, and remained apathetic and sullen. He only brightened when a gang of yelling boys came up; he ran off with them immediately, "charging around the house playing Indians." [72] Hitler himself, in a letter written after he had become Führer of his Party, recalled to a childhood friend "with endless pleasure" the war games they had played together as children.[73]

Contemporary letters and memoirs agree that Hitler was invariably the ringleader—in part because he was usually considerably older than his playmates—but that he carefully avoided all physical contact, preferring—as he would later in life—to dominate and command by means of his tongue.

Symptomatic irritability and temper tantrums associated with monorchid patients were also characteristic of the young Hitler. His half-brother, Alois Jr., gave the following report about him at the age of seven:

> He was imperious and quick to anger from childhood onward and would not listen to anyone. My stepmother always took his part. He would get the craziest notions and get away with it. If he didn't have his way, he got very angry. . . . He would fly into a rage over any triviality.[74]

The testimony of Alois Jr. may be suspect, but his description of Adolf's behavior up to the age of six or seven is so consistent with accounts of his adolescence and maturity that there can be little doubt about its accuracy. It is also supported by the testimony of Adolf's one close friend, who reported that Hitler could blow up over apparently trivial and insignificant things. One day, as the two friends were strolling along the Landstrasse in Linz, a boy of Adolf's age came up and, recognizing him as a former classmate, grinned and said "Hello, Hitler," took his arm in a friendly way, and asked how things were going. Instead of responding in kind, Adolf

> went red with rage. . . . "What the devil is that to do with you?" he threw at him excitedly and pushed him sharply away. Then he took my arm and went with me on his way. . . . It was a long time before he calmed down. . . . There was no end of things, even trivial ones, that could upset him. But he lost his temper most of all when it was suggested that he should become a civil servant. Whenever he heard the words "civil servant" even without any connection with his own career he fell into a rage. I discovered that these outbursts of fury were, in a certain sense, still quarrels with his long-dead father. . . .[75]

The prepubertal learning difficulties and academic troubles noted by Dr. Blos also plagued young Hitler. Through the years when he attended *Volksschule* (ages 6–11), Adolf's school record was excellent. Herr Lehrer Karl Mittermaier, his teacher in the little elementary school in Fischlam which he attended from the ages of six to eight, remembered him as the star of his school: "Full marks in every subject. . . . Mentally very much alert, obedient but lively." Similar reports have come down from the school at Lambach (ages 8–9). Here he was an excellent student and an asset to the boys' choir of the local monastery. Young Adolf also did very well in the *Volksschule* in Leonding, which he attended for half a year in 1899.

But when he entered the *Realschule* in Linz in September 1900 at the age of 11, striking changes appeared in his behavior. He now seemed unable or unwilling to concentrate on his studies. His first year went so badly and was so far "below standard" that he was obliged to repeat the form. The second year went rather better—since he was repeating all subjects—but during the third year (1902–1903) he failed in mathematics and his diligence was "variable." By 1904 he was doing so badly that he was passed only on the condition that he leave the Linz *Realschule*. His mother was obliged to send him to the school at Styr, about 15 miles from his home, where she rented a room for him. His report card (dated 16 September 1905) is still in existence. On a scale with 1 as excellent, 2 good, 3 satisfactory, 4 adequate, and 5 below standard, young Hitler received the following grades:

> Moral conduct—3
> Diligence—4
> Religious instruction—4
> German—5
> Geography—4
> History—4
> Mathematics—5
> Chemistry—4
> Physics—3
> Freehand drawing—2
> Gymnastics—1
> Shorthand [optional]—5

Since Adolf failed to reach the minimum standard in two required subjects, mathematics and German, he would have been obliged to repeat the form. Instead, he dropped out of school. His failure in German is not surprising to those who have read *Mein Kampf* or any of his adult letters in the original. His marks in history and geography scarcely support the boast in his memoirs that "by far my best work was in geography and better still in world history, my two favorite subjects in which I shot ahead of the rest of the form." [76]

Thus, by the age of 11, Adolf was no longer the obedient star pupil of previous years. Indeed, Dr. Huemer, one of his teachers during this period, described him as having been lazy, lacking in self-control, "argumentative, self-opinionated, willful, arrogant and bad-tempered. He had obvious difficulty in fitting in at the school. . . . He demanded of his fellow pupils their unqualified subservience, fancying himself in the role of leader. . . ." Another instructor at the Linz *Realschule*, Dr. Gissinger, reported strange activity on the part of his pupil. Gissinger said emphatically that he was not drawing on his own imagination but distinctly remembered "Hitler holding dialogue with trees stirring in the wind." One of Hitler's friends in Leonding confirmed this picture. He said his friends all considered Adolf quite strange and remembered that he liked to climb a hill to make speeches at night to nonexistent audiences.[77] Many other examples of Hitler's exaggerations and florid fantasies (including belief in his own magical powers, so typical of monorchids) are recorded by his admirers both in adolescence and during his mature years.

The age of 11–12, a time of resurgent sexual impulses and genital awareness, produces great anxiety in monorchid boys—an anxiety which in Adolf was almost certainly increased by the worries his over-solicitous mother had expressed through the years. Hitler's concern about his sexual development is indicated in a drawing he did at the age of 11 or 12 of a frightened *Realschule* teacher apparently caught in the act of masturbation. It seems likely that Adolf has projected his own anxiety and fears onto the teacher. (The cartoon is now in the Federal Government Archives in Coblenz.) A German biographer who reprints it thinks that the teacher is depicted as "overbearing," "suspicious," and "arrogant," and that he is holding an ice cream cone in his hand. But that cannot be an ice cream cone, since they made their first appearance at the St. Louis World's Fair of 1904—four years *after* Adolf drew the picture (p. 158) of his teacher.[78]

In order to help master the anxiety engendered by the anatomical defect, disturbed monorchid boys favor symbolic substitutes for the missing testicle. In addition to breasts, patients may be excessively concerned about eyes. Hitler's eyes were particularly important to him, and others began to notice them in early adolescence. His secondary school teacher, Dr. Gissinger, described Adolf's eyes as "shining"; when Kubizek first met him, he was particularly struck by Hitler's strangely compelling eyes and recalls that his mother was frightened by them. As we have noted, the adult Hitler was aware of their power and practiced "piercing stares" in front of the mirror. He also played games with his eyes. He would slowly cross them in looking at people, or he would stare them down. In effect, he may have been saying to them and to himself, "See, I do have two powerful (potent) testicles, and I can penetrate and dominate others." He was infatuated with the Medusa of the piercing eyes that could render others impotent. One might also consider Hitler's use of the extended, stiff-arm salute as a substitute for flawed genitalia. We have seen earlier how he boasted

that his ability to hold his arm stiff was proof of his masculine power and virility.

An American child analyst has reported that his young monorchid patients have a desire "of an almost frantic or feverish type" for redesigning and reconstructing buildings. They hope to quell their anxiety about defects in their own bodies by making other kinds of structures whole.[79] Hitler's lifelong preoccupation with replanning and reconstructing buildings and bridges in Linz, Vienna, and Berlin fits the pattern. Kubizek devoted two chapters to the subject in his memoirs: "Adolf Rebuilds Linz" and "Adolf Rebuilds Vienna." He recalled that "the first time I went to visit him at home his room was littered with sketches, drawings, blueprints. Here was the New Theatre, there the Mountain Hotel on the Lichtenberg. It was like an architect's office . . . he dragged me along wherever there was a building going up. . . . But even more than with these concrete examples was he taken up with the vast schemes that he himself originated. Here his *mania for change* knew no limit. . . . He gave his whole self to his imaginary buildings and was completely carried away by it. Once he conceived an idea he was *like one possessed*. Nothing else existed for him—he was oblivious to time, sleep and hunger. . . ." Finally, young Hitler decided that he could not rest until he had undertaken the "rebuilding of the entire city of Vienna, district by district." [80]

In a revealing and previously unpublished fragment of Hitler's *Tischgespräche*, Hitler shows that while he could take his adolescent paintings quite lightly, he was very serious indeed about the building and reconstruction plans of his youth. During the Third Reich, Hitler's sycophants searched all Europe for the watercolors their Führer had painted as a young man in Vienna and Munich. One day in March 1944 at the Obersalzberg the court photographer, Heinrich Hoffmann, triumphantly produced a water color his master had done in Vienna in 1910. Hitler's reaction is worth quoting at some length:

> Hoffmann, I hope you didn't buy that painting! Those things ought not to bring more than 150 or 200 RM even today. It is insane to pay a lot of money for them. I never wanted to become a painter. I only painted those things in order to stay alive and to study. For a picture like that I never got at that time more than about 12 RM. . . . I only painted enough to provide me with the bare necessities of life. I never needed more than about 80 RM a month. For lunch and for supper 1 RM had to do. I used to study all through the night. *The architectural sketches that I completed in those days, those were my most valuable possessions*, my own brainchildren which I would never have given away as I did the pictures.
>
> One should never forget that all my thoughts of today, all my architectural plans, go back to the drawings that I produced in those years of nightlong labor. When today I have the opportunity, for example, of drawing the ground plans for a theatre, it doesn't come from any trance-like fantasy. It is always exclusively and only the product of my previous studies. Unfortunately all of my former sketches have been lost to me.[81]

As Hitler's architect, Albert Speer, remembers so vividly, Hitler's mania for building and rebuilding lasted to the very end of his Reich. "The only time I saw him behave with genuine vivacity," Speer recalled in an interview, was ". . . when we were together, poring over architectural plans." Significantly, Hitler's relationship to Speer changed when they stopped talking about building plans: "Our rapport lasted only as long as I was his architect; once I entered his government as minister of armaments, everything began to change." [82] Hitler then went on by himself compulsively building bigger and bigger buildings to prove his strength, power, and potency. But no matter how much he built and rebuilt he could never rebuild enough. Always he felt inadequate.

In trying so desperately to correct the defects of the various structures that displeased him, Hitler seems to have been striving to undo the defectiveness of his own body. This frenetic effort—"this mania for change"—was of such vital significance to him that he gave himself to the task with utmost intensity. Small wonder that he would erupt in towering rages whenever his adolescent friend raised any question about problems of financing the grandiose architectural schemes. Much of this fury over the mere suggestion that a cherished wish might not be fulfilled may have derived ultimately from one all-important infantile hope: that his missing testicle would descend.

Predictably, boys who have genital defects as well as Oedipal problems develop castration anxieties of extraordinary dimensions. Hitler, we have noted, was beset by such fears. As Führer, the kind of punishment he chose to mete out reflects castration anxieties. Anyone found guilty of "causing ridicule of the Führer" was *beheaded*; artists who displeased him by using the wrong colors for skies and meadows were to be *castrated*.[83]

Hitler also showed his apprehension about his sexual adequacy in other ways. He was actually frightened by stallions and bulls, traditional symbols of masculinity. But he liked very much to gaze at statues or pictures of them, "enviously admiring their strength and yet actually afraid of the animals themselves, who possessed those qualities which he lacked but most desired." From the pictures he seems to have derived vicarious "sexual strength—satisfactory substitute—until faced with the real thing, when the satisfaction turned to hate and fear." [84]

For his new Chancellery, Hitler chose statues of stallions. Facing the garden and at either end of a colossal stretch of Egyptian-style columns were two gigantic prancing stallions by Josef Thorak; and the dominant statue in the cavernous "Marble Gallery" was a huge statue of a rearing stallion by Arnold Breker, the artist who also did the two heroic uncircumcised male nudes at the main entrance, symbolizing the Party and the Wehrmacht.

An American journalist who toured the building noted that stallions also figured prominently in the hall, whose enormous length contained 14 magnificent Gobelin tapestries, all personally selected by Hitler and all but four showing horses. If the sexual parts of the animals in the tapestries were covered by foliage or other objects, Hitler privately called in experts to determine the sex from the animal's mane, nostrils, bone formation, or musculature. Then, in entertaining guests, Hitler would point to a partially hidden horse and ask a visitor its sex. If the guest could not answer, Hitler pointed out the reasons why he knew it was a stallion, concluding, "But you don't know anything about horses." [85] By playing this game, was Hitler trying to reassure himself by saying, in effect, that as with horses, a man could be very masculine without revealing his sexual equipment?

Bulls were also a favorite virility substitute. As a boy in Vienna, we recall, Hitler had written a dramatic sketch involving a bull being held by the horns. When he decorated his new Chancellery he saw to it that the garden was dominated by a heroic uncircumcised Nordic nude wrestling a bull by the horns. Apparently Hitler thought that bulls helped him overcome fears of sexual impotence, for one of the

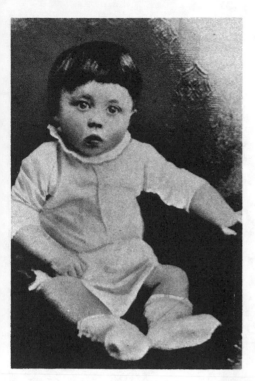

Adolf as a baby,
circa 1890.

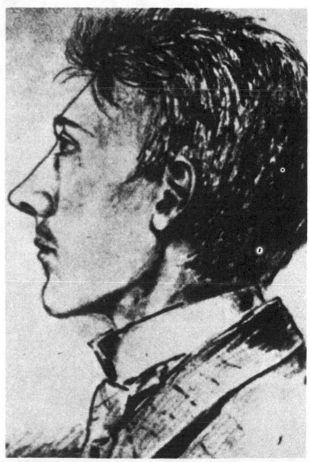

A schoolmate's
sketch of Hitler
at age sixteen.

Alois Hitler, circa 1890.

Klara Pölzl Hitler,
circa 1895.

Franz von Stuck's
painting of Medusa's head.
"Those eyes, Hanfstaengl!
Those eyes! Those are the
eyes of my mother!"
(For this picture's
significance to Hitler,
see pp. 6-7, 157).

The Ideal. Stefanie—The "Great Love" he never knew.

Geli Raubal, Hitler's niece—
"The only woman I could
ever marry."

Eva Braun—
the woman he married.

Der Führer just prior to
his "Seizure of Power," 1932.

Chancellor Hitler with
"Der alte Herr,"
President von Hindenburg, 1933.

Hitler near his
mountain retreat
on the Obersalzberg.

German artists often
went to extremes in
depicting their ruler.
One saw him as a cru-
sading knight. After
things took a bad turn
for the Führer, the
painting fell into the
hands of American GIs.
One of them spoke for
his comrades when he
rammed a bayonet
into Hitler's eye socket.

Hitler as Wagnerian hero.
The official portrait
of the Führer for 1938.
(See p. 102).

Franz von Stuck's *Wilde Jagd* ("The Wild Chase") was painted in 1889, the year Hitler was born. Hitler was a great admirer of von Stuck, knew this picture well and may have personally identified with the portrayal of Wotan as the god of destruction (see page 68). Used with permission of the Städtische Galerie im Lenbachhaus, Munich.

The Conqueror of Paris.

The last official portrait, 1944. Used as a propaganda poster, the caption read, "*Adolf Hitler ist der Sieg.*"

many injections which he pumped into his bloodstream was a concoction of syrup mixed with extract of bull testicles.[86]

He sought to reassure himself about his sexual powers in another way. His valet of many years was emphatic in reporting that Hitler kept two pistols near him: one, a 7.65 Walther, was always on his bedside table; the other, a 6.35 Walther, "ever since 1919 was always [*ständig*] carried in a specially made leather pocket which was sewn into all his trousers." [87] Thus, during his waking hours, when he entertained Chamberlain or the Duchess of Windsor, when he sat with Winifred Wagner listening to the *Götterdämmerung*, when he walked with little children, the pistol was in his pocket; when he orated to jubilant thousands, when he strolled the terrace of the Berghof, when he chattered gaily with movie starlets—always, a pistol was with him with its barrel pressed reassuringly against his thigh.

Let us return to Adolf's childhood. We have concluded that he was born with a sexual defect. The autopsy report, supported by psychological data and a consideration of his childhood and adult behavior, indicates that he was a monorchid. Further, we conclude that this physical condition, coupled with disturbed mother-child relations, shaped his attitude to his mother and contributed to his general psychological "modes" of mistrust and shame.

There is no direct evidence of the way Klara responded to her son's malformation. As with many questions raised by this book, we must speculate. It seems likely that she would have sought advice first from her aunts, who were experienced peasant women. There is no evidence that she consulted a physician. Probably her aunts assured her that little Adolf's condition was not at all unusual; she need not worry, since it was just a matter of time until the testicle "came down by itself." Thus the anxious mother—we are conjecturing—repeatedly reassured herself and her little boy that everything would be all right. If he waited patiently, surely the left testicle would, in due time, descend and everything would be normal. In this way, Hitler's childhood anxiety about time, and his impatience with waiting, were extended into a lifelong concern. He never trusted time again, and he developed a preference for watches whose faces were covered and clocks that were left unwound.

Time had always worked against him. In one of the last "Table Conversations" of which we have a record, that of 15 February 1945, he put it at the top of the list of those forces which had betrayed him and caused his defeat: "Time—and *it's always Time*, you notice—[is] against us." [88]

His mother's repeated and worried reassurances would have served not to alleviate little Adolf's apprehension but to intensify it. And her reminders would have further confused his ambivalent feelings about her. He did indeed love his mother, as he so often insisted. But she had done an evil thing to him, which he could never forget or forgive. She had given him a defect at birth that would mar him for life. And, as we are about to see, there was something else she had done to him that he resented bitterly.

HITLER'S "PRIMAL SCENE TRAUMA"

Alois Hitler was away from home for extended periods during the first three years of Adolf's life. In his absence, the little boy was drawn very close to his mother, who sometimes took him to bed with her "for company." * We may speculate that the closer little Adolf felt toward his mother, the more anxiety he felt about his father; the more he feared his father, the more he clung to his mother—and the circular anxiety of the Oedipal conflict was intensified. Fantasied incestuous relations would have sharpened his hatred of his father as a rival, as well as his fear of paternal vengeance.

Then one night, when he was about three years old, Adolf saw— or imagined he saw—a scene of horror: his inebriated father attacked his mother and did something terrible and strange to her. And, most awful of all, she seemed to enjoy it.

Once again the biographer is confronted with the question of whether his subject "actually experienced" an event or "merely imagined" it. And once again it must be emphasized that psychologically *it does not make much difference.* One of Freud's greatest contributions to a biographer's understanding is the insight that neurotic symptoms may not be related to any actual event at all. They are derived from what is often dismissed as "pure fantasy." But psychic reality is often more important than objective reality, and what a subject *imagines* to have happened must therefore be taken seriously. His fantasies, the words and turns of phrase he uses to describe them, the intensity of his imagery, the number of times he recounts them—none of this should be written off as accidental or arbitrary. These things are "unconsciously determined" and are very important indeed to the person involved. From a thousand other events in his life he has chosen these particular incidents; he has described them with these specific words, and not with the many alternative figures of speech available to him.

We shall never know with finality whether the infant Adolf actually saw the scene of sexual assault. But in his fantasy he did, and it was for him a "primal scene trauma." Parenthetically, it may be said that, in this instance, fantasy probably coincided with reality.

---

* Hitler told Hanfstaengl that one of his earliest and most pleasant memories was when he was permitted to sleep alone with his mother "in the big bed."

The Child As Father to the Man

The best historical source for the incident is Hitler himself. For quite unintentionally in his memoirs he has given us an eyewitness account of his own harrowing experience. Dr. Walter Langer and his psychoanalytical colleagues were the first to notice, in an OSS report of 1943, that a peculiar passage in *Mein Kampf* which ostensibly describes what happened to the little son of a "worker" is, in all probability, a thinly disguised autobiographical memoir. (For purposes of later discussion, some key phrases in the passage have been italicized and numbered.)

> Let us imagine the following: In a basement apartment of two stuffy rooms lives a worker's family. . . . Among the (1) *five children there is a boy, let us say, of three*. This is the age at which a child becomes conscious of his first impressions. (2) *In gifted people [bei Begabten]*, traces of these early memories are found even in old age. The (3) *smallness and overcrowding of the rooms* do not create favorable conditions. Quarreling and nagging often arise because of this. In such circumstances people do not live with one another, but (4) *push down on top of one another [drücken aufeinander]*. Every argument . . . leads to a never-ending, disgusting quarrel. . . . But when the parents fight almost daily, their brutality leaves nothing to the imagination; then the results of such (5) *visual education* must slowly but inevitably become apparent in the little ones . . . especially when the mutual differences express themselves (6) *in the form of brutal attacks on the part of the father towards the mother or to assaults due to drunkenness*. The poor little boy (7) *at the age of six*, senses things which would (8) *make even a grown-up shudder*. (9) *Morally infected* . . . the young "citizen" wanders off to elementary school. . . .
>
> The three year old has now become a (10) *youth of fifteen* who [has been dismissed from school and] despises all authority. . . . Now he loiters about and God only knows when he comes home. . . .[89]

The scene at the age of three does not seem at all improbable when one considers how little concerned Alois Hitler was about anybody's knowledge of his sexual life. He was unlikely to be embarrassed by the presence of a little child in the crowded living quarters, particularly if he thought the child was asleep.

The description as given by Hitler contains numerous phrases which reinforce the conclusion that the passage is autobiographical:

(1) *Five children*. For several years as a young boy, Adolf was one of five children, along with Paula and Edmund and his stepbrother and stepsister, Alois Jr. and Angela.

(2) *in gifted people.* He often referred to himself this way.

(3) *smallness and overcrowding of the rooms.* Not an inaccurate description of the close quarters in the inns and mill where the Hitlers lived during Adolf's early childhood.

(4) *push down on top of one another.* Description of the sex act?

(5) *visual education.* Once again, the importance to Hitler of the eyes.

(6) *brutal attacks . . . due to drunkenness.* These phrases and images are repeated several times in the chapter.

(7) *at the age of six.* Particularly important to Adolf because when he was six his rival, Edmund, was conceived.

(8) *make even a grown-up shudder.* Why should adults *shudder* at sexual intercourse? What kind of attacks was he imagining? Were they particularly sadistic? Would they possibly have been the kind of sadomasochistic sexual deviation which Hitler himself may later have indulged in? (See below, pp. 237–243.)

(9) *Morally infected.* Note that Hitler associates sexual intercourse with something morally infectious and repulsive.

(10) *Youth of fifteen.* The school dropout who despises authority, loiters about, and stays out until all hours is, as we shall see, an accurate description of Adolf's own life-style after the death of his father.

Of course, it is not always traumatic for a child to see parents engaged in sex. If it were, thousands upon thousands of Eskimos and Bedouins would, presumably, be a great deal more neurotic than they seem to be. The experience is traumatic only, as in little Adolf's case, if it reinforces other deeply disturbing childhood experiences.

In the midst of describing other dreadful incidents involving drunken husbands who are attacking their passive wives, Hitler stops to make a very important statement: *"I witnessed all this personally in hundreds of scenes . . . with both disgust and indignation."* [90] We must ask *where* young Adolf had ever personally witnessed such intimate and, to him, disgusting scenes. Certainly he had never seen them outside his own home. And he never showed any interest whatever in observing the workings of a three-year-old mind as it developed to the age of six and on to fifteen—that is, no such mind except his own. Then how could he have viewed these things himself "hundreds" of times?

It is possible that he may never actually have seen them at all, that it was "only a fantasy." But it seems more likely—given the specific details and turns of phrase in his description—that he did witness such a scene, and that he had relived the terrifying event hundreds of times in his imagination. Every psychoanalyst knows from clinical experience that when a patient constantly repeats an image or an association or has the same dream again and again, it is an "indication of the depth an impression has made and the intensity of what he wishes to communicate." [91]

The professional literature on primal scene trauma is extensive, but a few recurring symptoms may be summarized here. None of these by itself is decisive, but a combination of them does bespeak serious emotional problems in many patients as it did, we are suggesting, in Adolf Hitler. All patients show severe castration anxieties. Indeed, it is an established principle of analysis that severe castration anxiety is a common sequel to the observation of a primal scene under circumstances that are traumatic to the child. One of Hitler's most striking illustrations of this symptom was his lifelong preoccupation with decapitation in general and the Medusa's head in particular (see Chapter I, p. 21f). To decapitate is to castrate as well as to kill; the terror which the Medusa's head evokes is the terror not only of death but also of castration.[92] The castration fears which so frequently follow a primal scene trauma would have been particularly intense in young Adolf because of his monorchism, for monorchism represents the climax *in reality* of frightening Oedipal fantasies about paternal revenge. Thus, Hitler's anxiety would have been twofold: the actual body damage intensified castration fears, which were further stimulated by the primal scene experience.

Primal scene exposure also awakens in many patients, as it seems to have done in Adolf, incestuous fantasies and fears. The child is both repelled and attracted by the thought of incest, of replacing his father as his mother's sexual partner. Hitler expressed such horror—and infatuation—in many ways. First, as was his habit, he denied vehemently that he himself had any such desires by projecting them onto others. He insisted, for example, that it was not he but the Jews who were guilty of incest.[93] Or he would say that Vienna was "the personification of incest [*die Verkörperung der Blutschande*]." [94] The fact that his sexual affairs in later life were with mother substitutes is also strong evidence of incestuous feelings for his mother.

There is other indirect evidence that Adolf had incestuous fantasies about his mother, hated his father as a rival, feared him, and harbored a death wish toward the old man. This is hinted at in his adolescent drama about the Holy Mountain, in which a priest cuts off the head of a sacrificial bull. It seems likely that the bull, a traditional symbol of aggressive sensuality, was to young Hitler a father symbol in this context. Since Adolf was beginning to see himself as a Messiah, he may, unconsciously, have cast himself as the priest sacrificing his father to his own ambition and Oedipal fears.

We have seen that Hitler was also deathly afraid of strangulation. He had written about Dame Poverty as a snake that sought to throttle him. During one of his last "Table Conversations" he said, in an interesting turn of phrase, that the Jews sought to "asphixiate" him. He had nightmares about strangulation, drowning, and shortness of breath.

In a classic study of nightmares, Ernest Jones has shown that there is a direct connection between horror dreams of this kind and incestuous desires:

> *The malady known as Nightmare is always an expression of intense mental conflict centering about some form of "repressed" sexual desire. . . .* There is no doubt that this concerns the incest trends of sexual life, so that we may extend the formula just given and say: *An attack of the Nightmare is an expression of a mental conflict over an incestuous desire.*[95]

The peculiar biographical fact that both as a young man and as an adult Hitler prided himself on being a "wolf" may be tied-in with his infantile trauma. There are many examples of his identification with wolves, but most significantly, the tune he whistled often and absent-mindedly was "Who's Afraid of the Big Bad Wolf?" To those who are acquainted with Freud's celebrated case of the "Wolf-man" or the later publication of the Wolf-man's own memoirs, Hitler's infatuation with the wolf strikes a familiar note. Freud's patient, it will be recalled, had also as an infant watched his parents have intercourse; he subsequently developed a wolf phobia. While we do not know with certainty whether Hitler had a wolf or dog phobia as a child, the defiant tone of the Disney movie song suggests that he may have, and that he learned to defend against this anxiety by associating himself with the object of his fear, by deliberately cultivating it and surrounding himself with it. Familiarity, in this case, bred not contempt but a lessening of anxiety. In identifying himself as the wolf, he was reassuring himself by saying, in effect: "See, I don't need to be afraid of wolves, I myself am the Wolf." [96]

It is possible that the infant Adolf associated his father with the wolf, since it is known that Alois owned a large dog, possibly an Alsatian (in German, *Wolfshund*). As we have noted, Alois whipped the dog, and in calling for both his dog and his son he gave the same whistle.

There is no doubt that Hitler saw his father as an aggressor against him, as is shown both in the *Mein Kampf* passage and in his many references to the whippings he received as a boy. There is further evidence that Adolf identified with the aggressor-father. He sometimes treated his own *Wolfshund* in the brutal way that he had seen his father whip his own dog. One of the women with whom Hitler had intimate relations during 1926, Maria (or Mimi) Reiter, recalls that she saw him turn savagely on his own dog:

> He whipped his dog like a madman [*Irrsinniger*] with his riding whip as he held him tight on the leash. He became tremendously excited. . . . I could not have believed that this man would beat an animal so ruthlessly—an animal about which he had said a moment previously that he could not live without. But now he whipped his most faithful companion!

The Child As Father to the Man

When Mimi asked him how he could possibly be so brutal, Hitler replied grimly, "That was necessary." [97] In beating the dog, was Hitler punishing himself for his own guilt feelings, which he had transferred to the animal? He said that he knew his dog had "guilty feelings."

As in the case of Freud's Wolf-man, the horse seems to have replaced the dog or wolf as a phobic object. Hitler, it will be remembered, feared horses. But, as if simultaneously denying that fear and protecting himself from it, he habitually carried a riding whip and surrounded himself with pictures and statues of stallions.[98]

Among the long-range consequences of Hitler's infantile experience was the belief that coitus is brutal, infectious, and dangerous—so dangerous that the adult Hitler would liken it to going into battle on the Western Front (see Chapter 1, p. 52). The sex act also illustrates, as Hitler saw it, women's masochistic need to be overpowered by the audacious man; this reinforced his image of women as weak and deceitful creatures who were not to be trusted. His avoidance of genital intercourse with women may also have been a consequence of his unconscious association of all women with the one woman—his mother— who yielded deceitfully to his father-rival, produced deficient children (who died early in life or were mentally or physically defective), and then nursed them at breasts that later became diseased.[99]

His infantile experience seems to have had another long-range consequence. Phyllis Greenacre has shown that children to whom observation of parental sex was traumatic tend to become prejudiced toward minority groups. Such children emphasize the contrast between themselves and others, stare carefully at strangers, make special note of their physical appearance, and become radically antagonistic toward those whose appearance is different and repugnant to them.[100]

It is noteworthy that Hitler's most revealing expression of prejudice in his memoirs emphasizes visual scrutiny and physical appearance. He says that he suffered a profound shock when he first looked at an East European Jew:

> . . . One day when I was walking through the Inner City, I suddenly came upon a being clad in a long caftan, with black curls.
> "Is this also a Jew?" was my first thought.
> At Linz they certainly did not *look* like that. Secretly and cautiously I *watched* the man but the longer I *stared* at this strange face and *scrutinized* one feature after the other, the more my mind reshaped the first question into another form:
> "Is this also a German?" [101]

There is another reason why we have dwelt on this infantile experience: the way the mature Hitler remembered his parents' sexual relations reveals modes of thought that had historic consequences when he established his dictatorship. The words, images, and phrases he used in describing the event—or the fantasy—show a clear development of the mistrust and hatred that would determine all his interpersonal relations. His mental picture of the incident reveals that to his mind sexuality, power, aggression, and cruelty were all fused together in a dangerous, pathologic union: terror, brutalization, and ruthless power were to him the primary features of sex and life.

In short, attitudes revealed here characterized both his own personality and the political system he imposed on his country and much of Europe.[102]

LATER CHILDHOOD

Adolf Hitler's formative early years did not bode well for the development of the crucially important mother-child relationship. Maternal indulgence and paternal severity bound him excessively to his mother. Though tied to her emotionally, he was at the same time unconsciously repelled, for he blamed her for two things—his monorchism and the "primal scene"—which greatly complicated his Oedipal feelings. It is not possible to say which was the more important; indeed, we will probably never know. But it is less important to assign priority than to stress the cumulative effect of both experiences. That there was interaction and mutual reinforcement seems evident because the consequences of both experiences, as revealed in Hitler's later life, were far more intense than the symptoms observed in clinical cases where only one or the other trauma was experienced.[103]

Subsequent events of childhood served to strengthen his attitudes about himself and others. The beatings he had suffered from his father, for example, helped to justify his hatred of the old man; they also must have increased his ambivalence toward his mother, who was either unable or unwilling to protect him from his father's attacks. In his later recollections, Hitler was not very successful in justifying his mother's ineffectiveness and acquiescence to the beatings. "My poor mother was always afraid for me"—but was unable to protect him. "I knew my mother stood anxiously outside the door"—but did nothing to stop the torture.[104]

These childhood punishments, real and fantasied, intensified Hitler's Oedipal problem and may also have contributed to the later "splitting," so characteristic of the adult Hitler, between sadism and masochism, destruction and creativity, cruelty and kindness, love and hatred. As Freud pointed out in a famous study of sadomasochism, a sense of guilt for Oedipal desire is invariably present as the decisive force transforming sadism into masochism.[105]

An interesting line in *Mein Kampf* may or may not be autobiographical. If it is, we can speculate that Hitler may have developed profound guilt feelings for having once whipped his own mother. In this passage, he is continuing his description of the "worker's son," now age 15, and how he stays out to all hours of the night, showing total disdain for parental authority—a description, as we shall see, that fits Adolf's own behavior after the death of his father: "He loiters about, and God only knows when he comes home; for a change *he may even beat the poor creature who was once his mother,* curses God and the world. . . ." [106]

Key events of Adolf's later childhood appear to revolve around the birth and death of his brother Edmund. When, at the age of six, young Adolf saw the arrival of Edmund, it may be imagined that he resented this rival deeply and harbored death wishes towards him. If so, the wishes were fulfilled. For when Adolf was 11, his little brother died at the age of six. During the intervening years the two brothers seem to have grown close to each other, and it seems likely that Edmund's sudden death awakened guilt feelings in Adolf. Certainly the strange story of the little boy's funeral reinforced Adolf's belief that his mother could not be completely trusted. Like the fickle Goddess of Fate, she abandoned her sons in their direst need.

Neighbors of the Hitlers still alive in the village of Leonding in the 1950s shook their heads in incredulity when they recalled that when little Edmund Hitler died of complications following measles in March 1900 and was buried in the church graveyard, neither his mother nor father attended the funeral. They spent the day in Linz. Not even old Josef Mayrhofer, the usually outspoken village mayor and friend of Alois Hitler, could explain the curious behavior of the parents.

Neighbors suggested one possible explanation, but admitted that it was not very persuasive. They recalled that the anticlerical Alois Hitler had no liking for the village priest, whom he considered too "political." For example, the priest and a schoolteacher had the idea of organizing a soup kitchen for indigent wanderers and migrant farm laborers. Alois Hitler, the retired imperial official, as the most prestigious person in the village, became the leader of an anticlerical opposition which considered this church-school alliance to be "socialization and interference in local politics." If this were so, it would help explain why the mayor sided with Hitler *père* and was later so embarrassed about his absence from Edmund's funeral that he refused to talk about the matter. At any rate, it does seem possible that Alois could have become so furious with the local priest that he thumped the tavern *Stammtisch* and swore, in one of his fits of temper, that he would never enter the church of his enemy again, that he would be damned if he would ever hear that priest pray over his dead son. And so the stubborn old man refused to go to the funeral. Perhaps. But how explain Klara's absence? She was a devoted mother and a devout Catholic. And even if she were not, it seems passing strange that a mother would not attend her own son's burial. The only explanation that comes to mind, if valid, documents the tyranny of Alois over his wife. He flatly forbade her to go into "that priest's church" and thus embarrass him publicly. He ordered her, on the day of the funeral, to accompany him on a trip to Linz. Klara did not dare disobey.[107]

And so, abandoned by his mother, Adolf stood and watched in a driving snowstorm as his little brother was lowered into a grave for which the parents never supplied a marker.

The effect of this experience, it seems likely, was to increase Adolf's resentment against his mother. Consciously, of course, he continued to displace his resentment onto his father and to blame Alois for everything. For, as Menninger has noted, stern fathers help sons to justify feelings of antagonism and aggression. "But if we penetrate the many layers of hatred, we come eventually to the deepest hurt of all—'my mother failed me.' " [108]

Adolf already had reason to resent what his mother had done to him. In addition to equipping him with defective testicles and acquiescing in her own "rape" by Hitler's father-rival, she had given birth to another rival, Edmund, and abandoned Adolf to the care of his older half-sister, Angela. As Menninger notes, "When the child is turned over to a substitute mother at an early age, it often increases his burden of hate without expanding his capacity for love." By a great show of loving his mother a boy can "conceal his hostility to her . . . and avoid the consequences of attempting to express his masculinity in a normal way." [109]

Adolf's attitudes to his mother during his unusually difficult and disturbing prepubertal period, around the age of 12, were particularly confusing and complex. He was, we have surmised, burdened by guilt feelings for the death of his brother. It is possible that Klara's abandonment of both brothers at the funeral served to lessen Adolf's feelings of personal guilt by giving him the opportunity to project it. It was not he who should feel guilty about Edmund; it was his mother who was to blame for deserting them both.

But he could not afford to blame his mother too much. He was able to lessen hostile feelings toward her by transferring them to his father, and he may also have kept his feelings from becoming too negative by the defense Otto Kernberg calls "primitive idealization." In this defense, when a boy is confronted by a threatening father, he splits the parental relationship into the totally good and totally evil. He fantasizes an idealized mother who is a veritable paragon of love, tenderness, and strength—a defender who can protect him completely from the totally bad person who threatens him.[110] But in Hitler's case this defense was breaking down. Adolf's primitively idealized mother had not protected him from his father's whippings, and now she had apparently deserted him in abandoning his brother.

Edmund's death could have had another effect in reminding Adolf how many of his brothers and sisters had died: Gustav in 1887, Ida in 1888, Otto in 1888, and now Edmund. To his childish mind, the most natural explanation for his own survival would have been that he was allowed to live because he was under the special protection of Providence. Nor was it only a question of having physically outlived the other siblings. Adolf—apart from his monorchism—was also the only one of the survivors who was untainted by some obvious aberration. Rumor was correct in saying that the Schickelgrubers had a long history of mental and physical affliction. An affidavit in the local archives in Linz says that Klara's irascible sister Johanna was probably schizophrenic.[111] Hitler's first cousin, Edward Schmidt, the son of Klara's sister Theresia, was a hunchback with a speech defect. In the more immediate family, Adolf may have had a sister, older than he, who was an imbecile. At any rate, Dr. Bloch, the family doctor, when questioned by OSS personnel during World War II, said that he was "absolutely certain of this because he noticed at the time that the family always tried to hide the child . . . when he came to attend the mother." The younger sister, Paula, "is also said to be a little on the stupid side, perhaps a high-grade moron." [112]

Childhood knowledge of the deaths of his brothers and sisters, it seems likely, also produced feelings of "survival guilt" of the type that Robert Jay Lifton has described in his studies of psychological reactions to death. The "survival priority" manifested by those who live while others are dying forces the question, "Why have I been selected to go on living?" With it comes "inevitable self-condemnation in the face of other's deaths." The general feeling of guilt is notably increased in cases of sibling rivalry where death suddenly takes away the rival. The child may then have the feeling that his life is somehow controlled by destiny and hence not entirely his own. In Adolf's case, not only the deaths of his brothers and sisters but also his mother's fretful solicitude for him as the sole male survivor, as well as her compulsive concern for his health, would surely have strengthened his idea of his own privileged position.[113]

His mother's insistence that he was "special," her *Lieblingskind*, would have reinforced one of the common psychological defenses used by survivors: to justify their survival on the grounds that they have been specially selected by Fate or Destiny for a particular purpose. There is often an accompanying belief that as Destiny's choice, the survivor will somehow escape the death of mortals. Hitler, as we have seen, was convinced that he was spared because he was God's particular gift to the German people; he also believed that there was reserved for him a special place among the immortals of Mt. Olympus. Hitler was not unique in his intimations of immortality. One is reminded of Sigmund Freud's comment, "At bottom, no one believes in his own death, or to put the same thing in another way, . . . in the unconscious every one of us is convinced of his own immortality." Otto Rank, following Freud, argued that the motive underlying man's historic search for religion is "an assurance of eternal survival for his self." [114]

This broadly felt human desire is particularly acute for those who, like Hitler, survive when others have perished. Moreover, he was denied several of the usual ways that man has sought to achieve victory over the grave. His religious faith was not the kind that vouchsafed salvation in a Christian heaven; he could not live on in posterity through his children. He sought other solutions to his problem: he would erect imperishable buildings and monuments; he would perform military feats that would win him eternal fame as "the greatest field commander of all time." When that was denied him, in the end he may have hoped to achieve historical immortality through truly monumental destruction.

The feeling of special mission which, we are suggesting, resulted in part from his survival fantasies was also strengthened in childhood by the defense mechanism of omnipotence. This defense is often used by both monorchids and borderline personalities to counteract feelings of insecurity and inferiority. The imperiousness and insistence on having his own way which Adolf began to manifest in early childhood were evidences of the strong unconscious conviction such personalities often harbor: that it is their right as special and privileged individuals to expect gratification and homage from others.

Clinical studies of disturbed children who have survived the death of a sibling rival show another symptom which we have found in Hitler: his resistance to growing old, his difficulty in maturing. Child psychologists have found that sibling survivors may be so terrified by the thought of death that they seek to escape by remaining childlike and refusing to mature. The result may be a kind of "defensive regression" into infantilism. When the mother (like Klara Hitler) is excessively protective toward "the only little boy I have left," the death phobia and the desire to remain childlike are both intensified. Many survivors also try to surmount their fear of dying by insisting (as did Hitler) that they live a charmed life, that others can't kill them, that they alone would survive dangers fatal to other people.[115]

Hitler's lifelong fear of death had larger historical consequence. As his future career would show so clearly, he tried to exorcise personal death fears by killing others. The more power he had in deciding that other people must die—the more he commanded death—the less he felt its horror for himself. Apart from the calculated murder of millions of "inferior" people, we should note the way he received news late in the war that his personal SS division, the elite *Leibstandarte Adolf Hitler*, was being decimated on the Eastern Front. When a staff officer reported that the number of deaths in Hitler's personal division was very great, he was startled by his Führer's exultant reply, "Losses can never be too high!" [116]

We have been suggesting that the period 1900–1901, when young Adolf was in his 12th year, was unusually important to his personal development. The boy who had been the star pupil of village schools began to fail; the outwardly cocky, hyperactive ringleader of robust neighborhood games became the morose, self-absorbed, withdrawn preadolescent who talked to trees on lonely hills, orated to the winds, fought with his parents, caricatured his teachers, and hated the world. We can only guess at the reasons for these apparent changes. But we can be quite sure that they were not unrelated to his earlier life. For we know that the traumatic experiences of infancy have lasting repercussions. During Adolf's earliest years, attitudes of mistrust, shame, guilt, hatred, and fear had sent down deep and noxious roots. They were nourished during this bitter year by more baneful experiences: the sudden death and tragic funeral of his brother, with attendant feelings of guilt about his own survival; a reinforcement of his conflicting feelings about his mother; the transition from the familiar local school to the strange urban *Realschule*. And all these unsettling events took place at precisely the age when disturbed monorchids experience their most difficult period of development. It was a bad year. But with the death of his father, things began to look up.

"NEGATIVE IDENTITY": THE LINZ DANDY

Hitler remembered the years just after his father died in 1903, when his mother lived in a comfortable apartment in Linz, as the freest and happiest time of his life. The authoritarian old man could no longer whistle for him like a dog, demand obedient silence, or ask his infernal questions about schoolwork and plans for a career in the civil service. His doting mother drew on her comfortable pension and the profits from the sale of her house in Leonding to indulge Adolf's every wish. Glorying in a life of leisure as critic and patron of the arts in the provincial capital, he joined the local museum and library and rarely missed a performance of the Linz opera. He dressed immaculately in white shirts, flowing cravats with stickpins, a broad-brimmed black hat set at a confident angle, and well-cut tweed suits which were the envy of the young men of the town. In winter, he donned a silk-lined black overcoat. For the opera, he affected black kid gloves, an ivory-handled walking stick, and a top hat.[117]

Thus did Adolf assume what Erik Erikson has called a "negative identity"—that is, he took on a role which was the very opposite of what he knew his father would have considered "proper." In so doing, he showed active contempt for his father's ideals and values. Such role playing, as Erikson has shown, is not only a vindictive attack on the father but also a kind of personal defense. For it is much easier to fantasize one's self by assuming a negative identity than it is to struggle painfully for genuine self-definition and realization.[118]

Before he could indulge himself completely in his new role, however, he needed to free himself from the restrictive burden of education. He was already doing badly in school because—according to his own account—he was deliberately "sabotaging" his father's plans for Adolf's career in the bureaucracy. With his father dead, "suddenly an illness came to my aid, and in the course of a few weeks settled the perpetual arguments at home." Hitler says he suffered from "a severe pulmonary illness." But it was very much a blessing in very little disguise, for with it, "all that I had fought for, all that I had longed for in secret, suddenly became reality." [119]

It is not completely clear whether Adolf was in fact ill in 1905 or was malingering to impress his always indulgent mother and cajole her into letting him quit school. His friend Kubizek assures us—both in his memoirs and in a letter now in the provincial archives in Linz—that Adolf really was seriously ill during 1905–1906. But the family doctor, Eduard Bloch, could not recall any such serious illness, and when specifically pressed about it by an American interviewer, said he was very sure that "he never detected even the faintest traces of such a disease when he examined Hitler." Dr. Bloch repeated the assertion in a later memoir: "There was never anything seriously wrong with Hitler . . . I cannot understand the many references to his lung trouble as a youth. I was the only doctor treating him during the period. . . . My records show nothing of the sort." [120]

On the other hand, a cousin, Johann Schmidt, on whose mother's farm Klara and her children spent the summers, recalls clearly that in the summer of 1905, Adolf was so ill he was treated by a Dr. Karl Keiss in the neighboring village of Witra and Adolf's mother nursed him carefully with nourishing food and milk.[121] The indefatigable archivist Jetzinger insists that his subject simply feigned illness to get his way with his mother. He draws heavily on an interview he had with a man who, as a youth, had taken his meals at Klara Hitler's home in Linz. But, as an American biographer has pointed out, this man, Hagmüller, had only known Adolf *after* the summer of 1905.[122]

Let us conclude that Adolf's illness may not have been severe, but when combined with his very considerable dramatic talent, it was sufficient to alarm his mother. Once again indulging him, she let him quit school.

As he later confessed in *Mein Kampf*, now he really was "his mother's darling" who slept until noon in his "soft, downy bed." During the afternoons he would read, or copy with meticulous care, pictures of paintings or postcards, making many copies of the same picture. But his chief work was to draw and redraw architectural plans for the rebuilding of Linz. His friend of these years was struck by his terrible intensity and his absolute confidence that someday he would see all his plans carried out. And so they were. What the adolescent planned, the dictator executed—and in specific detail.

This happened with uncanny regularity, as though the fifteen-year-old had taken it for granted that one day he would possess the necessary power and means. . . . The plans which that unknown boy had drawn up for the rebuilding of his home town . . . are identical to the last detail with the town planning scheme which was inaugurated after 1938. I am almost afraid of giving, in the following pages, my account of these early plans, lest my veracity should be suspected. And yet every single syllable of what I am going to recount is true. . . . His belief that one day he would carry out all his tremendous projects was unshakeable. . . . This absolute faith was too much for my rational way of thinking. . . .

To young Hitler reality and fantasy were so interwoven that time and again he would go and visit the buildings which existed only in his mind's eye.[123]

During the evenings, often until past midnight, Adolf would attend the opera or go with his friend on long walks in which he would plan and replan more buildings or hold forth on the ills of the arts and society. He showed that his capacity for projection was already well developed. One day the two friends strolled by the Cafe Baumgartner and saw young men idly chatting as they sipped white wine at its marble-topped tables. Adolf was furious with those "stupid parasites" who wasted their time in idle chatter and gossip.[124] But as he vented his anger on these "parasites," he probably had his own life-style in mind, and he may have been angry with himself for being so dependent on his widowed mother. Such feelings would have increased his ambivalence toward her: he loved and needed her, but the very dependence made him feel guilty and resentful.

Yet he continued to let his mother indulge him. Thus, when Adolf decided that he might enjoy playing the piano, his mother bought him a Heitzmann grand and sent him to an expensive teacher, Josef Prevratsky-Wendt, who remembered him as a desultory pupil bored by finger exercises. After four months Adolf decided his talents lay elsewhere. It also seems likely that his mother financed him briefly in Munich, where, sometime during 1905, he took a few art lessons from a Professor Gröber in the Blütenstrasse in Schwabing.[125]

In the spring of 1906, Adolf thought it would be nice to visit Vienna, where he spent a fortnight attending the opera and examining critically the new buildings of the Ring. He was not pleased by the interior of the Imperial Opera, he wrote in a postcard he sent back to Linz. Another card told of attending *Tristan* one night, *The Flying Dutchman* the next, the municipal theater the next. Since it is unlikely that Klara could have financed these trips from her pension, she must have drawn heavily on the capital from the sale of her house.[126]

While such diversions were pleasant enough, Adolf's ripening tastes really required more financial support than his mother was able to provide. Having decided to win a very large amount of money in the national lottery, he made one of the many "great decisions" of his life and purchased one lottery ticket. There is of course nothing particularly unusual about a boy of 16 buying a lottery ticket and dreaming of how he would spend his vast winnings. What is striking about young Hitler is his absolute conviction that he would win. He therefore planned carefully how all the money would be spent. He decided that it probably would not be prudent to invest too much of the money on a new villa. Rather, he would rent a large flat and adapt it to his purposes. After extensive house hunting, Adolf and his friend "Gustl" Kubizek found a suitable apartment at 2 Kirchengasse in Urfahr, a suburb of Linz. Adolf made elaborate plans to furnish each room carefully and fastidiously. He would create an artistic salon in which the cultural elite of Linz might gather. Gustl would supply musical entertainment; Adolf would recite poetry and expound his views on aesthetics, culture, and history. The coterie would be presided over by a refined, dignified, and elderly gray-haired lady who would be decorative, charming, and witty—but not too clever. For, as Hitler later observed, women didn't need brains, since he could supply enough for any social gathering. During the summer, Adolf decided, he and his friend would make an extensive tour of Germany; he vowed to make an annual pilgrimage to the shrine of Wagner at Bayreuth, the source of his greatest ideas.

Once again one is struck by the way fantasy and reality mingled in Hitler's mind. It is also noteworthy that the woman who was to preside over his salon may have been a mother substitute; it was certainly not Klara Hitler, who died without a gray hair on her head. With all the money and with all his plans, his mother was not once mentioned. Nor did Adolf fantasize a beautiful and cultured wife to complement his artistic circle. Rather, he would have his friend Gustl live in celibacy with him.[127]

Adolf awaited the day of the lottery drawing with complete assurance. He simply could not believe that he had lost. In blind fury he rushed into the upholstery workshop of Kubizek's father:

> I have rarely heard him rage so madly as then. First he fumed over the State Lottery, this officially organized exploitation of human credibility, this open fraud at the expense of docile citizens. Then his fury turned against the State itself, this patchwork of ten or twelve or God knows how many nations, this monster built up by Hapsburg marriages. Could one expect other than that two poor devils should be cheated out of their last few crowns?

Kubizek is perceptive in noting that this apparently silly incident was shattering to Adolf because "he had been deserted by his willpower" and was unable through the force of his will to get his way, to make fantasy become reality.[128]

Boyhood Plans for a New *Reich*

During their long evening walks and daytime excursions into the hills, castles and monasteries surrounding Linz, Adolf talked interminably to his young friend about the social order he would establish in his new *Reich*. The concept was to him a holy mystery which he refused to profane by definition. But he was sure that one day a great *Reich* would be established under his leadership. The word itself was magic, its very incantation sufficient to the solution of any political, moral, or aesthetic problem. Dissatisfied with stage settings for a Wagner opera they had seen in Linz, Adolf assured his friend that in his government a "*Reich* Stage Designer" would create sets for provincial theaters throughout the vast extent of his empire.* Similarly, all difficulties with health, education, housing, and eugenics were assigned to the appropriate official of the *Reich*. "Whenever he had talked himself into a blind alley and was at a loss how to continue, he would say categorically, 'This problem will be solved by the *Reich*.' " [129]

One day in 1939 the Führer of the Third Reich made one of his many pilgrimages to the shrine of Wagner at Bayreuth. On that occasion he told Frau Wagner that his political career had been miraculously laid open before him one night in Linz when, as a boy, he attended a performance of Wagner's *Rienzi*. "That was the hour, it all began," he said.

The hour had struck one blustery day in November 1906, a day not unlike the raw March morning six years earlier when Adolf had watched the burial of his young brother and felt, as the survivor, the hand of Destiny upon him. Now at the age of 17 he sat enthralled as he listened to Wagner's music and watched the rise and fall of Rienzi, champion of his people, who had been goaded to political action after seeing his young brother killed by the plebeians of Rome.

The long opera was not over until well past midnight. Together the two friends went out into the dark and windy night. Usually Adolf gave a long and excited disquisition on the performance, the plot, the stage setting, and the genius of Wagner. But tonight he was silent as he trudged along the cold and deserted streets with his black overcoat collar pulled up against the chill. When his friend tried to break the silence with a leading question about the performance, Adolf threw him a hostile glance and told him to shut up. Instead of heading home, the two friends took the road west leading up the Freinberg. When they reached the top, the mist broke and stars spangled the sky. After gazing moodily at the distant heavens, Adolf suddenly wheeled around, grabbed his friend by both hands, and looked him searchingly in the

---

* After he came to power, Hitler appointed an official with exactly that title. Albert Speer recalls being present while Hitler discussed scenery for a Wagnerian production with Benno von Arent, the "Reich Stage Designer." Speer, *Spandau: The Secret Diaries* (New York, 1976), 102.

eye, his own eyes burning with passion. "He had never made such a gesture before," his friend tells us. But he certainly would again, for it was the characteristic gesture of the Führer in talking earnestly to his followers. After gazing intensely at his friend for a full minute, he began to speak. "Never before and never again have I heard Adolf Hitler speak as he did in that hour as we stood there alone under the stars as though we were the only creatures in the world." Kubizek thought there was something strange about Hitler that night. "It was as if another being spoke out of his body, and moved him as much as it did me. It wasn't at all a case of a speaker being carried away by his own words. On the contrary; I rather felt as though he himself listened with astonishment and emotion to what burst forth from him with elementary force. I will not attempt to interpret this phenomenon, but it was a state of complete ecstasy and rapture." What Hitler said that night has been lost, but one thing was burned into Kubizek's memory. Adolf did not speak of becoming an artist or an architect. Now he saw himself, like *Rienzi*, as the Messiah of his people. He spoke of a "*mandate* which, one day, he would receive from the people to lead them out of servitude to the heights of freedom . . . He spoke of a special mission which one day would be entrusted to him."

In silence Adolf and Gustl descended to the town. A neighborhood clock struck three as the two friends shook hands in front of Kubizek's house. Adolf started again in the direction of the mountain and in answer to an anxious question about his destination replied, "I want to be alone." [130]

Decades later, Hitler ordered that the enormous Party rallies of the Third Reich open with the overture to Wagner's *Rienzi*.

Stefanie: The Unapproachable Love

Fantasy again merged with reality in Hitler's first great love. His was an idealized, pure and unsullied passion which he did not dare to confront with the reality of physical contact. In a scene reminiscent of Dante's first sight of Beatrice, Adolf had seen his Stefanie one day, probably in the fall of 1906, as she strolled with her mother down the fashionable Landstrasse of Linz.

Every day thereafter, as long as he lived in Linz, Hitler stationed himself at five o'clock at the Schmiedtoreck in hopes of catching a glimpse of his beloved. If he imagined that she glanced at him and smiled, he was radiantly happy. If perchance she seemed to frown, he was crushed and threatened to destroy himself and the world. She was to him the paragon of all Teutonic and cultural virtues, a Wagnerian goddess of racial perfection, a "gem of purest ray serene." In point of fact, she really was a pretty girl. Her fresh, unaffected face, framed by blond braids, smiles at us from a picture taken by a local portrait photographer, one Franz Zuny of Linz-Urfahr.

Adolf spent many happy hours casting Stefanie in various

The Child As Father to the Man

Wagnerian roles. He worried about her voice and musical talent and was overjoyed when his friend found out from a cellist who knew Stefanie's brother that she did have a good voice. But he was devastated to hear that she enjoyed dancing and was often seen in the arms of handsome lieutenants of the guard. When Gustl suggested that he might learn to dance in order to win Stefanie, Adolf flew into a rage which his friend considered an excessively violent response to so modest a suggestion: " 'No, no, never!' he screamed at me. 'I shall never dance! Do you understand! Stefanie only dances because she is forced to by society on which she unfortunately depends. Once she is my wife, she won't have the slightest desire to dance!' " [131] So repugnant to the young Hitler was the thought of holding an attractive young woman in his arms.

Adolf wanted Stefanie for himself and was furiously jealous of her social life. To keep her from dancing with the handsome lieutenants he worked out detailed plans for kidnapping her. Then, one day as she passed the Schmiedtoreck and seemed to avert her eyes without looking at the anxiously awaiting Adolf, he was frantic and cried, "I can't stand it any longer! I will make an end of it!" He then plotted suicide, insisting that Stefanie would have to die with him.

Although he cast her in operatic roles, wrote long heroic poems in which she was the heroine, and designed a magnificent villa for her— "I have decided to do her house in the Renaissance style"—he could always think of many reasons why it was not possible for him ever to meet her. Extraordinary human beings like Stefanie and himself, he observed, do not need to converse in the usual way. He knew clearly that she shared all his artistic tastes and secret thoughts. When his friend suggested that she might not really share all his ideas and interests, Adolf was furious: "You simply don't understand because you can't understand the true meaning of extraordinary love." [132]

Thus did Adolf adore from afar. Stefanie never knew of his great love for her—indeed, she never remembered having seen Adolf Hitler. Years later the still beautiful woman, now the elderly widow of a colonel living in retirement in Vienna, said that she had no knowledge that the famous Führer had once been her great admirer. When pressed, a light came to her eyes and she gasped, "*Jetzt weiss ich was!* He must have been the one who wrote that letter!" She went on to recall that one day in Linz she had received a strange unsigned letter from an art student who spoke of solemn vows and begged her to wait four years for him until he had finished his training. Then he would return to marry her. She and her mother had laughed at the awkward letter by the terribly serious and completely anonymous admirer.[133]

There seem to have been several reasons why Adolf was so insistent that he never actually meet her. Since the Stefanie of his imagination was the incarnation of all Germanic virtue, he must have feared that the Stefanie of reality might fall short of that standard. But to him she was more than an abstract ideal. She was, almost in a literal sense, his alter ego, an idealization of himself. "There was no other person apart from himself," the observant Kubizek wrote, "whom he credited with so much knowledge and so many interests." If he had met her and discovered that she did not really share his intimate concerns, indeed was uninterested in them, the disillusionment would have been unbearable. The destruction of his idol would have meant the destruction of self. It was too great a risk to take. His friend was right: "Only the most rigid separation could preserve his idol." [134]

Then, too, Stefanie served as a defense against feelings of sexual inadequacy. Since, in his fantasy, he had plighted his troth to her alone, he had an excellent reason why he could never approach any other female. He must preserve the "sacred flame" of his love, a love that was never to be extinguished, touched, or tested. From his ethereal love for the inviolate Stefanie he could make a virtue out of his psychological necessity of avoiding physical relations with women.

THE DEATH OF KLARA

The most formative psychological experience of Hitler's youth was associated with the illness and death of his mother. As we shall see, during and immediately after this event Hitler underwent a crisis in self-identity and found the ideology that would govern both his personal life and his political career.

After Klara Hitler's illness was diagnosed as cancer of the breast, a mastectomy was performed at the Sisters of Mercy Hospital in Linz on 18 January 1907. The surgeon was Hofrat Dr. Karl Urban. He was assisted by the family doctor, Eduard Bloch. Klara's private room, number 16, afforded a pleasant view and she had excellent nursing care.[135]

Hitler wanted people to believe that his mother's illness "had almost exhausted the meager funds" left by his father and that he was therefore constrained as an impoverished orphan at the age of 17 "to earn my own daily bread." [136] As a matter of fact, Klara's finances were in such excellent shape that there was little trouble in meeting medical expenses. Costs for the operation and hospitalization amounted to 100 kronen—about the amount Adolf had cost his mother for his fortnight excursion to Vienna the previous year. He would reach the age of 22 before he earned the price of even one loaf of bread.[137]

For a time after her operation, Klara seemed to recover. Neighbors saw her taking short walks in the neighborhood, and she agreed to let Adolf go to Vienna to apply for admission to the Academy of Fine Arts. Then, sometime late in November 1907, she had a serious relapse and suffered excruciating pain which Dr. Bloch could only temporarily alleviate by daily shots of morphine.[138]

Adolf's conduct during his mother's fatal illness is in dispute. Kubizek, the always loyal friend, insisted that throughout her ordeal Adolf showed himself to be a totally dutiful and loving son. When she was in the hospital in January 1907, Adolf "visited her every day" and gave his friend detailed reports.[139] According to Kubizek, Adolf left for Vienna only because he thought the operation had been successful. As soon as he heard of her relapse in November, he hurried home and manfully took over all the household chores and responsibilities. He tutored his rather backward sister Paula. He donned a huge blue apron to keep his clothes clean as he swept the walks and scrubbed the floors on his hands and knees; he cooked his mother's favorite dishes and read aloud to her the maudlin novels she loved and he despised; he sat by the hour holding her in his arms in an effort to ease the pain; he moved a couch beside her bed so that he could sleep near her. "I didn't trust my own eyes and ears," his friend later wrote. "Not a cross word, not an impatient remark, no violent insistence in having his own way, he forgot himself entirely in those weeks and lived only for his mother . . . an atmosphere of serene contentment surrounded the dying woman." [140]

Franz Jetzinger, the careful Linz archivist who enjoys correcting Kubizek and is never averse to putting Hitler in an unflattering light, tells a very different story. Adolf, he says, callously left his desperately ill mother to pursue his own pleasures in Vienna and returned to Linz only in time for his mother's funeral. Jetzinger is quite right in noting that Kubizek's memoirs are sometimes mistaken about chronology, and he finds other flaws in Kubizek's glowing account of Hitler's filial devotion. He notes that there was no need for Adolf to do any of the housework, since there is incontestable proof that Adolf's aunt Johanna was living in the house during Klara's illness and that, "unlike Adolf, she knew how to cook and scrub." Jetzinger corrects Kubizek's memory on other points and presses an assertion which is based on secondhand testimony. A postmaster's widow who lived in the same house as Frau Hitler, at 9 Blütengasse in Urfahr, was a good neighbor and very helpful during Klara's illness. Years later, in 1938, Hitler wrote a letter thanking her warmly for her help during his mother's last illness. When the widow herself fell ill, the Führer saw to it that she was given the best available medical care and a private room in the Linz Municipal Hospital. While she was there, according to Jetzinger, several people questioned her about Adolf's conduct during Klara's illness. Jetzinger says she told them it was only *after* Klara's death that Adolf had arrived from Vienna. She remembered that distinctly because she felt sorry for the boy for having arrived too late to see his mother alive.[141]

Hitler's own account of the period is typically vague about details and chronology. He does not say when he returned from Vienna, but, rather surprisingly, he makes no effort to present himself as a dutiful son. Indeed, one sentence can be read to support Jetzinger's conclusion: *"During the last months of her suffering I had gone to Vienna* to take my entrance examination at the *Akademie."* He then hurries on to describe his heartfelt disappointment at his rejection.[142]

The most reliable testimony comes from three people who would have been in a position to know about Adolf's conduct: the family physician, the helpful neighborly woman, and Hitler's sister. In November 1938, Dr. Bloch was asked by a Nazi Party archivist to write a memoir of Klara Hitler and her son. The statement, which may now be found in a file marked Gestapo Reports in the Party archives, asserts that young Hitler did indeed return from Vienna to nurse his mother: "During my house calls [on Klara Hitler] I had many opportunities to observe the Führer. He stayed close by his mother's side, with the deepest love, watching her every movement in order to be able to extend to her quickly little services that might help alleviate some of her pain. His usually saddened eyes lit up when his mother was not suffering." And he was present at her death bed. Indeed, Bloch clearly remembered that Adolf stayed alone in the room to draw a picture of her emaciated body; and Dr. Bloch concluded, "In my nearly forty years of medical practice I have never seen a young man so heartbroken and filled with sorrow as the young Adolf Hitler was in the days after the burial of his beloved mother, when he came to thank me for my care."

When Adolf went back to Vienna after the funeral, he did not forget the doctor's kindness and sent him two carefully painted postcards expressing his gratitude. Dr. Bloch noted that over the years he had received countless thank-you notes from grateful patients, and he asked rhetorically why he had kept and cherished these particular cards. He answered, "Because I saw in them the signs of the future greatness of the Führer? No! I kept them as souvenirs of a fine and exemplary son who bore such a deep love and concern for his dear mother which one finds on this globe only in extremely exceptional cases." [143]

It may well be objected that the statement made by the intimidated Jewish doctor in 1938 was a futile and pathetic attempt to ingratiate himself with the Nazis by painting their Führer in the most flattering light. Yet in the safety of his American exile in 1943, when he had no reason whatever to please the Nazis, Dr. Bloch still stood by his story of the solicitous Adolf who loved his mother with such great devotion.[144]

We also have the testimony of the postmaster's widow, whose name seems to have been Frau Prezemeyer. In an interview with a Nazi reporter, she recalled that she too had received a thank-you letter from the Führer and that he had helped her when she was ill. In important lines that biographers may have missed because they are blurred by a fold in the paper, she also asserted that it was she who had written Adolf in Vienna about his mother's relapse and that Adolf immediately "interrupted his studies and *hurried to the sick bed of his mother."* [145]

Again, it may be objected that Frau Prezemeyer's testimony should be discounted as an effort to curry favor with the Nazis. But it was unnecessary for her to do so, since the Führer himself had already documented his gratitude to her in a personal letter. Moreover, she could easily have paid general tribute to the Führer's kindness as a boy without making specific reference to the timing of his return.

The third witness was Hitler's sister Paula, who, in an interrogation conducted by U.S. Army intelligence officers after the war, testified that "Adolf . . . stayed at home until [Klara's] death."[146]

Psychological evidence, while it does not resolve the issue, would seem to support the story of the solicitous son who was seen cleaning the house and the walk. Hitler's ambivalent feelings toward his mother would, at the time of her imminent death, probably have reactivated acute guilt feelings. He could be expected to defend against those feelings by a visible display of solicitude and concern. His talents as an actor, in addition to his genuine love and remorse, would have helped convince himself and others that he really was an extremely devoted and dutiful son.

He composed the death notice printed by the Linz firm of Kölndorffer:

> Adolf and Paula Hitler, in their own behalf and in the names of the surviving relatives, announce the death of their deeply loved and unforgettable mother, step-mother, grandmother, and sister, Frau Klara Hitler, Royal and Imperial Senior Customs Inspector Widow who was taken from us on 21 December 1907 at 2 A.M.[147]

The funeral took place two days later. As she had wished, Klara was buried at the side of her husband in a little church cemetery in Leonding. Relatives had asked Adolf to spend Christmas Eve at their home, but the miserable youth was in no mood for Christmas conviviality. He confided to Kubizek that he much preferred "to go to Stefanie"—that is, to be completely alone with his fantasies. He stayed alone all evening, as he would every Christmas Eve of his life.[148]

His mother's death seared his memory in other ways. Ever afterward, he said, he hated snow because it reminded him of his mother's shroud.* When he became Führer, he planned to transform the celebration of Christmas into a day to worship mothers. Even the name of the holiday was to be changed from "Holy Night" (*Weihenacht*) to "Mother-Night" (*Mutternacht*).[149] Yet curiously, Hitler never took advantage of an obvious and traditional way of displaying his love visibly and permanently for all to see—namely, by erecting an impressive tombstone. It is strange that this devoted son never put a marker of any sort on his beloved mother's grave. This omission is particularly surprising because

---

* It may also have reminded him unconsciously of his little brother Edmund's shroud. We know that there was a heavy snowfall in Upper Austria on 30 March 1900, the day young Hitler stood alone beside his brother's open grave.

he often talked about memorializing death and personally designed tombstones for himself and other people he admired. But nothing for his mother. Was he avenging his brother Edmund's lack of a grave marker by denying one to his parents? Was he expressing his desire to keep his family background obscure?

Even after he came to power and was a man of wealth and influence, the graves of his parents went neglected and unmarked until local Party functionaries intervened. A Party archivist wrote with pained surprise, after visiting the Leonding cemetery in 1938: "The parents' grave of the Führer would be no longer maintained today if, at the last moment, it had not been for the Linz NSDAP. For many years their membership, apparently, have been paying the costs. I have the relevant document." [150]

During a hurried visit to Leonding in 1938, Hitler did go to the cemetery to see the graves and the new marble tablet which contains a picture of Alois and the inscription:

Here rests in God
Herr Alois Hitler
Royal and Imperial Senior Customs Inspector, Retired
and Householder
Died 3 January 1903, in his 65th year
and his wife
Frau Klara Hitler
Died 21 December 1907 in her 47th year

R.I.P.

The Führer glanced perfunctorily at the gravestone, turned quickly without comment, and left the cemetery. He never returned.[151]

IDENTITY CRISES, 1908–1918

Erik Erikson's studies of the human life cycle give us a clearer understanding of Adolf Hitler's late adolescence and early manhood. Erikson has shown that personality development continues through the whole cycle of life and is not crucially determined by age four or five, as traditional psychoanalysis had tended to insist, nor indeed by any one period of life: "What a man adds up to must develop in stages, but no stage explains the man." There is, however, one period of life that is particularly important to the consolidation of personality. It occurs at the end of adolescence and is associated with the "identity crisis." Erikson has been careful to point out that two of his distinctive terms, "identity crisis" and "identity formation," should not be confused or used interchangeably. In late adolescence the individual experiences the identity *crisis*, but identity *formation* neither starts nor ends with adolescence. Identity formation is a "lifelong development largely unconscious to the individual," going all the way back to babyhood. It is a complex process, "an evolving configuration" that may be altered or changed at any time during the life span of an individual.[152]

During a discussion in which questions were raised about whether there is only one identity crisis in life or repeated crises in the search for identity, Erikson replied, "Let me try to clear this up once and for all. Everybody has repeated identity crises . . . but there is only one basic identity crisis which may be called *the* crisis, and it does happen in adolescence/young adulthood. But there may be a whole series of lesser crises—I would put them in quotation marks. They may stretch from early childhood . . . to later life." [153]

During this major crisis of late adolescence, a person tries, as the phrase goes, "to find himself"—to work out some fundamental definition of self, some core of personal meaning, some central purpose and direction. And in this painful process there is often a considerable amount of "identity confusion"; that is, the adolescent may try out several identities by playing different roles, none of which may be truly himself. Thus we have already seen young Hitler as leader of war games; as mother's darling; as builder of new cities; and as artistic dilettante and dandy. Later he would become a dropout, a derelict in a Viennese flophouse, before turning into a "writer" in Munich, a war hero, and finally the Führer of all Germany.

During the identity crisis a person may adopt a "negative identity" as a means of attacking a hated father. Indeed, Erikson believes that when a son takes on an identity radically different from one his father intended for him—and this is certainly what Adolf did—he is showing a "paranoid form of a powerful death wish (latent in all severe identity crises) against [his] parents." [154]

Erikson has also described other behavior patterns shown by young people struggling with identity. All are familiar to those who know about young Adolf Hitler. There is a "mistrustful difficulty with mere living in time. Time is made to stand still by the device of ignoring the usual alternation of day and night"—or by ignoring watches or keeping them unwound.[155] During such a crisis, a young man often shies away from heterosexual intimacies because he is unsure about his sexual effectiveness. Alternatively, he may choose one person whom he feels he can dominate completely—apt descriptions of Adolf's relationships with Stefanie and Kubizek. For long periods of time there is tortuous self-consciousness and inability to work. Noteworthy also is snobbish disdain for other people. The troubled youth may become a dropout and seek anonymity so that no one can tell whether he has succeeded or failed. Music can become very important for such a person, as a means of expressing his own inarticulate feelings and communing with his emotions. For Hitler, music served to verify and express his turbulent inner life. He needed the heroic fantasies of Wagner, not the measured serenity of Mozart or Haydn. Hence his belief that Wagner was one of the few people who ever understood him.

A main element in the identity crisis is the "moratorium," a period of withdrawal before a person sets forth on the career that "makes his name": Luther in a monastery, G. B. Shaw in business offices, Winston Churchill in the Indian Army, Bismarck in the bureaucracy, Jesus in the wilderness, Gandhi and Lincoln practicing law. Hitler would find his moratoriums both in Vienna and at the front in World War I. The moratorium period is paradoxical. All the people mentioned, though vastly different in temperament and accomplishment, were all men of historic achievement, yet their early careers gave little indication of future greatness. They all looked like failures at this stage of their lives. Do *all* great men experience a moratorium? If so, what brings them out of it? Many questions are still open, but Erikson has suggested that great men have some dominant faculty, some special gift which enables them to emerge from the doldrums of their lives. Among ideological innovators such as Luther (and Hitler), Erikson notes a remarkable effectiveness with words: "above all else, such people do not need simply to talk: they need to *talk back.*" It is not merely a matter of facility with words. At a deeper level, they really mean what they say. There is a need to settle a score. This is the real "Meaning of Meaning It"—as Erikson entitled a chapter on Luther.

In studying the identity crises of Luther and Gandhi, Erikson also found that as young men they both had a sense of their own toughness, a certain "inviolability of spirit," a realization of "special mission." However distasteful it may seem to compare Hitler with either of these men, the fact is that Hitler too demonstrated this quality. During the dark days after the death of his mother, at the front during the war, after the disintegration of his Party in 1924, and in the political crisis of 1932–1933, Hitler displayed a toughness and resiliency—an "inviolability of spirit"—that was remarkable. His movement was, in many ways, the triumph of his personal will.

The Onset of Anti-Semitism

During the identity crisis of late adolescence, Erikson has found an acute need both to repudiate and to affirm. And often—as in Gandhi, Luther, and Hitler—there is a hunger for an ideology, a total commitment, that will answer all the vague but "urgent questions which arise in consequence of identity or conflict." [156] Hitler found his faith in anti-Semitism and racial nationalism. For him it met all of Erikson's requirements for an overarching ideology that is total, uncompromising, vivid, complete.[157] It became the ground of his being and the core of his political philosophy. It allowed him to repudiate and to affirm, to destroy and to create. It required that he destroy the "Jewish peril" and create a racially pure Motherland.

The Child As Father to the Man

Anti-Semitism was deeply satisifying to Hitler for psychological as well as historical or philosophical reasons. He embraced anti-Semitism at a highly vulnerable point in his life. Even before his mother died, Adolf had experienced one of the most shattering events of his life: he was rejected by the Viennese Academy of Fine Arts, apparently smashing his cherished ambition to become an artist. Each applicant, in addition to his own portfolio, was obliged to submit two set drawings: "Expulsion from Paradise" and "An Incident from the Flood." The judges found Adolf's drawings unsatisfactory for a reason that would surprise anyone who has seen his later compulsive doodlings: "Too few heads." [158]

The timing of Klara's death was important; so too were its causes and conditions. Klara died of breast cancer while being attended by a Jewish physician. After the funeral, Hitler returned to Vienna. It was during this period—in early 1908—that he became an anti-Semite. Other writers have set different dates for the genesis of his racist doctrine, but there seems no reason to dispute Hitler's own testimony, given most clearly in *Mein Kampf*. "This was the time," he wrote, "in which the greatest change I was ever to experience took place in me. From a feeble cosmopolite I had turned into a fanatical anti-Semite." [159] Further emphasis on the year 1908 was given in a rambling and ungrammatical letter now in the so-called *Gestapo Berichte* of the former Party Archives. In it Hitler wrote that "within less than a year" after the death of his mother he had become a violent anti-Semite. Years later he confirmed the date when he told Neville Chamberlain that he had begun his racist thinking during his "nineteenth year"—that is, in 1908. [160]

A leading German biographer disagrees, contending that Hitler was already an anti-Semite while living in Linz. He relies heavily on the testimony of the editor of an anti-Semitic newspaper who told Party officials in 1938 that the Führer had read his paper as a boy. [161] But this evidence is not persuasive: it is understandable that the editor should seek to ingratiate himself with Nazi officials by boasting of his contribution to the Führer's intellectual development. The only anti-Semitic journals Hitler himself mentions are those he read in Vienna.

Other historians insist that the genesis of his political anti-Semitism came much later. Rudolph Binion dates it at 1918; George Mosse believes that the real onset came only with the influence of Dietrich Eckart and others of the Thule Society after 1919. [162] There can be little doubt that the postwar Munich experience was important, but chiefly because it reinforced ideas Adolf had already picked up in Vienna. In a revealing passage in *Mein Kampf*, Hitler himself gives support to this view, stating that when he was handed a racist pamphlet in Munich in 1919 he was immediately reminded of a similar event that took place a decade before in Vienna: "Involuntarily I saw thus my own development come to life again before my eyes." [163]

It is true that August Kubizek remembers his boyhood friend expressing anti-Semitic sentiments as early as 1904 or 1905, but Hitler did not work out his political program of anti-Semitism until his Vienna period. In an unpublished memoir, Kubizek himself gives a date when Hitler's serious interest in the ideology of anti-Semitism began. One day in 1908, Hitler came bursting into their room to announce, " 'Hey! Today I became a member of the anti-Semitic Union and I enrolled you too.' " [164] It was during this year, as we have seen, that Hitler devoured the racist pamphlets of Lanz-Liebenfels, List, and Fritsch along with Wagner's diatribes against the Jews.

It is difficult to overstate the importance to Hitler of his commitment to anti-Semitism. It meant almost everything to him. He looked back on this year in Vienna as the time in which *the greatest change I was ever to experience* took place—the time when he became *a fanatical anti-Semite.*

The close association between the onset of Hitler's fanatical hatred of Jews and the death of his mother seems clear. It is of course possible that the connection is purely coincidental. But appeals to coincidence are not generally satisfying when there is the possibility of a causal connection. The Freudian interpretation which follows was first suggested in a brilliant article by Gertrud Kurth, "The Jew and Adolf Hitler," which appeared in the *Psychoanalytic Quarterly* in 1947. Dr. Kurth's assumption that Hitler had an unreconciled Oedipal complex is manifestly valid. As has been noted, Adolf showed deep ambivalence toward his father. Consciously and publicly he always spoke well of "the Old Gentleman," but unconsciously he hated and feared him as the rival for his young mother's love.

The father had died, but now the Jewish family doctor, Eduard Bloch, arrived and reawakened the former conflict with his father. Through the process of displacement, Dr. Bloch became a substitute for Adolf's own father. Adolf was ambivalent toward Dr. Bloch, as he was toward his real father: he was at once deeply appreciative and bitterly resentful. His gratitude is attested by hand-painted postcards sent from Vienna with the inscription "From your ever-grateful patient, Adolf Hitler." But unconsciously, Adolf feared Bloch as a new rival. For this Jewish doctor had done many of the things young Adolf had seen his father do in reality or in fantasy: he too had entered his mother's bedroom; he too had undressed her; he too had examined her breasts. Other medical intimacies could have become associated in Adolf's mind with his image of his father as the lecherous attacker of his mother. Brutality and mutilation were now represented by the ablation of the breast. The poisoning of the blood, which he feared so much and for which he blamed his father, was now represented by the doctor's almost daily hypodermic injections of morphine into Klara's bloodstream in order to alleviate the woman's suffering. Thus, though he consciously expressed his gratitude to the kindly family doctor, Adolf unconsciously perceived this Jew as the brutal attacker who had finally mutilated and killed his beloved mother.

An American historian has discovered something else about Klara Hitler's medical treatment that might have contributed to Adolf's hatred of the Jewish doctor and hence to his rapidly developing anti-Semitism. As a dressing for the postoperative wound, Dr. Bloch apparently applied iodoform, an iodine derivative. Although it is unlikely that the iodoform was either excessively painful or lethally toxic, Adolf may have *believed* that it was.*

It seems plausible that Adolf would have associated himself with his mother's suffering at the hands of a Jew. Throughout his life he had identified with his mother in many ways: her eyes, he had noticed, were the same as his; the loss of her left breast was a kind of complement to his missing left testicle; he identified her with the German Motherland it was his life mission to save. She was, he said, a woman who had given Germany one of her greatest sons. A psychiatrist agrees with this association: "It is quite valid . . . to assume that his mother's sufferings, for which Adolf unconsciously held Dr. Bloch responsible, were experienced by Hitler as though they had been inflicted on himself." [165]

There is also the possibility of a further and historically more consequential displacement. The individual Jew, Dr. Bloch, was not merely the blood poisoner of Hitler's mother; by association with the Motherland—and it is worth emphasizing that Hitler used this term rather than the more usual Fatherland—Jews in general became the seducers and blood poisoners of the entire German nation. Thus Hitler would write that he had learned to know the Jew as "the *seducer* of our people," and he promised to "smash the *seducer* and *corrupter* against the wall." [166] There were two parts to this ideology, this *idée fixe* that

---

* Rudolph Binion has attempted to prove that the treatment was excrutiatingly painful, that it produced psychosis in Klara, and that iodoform, rather than cancer, was the actual cause of her death. ("Hitler's Concept of *Lebensraum*: The Psychological Basis," *History of Childhood Quarterly*, Vol. 1, No. 2 (Fall, 1973) and *Hitler Among the Germans* (New York, 1976), 14–21; 138–143) It is true that excessive use of iodoform bandages may, in rare cases and with allergic patients, result in poisoning and death. (*Lancet*, II (1933), 250, cited in *United States Dispensatory*, 27th ed., 1973, p. 630; see also *Pharmacology and Therapeutics*, 7th ed. 1970) But several things make it unlikely that this happened to Klara Hitler. Reactions to the use of iodoform dressings vary enormously: some patients experience no adverse effects whatever; others react violently showing immediate and clear symptoms of toxicity: burning pain, vomiting, delirium, convulsions, a faint and rapid pulse-rate that may go up to 180, *etc.* There is no evidence that Hitler's mother exhibited the gross physical and mental symptoms which Binion's argument requires. If she had, the few women who knew her well in Urfahr would certainly have mentioned them. It can also be assumed that Dr. Bloch would have observed such violent reactions and immediately stopped using the bandages. He was neither an incompetant nor a sadist. Indeed he enjoyed a reputation as a fine physician and a kindly man, widely known as the "Doctor of the Poor." If Klara had suffered extreme toxic reactions to iodoform as Binion insists, Dr. Bloch would not have continued to use the bandages. Furthermore, Bloch already knew that the operation had shown Klara's cancer to have metastasized into the pleura. (Bloch interview with US officials, 4 March 1943, OSS Source Book, 21) He would not have tried to cure it with superficial bandaging. Even Gestapo investigators of Klara's death had nothing but praise for Dr. Bloch. Surely the Nazis would have been delighted to have found any evidence suggesting that a Jewish doctor was guilty of malpractice in the death of the Führer's mother. They could find no such evidence.

was to dominate his life, and both seem to have been associated with his parents: the German Motherland became a substitute, through displacement, for his own mother; and the Jews, also through displacement, became a father substitute—a substitute made more real in his mind by his suspicion that his father's father might actually have been a Jew.

Commitment to an ideology of anti-Semitism and racial nationalism was also Hitler's way out of the depression which had swept over him after his return to Vienna following his mother's funeral. Kubizek had long known that his friend was a moody and volatile person, but now he was really concerned for Hitler's mental health:

> Altogether, in these early days in Vienna, I had the impression that Adolf had become unbalanced. He would fly into a temper at the slightest thing. . . . I did not know to what this present mood of deep depression was due. . . . He was at odds with the world. Wherever he looked he saw injustice, hate, and enmity. Nothing was free from his criticism; . . . Choking with his catalogue of hates he would pour his fury over everything, against mankind in general who did not understand him, who did not appreciate him and by whom he was persecuted. . . .
>
> Suddenly, however, in the middle of this hate-ridden harangue where he challenged a whole epoch, one sentence revealed to me how deep was the abyss on whose edge he was tottering.
>
> "I shall give up Stefanie." These were the most terrible words he could utter, for Stefanie was the only creature on God's earth whom he excepted from this infamous humanity. . . .[167]

To keep his sanity, Adolf drew on two main defenses: displacement and projection. He found in the Jews an explanation for all his difficulties and the reason for his feelings of guilt and despair. It was very simple: Jews were to blame for everything. They and not he were social parasites; it was they who practiced incest. A Jew had killed his mother. And now he discovered the real reason why he had failed his entrance examination: Jews were to blame for that too. Many years later he told friends that after his rejection he had investigated the members of the art jury who had ruled against him. As soon as he found out that four of the seven were Jews, he sat down and wrote a letter to the director of the Academy which ended with the threat, "For this the Jews will pay!" [168]

Religious festivals also seem to have had a bearing on Hitler's conversion to anti-Semitism. We do not know the precise day in 1908 that he made his decision, but it was probably just before or just after Easter. It could not have been during the holidays, since Kubizek was home in Linz visiting his parents; and by the end of June the roommates parted company. The timing of Easter is important. That day, which commemorates the resurrection of Christ, obviously brings to mind His death—and anti-Semitic Vienna offered many reminders that the Jews had killed Jesus. The idea of Jewish deicide meant more to Hitler personally than it did to others. At this time it seems likely that he was beginning to identify himself with the Messiah. He had felt an intimation of his messianic mission the night of *Rienzi*, and as the years went by he would speak more and more clearly about the matter, comparing himself directly to Jesus and speaking His very words.

Easter came late in 1908, which was a leap year. And Easter Monday actually fell on Hitler's own birthday, 20 April.[169] It is unlikely that Hitler, who was prone to find hidden meanings in apparently coincidental dates and anniversaries, would have missed that fact. By yet another accident of the calendar—which Hitler could have seen as divine plan—he himself had actually been born on Easter Eve, 1889. Now, at Easter in 1908, he, like Jesus, would be resurrected. He would arise from the depth of his depression and became transformed by a new doctrine that "opened [his] eyes for the first time" to the cause of all his problems.

The association in his mind between Jews and Christian festivals may have been reinforced by another coincidence which he was likely to find portentous. His "sainted mother" had been buried the day before Christmas Eve; a Jew had failed to save her life, and that, to his mind, was tantamount to murder. It would be his mission to punish the Jews, for in Vienna he had become convinced that *"by warding off the Jews, I am fighting for the Lord's work."* [170]

Thus, during his identity crisis of late adolescence, for reasons conscious and unconscious, Hitler embraced the ideology which was to become so important to his career and so fateful for the lives of millions.

Life in Vienna, 1908–1913

After he had buried his mother, Adolf returned to Vienna, where— at least in his own account—he would meet one of his more unpleasant images of motherhood: "The milksop was thrust out of his downy nest and given over to the care of Dame Sorrow, *his new mother.*" [171] Stefanie was part of the reason he left Linz. Although he could never bring himself to meet her, neither could he bear any longer to live in the same town. "There's only one thing to be done," he said. "I must go away—far away from Stefanie." [172] Other things about Linz had also become intolerable. His relatives kept asking carping questions about his plans for a career and reminded him that he had not earned a penny for his own support. And he must have heard the ominous rumor that his guardian, old Mayrhofer, was making arrangements to apprentice him to a baker. Impossible! The sooner he left, the better.

Vienna had other appeals. In his imagination he had already reconstructed—over and over again—every bridge and public building in

Linz. The capital of the empire offered new architectural challenges. And, of course, Wagner was better performed there. He also went to Vienna to prove something to his dead father:

> Always bearing in mind my father's example. . . . I too hoped to wrest from fate the success my father had met fifty years earlier. . . . I, too, wanted to become "something." . . .[173]

Alois had run away at the age of 13 and made good in the capital. Adolf would do even better. He described his conquest of real and imagined obstacles in a turgid and awkward letter of 29 November 1921 to the director of the Archives of the new Nazi Party, who had asked for a memoir of the Führer's life:

> I was orphaned with no father or mother at seventeen and left without any financial support. My total cash at the time of the trip to Vienna was about 80 *kronen*. I was therefore forced immediately to earn my bread as a common laborer. I went, as a not yet eighteen year old, as a worker's helper on construction jobs and had in the course of two years experienced almost all types of work of the common daily wage earner. . . .
>
> After indescribable effort, I succeeded to educate myself so well as a painter that I, through this activity from my twentieth year on, was able to make out in this work even if at first scantily. I became an architectural draftsman and architectural painter and was practically completely independent by my twenty-first year. In 1912 I went in this capacity to Munich.[174]

Adolf was too modest about his financial resources. Ever since his 18th birthday (April 1907) he had received his share of his father's inheritance, which had been drawing interest since 1 February 1904 at the mortgage bank for Upper Austria. The total amount was 700 kronen. In addition, he now received an orphan's pension. He also received an inheritance from a great aunt, Walpurga Hitler. Thus, far from being the impecunious orphan forced to earn his daily bread as a common laborer, he was comfortably off financially. He had neither the need nor the inclination to do any work at all. His total income exceeded 85 kronen per month—rather more than the average schoolteacher or postal official.[175]

He could have supplemented his income by doing odd jobs, but in the whole time that he lived with Kubizek in Vienna he earned no money whatsoever—he did not even paint and sell postcards during this period. Kubizek wrote: "As long as I was with him [February through June 1908] he painted no pictures. . . . I suspect that after he had been denied admission to the Academy he lost his pleasure in painting. . . . He sold no pictures therefore during this period and indeed had no employment of any kind the whole time we were together." [176]

The Child As Father to the Man

In Vienna, Adolf found a room in the Sixth District in the Mariahilfe, at Stumpergasse 29, in a building which later became a small linoleum factory. He invited his friend Kubizek, who had been accepted at the Conservatory of Music, to live with him. "Gustl" was greeted at the railway station by a dashing and debonair Adolf in dark overcoat, kid gloves, and ivory-handled walking stick. Since his quarters were too small for two, Hitler managed to inveigle the landlady into moving out of her own room, and the two young men moved in. There was now room for Gustl's piano and, most important to Hitler, space for him to stride diagonally back and forth across the room, as he had in the Blütengasse in Urfuhr and as he would during his conferences as the Führer.[177]

Normally Adolf slept until noon. His afternoons depended on the weather. If it was rainy or cold he would either go to the *Hofbibliothek* to read or stay home to work on outlines for plays or plots for operas. But normally, since Kubizek had to practice, Adolf would storm out. On pleasant days he would examine the buildings he planned to rebuild or sit reading in the Schoenbrunn. His favorite spot was a stone bench in the woods to the left of the Gloriette. But he would not go there on Sundays. He didn't like big crowds, and he despised the officers and carefree, stupid citizens.

Every evening the two young artists went to the theater. Kubizek insisted on this point in a later conversation with the archivist Jetzinger:

How often?
Every day!
O come, nobody will believe that!
We went out every evening almost without exception, usually to the Burgtheater or the Opera and sometimes to concerts when as a music student I got free tickets.[178]

They did not miss a performance of Wagner. Since Adolf would not go to the gallery of the opera because of the women, they stood in the pit where women were not admitted.

For several weeks, day and night, Adolf's energies were taken up with plans for a "Mobile Reichs Orchestra" which he would establish when he founded his new Reich. This huge orchestra would bring music to the remotest city of Hitler's vast empire. In these plans, as in all others, Hitler brought together sweeping ideas and minute detail. He thought of everything. The first cellist would not leave his seating arrangements to chance. His chair would travel with him. Should the dress be formal, or perhaps a type of uniform? Adolf decided on dark suits, "distinguished but not obtrusive." Where would the orchestra perform? Few town halls could accommodate 100 musicians and large audiences. He thought of outdoor performances—Wagner was magnificent under the stars—but it might rain, and acoustics were always difficult. His solution: the Reich orchestra would play in local churches. He told Kubizek to petition ecclesiastical authorities for permission to use the churches of Germany and Austria for the orchestra. Adolf devoted many hours to programming the concerts: only German composers would be played, and Wagner most of all. For weeks he kept a little black notebook in which, after every concert, he would jot down the works played, the name of the composer, the conductor, the time it took to play each piece, and his evaluation of the performance. The highest praise he could give was to say, "This will be included in our program."

Through it all, there was never a rueful admission that his plans were really an adolescent dream. He was absolutely convinced that the "Mobile Reichs Orchestra" would in fact come into being. He brushed off all queries about finances. Everything would be solved in his new Reich. He was "absolutely certain that one day he, personally, would give commands whereby the hundreds and thousands of plans and projects he had at his fingertips would be carried out." [179]

In the beginning of July 1908, Kubizek, who had finished his course at the Conservatory, left Adolf in Vienna to work in his father's upholstery shop in Linz. The roommates decided to return to their life of art and music at the end of the summer. Meanwhile, they kept in touch. Sometime in July—the postmark is not completely legible—Adolf sent a postcard of the Trinity Column which commemorates the plague of 1679: "Since your departure I have been working very hard often until 2 even 3 in the morning again." He planned to spend part of the summer on his aunt's farm at Spital, but added "shan't want to go at all if my sister will be there." A letter dated 17 July complained that Frau Zakreys insisted on drumming him out of bed too early in the morning. One peculiar line reads "I caught a whole mass of bugs which were soon swimming around dead in 'my' blood." As in all other correspondence of the Vienna period, there is no mention of the strenuous manual labor Hitler would talk about later.

When Kubizek returned to the Stumpergasse in the fall, Adolf had disappeared without leaving a forwarding address. "I have often racked my brains," Kubizek confided in a personal letter, "over why our long-standing friendship was so completely and suddenly broken off without any reason. But I cannot find a satisfactory answer." [180]

In his later memoirs, however, Kubizek himself has provided an explanation. Prior to leaving Vienna in early July, Kubizek—whom Hitler always considered his inferior—had graduated from the Conservatory with high honors. Adolf had stood by and watched as he was congratulated by the professor of composition, the head of the conductor's school, and the director of the conservatory himself. [181]

Like other young men who have undergone a difficult identity crisis, Adolf preferred to drop out and seek total anonymity rather than accept his own failure and his friend's success. In October 1908, Hitler tried once more for admission to the Academy of Fine Arts, with results even more disastrous than the first application: his talent was considered so minimal he was not even admitted to the examination.

Little is known about Hitler's activities during the 15-month period from late September 1908 to December 1909. We can trace where he lived through police registration records. But house numbers reveal little of the life of the lonely young man who dwelt at those addresses. At least five moves within a little over a year suggests that he shared something of his father's restlessness. After leaving Frau Zakreys, he stayed for a time in a pleasant, bright room across from the West Railway Station, at Felberstrasse 22; there, it seems likely, he read *Ostara* pamphlets avidly. In September he was living at Sechshauserstrasse 58. In November he roomed for a time in the Simon-Denkgasse, and there may have been other addresses. At this point, money from his father's and great aunt's inheritance seems to have run out, for we find him, by late November, in the Hostel for the Homeless (*Obdachslosenasyl*), a charitable institution in the Meidling District which had been made possible by the generosity of the Jewish Epstein family. Here, free of charge, he could get soup and bread and a bed for the night. Similarly, free food was available from the Warming House on the Erdbergstrasse, thanks to the generous endowment of another Jew, Baron Moritz Königswarder.[182] Since the hostel had to be vacated during the day, it is possible that now in November and December 1909—for the first and last time in his life—he may have done a few odd jobs such as shoveling snow. He certainly did not paint houses or hang wallpaper or work as a construction worker, as later accounts alleged. The fact that during the entire Third Reich not one workingman ever came forward to boast that he had labored side by side with the Führer during his Vienna years strongly suggests that he never worked anywhere for any length of time.

Just before Christmas 1909, Hitler apparently received money from his Aunt Johanna and moved to the comfortable Home for Men (*Männerheim*) at Meldemannstrasse in the Brigittenau District next to the Jewish quarter of Leopoldstadt near the Danube. Here he would live until he left for Munich, as the police records show, on 24 May 1913.[183]

The Home for Men provided separate bedroom cubicles, with the luxury of a weekly change of linen; there were washing facilities in the basement. Food was plentiful and inexpensive. More significantly, Hitler was able to commandeer a corner of the large writing room where he made dozens of copies of the same watercolors which he sold to art dealers and picture frame manufacturers in the Jewish quarter. During the Third Reich, great effort was made to recover the Führer's own paintings. One of the Party archivists, in a letter of 17 May 1938, noted the "very unpleasant" fact that many of the Führer's paintings were in the hands of Jews.[184] Among the many Jewish dealers and collectors who befriended Hitler and paid generously for his copies of copies of the

Gloriette or the churches of Vienna and other tourist attractions were such men as Altenberg, Neumann, Feingold, Morgenstern, and Landesberger.[185]

The modest and sporadic income Hitler received from selling his paintings was probably enough to pay for his room and board. It was not sufficient to fund the concerts, opera and other diversions to which he had become accustomed. The rest of his income came from two sources —not mentioned, understandably, in any of his later reminiscences. All this time he had been receiving an orphan's pension under the fiction that he was an art student duly registered at the Academy of Fine Arts. By this deception he deprived his younger sister Paula of the full orphan's pension that should have come to her as a dependent child. Hitler accepted the orphan's pension of 25 kronen per month until he was forced to give it up by court order of May 1911, shortly after his 22nd birthday. He could afford to do so because he had cajoled his crippled Aunt Johanna into "lending" him large sums of money from her life savings and inheritance to support his career as a professional artist. When she died in March 1911, she left him the handsome sum of 3,800 kronen, according to the records of her will probated in the District Court of Linz.[186]

Thus, while life in Vienna may have been lonely and aimless, there was no reason why he was compelled to suffer the privation and misery which, he later insisted, had been his melancholy lot.

Escape to the Motherland, 1913–1914

In writing his memoirs, Hitler spent an extraordinarily long time explaining why he fled from Vienna to Munich.* Over six pages of turgid prose set forth his reasons for the momentous move—a departure which Austrians, prior to the *Anschluss*, sardonically called their revenge for defeat in 1866. "I left Austria first and foremost," Hitler wrote, "for political reasons. . . ." He despised the Austrian state and all it stood for, and he was glad to leave that sinking ship. Artistic considerations were also important. After the completion of the Ring, he could expect no great architectural commissions; and anyway, Germany offered a far better future for the "new architecture" he was creating. In general, Austria could only frustrate both his political and artistic genius: "I was convinced that this State was bound to oppress and to handicap every really great German. . . ." There was also a racial reason: "I detested the conglomerate of races that the realm's capital manifested." Then, too, there was the matter of dialect: "The German language of my childhood was the dialect that was spoken in Lower Bavaria; I was neither able to forget it nor to learn the Viennese jargon."

But he may also have left Austria and fled to Germany because he was fleeing to a substitute mother, a mother who, though separated

* He also predated the move by more than a year, claiming that he left Austria in the spring of 1912 when in fact it was May 1913.

from him, was still faithful and beckoned him back to her breast. In Hitler's imagery, his degenerate and racially corrupt father was Austria; his mother was Germany. Passion for the Motherland pulsates through his prose:

> The longing grew stronger to go there where, since my early youth, I had been drawn by secret wishes and secret love. . . . But finally I wanted to share the joy of being allowed to work in that place where the most ardent wish of my heart [*brennendster Herzenswunsch*] was bound to be fulfilled. . . . There are many even today who are unable to understand the intensity of such a longing. . . . I appeal to all those who, severed from the Motherland, . . . now in painful emotion [*im schmerzlicher Ergriffenheit*] long for the hour that will permit them to return to the bosom of their faithful Mother [*an das Herz der treuen Mutter*].[187]

A more prosaic and pressing reason lay hidden behind the smoke-screen of rhetoric: he left Austria because he was being sought as a deserter from the Austro-Hungarian Army.*

Hitler arrived in Munich on 26 May 1913. On the registration form where an official had originally listed his profession as that of artist, Hitler himself wrote in "writer" (*Schriftsteller*), and where the official had listed his home district as Linz, Hitler had written, and misspelled, the word "stateless." [188]

Meanwhile, Austrian officials began a desultory search for the deserter. After some five months they finally located him in a room in the Schleissheimerstrasse. The actual summons was not served until Sunday afternoon, 18 January 1914, when he opened his door to be confronted by the police. Next morning he was taken to the Austro-Hungarian consulate.

Here Hitler's vaunted persuasiveness stood him in good stead. He apparently got through to the consul-general himself. This gentleman was obviously impressed by the intense young man's sincerity, and advised him to write a letter of explanation to the authorities at Linz.

---

* According to the Conscription Act of 1889, Hitler should have gone to the authorities in late autumn 1909 to have his name entered in the roster for military service. In the spring of 1910, at the age of 21, he should have reported personally to begin military service. This was general public knowledge; information about conscription appeared in newspapers and placards so that no one could plead ignorance. Between 1909 and 1912, when he was of military age and living in Vienna, Hitler did not enter his name in the registry, nor did he report for military training in any one of the subsequent years. In the recruitment list of men due for military service from Linz the following notation was placed opposite his name: "Failed to report. Address not known." Hitler may have waited until May 1913 before leaving Austria because he thought that after his 24th birthday he was no longer liable for the draft and could safely cross the border. Or he may have fled because he was told at the Home for Men that he might still be arrested as a deserter because he had failed to report during the years when he was liable for service. See Jetzinger, *Hitlers Jugend*, 253–272; *Hitler's Youth*, 144–154.

The consul-general himself transmitted this letter on 23 January, along with a personal note endorsing Hitler's petition. He wrote that he was convinced that "Hietler [sic] . . . was suffering from a complaint which renders him unfit for military service and at the same time removes all motive for evading it. . . .He seems very deserving of considerate treatment."

Hitler's important letter of apology and explanation to the Linz authorities covered three and one-half pages of foolscap. He first expressed surprise and shock that he should be arrested and ordered to report so soon that "I would barely have had time even for the most basic bodily cleansing, such as taking a bath." He noted that he was correctly described in the summons as an artist, yet "though this title is mine by right, it is nevertheless only in a limited sense correct." He went on to say that he was barely able to support himself by painting and would have great difficulty raising money for his transportation back to Linz. "Now certainly in all this there is some fault of mine. I omitted to report in the autumn of 1909." He then went on to lament his miserable existence in Vienna and to cite his alleged poverty as the reason for this "sin of omission."

There can be little doubt that Hitler had experienced difficult months in Vienna during 1909. But the claim that he suffered abject poverty "for two years" is fiction. He was not too proud to bilk his young sister out of a share of her orphan's pension or to persuade a crippled Aunt Johanna to give him money and leave him her life savings.[189]

One of the interesting things about the incident is the remarkable leniency of those Austrian bureaucrats whom Hitler so thoroughly despised. He received sympathetic help from the consul-general in Munich; the officials in Linz granted his request to appear in Salzburg rather than requiring him to return to Linz; and he was allowed to go as a regular recruit, not as an apprehended deserter. Most significantly, he received no fine or punishment of any kind. On 5 February 1914 he reported to the Standing Military Commission in Salzburg. The commission found him "unfit for combatant and auxiliary duties, too weak. Unable to bear arms." He returned to Munich a free man.

We get only brief glimpses of Hitler's life in Munich from the fall of 1913 to August 1914, when he went away to war. What evidence we have suggests that this year was pretty much a continuation of the lifestyle he had developed in Vienna. He continued to enjoy relative ease and comfort. He himself called this period one of "the happiest and most contented" of his life.[190]

Hitler's room in the Schleissheimerstrasse had the sentimental advantage of being in Schwabing, the artistic center of Munich. The street was only barely within the district, but that was enough to provide an address that gave his artist's pose a pleasantly authentic touch.

The Child As Father to the Man

Hitler lived on the extreme western fringe of Schwabing not far from the Dachauerstrasse—the road that leads to Dachau.

Materially he seemed to be quite comfortable. His letter to the Linz authorities reported an income from his paintings of 100 marks each month, and he later told an associate that "I never needed more than 80 marks a month." [191]

The room, which he rented from a tailor, Josef Popp, cost him only 20 marks a month. It was pleasant, well furnished, and had a private entrance from the street. Hitler could easily have entertained, since the Popps had no objections. Yet as they both recalled with some surprise, Hitler never once invited either a male or female guest to his room. Popp had been trained in Paris and prided himself on being a master tailor of modish fashions. Since he was also a kindly man, he saw to it that his tenants' clothes did not cast adverse reflections on his business. Hitler was supplied with well-cut suits and an overcoat. The Popp children, Josef Jr. and Elisabeth, liked the nice man who lived upstairs. But he always remained a little aloof and never wanted to talk about his family background. "We never knew," they said in an interview in 1967, "what he was really like." The younger Popp later recalled especially that their tenant "spent a lot of time in keeping his body clean." [192]

Hitler was also befriended by a kindly baker just around the corner, on the Gabelsbergerstrasse 66, who sold him slightly stale rolls and cakes for a few pennies. This baker, Herr Heilmann, reported in a 1952 interview that "Hitler never did any manual work" and always appeared clean and neatly dressed.[193]

The baker also said that Hitler sold his paintings for 10 to 20 marks each and that he himself purchased two. We have other evidence of sales. A certain Doctor Schirmer recalled that "sometime before the war," as he sat sipping a beer in the garden of the Hofbräuhaus one summer evening, "a neatly dressed young man" politely asked him if he would be interested in purchasing a painting. The doctor bought the small oil Hitler was carrying and asked him to copy in watercolor two favorite postcards of Bavarian mountain lakes. Hitler fulfilled his commission within the week. A Herr Würsler remembered that he had paid Hitler 25 marks for a small painting in oil.[194]

As in Vienna, Hitler spent his mornings in bed. His afternoons were free for general cultural activities. He could stay at home and paint, or he could go to read in the Bavarian State Library, about a 15-minute walk from his room. His impressive knowledge of art history shows that he must have spent many hours in the excellent art museums within easy walking distance: the Alte Pinakothek and Neue Pinakothek, the Glyptothek, and the collection of modern paintings at the Glass Palace. In the Neue Pinakothek in 1914 he would have seen, again and again, some of his favorites: Böcklin's voluptuous *Spirit of the Waves,* Makart's *Abundantia,* and von Stuck's sensuously daring *Sin*. It was an easy if lonely life, but Hitler had always been a loner.[195]

These were, as he said, happy days. But one suspects that he felt stirrings of uneasiness tinged with guilt. For while the world throbbed with excitement and exhilarating portents of change, during that summer of 1914, there was Adolf Hitler living his placid and aimless life. He was doing nothing to fulfill the great mission presaged to him the night of *Rienzi* in Linz, nothing to carry out those magnificent plans for a new Reich he had formulated in Vienna. He felt deeply the need for "deliverance" or "redemption" from the frivolous and vexatious feelings of youth. He needed some great catalytic force to give him the sense of identity, direction, and purpose that had so far eluded him.

Then suddenly, in August 1914, like a bolt from heaven, like a gift from his Goddess of Destiny, came the declaration of war. It was the call he needed. Thousands upon thousands of patriotic young men in Europe cheered the coming of the war, but few with such a sense of *personal* need. For the war meant two things to young Hitler: a destiny-directed solution to the problem of his personal identity and a chance to defend his beloved Motherland. No wonder he welcomed the war with such great expectations. We have the famous picture of the fashionably dressed young man in the Odeonsplatz, his eyes shining, doffing his hat and hailing the war. We also have the revealing personal confessions of his memoirs:

> To me personally those hours appeared like a *deliverance* from the vexatious moods of my youth. I am not ashamed even today to say that, overwhelmed by impassioned enthusiasm, I had fallen on my knees and thanked Heaven out of my overflowing heart that it had been granted to me the good fortune of being allowed to live in these times.[196]

He had been a deserter from the army of his father's Austria, that "racial cesspool." But to fight for his German Motherland, in this "struggle for her existence," was very different. He was overwhelmed with gratitude at the chance to defend her personally from the evil forces that sought to attack and abuse her.

Hitler As War Hero, 1914–1918

The war on the Western Front was everything Hitler had hoped for. Here was escape from failure and frustration in a philistine world that refused to recognize genius and had called him "inadequate." Here he could enjoy a moratorium from its asinine demands. No longer was he a miscast failure. Now he belonged. He was an integral part of the most powerful war machine in the history of the world. In it he found the direction, purpose, and power that he lacked in himself. He felt the exhilaration of being militarized; he would, one day, militarize a society.

His job in the army increased the feeling of participating in power, for he was assigned to regimental headquarters as a *Meldegänger* (dispatch runner). As such, he carried messages from regimental to company headquarters. He remained a runner throughout the war. The highest rank he attained was *Gefreiter*—roughly equivalent to private first class in the American Army. There is no evidence of his "bucking" for a noncommissioned officer grade or for a transfer. He liked his job. Living conditions were relatively comfortable and clean at regimental headquarters. But, more important, the position gave him a feeling that he was helping to make significant military decisions. "The orders he carried set battalions in motion, started artillery barrages, or sent further orders down the line to hold ground regardless of losses." [197]

In the archives of the National Socialist Party there is a folder marked "Hitler as Soldier—Letters about Him, Experiences at the Front." The most striking thing about all these letters and later reminiscences of men who were in his regiment is that they say so little about what kind of person this soldier was. No one really knew him. For at the front he continued to be a loner and something of an oddball: a soldier who neither drank nor smoked, who didn't to talk about women, who said he wasn't interested in letters or packages from home, who loved the army and gladly took on extra duty—particularly at Christmastime, when he didn't want to go home or join in celebrations.[198] When the Munich baker Franz Heilmann sent him a food package, he got a stiff note back thanking him but saying that "under no circumstances" was he to send any more packages. Adolf wanted to be left alone.[199]

Generally Hitler left his mail unanswered. But we do have a few postcards, two long letters he wrote to Josef Popp, his landlord in Munich, and one to a certain Assessor Ernst Hepp. These letters, however, seem contrived to reveal as little as possible about the personal feelings of the writer. They are curiously wooden set pieces written by a depersonalized German soldier commenting on "life at the front." The writer is a dutiful patriot who warns against "a world of enemies," distrusts Austria, and glories in the battle to save the German Motherland. He describes in excessive detail the slaughter of men and horses. Soldier Hitler is deferential to authority and very proper and formal. His landlord, with whom he had spent many an evening talking politics, is addressed as "Honored Sir." The letter to Hepp ends "with most respectful greetings to your highly esteemed Mother and Wife from your very respectful and grateful Adolf Hitler." [200]

A soldier who later became a Franciscan monk reported that Hitler was none too popular with his comrades. He let it be known that their patriotism and devotion to duty did not measure up to the standards he set for them: "Always deadly serious, he never laughed or joked." He answered the usual soldier's gripes with furious fulminations about patriotism and a soldier's responsibilities. "We all cursed him and found him intolerable," another comrade recalled. "There was this white crow among us that didn't go along . . . when we damned the war to hell." [201] Hitler had no use for women. When a buddy, Hans Mend, made out rather well with a pretty French girl, Hitler preached him a homily on the evils of interracial liaisons and the importance of keeping German blood pure and undefiled. He was known in the regiment as "the woman hater" (der Weiberfeind). His one indulgence continued to be a desire to suck on sweets. It became another joke of his outfit: "If he found a tin of artificial honey, nothing could get him away from it, shells or no shells."

There was something else Hitler was remembered for in his regiment: he lived a charmed life. Time after time he seemed to court death, but when bullets claimed a comrade, he escaped unscathed. After one notable attack which left the regiment decimated, someone turned to Hitler and said, *Mensch für dich gibt es keine Kugel!"* ("Man, there's no bullet made with your name on it!") Successive letters to the Popps read: "It is an absolute miracle that I was not injured . . . I myself am, through a miracle, still alright . . . Through a miracle I remain well and healthy." [202] Thus was reinforced Hitler's conviction that he had been miraculously spared—unlike his brothers and sister and so many comrades in arms—for a special mission.

Though he spent most of his time in lonely, brooding silence, he could be drawn into excited barrack-room orations in which he held forth on the sinister conspiracies he knew about from reading Lanz-Liebenfels, List, and Fritsch: the menace of Freemasons, Catholics, and Marxists. But now, as later, he pointed to the Jews as the archenemy of the Motherland. When his comrades laughed, Hitler furiously promised that one day he would show them! When he came to power, he would rule over them all and get rid of the Jews.

Hitler's humor ran to *Schadenfreude* and mockery. For security reasons, dispatch runners went in pairs. Hitler's colleague for over 32 months, Hans Mend, had been a riding instructor in civilian life. Mend recalled that Hitler enjoyed embarrassing him by affecting mock formalism and humility: "Is it permissible to wish the Immortal Horseman a Happy New Year?" [203]

His comrades exaggerate slightly when they testify that Hitler "never once took a furlough." [204] There is evidence of at least one furlough as testified by a postcard (with typical misspellings) sent from Berlin 6 October 1917 to one Ernst Schmidt in Wurzbach, Thuringia:

Dear Schmidt:

Got here first on Tuesday. The Arendt family is very nice. I will not have wished for anything better. The city is great. . . . I now

have finally opportunity to study the museums a bit better. In short I am mising [sic] nothing.
  Es gruss [sic] *dir* [sic] *dein,*

A. Hitler [205]

All Hitler's commanding officers agreed that he was a brave and exemplary soldier. Testifying in 1922, before it was obligatory to praise the Führer, an officer recalled his courage and noted particularly that he somehow managed always to keep himself scrupulously clean.[206]

Hitler had been awarded the Iron Cross, Second Class, as early as December 1914. In March 1932 he sued a German newspaper for libel after it wrote that his conduct in the war was cowardly. A former commanding officer at regimental headquarters, Lieutenant Colonel Engelhardt, convincingly testified to his bravery. Hitler won the case.[207]

He was wounded for the first time on 5 October 1916 at 5:00 A.M., near Le Bargué, when he caught shell fragments in his left shoulder. Hospitalized in Beelitz-Berlin, he petitioned to be returned to the front so that he could spend Christmas alone there.[208]

Hitler was one of the very few common soldiers of World War I to be awarded the Iron Cross, First Class. There are differing and improbable accounts of how he won the great distinction,* but three things seem clear. First, he was entitled to the honor. Second, it was enormously important to him both personally and politically. He wore the Iron Cross constantly, for it was visible proof of his claim that he was the "unknown hero of the Great War." Third, the award shows that once again he had reason to be grateful to a Jew. As his commanding officer has written, Hitler never would have received the honor had it not been for the efforts of the regimental adjutant, Hugo Gutmann, a Jew.[209]

Hitler was wounded a second time when, on 15 October 1918, he was gassed on the southern front of the battle of Ypres. Records from the military hospital of Pasewalk near Berlin where he was evacuated simply say that he was gassed (*gaskrank*); but Hitler—hence all official biographies—always insisted that he was blinded by mustard gas. That he exaggerated the extent of his injury seems clear not only from the army records but also from two other facts. First, within one

---

* It has been said that he won it by his heroic, single-handed capture of seven Englishmen, or 12 (or 20) Frenchmen; or by luring an English tank to its destruction; or "for general bravery." An uplifting biography of Hitler written for schoolchildren of the Third Reich finds a moral in this incident in the life of the Führer: he had studied so hard in school that he spoke perfect French and thus could command 20 French soldiers to surrender. The book is aptly titled: *Unser Führer: ein Jungen- und Mädchenbuch* (*Our Leader: A Book for Boys and Girls*). The same edition of the offical Nazi newspaper *Völkischer Beobachter* (14 August 1934) gives two different dates for the heroic exploit: 4 August 1918 and 4 October 1918. Surprisingly, the official history of the List Regiment is silent about Hitler's citation.

month after his discharge he was accepted for reenlistment into the army—at a time when there was great competition for the few places available. Second, though in need of money, he never applied for a disabled veteran's pension. It seems apparent that he knew army hospital records would not support his claim.[210]

It is quite possible that Hitler's blindness, while real, was psychosomatic in origin, a form of hysteria produced by the trauma of Germany's defeat. Certainly news of the armistice was a shattering experience, and there is no reason for doubting the sincerity and intensity of his description of the event:

> Everything began to go black again before my eyes. Stumbling, I groped my way back to the ward, threw myself on my bed, and buried my burning head in the covers and pillows. I had not cried since the day I had stood at the grave of my mother.[211]

Something else may have reminded him, unconsciously, of his mother. As a little child, he had shut his eyes to avoid seeing his beloved Klara ravished by a father whom he was to suspect of being half-Jewish. Was he now blinded because he could not bear to see his Motherland defeated and humiliated by the Jews?

Hitler was certainly not the only German soldier to be appalled by the defeat and shocked by the "stab in the back" of the armistice and proclamation of a republic. But one has the feeling that for him there was something very personal about it, for he could never speak of the defeat of Germany without succumbing to paroxysms of hatred. Over and over again, for the rest of his life, he would rain a torrent of vituperation on those "traitors" who had "betrayed the Motherland" and committed "the greatest villainy of the century." This was the "November shame," perpetrated by the "November criminals" who had produced the misbegotten "Jew Republic." [212]

Something clicked in the Pasewalk Hospital. It was there at the turn of the year 1918–1919 that Hitler resolved his identity problem and reached what he called "the most decisive decision of my life." For now, finally, he knew who he was and what he must do. He was the leader sent by destiny. He must answer the "voices" that he said he heard—like Joan of Arc—distinctly calling him as he lay in his hospital bed. The voices told him to rescue his Motherland from the Jews who had violated her. He ends his chapter:

> With the Jews there can be no bargaining. There can only be the hard either/or.
> I had resolved to become a politician.

In this decision, the central position of anti-Semitism should be noted. Hitler's fight against the Jews who menaced the Motherland had become the central, driving force of his political mission.[213]

The Child As Father to the Man

Years later he would remind his followers that when he started his mission to the German people he was 30 years old, exactly the same age that another Messiah began His ministry.

MISSION IN MUNICH, 1919–1933

The Munich to which Hitler returned in the spring of 1919 seemed to be fulfilling the direst predictions of the Viennese pamphleteers. The graceful capital of the Wittelsbachs, the home of *Gemütlichkeit* and good-humored apathy, was being taken over by foreign radicals, Jews, and other Dark Ones.

The postwar history of the city is a sorry tale of regimes which were, in turn, inefficient, daft, corrupt, and terroristic—a history which served as excellent grist for the mills of Hitler's later propaganda. He did not allow the German people to forget that he had saved the Motherland from the horrors of democracy—from the time, for example, "when Israel was king of Bavaria." [214]

After the collapse of the Imperial German Armies on the Western Front, Kurt Eisner, a Jewish journalist recently released from prison and considered a "foreigner" because he spoke with a Berliner accent, had become leader of the Bavarian Independent Socialists. He raised the old cry of *Los von Berlin!*, and on 8 November 1918 proclaimed a socialist republic in conservative, Catholic Bavaria.

His support dwindled rapidly during the three short months of his regime. After the disastrous elections of January 1919, in which he received less than 3 percent of the popular vote, he was shot down as he was on his way to tender his resignation. His assassin, Count Arco auf Valley, was a young man who had been rejected for membership in the racist Thule Society because of a Jewish grandmother. The founder of the society paid him a twisted tribute for the murder: "He wanted to show that even a half-Jew could carry out an act of heroism."

Eisner's confused political inheritance was seized by a motley group of radical intellectuals who, after setting up headquarters in the queen's bedroom of the Wittelsbach palace, began the most bizarre governmental experiment in European history. The poet Ernst Toller was president of the Executive Council. While Munich faced starvation, he issued decrees announcing that the regeneration of the human soul was to be sought in art and free love. Silvio Gesell, leader of a free-money clique, found ample opportunity to experiment with his theories as minister of finance. A Dr. Franz Lipp, the new commissar for foreign affairs, was thoroughly enjoying a full-blown psychosis. His foreign policy consisted largely in writing a series of remarkable letters, including one to Pope Benedict XV to lodge a formal protest that someone had stolen the key to his toilet. The commissar for public housing decreed that henceforth no home in Bavaria could contain more than three rooms and that the living room must always be placed above the kitchen.

The happy, irresponsible government of these "coffee house anarchists" did very well to last for six days. It was succeeded on a lovely Palm Sunday in April 1919 by a group of Communists who established a Republic of Soviets (*Räterepublik*). Leadership was vested in three Russian emigrés—Leviné, Axelord, and Levien—whom Hitler would later castigate as the "Jewish kings of Munich." Their arrival brought a reign of terror that was mitigated only by confusion and inefficiency. Decree followed violent decree; soldiers of the "Red Army" ran drunkenly through the streets on plundering expeditions; schools, banks, newspaper offices, and the theater were closed; prisoners were released from jails, and police dossiers were burned.

Fed up with the chaos and terror of radical political experiments Müncheners finally called for help from the central government, which in May 1919 dispatched volunteer bands of soldiers to "liberate" the city and "restore order." These were the so-called Free Corps, who preferred to dub themselves Freebooters. Their contribution to the rise of Hitler will be discussed in a later connection (see Chapter 5, pp. 312–314), but it may be noted here that they established a reign of terror in Munich which made the "Red Terror" of preceding weeks look pale. Only relative political stability followed the Free Corps occupation in 1919. A year later, during unrest occasioned by the Kapp Putsch in Berlin, military leaders installed Gustav von Kahr as the virtual dictator of Bavaria. (This, substantially, was the government Hitler would try to overthrow in his Beer Hall Putsch of November 1923.) But in the meantime, Munich had become a haven for dozens of militant rightist and racist groups, all trying strenuously to save Germany from the evils of democracy.

Political Skirmishes

The crowded historical stage had been set for Hitler's appearance as Messiah. But the future Führer still stayed in the wings, hesitant and unsure. He did not yet know how to play the role destiny had assigned him. As would happen often in his life in moments of personal crisis, he was assailed by feelings of anxiety, inadequacy, and self-doubt. Thus, month after month, as the turbulent events of revolution, Soviet-style government, and Free Corps occupation swirled about him, he stood aloof, unsure of what to do. Yet through it all he was sustained by the conviction that he had been chosen; that somehow, someday, he would become leader of Germany. Belief in himself and his mission never left him. He must keep the faith and wait for the Goddess of Fate to guide him. And soon she did.

The Child As Father to the Man

His first steps led him back to the army. He was assigned to a special new department (Abteilung I S/P) which, after the recent events in Munich, had been established to investigate offbeat or subversive political groups. Hitler later styled himself the "educational officer" of the regiment. Actually he was a "V-Mann" (the abbreviation for *Vertrauensmann*), or undercover agent. His job was to act as a spy and report "reliable" and "unreliable" political movements.[215]

As part of his training, he was required to attend a series of indoctrination lectures given by patriotic professors at the University of Munich. One of his instructors, Professor Karl-Alexander von Müller, recalled that after a lecture he noticed that "the men seemed spellbound by one of their number who was haranguing them with mounting passion in a strangely guttural voice. I had the peculiar feeling that their excitement derived from him and at the same time they, in turn, were inspiring him." [216] This giving and receiving, this mutual nourishment between Hitler and his audience, would remain characteristic of his relationship to a crowd.

The professor was so impressed he recommended that Hitler be assigned to promoting patriotism in the ranks of the army. Hitler himself remembered the incident clearly and gloried in the power and personal satisfaction he felt in moving a crowd through the spoken word:

> I started full of ambition and love. For thus I was at once offered the opportunity to speak before a large audience. . . . What previously I had always assumed to be true out of pure feeling without knowledge, became clear now: I could "speak" [*Ich konnte "reden"*]. . . . No other task could make me happier than this one.[217]

He was about to illustrate this power at a fateful moment in history. For one day in September 1919, either because his job as an army informer required it or—as he preferred to believe—because the Goddess of Fate directed him to do so, he investigated a meeting of the struggling racist party founded by a railway mechanic named Anton Drexler. The little group, which called itself the German Workers' Party, gathered in the Sterneckerbräu tavern in the Tal. The meeting, in a back room that reeked of good beer and bad cigars, was moribund until the stranger with the flashing eyes and compelling voice rose in anger to answer a professor who had suggested that Bavaria should break away from the Reich. So furious and effective was Hitler's attack that the demolished opponent left the meeting. Drexler was impressed.

Hitler subsequently wrote a report to his superior officer, Lieutenant Mayr, warning of the "Jewish racial tuberculosis" and insisting on the need for immediate "*Progroms* [sic]" and "the removal [*Ent-*

fernung] of absolutely all Jews." His report must have persuaded his superior, for he appended a note and endorsed Hitler's metaphor: "I am in agreement with Herr Hitler . . . all dangerous elements must, like disease carriers, be either 'isolated' [literally, encysted, *verkapselt*] or eliminated. That includes Jews." [218]

A few days later, Hitler made another of "the greatest decisions" of his life: he joined the German Workers' Party. At a subsequent meeting he listened as a dutiful treasurer reported with pompous pride that the Party now had total assets of 7 marks, 15 pfennig. It was suggested that it might invest some of its money in three rubber stamps to improve its office equipment.[219]

This was the group that Hitler would transform into one of the most effective political movements of modern history. He did it largely through the force of his personality and the power of the spoken word. His effectiveness as a demagogue is attested by nearly everyone who heard him. The Munich police reports for November 1919 describe his performances as Party orator as "masterful" and note time and again that he was received with "tumultuous applause." Ernst Hanfstaengl, a sophisticated Harvard graduate, found Hitler "absolutely irresistible . . . a master of the spoken word." Konrad Heiden, then a university student and political opponent of Hitler who had heard him dozens of times, put his finger on a source of Hitler's effectiveness: he played the role of man of destiny with such fidelity that he actually became the part he played. In transforming himself, he transformed his audience:

> . . . suddenly this man, who has been awkwardly standing around . . . begins to speak, filling the room with his voice, suppressing interruptions or contradictions by his domineering manner, spreading cold shivers among those present by the savagery of his declaration, lifting every subject of conversation into the light of history . . . the listener is filled with awe and feels that a new phenomenon has entered the room. This thundering demon was not there before; this is not the same timid man with the contracted shoulders. He is capable of this transformation in a personal interview and facing an audience of half a million.[220]

Other opponents observed the same phenomenon: a limp, little man changed into a force of overwhelming power, the stream of speech stiffening him "like a stream of water stiffens a hose." Otto Strasser gave one of the most graphic descriptions of the rhetorical skills that were to make Hitler master, first of the Party, and then of Germany:

> Adolf Hitler enters a hall. He sniffs the air. For a minute he gropes, feels his way, senses the atmosphere. Suddenly he bursts forth. . . .

His words go like an arrow to their target, he touches each private wound on the raw, liberating the mass unconscious, expressing its innermost aspirations, telling it what it most wants to hear.[221]

Oratorical ability is often important to a revolutionary leader, but it is never enough in itself. Stalin, an indifferent speaker, ousted Trotsky, the best orator produced by the Russian Revolution. A part of Hitler's success must also be attributed to his organizational ability and his capacity for ruthless political infighting.

He soon had need for all these skills, for his control of the Party did not go unchallenged. A crisis of leadership developed in 1921, a crucial year in the life and political fortunes of Adolf Hitler. Toward the end of July an anonymous pamphlet opposing Hitler was circulated among Party leaders and published in a special edition of the *Münchener Post*, 3 August 1921.[222] The pamphlet bore as its title the suggestive question, *Adolf Hitler—Verräter?* (Adolf Hitler—Traitor?). It spoke of Hitler's "lust for personal power"; it asked pointed questions about his personal finances and expensive tastes, particularly in clothes and women. Did he see himself, it was asked, as the leader of a working-class party or as "Adolf I, King of Munich"? The pamphlet complained that Hitler treated his colleagues as lackeys and maligned them as "common dogs"; it gave instances of how he twisted facts to suit his own purpose "in a typically Jewish way." It resented Hitler's claim to "infallibility" as the "so-called spiritual leader" of the Party. Finally, it appealed to all decent members of the Party not to be misled and deceived by this "megalomaniac and demagogue" and urged that he be removed from office.

Hitler, who sometimes dawdled and delayed when confronted by a crisis, showed in this instance that he could meet a direct challenge with immediate and effective action. He called a meeting of all Party members for 29 July in the Hofbräuhaus, the same evening the original pamphlet had appeared. We have a full report of the meeting thanks to the Munich Police Department's *Politischer Nachrichtendienst* (Political Reporting Service).

About 1,200 members of the Party attended. Hitler saw to it that he was introduced with fulsome praise by a Party member whom everyone had assumed was his political enemy; he lavished compliments on Drexler, whom the pamphlet had hinted was disenchanted with him; he then launched into a stirring speech which had the whole crowd cheering. The meeting was a tremendous personal triumph. A formal resolution made him, in effect, the undisputed leader of the Party. Key figures of the movement rallied to his support and hailed him as their personal and national savior.[223] As the closest student of this important event has concluded, "From this day on, the National Socialist German Workers' Party had become a one-man party with Hitler its dictatorial Führer." [224]

The Beer Hall Putsch

Hitler's first attempt to seize power in Germany, the Beer Hall Putsch of November 1923, casts special light on his personality. He showed a combination of decision and irresolution, effectiveness and ineptitude, and—as we shall see in a later connection—a curious impulse to flirt with disaster.

The historical background for the famous event can be quickly sketched. After Munich was "liberated" from the Communists in the Spring of 1919, Free Corps fighters by the hundreds flocked to the city where sympathetic officials gave them haven.* Two political leaders sought the support of these militant, unruly veterans and racist activists: the "strongman" of Bavaria, Gustav von Kahr, and Adolf Hitler. Kahr was a ponderous, stubborn, uninspiring bureaucrat who had just been made state commissioner general [*Generalstaatskommissar*]— a post whose powers were well beyond his ability. Both men were uncomfortable with their restless supporters who demanded action and the immediate overthrow of the hated Weimar Republic.

Hitler in particular was uncertain and hesitant. He did not quite know what to do with a political situation which seemed so propitious for political upheaval. By the late summer of 1923, Germans were stunned and shaken by the recent French invasion of the Ruhr; runaway inflation was wiping out people's life savings; unemployment grew unchecked; thousands went hungry. In addition to economic distress, there seemed to be political crises everywhere. Radical socialists seized the governments of Saxony and Thuringia. A Red uprising in Hamburg was put down only after vicious street fighting. In the Rhineland, separatists proclaimed an independent Rhenish Republic. Everywhere, it seemed, "things were falling apart." And nowhere was there more happiness than in Hitler's headquarters.

Destiny seemed to be calling him. But he was not quite sure. He got no clear message. For weeks he had talked loudly and often about overthrowing the government of "Jewish traitors" and "November Criminals." But he was disconcerted when militant veterans began to take him literally. They wanted action, and he was disappointing them. They began to mutter about the leader "who makes revolution with his mouth." In a secret session of Hitler's subsequent trial, Wilhelm Brückner, then the leader of the Munich Brownshirts and later Hitler's personal adjutant, testified, "I also personally told Hitler that the day was

---

* The tone and political bias of the city is shown in an incident recalled by Ernst Röhm, a right-wing militant and early supporter of Hitler who was later gunned down on his Führer's orders. "One day an alarmed statesman went up to the Police President [Ernst Pöhner] and whispered in his ear, 'Herr President, political murder organizations actually exist in this country!' Pöhner replied, 'Yes, I know—but not enough of them!' [*So, so, aber zu wenig!*]" Röhm, *Die Geschichte eines Hochveräters*, 7th ed. (Munich, 1934), 131.

near when I could no longer restrain the men. If nothing happened now, the men would drift away from him." [225]

Nor could Hitler be comforted by the memory of a promise he had recently made to the Bavarian minister of the interior. When the minister had called him to his office and expressed concern over rumors that he and his men were about to try to seize power, Hitler "jumped up from his chair, beat his breast, and cried: 'Herr Minister, I give you my word of honor, never as long as I live will I make a *Putsch*!' He repeated: 'My word of honor, I will never make a *Putsch*!' " [226] It was Hitler's first formal political promise.

Kahr was equally torn and embarrassed. He certainly did not want a revolution, but he needed to carry Freebooter support for his program of conservative restoration. He could not afford to let the angry veterans gravitate to Hitler. In the beginning of November, Kahr invited the leading nationalists of Bavaria and the Reich to a meeting which was to be held on 8 November 1923. It is not clear what Kahr intended, but Hitler was afraid that his rival was about to make a dramatic announcement—perhaps proclaim the restoration of the Wittelsbach monarchy. At any rate, the Nazi leader could not let the initiative pass to Kahr. After sleepless nights of indecision, he decided that the time had come to act "decisively" and with "ice-cold finality."

On the evening of 8 November 1923, Kahr addressed leading conservatives of Bavaria as they sat around the tables of the eminently respectable Bürgerbräukeller drinking beer. The pompous bureaucrat was reading falteringly and badly from a prepared manuscript. He had reached a passage asserting his opposition to Communism. As his voice droned on, the assembled dignitaries were startled by a commotion near the center of the hall. A ludicrous figure in an ill-fitting morning coat had jumped to a chair or table—the matter is in dispute —fired two shots into the ceiling, and with blazing eyes announced that the national revolution was taking place.

Hitler did not look like a revolutionary leader. Indeed, he did not cut a very imposing figure at all. Admiral von Hintze, the last Imperial secretary of state for foreign affairs, who was present at the beer hall that night, recalled that Hitler was "dressed in a morning coat, the most difficult of all garments to wear, let alone a badly cut morning coat, and let alone a man with as bad a figure as Hitler with his short legs and his long torso. When I saw him jump on the table in that ridiculous costume I thought, 'The poor little waiter!' " [227]

After firing his shots, Hitler rushed to the platform and at pistol point commanded the three most powerful men in Bavaria, Kahr, Lossow, and Seisser * to go with him to a side room. There he briskly

---

* Kahr, as noted, was the state commissioner general. General Otto von Lossow was commander of the Bavarian Reichrwehr Division. He was an affable, intelligent man with wry wit but little resolution. Colonel Hans Ritter von Seisser, commander of the Bavarian State Police, was a resolute and humorless person of independent mind and proven courage.

ordered a glass of beer for himself—at a cost of 500,000 inflated marks. (When he flung the glass away later in the evening, his devoted followers carefully picked up the shards and preserved them as relics.) He then turned to his hostages and either cajoled or threatened them into supporting him in the formation of a national government. He returned with them to the hall and announced that General Ludendorff, the hero and military dictator of the war years, would lead a new National Army; Hitler would take over the political leadership. Kahr, Lossow, and Seisser, along with other Bavarian rightists, would have positions of responsibility in his new administration. When each of the hostages spoke to the crowd and apparently supported him, Hitler was delighted. He reminded the historian Karl-Alexander von Müller of a little child "beaming with joy, overjoyed at his success; he had a childlike, frank expression of happiness I shall never forget." [228]

Hitler then launched into an oration which electrified the crowd of 3,000 people. He ended dramatically with the promise that "tomorrow will find either a nationalist government in Germany or us dead." Actually, on the morrow he would seek a third alternative. But for the moment his speech was effective, and a sullen and uncertain crowd was turned, as a listener described it, "inside out, like a glove." [229]

After this smashingly successful speech, Hitler sank into lethargy and into the strange, self-defeating behavior we shall examine more closely in the concluding chapter. He allowed the whole situation to disintegrate until it reached its disastrous climax. It was Ludendorff, not Hitler, who took the initiative in ordering a march on the center of the city for the next morning. The Führer was shamed into action. As his uncertain followers approached the Bavarian Provincial Police drawn up in front of the Odeonsplatz to stop them, Hitler suddenly hooked his arm in that of the person marching next to him. It was, as Heiden observed, "an astonishing gesture of uncertainty and helplessness." [230] After the usual "unknown shot," the police opened fire.

Once again, as so many times during the war, Hitler miraculously escaped death in the fusillade that killed about 20 people in his immediate vicinity. He either fell to the ground or was pulled down by the dying body of the man he had linked arms with. The place where he lay was very close to the stone Bavarian lions guarding the Feldherrenhalle—almost exactly the spot on which he had stood on that August day in 1914 to hail the coming of the war.

Hitler's immediate reaction was to run away—as he tended to do whenever a situation became intolerable. As a boy in Leonding, he had run away when the woods where he was playing cowboys and Indians were set on fire. At the age of 19, when relatives suggested that he take up some meaningful work after his mother's death, he ran away to Vienna. When his friend Kubizek successfully earned his diploma, Adolf Hitler hid from him; when he was threatened with arrest for desertion from the Austrian Army in 1913, he ran away to Munich. And at the end, in 1945, he sought escape in death.

The Child As Father to the Man

Now, on 9 November 1923, he did not—as the Nazis later claimed —heroically carry "a small boy out of the hail of fire," or try to rally the resistance.[231] At the first opportunity, he jumped into a little yellow—or was it red?—Fiat belonging to an SA doctor and ran away to hide in the attic of Ernst Hanfstaengl's country home on Lake Staffel, about 35 miles south of Munich. He must have been experiencing considerable physical and mental pain, for the prison doctor at Landsberg, Dr. Brinsteiner, stated in a report on 8 January 1924:

> During the Putsch of 8 November, Hitler suffered a dislocation of the left shoulder with a fracture of the upper arm socket. And subsequently from very painful traumatic neurosis [*eine traumatische Neurose*]. Hitler continues to be under continual medical treatment and will probably continue to suffer partial stiffening and painful effects in the left shoulder. It is not expected, however, that he will lose motor functions.[232]

When he arrived in the Hanfstaengl home the night of 9 November he was, according to Mrs. Hanfstaengl, completely despondent and "almost incoherent." He wanted to be left alone, and spent the next day hiding in the attic under two English blankets, one of which Hanfstaengl treasured for decades as a kind of relic. He kept threatening suicide until Mrs. Hanfstaengl disarmed him and threw his pistol into a barrel of flour she was hoarding. On 11 November he surrendered to the Bavarian police while screaming threats of revenge.[233]

After the fiasco of Hitler's first attempt to seize power, observers generally agreed that his movement had collapsed. But as the American military attaché in Munich, Captain Truman Smith, reported, "Only a miracle could save him, but the miracle happened." [234] The miracle was the way Hitler extricated himself by making brilliant use of his trial for high treason in late February and March 1924. He was given every assistance by the court. The prosecuting attorney, a man by the name of Stenglein, sounded very much like the defense attorney as he called Hitler an admirable person, a brave soldier, and a selfless patriot who had broken the law only because he had been driven to do so by the enthusiasm of so many supporters: "We cannot reproach him with selfishness. His actions were not prompted by personal ambition but enthusiasm for the cause. . . . We cannot deny him our respect." The judge nodded sympathetic agreement. Hitler was in command throughout. As the transcript of the trial shows, he kept interrupting and haranguing government witnesses so loudly that the judge on several occasions plaintively asked if he could not perhaps lower his voice.[235]

Hitler's final plea was a masterpiece of invective, serving as a harbinger of orations to come. He spoke for four hours. When the judge was later asked why the defendant was given such liberty, he replied that he found it impossible to interrupt the swell of Hitler's patriotic oratory. Instead of accepting the role of defendant charged with treason against the state, Hitler put the entire government of the republic in the dock, accusing President Ebert and Chancellor Scheidemann and all their supporters of high treason against Germany.

In this most important speech in which he was fighting for his political life, Hitler's thoughts turned to Wagner and to mothers. He aspired, he said, to no special title: "As I stood for the first time at Wagner's grave, my heart overflowed with pride that here lay a man who had forbidden it to be written: 'Here lies Privy Counselor Music Director, His Excellency Baron Richard von Wagner.'" His final appeal involved mothers. The deed of 8–9 November, he proclaimed, could not be considered a failure. The only possible way he himself could have looked upon it that way would have been if "a mother had come to me and said. 'Herr Hitler, you have my son on your conscience.' No mother came to me." Which is to say, his own mother did not blame him; his own conscience was clear. Indeed, at the end of the speech a mother figure—once more appearing as a benevolent goddess—smiled benignly upon him. He turned to the judge and said:

> You may pronounce us guilty a thousand times, but the Goddess of the Eternal Court of History will smilingly tear up the indictment of the prosecutor and the verdict of the judges and set us free! [236]

At the close of the trial, thousands upon thousands of supporters jammed in front of the Ministry of Justice. In a preview of coming years, they kept yelling "Heil Hitler!" until he appeared on a balcony to accept their homage. Overnight the obscure Munich street agitator, who had failed so lamentably a few months before, had become a national hero and martyr to the cause of a resurgent Germany.

His sentence was about what could be expected from the sympathetic court system of the Weimar Republic. He was not deported to Austria, as the law for treason clearly required; a judge ruled that though technically he might be an Austrian, he certainly *thought* like a German." Formally he was sentenced to five years of fortress confinement at Landsberg am Lech; actually he served less than nine months, from 1 April to 20 December 1924.

Hitler in Prison

With the approval of indulgent guards, Hitler's suite in the Landsberg fortress, which he shared with Rudolf Hess, was converted into what was laconically called "the first Brown House"—the later headquarters of the Nazi Party. Party emblems, pictures, and a huge swastika covered the walls. The state's attorney made a special concession on 3 December 1923: "Hitler's shepherd dog may be present during interviews." He was permitted to read or talk until midnight and to sleep late in the morning. His breakfast was served in bed by regular prisoners who were assigned as his servants. He dictated the memoirs which were to make him wealthy. He wrote editorials and drew cartoons for the prison newspaper, the *Landsberger Ehrenbürger*; these issues have regrettably been lost.[237]

On his 35th birthday (20 April 1924), military airplanes circled the fortress and dipped their wings in salute to Hitler. Hanfstaengl, who called to congratulate him on the day, found that "the place looked like a delicatessen store. You could have opened up a flower and fruit and wine shop with all the stuff stacked there. People were sending presents from all over Germany, and Hitler had grown visibly fatter as a result." When it was suggested that he really ought to participate in the prison games to take off excess weight, Hitler replied, "No. I keep away from them. It would be bad for discipline if I took part in physical training. A leader cannot afford to be beaten at games." [238]

On the day of Hitler's release, 20 December 1924, Putzi Hanfstaengl arranged a quiet celebration dinner in his new Munich home in the Pienzenauerstrasse in the fashionable Bogenhausen District of Munich. Hitler arrived in his bourgeois blue serge suit, now pulled tight by the weight he had added at Landsberg. In this moment of apparent triumph, Hitler was ill at ease. His first thought was of Wagner—and of death. "Hanfstaengl, play me the *Liebestod*!" he said. Hanfstaengl obliged by hammering out with his huge hands Hitler's favorite aria from *Tristan und Isolde*. After a banquet ending with his favorite Austrian pastries, Hitler was in high good humor and started his imitations. Striding diagonally across the room, he talked of war and his memories of the Western Front and began imitating artillery barrages: "He could reproduce the noise of every imaginable gun, German, French or English, Howitzers, 75's, machine guns, separately and all at once. . . . We really went through about five minutes of the battle of the Somme." The virtuosity of the performance suggests that he had rehearsed his imitations many times. He enjoyed the adulation of an audience. It was also on this—or perhaps a later occasion—that Putzi did piano portraits of leading Nazis: quiet runs for Himmler sneaking across the carpet; ponderous passages for the heavy Göring; limping, fractured melodies to imitate the club-footed Goebbels. Hitler, who always enjoyed the infirmities of others, found it all terribly funny. He covered his mouth and bad teeth with his hand and shook with laughter.[239]

Reassertion

The political situation Hitler faced after returning from Landsberg was not so amusing. His political movement, officially dissolved by government decree, was rent by a dozen petty feuds. He had no party. Yet within ten years (1924–1934) he had crushed all opposition and had become undisputed leader of National Socialism and dictator of the German nation. It was a political feat matched in modern history only by Lenin's triumph in the decade from 1908–1918, when he moved from the position of outcast wanderer in Stockholm, Berne, and Zurich to become master of the Kremlin and ruler of Soviet Russia.

The two men had much in common. Both had more than a touch of political genius. Both met Machiavelli's requirement for the ideal Prince: each was part lion, part fox, combining commitment with cunning. Both were "terrible simplifiers" who were masters of propaganda. Lenin, like Hitler, was sustained by faith in himself. He, too, had the capacity to convince.

A quirk of fate had brought them both to Munich, where both had lived in Schwabing in the Schleissheimerstrasse. A dozen years before Hitler arrived, Lenin had rented a room up the street from Popp's tailor shop at 106, above a cabinet maker. There, in 1902, he had written the most important political pamphlet of the 20th century, *What Is to Be Done?* In it he inverted Marx and set forth in clear and specific prose how a political elite of professional revolutionaries could seize power and determine the economic and social structure of a country and the world. Both men had bought their bread at Herr Heilmann's bakery. Lenin, too, had eaten meals in the Osteria Bavaria and had drunk beer at the Hofbräuhaus, the scene of Hitler's early party triumphs.*

Hitler's reassertion of power over the Party in 1924 was achieved not only through political acumen, dedication, and faith in himself, but also by the cultivation of influential friends. Captain Ernst Röhm, for example, was of inestimable value for his connections with the army, disgruntled veterans, and former members of the Free Corps. Dietrich Eckart, probably the most influential intellectual in southern Germany, became Hitler's patron and introduced him to racist circles. Eckart, as we have noted, had established a racist-nationalist journal, *Auf gut Deutsch* (In Plain German), which he edited until he took over Hitler's own newspaper, the *Völkischer Beobachter*, in 1921. Like Hitler, Eckart had been heavily influenced by Lanz-Liebenfels; and he too had a simple solution for the "Jewish problem." The best thing to do with the Jews, he said, was to load them all in railway boxcars "and dump them into the Red Sea." In an issue of *Auf gut Deutsch* of March

---

* In 1960 the ancient but still spry little man who had been Lenin's landlord recalled in conversation that his famous tenant had always been polite, kind to children in the block, gallant to the ladies, and prompt with his rent. He worked very hard and seldom took time off to relax. One evening, however, he and Krupskaya joined the landlord and his wife for a convivial evening in the Hofbräuhaus. Lenin laughed and nudged his wife as they all linked arms and sang the old drinking song, "In München steht 'n Hofbräuhaus . . ." as they raised their liter steins decorated with the crown of Bavaria and the initials HB. But Lenin was not toasting the royal brewery. He was drinking to a different H.B.: the letters in Russian are the initials of N.V.—*Narodnaya Volya*, the revolutionary "will of the people." Lenin was illustrating Axelrod's comment that the reason Lenin excelled all other Russian revolutionaries was this: "He is the only one of us who works at revolution twenty-four hours a day: the twenty hours he's awake; the four hours he is sleeping when he dreams of revolution"—and, one might add, the few hours he spent drinking beer.

The Child As Father to the Man

1920, Eckart had asserted his faith in the coming of a powerful Teutonic leader, but he was uncertain who he would be:

> A Cincinnatus was called from his plow to save his Fatherland . . . whether it will be a soldier or a farmer or a worker who will come to lead us doesn't matter. All he needs is a soul—a bold, selfless, German soul. . . . Do not ask where: believe!

A year later, January 1921, Eckart had found the leader he and Germany craved, a new German Cincinnatus: "Of such stuff is Hitler, the passionate leader of the German Workers' Party." [240]

Hitler was genuinely grateful for Eckart's patronage. Of all the people to whom he was indebted, he paid special tribute only to Wagner and Eckart, going to the unusual length of dedicating the second volume of his memoirs to "that man, who, as one of the best, by words and by thoughts and finally by deeds, dedicated his life to the awakening of his, of our nation: Dietrich Eckart." [241] And in private conversation he referred to him as the "loyal Ekkehard," his one true friend. Hitler's secretaries concluded that "Dietrich Eckart [was] the single person in his life he . . . looked up to." [242] They should also have included Richard Wagner.

Another of Hitler's political assets was his ability to convince many different people that each alone enjoyed the special confidence of the Führer. All in the end were deceived, for Hitler could give himself in confidence and in trust to no human being. From infancy on, his life was characterized by basic distrust of others. In this—as in many other things—the child was father to the man. As Führer he so distrusted others that he made sure his thoughts were concealed from his closest advisers. And when he began to suspect that someone might be penetrating his defenses, he would reinforce them through deliberate dissimulation.

In an interview after the war, General Halder, the perceptive and intelligent Chief of the General Staff, remembered the following revealing conversation with Hitler:

> Hitler: You should take note of one thing from the start, that *you will never discover my thought and intentions* until I am giving my orders.
> Halder: We soldiers are accustomed to forming our ideas together.
> Hitler: (smiling and with a negative wave of his hand) No. Things are done differently in politics. *You will never learn what I am thinking and those who boast most loudly that they know my thought, to such people I lie even more.*[243]

This quality of distrust, aloofness, and impenetrability, so important to his psyche, was of considerable political advantage. True, in the long run—as we shall see—it would work against him; but in his rise to power it helped him play to perfection the role of the inaccessible and infallible Leader operating in a realm far removed from petty political or personal squabbles.

Aloofness was coupled with another characteristic of inestimable value. Hitler, like Lenin, possessed in abundance that indefinable but essential quality of political leadership which Max Weber called charisma. But there was one significant advantage the Nazi dictator had over his Communist counterparts: Hitler's theory institutionalized personal charisma in a way that Weber never contemplated and Lenin and Stalin could never practice.

The adroit use of personal charisma was of crucial importance to Hitler's success in the years following 1924. Rudolf Hess put the matter in a sentence: "Adolf Hitler is the Party; the Party is Adolf Hitler." This statement of fanatical adoration and hard political fact was made at the victorious Nazi Party rally at Nuremberg in 1934, after Hitler had consolidated his power over Germany. But the principle of the myth-person had been a political fact of life under Hitler ever since his return from Landsberg in 1924. It shines as a clear and guiding light through the entire labyrinth of political squabbles during that decade. We can clearly see it in operation in three notable instances.

While Hitler was imprisoned, two wings of the Party started to grow: the more conservative group called itself the Greater German People's Community, while the majority of the more revolutionary members formed the National Socialist Freedom Party. But neither of these groups was a threat to Hitler because neither could exist without venerating his person as the Führer. Hitler merely waited for an opportune moment to dissolve both of them, and their members then reaffirmed their allegiance to him. Problem solved.

The practical impossibility of successful factionalism within the Nazi party was again shown in 1926 when there developed the so-called "Northern Faction" of the "Working Association" of Gregor Strasser and Joseph Goebbels. Historians who assert that these groups were directed against Hitler are mistaken. "Nothing was further from their minds than challenging Hitler's leadership. Hitler remained the only concrete point of unity in the heterogeneous movement. He was above the conflicts, and he was regarded 'as something mystical, unreal.' " [244] Gregor Strasser, it is true, left the Party in 1932 and was murdered in the Blood Purge two years later. But he remained loyal to Hitler. A few days before he was shot on Hitler's orders, he had received from his Führer's hands the golden *Ehrenzeichen* of the Party. His statement that Hitler was "the unchallenged and sole leader of the NSDAP" was both an expression of personal loyalty and a realistic appraisal of a fact of life in Hitler's party.

Again, in the better known and bloodier incident of 1934 variously called the "Röhm Revolt," the "Blood Purge," and the "Night of the Long Knives," Röhm and his followers in the SA may have disagreed with their Führer's social policies, but they had no intention whatever of leading a revolt to seize power from him. Hitler himself, for political reasons, had manufactured the rumors of rebellion. He knew that the military and industrial leadership of Germany was alarmed by radical social ideas which were spreading through the SA. Since he needed the support of influential conservatives in order to gain power after the death of Field Marshal–President Hindenburg, he decided to placate them by sacrificing hundreds of his old comrades. Röhm and the SA remained loyal to Hitler throughout. Indeed, many of them believed they were dying for him in an SS plot engineered by Göring and Himmler against Röhm and Hitler. Gunned down by Hitler's orders, they shouted "Heil Hitler!" defiantly to their executioners as they died.

In no important instance was factionalism within the Nazi Party a serious threat to Hitler's position or a danger to the unity of the Nazi movement. Indeed, Hitler actually encouraged factions for two reasons. First, they represented diverse classes and interests which Hitler needed to cultivate. Röhm—at least up to 1934!—had attracted the veterans and Free Corps fighters; Strasser appealed to many Socialists; Baldur von Schirach was attractive to the youth. Second, Hitler encouraged factionalism because he discovered that his refusal to commit himself to any one group increased his authority over all. Each faction sought to outdo its competitor in the homage it paid to him. Once a faction failed to win Hitler's personal stamp of approval, it was finished, for it had no other court of appeal.[245]

LIFE-STYLE OF THE FÜHRER

There were obvious political advantages in leadership by personal charisma, aloofness, and delay in making policy decisions. But Hitler also liked the method because it suited his lifestyle. Once the *Führerprinzip* was firmly established by 1925, political leadership required a minimum of effort on his part. Hitler did not allow politics to interrupt the routine of his private life. It is true that upon occasion—such as the leadership crisis of 1921, the Reichstag elections of 1932, or the Blood Purge of 1934—he could show bursts of energy. Generally, however, he preferred a lazier pace. His personal habits as Party Führer and chancellor did not change very much from his adolescent years when, after the death of his demanding father, he enjoyed the life of a dilettante with Kubizek in Linz and Vienna. Now, as then, he slept late and occupied most of his day with desultory talk, picnics, excursions, and other diversions. After leaving Landsberg, he returned to his tiny apartment above a *Drogerie* at 41 Thierschstrasse. As a marble plaque in the wall during the Nazi period proclaimed, "Adolf Hitler lived in this house from 1 May 1920 to 5 October 1929." The main room was about nine by ten feet, the floor was covered with worn linoleum and a few scatter rugs. There were a chair, a table, a makeshift bookcase, and, above the bed, his mother's picture. The room was small, but there was space for him to stride diagonally back and forth in carpet slippers as he solved the problems of the day.

Increasingly, however, Hitler spent his time in the neighborhood of Berchtesgaden in the Bavarian Alps close to the Austrian border. First he stayed at the Pension Moritz, then in Berchtesgaden itself in a hotel, the Deutsches Haus. Here he finished the second volume of *Mein Kampf* and wrote newspaper articles. As he later recalled, "I lived there like a fighting cock. . . . I wrote the second volume of my book. I was very fond of visiting the *Dreimädlerhaus*, where there were always pretty girls. This was a great treat for me. There was one of them especially who was a real beauty." [246]

In 1928 he began renting a house high in the mountains with a commanding view of the Obersalzberg. A few years later he bought the property, had it completely rebuilt, and called it his *Berghof* (Mountain Farm). Expensive furnishings were contributed by his motherly benefactors, Frau Hélène Bechstein, widow of the piano manufacturer, and Frau Winifred Wagner. Among the gifts were rare porcelain, books (including the complete works of Richard Wagner), and a manuscript page of *Lohengrin*.[247] During this period he also changed his residence in Munich, moving into an impressive nine-room apartment at 16 Prinzregentenplatz in the fashionable Bogenhausen part of town, a household which he maintained until his death. Here he was near two of his favorite artists. The villa von Stuck was just down the street, as was the *Prinzregententheater,* built in 1900–1901 especially for Richard Wagner, whose marble statue dominates its gardens.

He could afford these luxuries because his finances had improved, thanks, in large part, to social connections. As Ernst Hanfstaengl recalled with considerable pride, "Mine was the first Munich family of standing into which he was introduced." He brought Hitler into the "best" society—at any rate, people of influence and money. They included the family of Fritz-August von Kaulbach, the Bavarian artist, and the Bruckmanns, wealthy Munich publishers who had among their authors Houston Stewart Chamberlain. Elsa Bruckmann, the former Princess Cantacuzéne, a considerably older woman, made something of a protégé of Hitler, as did Gertrude von Seidlitz and yet another older women, Carola Hoffmann, who called herself "Hitler's Mommy" (*Hitlers Mutti*). Frau Bechstein, who called Hitler "my little wolf," also developed a motherly interest in him. She wanted her daughter Lotte to marry the charming Austrian.

The value of wealthy female admirers is shown graphically in the inventory Hitler used as security for a loan in the summer of 1923. For an undisclosed purpose, he borrowed 60,000 Swiss francs from the coffee magnate Richard Frank of the Korn-Frank Company in Berlin. The note reads:

> As security for the loan, Herr Adolf Hitler transfers to Herr Richard Frank valuables to the banking house of Heinrich Eckert in Munich . . . the following . . . articles of value: 1 emerald pendant with platinum and diamonds and platinum chain . . . one platinum ruby ring with diamonds . . . one sapphire ring in platinum with diamonds . . . one solitaire diamond ring . . . one 14-carat gold ring . . . one seventeenth century Venetian lace, hand made, 6½ meters long, 11½ centimeters wide . . . one red silk Spanish piano shawl with gold stitching (size 4 × 4 meters). . . .[248]

Hitler's income tax statements filed with the Munich Finance Office for the years 1925–1935 fail to do justice to his style of life.[249] They do, however, reveal something about the personality of the man filing the return. It is clear, for example, that the political leader who paraded his patriotism did not make the personal sacrifices he demanded of his countrymen and was not averse to cheating the government of tax revenue. In May 1925, for example, he reported no income whatever for 1924 and the first quarter of 1925. Yet in February 1925 he was somehow able to buy a custom-built, supercharged Mercedes.

Hitler tended to lump tax collectors, judges, clergymen, and prostitutes together as the dregs of society. But with regard to his own taxes, he had little to complain about. Officials never investigated his actual income and with surprising equanimity accepted all his declarations as valid. Later, the delicate question of the Führer's back taxes from sales of *Mein Kampf* was solved by declaring him exempt from taxation.

Hitler's income from *Mein Kampf* served as a negative barometer of the Weimar Republic. Sales went down as prospects for democracy improved; they went up with the economic and political crisis of 1930. After Hitler came to power, when it was advisable for everyone to own the book—if not to read it—the author's income skyrocketed. He was quite accurate in announcing in 1943 that his book was right next to the Bible in total sales, having finally overtaken Grimm's Fairy Stories.

Hitler's valets, secretaries, and other associates have given a clear picture of the daily pattern of his life after he became chancellor, which did not differ significantly from patterns established during the previous decade. Normally he began getting up between 11 o'clock and noon. His valet (Karl Wilhelm Krause, 1934–1939; Heinz Linge, 1939–1945) watched for the first signal: an arm clad in a nightgown would be seen reaching out to the chair outside his bedroom door for morning newspapers and important telegrams and messages. The arm would quickly withdraw as its owner returned to bed to read his papers. Hitler would bathe and shave himself, always using two blades for each shave. One hour after the first signal, if Hitler did not feel like playing his dressing game, his valet would knock on the door and say, *"Guten Morgen, mein Führer. Es ist Zeit!"*

Breakfast consisted of milk, rusks, peppermint or camomile tea, sometimes an apple and cheese. (After 1944 he added chocolates to his breakfast menu.) Lunch, at two or three or four o'clock, if eaten at home, consisted of vegetable soup. Very often he would take his lunches either at the Cafe Heck at the Hofgarten or at the Osteria Bavaria. When he ate out, lunches could last for three or four hours. What was left of the afternoon was spent in dictating speeches or making decisions or going on picnics. Suppers would usually begin at about ten o'clock and last until very late. They were followed almost invariably by movies and more talk, so that the day ended anytime from three o'clock to six o'clock in the morning. (After Stalingrad he often took one or two glasses of beer before going to bed in order to induce sleep.)

His press adjutant of many years recalled that Hitler spent dozens of hours a week in automobile travel: "He constantly sought pretexts for moving from place to place. Up to 1939 he was everywhere and nowhere at home. . . . He covered hundreds of thousands of kilometers by automobile and kept his adjutants busy planning his private journeys." [250]

Hitler was fond of designing office desks, but he seldom used them. At the Party headquarters, an associate recalled, "the desk was empty and the room had the atmosphere of one that had never been used. I had the same impression in all of Hitler's offices—in his apartment, in the Braunhaus, and in the Chancellery. Never have I seen him working at his desk. Desks were for him only decorations. Never did he keep office hours. 'If you want to meet Hitler you must go about three o'clock to the Cafe Heck, Hess called to me.' " [251] Oswald Spengler, who was at first attracted to Hitler as one of his men of destiny but was soon disabused, told a German psychiatrist just before he died: "If Hitler is not defeated by anything else he will be defeated by this: he cannot really work." [252]

As early as 1923 a close associate had become disturbed by Hitler's luxurious life-style and slovenly work habits. He wrote a warning letter telling him that many of the old Party comrades felt he was deserting the working class for the champagne and caviar set to which "Mister" Hanfstaengl had introduced him. The writer, Gottfried Feder, continued, "I certainly don't begrudge you the leisure time you spend away from your demanding work in the company of artists and the circle of beautiful women. But there is an urgent necessity of filling the gap between you as leader of those who wish to be your followers and a movement for German freedom." The writer went on to complain, "We never see you personally," and repeated his charge about "the anarchy of the allocation of your time." [253]

But Hitler could not or would not break the habit patterns of his youth. There was a brief change just after he became chancellor, when he had his office in the Wilhelmstrasse very close to that of the old Field Marshal–President von Hindenburg. While he was under the watchful eye of Hindenburg, Hitler felt—as he had with his own father—that he must toe the mark. His press attaché, Otto Dietrich, recalls that while Hindenburg was alive Hitler was punctual and even held cabinet meetings in the morning. But as soon as "the Old Gentleman" died he reverted to the life-style he had adopted after the death of his "Herr Vater."

Albert Speer was appalled by the sheer waste of time. Hour after hour and day after day of planning fantastic buildings; hundreds of picnics and pleasure trips in his car; fatuous nightly soliloquies filled with trivia about theater and diet and the training of dogs and misconceptions of history; one or two movies a night, followed by conversations of the most striking mediocrity. Speer himself often called on Hitler once or twice a week at midnight and, after the last movie run, chattered about art until three or four in the morning. After thus cataloguing the empty hours, Speer asks a sensible question: "When, I would often ask myself, did he really work?" [254]

HITLER'S LOVE AFFAIRS

During all these years, Hitler's relations with women continued to be influenced by his love for the woman whose picture hung over his bed in all his bedrooms. All his serious affairs involved mother substitutes who played the role of Klara to Adolf's Alois. Each of these women was as young in relation to Hitler as Klara had been in relation to her husband. In each case Hitler seems to have been attracted to the young woman because there was something else about her that reminded him of his mother. And in each case, there were manifestations of the sadomasochism which, to his mind, characterized his parents' relationship to each other.

Mimi Reiter

The memory of his vicarious adolescent love affair with Stefanie faded slowly over the years. There is no reliable record of Hitler's interest in a woman until 1926, when he was 37 years old. Then, while staying in the lovely Alpine village of Berchtesgaden, he was attracted by a pretty blond girl who clerked in her mother's dress shop on the ground floor of his hotel. She was 16. Her name was Maria Reiter, though Hitler, who preferred Austrian diminutives, called her Mimi, Mizzi, or Mizerl.[255]

They had met while walking their dogs. Hitler was drawn to her for several reasons besides their common interest in animals. Her light blue eyes, she remembers him saying, reminded him of his mother's. And when her mother suddenly died, Hitler was quick to point out that he too had "suffered terribly" at his own mother's death and had also been left an orphan at the age of 16. (Actually, at 18.) Hitler also found it more than coincidental that Mimi had been born on the anniversary of the day his mother had been buried. He kept thinking of his mother.

For a long time Hitler could not summon the courage to ask her for a date. Finally, he sent an aide to inquire if she and her sister would go with Hitler and his friend for a walk. Mimi refused but accepted a second invitation, also made formally and through an intermediary, to attend a Hitler speech at the hotel Deutsches Haus. He was anxious that she hear him give an oration.

Mimi was acutely uncomfortable during the course of his passionate harangue. She remembered that he "kept looking over at our table and fixed his eyes directly on me." When she later told an anxious Hitler that she had enjoyed his speech, he was as happy as could be, and immediately began addressing her in language normally reserved for children. He then took his fork and playfully fed her cake as if she were a little child. Suddenly he became very serious, spoke gently of her mother's death, and asked if he could go with her to the grave.

That evening they walked their dogs. When Hitler's Alsatian refused to obey him, he gave a demonstration of his idea of masculinity, mastery, and power by brutally whipping the animal. Later that night, when she refused his request for a good-night kiss, he was furious but kept his anger under control. Again he demonstrated his masculinity: he drew himself up to his full height, thrust out his arm stiffly in the Nazi salute, and said in a deep voice, "Heil Hitler!"

On their second double date, they went for a ride in Hitler's impressive supercharged Mercedes. Mimi recalled that Hitler sat in the back seat with her and "kept wanting to close my eyes with his fingers, saying that I should sleep and dream." He assured her that he would watch over her carefully. (Was he watching her as he had watched over and sketched his dead mother after he had gently closed her staring eyes with his fingers?)

On the third date, in the graveyard, Hitler said something Mimi was never able to forget or to understand. As he stared down at her mother's grave he muttered, "I am not like that yet! [*Ich bin noch nicht so weit!*]" He then gripped his riding whip tightly in his hands and said, "I would like you to call me Wolf."

On another occasion the two went for a walk in the woods where they "romped like children." Then Hitler grew very serious and led her to a huge fir tree:

> He placed me in front of it, turned me left and right. He stepped back and warned me to stay perfectly still like an artist's model.

Then he dropped his arms, silently shook his head as if there were something he could not comprehend. . . . "A magnificent picture!" he exclaimed. . . . He stood back about ten paces from me. . . . He looked at my legs and at my face. His gaze went up to the top of the tree behind me. Then he stretched both arms out beckoning me to him. "Do you know who you are now? Now you are my woodland sprite [*Waldfee*]."

When Mimi laughed and asked what that was supposed to mean, Hitler interrupted her sternly: "That you will understand much better later, Mimi my child. You must never laugh at me!" He then smothered her with kisses and said, "Child, I could just squeeze you to bits now at this very minute!"

The stories of Hitler's affair with a teen-aged girl did little to help him politically, and he suddenly broke off his relations with Mimi in 1928. That same year she tried to kill herself by hanging. After recovering, she married a hotelkeeper in Seefeld.

Years passed, and late in 1931 or early 1932, Hitler sent an emissary, Rudolf Hess, to ask her to come to visit him. She packed her bags, left her husband, and spent one memorable night with Hitler in his apartment in the Prinzregentenplatz. She later recalled "I let him do whatever he wanted with me. [*Ich liess alles mit mir geschehen.*]" Hitler promised her anything if she would be his mistress but flatly refused the marriage she demanded. Once again in 1934 she came to him; they relived the experience of that earlier night, but again he refused to marry her. They never saw each other again. Maria divorced her first husband and, in 1936, married an SS officer named Kubisch. Hitler sent her 100 red roses in 1940 when her husband was killed in battle.

She never heard from him again, but she kept his letters and the wristwatch he gave her for her birthday, 23 December, the day his mother had been buried.

Geli Raubal

Hitler often told intimates that there was only one woman he really loved or could possibly have married: his niece, Geli Raubal.

After he had moved into his large Munich apartment during the fall of 1929, he asked his half-sister Angela, who years before had been his little substitute mother, to come and be his housekeeper. She arrived with her two daughters. One of them, also named Angela but called "Geli" by everyone, caught his eye. She was much younger than he— about as young as his mother had been when she married his father. And just as his own parents had called each other "uncle" and "niece," Hitler asked Geli to call him "Uncle Alfi"; he always referred to her as "my niece Geli." He was pleased to notice that, like his mother, she was a deeply religious person who attended mass regularly.

There is almost universal agreement about Geli's personal qualities. The leader of the Nazi Youth Movement and his wife, who knew her well, found her to be sweet, unaffected, "irresistibly charming." Hitler's chauffeur said she was "a princess . . . people in the street would turn around to take another look at her—though people don't do that in Munich." Hitler's close associate and official photographer remembered her as "an enchantress":

> In her artless way and without the slightest suspicion of coquetry she succeeded by her mere presence in putting everybody in the best of good spirits. . . . Geli was deeply revered, indeed worshipped, by her uncle. . . . To him she was the personification of perfect young womanhood—beautiful, fresh and unspoiled, gay, intelligent, as clean and straight as God had made her. He watched and gloated over her like some servant with a rare and lovely bloom, and to cherish and protect her was his one and only concern.[256]

The one jarring note in this symphony of praise is struck by Hanfstaengl. For some reason he despised her:

> She was an empty-headed little slut, with the coarse sort of bloom of a servant girl without either brains or character. She was perfectly content to preen herself in her fine clothes, and certainly never gave any impression of reciprocating Hitler's twisted tenderness.[257]

Everyone, including Hanfstaengl, agreed that Hitler was completely captivated by the girl. He became irrationally jealous and watched over her constantly, regulating her life, choosing her clothes and the company she could keep. He went everywhere with her, accompanying her on window-shopping trips, excursions, and picnics, and to movies and the opera. When he was with her, one observer noted, he became a different person, invariably happy, relaxed, gentle; another found that "she made him act like a seventeen year old." Geli became for him—as Stefanie had once been—"the complete embodiment of his ideal of womanhood." [258]

It seems clear, however, that Geli did not reciprocate her famous uncle's feelings. A close observer admitted that he was baffled by the relationship, but there was "something very unusual about it which made a life together unbearable for her." Another, who claimed to have been her confidant, testified that she was desperately unhappy because she could not bring herself to do "what he wants me to." [259] That life with Hitler had become quite literally unbearable to her became apparent in late afternoon of 18 September 1931: Geli shot herself with Hitler's 6.35 Walther pistol. The wound was near her heart; she slowly bled to death.

The Child As Father to the Man

To all her friends, the suicide seemed incomprehensible. Geli was not a brooding, remorseful, or hysterical person. She was an attractive young woman who was, to all appearances, looking forward to a trip to Vienna where her uncle had finally allowed her to go to take music lessons. The note she left behind in her room only deepens the mystery of her death. It was addressed to a young friend in Vienna and ends:

When I come to Vienna—hopefully very soon—we'll drive together to Semmering, an . . .

She never added the final "d" to the *und*.[260]

Geli's sudden and apparently inexplicable death has challenged the imagination of contemporaries and later historians. Hitler attempted to stop some of the ugly rumors by making statements to newspapers. The *Münchener Post* reported in its edition of 22 September 1931 that it had received the following statement from Adolf Hitler: " 'It is untrue that I and my niece had a quarrel on Friday 18 September; it is untrue that I was violently opposed to my niece going to Vienna; it is untrue that my niece was engaged to someone in Vienna and I forbade it.' " [261]

Hanfstaengl claimed that Geli killed herself after "a flaming row" with Hitler after he discovered that "she was pregnant by a young Jewish art teacher from Linz." But another intimate gave a very different story. He testified that the physician who examined Geli's body said she had died a virgin.[262]

Others darkly suspected not suicide but murder, committed, in the most popular account, by Heinrich Himmler who—for undisclosed reasons—saw Geli as a threat to his ascendancy within the Party. Still others, including the redoubtable Greiner, had Hitler—though in Nuremberg at the time—somehow spirit himself back to his Munich apartment to pull the trigger.[263]

All responsible evidence, however, indicates that Geli died by her own hand. While historians must guess at the reasons for her suicide, there can be no doubt whatever that Hitler was shattered by the news. As soon as he heard it, he hurried back from a political trip to Nuremberg and spent two days in isolation. He and a close associate went to a Party member's summer home on the Tegern Lake and there, as he would do in moments of turmoil throughout his life, he paced the floor:

In my own room I stood in the window, listening to the dull rhythmic sound of the pacing feet over my head. Hour after hour, ceaselessly and without pause, it continued. Night came, and I still could hear him, pacing up and down, up and down. . . . And so it continued, hour after endless hour, throughout the long night. . . .
He spent another day pacing and then drove all night until he

arrived at the Vienna Central Cemetery where he stayed thirty minutes alone by the grave.[264]

For a week he seemed on the brink of total collapse. Over and over again he said that he must give up politics, that he would never look at another woman, that his career was ruined, that he must kill himself. Geli became for him a kind of personal cult. He locked the door to her room and would allow no one to enter except Frau Winter, the motherly servant who was instructed never to change anything in the room but daily to place a bunch of fresh chrysanthemums there. He commissioned a bust and portraits to be made from a variety of photographs. Along with portraits of his mother, he kept a portrait or a bust of Geli in every one of his bedrooms. In his entourage there was an unwritten rule that no one was ever to mention her name. And when Hitler himself spoke of her, tears would come to his eyes. Years later, during the Nuremberg trials, Hermann Göring told a defense attorney that Geli's death had had such a devastating effect on Hitler that it had changed his relationship to all other people.

One can only wonder at the reason for Hitler's extraordinarily intense reaction. With the single exception of his mother's death, no other event in his personal life had hit him so hard. One of Hitler's assistant valets, Willie Schneider, recalled that for many years after the death of Geli, Hitler spent Christmas Eve alone in the room where she had died.[265] That is to say, he stayed in the death room in Munich just as in Linz, years earlier, he had spent Christmastime watching over the corpse of his mother. Thus, it seems likely that the loss of Geli was so overwhelming to Hitler because in her death he suffered anew the death of Klara.

Eva Braun

One day in 1930, Hitler wandered into the Schwabing photography studio of Heinrich Hoffmann, an avid Nazi who had joined the Party in 1929 and was rapidly becoming wealthy as a result of the monopoly he enjoyed on all official photography done for the movement. Hitler struck up a conversation with Hoffmann's new employee, Eva Braun, who served as a clerk and photographer's model. Thus began Hitler's most publicized love affair.

Eva had a kind of "impersonal chocolate-box type of prettiness" and an attractive, if slightly plump, figure which occupied her daily attention. She seemed to Hitler to be just the right age: at 18 she was 23 years younger than he. And her eyes were exactly the color he always found compelling. A friend called them "limpid, porcelain blue"—exactly the color of Klara Hitler's.

Not everyone was impressed with Eva. Her employer considered her "frivolous, vain, feather-brained, inconsequential . . . flattered and thrilled beyond words at the attention and compliments which this rising power in the land was paying her." One of Hitler's physicians thought her "cheap, arrogant and selfish," but always compliant and sweet in Hitler's presence.[266]

Hitler showed only intermittent interest in Eva until she tried to commit suicide. On 11 August 1932 she shot herself over the heart, as Geli Raubal had almost a year earlier. Hitler at first suspected that she was faking the act to gain his attention, but when the surgeon, a Doctor Plate, assured him that she had come, quite literally, within an inch of her life, Hitler was favorably impressed; he began to see a good deal of her.

Their relationship was not so placid as has sometimes been pictured. Eva attempted suicide once more in May 1935, this time with 20 tablets of Vanodorm. She was saved at the last minute by her sister Ilse, a medical technician.[267] After this second effort, Hitler took her seriously. He set her up in a house near his own apartment and, after the 1936 remodeling of his Berghof, provided her with rooms connecting directly with his own.

To Hitler she seemed to be a living doll, the embodiment of the ideal woman he had often described: cute, cuddly, naïve, tender, sweet, and stupid. He found her a relaxing and pleasantly undemanding companion on picnics and at motion picture shows. Totally ignorant of politics, she listened avidly to Hitler's ideas and agreed with them all. He saw to it that she was kept out of sight and excluded from all public functions, but at the Berghof she played a larger role. There, Albert Speer told an interviewer, "Hitler kept his Eva like a puppet in a doll's house. She was a part of the ambience, like the canary cage, the rubber tree . . . and the kitschy wooden clocks." [268]

Over the years Hitler really became very fond of Eva and took to addressing her, both in private letters and within the intimate circle at the Berghof, with tender Austrian diminutives. But he chose rather curious words to express his affection—*Tschapperl, Hascherl,* and *Patscherl.* The terms are asexual and neuter-gendered, as well as quite untranslatable. But to the Austrian or south German ear, their meaning and flavor seems inappropriate for adult lovers. The words have a condescending tone, with a slight echo of derogation. They express intimacy and endearment, but in the way a mother would talk to her baby. *Patscherl,* for example, is derived from the Austrian equivalent of the baby game "Pat-a-cake, pat-a-cake, baker's man. . . ."

Why did the adult Hitler consider these terms an appropriate way to express affection to a woman? Was it because they stirred memories in his unconscious of the first words his beloved mother had murmured to him as an infant? A remark made by one of his secretaries gives some support for that suggestion. In an interview after the war, she remembered vividly how often Hitler called Eva Braun by that diminutive in urging her to eat food—much as Adolf's mother had forced food upon her sickly little boy: "He patted her hand, calling her 'my *Patscherl.*' . . . He always urged her to eat this or that, saying, 'Now, my *Patscherl,* eat this little morsel that is good for you.' " [269] Eva's own feelings about Hitler were revealed in a private diary and in letters which were discovered after the war.* The diary is that of an immature and limited young woman whose love for Hitler is unmistakably sincere.

As the years passed, Hitler too felt more and more bound to Eva. During the war he telephoned her almost every night, and we have a letter he wrote to her just after the attempt on his life in the "Bomb Plot" of 1944. The letter, pecked out on a typewriter and pocked with errors, contains awkward and stilted phrases of the kind Hitler had used 35 years before in his correspondence with Kubizek. One must conclude that while it may not have been possible for Hitler to love anyone, he did, after his fashion, feel genuine and tender concern for Eva Braun:

> *Mein liebes Tschapperl,*
>
> Don't worry about me. I'm fine though perhaps a little tired. I hope to come home soon and then I can rest in your arms. I have a great longing for rest, but my duty to the German people comes before everything else. Don't forget that the dangers I encounter don't compare with those of our soldiers at the Front. I thank you for the proof of your affection and ask you also to thank your esteemed father and your most gracious mother for their greetings and good wishes. I am very proud of the honor—please tell them that—to possess the love of a girl who comes from such a distinguished family. I have sent to you the uniform I was wearing during the unfortunate day. It is proof that Providence has protected me and that we have nothing more to fear from our enemies.
>
> From my whole heart, your A.H.

He enclosed in the letter a sketch he made of the barracks after the explosion.

We also have Eva's reply:

> *Geliebter,*
>
> I am beside myself. I am dying of anxiety now that I know you are in danger. Come back as soon as possible. I feel as if I am going insane.
>
> The weather is beautiful here and everything seems so peaceful that I am almost ashamed of myself [for enjoying such tranquillity]. . . . You know I have always told you that I would die if

---

* There are two versions of the diary. One is a fraud. An authentic, unpublished version is deposited in the National Archives. This diary covers only the period from 6 February to 28 May 1935, the time when Eva's attraction for Hitler was ripening into love. Eva's younger sister, Ilse Fucke-Michels, has vouched for its authenticity. See Appendix, "A Note on Spurious Sources."

anything happened to you. From our first meeting on, I have promised myself to follow you wherever you go, even to death. You know that I live only for your love.

Your Eva

In the end, as we shall see, she flew to crumbling Berlin to die with the man she loved. Amid the bedlam of the last days in Hitler's air raid shelter, while others faced death with varying degrees of cowardice, panic, and histrionics, Eva Braun grew in stature. There was about her a quiet inner strength. Even someone who had cordially disliked her said at the end that "she attained heights which more than atoned for the vanities and frivolities of the past."[270]

Affairs with Other Women

Though he could not possibly have had the number of sexual liaisons with beautiful young women that rumor and conjecture have claimed, Hitler apparently had a number of fleeting affairs or overnight experiences during the years that he lived with Geli Raubal and Eva Braun.

A German film director testified to OSS officers during the war that he had helped supply Hitler with attractive starlets for the night.[271] He had been infatuated with the famous movie director Leni Riefenstahl, who filmed both the Berlin Olympic Games of 1936 and the effective propaganda film *The Triumph of the Will* in 1934. Fräulein Riefenstahl later denied having anything more than a platonic relationship with the Führer. The Italian foreign minister believed that Hitler had had intimate relations with a Sigrid von Lappus, whom he described as 20 years old with "beautiful quiet eyes."[272] U.S. Military Intelligence found evidence of intimate affairs with two young Munich women, Fräuleins Abel and Haue.[273] Ernst Hanfstaengl reported that, while entertaining Hitler in his home one evening, he returned from calling a taxicab to stumble upon an awkward scene. Hitler was down on his knees in front of Hanfstaengl's beautiful wife, Hélène. He was proclaiming his love for her, saying that it was a shame he had not met her while she was still free and declaring himself her "slave." He made a similar declaration in Berlin to one of the daughters of a benefactor, again going down on his knees in front of the embarrassed young woman.[274]

According to another intimate, Hitler had an affair with a young married woman, Suzi Liptauer, who, after one strange encounter, tried to hang herself in a Munich hotel. The last wife of the leader of the Labor Front, Frau Inge Ley, committed suicide, it is reported, after having an affair with him. The German film star Renaté Mueller also killed herself, reportedly after a harrowing sexual experience with him.[275] Hitler himself claimed that Frau General Ludendorff was quite mad about him, and that shortly before she married the general she had entreated the Führer to be her lover.[276]

There can be no doubt that Hitler was impressed by Miss Unity Walkyrie Mitford, the daughter of Lord Redesdale. Often, and in front of Eva Braun, he extolled her as the "perfect Germanic woman." Miss Mitford, who had long enthused over Hitler's ideas, developed a cloying devotion to his person. She and her sister, who later married Sir Oswald Mosley, the British fascist leader, would haunt the Osteria Bavaria first to gaze at their hero and then, after they had been welcomed to the group, to spend hours listening with rapture to his table conversation.

On one occasion Miss Mitford astonished the British ambassador, Sir Neville Henderson, by greeting him in public with the Hitler salute and a loud "Heil Hitler!" Sir Neville was so dumbfounded he forgot his usual response to such greeting: snapping to attention, giving a crisp British Army salute, and proclaiming, "Rule Britannia!"[277] Miss Mitford's car was emblazoned with both a swastika and a Union Jack. She drove through her adopted Fatherland breathlessly and indefatigably preaching the message of the flags and the symbol of her name: the unity between the "Lord of the Land and the Ruler of the Seas." For this faith and this mission, she said, she would gladly die. She very nearly did.

On 3 September 1939, when Britain entered into a state of war with Germany, Unity Mitford saw the dream of her life shattered. In despair, she went to the English Garden in Munich and shot herself in the head. Adolf Hitler sent for the best physicians, brought her flowers in the hospital, held her hand, and signed a portrait of himself which she kept at her bedside table. On his orders, she was escorted by his personal physician to Switzerland, where she recovered. She died in England in 1948.[278]

HITLER'S SEX LIFE

No area of Hitler's life has been the subject of more controversy and speculation than his sexual practices. It has been asserted, variously, that he was absolutely normal, that he was a homosexual, that he had no interest whatever in sex, that he engaged in a particularly gross form of perversion.

Serious students of his career will wish to pursue this matter in some detail—not in order to indulge prurient interests, but because of its redeeming historical value. For one major contribution that psychoanalysis made to historical biography is the demonstration that sexual attitudes and practices play an important and integral part in personality development. Moreover, they help shape a person's social thinking. As Theodor Reik has noted, "Whoever has had the opportunity to observe persons analytically for any length of time is bound to receive the distinct impression that the intimate sexual life definitely marks the individual's attitude toward society." [279]

It is probable that we shall never know all the intimate details of Hitler's sex life. But of one thing we may be sure: those associates and biographers untrained and disinterested in psychology who assure us that Hitler was "in all respects sexually normal" are mistaken.* There is simply too much evidence against that conclusion.

Ever since the trauma of his infantile experiences, normal sexual intercourse had seemed frightening and repulsive to him. And yet, while repelled by sex, he was also intrigued by it. His absent-minded doodles and sketches are replete with sexual symbolism. *Mein Kampf* is filled with sexual imagery. Every chapter bespeaks a mind that is inordinately excited by rape, prostitution, syphilis, and "the most disgusting" sexual practices. He wanted to look at sex. He was infatuated with von Stuck's sensuous paintings; he had a library of pornography; he had "blue" films made especially for his private viewing; and he drew pictures which "only a perverted voyeur could have committed to paper." [280]

The amount of time he devoted to talking about sex is a further indication that the subject was often on his mind. "Depraved" sexual practices were among his favorite topics of conversation as a young man; as chancellor, he would invite young women to confide in him about their sexual experiences, urging them to give him detailed descriptions. His own contribution to these conversations was to speak at length and with increasing excitement about his historical importance. Several of the chorus girls who spent nights with him reported that nothing much happened except that "Hitler sat around bragging the whole evening . . . of his greatness and power." [281]

Much as he enjoyed seeing, hearing and, talking about sexual activity, he was usually careful to avoid physical contact with women of his own age. He delighted in caressing little girls, and he allowed motherly older women to stroke his hair or pat his cheek. But as a youth he had been outraged when it was suggested that he learn to dance; later, as chancellor, he refused to dance with anyone either in private parties or at state functions. He was horrified when a woman kissed

---

* Proponents of this view include Werner Maser (*Hitler*, 320, 431–438 and *passim*) and John Toland (*Adolf Hitler*, 137, 827, 892–893). Hitler's secretaries and valets also believed that rumors about sexual aberrations were "completely false." (Zoller, *Privat*, 107; and Linge, *Revue*, 26 December 1955). Eva Braun herself apparently told her sister that her sexual relations with Hitler were "completely normal." (Nerin Gun, letter to the editor, *Der Spiegel*, 11 December 1967). But she gave a very different impression to a close friend whom she had known since their schoolgirl days. To this friend, who became the wife of Hermann Esser, she confided disgustedly, "As far as his manhood is concerned, I get absolutely nothing from him. [*Als Mann habe ich von ihm überhaupt nichts*]." (Hanfstaengl interview, April, 1967).

him lightly and good-naturedly under the mistletoe during a Christmas celebration.

When he confessed to Kubizek that he could never have intimate relations with a woman because he did not want to become "infected," he seems to have had two kinds of infection in mind. Certainly he was terrified at the thought of syphilis—though he was also fascinated by it, as the many pages on the subject in his memoirs attest. But ever since his primal scene experience as an infant, he had felt that sexual intercourse was "moral infection"—something corrupting and evil. In particular, he associated copulation with capitulation. This may help explain why he had such an absolute horror of military capitulation, saying explicitly on many occasions, "There is one word I can never use and that is *capitulation*. . . . There is one word that does not exist in my vocabulary: *capitulation*. . . . I prefer to die in order to escape the shame of *capitulation*." [282]

Over the years, Hitler thought of many reasons why he could not possibly get married: his offspring might be imbeciles; he had only one bride, his Motherland; the only person he could have married was Geli, and she was dead. He also noted that an earlier Messiah had never married. At times he urged the pragmatic political importance of preserving the image of the bachelor patriot: "If I married, I'd lose five million votes of German women." A wife would interfere with his mission. Perhaps he could never find a woman worthy of his genius, or, conversely, insignificant enough to complement his stature; it was one of his aphorisms that "the greater the man, the smaller the wife should be." But whatever the reasons he gave, the thought of getting married and of having genital sexual relations with a wife did not appeal to him.

Homosexuality?

There is insufficient evidence to warrant the conclusion that Hitler was an overt homosexual. But it seems clear that he had latent homosexual tendencies, and it is certain that he worried a great deal about them.

He was terribly concerned, for example, lest he give the impression of showing feminine traits—which, indeed, he did. The noted English diplomat and historian Sir Harold Nicolson, who was himself a practicing homosexual, was particularly interested in Hitler's femininity. He records in his diary a conversation with a colleague who told him that Hitler "is the most profoundly feminine man that he has ever met and there are moments when he becomes almost effeminate." [283] The American journalist, William L. Shirer, who watched Hitler closely one day in September 1938 as he came out of a hotel in Bad-Godesberg on the occasion of meeting Chamberlain, wrote in his diary: "It was a very curious walk indeed . . . very ladylike. Dainty little steps." But a German doctor who had very personal reasons for wondering about Hitler's sexual preferences reached a different conclusion:

As a homosexual, I was fascinated by Hitler's eyes, speech and walk. But I sensed immediately that he is not one of us.[284]

Direct evidence from people who knew him well does not support a claim of overt homosexuality. The recollections of his roommate, for example, may be suggestive, but they are only that. Kubizek recalled that when he met his friend at a railway station in Vienna one foggy February night in 1908, Adolf "greeted me with a kiss and led me to the lodging where we would spend the night."[285] Kubizek also reported several occasions when adult homosexuals attempted to seduce Adolf, but his friend "scrupulously avoided all personal contact with such men" and talked about homosexuality as one of the "social problems" he would solve when he established his Reich.[286]

It is true that Hitler was closely associated with Ernst Röhm and Rudolf Hess, two practicing homosexuals who were among the very few people with whom he used the familiar *du*. But one cannot conclude that he therefore shared his friends' sexual tastes. Still, during the months he was with Hess in Landsberg, their relationship must have become very close. When Hitler left the prison he fretted about his friend who languished there, and spoke of him tenderly, using Austrian diminutives: "*Ach mein Rudi, mein Hesserl,* isn't it appalling to think that he's still there."[287] One of Hitler's valets, Schneider, made no explicit statement about the relationship, but he did find it strange that whenever Hitler got a present he liked or drew an architectural sketch that particularly pleased him, he would run to Hess—who was known in homosexual circles as "Fräulein Anna"—as a little boy would run to his mother to show his prize to her.* Another valet, Krause, agreed that the relationship with Hess was very close indeed—but that was all he said about it.[288] Finally, there is the nonconclusive but interesting fact that one of Hitler's most prized possessions was a handwritten love letter which King Ludwig II had written to a manservant.

A different kind of evidence indicates that Hitler was personally concerned about latent homosexuality and struggled against it. There is a remarkable similarity between his attempts to deny any suggestion of homosexuality and his efforts to prove that he could not possibly be tainted by Jewish blood. In both cases he used the same defense: he denied that he was Jewish by persecuting the Jews; he denied that he was homosexual by attacking homosexuals. Indeed, he made a special point of doing so.

After he came to power, his government moved immediately against all types of sexual deviation and sex crimes. But the sharpest rise in prosecutions was for homosexuality: the number of prosecutions increased from 3,261 for the years 1931 through 1934 to almost 30,000 between 1936 and 1939.[289] It is also suggestive that Hitler grouped

---

* By 1941, Hitler had revised his high opinion of Hess and declared him officially insane, damning him publicly as a traitor for his mission to England on Hitler's behalf but without Hitler's knowledge.

homosexuals with Jews and Communists as "enemies of the state," and set up a special section of the SS to root them out.[290] Apparently his campaign to destroy homosexuality was not entirely successful, for on 15 February 1942 he felt it necessary to set forth a decree punishing homosexuality within the SS with death.[291]

Hitler also revealed fears of homosexuality by protesting so much that he had absolutely no feminine characteristics whatever. He was, he kept insisting, not soft or weak. He was totally masculine—tough, hard, cold, ruthless, brutal. His tendency to think in terms of disjunctive stereotypes about men and women (strong, iron-willed, effective male vs. weak, emotional, incompetent female) is in itself revealing. Such thinking demonstrates a strong conflict and confusion between masculine and feminine natures. To him, sexual differences appeared as exaggerated and mutually exclusive opposites, as roles to be played, rather than as natural attributes of human personality. In Hitler's case —as in Himmler's—the fantasied tough male sex role developed into sadism, murder, and destruction.[292]

The question of Hitler's latent homosexuality can also be approached indirectly. It can be stated with some confidence that Hitler must have had latent homosexual tendencies because he showed clear indications of paranoia. This does not mean that all homosexuals are paranoid, but it does mean that all paranoids have fears of homosexuality. The direct connection between homosexuality and paranoia was first noticed by Freud, who concluded that paranoia "invariably arises from an attempt to subdue an unduly powerful homosexual wish." [293] A distinguished American psychiatrist, Robert P. Knight, after years of research on the problems of homosexuality, concluded that "no psychoanalytic theory . . . rests on firmer foundation or has been less frequently attacked by critics of Freud" than the assertion that "an intense homosexual conflict is never absent in a male paranoic. . . ." [294]

In his study of paranoids, Dr. Knight found specific consistent characteristics, all of which fit Adolf Hitler. There is a "terrifically strong" need to deny homosexuality; the very thought of homosexual contact with another man is "completely intolerable." Moreover, the need felt by a paranoid for approval is especially acute; his megalomania is in itself an expression of his need for proof that he is important. There is a high incidence of constipation in paranoid individuals. All paranoids have strong anal components, problems with order and cleanliness, and obsessions with purity and vice and with the impurity or infections of others. Anal sadistic fantasies are directed against the father because he is seen as the rival for the mother's love; the intensity of the drive to be loved is supported mainly "by the intense need to neutralize and eroticize a tremendous hate." When the unconscious hate is so great, the attempt to eroticize it fails and the individual turns to sadism.[295]

As Knight has pointed out, while homosexual feelings and paranoid delusions may be in bitter conflict, both are, in a sense, dependent on each other and are defenses against one another. Thus, it seems quite possible that Hitler developed paranoid delusions, in part, to fight his homosexual feelings. As long as he prosecuted and attacked homosexuals, he felt he was successfully combating his own inadmissible inclinations toward homosexuality.

Perversion?

The question of Hitler's sexual perversion is a matter of concern to those interested in his personality. It is also a matter of considerable dispute. Many responsible observers who knew him well are emphatic that there was no perversion; later historians are not at all persuaded either of its existence or its importance.

The first published statement that Hitler may have had a perversion was made in an article appearing in 1971 and drawing on a valuable psychological investigation of Hitler prepared for the OSS in 1943 by Dr. Walter C. Langer and other American psychoanalysts and clinical psychologists.[296] This wartime report, subsequently published in 1972, reached the following conclusion with regard to Hitler's aberrant sexual activity:

> It is an extreme form of masochism in which the individual derives sexual gratification from the act of having a woman urinate or defecate on him.[297]

Historians were not slow in responding. The Regius Professor of History at Oxford University, for example, found the discussion of Hitler's perversion outrageous, irrelevant, and totally unsubstantiated. He concluded roundly and with conspicuous confidence, "There is not a shred of evidence on any of these matters." [298]

It is important to emphasize that a historian dealing with an emotionally disturbed subject is obliged to use two quite different types of evidence. There is, of course, the familiar kind of testimony which is often thought of as being "solid," objective, rational, or factual. This sort of historical fact is important and should be evaluated very carefully. But another category of evidence, psychological data, may prove equally valuable when handled with discernment. Historians who feel professionally ill equipped to interpret such data may find it advisable to consult professional psychologists.

With regard to Hitler's alleged perversion, the traditional kind of direct evidence is not entirely convincing. It comes largely from a former intimate of Hitler's, Otto Strasser, who told OSS officials during an interview in Montreal on 13 May 1943 that he had learned about Hitler's perversion from Geli Raubal herself. He said that "after much urging" concerning the nature of her relationship with her famous uncle, she said:

Hitler made her undress. . . . He would lie down on the floor. Then she would have to squat over his face where he could examine her at close range and this made him very excited. When the excitement reached its peak, he demanded that she urinate on him and that gave him his sexual pleasure. Geli said the whole performance was extremely disgusting to her and . . . it gave her no gratification.[299]

One might well raise questions about the reliability of Otto Strasser's testimony on anything. In particular, one might well wonder whether Geli would be likely to confide in him over such intimate matters. Langer and his associates, however, reported that other informants —whose names are not mentioned—gave similar testimony about Hitler's perversion.[300]

Long before Dr. Langer and his colleagues drew up their report, a Catholic priest provided evidence which tends to support their findings. This priest, Father Bernhard Stempfle, had befriended Hitler and helped edit *Mein Kampf* for publication. He asserted that in 1929 Hitler had written Geli a shockingly compromising letter which explicitly mentioned his masochistic and coprophilic inclinations. Geli no doubt would have been repelled by the letter, but she never received it. It fell into the hands of Hitler's landlady's son, a man named Rudolph. Hitler was saved from embarrassment—and conceivably from political disaster— by a remarkable person, a gnomelike eccentric named J. F. M. Rehse. For years this indefatigable little man, who was a close friend and confidant of Father Stempfle, had collected political memorabilia. His rooms were packed to the ceiling with cartons containing copies of official decrees, pictures, political advertisements, and thousands of newspaper clippings. One day Hitler sent the Party treasurer, Franz X. Schwarz, to Rehse and asked him to buy Hitler's incriminating letter from Rudolph with the excuse that he needed if for his collection. But Rehse, on the advice of Father Stempfle, saw an opportunity to profit from Hitler's embarrassment. He demanded that the Nazi leader assume financial responsibility for his beloved collection. Hitler yielded to this extortion and found the money to underwrite the Rehse collection, which still may be found in the archives of the Nazi Party, now largely on microfilm in the Hoover Institution and in the National Archives.

At any rate, the compromising letter—which probably never went through Rehse's hands at all—was delivered by Father Stempfle to Schwarz, who gave it to Hitler. It may well be that this service to Hitler helped make Schwarz one of the more influential though publicly obscure figures within the Nazi Party. Hitler further testified to his confidence in Schwarz when he made him sole executor of his personal will of 2 May 1938.

There is another bit of evidence that would seem to support Father

Stempfle's story of Hitler's perversion. In June 1934, during the so-called Blood Purge, when Hitler settled his accounts with people who were in a position to embarrass him politically, Father Stempfle was found dead in the forest of Herlaching near Munich, with three shots through his heart.[301]

The idea that Hitler had a sexual perversion particularly abhorrent to women is further supported by a statistic: of the seven women who, we can be reasonably sure, had intimate relations with Hitler, six committed suicide or seriously attempted to do so. Mimi Reiter tried to hang herself in 1928; Geli Raubal shot herself in 1931; Eva Braun attempted suicide in 1932 and again in 1935; Frau Inge Ley was a successful suicide, as were Renaté Mueller and Suzi Liptauer. Unity Mitford's attempted suicide seems clearly to have been prompted by political reasons.

But these are only shreds of evidence, insufficient in themselves to support a conclusion that Hitler had a masochistic, coprophilic perversion. Equally important to this conclusion is a different kind of historic fact: he displayed other behavior patterns thoroughly consistent with this kind of perversion, which is quite well reported in the literature.[302]

Specialists in these matters have shown, first, that sadomasochistic traits are a prerequisite for such a perversion. Indeed Phyllis Greenacre has concluded that they "are characteristic of *all* perversions."[303] Hitler's sadism scarcely requires further documentation. What is less widely recognized is that from adolescence on he displayed moods of deep depression and self-loathing which indicate masochistic feelings. As his worried friend August Kubizek noted, he would "torment himself" and wallow "deeper and deeper in self-criticism . . . and self-accusation," until finally, after his mother's funeral, he lacerated himself with the most awful punishment he could devise: he said that he would "give up Stefanie!"—that is, he would give up his fantasies about her.[304]

As we noted in discussing his latent homosexuality, Hitler showed a tendency to stereotype male and female traits which is a complement of sadomasochistic impulses. In private conversation and public speeches he revealed how constantly his mind swung between masochism (weakness, submission) and sadism (brutality, strength, mastery). He would speak, typically, of the necessity to exalt "the victory of the *better and the stronger* and to demand the submission of the *worse and weaker*."[305]

When told of Hitler's infatuation with the movie *King Kong*, an experienced analyst found that fact to be a revealing expression of Hitler's sadomasochism: "The image for me that is the most startling is *King Kong*. It's easy to read Hitler as the huge gorilla—but he was only that in part. He was also, at the same time, the helpless, sweet little blonde. He was so infatuated with the image because he yearned to be helpless (masochistic), to be overwhelmed by the powerful (sadistic) ape who at the same time sought to protect him. King Kong is thus a very effective expression of his sadomasochism." [306]

Hitler's childlike game of having his valet tie his tie for him and tighten it while he counted to ten is, psychologically, a rather complex phenomenon. It speaks of many things. One of them is revealed in the research of psychoanalysts who have discovered that playing games involving ropes around the neck—or, presumably, neckties—is a form of eroticism and masturbation. As noted earlier, the game is also a way of acting out, and thus rendering more innocuous, fears of death by strangulation or suffocation. Often in these games patients reveal incestuous desires and Oedipal guilt, which are "assuaged through the masochistic brush with death." But for present purposes let us emphasize that one of Hitler's favorite games was a kind of substitute suicide, the ultimate masochistic resolution. [307]

Hitler's generalized sadomasochistic impulses were carried over directly to his conduct with women. The whip that he habitually carried for many years is, of course, a traditional symbol of sadomasochism. Hitler's whips were associated with mother substitute figures; his three favorite ones were all given to him by motherly women. We also know that he used whips violently in scenes involving women who were about as young as Klara had been when she married Alois. Heinrich Hoffmann's daughter, for example, remembered clearly that when she was a 15-year-old girl in pigtails and flannel nightgown, Hitler, who was visiting their home, asked for a good-night kiss. When she refused, he beat his hand viciously with his whip. [308] In 1926, apparently in order to impress Mimi Reiter, a 16-year-old girl, he whipped his dog so savagely that she was shocked by his brutality.

Another curious episode took place in June 1923 in Berchtesgaden, where he was staying at the Pension Moritz. Frau Büchner, the wife of the proprietor, was a striking, six-foot-tall, blond Brünnehilde who towered over Hitler and inflamed him sexually. He tried repeatedly to attract her attention by striding up and down in front of her as he swung his whip and beat it against his thigh. The more she ignored him, the more agitated he became. Almost beside himself, he spoke loudly about an experience he had had in Berlin which showed, he said, the decadence and moral depravity of the Jews. As he lashed about him with his whip, he cried, "I nearly imagined myself to be Jesus Christ when He came to His Father's temple and found it taken over by the moneychangers. I can well imagine how He felt when He seized a whip and scourged them out." This story was told by Dietrich Eckart, the close friend and admirer of Hitler. [309]

Thus, while Hitler used his whip in lashing out at others, he also—according to this testimony and that of his private pilot—whipped himself, beating his boots or thighs in moments of excitement. Even after he stopped carrying it, he told his valet that he considered the whip to be his personal symbol. [310]

The Child As Father to the Man

There is other evidence of Hitler's masochistic impulses. He liked to talk about physical punishments and he liked to act them out. The German film star Renaté Mueller reported that when she was invited to spend the night with Hitler in the Chancellery, he first described in great detail the medieval and Gestapo techniques of torturing victims. Then, after they were undressed, Hitler "lay on the floor . . . condemned himself as unworthy, heaped all kinds of accusations on his own head, and just groveled around in an agonizing manner. The scene became intolerable to her, and she finally acceded to his wishes to kick him. This excited him greatly; he became more and more excited." [311]

Hitler's sadomasochistic tendencies, we are suggesting, are consistent with a coprophilic perversion, for in it masochism and sadism are united. By having young ladies defecate or urinate on his head, Hitler degraded both himself and others. In this act he could unite with his victims, "who became the personification of [his own] depraved self, as the persecutor who attacks a part of himself in his victims." [312]

Hitler's fixation on the anus, and his special interest in feces, filth, and urine (see p. 148f) coincide with this sexual perversion. Sexual pleasure can be stimulated by the rectal mucous membrane and by the retention or expulsion of the feces. We know that Hitler liked to give himself enemas; it seems quite possible that his sexual behavior was similar to those patients with anal interests who, Otto Fenichel has shown, find it pleasurable "to defecate on another person or to have another person defecate on oneself." [313] Hitler apparently enjoyed the reaction he got from women when he talked about "sewer water," which seems to have been his euphemism for urine. His secretaries were appropriately shocked, for example, when he told them that their lipstick was made from Parisian *Abwasser.*" [314] To compensate for this fascination with feces and filth, Hitler practiced, as we have noted, the most punctilious personal cleanliness.

He enjoyed talking about sex in general, but he was particularly interested in deviate sexual behavior. In a private letter, Kubizek reported that his friend chattered "by the hour" about "depraved [sexual] customs." [315]

He employed the same psychological defenses against perversion that he used against feelings of latent homosexuality and fears of Jewishness: denial, projection, and punishment. Only two examples of projection can be given here. In one particularly revealing turn of phrase, he accused Jewish journalism and literature of *"splashing filth in the face* of humanity." And his immediate reaction on seeing photographs depicting gross types of deviate sexual activity is worth remembering. He said that the males involved could not possibly be Germans: *they must be of Jewish extraction.*[316]

In a table conversation of 22 May 1942, he made a special point of lashing out against sexual deviants, insisting that they were a threat to society and "public decency." They should all be handed over to the Gestapo and severely punished:

> Experience shows that unnatural offenders generally turn into homicidal maniacs; they must be rendered harmless however young they may be. I have therefore always been in favor of the strongest possible punishment of these antisocial elements.[317]

Other aspects of Hitler's personality also fit what we know to be true about the psychopathology of sexual perversion. The infantilism we have found in him is one necessary ingredient. For as Freud was first to notice, "perverted sexuality is nothing else but infantile sexuality, magnified and separated into its component parts." Infantilism is clearly marked when, as with Hitler, the perversion involves a reversion to the anal stage.[318] Hitler's harrowing childhood memories of his primal scene experience and his monorchism clearly qualify as prerequisites for adult perversion, as set forth by the distinguished child psychoanalyst Phyllis Greenacre. "If I were to attempt a formula describing the development of perversion," she has written, the primary cause would lie in a disturbed mother-child relationship, "especially [one] involving the genitals. This becomes most significant . . . when castration anxiety is extraordinarily acute." [319]

Psychoanalysts have shown that the mothers of boys who become sexual perverts often were overly stringent about toilet training. As we have noted, Klara Hitler had a reputation in Leonding and Linz for having had "the cleanest house in town" and keeping her children "absolutely spotless." It is interesting, and perhaps in this connection suggestive, that in one case of perversion described by an American analyst, the patient showed an identification with his mother: he displayed a desire "to have his sweetheart urinate in his presence while he encouraged her in a friendly way. He was playing the role of his mother who used to put him on the chamberpot when he was a baby." [320]

In his chapter on perversion in his standard work on psychoanalytic theory, Otto Fenichel lists three basic characteristics: patients with perversions tend to be infantile; they have unreconciled Oedipus complexes; and they all display castration anxiety. Indeed, Fenichel concludes: "*Castration anxiety* (and guilt feelings which are derivatives of castration anxiety) must be *the* decisive factor." [321] Adolf Hitler's lifelong concern about castration has already been mentioned perhaps too often.

If the clinical literature is correct in concluding that Oedipal problems, sadomasochism, infantilism, and castration anxiety are the marks of perversion, then Hitler certainly had all the chief symptoms. But there is a more specific reason why Adolf's symptoms were so intense and why a sexual perversion of the kind described was, psychologically, an appropriate response to sexual problems dating from his earliest years. The combination of monorchism and primal scene trauma had given Adolf Hitler a lifelong fear and abhorrence of genital sexual intercourse. He saw it as dangerous, evil, depraved, something that must be avoided. He could avoid genital intercourse by redirecting his sexual energies in deviate ways.[322]

As with other issues raised in this book, we cannot be absolutely certain that Hitler had the perversion described here. It must be admitted that traditional historians who reject this hypothesis are correct in saying that they can find evidence to support their assertions that he was sexually normal. But that conclusion is also based on fragmentary evidence of uncertain reliability. And it simply does not fit the psychological data.

In short, we conclude that Adolf Hitler, upon occasion, had young ladies urinate or defecate on his head. We are persuaded that he had this perversion not because the traditional type of evidence is completely convincing but because it is reinforced by psychological evidence. The perversion fits all that we know about Hitler's private life and public performance. It was an expression of the fetid underside of his grandiose, moralistic public image, it expressed the degraded, guilt-ridden self which pleaded for punishment and humiliation. This impulse for self-punishment, we shall suggest in the concluding chapter, was to have historic consequences.

Thus did the evils done in childhood visit themselves upon the man. We leave him now to look at the larger historical picture, the conditions which helped bring him to power. For no historical leader can achieve a political goal without the assistance of forces congenial to his personality, time, and place. No man or nation can escape history, and none can be understood apart from it.

In following the course of German history as it moved toward its fateful meeting with Adolf Hitler in 1933, we shall want to know what there was in the past that he could bend to his purposes; and how, in the context of his times, the very pathology of this flawed and unbalanced man became a political asset.

CHAPTER 4

The Past As Prologue: Hitler and History

What's past is prologue.

—William Shakespeare

Accurate scholarship can
Unearth the whole offence
From Luther until now
That has driven a culture mad. . . .

—W. H. Auden

I do not believe that a historian should either excuse or condemn. His duty is to explain.

—A. J. P. Taylor

NO HISTORIAN can hope to "unearth the whole offence"—nor can he begin the task of digging into German history without an uncomfortable feeling that he is not being quite fair to the past. For to some extent he knows in advance what he is looking for; and however careful his scholarly excavations may be, he realizes that they are selective. Vast areas of a rich and varied field must remain neglected.

Such is true of these pages. This commentary on the history of Germany up to 1933 obviously will not do justice to the whole complex story, for it will concentrate only on those developments which help explain how it was possible for a gifted and cultured people to accept Adolf Hitler as their leader and to follow him to destruction. They did so, in part, because of the adroit way in which he joined his own movement of political and social cannibalism with certain pernicious tendencies of the German past. The union produced a system which, in very truth, drove a culture mad.

It may well be protested that the kind of selective historical writing found in this chapter exploits the past for purposes of illuminating present problems. And in a sense it does. But the present is always involved with the past: the past shapes the present, and the present may determine, if not the past, at least our understanding of it. For our view of history will be greatly affected by what we seek from it. If we wish to find out why something turned out the way it did, we search past experience for answers to present problems—whether we lie on the analyst's couch, sit in a research library, or attend a session of the local Monday Morning Quarterbacks. In so doing, we exploit history by selecting from it what is useful to us at any given moment.

We take advantage of the past in another way. Since we know in advance how things have turned out, we can tell what tendencies and movements are going to be "historically important." To the extent that we emphasize these developments and neglect others which may have seemed equally important to people in their own era, we distort the picture of their lives and times. The point was well made by the great English historian Maitland, in words that seem fatuous when first read but which grow in subtlety and meaning: "It is very difficult to remember that events now in the past were once far in the future."

We of the future, wise both before and after the event, write histories that are affected by our foreknowledge. Present-day historians, for example, who write books about the social structure and political institutions of 18th-century France are aware that a great social and political upheaval took place by the end of the century. Their accounts of the preceding decades would be very different if the immediate future had been different: if Louis XVI had taken better advice, if Marie Antoinette had developed different habits, if the taxation system had worked better. . . . But these things did not happen, and the French Revolution took place—a revolution that shaped both the future of France and our view of preceding French history. Similarly, intellectual historians who trace Russian social thought of the 19th century know what happened in 1917. And their histories show it. If Lenin had not been permitted to arrive at the Finland Station that April, or had fallen through the ice of the Neva River—as he very nearly did—or if Kerensky had stabilized the Russian Republic during the summer and fall, history books entitled *Sources of the Russian Liberal Tradition* might be assigned to undergraduates instead of books with titles like *Russian Revolutionary Thought of the 19th Century.*

As things turned out, Hitler helped dictate the contents of this chapter. He might easily have been denied that opportunity. If the Weimar Republic had been successful and if the Viennese vagabond, after his attempt to overthrow it, had been permanently banished to Austria in 1924 (as the law clearly required), this discussion of important tendencies in German history would have been radically different. It would have concentrated on the humane and liberal traditions that contributed so positively to Germany's first successful experiment in democracy. But it did not happen that way. The Weimar Republic failed;

Hitler established a pitiless yet popular dictatorship and, inevitably, history will be asked to explain how that was possible.

And history is full of explanations. Indeed, knowing what the future had in store, one can search the past and find so many explanations and write so confidently and persuasively about them that it is quite easy to convince oneself that Hitler was *bound to happen*. Thus one can conclude, in the words of one popular history, that "Nazism and the Third Reich . . . were but a logical continuation of German history." [1]

Most historians are leery of this kind of logic. But that it is quite possible to go too far in another direction has been demonstrated convincingly by an English historian who has argued that while there was one chain of events in German history that led to Hitler, "there was also a chain of events which did not." [2] Perhaps so. But we shall never know where all those other events might have led. What we do have is the certain knowledge that by 1933, German history had arrived at Hitler's dictatorship. And we are back to the problem of trying to explain how that happened. Hitler was neither a historical necessity, the inevitable and logical result of the past, nor an accident, totally estranged from past German experience.

The history of any country may be recorded on several different levels. There is a kind of pure history, the complete story of "what actually happened," in all its fullness and detail. But only God—and perhaps Clio—knows such "total" history. It is not accessible to mortals. There is also the history preserved in scholarly monographs and erudite cooperative studies which, professional historians sometimes like to think, approximates the first kind. Most members of the guild, however, recognize that their knowledge of the past must always be incomplete and their insights limited.

Then there is the kind of history that probably does the most work in the world and has the most influence: what large numbers of people over a long expanse of time *believed* happened. This is important history, for beliefs—whether true or false—are sometimes stronger than fact, more tenacious than truth, more influential than erudition. Popularly remembered history has been memorialized in that priceless essay on historiography *1066 and All That*. One paragraph of the "Compulsory Preface" is eminently memorable—and probably right: "History is not what you thought: *It is what you can remember*. All other history defeats itself." [3]

In what follows here, stress will be placed not so much on what actually happened as on what many Germans remembered about their history—the memories which helped Hitler come to power. For well he knew how to exploit popular history for his own purposes. Our attention will also focus on the *results* of ideas and actions: on the legacy of Luther and Nietzsche rather than on what they may actually have thought or intended; on the consequences, rather than the causes, of World War I and the Great Depression.

The Past As Prologue: Hitler and History

THE FIRST REICH, 800–1806

> The path to dictatorship in Germany was long,
> tortuous, and amazingly crowded.
>
> —Fritz Stern

To most Germans the medieval past was an indistinct shimmer, a romantic haze through which resounded the reassuring phrase all schoolchildren learned: *Das heilige römische Reich deutscher Nation.* Of course Voltaire was right in asking his questions: "In what respects, Monsieur, was it Holy? or Roman? or an Empire? or a Nation?" In point of historic fact it was none of these, but it left a glorious memory, a lasting myth, and a longing for the future—for a time when there would indeed be one German nation and a mighty Reich. The untranslatable word "Reich" would have continuing appeal to Germans across the centuries. To the Romantics, to Pan-German nationalists, and eventually to the Nazis it would express a mystical and "eternal" Germandom (*Deutschtum*).

"Reich" was not only a favorite word of German intellectuals, but it also entered into popular culture. A student who has traced the power of myth in German history has written that belief in the Reich was "so deeply implanted in the German people through the schools and universities and as a result of the monotonous repetition of its themes that through the force of habit the German people came to accept it as the truth." In order to understand its power to attract, one must remember that this beautiful little word of Celtic origin has to the German ear a sacred and religious tone. To Catholics and Protestants alike, it is a cherished word in their most familiar prayer: *Dein Reich komme, dein Wille geschehe. . . .* The word also conjures up romantic glories in a dozen fairy tales. "When one pronounces the word," a German has written, "a picture book of enchanted centuries flashes before the mind's eye." [4]

Hitler, with his remarkable ability to respond to the myths and aspirations of the German people, had planned to paraphrase the expression in a book he thought of writing in 1919, the "Monumental History of Humanity." The German task, he said at that time, was to establish a new and racially pure Reich: "The Germanic Reich of the German Nation" (*Germanisches Reich deutscher Nation*). The book of 1919 did not materialize. But his Reich did, and it preserved the cadence of the ancient phrase in its title *Das dritte Reich deutscher Nation.*

The writers of school textbooks also took the concept of the Holy Roman Empire much more seriously than did Voltaire. A widely used geography of 1913, for example, claimed this "first German Reich" to be the predecessor of the "Second Reich of Bismarck and our Kaiser." It listed all the lands that "belonged to Germany" during the First Reich, noting pointedly that Switzerland, Liechtenstein, Belgium, the Netherlands, and Luxembourg were inhabited by German-speaking people, even though "they are now detached almost entirely from the old German Reich to which they once belonged." The acquisition of Alsace-Lorraine in 1871 and the prospects of adding Belgium and the Netherlands to the new Reich were defended on the grounds that they had all been a part of the "Old German Empire." [5]

The most memorable Holy Roman Emperors were not lawgivers and statesmen like their contemporaries, William I, Henry II, and Edward I of England or Louis IX and Philip Augustus of France. The greatest German hero of the period was the emperor, crusader, knight errant, and warrior with that splendid sobriquet, Friedrich Barbarossa. The legend of Barbarossa, alive in generation after generation of memories, was that of the heroic leader who never died. Even now, it was said, he still sits at a huge oaken—or is it marble?—table in a secret cave, deep in enchanted slumber. While Germany is troubled, disunited, despised, his red beard keeps growing. But one day, when the beard has encircled the entire table—and when Germany needs him most—the great leader will shake off the sleep of the centuries, arise in glory, and establish a magnificent, all-powerful Reich. Some said the cavern was located in the Kyffhäuser at the edge of the Harz Mountains. Others said that it was in the Bavarian Alps near Berchtesgaden. Hitler preferred the second alternative.

The Führer was so taken with both the successes and failures of the medieval hero that he would call his most important military campaign, the invasion of Russia, "Operation Barbarossa."

A Legacy of Luther

> The outstanding event of our history is still Martin Luther.
> —Friedrich Nietzsche

> Side by side with Frederick the Great stands Martin Luther as well as Richard Wagner.
> —Adolf Hitler

The towering figure of Martin Luther dominates the period known as the German Reformation and casts a shadow across the following centuries. Popular German history tends to neglect his theological achievements and remembers him as the national hero who broke the universality of the Western church, almost single-handedly established the German language, insisted on obedience to the state, and demanded that the Jews be harried from the land.

Heinrich Heine called Luther "the most German man of our history." He was typical of his countrymen, Heine thought, in being a man of striking contrasts:

> He was at the same time a visionary mystic and a practical man of action. His thoughts not only had wings; they had hands. . . . The

man who could curse like a fishwife could be tender as a young virgin. After spending a day working out rigorous scholastic distinctions, he took up his flute at night and lost himself in melody and reflection among the stars. Often he was as wild as the storm that uproots oaks, then gentle as the zephyr that strokes the violets. He could become completely absorbed by spirituality; . . . his was the motto, 'Who loves not wine, women, song/ Remains a fool his whole life long. . . .' In his character was combined, in the most magnificent way, all the virtues and vices of the Germans.[6]

Few thinkers have been so revered and so maligned. He has been called a forerunner of Nazism or, as the title of a war book would have it, *Martin Luther—Hitler's Spiritual Ancestor*. The title is a calumny. A spiritual universe separates the Christian leader from the racist demagogue. Luther would have been appalled by the Third Reich; with magnificent moral courage, he would have denounced Hitler as the Antichrist incarnate; he would have been among the first executed by the Gestapo. Yet having said that, we must also say that the great religious reformer did unwittingly help pave the way for Hitler. First and foremost he himself preached—and generations of Lutheran pastors echoed his words—that the Christian owes absolute obedience to the state, "whether it does right or wrong." Luther demanded not merely obedience to those in authority but *Staatsfrömmigkeit* (literally, piety toward the state). His respect for rulers was increased by his distrust of the common people:

> The princes of this world are gods, the common people are Satan, through whom God sometimes does what at other times he does directly through Satan, that is, makes rebellion as a punishment for the peoples' sin. . . . I would rather suffer a prince doing wrong than a people doing right.[7]

The inevitable corollary to such obedience to the state was the belief that individuals had no political rights, only political duties.

Luther's anti-Semitism also had lasting consequences. It was set forth most notably in a scurrilous pamphlet entitled *On the Jews and Their Lies*. Virtually unknown to the English-speaking world until 1971, the tract was widely circulated in Germany and quoted, through the centuries, in dozens of anti-Semitic pamphlets, typically by such influential Jew-baiters as Theodor Fritsch, Guido von List, and Richard Wagner. The American editors of Luther's collected works are understandably disconcerted by the essay. Before presenting their dutiful and accurate translation, they comment regretfully: "One hardly knows whether to be more astonished at the crudity of Luther's language or at the cruelty of his proposals."

Centuries before Hitler, Luther was convinced that the Jews were pernicious parasites who exploited and enslaved honest Germans. While

Germans toiled by the sweat of their brow, Jews "stuff themselves, guzzle and sit around the stove . . . fart and roast pears [a proverbial expression for laziness] . . . they fleece us of our money and goods." He had specific ideas for dealing with "this depraved and damned people of the Jews." Luther's program, which Hitler would carry out in every detail, was set forth in 1543:

> First, to set fire to their synagogues or schools. . . .
> Second, I advise that their houses also be razed and destroyed. . . .
> Third, I advise that all their prayer books and Talmudic writings, in which such adultery, lies, cursing and blasphemy are taught, be taken from them. . . .
> Fourth, I advise that their Rabbis be forbidden to teach henceforth on pain of loss of life and limb. . . .
> Fifth, I advise that safe-conduct on the highways be abolished completely for the Jews. . . .
> Sixth, I advise that . . . all cash and treasure of silver and gold be taken from them. . . .
> Seventh, . . . Let whosoever can, throw brimstone and pitch upon them, so much the better . . . and if this be not enough, let them be driven like mad dogs out of the land. . . .[8]

It is one of those jarring accidents of chronology that Hitler launched his first pogrom against the Jews, known as *Kristallnacht*, setting fire to their synagogues and schools, on the night of 9–10 November 1938—on Luther's birthday.

As far as Germany's future political health was concerned, Luther's most baneful legacy was his conception of the dual nature of man and, correspondingly, the necessity for two governments—one secular, one spiritual. Man was both physical and spiritual, "outer" and "inner." The outer person was subject to the physical environment and earthly powers. In this world man was never free. Spiritual, "inner" man, however, could—through faith—be set free, justified, and saved. The state ought not to intervene in this world of faith and the inner man.

As the doctrine was preached in Germany by generations of Lutheran pastors and practiced by Lutheran statesmen, this dualism entailed a separation between private and public morality. The individual Christian believer should practice the beatitudes and be loving, kind, forgiving, and honest in his private and personal life. But there was also an external kind of public morality: the state, for "reasons of state," might be crafty, ruthless, harsh, and cruel. As long as the state did not interfere with the spiritual life of the "inner man," it must be obeyed. A student of the Resistance Movement to Hitler has concluded that this doctrine had the effect of deterring Lutheran opposition to Nazi tyranny.[9] Certainly there were many individual acts of heroic resistance among German Protestants, as there were among Catholics. But the Lutheran Church as such did not protest when Nazis carried out pernicious programs affecting wide areas of life. The reason given was that such actions touched only the "outer man." And that, it was said, was the legitimate concern of the Secular Kingdom—the word, once again, is "Reich." The problem in Hitler's Third Reich was that the secular realm was totalitarian in its claims. Thus, in the name of Luther, Protestant Christians preached obedience to the state and found themselves acquiescing in a thousand inhumanities to man on the morally grotesque grounds that Nazi persecutions, atrocities, and murder had nothing to do with the inner spiritual life of the devout Christian.

Martin Luther was a Christian theologian who made imperishable contributions to the religious life and thought of the Western world—contributions far greater than can be acknowledged here. But there is another legacy pointed to by a thoughtful German, who, writing after Hitler's Holocaust, concluded that "without any question, Lutheranism influenced the political, spiritual and social history of Germany in a way that, after careful consideration of everything, can be described only as fateful."[10]

The Thirty Years War and the Call for a Führer

> I will awaken a German Hero.
> —Grimmelshausen (1669)

Amid the disasters of the Thirty Years War, Germans heard one of the first and clearest calls for a new Barbarossa, a powerful Leader who would rescue their tortured and divided Fatherland and establish a mighty Reich of the German nation.

During three terrible decades, "the Germanies" had been the battle-ground for pillaging armies from Spain, Denmark, France, Flanders, and Bohemia. When the Peace of Westphalia was signed in 1648, the land lay in ruin, farms had been abandoned, and once thriving towns had simply disappeared from the map. Uncounted thousands had died of battle, hunger, disease, and cold. Indeed, more people perished during the Thirty Years War than had died in the Black Death.

The entire population suffered, but the hardest hit was the middle class, which in happier lands like England and the Netherlands was strengthening the economy, contributing to culture, and building solid political bulwarks against the threat of dictatorial government. The Netherlands prospered mightily under those portly burgers who still smile down from the canvases of Franz Hals and Vermeer. Known officially and collectively in the 17th century as "Their High Mightinesses [*Hooge Moogende*], The Estates General of the United Provinces," they had good reason to be proud. They had beaten back foreign invaders, established stable and representative government, and provided perhaps the most civilized society of the century.

England too was enjoying one of her finest hours. The middle class and the squirearchy had challenged Stuart pretensions, set forth great principles of free government and accomplished a peaceful Revolution still remembered as Glorious. It was an age graced by the buildings of Sir Christopher Wren, the genius of Newton, the letters of Milton and John Donne, and the political theory of Halifax and Locke—which, by the end of the century, was pointing the way to contractual government, and inspiring the constitution makers of the New World.

Across the Channel and the Rhine, the political legacy of the 17th century was sharply different.* The Thirty Years War had left the German middle class politically ineffective and the petty princes ensconced in arbitrary power, unrestricted by constitutions and preoccupied with divisive feuds.

The war served to increase the longing for a mighty Leader who would bring stability and order to a devastated land. Articulation of these hopes was provided by Germany's enormously popular writer, Hans Jakob Christoffel von Grimmelshausen (1625?–1676). His stories and picaresque novels went through dozens of editions and sold thousands upon thousands of copies through subsequent centuries. His novella, *Die Landstörzerin Courasche* (The Vagabond, Courage) inspired both Bertolt Brecht's *Mother Courage* and Jerzy Kosinski's *Painted Bird*, the searing adventures and sufferings of a young boy who wandered through the same lands of Central Europe during a later period of holocaust and terror—the Nazi occupation of World War II.

Grimmelshausen's most famous work, *The Adventurous Life of Simplicius Simplicissimus* (1669), describes graphically and with bawdy humor scenes of pillage, whoring, torture, and death—scenes which the author himself had witnessed as a boy. Through it all, the hero, the abysmally ignorant Simplicius, is sustained by the faith that one day the tortures and travail of Germany will end. The day of deliverance will come only with the arrival of a national leader:

> I will awaken a German Hero who will consummate all this with the strength of his sword; he will slay all wicked men and protect and exalt the good.

In this version of the Barbarossa legend, Grimmelshausen made an important contribution to the Führer mystique. His German Hero was a man of charisma who would bend the world to his will. "Every

---

* It is true that during these and subsequent years influential Germans wrote eloquently about individual and natural rights. But such writers as Samuel Pufendorf, Christian Thomasius, and Christian Wolff were disinterested in developing constitutional institutions to protect those rights. Indeed, they believed that freedom could be attained only through subservience to the state to which they assigned absolute power. Immanuel Kant disliked tyranny but he disdained democracy. He was unable to reconcile his concern for individual liberty with his commitment to royal absolutism. A very great philosopher, his political thinking ended in virtual "political paralysis." (See especially Leonard Krieger, *The German Idea of Freedom: History of a Political Tradition* (Boston), 1957, 50–53, 65–66, 87–90, 124).

great city shall tremble before him . . . he shall command the mightiest ruler of the world and reign over earth and sea." Woe to those who refuse obedience to this German Leader, for these "he will exterminate [*ausrotten*]. . . ." He would establish a kind of crude socialism, and people of German blood would live together in one harmonious *Gemeinschaft*. His Greater Reich of the German Nation would extend far beyond the borders of Germany, for he would be a mighty conqueror. All of Central and Eastern Europe was to come under his direct control. Western lands would also feel his power: "The Kings of England, Sweden and Denmark, being of German blood . . . will receive their crown and kingdoms as fiefs of the German Nation." To consolidate his vast dominion, the German Hero would build a magnificent new capital of Germania, "the city in the middle of Germany greater than Manoah in America and richer in gold than Jerusalem at the time of Solomon." [11]

A British authority on Grimmelshausen, writing smugly in 1931 at a time when the German Republic was struggling for survival, found the fantasies of Grimmelshausen and his dreams of conquest really quite diverting. "One can smile," he said, "at the idea of other European countries as vassals of Germany." [12] Just ten years later, he would have found the prospects neither preposterous nor amusing.

The Contributions of Prussian Kings

> Two souls lived in the Prussian state of Frederick William I and Frederick the Great. One soul was capable of culture; the other was hostile to it.
> Friedrich Meinecke

Two centuries before Hitler was born, two Prussian kings—father and son—were building institutions and leaving memories which the Austrian would find of inestimable value in creating his dictatorship. Both monarchs would probably have been appalled by their contributions to his success, yet they provided Germany with an early model of "a well-ordered police state." Word for word, a scholar's description of their government can be applied to the Third Reich. Like Hitler, they demanded "tyrannical control and supervision of every facet of public and economic life," and exactly as in Hitler's Reich, there was a "downgrading of the individual in favor of the community, as personalized by the ruler." [13]

Frederick William I (1688–1740), laid the foundations upon which Hitler would build a militarized society. He was the creator of the Prussian Army—or rather, as Mirabeau commented in a memorable *mot*, "Prussia is not a country that has an Army; it is an Army that has a country." The king's demand for devotion was not very different from the fanatical commitment the Führer required of those who swore a sacred oath to him on the Blood Flag of 1923. The oath to

Frederick William as set forth in army regulations of 1726 was a preview:

> When one takes the oath to the flag one renounces oneself and surrenders entirely even one's life and everything to the monarch. . . . Through this blind obedience one receives the grace and confirmation of the title of soldier.

The king's bureaucracy, less well remembered in popular history, had at least as much historical importance as the army. Indeed, the two institutions were related in spirit and form. The civil service was operated like the army, with the same bristling discipline, absolute subordination, and complete centralization. Both institutions were calculated to eliminate all personal opinion and initiative and to make officials subordinate to the king alone.[14]

The king's control over the private lives of his subjects often seemed to fulfill the royal boast that "salvation is God's affair; everything else belongs to me." His chief means for enforcing that claim was his formidable and ubiquitous army of state officials who "wore the king's coat." They spread his autocratic system into every hamlet of the realm. Along with army veterans and elementary school teachers (who were usually army veterans), they inculcated the "correct attitudes" associated with what have become known as the "Prussian virtues" of obedience, discipline, industry, and thrift.*

Frederick William's influence was felt by generations of his countrymen. Writing in 1914, a leading historian said that Germany "still carries the . . . ineradicable stamp of his personality." In 1933, Oswald

---

* The monarch practiced the virtues he preached. His marginalia on requests for money, for example, bear witness to the royal frugality—as well as his penchant for writing doggerel and thinking about excrement. On one occasion, he noted that he could not fulfill a petitioner's request because he had to feed 100,000 men, and not even the king of Prussia was able to shit gold:

> *Eure Bitte kann ich nicht gewähren*
> *Ich habe hunderttausend Mann zu ernähren*
> *Gold kann ich nicht scheissen*
> *Friedrich Wilhelm, König in Preussen.*

The royal concern about feces and flatulence was shared by other famous Germans. Hitler's anal fixation has been noted (see Chapter 3, p. 148), and Martin Luther believed that the products of the anus provided the best defense against the Devil. He could render the Devil helpless, he firmly believed, if he could but "fart into his nostrils." He wrote a message personally addressed to the Devil saying, "Note this down: I have shit in my pants, and you can hang them around your neck and wipe your mouth with it" (Erik Erikson, *Young Man Luther*, 61, 245). One of Frederick William's descendants, Emperor William II, wrote in a marginal note on a state paper that the best thing to do with the suggestions of the Hague Conference of 1899 with regard to restrictions on the conduct of war was to "shit on their resolutions"; see *Die grosse Politik der Europäischen Kabinette* (Berlin, 1924), 4: 306.

The Past As Prologue: Hitler and History

Spengler called the king the first national socialist. The Nazis accepted him and his son as their spiritual ancestors and proclaimed them "the conscience" of National Socialism.[15]

Frederick II, called Frederick the Great (1712–1786), had an even greater impact than his father upon Germany history and upon Adolf Hitler. Certainly no one in German history—before the advent of the Austrian—was hailed with such panegyric. He was *Friedrich der Einzige* (Frederick the Unique), who was "not merely the patron saint of Germany but the greatest monarch in modern history, with an honored place in the German Valhalla beside Luther and Goethe, Kant, Beethoven and Bismarck." Neubauer's *Lehrbuch*, a popular textbook which went through many editions between 1890–1914, taught German children to honor him as the ideal leader—a veritable paragon standing "on a solitary height above his people: the war lord and statesman, the philosopher and historian, the most powerful example of unqualified and complete devotion to the State." [16]

The reign of the famous son saw the continuation and intensification of attitudes and institutions associated with his father. Under Frederick the Great, the army and the bureaucracy, if anything, increased in social importance. But there was a notable difference. Unlike his father, the son exulted in war. In 1740 the father had signed a document giving the "sacred word of Prussia" that his country would not invade young Maria Theresa's province of Silesia. With the old man barely in his grave, Frederick attacked. His justification for the unprovoked assault on a neighbor's land was worthy of Adolf Hitler:

> Let the ignorant and envious babble; they shall never form the compass by which I shall steer. . . . My object is glory; of this I am more enamoured than ever.[17]

This "rape of Silesia" helped to produce the Seven Years War, a war that would give Frederick an imperishable reputation as a field commander. His brilliant victories at Rossbach, Zorndorf, and Leuthen would be studied in the principal military academies of the world as examples of superb generalship. Napoleon called Leuthen an absolute "masterpiece . . . which would alone have sufficed to make Frederick immortal." Popular history added more accolades. He was remembered as the intrepid national hero who, although outnumbered 12-to-1 and surrounded by "those damn women" (Maria Theresa, Elizabeth of Russia, and Madame de Pompadour), proved that he could still conquer though half the world opposed him.

This is the memory that sustained Adolf Hitler in his last desperate days in the Berlin air raid shelter during the darkening spring of 1945, as he sat before the candlelit portrait of Frederick the Great frantically reading the German translation of Carlyle's multivolume biography hoping to find inspiration and waiting for a sign of deliverance.

And, miraculously, it came! For on 12 April there was suddenly announced the death of Franklin Roosevelt. Champagne corks popped in Berlin and Hitler's entourage rejoiced with their Führer; for just as Frederick in his extremity in 1762 was saved by the sudden death of the Tsarina Elizabeth, Hitler too had received deliverance through the death of his enemy.

Besides identifying with the beleaguered Frederick of the Seven Years War, Hitler believed that he and the great Prussian king had many other things in common. Both men as children had good reason to respect and to despise fathers who had hurt and humiliated them.* Both rulers, Hitler was convinced, had strikingly similar skull measurements and hand structures. He also thought that their eyes were very much alike; in 1934 he bought Anton Graff's portrait of Frederick in a powder blue uniform which set off "the startling clear blue of his eyes." Hitler took the portrait with him as a kind of talisman wherever he set up residence and gave specific orders at the close of his life that all his personal effects should be destroyed, but not the portrait of Frederick the Great.[18]

Hitler was also persuaded that he and the Prussian king were alike in other respects: they shared the same attitude toward Jews; both showed a mastery of the arts of politics, music, and war. And—according to Hitler—they had strikingly similar intellectual capacities. "Over and over again," Hitler remarked, he was delighted to find that his own ideas "were so very similar to the thought processes of *Der alte Fritz.*" As an example, Hitler noted that he too was really a very tolerant person who believed in the candid give-and-take of ideas and was convinced that truth would ultimately prosper. In a passage in the *Tischgespräche* which reads like Frederick—and even more like J. S. Mill's *Essay on Liberty*—the Nazi dictator observed:

> I do not believe that the truth can be suppressed for any length of time, Truth must in the end be victorious! . . . I foresee a time of absolute tolerance. I can only say [with Frederick the Great] that everyone should be permitted to save himself according to his own fashion.

The man who established one of the most extensive and heinous secret police systems in history said that he was very like Frederick

---

* Frederick the Great never forgot one childhood incident which was typical of the way his father had treated him. Frederick William, before retiring for the night, would line up his family and order them to kiss him. One day the little prince, who had just been brutally and unjustly whipped by his father, demurred. The king grabbed him by the hair, threw him to the floor, and ordered him to kiss the royal boot. As an adolescent and young man, the son was publicly whipped, imprisoned, and forced to watch his closest friend beheaded at his father's orders. An additional turn of the screw was given when the king ordered that the decapitated body be left where it fell from eight in the morning until two in the afternoon. Fritz stood and gazed at the corpse for hours.

in his dislike of spying on other people. During one of his nightly conversations he told "a delightful little story" of how Frederick the Great had refused to use secret police to ferret out the thoughts of his subjects. The Führer concluded by saying that he too found the idea of spying completely "repellent" (*abstossend*). Hitler's own comparisons with Frederick were not always flattering to himself, however. In an unguarded moment he remarked that the level of conversation at Sans Souci between Frederick the Great and Voltaire was such as "to make one ashamed of the depths of our present day conversations." (Anyone who has struggled through Hitler's "Table Conversations" is constrained to agree with him.) Hitler also suggested—indirectly—that Frederick was the greater military commander. On 28 January 1942, in his headquarters at the *Wolfsschanze*, he observed:

> When one recalls that Frederick the Great was confronted by a force twelve times greater than his own, one realizes what a shithead [*Scheisskerl*] one is! We ourselves this time have numerical superiority! Quite frankly, isn't it a disgrace? [19]

As he hid in his shelter in Berlin in 1945, Hitler may have recalled that Frederick had also viewed the collapse of his country with equanimity. Finding himself in desperate circumstances during the Seven Years War, the Prussian king wrote in 1757, "If everything collapses, I should calmly bury myself beneath the ruins." [20]

The royal absolutism established by the early Hohenzollerns provided efficient government. Indeed, it was too good for the future political health of the people. Nations may have reason to look back with a feeling of gratitude for the bad governments they experienced in their historic past. America owes a good deal to George III and Lord North; Frenchmen are indebted to the errors in judgment of Louis XVI; and Englishmen continue to be blessed by Bad King John, who gave them the Magna Carta, by James II, who inspired the Glorious Revolution, and by the kind of government provided by the first four Hanoverian Georges. With rulers like these, parliamentary government was not merely possible, it was downright necessary.

The Prussian kings left a different legacy to German history: the conviction that the best government is authoritarian government, and that those in authority must be obeyed. Religion demanded obedience to the *Obrigkeit*, but experience had also shown that paternal government was good government—so good, so efficient, and so just that there was need neither for revolt nor for political participation. Thus it came about in Prussia that a religious assertion of the Lutherans became a political statement of faith that was to resound in the future: "Everything comes down from above" (*Alles kommt von oben herab*).

It was a political legacy upon which Hitler drew heavily.

GERMANY WITHOUT A REICH, 1806–1871

Napoleon and the "War of Liberation"

> It was at this time that Germany departed from
> the mainstream of European political thought.
> —Hajo Holborn

Germans had mixed reactions to Napoleon, the man who conquered their lands and dissolved their first Reich. He was hated as the
"Enlightenment on horseback" who brought with him Western ideas
of liberty and equality, constitutions, codes of law, and other concepts
foreign to the German experience. Yet there was grudging admiration for this man of power and *Obrigkeit*. "Rattle your chains as you
will," said Goethe, "he is too strong for you." Hegel hailed him as a
"world historic hero." The most influential historian of the day, Johannes von Müller, extolled him as "a hero whose equal is not to be
found in the memory of the centuries." After receiving a personal
audience with the French conqueror of his native land, Müller wrote
ecstatically, "It was one of the most remarkable days of my life. By
his genius and his unconstrained kindness, he has conquered me." [21]
The "war of liberation" against Napoleon illustrates the tenacity
and power of myth in history: what is formative in the life of a nation—
as in personal lives—is not so much what actually happened as what
people believe took place. And what generations of Germans believed
about their *Befreiungskrieg* was pretty much what Germany's most
popular historian told them it was. Heinrich von Treitschke, "School-
master of Germany," * enjoyed an influence over his countrymen
unmatched by any other modern historian. For generations, the
history taught in German schools was Treitschke's *History of Germany*.
Indeed, his book was so widely accepted that it was often cited as the
Deutsche Geschichte, without the name of the author being given.
In every school and university lecture hall the message was proclaimed: Prussia and the "North German stock," through glorious victories over Napoleon, had won the moral right and historic mandate
to unite the Fatherland and impose the Prussian system on a new and
militantly powerful Germany. Treitschke hailed the glories of Prussian
power in memorable—if not always accurate—prose:

> The common people . . . had, amid need and suffering, rediscovered
> their love for the Fatherland. Their souls were stirred . . . they
> stormed forward irresistibly and then they broke loose the old
> *furia tedesca*, the savage wrath of the Northern berserkers. . . .
> What a wonderful sight it was when the peasants rushed upon
> the compact square of the French infantry at Hagelberg, advancing

* For Treitschke's influence on other aspects of German thought, see pp. 272–
286.

silently, pitilessly, in unspeakable wrath; when the dull crackling of the musketry ceased, there lay a horrible heap of corpses piled up to the level of the top of the wall, with the brains oozing out of the smashed skulls of the dead.[22]

It was a scene that would be repeated in German history.

German Romanticism

> National Socialism fused and transformed . . . Prussianism and Romanticism. It was their illegitimate offspring.
>
> —Hans Kohn

Smashing military victories over Napoleon formed the setting for Romanticism. Although it was primarily a literary and artistic movement, as it developed in Germany it would have profound and protracted political consequences. One of them is set forth in Hans Kohn's arresting aphorism.

As in all acts of human procreation, the father (Prussianism) played an important role. But it was not enough in itself to produce this child. For Prussianism was too cold, elitist, and withdrawn to have wide popular appeal. Nazism electrified the masses with emotion, yearning, and myth—the kind of things supplied by Mother Romanticism. She, according to Kohn (as well as Sigmund Freud), was the more important parent in the child's gestation and early development.

Among others who gave memorable expression to concepts of German Romanticism which would be taken over—and traduced—by the Nazis was the poet Ernst Moritz Arndt (1769–1860).* Arndt illustrates the power of song to form and shape the attitudes of a nation, and the truth of the Scotish balladeer's boast: "Let me write the songs of a country, and I care not who writes its laws." Arndt was the author of Germany's most popular patriotic song until *Deutschland über Alles* later in the century. For generations, Arndt's hymn, *Das deutsche Vaterland* (1813) gave voice to the expansionist dynamic of German nationalism. It raised and answered a rhetorical question about the Fatherland by saying that Germans would never feel fulfilled until all German-speaking people were united in an enormous new *Reich* of the German nation:

> What is the German's Fatherland?
> The Prussian, or the Swabian kind?
> Where Rhenish grapes bloom ripe and full,
> Where curves his flight the Baltic gull?

* The most influential Romantic of all, Richard Wagner, had such special personal importance to Adolf Hitler that he has been discussed with those who directly shaped his life and thought; see Chapter 2, pp. 103–113.

Ah, no! No! No!
His Fatherland must greater grow!

Arndt and his fellow Romantics demanded a new and portentous form of nationalism. English, French, and Russian nationalists emphasized the alleged political, cultural or religious superiority of their countries over others; Arndt called for a nationalism that was *racial*. His specific terminology, "racial purity" and "bastardization" and "mongrelization," would appear again in Germany. A century and a half before Hitler, for example, he insisted that "the Germans are not *bastardized* by alien peoples, they have not become *mongrels*, they have remained more than any other peoples in their original *purity*." And he preached the messianic mission of the race: "The German is a universal man [*Allerweltsmensch*] to whom God has given the whole earth as a home . . ."

Arndt also preceded the Nazis in exalting the Leader as the incarnation of a mysterious power which united the *Volk* with "the invisible majesty of the nation." And he agreed with Hitler about the positive values of battle: "War and struggle, the live moment of live forces—that is my lust, thus my name is called, that is myself, I God the Lord." [23]

Arndt's patriotic verse appeared in a dozen anthologies used in the schoolrooms of Germany during the Empire, Republic, and Third Reich. For example, Scheel's widely read *Lesebuch*—a kind of German *McGuffey's Eclectic Reader*—contained the following poem which children in the *Volksschulen* of 1900–1914 were obliged to memorize:

> We'll redden the iron with blood
> With hangman's blood
> With Frenchmen's blood;
> Oh sweet day of Revenge! [24]

Heinrich Wilhelm von Kleist (1777–1811), like many of his fellow Romantics, was torn between a sentimental longing for "a higher peace" and a delight in war and carnage. He was one of the authors of those poems which Treitschke would later call "the most beautiful political poetry in which any race could pride itself." One such poem of 1809 was entitled "*Germania an ihre Kinder*." The attitudes Mother Germany encouraged in her children with respect to the treatment of her enemies would be developed further in the *Hitler Jugend*:

> Color all the pastures, all the steads
> White with their bones
> Those which the raven and the fox disdain
> Deliver them over to the fish;
> Dam up the Rhine with their corpses. . . .
>
> *Chorus*:
> A joy-hunt as when marksmen are on the track of the wolf!

The Past As Prologue: Hitler and History

> Strike him dead! At the last judgment you will not be
> asked for explanations.[25]

Kleist's call for revenge against the West was heard not only during the Napoleonic wars but again after the defeat of Germany in 1918. One of the striking facts about the intellectual history of the Weimar Republic was the revival of Kleist's popularity. During this period, "Kleist scholarship became a passion, the cult a crusade." [26] Kleist and Arndt both said a great deal more than has been quoted here. But these things they did say—and they were long remembered.

Not all German Romantics delighted in conquest and carnage. One of them, Heinrich Heine (1797–1856), after listening to some of Kleist's and Arndt's "beautiful political poetry," gave a warning and penned a prophecy in 1834 which was to be fulfilled almost exactly a century later: "These doctrines have developed revolutionary forces which only await the day to break forth and fill the world with terror and astonishment." The Christian cross had for centuries kept "that brutal German joy in battle" tamed. But, Heine concluded,

> Should the subduing talisman, the Cross, break, then will come roaring forth the wild madness of the old champions, the insane Berserker rage of which the Northern poets sing. That talisman is brittle, and the day will come when it will pitifully break. The old stone Gods will rise from the long-forgotten ruin and rub the dust of a thousand years from their eyes; and Thor, leaping to life with his giant hammer, will crush the gothic cathedrals! [27]

Few Germans at the time listened to Heine. He was too much the humanitarian cosmopolite, too much at home in Paris. And he was a Jew.

A Romantic who had more influence on later generations than on his own was the nationalist philosopher Johann Gottlieb Fichte (1762–1814). He is best remembered by generations of German patriots for his stirring *Addresses to the German Nation* (1807–1808), which proclaimed the German people to be unique, the primal people (*Urvolk*), and endorsed racial nationalism:

> To have character and to be German [*Charakter haben und deutsch sein*] undoubtedly mean the same. . . . All comparisons between the German and the non-German are null and void. . . . We are the chosen people. Chosen by God . . . with a moral right to fulfill our destiny by every means of cunning and force.

Fichte made contributions not only to the cult of the *Volk* and Teutonic messianism but also to the idea of national socialism. In his influential book *Der geschlossene Handelsstaat* (The Closed Commercial State), published in 1800, he attacked the Western liberal economics of his day and demanded that Germany create a completely self-sufficient, state-regulated economy and expand to provide "living space" for the *Volk*.[28]

Among the most influential of all Romantics were the collectors of fairy stories, the famous Brothers Grimm, Jakob (1785–1863) and Wilhelm (1786–1859). Both were distinguished scholars and philologists. Their popular fame, however, rests on the results of their typically Romantic impulse to rediscover the distant past by gathering ancient stories and legends of the German people. Their edition of these *Volk*-stories had an enormous impact. By 1815 it had sold more copies than any other book with the single exception of the Lutheran Bible. For a 150 years and more, German children were lulled to sleep as the lessons of these stories sank deep into their little heads. Modern child psychologists have learned that Schiller was quite right: "Deeper meaning lies in the fairy tale of my childhood than in the truth that is taught by life." [29]

The first lesson of the Grimm tales is that little children must respect authority and be very obedient. Such is the message of a frightening story entitled "The Girl Without Hands." In it, the devil orders a father to cut off the hands of his little daughter. The father asks the little girl if she understands his predicament: he certainly doesn't want to cut off her hands, but he has been given orders by authority. The daughter responds dutifully: "Father Dear, do with me what you will, for I am your child." Thereupon she lays down both her hands, and her father hacks them off at the wrists.

Obedience and discipline are also driven home in one of the shortest and most memorable of these bedtime stories, "The Willful Child":

> Once upon a time there was a child who was willful, and would not do what her mother wished. For this reason God had no pleasure in her, and let her become ill, and no doctor could do her any good, and in a short time she lay on her death-bed. When she had been lowered into her grave, and the earth was spread over her, all at once her arm came out again, and stretched upwards, and when they had put it in and spread fresh earth over it, it was all to no purpose, for the arm always came out again. Then the mother herself was obliged to go to the grave, and strike the arm with a rod, and when she had done that, it was drawn in, and then at last the child had rest beneath the ground.[30]

To be sure, there are some sweet and charming little stories, but the number of tales involving bizarre physical and psychic cruelty is appalling. Let us consider the following scenes taken from a dozen or so of the stories, and note particularly the visual imagery they evoke in a child's mind: a queen boils and eats her own children; a young man is required to sleep with a corpse to keep it warm; a king's daughter is torn apart by bears and her mother is roasted alive; a wicked stepmother (Grimm's stepmothers are always wicked) is put into a barrel filled with venomous snakes; a little girl's tongue and eyes are cut out; a pretty young girl is hacked to pieces and thrown into a vat filled with putrefying human remains; a little boy is chopped up, put into a pan, and made into a pudding which is eaten by his father; a stepmother plans to eat the lungs and liver of her children; an old women cuts off the head of her beautiful stepdaughter, whereupon drops of blood from the girl's head carry on a conversation. In the original version of "Cinderella," not used by Walt Disney, her sisters cut off their toes and heels in an unsuccessful effort to wear the slipper, and their eyes are pecked out by a pigeon. The fate that awaited Hansel and Gretel, it will be recalled, was to be roasted and eaten.[31]

Little Germans of many generations also learned from these stories to admire racial purity and to distrust Jews. The attitude toward outsiders—such as stepmothers—is usually one of suspicion and animosity. But hatred for the Jew as an outsider is so general and so intense that the Grimms assumed it to be a "natural sentiment." In their stories, the heroes are usually peasants or knights and noblemen. The middle-class merchants tend to have a bad time, but this is particularly true of the Jew. He is a foreigner, a product of non-Teutonic culture; he dresses badly, his teeth are yellow, his smile sinister. He is a miser who delights in fleecing the good, naïve peasants; he is a coward who whines when punished. Given the content and the lessons of these bedtime stories, it is not surprising that Hitler chose a special edition as prizes for the younger children of the *Hitler Jugend*.

Another of the well-remembered Romantics of the period was the founder of German gymnastic societies and organizer of a *Freikorps* of 1813, Friedrich Ludwig Jahn, affectionately called "Turnvater Jahn" (1778–1852). One of the first "*völkisch* Nationalists," he preached the concept of *Volkstum*—the mysterious racial force that shapes all history—and in 1813 he called for a national leader, "a great Führer, cast of Iron and Fire . . . The *Volk* will honor him as savior and forgive all his sins." [32]

Of course, it must not be thought that Romanticism was the only current running in the turbulent stream of German life and letters during the Napoleonic era. Immanuel Kant (1724–1804), one of the world's most creative philosophers, was widely read at this time; Goethe (1749–1832) and Schiller (1759–1805) were gracing world letters with magnificent expressions of the human spirit; Friedrich Schleiermacher (1768–1834) and his fellow Pietists were preaching the sanctity of the individual personality; and Wilhelm von Humboldt (1767–1835) was calling for civil rights and constitutions. But none of these writers had the impact of these political Romantics. None contributed so much to the historic forces that pushed Germany away from its own humanist tradition toward militant, racist nationalism, and toward an exaltation of power and aggression that was not uncongenial to the political and social program set forth by Adolf Hitler.

1848: The Failure of a Democratic Alternative

> The German generation that came of age in 1848 rode forth on a romantic quest to rescue liberty. They turned back to marry power.
> —Geoffrey Bruun

The failure of Germany to develop a democratic alternative to dictatorship was one of the key reasons for Hitler's rise to power. No single event in German history was more important to the fortunes of parliamentary government than the Revolution of 1848. As two memorable clichés have put it, that was the "Year of Decision" and "the turning point in German history, where history refused to turn."

After the defeat of Napoleon, an age of restoration and reaction set in, as the princes of the Germanies cooperated with Count Metternich (1773–1859) in reestablishing old governments and crushing nationalist movements. Metternich's system required the support of the Prussian power structure. This he received in full measure, for the Prussian aristocracy, army, bureaucracy, and warlord king were all as anxious as Metternich to preserve Prussian absolutism. They were particularists to the core and wanted no nonsense about civil liberties, parliaments, or national unification. Treitschke could weave his glowing myths about Prussian support of German nationalism, but in fact the people who counted in Prussia ridiculed the idea. They imprisoned or hounded the Prussian reformers into exile, along with the poets of *Gefühlspolitik* and nationalism.

With Prussian help, Metternich's system was effective in the Germanies until the fateful year 1848, when Europe was swept by revolution. In France the "Banquet Campaign" of February and the aftermath of street massacres drove King Louis Philippe and his chief minister, the well-hated historian François Guizot, into exile. The contagion spread—for "when France sneezes all Europe catches cold"—to Hungary, Spain, Italy, and the Germanies. Even in Prussia and Austria the old order suddenly seemed to be tottering. Among liberals everywhere, hope quickened that a brave new world would arise from the aristocratic ruins of the *ancien régime*. Many German patriots saw a splendid opportunity to unify the Fatherland as one great national state dedicated to liberty and established on the foundations of a democratic constitution.

The expectations, sincerity, and naïveté of a generation were expressed by the youthful Carl Schurz (1829–1906), whose own life is a poignant commentary on the course of the revolution. Like dozens of students of his day, as an undergraduate at the University of Bonn he took up the cause of revolution. After its failure he was driven into exile by Prussian authorities. He returned in 1850 to rescue his old teacher, who had been imprisoned by the Prussians. Again exiled in 1852, he and his wife—along with thousands of other disappointed German liberals—immigrated to the United States. In America he found opportunity, denied him in his native land, to contribute his talents to the service of democratic political ideals. He became one of this country's most honored and productive citizens.

But in 1848 he was a German undergraduate caught up in the fever of revolution and filled with high expectations for his Fatherland:

> The word democracy was on all tongues. . . . Like many of my friends, I was dominated by the feeling that at last the great opportunity had arrived for giving to the German people the liberty which was their birthright and to the German fatherland its unity and greatness, and that it was now the first duty of every German to do and to sacrifice everything for this sacred object. We were profoundly, solemnly, in earnest. . . .[33]

Such was the spirit of 1848—a year its leading German historian, with forgiveable exaggeration, considered to be the most important single year in the history of Germany.[34]

It was certainly both an important and a symbolic year. For the first—and to date, the last—time in German history, delegates from all the Germanies met in an effort to establish unity for Germany on a democratic basis. That these liberal patriots failed in 1848 is one of the greatest tragedies in German history, for their task of nation-building was left to others who despised their humane idealism.

Reasons for their failure have formed the subject of a dozen scholarly monographs. More important, however, for the future of Germany than the causes was the bare fact of failure itself. Something akin to a feeling of group inferiority beset the German liberals. They had tried and they had failed. The middle class, they concluded, was incapable of political leadership. Nothing could be accomplished in politics by discussion and parliaments; only military force could solve the German problem. Thus, after riding forth gaily and expectantly "on the romantic quest to rescue liberty, they turned back to marry power."[35]

Julius Froebel, a disappointed liberal, caught the mood perfectly when he wrote after the failure of 1848:

> The German nation is sick of principles and doctrines. . . . What it wants is power, power, power! And whoever gives it power, to him will it give honor, more honor than he can ever imagine.[36]

The epitaph for mid-19th-century German democracy was provided by F. T. Fischer, another liberal who looked back at the failures of his colleagues at Frankfurt and concluded: "Freedom and unity cannot come together. Unity must come first and can only be achieved by a tyrant. . . . Freedom can come later, after unity has been imposed on us by Prussia." [37]

This was the tragedy of 1848: the conviction that tyranny would bring unity and freedom to the German people.

THE SECOND REICH, 1871–1918

Bismarck

> Come, Savior, if already born
> Step forth, we'll follow in thy tread!
> Thou, last of all dictators,
> Come, bring the last dictatorship! *
> —J. G. Fischer, 1848

In founding the Second Reich of the German nation, Otto von Bismarck (1815–1898) fulfilled the fondest dream of disillusioned democrats of 1848. Summoned to Berlin in the fall of 1862 by the Prussian king to put down parliamentary pretensions, he quickly set forth his program in a self-fulfilling prophecy: German unity, he predicted, would not come through parliament but through power, through iron and blood. He was not "the last dictator," but he reinforced a tradition and left an inheritance which were immensely helpful to the dictator who would one day be hailed as savior and worshipped as a god.

In popular portraiture, Bismarck appears as the massive paragon of political ability, the cold master of *Realpolitik*. Indeed, the very word is identified with Bismarck, and no one described the concept better than he. It is entirely appropriate that Bismarck should be quoted on Bismarck by an admirer and latter day *Realpolitiker*, Henry Kissinger:

> For heaven's sake, no sentimental alliances. . . . Gratitude and confidence will not bring a single man into the feud on our side; only fear will do that, if we use it cautiously and skillfully. . . . Politics is the art of the possible, the science of the relative. [38]

Hitler liked to imagine that he and Bismarck were very much alike. He noted that they both had delicate, artistic hands and pale blue eyes, and that their cranial measurements were very similar. By any test of intellect, culture, and statecraft, a vast gulf separates the creator of Germany from its destroyer. And yet the personalities of the two men do show surprising parallels. For Bismarck was far

---

* The German verse reads:
> *Komm, Einzger, wenn du schon geboren*
> *Tritt auf, wir folgen deiner Spur!*
> *Du letzter aller Diktatoren*
> *Komm mit der letzten Diktatur.*

from the emotionally stable person his traditional image suggests. He too was a man in deep conflict with himself.

The "Iron Chancellor" was, as he himself confessed, "all nerves," a whining hypochondriac * who often sobbed uncontrollably. The soul of grace and thoughtfulness one moment, he was viciously vengeful the next. He despised intellectuals and used the word "professor" like an epithet, yet he could have given university lectures on Goethe or Shakespeare and he wrote in six languages. He indulged himself, drinking gallons of "Black Velvet," a mixture of Guinness and champagne; he also denied himself, living for a year on a diet of raw herring. The man who boasted of his *Herrschernatur* (commanding presence) could not sleep at night until he was tucked in by his favorite doctor, who held his hand "like a mother with a restless child." Comforting the Iron Chancellor and putting him to bed became a nightly routine.[39]

Adolf Hitler may or may not have recognized in Bismarck a kindred psychological spirit; he was certainly impressed with the Iron Chancellor's political performance and spoke admiringly of his "brutal will," noting that he was "absolutely right" in ordering the slaughter of French civilians during the seige of Paris in 1870 and in requiring the death penalty for a wide range of crimes. The Führer could not help feeling, however, that he was superior to his predecessor in many ways. Bismarck, he said, was incapable of understanding the Catholic Church; he had been much too lenient with Austria; he was ineffective in handling socialism; he lacked "a really spiritual foundation." Above all, "Bismarck did not recognize the impending danger" of economic materialism, "the worship of Mammon," and the evil machinations of Jewish bankers.[40]

But all in all, Hitler was generous and concluded that as statesmen the two had a great deal in common. In this the Führer was mistaken. Of the many differences between them, two are particularly striking. Unlike Hitler, Bismarck had the capacity for growth, for change and maturation. He also knew how to set limits, to recognize that politics was indeed "the art of the possible." One of his favorite quotations from Goethe was one that Hitler could never understand, let alone practice: "Genius is the art of limitation" (*In der Begrenzung zeigt sich der Meister*).

Bismarck demonstrated the art in foreign policy. Having attained his goal of creating a strong Germany through war, he announced that "we are satiated" and used all his enormous diplomatic skill to preserve his empire by keeping the peace. Thus he created his intricate system of alliances, which he liked to refer to as "My League for Peace" (*Mein Friedensbund*). Unlike Hitler, and like a good poker player, Bismarck knew when to quit.

Bismarck's domestic policy also shows the touch of the master. It is best seen in the way he handled four groups who sought to dispute

---

* His list of real and imaginary ills included gout, migraine headaches, insomnia, gallstones, neuralgia, diarrhea, constipation, and, worst of all, "bad nerves."

his power: liberals, Catholics, Social Democrats, and conservatives. By the adroit balancing of one group against another and by satisfying the basic needs of each, he converted opponents into supporters of his empire and its system of authoritarian paternalism. The opposition of the liberal middle class was swept away by an exultant tide of patriotism hailing Bismarck's military victories and the proclamation of a united Fatherland. Bismarck also was given credit for economic reforms, stable currency, and concessions to industry, which was making Imperial Germany incomparably the strongest economic power on the continent. As for the Catholics, after an ill-advised conflict with their Church and with the Catholic Center party, Bismarck—unlike Hitler—recognized his mistake, retreated adroitly, and gained Catholic support for his domestic and foreign policy. Future history would show a continuation of the Catholic Center's preference for authoritarian government to democracy. In a crucial vote in 1933 over whether the new chancellor, Adolf Hitler, should be given dictatorial powers, the Center cast the decisive vote for the "Enabling Act" which provided the legal basis for Hitler's dictatorship. Thus, in the Third Reich, as in the Second, the Catholic Center was not conspicuous for its defense of democracy.

Other opponents won over to Bismarck's Reich were the Marxian Social Democrats. Bismarck's method with them was similar to the technique he had used so successfully with the liberals. He gave them what they wanted; he killed them with kindness. He pushed through parliament the most sweeping social legislation in the contemporary world. This vaunted conservative became a pioneer of state socialism and thus sustained the paternalistic tradition of the authoritarian state (*Obrigkeitsstaat*), which would be extended in the National Socialism of the Third Reich. It is true that the Marxists continued to grow in numbers throughout the empire. But they were no longer a revolutionary party. Their words were the words of Marx, but their deeds were the actions of patriots.

In consolidating his Reich, Bismarck also confronted opposition from conservative Prussian particularists. He reassured them by promising that Prussian interests and attitudes would continue to dominate the power structure of the state—army, bureaucracy, industry, agriculture, banking, and the educational system. He kept his promise. The result was a conversion as remarkable as that of Marxian labor, Catholic Center, and the liberal middle class. Prussian conservatives for the first time became supporters of the idea of empire. National patriotism had become respectable. Indeed, it was now endorsed by so many diverse and influential groups that it was soon to become lethal.

Bismarck's legacy to the German people can be assessed in many different ways. It is certainly true that under the benevolent system of government he established, millions of people lived out their lives in relative comfort, security, and freedom from want, that German industry reached remarkable heights, that arts, letters, and science flourished in a world at peace. These were indeed, as the emperor proclaimed, magnificent times (*herrliche Zeiten*). Most Germans agreed with the author of a widely read book, entitled *Government and the Will of the People*, that their country had the best form of government ever devised by modern man.[41]

Yet it is also fair to say that this paternalism had a price. The political cost to the German people was well expressed by two of Germany's most perceptive observers. The historian Theodor Mommsen said that Bismarck had "broken the political backbone of the nation." The sociologist Max Weber agreed. Bismarck, he concluded, had left behind a nation without the rudiments of political education: "He taught us to distrust our own political intelligence. . . ."[42] Bismarck would have smiled knowingly and agreed with both criticisms. He wanted it just that way. Subjects should learn that the arts and wiles of government were so intricate that only a few great leaders could master them and run the affairs of state. He was directly in the tradition of Frederick the Great: "The ruler rules, the subject obeys." It was an aphorism that admirably suited Hitler's *Führerprinzip*.

The "German Condition": Formative Influences

> Hitler and National Socialism were in a long-standing tradition. . . . They were not unfortunate accidents, not incomprehensible derailments in the path of German history; they were, as Konrad Heiden said, a "German condition."
> —Karl Dietrich Bracher

At the height of the Second Reich, during the decades from 1890 to 1910, a generation was born and raised that was to play a decisive role in bringing Adolf Hitler to power. The formative influences on their lives invite our attention.

This generation was affected by what has been broadly called the "German condition"—a tradition hostile to democratic government and congenial to the acceptance of National Socialism. Specifically, it included glorification of the authoritarian state and denigration of democracy; belief that the Jewish people were a clear and present threat to *Kultur*; endorsement of racial nationalism and aggressive expansion in the name of a Germanic mission; insistence that the claims of the *Gemeinschaft* take precedence over the rights of the individual; and exaltation of military power. This "condition" had long been present in German history, but it became acute during the years that shaped the lives of young Adolf Hitler and his generation.

Of particular importance to the German political tradition was an attitude of mind which extolled the power of the state and derided parliamentary government. This attitude fostered what Fritz Stern has called "illiberalism" and "formed it into a habitual response" to all political and social problems. Glorification of the state was encouraged by the historic achievements, vividly memorialized in popular history, of such authoritarian political rulers as Frederick the Great and Bismarck. Political theory also helped in the sanctification.[43]

The German theory of the state differed strikingly in two respects from that of other Western nations. A persistent characteristic of Western thought, particularly in England and America, has been an emphasis on moderation, a distrust of political extremes. From the great theorists of the Middle Ages through Halifax in the 17th century, Locke and Jefferson in the 18th, and the political practitioners of the 19th and 20th centuries—whatever their political party—English and American political leaders have accepted parliamentary government and publicly endorsed political moderation. In Germany, by contrast, influential political thought has run to extremes—from the exaltation and near deification of the state found in Hegel to the revolutionary theory of Marx and Engels, who wanted to destroy all traditional forms of political organization.

Germans also held a dramatically different conception of the nature and purpose of the state. To such leading political theorists as John Locke, Jean-Jacques Rousseau, and Thomas Jefferson, the state was created by man to serve his needs. If a particular creation failed to live up to contractual expectations, citizens had the right to abolish that state and create another. Man, not the state, was the master. The idea is made clear in these familiar and beautiful words:

> To secure these Rights, Governments are instituted among men . . . that whenever any Form of Government becomes destructive of these Ends, it is the Right of the People to alter or abolish it, and to institute new Government . . . on such Principles . . . as to them shall seem most likely to effect their Safety and Happiness.

Throughout the 19th century, German theorists rejected democratic ideas so commonplace and essential to the Western tradition. To them, the state was so sacred, so miraculous that it could not have been the work of mere man; it must have been created by the unfathomable forces of nature or by an inscrutable Providence. Thus Adam Müller, the political philosopher of the Romantics, proclaimed —in striking contrast to the thought of Locke and Jefferson—that "the State was not established for the benefit of the individual" but for its own mysterious purposes.[44]

GEORG WILHELM FRIEDRICH HEGEL

Germany's most influential 19th-century political theorist was Georg Wilhelm Friedrich Hegel (1770–1831). He wrote and lectured early in the century, but his influence reached its climax during the Second Reich, when his philosophy of the state became virtually the official faith of all German political theorists. Hegelianism conquered key positions in every field of thought: political theory, ethics, philosophy, aesthetics, historiography. For decades none but Hegel's disciples occupied chairs of philosophy and political economy in all the universities of Prussia.[45]

Hegel's writings are difficult, abstruse, often incomprehensible to all but the initiate. About one thing, however, he is very clear indeed: the state must be revered above all institutions. For it is no mere human creation—it is an act of God. Indeed, it is "the movement of God through history" and the "institutionalization of God." In Hegel's special formulation—the Hegelian dialectic—the state is the higher *synthesis* which evolves from the clash of *thesis* and *antithesis*. The state synthesizes individual will and collective will, power and justice; it combines both moral right and physical force, freedom and authority. In fact, according to Hegel, freedom can fully exist only in a national state, and only in the state can moral purpose be fulfilled: "The State is the true embodiment of mind and spirit. And only in it . . . [does] the individual share in truth, real existence and ethical status."

The state is not a means to an end, as in Locke and Jefferson; rather, it has its own moral end. But what the true nature of this purpose is very difficult to get from Hegel, for his mysticism leads to mystification:

> The State is the reality of the moral idea—the moral spirit as the revealed will apparent to itself, substantial, which thinks and knows itself and accomplishes that which it knows and insofar as it knows it.

As Ralf Dahrendorf well asked, what is really meant by all this, what is being said here? Who and what is the state? It is difficult to tell, for the state is beyond comprehension, hence beyond rational criticism. And from that point it is not a long step to the conclusion reached by latter-day Hegelians that "the State can do no wrong." [46]

Hegel's emphasis on the *Gemeinschaft* shows his indebtedness to the political Romantics. Apart from the state, people have no moral meaning and no political form. They are a shapeless mass until welded into "the community of the state."

The flavor of Hegel and the intensity of his adoration of the state are best conveyed in his own words:

> The State is divine will . . . the State therefore knows what it wants, knows it in its generality as thought, and it acts therefore according to purpose. . . .

> One should therefore revere the State as something divine upon earth [*irdischgöttliches*] and realize that if it is hard to understand nature, it is immeasurably more difficult to grasp the State.

Again and again, Hegel insists that the state is not comprehensible, that the people should not try to understand it, they should simply obey its dictates:

> The people . . . are that part of the State *which does not know what it wants.* For to know that is the fruit of deep knowledge and insight which is not the people's affair. . . .

> Sacrificing oneself for the individuality of the State is . . . a *general duty.*[47]

Even more important to Hegel than the State was the *Volk.* For it was the *Volk* which was the primary agent of his historical dialectic or the means by which the freedom of the individual was reconciled with the authority of the State.

Hegel had no confidence in parliaments, "the incompetent and ignorant." He placed his trust in great men. His message about them would be repeated often in the ensuing years, until it reached its final bastardized and disastrous culmination in the *Führerprinzip.* "In public opinion all falsehood and all truth is contained, but to find the truth is the task of the Great Man. He who says and accomplishes what his time wants and desires is the Great Man of that time. He does what is the inner essence of his time, he realizes it, and yet he who does not know how to despise public opinion . . . will never accomplish anything great." [48]

Like every other responsible German philosopher, Hegel would have been appalled by Hitler's brutal dictatorship. But his endorsement of the concept of a "World Historic Leader," the "World Spirit Incarnate," and the "World's Soul" (as he called Napoleon) helped create a tradition of political hero worship in Germany that was not uncongenial to Hitler's concept of the Führer.

One of the most influential popularizers of Hegel's thought was the historian Heinrich Treitschke, who also provided "the ideological underpinnings of Bismarck's *Realpolitik.*" Over and over again, in his immensely popular lectures at the University of Berlin, Treitschke roared in his deafness to wildly cheering students:

> Power, within and without, is the very essence of the State. . . .

> Since the State is power, it can obviously draw all human actions within its scope. . . . The State can overshadow practically the whole of a people's life . . . no limit can be set to the functions of the State.[49]

Treitschke turned his back on his earlier liberalism to hail the triumphant march of Bismarck's *Machtpolitik.* "Liberalism," he decided, "is merely the embodiment of social selfishness"; he now put his faith in "the mystery of the Great Man." After arguing that the state should regulate all aspects of a people's life, he added, "It does not ask for opinion but demands obedience. . . . Submission is what the State primarily requires; it insists upon acquiescence; its very essence is the accomplishment of its will." [50]

Adolf Hitler had little need to expand on this conception of obedience.

FRIEDRICH LIST

Economic theory in Germany, as well as political theory and historic practice, endorsed state control of the economy and thus set important precedent for Hitler's National Socialism. Friedrich List (1789–1846), incomparably the most influential German economist of the 19th century, directly and vehemently attacked Adam Smith's *Wealth of Nations,* whose theory of laissez-faire economic individualism was accepted as orthodoxy in the English-speaking world.

List's immensely influential book championing state intervention and control was accurately entitled *Das nationale System der politischen Oekonomie.* First published in 1841, it was as important to Germany as Adam Smith's ubiquitous classic was to England and America. By 1890 it had gone through a dozen editions and had been the subject of literally thousands of books and articles.

List took violent issue with all of Smith's convictions. Where Smith was a liberal cosmopolitan, List insisted that the very idea of internationalism was dangerous to the growth of a vigorous Germany. Where Smith stressed individualism, List sought something between individualism and internationalism and he found it in the nation, which he considered far more important than either the individual or humanity.

Two terms would predominate in German expansionist rhetoric of the 20th century: *Drang nach Osten* (push toward the East) and its corollary *Mitteleuropa,* a concept particularly dear to the hearts of Nazi geopoliticians who argued that he who could control the heartland of Central Europe could control the continent. The terms were not invented in the 20th or 19th centuries, nor were they original to List —some of the thinking is as old as the Teutonic knights' mission to the East—but List's system embodied both concepts. He added a *Drang nach Westen,* proclaiming that the German nation could not be complete so long as it did not extend "over the whole coast from the mouth of the Rhine to the frontier of Poland, including Holland and Denmark. A natural consequence of this union must be the admission of both these countries . . . into the German nationality . . . both of these nations belong, as respects their descent and whole character, to the German nationality." All these countries must be consolidated into one "mighty body" which Germany would control by establishing a *Pax Germanica* on the continent.[51]

Adam Smith had supported free trade among all nations; List urged the lowering of tariffs within the Germanies in a national customs union (*Zollverein*) with a high tariff wall protecting the Fatherland against encircling economic threats. Where Smith favored the freeing of colonies from the mother countries, Friedrich List demanded "supplementary territories" (*Ergänzungsgebiete*). When asked why Germany should dominate so many other countries economically and politically, he replied in a manner familiar to those who considered it Germany's mission to civilize the world: "It is hardly subject to doubt that Providence has by preference dedicated the Germanic races, by means of their nature and character, to the solution of the great tasks of leading world affairs. . . ." [52]

Adam Smith, like many other liberals, had insisted that government should not impinge upon individual rights and should regulate the social and political order as little as possible. List demanded that the state control not only the economy but also education, art, music, literature, and culture. He called for "a royal dictatorship" (*königliche Diktatur*) to carry out his plans.[53]

LAGARDE AND LANGBEHN

The names of Lagarde and Langbehn are scarcely household words today, but at the height of the empire they were enormously influential in shaping the thought of a generation. Both used their impressive talents to denigrate democracy, applaud racist nationalism, and endorse the need for a mighty Führer of the Germans.[54]

Paul Anton de Lagarde (1827–1891) was a scholar of staggering productivity * whom Thomas Mann regarded as "one of the giants of our people," along with Nietzsche and Wagner. By far Lagarde's most influential book was a mystical hypernationalist work entitled *Deutsche Schriften* (German Writings). First published in 1878, the work went through dozens of printings and was widely anthologized. "Pithy, patriotic passages" taken from his writings also appeared on picture postcards.

Lagarde was repelled by democracy and by the entire liberal, rational outlook which, he saw quite correctly, was an important underpinning for parliamentary government. His pronouncements, such as "democracy and culture are mutually exclusive," became popular aphorisms among German intellectuals.

A main purpose of Lagarde's political writings was to sound the call for a new Reich of a racially pure *Gemeinschaft*. The *Volk*, once freed from the pernicious influence of the Jews, would experience a tremendous cultural and spiritual revival. This Reich could only come about, he believed, with the advent of a Führer who would preach power and a new religion of mystical nationalism. Lagarde is explicit

---

* In the course of one decade he produced, among other writings, the following: 25 books on general philology, 22 on Hebrew, 26 on Greek, 8 on Latin, 6 on Arabic, 19 on Syriac, 2 on Persian, and 5 on Coptic and Egyptian. His other interests ranged from strident anti-Semitism to the origins of hard cider, from a critique of the government of Louis Philippe to the mathematical concept of X.

about the need for a Führer who "senses the nation's will . . . foresees its needs—or, better still—by some mysterious intuition, educates his nation in its needs. . . . Only the . . . , strong will of a Single Man can help us, . . . not parliament nor statutes nor the ambition of powerless individuals." As his disappointment in Bismarck's Germany grew, so did the intensity of his faith in a new Barbarossa, "a Führer who would so completely represent the people that in him they would be united and his command would be their will." This statement, first written in 1878, is an accurate description of Hitler's theory of the relationship between Führer and *Volk*.[55]

According to a popular German encyclopedia, Julius Langbehn (1851–1907) had "far-reaching influence" through his work *Rembrandt als Erzieher* (Rembrandt as Educator), first published in 1890.

He most certainly did. The remarkable popularity of his book is mystifying, since its prose is as turgid as its thesis is absurd. Somehow, through a thought process that is obscure, Langbehn hit upon the strange notion that the humane Dutch painter was the source of racist nationalism.* It is not at all clear why Langbehn was so influential. Perhaps, as Fritz Stern has suggested, it was because "chaos and absurdity may suggest great impenetrable depth, and repetition may weary the reader into belief."

Whatever the reasons, the book sold by the thousands and had enormous impact on German thought. The publishing sensation of the 1890s, it went through 40 printings in the first two years. It was particularly influential in the youth movement prior to World War I, where it was as popular as Nietzsche's *Zarathustra*. Sales eventually dwindled, but they revived in the 1920s when it became, as one critic noted, "a mighty force in German life."

Langbehn was particularly noted, as we shall see, for his virulent anti-Semitism. But he also served as a bridge to Hitler in another way. Like Lagarde, he made racist nationalism "respectable" in intellectual circles. Like many influential German intellectuals, he disdained politics and ridiculed democracy in vastly popular writings. Only a dictatorial leader, he insisted, could rescue the Fatherland from the swamp of civil rights, racial pollution, and cultural mediocrity in which it was floundering. Thus he called stridently for "a New Barbarossa . . . a Great One . . . a Leader of Genius with artistic temperament . . . a Caesar-Artist . . . whose fire of . . . spirit and strength of arm will fulfill our ancient, victorious longings." [56]

FRIEDRICH NIETZSCHE

One day within the year preceding Hitler's birth, Friedrich Nietzsche (1844–1900) jotted down a prophecy in his notebooks which would be fulfilled in the Third Reich. "I know my destiny," Nietzsche

---

* He called Rembrandt "the most German of all German painters" and Hamlet "the most outstanding example of the German spirit." See *Rembrandt als Erzieher* (Leipzig, 1890), 9, 44.

wrote. "Someday my name will be associated with the memory of something monstrous [*Ungeheures*]." [57]

That one of the most brilliant and creative minds of the 19th century was appropriated by the Nazis—who grossly distorted his thought —is one of the tragedies of intellectual history. One may well agree with Albert Camus: "We shall never finish making reparation for the injustice done to him." [58] Yet Nietzsche himself bears heavy responsibility for that injustice and for helping to create the monstrosity he would have abhorred. He was distorted because he was eminently distortable.

Nietzsche's real meaning was often, as he said, "hidden behind a mask"—stated obliquely or in poetic images. There are parts of his message, however, that come through with glaring clarity. In particular he loathed Christianity and all it stood for. In a work he gloried in calling *The Antichrist*, he wrote, "I call Christianity the one great curse, the one innermost perversion. . . . I call it the one immortal blemish of mankind. . . . One does well to put on gloves when reading the New Testament—the proximity of so much filth almost forces one to do this. . . . I regard Christianity as the most fatal, seductive lie that has yet existed." To him, Christianity was a kind of defense mechanism used by the ineffectual and the cowardly, who, in their weakness, proclaimed meekness a virtue. It was, he said, the means by which "the weak take revenge on the strong . . . the morality of slaves." It is not the meek who will inherit Nietzsche's earth; it is the powerful, the ruthless, the hard. Not only did he despise the morality of Christianity, he also accused it of spreading "the poison" of the doctrine of human equality in the sight of God.[59]

Nietzsche also mounted a frontal and sustained attack on many other things dear to the Western world. Indeed, his was the heaviest assault ever made by a first-class mind from within the gates of Western civilization. With blazing contempt he attacked those who believed that freedom can be gained through constitutions and the rule of law: "The human being who has become free . . . spits on the contemptible type of well-being dreamed of by shopkeepers, Christians, cows, females, Englishmen, and other democrats. The free man is a warrior." [60]

To Nietzsche, the whole concept of democracy was a disaster. It mouthed the stupidity "Everyone is equal to everyone else," and that meant "At bottom we are one and all self-seeking cattle and mob." He indicted democracy as a confession of the decadence of man consummating his diminution (*Verkleinerung*), mediocrity (*Vermittelmässigung*), and degradation of value (*Wert-Erniedrigung*). Over and over again he repeats the phrase "parliamentary drivel" (*Blödsinn*).[61]

Nietzsche challenged the youth of Germany to surpass the democratic herd and become Supermen or Overmen (*Übermenschen*). Since it was never very clear what he meant by the concept, many different aspirants could claim membership in this elite. In one regrettable passage, later appropriated by the Nazis, he had talked of "the magnificent blond beast, roaming wantonly in search of prey and victory."

Nietzsche's defenders have been quick to emphasize he did not mean the concept as racial, and the victories were cultural, not military. Nevertheless, the words easily lent themselves to misinterpretation.

Though he almost certainly did not intend it, Nietzsche provided an ethic for aggression and exploitation. His tirades against softness and pity, as well as his call for hardness and brutality, served as the rationale for aggression in both the Second and the Third Reich. Nietzsche should not be maligned or misquoted; but as Georg Lukács has written, neither should he be bowdlerized and prettified. "He was an honorable thinker, neither hypocrite nor pussy-footer [*Schleicher*]," and he sometimes meant precisely what he said. Read in context, Lukács argued, Nietzsche gave direct and explicit endorsement for exploitation and ruthless brutality. The point can be illustrated from Nietzsche:

> The beast of prey and the jungle prove that evil [*Bösheit*] can be very healthy and develop the body magnificently. . . .
>
> They shall become better beasts of prey, finer, slyer, more like humans [*Menschen-ähnlicher*]; for men are the best predators.[62]

Hitler's New Order would make passages in Nietzsche ring with prophecy fulfilled. In place of "parliamentary drivel," Nietzsche had called explicitly for a

> New Order . . . One Will to dominate and rule Europe—a frightening individual Will . . . [that] will bring an end to the long spunout comedy of little states . . . as well as democratic many-willedness [*Vielwollerei*]. The time for petty politics is past: the next century will bring the battle for the domination of the earth [*Erd-Herrschaft*]; the urge for politics on the grand scale [*den Zwang zur grossen Politik*].[63]

Nietzsche longed for the coming of a powerful leader who would be the "Master of the Masses" (*Herr der Herden*) and who would set forth "new philosophies" of power and control. "For that purpose," Nietzsche concluded, "a new kind of philosopher and commander [*Befehlshaber*] will be required." [64]

Walter Kaufmann and many other defenders of Nietzsche have rightly emphasized that he would have been adamantly opposed to Nazi ideology. He despised the anti-Semitism and racism of his own day and excoriated both Treitschke and Wagner for their Jew-baiting. He had high praise for the Jews and only one major criticism: they produced Christianity. His notebooks show his feelings with unmistakable clarity:

> Maxim: associate with no man who is a part of the lying race-swindle.

What differentiates a Jew from an anti-Semite: if a Jew lies, he knows he is lying; the anti-Semite does not know that he is always lying.[65]

His revulsion at being associated with anti-Semites was so great it made him physically ill, as he noted in a bitter letter to his sister, who had married a racist and was misusing his work:

> . . . You have committed one of the greatest stupidities—for yourself and for me! Your association with an anti-Semitic chief expresses a foreignness to my whole way of life which fills me again and again with ire or melancholy. . . . It is a matter of honor with me to be absolutely clean and unequivocal in relation to anti-Semitism, namely, *opposed* to it, as I am in my writings. . . . That the name of Zarathustra is used in every *Anti-Semitic Correspondence Sheet,* has almost made me sick several times. . . .[66]

Far from exalting the state, Nietzsche feared and opposed its encroachments on the freedom of man. He was appalled by the power of the military-industrial complex of Imperial Germany and despised the whole cult of Germandom: "Behold the Germans, the lowest, most stupid, most common race that exists on earth, now hohenzollerned [*verhohenzollert*] to hate spirit and freedom."[67]

Finally, in mind, character, and intent, Nietzsche was a world apart from Hitler. Nietzsche would destroy in order to create a finer order; he dreamed of new beginnings and higher creative purposes; he was "boundlessly honest," with a courageous commitment to self-awareness and truth. Hitler had no vision beyond his lust to brutalize and dominate other men in a racist dictatorship. Nietzsche was a courageous and instinctive heretic. When he cried out that God was dead, he meant that all systems of authority were dead. He would have joined Luther as one of the first victims of Nazi tyranny.[68]

All this needs to be said. But his admirers are unable to make a persuasive case that Nietzsche was "a good European" who had no connection whatever with the rise of Hitler to power in Germany. True, Nietzsche himself had said he was a "good European," in part to dissociate himself from the noisy nationalists of his day. But he was not being a good European when he sought to destroy the European heritage: rights of citizens protected by laws and constitutions; the conviction that people could shape their own social and political future through parliamentary government; a code of ethics and morality based on Judeo-Christian and humanist principles. All these things Nietzsche despised and ridiculed. Certainly he sought to build new forms in the rubble of destruction, but the lust to destroy was more potent than the hope of creation.

Nietzsche's unintended contribution to the coming of Nazism was twofold: negative and positive. By the turn of the century, his call for "triumphant negation" was being listened to by thousands of young Germans. It is noteworthy that when Adolf Hitler and his generation went to war in 1914 they took Nietzsche with them in their knapsacks— along with Luther's translation of the New Testament, a book Nietzsche so thoroughly despised. A wartime edition of *Also sprach Zarathustra* was specially printed, bound in durable field-gray, and sold to tens of thousands of German soldiers.* How many young volunteers, including Adolf Hitler, read and remembered Nietzsche's lines hailing negation and announcing the coming of "the last man . . . the *most despicable man* [*der verächtlichste Mensch*]" ?

> Alas! The most despicable man is coming,
>   he who can no longer despise himself.
> Behold! I show you the last man.
>
> What is love? What is creation? What is longing?
> What is the star?—
> Thus asks the last man and blinks.

How many young minds responded to Nietzsche's defiant rejection of traditional ethical values, his exaltation of brutality and destruction, his sneering references to pity and the teachings of Jesus?

> You say a good cause can even sanctify war?
> I say unto you: it is a good war that sanctifies
>   any cause.
>
> You shall love peace as a means to new wars,
> And the short peace more than the long!
>
> For a sword wants to drink blood
> And glistens with desire [*funkelt vor Begierde*].
>
> I sing and I mock all pity . . .
> God is dead . . .
>
> "Man is evil," so spoke all the wisest to
>   comfort me . . .
> "Man must become better and more evil," so I teach.
>
> The greatest evil is necessary for the Superman's
>   best
> [*Das Böseste ist nötig zu des Übermenschen Bestem*].
>
> It may have been good for that Preacher of the
>   little people

---

* The title page of the copy before me as I write reads: 141–150 *Tausend, Kriegsausgabe.*

That He suffered and bore the sins of man.
But I rejoice over great sin as my great comfort . . .

Thus spake Zarathustra.[69]

Nietzsche's emphasis on negation fit the mood of disillusionment which swept postwar Germany. His slashing attacks on all systems of politics and morality continued to make him far and away the most widely read philosopher among the youth of Germany during the decade prior to Hitler's accession to power. Nietzsche did as much as any single writer to destroy a moderate alternative to political extremism. For he would tolerate no half-measures; he demanded totality—total destruction and total creation. He despised Heinrich Heine's "subduing talisman of the Cross"; he rejected Goethe's sense of restraint and limitation; he ridiculed political moderation; he trumpeted "the magic power of extremes." His invitation to live dangerously—"Build your cities under Vesuvius! . . . Live at war! . . . Be robbers and conquerors!"—was taken up with enthusiasm by those who would come of age in 1933.

Nietzsche also made a positive contribution to Hitler's receptibility. His most persuasive call had been the power of the will and the Will to Power—a will that was self-justifying, with no reference to any recognizable external standard. The last sentences of his notes, collected as *Will to Power*, took on an ominous sound as they reverberated in the Third Reich. After talking of his "mystery world of . . . voluptuous delight," of a world "beyond good and evil . . . without goal," Nietzsche concludes:

Do you want a *name* for this world? A *solution* for all its riddles?
A *light* for you, too, you best-concealed, strongest, most intrepid,
most midnightly men?—*This world is the will to power—and
nothing besides*! And you yourself are also this will to power—and
nothing besides! [70]

The single principle to which he reduced life was the irrational Will to Power, a slogan he did not mean politically but one which was easily distorted and appropriated by Hitler's brutalizing politics. So was the final commandment Zarathustra gave to his followers: "This new tablet oh my brothers, I place over you: *become hard!*" [71]

There can be no doubt that, using the same words, Nietzsche and Hitler meant quite different things. But the words *were* the same. On occasion, Nietzsche could seem to glory in brutality with the relish of an SS officer. Again, it may be said that he did not really mean what he wrote. But if he was misinterpreted by the Nazis, he had no one but himself to blame:

To witness suffering is pleasant, to inflict it even more so. . . .
There is no festivity without cruelty; so teaches the longest, old-

est history of mankind. Even in punishment there is something very *festive*!

Nietzsche, like the Nazis, talked of two "species" of men with two systems of morality and modes of conduct: masters and slaves. True, he was thinking in neither racial nor social terms, but his attitude toward "inferiors" would not have seemed strange to a guard at Auschwitz. Nietzsche's Superman had elitist contempt for "Undermen." From his perspective, the inferior beings were simply those who did not measure up to his standards. They were to be treated like chattel.[72] Hitler felt the same way about Poles, Russians, Gypsies, and Jews.

There is one arresting paragraph in Nietzsche's notebooks, posthumously published, which demands commentary. Anyone who admires Nietzsche must find the thought appalling, but if words mean anything, these words mean that this sensitive poet and philosopher sometimes thought in patterns not dissimilar from the brutal demagogue and dictator. In contemplating a new order of society Nietzsche wrote:

> The Great Politics [*Die grosse Politik*] intends to make physiology the mistress over all other questions. She will create a power strong enough to *breed* [*züchten*] a more complete and higher form of humanity with merciless hardness [*schonungsloser Härte*] against the degenerate and parasitic in life—against that which corrupts, poisons, defames, and destroys . . . and which sees in the annihilation of life the mark of a higher form of the soul.[73]

Predictably, the Nazi "philosopher" Alfred Rosenberg quoted this passage to demonstrate his thesis that the Nazis and Nietzsche were "spiritual brothers." [74]

It cannot be emphasized too strongly that the "New Order" which Nietzsche sought was to be directed by a philosopher, not a demagogue; that his enemy was not the Jewish people; that by physiology he did not mean racist biology. Nevertheless, Hitler would use *precisely the same terminology* in setting forth his ideology for the Third Reich: he too demanded that his followers be "mercilessly hard" in crushing a group of people he considered to be "degenerate and parasitic"—those he accused of conspiring to "corrupt, poison, defame, and destroy" a higher breed of men.

The greatest irony of Nietzsche's life and thought was noted by one of his most distinguished admirers, Thomas Mann. In one of his last essays, entitled "Nietzsche's Philosophy in the Light of Recent History," Mann summarized Nietzsche's contribution to Hitler's Germany. He first recalled how the philosopher had criticized his fellow Germans and held their traditions in contempt. "But who, in the end," Mann then asked, was more German than he; who served the Germans as still another model for those traits which made them a disaster and terror to the world, and led them ultimately to ruin themselves: romantic passion; the drive to eternal expansion of the self into space, without any fixed object; will which is free because it has no goal and aspires to the infinite. . . . In more than one sense Nietzsche has become historic. He made history, frightful history, and did not exaggerate when he called himself "a nemesis." [75]

We are left with the question posed by Karl Jaspers: "Is he the one who wanted the highest, who yearned for the impossible, who against his will became a power which unleashed among us all the devils of hell?" [76]

Regrettably, the answer is yes, he was such a one.

OTHER ANTIDEMOCRATIC INTELLECTUALS

Even those intellectuals who were critical of Imperial Germany had nothing but scorn for parliamentary democracy. Priding themselves on being "unpolitical," they forfeited the political game to others. Many called explicitly for a Führer to rescue Germany from the confusions which their disdain for democracy had done little to alleviate. When the young Thomas Mann professed his admiration for Lagarde, Nietzsche, and Wagner, it was because, Mann said, they had performed the service of proving that "democracy is alien to us."

The attitude of German intellectuals during the Second Reich was given classic expression in a long and important essay written by Mann and proudly entitled *Betrachtungen eines Unpolitischen* (Reflections of an Unpolitical Man). In this influential book, Mann urged his fellow Germans to be nonpolitical because politics was associated with democracy and democracy was deeply un-German. Freedom from politics, he argued, constituted the basic foundation stone of German *Kultur*. A typical passage reads:

> I declare my deep conviction that the German people will never be able to love political democracy for the simple reason that they cannot love politics and that the much decried *Obrigkeitsstaat* is and will remain the form of government suited to, deserved, and basically desired by the German people.[77]

In fairness to the memory of the great novelist and humanist, it must be reported that Mann later regretted having written the essay. When he recognized the menace of Hitler, he urged his countrymen to participate in politics and to support the Weimar Republic. But the hour was then very late. His influential statement, widely publicized at the birth of the republic, expressed the sentiments of most German intellectuals of the pre-Hitler period.

Another seminal thinker, Max Weber, provides an additional example of the forces that stunted the growth of German democracy. The noted sociologist often spoke in favor of democracy; indeed, he would help to establish the Democratic Party just after the war. But his understanding of the term was peculiar. When it was clear in 1918 that Germany would be defeated, he spoke directly to General Ludendorff urging that he sign a peace treaty and establish a democratic government. The following conversation took place:

> *Ludendorff:*   Then what do you mean by democracy?
> *Weber:*   In a democracy, the people choose a leader in whom they trust. Then the chosen leader says, "Shut up and obey me." The masses and political parties are then no longer free to interfere with the leader.
> *Ludendorff:*   I could like such a democracy.

That Weber meant what he said in this conversation became apparent when, after the Weimar democracy was established, he used his very considerable influence to undercut its effectiveness because it failed to produce the "chosen leader" he had mentioned to Ludendorff. In a lecture to Munich students in 1919 on the subject of politics as a profession, Weber paid special tribute to government that demanded the devotion of the masses to a "charismatic leader." He concluded his lecture by saying that Germans had a choice between an effective Führer and the present leaderless democracy, which had created "a carnival," not a true German government.[78]

Anti-Semitism in the Second Reich

> In plain words, the Jew has always been an element of national decomposition. . . . The Jews are our misfortune.
> —Heinrich Treitschke (c. 1875)

> Fundamentally, only the complete disappearance of the Hebrew can be called a worthy solution to the Jewish Problem.
> —Eugen Dühring (1880)

Something of the long and tragic history of German anti-Semitism is caught in the following vignette from the 18th century:

In October 1743, a boy stood at the gates of the city of Berlin, asking permission to enter. He was only 14 and a hunchback, and he had to ask permission to enter because he was a Jew. Jews not only were required to enter cities through a designated gate, but they had to have a permit to travel the country's roads. This hunchback Jewish boy had grown up in the restricted circumstances of the ghetto, and he knew only a few words of German. One of them was "Dessau," the city from which he had walked, alone to Berlin; the other word was "lernen"—the reason for his trip—"to learn," to study the Talmud with the rabbi of Berlin. The soldier on guard, in going off duty, wrote in his log, "Today there passed through the Rosenthaler Gate six oxen, seven swine, and one Jew." [79]

That hunchbacked little boy would one day become so famous as a philosopher and humanist that he would be known as the "Jewish Socrates." His close friend Lessing would immortalize Moses Mendelssohn as the central figure of his play *Nathan der Weise*.

Jews continued to be persecuted in Germany—as in many other countries—for centuries. During the "war of liberation" against Napoleon, Prussian patriots talked of driving out Jews along with other foreign influences. The democratic revolution of 1848 saw a rise of popular anti-Semitism; a contemporary pamphlet from Baden, for example, called for the deposal of kings and the expulsion of Jews. "Not infrequently, the leveling of castles and the looting of Jewish homes took place together." [80]

Racial anti-Semitism of a kind clearly anticipatory of Nazism, however, began to develop in Germany only during the Second Reich. The high tide of nationalism that swept Germany after the founding of the empire encouraged an emphasis on German *Kultur* and a disposition to look upon Jews as "outsiders." Periods of extreme nationalism may produce anti-Semitism in any country—as in Spain during the 15th century and in France during the Dreyfus affair—but the connection was particularly strong in Germany where, since the days of the Romantics, nationalism had acquired a distinctly biological emphasis. Fascination with sexual relations and emphasis on "blood pollution" were particularly marked. A typical expression of the concern is found in the third of the new Ten Commandments as set forth by the influential anti-Semitic pamphleteer Theodor Fritsch in his pamphlet *Anti-Semiten-Katechismus* of 1893: "Thou shalt keep thy blood pure. Consider it a crime to soil the noble Aryan breed of thy people by mingling it with the Jewish breed. . . ." [81]

Anti-Semitism was initiated or sustained by other influential writers of the period. During the economic panic of 1873, a leading journalist, Wilhelm Marr, published a hysterical pamphlet entitled *Der Sieg des Judentums über das Germanentum* (The Victory of Judaism over Germandom). It went through 12 editions in six years. Marr's success encouraged him, in 1879, to establish the first organization in any country to bear the title "The Anti-Semitic League." He was the first to introduce the term "anti-Semitism" to the German people and to insist that the "Jewish problem" was not religious; it was racial. He demanded that "Germandom" gird its Aryan loins against the "world domination of international Jewry." The only way to halt the "Jewification of society" was by unbridled pogroms. [82]

The blind anarchist philosopher Eugen Dühring lent a type of intellectual respectability to the hatred of Jews. His influential book, which first appeared in 1880, bore a title that summarizes much of its contents: *Die Judenfrage als Frage Rassencharakters und seiner Schädlichkeiten für Existenz und Kultur der Völker* (The Jewish Question as a Problem of Racial Character and Its Dangers for the Existence and Culture of the People). In the sixth edition, published after World War I, Dühring confessed that he had been much too moderate with regard to the Jews who had caused the war and were responsible for Germany's defeat. He now realized that "only the complete disappearance of the Hebrew can be called a worthy solution to the Jewish Problem." And only a dictator could establish the racially pure *Gemeinschaft* necessary for the salvation of Germandom.[83]

Paul de Lagarde also lent his name to the effort to make mindless prejudice intellectually acceptable. His specific contribution was to provide slogans and ugly metaphors which would be picked up by dozens of racists from Fritsch and Wagner to Hitler and Goebbels. He warned that Germany was becoming "Jewified" (*verjudet*); the Jews were "decayed parasites," "diseased," and "usurious vermin." He noted ominously that "with trichinae and bacilli one does not negotiate, nor are trichinae and bacilli subject to education; they are exterminated as quickly and thoroughly as possible." Hitler carried out that injunction. In 1944, in the midst of the mass extermination of European Jews, the Nazis brought out an anthology of Lagarde's anti-Semitic pronouncements and demands for wholesale murder. The little book was published under the graphic title *Ich Mahne und Kunde* (*I Warn and Proclaim*).

Lagarde had presaged Hitler's policy for Central Europe with remarkable foresight. Like so many intellectuals before him, he preached a *Drang nach Osten* and the creation of an enormous *Mittleleuropa*. His particular program of colonization, however, was more brutal than that of many others who preceded Hitler. He demanded the expulsion or extermination of Polish Jews, so that there could be a "Jew-free" land for Germans to dominate in Central Europe. As Fritz Stern has noted, "Few men prophesied Hitler's work with such accuracy—and approval." [84]

Julius Langbehn's incredible best-seller *Rembrandt als Erzieher* also served as a preview of things to come. He recommended that *Ahnenprobe* (proof of ancestry) be instituted in Germany as a condition of citizenship; it was an idea that Hitler put into practice. He also demanded extermination of the Jews: "They are poison for us and must be treated as such. . . ." In 1891 he called for a "Secret Emperor who will intervene actively . . . in the Jewish question. . . ." By 1892 he was listing the enemies of his Reich as "Jews and idiots, Jews and scoundrels, Jews and whores, Jews and professors, Jews and Berliners." By this time, Langbehn had moved into what must be considered the final stage of anti-Semitism: the bacteriological phase. The Jews had become a "cholera" that must be destroyed.[85]

Germany's most popular novelist of the last half of the century, Gustav Freytag, also made an important contribution to anti-Semitism in his novel *Soll und Haben* (*Debit and Credit*). First published in 1855, it was to go through dozens of editions. In this novel, Freytag introduced

Veitel Itzig, a character who became the stereotype for "the Jew" in virtually all anti-Semitic literature. Itzig was slovenly, slack-jawed, with greasy hair and yellowed teeth; he was dirty, unkempt, and sloppy in his clothing and habits; his voice was whining and nasal. Freytag considered himself to be a liberal because he had no objection to "good Jews." His battle was against "bad Jews" who refused to be assimilated or to accept "German Christian ways." These, he said, were the "sick part of our people" who must not be allowed to "infect" healthy Germans.[86]

Heinrich von Treitschke was also a notable anti-Semite whose attitude toward the Jews was summarized in his immensely popular lectures: "In plain words, the Jew has always been an 'element of national decomposition'; . . . Whenever [the German] finds his life sullied by the filth of Judaism, [he] must turn from it and learn to speak the truth boldly about it." Treitschke seems to have been the first to coin the slogan, which would become a battle cry for the Third Reich, "The Jews are our misfortune."[87]

One of the most effective agencies for spreading fear and hatred of the Jews was the prestigious and influential Pan-German League (*Alldeutscher Verband*). Throughout the 1890s its powerful press warned members of Hitler's generation to watch out for the "Jewish menace," and it set forth solutions for the "Jewish problem." It demanded rigorous restrictions on the "Jewish press" (including the *Berliner Tageblatt* and the *Frankfurter Zeitung*); the enactment of laws which would bar Jews from key professions, treat them as "aliens," and tax them double the amount paid of "real Germans"; and the promulgation of racial laws which would prohibit Jews from mixing their blood with the "Germanic race."[88]

The ideals of the anti-Semitic theorists and the warnings of the Pan-Germans were taken seriously by the social institutions of Imperial Germany, which placed both formal and informal restrictions on Jews. Few Jews, for example, could look forward to a career in the universities of Germany. In 1910 fewer than 3 percent of all professors were Jews; at the University of Berlin, the biggest and most prestigious university of the empire, in the first decade of the 20th century not one Jew was a full professor. The student organization, *Verein deutscher Studenten* (also known as the *Kyffhäuserverband*), in 1896 adopted this principle: "Jewish citizens of the Reich are not to be regarded as Germans."[89]

Neither the Catholic nor the Protestant church was interested in taking position against the anti-Semitic movement. The Lutherans in particular, following the advice of their founder, became directly supportive of anti-Semitism in politics. In addition to the notorious Jew-baiter, the court chaplain Pastor Adolf Stöcker (1835–1909), four other Lutheran pastors sat in the Reichstag as anti-Semites and another was a member of the Prussian Diet.[90]

Jews had difficulty finding a career in the Imperial Army. In contrast with other countries of Europe on the eve of World War I, whose armies were officered by Jews,* there was not one Jewish officer in the Imperial German Army in 1910. Even Jews who had made extraordinary contributions to their country could not find access to its peacetime army. The distinguished industrialist who did more for Germany's war effort than anyone else, Walther Rathenau—to take one example—wrote to Frau General von Hindenburg in December 1917: "Even though my ancestors and I served this country . . . I am, as you should well know, as a Jew a second-class citizen. I could not become a political civil servant then in peacetime, not even a lieutenant." [91]

The anti-Semitic practices of the Third Reich thus had pernicious precedents in the Second.

Racial Nationalism and the Cult of Force

> Everything that is great, everything that is thorough, everything that is enduring in European institutions is German.
> —Adam Müller (c. 1810)

> Our race with its culture is superior to all other nations and races on earth.
> —Statement of Pan-German League (c. 1910)

In the decades prior to World War I, the German people had no monopoly on patriotism. *Chauvinisme*, we are reminded, is French; jingoism is English. But four interconnected tendencies combined to make German nationalism particularly powerful and peculiarly receptive to Hitler.

First, the Nazis were justified in thinking that racial nationalism and belief in the superiority of the German people were traditions of long standing. The arguments of racial superiority set forth by the Romantics at the beginning of the 19th century, as Karl Dietrich Bracher has pointed out, provided "the basis for *völkisch* ideology . . . which was to become the governing principle of the National Socialists' *Weltanschauung*." [92] Proclamations of racial superiority continued to be made throughout the century and reached some sort of climax in 1914 when Ernst Haeckel, a famous biologist, delivered this highly unscientific pronouncement: "One single highly cultured German soldier . . . represents a higher intellectual and moral life-value than hundreds of the uncivilized human beings whom England and France, Russia and Italy oppose to [him]." [93]

Second, a corollary of racial superiority was the conviction that it was Germany's destiny to conquer and control vast areas of *Lebensraum*, particularly in Eastern Europe, where German *Kultur* was destined to replace that of the inferior Slavic people. Lagarde, for

---

* In Austria-Hungary there were over 2,000 Jewish officers, including one field-marshal; in Italy there were 500; and in France, in spite of the Dreyfus Affair, 720.

example, had announced that Germany should annex Austria and colonize all of Central Europe, arguing that "Magyars, Czechs and similar nationalities . . . are a burden on history," and that Polish Jews need to be "rooted out." [94] Germany's most distinguished sociologist, Max Weber, was furious when a friend criticized the government's policy toward Polish subjects as an infringement on human rights. Weber's reply was worthy of Hitler: "It is only thanks to us that Poles are human beings!" (*Wir haben die Polen erst zu Menschen gemacht*) [95]

A third characteristic separated German nationalism from its Western counterparts and made it particularly receptive to Hitler: it was heavily influenced by myths of German antiquity and sought to justify itself by evoking nationalistic urges it found in pagan prehistory. German mythology was filled with pagan gods like Wotan and Siegfried and half-legendary figures of supernatural powers such as Barbarossa. In popular imagination these gods and demi-gods had all become national heroes. This kind of nationalism, with its stress on myth, mystery, and magic was only a step away from Nazi ideology and the mystical powers it assigned to Führer, *Volk,* blood, and soil.[96]

The word *Mythos,* which has had a peculiar attraction to Germans, carries a different meaning from the English *myth.* In English usage the word suggests little more than a fairy tale, or a nonexistent person or event. A definition in a standard German dictionary, *Der Sprach-Brockhaus,* is jarringly different: "*Mythos*: a symbolic idea with life-renewing force." This was certainly the conception of influential German writers for many generations. Like their Romantic predecessors, the intellectuals of the Weimar Republic who called themselves Conservative Revolutionaries boasted of their commitment to *Mythos* rather than rationality. One of them wrote in 1920: "Myth is the word and the vision which tells about *Volk* and God, about what has actually happened [*von wirklichem Geschehen*]." Another, writing in 1923 in a book he entitled *Das dritte Reich,* warned his readers that the idea of the coming Reich was filled with "myth and mystery . . . charged with feeling not of this world but of the next." [97] Hitler exploited to the fullest this emphasis on myth and mystery. Indeed, he institutionalized these ideas and became himself the "myth-person" whom many German thinkers had foretold.

A fourth characteristic of German nationalism, as it developed in the 19th and 20th centuries, was the exaltation of power and war. Of course, one can find strident proponents of national power in other countries. But in no other nation of the world did so many respected leaders in so many different walks of life over so long a period of time proclaim that might made right and preach the moral justification of war; their words would be echoed in Hitler's evocation of power, brutality, and battle as the law of life. Germany's most influential 19th-century philosopher, for example, insisted that "war has the higher meaning; through it . . . the ethical health of nations is maintained . . .

just as the motion of the winds keeps the sea from the foulness which a
constant calm would produce—so war prevents the corruption of nations which a perpetual . . . peace would produce." [98]

One of Julius Langbehn's favorite arguments was that war was
creative and necessary for cultural advance. Treitschke, too, in dozens
of impassioned lectures, glorified war with a fanaticism worthy of
Hitler: "War is political science par excellence . . . only in war does a
Volk become in very deed a *Volk*. . . . The idea of perpetual peace is
not only impossible, but immoral as well. . . . War is the very sphere in
which we can most clearly trace the triumph of human reason. . . . The
army, not parliament, is the most valuable institution of the State." [99]
Oswald Spengler was equally enthusiastic about the benefits of battle,
finding it "the eternal form of higher existence" and concluding that
"states exist for the purpose of waging war." [100]

The elder von Moltke (1800–1891), the famous chief of the Prussian General Staff, was not interested in politics. Yet he influenced
political developments by placing his enormous prestige behind the
doctrine that war was both inevitable and beneficial. His words were
remembered and widely quoted: "Eternal peace is a dream and not even
a very pleasant one, and war is a part of God's creation. It has enfolded
the noblest virtues [*Tugenden*] of man: courage and self-renunciation,
loyalty to duty and willingness to sacrifice with one's life. Without war
the world would sink into materialism." [101]

One of the most influential books published in Germany during the
immediate prewar years was prophetically entitled *Germany and the
Next War*. It first appeared in 1911 and quickly went through seven
huge printings. The author—who had been a student of Treitschke's—
set forth a simple thesis: "War is a biological necessity of the first importance. . . . The efforts directed toward the abolition of war must not only
be termed foolish, but absolutely immoral, . . . unworthy of the human
race. . . ." He closed his first chapter, entitled "The Right to Make War,"
with Goethe's "manly words":

> Dreams of a peaceful day?
> Let him dream who may!
> "War" is our rallying cry,
> Onward to victory! [102]

The emperor himself made notable contributions to the cult of
force. No head of state in any other country reveled in such brutal
exhortations. Indeed, his speeches on the eve of battle served as remarkable precedents to the orders later given by Hitler. For example, in
launching the Polish campaign which started World War II, the Führer
told his commanders to "close your hearts to pity . . . act brutally."
Decades before, in sending German troops to China to put down the
Boxer Rebellion in 1900, William II had issued orders which were to
give the name of "Hun" to German soldiers during World War I:

No quarter will be given. No prisoners will be taken. Whoever falls into your hands, let his life be forfeit!

The Huns under King Attila a thousand years ago made a name for themselves that has remained mighty in tradition and tale to this day; may you make the name of German a thing to conjure with. . . .

Well in advance of Hitler, the emperor had spoken of providing "blood-baths" for those who opposed him, and prescribed wars of conquest for the general health of the German people. During the Christmas season of 1905, for example, he communicated the following sentiments to his chancellor:

First shoot down, behead, and eliminate the Socialists, if necessary by a bloodbath, then go on to a foreign war. But not before, and only at the proper time.[103]

The Pan-German League was extraordinarily effective in spreading the cult of nationalism and force throughout Imperial German society. The extent of the league's commitment to power is suggested by the fact that, try as he might, William II was never able to measure up to the Pan-German standard of bellicosity. From 1911 on, their press continued to call him *Guillaume le timide*.[104]

The League's program differed in no essential way from Hitler's. At a time when Klara Hitler was nursing the future Führer, the Pan-Germans were proclaiming their doctrine of Aryan racial superiority and their right to conquer the East and to use "inferior races" as slave labor. They also called for a Führer who would establish a dictatorship and rid the Fatherland of the "Jewish menace."

It is of course true that nationalistic societies existed in other European countries on the eve of World War I. But the societies of no other country preached a program so clearly anticipatory of Nazism, and none had the influence of the Pan-German League. In Russia, the Pan-Slavs lacked an effective organization, and their influence upon their government was negligible; in France, Déroulède was driven into exile and his League of Patriots declared illegal. By contrast, the program and war aims of the Pan-German League, as Fritz Fischer has shown, became the official war aims of the Imperial German government.

The Pan-German League was founded in September 1890 by the influential publicist Alfred Hugenberg. Its total membership during the empire never reached more than 40,000; but the names were impressive. They read like a "who's who" of German academic, industrial, and political life. There were 60 members of the Reichstag, leading editors and publishers, key landowners and industrialists, the distinguished scientist Ernst Haeckel, historians and social scientists such as Karl Lamprecht, Dietrich Schäfer, Max Weber, and many others. The list for

1906 shows that 36 percent of all members in local groups belonged to the teaching profession, and of these almost 60 percent were professors. Members were thus well qualified to fulfill what the league considered to be its primary obligation: to "educate the people of Germany" in racial nationalism.[105]

When the long-awaited war finally came, leaders of Germany's intellectual community on 8 July 1915 drew up the "Petition of the Intellectuals" (*Intellektuelleneingabe*) which supported German annexationist plans so completely that the president of the League said it was "in complete agreement" with his war aims. The petition demanded that Germany retain the conquered parts of northern France, that Belgium be occupied by German arms, that a high indemnity be imposed "without mercy" upon the defeated countries, and that a vast expanse of territory in Eastern Europe come under German control. Within a very short time, 1,347 intellectuals signed the petition. There were 352 university professors (these formed by far the largest single professional group), 252 journalists and writers, and 158 clergymen and teachers. It is true that a more moderate petition was circulated by Hans Delbrück, but he got a total of only 141 signatures. The overwhelming majority of the intellectual and spiritual leaders of Germany supported the expansionist demands of the Pan-German League.[106]

The cult of force was certainly not the only attitude discernible in Imperial Germany. There was a sizable pacifist movement, and the largest political party in the country, the Marxian Socialists, stated its theoretical opposition to wars of aggression. Yet the demands for military expansion were so dominant, and its supporters so persistent and powerful over so many years, that a discerning historian in noting the way aggressive tendencies flowed from the Second to the Third Reich has asked, "Is the continuity of intentions and hopes; of style and aims not altogether amazing?" [107]

It is indeed.

The Militarization of Society: From Second Reich to Third

> In the nineteenth century . . . in the West the Army was a sort of necessary evil; but with us it formed the highest pride of the nation.
> —Gerhard Ritter

> One key to understanding the *Weltanschauung* of the Germans is to realize that the entire spirit of the Army is moved, lock, stock, and barrel, into civilian life.
> —Werner Bruck

The complete and brutal militarization of German life came only with the Third Reich. But here, too, the past was prologue to Hitler's present. For the Imperial German Army made major and pernicious contributions to the "German condition" as it affected the generation born in the 1890s. Hitler was probably correct in saying in 1933 that he could not have come to power without the help of the army and its traditions.

The glories of the Prussian Army and its heroes from Frederick the Great to Blücher, Scharnhorst, and Moltke had long been celebrated in Germany. But the ubiquitous power which the army exerted over German society became particularly evident after 1871, with the triumphant military victories that established the Second Reich.

Exaltation of military values was greatly aided by the country's most popular historian, Heinrich von Treitschke, who lectured a generation on the "Godlike majesty of war," the duty of absolute obedience, and the notion that the German Officer Corps was "a careful selection of the most exalted human beings on earth." Emperor William II, who boasted that he had never read the constitution of Germany, also lent the prestige of his position to acclaiming the army and denigrating parliament: "The soldier and the Army, not parliamentary resolutions, have welded together the German Empire. My trust is in the Army." William had the habit of using one particular phrase in referring to nonmilitary people: they were "slovenly civilians" (*schlappe Zivilisten*). Any officer of the guard, he believed, was "the quintessence of all virtue, education and intellectual attainment." [108]

The German Officer Corps made special and successful efforts to emphasize its exalted position in society. Crucial to the distinction between German officers and "mere civilians" was the Code of Honor, which was preserved very largely through the dueling system and the privilege it gave of "giving satisfaction" (*Satisfaktionsfähigkeit*). It was felt that an officer who had that honor must defend it; conversely, a man without honor had nothing to defend. This meant, for example, that an officer could insult a workman with impunity, for the workman was not *Satisfaktionsfähig*. As the century wore on, although protests were made against the folly and cruelty of dueling, it persisted in the army and in university fraternities. Dueling scars—genuine and self-administered—continued to be a mark of honor well after World War I.

As a result of the training and the pronouncements of those in authority, officers in the Imperial Army were encouraged to believe that they were above the civilian government. The oath they swore was not to the country or the constitution but to their Supreme Warlord. The army, it was said, was a "state within a state"; but it was more than that. Its position was perhaps most clearly expressed by the imperial general who was to serve as a transitional commander between the Second and Third Reichs. General Hans von Seeckt concluded in his book *Gedanken eines Soldaten* (Thoughts of a Soldier):

I have tried to treat my theme from a purely political point of view. In the sense in which I understand the word, the Army must be "political," that is, it should grasp the concept of the State. But it certainly must not be "political" in the usual sense of party politics. "Hands off the Army!" is my cry to *all* parties. The Army serves the State and only the State because the Army is the State.*

The disdain for parliaments felt by members of the army command was pungently expressed in parliament itself by the old Herr von Oldenburg auf Januschau, who told his fellow members of the Reichstag: "The King of Prussia and the German Emperor must always be in the position to say to any lieutenant: 'Take ten men and shoot the Reichstag.' " His fellow Conservatives greeted the speech with a standing ovation.[109]

Military values and modes of conduct were disseminated throughout Imperial German society in a number of ways. The army saw to it, for example, that veterans received preferred positions in the civil service. In 1897, half the jobs open in the Department of Justice went to army veterans, and the Foreign Office was particularly prone to recruit young officers of promise. Soldierly values and experiences were also preserved through dozens of veterans' associations. The *Kyffhäuser Bund* alone by 1910 had a membership of well over 2,500,000. One of its stated objectives was to combat democracy.

The army saw to it that German children learned military values. In ways that paralleled Hitler's later youth organizations, children of the empire were indoctrinated in a dozen militarized youth groups. "In one way or another," a military historian has concluded, "nearly five million Germans were either directly or indirectly connected with the Army." [110]

And beyond sheer numbers, the army exerted its influence by setting a military tone in society. Military standards were reflected in institutions that would seem least likely to cultivate soldierly values: the university and the parlors of Imperial Germany. In German fraternities from Berlin to Munich the point of emulation, the ideal to copy, was a military man, a Prussian officer. The criterion of selection for university fraternities was a military criterion: ability to fight a duel. Duels were called *Mensuren*; that is to say, the true measure of a man was his capacity to give "satisfaction" with a saber. Those who were not *Satisfaktionsfähig* were called "finks" (*Finkenschaft*) and treated with contempt.

The military standards and values were carried over into civilian life in the machinery of imperial social etiquette, hierarchy, rank, and status. Militarism entered the parlor, where the woman whose husband held the highest rank commanded that seat of honor, the sofa, and those of lower status were assigned to lesser pieces of furniture. A German social historian has concluded, "This idea of military machine permeated the whole social life . . . militarism has rightly been called

---

* It is not surprising that in an edition of Seeckt's book, published after Hitler came to power, the sentence " '*Hände weg vom Heer!' ich rufe allen Parteien zu*" was deleted. Compare 1st ed. (Berlin, 1921) with rev. ed. (Leipzig, 1935), 116.

the cement that bound the whole structure of society into an entity. . . ." In school, in a tavern, in street cleaning, in the mayor's office, one found the same bristling efficiency; the same rigorous discipline, and the same hierarchical consciousness.[111]

One of the most important means of impressing German citizens with military ideals was through the Reserve Officer Corps. Traditionally the Officer Corps had been the preserve of the agrarian Junkers, and during the empire they continued, by and large, to supply officers to the army. But selected members of the middle class were now given the privilege of participating in the "highest pride of the nation" by becoming reserve officers. So great was the status value that many middle-class fathers impoverished themselves to get their sons into the reserve of a prestigious regiment and thus to become a "privileged man" (*Vornehmer Mann*). No liberals or Jews or other "unreliable elements" were permitted to enter.

The attitude of civilians to reserve officers was given classical expression in Zuckmayer's play *Der Hauptmann von Köpenick*. The hero listens with approval to a tailor's observation:

Na, so you have managed to become a Reserve Lieutenant—that is the chief thing—that is the thing you must be these days—socially, professionally, in every connection! The doctorate is the visiting card, but the Reserve Commission is the open door—that's the essential thing these days! [112]

Two incidents in the lives of distinguished Germans illustrate the importance to them of a reserve officer's commission. A professor who was to be given a high honor on the occasion of his 75th birthday was asked what gift would give him the most pleasure. It was supposed that he would wish to attain the rank of privy counselor (*Wirklicher Geheimrat*), a position that carried the title of "Excellency" and the highest civil distinction of the time. But the professor had no such honor in mind. The learned old gentleman wanted above all to be promoted from first lieutenant to captain in the Army Reserve. In the second case, the chancellor of Germany, Bethmann-Hollweg, thought it appropriate to don his uniform of reserve major in making his first appearance before the parliament of his country. These, and many other civilians, were showing that a staff officer of the Imperial Army was quite correct in observing that "militarism is the state of mind of the civilian." [113]

A contrast in political and social attitudes between England and Germany is suggested in the different classes each nation tended to emulate. The English aristocracy and royalty of the 19th century adopted the standards and manners of the middle class. Victoria became the "British Empire's number one bourgeoise," and her son Edward was as *bürgerlich* as he could possibly be. In Germany, however, the middle class enjoyed no such pride of place or self-confidence. They sought their social norms outside their own class; they emulated the Army and the Junker aristocracy.

The Imperial Army's influence over German life went beyond social values to include foreign policy. Military leaders simply assumed that "they alone had the right to determine the foreign policy of the Empire." [114] The military elite became the effective rulers of Germany in 1917 when Generals Ludendorff and Hindenburg established a virtual military dictatorship. Ludendorff in particular got that thirst for political power he would later try to slake when he marched in 1923 with Hitler in their effort to seize the government of Germany. Now, in 1917, he determined foreign policy—dictating draconian terms of peace with the Soviet Union; he dismissed and replaced chancellors and judges; he determined wages and hours; he chose the emperor's personal entourage. In short, "the Army, hitherto a State within a State, had become the State." [115] But the Army's contribution to Hitler went beyond setting a general precedent for authoritarian government. Members of the High Command wanted a particular kind of dictatorship. Their thinking was so distinctly proto-Fascist that it made Hitler's ideology seem familiar to important segments of German society.*

This military dictatorship of the war years marked the effective end of Bismarck's Second Reich and, in important ways, prepared the way for the more vicious militarism of the Third.

Family Life and Education of the Hitler Generation

> The Germans have always sought a father, indeed . . . [their] conception of the State is generally patterned after the model of the family.
> —Wolfgang Sauer

Family life and public education were of obvious importance in shaping the attitudes of mind of Hitler's generation. These Germans, born and raised at the zenith of the Second Reich, would suffer defeat in the Great War and form a large cadre of Hitler's movement, for it appealed particularly to those whom Konrad Heiden would call "the generation of the uprooted and disinherited."

The family experience of that generation was strikingly similar to Adolf Hitler's. An authoritarian father dominated the family; the mother, like Klara Hitler, was confined to *Küche*, *Kirche*, and *Kinder*, often trying ineffectively to shield her children from the demands and punishments of the awe-inspiring "Herr Vater."

---

* Specifically, leaders of the High Command endorsed racial anti-Semitism, primitive nationalism, and leadership as an end in itself. They demanded a totalitarian state in the name of *Volksgemeinschaft*—a perverted socialism which appealed to the masses but preserved the power of the industrial, military and agrarian elite. (See especially Martin Kitchen, "Militarism and the Development of Fascist Ideology; The Political Ideas of Colonel Max Bauer, 1916–1918," *Central European History*, 8 (September 1975), 216–219)

Although it is obviously risky to generalize about life-styles in the homes of any country, two observations about the German family can be made. Students of comparative family life have shown that German families tended to be more authoritarian than those of other countries and that authoritarian values were maintained over a longer period of time. A careful sociological study based on interviews with many different age groups of Germans who spent their childhood, variously, under the Empire, the Republic, and the Nazis concluded that "the basic premises of German family life show no significant difference during these 76 years [1870–1946]. . . ." [116]

Ehrfurcht, the German word used to express the proper and traditional attitude towards the father of the family, is normally translated "respect." But it connotes far more than that, for it combines, quite literally, "honor-fear." The continuing force of the idea is suggested by the fact that even after the collapse of Hitler's dictatorship, 73 percent of the 2,000 Germans questioned in 1946 agreed with the following statement: "The word of the father has to be an inflexible law in the family."

The passive mother was expected to devote her life to her "three K's." She should show affection and concern for her children, but she was not to interfere with the father's prerogative of determining family policy and dominating the group. After World War II, 70 percent of German women chose the words "a bad wife" as the best way of completing the sentence "A mother who interferes when a father is punishing his son is. . . ."

Additional features of German family life should be noted. There was a tendency to adhere to set patterns and to feel uncomfortable when obliged to deviate from a position once taken. The German father found it very difficult to admit mistakes or to yield a point in discussion. To do so was generally considered *weiblich* (effeminate). The father also asserted his masculine power by insisting that the children live up to his demanding expectations. Since the child was afraid of failure, he tried to avoid mistakes by constant repetition and compulsive thoroughness in performing household tasks.

Obedience was the greatest virtue in the family, but it was also a defense. From his earliest years, the German child learned that compliance was the key to safe relationships with his parents. Hence he tended to feel comfortable in yielding to authority and uneasy when given too much freedom. The importance of obedience in family training was emphasized by Rudolf Hoess, who, under Hitler, became commandant of the death camp at Auschwitz. He also spoke for many of his generation in emphasizing the virtues of cleanliness:

> I was perpetually washing and bathing . . . this passion for water remains with me to this day. I had been brought up by my parents to be respectful and obedient toward all grown-up people . . . it

was constantly impressed upon me in forceful terms that I must obey promptly the wishes and commands of my parents, teachers, and priests. . . . Whatever they said was always right. . . . These basic principles on which I was brought up became part of my flesh and blood. . . . From my earliest youth I was brought up with a strong awareness of duty. In my parents' house it was insisted that every task be exactly and conscientiously carried out. . . . My father took particular care to see that I obeyed all his instructions and wishes with the greatest meticulousness.

Hoess has provided statistical proof on his capacity to obey instructions:

I personally arranged for . . . the gassing of 2,000,000 persons between June–July 1941 and the end of 1943, during which time I was Commandant of Auschwitz.[117]

Respect for *Ordnung*—a favorite German word—was taught, not only by threat of punishment but also by ritual: the child learned to keep his hands *on* the table, never indecently in his lap; to go to sleep lying on his back with hands *outside* the covers. Closely associated with order was cleanliness, which the child was taught to associate with purity. Indeed the German word *rein* is applicable to both. He learned that to be dirty (*schmutzig*) was to be bad. Thus the association: order and cleanliness, dirt and evil. It was not a difficult transition to believe that the blond and white-skinned Germans were cleaner and purer than other people—hence better than those of "mixed" races, who were impure-dirty-inferior-bad.

The family experience put heavy emphasis on status and rank. Respect for hierarchical order was strengthened by the military tradition, but it started very early in family life. A child attained status in the home not just on the basis of age, complexion, or physical size but on whether he had earned the title of *Lieblingskind* (favorite child). When he went to school he was seated in order of his performance, starting at the top in the back seats and proceeding methodically downward in rank toward the front. At the age of ten a major status decision in his life was made: either he would become a member of the elite group bound for the university and a profession—perhaps with a coveted doctorate—or he would join the "masses" who terminated their academic career with the *Volksschule* certificate.

It seems likely that one of the reasons German consciousness of rank was so prevalent was because it was comforting. A father knew what he could demand from his family merely because he was the father. A wife and son and daughter knew exactly what their duties were, simply because they were wife and son and daughter.

Strong feelings, both passive and aggressive, were developed in the family. A son's attitude toward his father necessarily was passive, but he knew that when he reached maturity he could treat his children just as his authoritarian father had treated him. Thus was the system perpetuated. Attitudes initially developed in the family reflected one of the striking qualities of German life and letters, a kind of tension between extremes. A word often used in essays on German character is *Zerrissenheit*, the sense of being torn apart by conflicting values. Many leaders of German thought have been intrigued by this conflict of opposites. Goethe spoke of "two souls, alas, within my breast"; Hegel's system moved by the clash of thesis against antithesis; Nietzsche thought in terms of Apollonian harmony versus Dionysian frenzy, and he hailed "the magic power of extremes." German political theory tended to deride moderation and call either for complete obedience to the state or for revolution to overthrow it. In the popular stereotypes, Germans have been noted for both sentimental romanticism and cold efficiency. It seems likely that early family experience contributed to these attitudes by emphasizing the great difference in the treatment the child received from the father and the mother; their behaviors diverged so sharply that it was difficult for the youngster to identify with both parents. Yet to choose one and not the other was to invite further conflict. One unsatisfactory solution was to alternate between them, so that "at one time [the child] will behave like his aggressive, dominating father; at others like his submissive, loving . . . mother." [118]

Hitler appealed to the Germans in part because he appealed to values that were deep-rooted in the traditional authoritarian family. Specifically, he promised an orderly government that would be a model of the same principles that the Germans were accustomed to find in proper family life. He promised security, work, food, and clothing if they granted him authority. He offered himself as a German father figure who inspired *Ehrfurcht* and obedience; he promised to provide a clean and racially pure family, a *Volksgemeinschaft*; he would reunite all Germans and bring them back into the family fold. Hence the particular appeal of his slogan: *Heim ins Reich*. In contrast to the freedom which was uncomfortable to many Germans and associated with the failures of the Weimar Republic, Hitler offered the security of authority: "To a large percentage of Germans this was neither absurd nor dangerous, but a natural arrangement between a leader and his subjects; a situation to which they had become accustomed from infancy on in their home life, schools, work experience, and military service." [119]

Emphasis on the appeal of the father image has not been confined to sociological studies. The political historian Wolfgang Sauer has noticed how much his fellow Germans have been attracted by the idea of a paterfamilias for their country: "From Bismarck to Adenauer, the Germans have always sought a father, indeed it appears as if the German conception of the State is generally patterned after the model of the family." [120]

The German educational system reinforced the basic system of values first learned in the family. Training tended to be specialized, with little effort at dealing with the "whole person." There was, for example, "only the most primitive preparation for civic responsibility." [121]

Public elementary schools tended to emphasize Luther's dualism of the two kingdoms: the *private virtues* of honesty, sobriety, obedience, compassion, and cooperation were not translated into the *public values* and civic responsibilities important for self-government. Instead, as in the home, the child was taught to obey authority, not to participate in making decisions.

The highly selective humanist *Gymnasium* also encouraged aloofness from public life and politics. The humanist curriculum certainly emphasized a general cultural education (*allgemeine Bildung*) and the ideal of the "universal man".—but not the public-spirited citizen. Indeed, the graduate of the *Gymnasium* felt himself to be a member of the cultural elite; he fixed his gaze far above the sordid world of politics, on the lofty peaks of the German spirit.

While encouraging nonpolitical attitudes, the imperial educational system also fostered obedience to authority and a nationalism more bellicose than that found in the schools of any other country in the Western world. It is true that young French pupils were imbued with the glories of French history and with the national humiliation at the loss of Alsace-Lorraine. But an American observer of French and German education in the decade prior to 1914 found that French education lacked the aggressive nationalism and militarism he found east of the Rhine. His conclusions are supported by the most widely used French history textbooks, written for the public schools by distinguished historians. Lavisse's *L'Histoire de France,* it is true, urged pupils not to forget the loss of Alsace-Lorraine and said that Frenchmen ought to be prepared for any further invasions from Germany; but the tone was not belligerent. Aulard and Debidour are even more low key in their popular textbook *Notions d'histoire générale.* While stressing the glories of French history since the revolution, the authors warned against the dangers of militarism and called nationalism a dangerous reincarnation of Boulangerism. War in the future, they said, would be so terrible that people must foster the fraternal spirit of international brotherhood engendered by the great principles of 1789. Thus, French patriotism was balanced by a considerable amount of outright pacifism.[122]

By contrast, German schoolchildren were subjected to strident nationalism and the exaltation of war. The same American observer concluded: "I have found nothing approaching pacifism in the German textbooks. . . . Rather there is a tendency to foster militant and exaggerated race-consciousness which has been shown to be *the* characteristic of the German system of education." Passionate selections from such racial nationalists as Arndt, Kleist, and Treitschke were incorporated into all the common school history textbooks and reading materials. The idea of Germandom was to be spread far beyond the borders of Europe, as is shown in the treatment given the American Civil War in Schenk-Koch's widely used *Lehrbuch der Geschichte.* German children were taught that the reason the North won was because "the blood of the North came from German stock." They were also encouraged to believe that German emigrants to America in the decades following the Civil War still considered themselves German and "have become more deeply conscious of their Germanism [*Deutschtum*] and of their connection with the Unified Fatherland." [123]

Of course, not all German youth complacently accepted the social values taught by family, school, and society in Imperial Germany. Indeed, one of the most formative experiences of the generation born in the decade prior to World War I was participation in the youth movement, which was, in many ways, a revolt against traditionally accepted values. But this kind of rebellion did little to support a democratic alternative to dictatorial government. On the contrary, it encouraged belief in mystical nationalism, expectations of a new and racially pure *Volksgemeinschaft*, and faith in the coming of a powerful political Führer.

The youth movement had started obscurely and quietly in 1897 when a schoolteacher named Karl Fischer began taking his pupils on weekly hikes into remote and wild country. Fischer was called the Führer, and his youthful followers greeted him with *"Heil!"* In 1901 the small group expanded into the *Wandervogel*, and within a decade the movement swept Germany.

The most revealing picture of the German Youth Movement would show a group of suntanned young Nordics wearing leather shorts, tramping through the woods, and singing the "Song of the Freebooters" (*Landsknechtslied*). A popular time for these *Fahrten ins Blaue* (expeditions with no set destination) was the summer solstice. Langbehn, one of the movement's patron saints, sensed peculiarly significant Germanic emanations at that season of the year.

Picture such an exhibition. After tramping all day, the leader gives a signal, and his group stops at dusk to build a great fire. They sit in silence listening for "the messages from the forest" and feeling the mystic stirrings of the *völkisch* soul. Their tense young faces light up as someone recites from a favorite author: Langbehn, Lagarde, Nietzsche, or perhaps Stefan George, who as early as 1907 had pleaded: "*Volk* and high council yearn for The Man!—The Deed! . . . Perhaps someone who sat for years among your murderers and slept in your prisons will stand up and *do the deed*." One of the group who has obviously heard the forest message jumps up. Like his comrades, he professes disdain for politics, for he is proudly "nonpolitical," yet his exhortation affirms two essentially political attitudes characteristic both of the youth movement and of Nazism: the eagerness to submit to a leader, and lust for action—action simply for its own sake. He cries out:

Leaders, Leadership, that is our need; and obedience and great wordless activity. . . . Discussion can be left to leaders around the council fire. . . . The new religion must be inarticulate. . . . Convictions must be sealed in the dark. . . .

I want the fight, and man naked and unashamed with his sword in hand; behind, the stars sweeping westward, and before, the wind in the grass. It is enough, Brothers. Action! The word is spoken.[124]

Like the Nazis after them, the youth movement found it difficult to articulate the concept of the *Führerprinzip*. But a part of the mystery is penetrated in the following description, as given in a contemporary pamphlet:

To be Führer means to be the revealer of the goal, indicator of the way, awakener of the will, and of the powers, and the ideal of its desires.

[*Führer sein heisst Künder des Zieles, Weiser des Weges, Wecker des Willens und der Kräfte und ein Vorbild seines Wollens.*] [125]

The prewar youth also emphasized the mystic fellowship of the *Volk*, as opposed to the rights of the individual. An incessant refrain throughout the literature of the movement was one that would be later taken up by Hitler's propaganda machine: The individual is nothing; the *Volk* is everything. This emphasis on the *Volksgemeinschaft* inevitably led to an attack on the democratic processes which were struggling for expression in Imperial Germany. It also led to racism.

The young people who longed for a new *Volksgemeinschaft* were not very specific about the term, but a few things were clear. This "New Order" would not be liberal-democratic, nor would it be Marxist. Rather, it would be a kind of German national socialism. Only a mighty Führer could bring all Germans together into this "racial community of true socialism"; Jews were not wanted.[126]

Of all the words that echoed with mysterious meaning around the campfires, the most compelling was "Reich." Youthful worshipers did not want to profane so sacred a concept with a definition. But it is clear that *Das neue Reich* of their dreams "was neither Luther's realm of God nor a political German Empire, though it contained elements of both; rather it was primarily a symbol of the new attitude of a new generation. . . ." After the war the word was taken up again, and in the 1920s one youth organization called its periodical *Das dritte Reich* Another youth group published a glowing essay with the same title, in which the author looked forward to deliverance from the democracy that was stifling him: "The *Reich* we seek with our inner eye and to which we pledge our hearts and our vows is not of this time. . . . We are convinced, even possessed, of the certainty that a day of reckoning will come. . . ." [127]

In all fairness, it must be said that there were other tendencies in the prewar Youth Movement. One was characterized by high idealism and gentle good will, best expressed by the pacifist Friedrich Wilhelm Foerster:

> The Youth Movement is the snowdrop on the hard German winter snow. . . . The *Jugendbewegung* is a moral rejuvenation of the German people; the return of the German soul to its best traditions.[128]

In point of historic fact, however, the future would belong to those who pursued power, not to those who formed snowdrops on the hard German snow. It was not the gentle aspects of the movement which conditioned thousands of Germans in the impressionable days of their youth.

One man who was active in the *Wandervogel* and later joined the Nazis has shown the connection between the experience of his boyhood and his subsequent participation in the Nazi Party. "The youth movement which we all knew, the movement to which we all belonged in our time as senior school boys, was the first start of the revolutionary dynamism . . . which culminated in Hitler's more ruthless revolution." [129]

But that brutal revolution awaited Hitler. Meanwhile, members of his generation were to undergo the most shattering experience of their young lives: the trench warfare of World War I.

THE COMING OF THE THIRD REICH, 1918–1933

> All who feel Germany's need deep within their hearts await a Savior [*Erlöser*]. With the greatest longing thousands upon thousands of minds imagine him; millions of voices call unto him; one single German soul seeks him.
> —Kurt Hesse (1922)

> That is the miracle of our time, that you have found me—that among so many millions you have found me! and that I have found you! That is Germany's good fortune!
> —Adolf Hitler (1932)

Germany's experiences during World War I and its aftermath were of vital importance to Hitler's rise to power. His ideology of hatred and racist nationalism, germinating since his Vienna days, would find well-fertilized soil in a disordered and embittered postwar society seeking revenge and a savior to replace a republic despised as traitorous and ineffective. The battles of the war and the postwar

years also provided Hitler with the "New Men" who formed the vanguard of Nazism.

Legacies of World War I: Nationalism, Socialism, Totalism, and the "New Order"

> In the battle for the existence of our *Volk*, the
> new idea of 1914 was born, the idea of German
> *Volksgemeinschaft*, of a national socialism.
> —A German soldier (1918)

Shortly after the death of Hitler and amid the ruins of World
War II, Germany's greatest living historian wrote a thoughtful essay
which attempted to answer his own poignant question, "Will anyone
ever fully understand the monstrous experience which befell us during
the twelve years of the Third Reich?" [130] Meinecke concluded that a
key reason for Hitler's success lay in the adroit way in which he
utilized two legacies of World War I: he identified himself with socialism and nationalism, the two most powerful forces in contemporary European history.

Socialism in one form or another was on the rise in Europe during
the first third of the 20th century. Demands for total mobilization during the long war and the social and economic dislocations of its aftermath posed problems too big and too complex to be solved by 19th-
century laissez-faire economics. Everywhere government regulation and
control increased either in the name of "war economy" or as socialism
or some variant of the welfare state. And everywhere, the nationalism
that had been intensified by the passions of war and the frustrations
of peace shaped the domestic and foreign policies of victors and vanquished alike.

With remarkable insight into the mood of the historic moment,
Hitler offered the distraught German people something that his political
rivals on the left and right were unable to provide. The Communists
were not nationalists; the conservative nationalists were not socialists.
Hitler proclaimed that he was both. His was the only mass party in
postwar Germany which promised the best of both worlds. He combined socialism with nationalism in a program which was at once
radical and conservative. The name he gave to his movement is a
measure of his political acumen. He called it National Socialism.

Incipient totalitarianism was another legacy of the war which
Hitler used to his own advantage and brought to awful completion.
Twentieth-century totalitarianism involves many things, but one of
them is a habit of mind that rejects moderation and exalts totality.
The habit was well developed during World War I, when people became accustomed to thinking in terms of "total war" and "total mobilization," which were guaranteed to bring "total victory." When the Versailles Treaty seemed to bring complete disaster instead of the expected
triumph, Germany experienced a terrifying emptiness—a vacuum

which totalitarian ideology rushed in to fill. The call for immediate solutions to complex problems was a call to which Hitler, the century's most notable *simplificateur terrible*, gave brilliant response.

Totalitarianism also specializes in techniques to control the masses through calculated manipulation of their emotions. During the war, nations had discovered anew the ancient wisdom attributed to Thucydides: "In war, reason is the first casualty." All countries experienced on a huge scale the power of the irrational to move men. War propaganda everywhere stressed mass emotional commitment: to love one's country with unquestioning devotion, to hate the enemy passionately.

As the horrendous toll of death and destruction mounted, year after anguished year, each belligerent sought to justify the carnage by proclaiming the complete rectitude of its own cause and the total depravity of the foe. Mankind witnessed a "mobilization of hatred" on a scale never known before. It was "the first modern effort at systematic nation-wide manipulation of collective passions." [131]

Hitler was fascinated by this process. In *Mein Kampf* he showed how much he had learned from studying it closely. He devoted a chapter to "War Propaganda" and concluded that "it was shown only during the War to what enormously important results a suitably applied propaganda may lead." [132] He was to make very effective use of those lessons.

Systematic manipulation of collective emotions points to another way in which World War I contributed to totalitarian government. For one of the characteristics of modern totalitarianism is that, unlike older forms of tyranny, it gains legitimacy from mass support and mass approval.[133] The war saw the early but clear development of a concept which would be perfected in Hitler's Reich: the "voluntary compulsion" of the masses. In time of war, the phrase was associated with the performance of patriotic duty; under Hitler, it became an ominous euphemism for oppression, as citizens were compelled to volunteer enthusiastic endorsement of a thousand forms of tyranny. As institutionalized by Hitler, "voluntary compulsion" blurred conventional notions of the difference between coercion and consent. Through adroit use of terror coupled with "the high art of propaganda," he gained such control over the masses that they not merely acquiesced to oppression, they roared their approval.

"Total mobilization" was economic as well as psychological, and it led to government regulation of both the public and private sector. Although this was true of all warring countries, nowhere was government intervention so comprehensive and effective as in Germany, where the system was called "war economy" (*Kriegswirtschaft*) or war socialism (*Kriegssozialismus*). "From a relatively free economy in 1914," a distinguished historian has written, "Germany emerged in 1918 with a thoroughly militarized economy of state socialism in which government controls and regulation covered all phases of economic life." The precedent was important for the future; the Nazi economic system profited enormously from the wartime experience.[134]

Thus, during the years from 1914 to 1918, Germans experienced three essentials of Nazi totalitarianism: totality of commitment; the power of the state to coerce and control the lives and fortunes of its people; and a new form of autocracy basing its legitimacy on the will of the masses, which it manipulated through advanced technology.

Moreover, extremism, which flourished in every belligerent country, seemed to grow with particular virulence in Germany, which had already shown a tendency to succumb to "the eternal either/or." The pull of opposites was felt particularly in the last phase of the war and its immediate aftermath. Feelings of desperation and despair, with the impulse to smash all social systems, vied with vaulting hopes that a "New Order" would bring complete solutions to all Germany's problems. Neither attitude was helpful to the struggling young republic.

After the catastrophic defeat of 1918, many Germans came to hope that the destruction prescribed by Nietzsche had been accomplished. They swung from depression to euphoric expectation that the revolution would establish the long-awaited Reich of the patriots' dreams. The tenacious myth of the coming of a new Barbarossa was renewed with unusual fervor during the dark days of defeat and revolution. And the experience of the war fostered chiliastic thinking in other ways. The sheer horror of war and the enormity of the sacrifice could be justified only if one could believe that a splendid new society would come into being—a society that would preserve the wartime experience of comradely sacrifice and cooperation. Economic mobilization of the war years contributed to the idea of a patriotic socialism which was to be expected in the New Order, where an economy of "service to state and *Volk* would form the material foundations for the social and moral edifice of a new Germany."

Life in the trenches—at least in retrospect—had also made a positive contribution to the hopes of a new social order based on what was called "front socialism." For at the front, it was said, soldiers experienced a "close, warm feeling of belonging together, a deep solidarity of all members of the *Volk* . . . a common life in which all social, political, religious and cultural differences either virtually disappeared or sank into insignificance." One writer saw in this "socialism of the trenches" a true revolution—a German counterpart of the French Revolution of 1789: "In the battle for the existence of our *Volk*, the new idea of 1914 was born, the idea of German organization, of *Volksgemeinschaft*, of national socialism."[135]

Faith in a coming New Order, in a new Reich, and in the establishment of a *Volksgemeinschaft* was held with religious intensity. The political romantics of 1918—much like the Romantics of an earlier generation—longed for a new kind of religion, "the spiritual organization of the German *Volk*, of the German nation: the *corpus mysticum*

Germanicum." In this new religion, concepts of sin and responsibility would be collectivized. "It will not be as individuals that we stand before God to be judged," a neo-Romantic wrote, "but as a Community of Fate, of Race and Blood." [136]

As hope and expectations soared ever higher, all the more sordid seemed the bleak reality of the Weimar Republic, born of defeat and national humiliation and staggering under economic and psychological burdens it was too weak to bear.

THE "NEW MEN" VS. THE "NOVEMBER CRIMINALS"

World War I contributed to the receptibility of Hitler's totalitarian ideology. It also provided his movement with a particular kind of personnel: the "New Men" who, like Hitler, had fought on the Western Front and who would form the overwhelming majority of the leadership group of the Nazi Party.[137]

In August 1914 a young law student who was soon to die at Châlons-sur-Marne wrote these lines in a letter to his family:

> Hurrah! At last I have my orders. I report tomorrow morning at 11 o'clock. . . . We are bound to win! Nothing else is possible in the face of such a determined will to victory. My dear ones, be proud that you live in such a time and in such a nation and that you too have the privilege of sending those you love into so glorious a battle.[138]

Thus the unknown Austrian volunteer who was "overwhelmed by impassionate enthusiasm," and who fell on his knees and thanked God for the coming of the war, was no exception. German youth by the thousands welcomed the war and eagerly grasped the opportunity to defend their Fatherland. To a man they were convinced of the righteousness of their cause. Even the pacifist poet Ernst Toller wrote in his memoirs, "I was proud. I was a soldier at last, a privileged defender of the Fatherland." [139]

As the jubilant, singing throng left for the front, only one thought disturbed them. The war, everyone knew, would be over in a month or so, and they might be too late to share in the glory of the hour. As the war dragged on year after year, youthful enthusiasm vanished. The war diary of Ernst Jünger records a terrible transformation. As a sensitive, idealistic volunteer he was nauseated by the sight and stench of rotting corpses, and on a lovely April day he wrote that his sympathy was with the poet:

> Surely this day that God has given
> Was meant for better uses than to kill.

In the course of two war years, that boy of 19 was changed into a hard and ruthless killer, the veteran of 20 wounds, the proud wearer of the *Pour le Mérite*, the commander of a Storm Battalion. He now wrote in memoirs which sold tens of thousands of copies in the postwar period:

> The turmoil of our feelings was called forth by rage, alcohol, and thirst for blood. . . . I was boiling over with a fury which gripped me—it gripped us all—in an inexplicable way. The overpowering desire to kill gave me wings. Rage squeezed bitter tears from my eyes. . . . Only the spell of primeval instincts remained.

And he acclaimed what he called the "New Man" born in battle on the Western Front. Since we shall meet him again in the Free Corps and among the Nazis, we had better be introduced:

> This is the New Man, the storm soldier, the elite of Central Europe. A completely new race, cunning, strong, and packed with purpose. Far behind them awaits . . . the nations whose inner foundations will be torn asunder by the attacks of this New Man —of the audacious, the battle-proven, the man merciless both to himself and to others. This war is not the end. It is only the call to power. It is the forge in which the world will be beaten into new shapes and new associations. New forms must be molded with blood, and power must be seized with a hard fist.[140]

Of course, it should not be suggested that the attitude of these "New Men" is typical of all German soldiers in World War I. A convenient antidote to Jünger can be found in Erich Maria Remarque's *All Quiet on the Western Front*. But the popularity of Remarque belongs to a later era. He was no spokesman for the war veterans of the immediate postwar years. His was a statement of a humane spirit looking back from the relative peace of 1928.[141]

Germans were totally unprepared for the sudden news of defeat in 1918. Patriots spread the story that the army had never really been defeated in the field. Rather, like Wagner's Siegfried, the Fatherland had been betrayed and given a stab in the back (*Dolchstoss*) by the "November Criminals"—that is, by traitorous Jews and other revolutionaries at home. The story was a myth. Time and again it has been pointed out that the Supreme Command threw in the towel well before the revolution; that during the war years it had exercised military, political, and economic control over the civilian government; and finally, that it was General Ludendorff who forced an unwilling civilian government to sue for peace. Yet the historical importance of the legend is not that it was false but that it was *believed to be true*. By a process of rationalization born of humiliation and wounded pride, German patriots believed, or came to believe, completely and thoroughly, that the army had never been defeated after all. Apart from the very real fact that the soldiers wanted desperately to believe it, the patriotic myth-makers were aided by two other factors: effective and widespread propaganda disseminated by the Army, and the bungling attempts of the civilian government to win the support of veterans by flattery. One of the new government's incredible pamphlets told the soldier:

> A new Germany greets you! . . . Perhaps you do not return as victors who have completely crushed the enemy to the ground . . . but neither do you return as the vanquished, for the war was stopped at the wishes of the leadership of the country [*Reichsleitung*] . . . so you can hold your heads high.[142]

It was not difficult to predict the attitude of the front-line soldier when he returned home. He was convinced that the Army, which had fought through four years of cruel war, had been stabbed in the back by cowards and pacifists on the home front.

"TREATY OF SHAME"

In the eyes of the soldier-patriots, the Republic renewed its treason by signing the Treaty of Versailles, a treaty despised by all Germans. When its terms became known in May 1919, mass demonstrations were held; a period of mourning was declared; and cinemas, theaters, and other places of amusement were closed. Throughout the Republic on "*Versailles-Diktat* Day" the schools of Germany were draped in black.

In retrospect, it seems likely that the primary political reason for the failure of democracy in Germany and the rise of militant dictatorship during the interwar years was German reaction to this "Treaty of Shame," this "Treaty of Treason." With sure political instinct Hitler, in dozens upon dozens of impassioned speeches, played on a constant theme: the betrayal of the Motherland, the direct responsibility of the "November Criminals" for the humiliation of Versailles. "How many times, oh how many times," he later mused, "did I speak about the *Versailles-Diktat?*"

It has often been suggested that the treaty was not in fact so harsh as the lamentations of German patriots proclaimed, and that if Germany had won World War I, the treaty imposed upon the Allies would have been infinitely harsher. Support for this view may be found in the Treaty of Brest-Litovsk, which Germany dictated to Russia in February 1918. According to its terms, Germany seized control of a vast sweep of land from the Arctic to the Black Sea. It was planned that German dynasties would be established in Finland, Estonia, Latvia, Lithuania, Poland, and possibly in the Ukraine and in Georgia. By the treaty, Russia lost 25 percent of its territory, over 40 percent of its population, and more than 70 percent of its industrial capacity. "Never in the history of the world," a member of the Reichstag admitted, "has there been an instance of greater annexationist politics. . . ." And seldom has a treaty been so widely acclaimed. A leading Christian newspaper, *Allgemeine Evangelisch-Lutherische Kirchenzeitung*, reflecting the enthusiasm of the nation, rejected the idea of peace without annexation and hailed the treaty as evidence of God's special will for Germany:

> Peace without annexations and reparations! Such was man's resolve. . . . But here, too, God willed otherwise. . . . And Russia finally had to give up immense booty: 800 locomotives and 8,000 railroad cars filled with all manner of goods and provisions, God knew we needed this. We also needed cannon and munitions. . . . God knew that, too. So out of His generosity—for God is rich— He gave us 2,600 cannons, 5,000 machine guns, 2 million rounds of ammunition for the artillery. He also gave us rifles, airplanes, trucks and much more.

The stated war aims of German political and military leaders also provide evidence of the kind of treaty a victorious Germany would have exacted from the defeated Allies. The war aims called not only for conquest of Eastern Europe but also for domination of the West. Belgium, the Low Countries, and industrial France would all come under German control, as would the British Empire and huge tracts of land in Africa.[143]

But Germans forgot their own precedent and expected for themselves a strict application of Wilsonian ideals of reconciliation and "peace without victory." They were soon disabused. The victors, while paying lip service to the right of "self-determination of nationalities," ignored the wishes of German inhabitants and transferred land to Poland and Czechoslovakia. The treaty promised impartial solutions to colonial claims, yet all German colonies were seized by the victors. The treaty set up a new world organization, but Germany was excluded as unworthy of membership. The treaty talked about disarmament, but only Germany was forced to disarm. The most galling section of the treaty was Article 231, in which the Germans were required to confess what was patently untrue: that they were solely responsible for causing World War I. Germany was threatened with a blockade until she signed the treaty.

The result of all this was that Germans—all Germans—considered themselves betrayed. If any one speech can convey the attitude of an entire country, that speech was given by the German foreign minister, Count Brockdorff-Rantzau, when he received the terms of the Versailles Treaty. Refusing to stand as a penitent in the dock, he remained seated to deliver the following memorable commentary:

> We are under no illusions as to the extent of our defeat and the degree of our powerlessness. We know that the strength of the German arms is broken. We know the intensity of the hatred which meets us, and we have heard the victor's passionate demands that as the vanquished we shall be made to pay, and as the guilty we shall be punished.

The demand is made that we shall acknowledge that we alone are guilty for having caused the war. Such a confession in my mouth would be a lie. We are far from seeking to escape from any responsibility for this World War, and for its having been waged as it was. . . . But in the manner of waging war, Germany was not the only one that erred. . . . I do not want to reply to reproaches with reproaches, . . . crimes in war may not be inexcusable, but they are committed in the struggle for victory . . . When we . . . are in such passion as makes the conscience of peoples blunt. The hundreds of thousands of noncombatants who have perished since November 11, because of the blockade, were destroyed coolly and deliberately, after our opponents had won a certain and assured victory. Remember that, when you speak of guilt and atonement.

Wilson listened attentively to the speech, Clemenceau flushed with anger, Lloyd George laughed, Bonar Law yawned.[144]

One of the more interesting psychological phenomena of recent history is the remarkable hold that the "war guilt question" (*Kriegs-schuldfrage*) had on the German mind. Germans seemed absolutely fascinated with the problem. Long after Western historians and Allied statesmen had abandoned the untenable thesis of Germany's sole guilt, Germans still insisted on belaboring the issue; they kept thinking, writing, and talking about it.[145] In 1925, for example, a German book dealer issued a catalogue of no fewer than 2,300 titles concerned with the causes of World War I. One German periodical, entitled *Die Kriegs-schuldfrage*, was devoted exclusively to denying German "guilt" and vindicating Germany by indicting the Entente. This periodical, started in 1923, kept publishing until 1934. For those who preferred less heavy reading, the question was kept alive by popular gimmicks. One publisher sold a tear-off calendar which advertised that "this calendar shows every month in words and pictures the rape of Germany . . . the lies of 'war guilt' are sharply refuted by daily slogans." Another enterprising entrepreneur capitalized on the popularity of the war guilt issue by selling strings of rosary-like beads, each devoted to a "prayer" proclaiming Germany's innocence. Why this continued fascination with the issue long after it had been dropped by every responsible Allied statesman and historian? It should be emphasized that it was the Germans themselves who insisted on casting the issue in stridently moral tones.

Why? Once again, this obvious yet difficult question poses problems and invites speculation. It seems likely that the underlying reason for the surprising popularity and longevity of the war guilt debate was psychological. Like the legend of the stab in the back, it could not be sustained by rational argument. But the depth of commitment to both of these myths suggests that they served the important psychological function of displacing a national sense of shame and shock. Not shame at having caused the war, for the Germans were convinced they were innocent of that charge. Rather, their shame was in having lost it. Sudden, unexpected, and humiliating defeat produced intense feelings of confusion, shock, and self-accusation which were displaced by taking up the charge of war guilt and defiantly rejecting it. The issue, we are suggesting, was embraced so fervently for so long because it diverted attention from the real cause of anxiety: personal and national failure. It was easier and more gratifying to disprove a false moral accusation than it was to confront the reality of defeat and the humiliation of failure. Thus, the war guilt myth joined the *Dolschstoss* legend as a means of preserving national self-respect by convincing German patriots that they were innocent victims of unprovoked aggression as well as heroic victors who had been treacherously stabbed in the back.

It is not surprising that the diaries and memoirs of returning veterans—the "New Men" born in the trenches—are a veritable hymn of hate directed against the Republic. Only two examples out of dozens can be given here. A hardened soldier, who had been a teenage volunteer in 1914, recorded in his diary on 21 January 1919:

> I will set down here in my journal . . . that I will not forget these days of criminals, lies, and barbarity. . . . The day will come when I will knock the truth into these people and tear the mask from the faces of the whole miserable, pathetic lot. . . .[146]

Another veteran, who joined the Ehrhardt Brigade to fight in the Baltic and would later march with Hitler on the Feldherrnhalle in Munich in 1923, set forth his faith in burning prose:

> The state, born of this Revolution—whatever constitution it gives itself, and whoever is at the head of it—this state will forever be our enemy. The strength of its first year was treason, cowardice, lies, corruption, weakness and selfishness. . . . *Out of the experience of the Revolution came the conviction that our task for the next decade would be: for the Reich! for the Volk! fight the Government! Death to the democratic Republic!* [147]

Such was the attitude of those who could not demobilize psychologically. History records few ironies more bitter than this one: the Weimar Republic would hire these men to save it from destruction.

From Revolution to Republic to Dictatorship

> This Revolution without revolutionaries . . . produced a Republic with few republicans.
> —Anonymous

Germany's first experiment in democracy began with the Revolution of 1918. As revolutions go, this was a rather disappointing affair, lacking almost all the characteristics of the *genre*. The inefficiency and corruption which plagued other governments on the eve of revolution were not hallmarks of the Hohenzollerns. Moreover, German intellectuals, unlike such thinkers as Locke, Rousseau, Jefferson, Herzen, or Mao, had not deserted the establishment; they still endorsed it. Normally, revolutions veer sharply to the left; but this one moved steadily to the right. It was a revolution without joy and without song—perhaps the only songless revolution in history.

Revolutionaries, normally required by successful revolutions, could not be found among the leaders of the new German government. Friedrich Ebert (1871–1925)—who looked and acted like the successful small businessman he was—was the leader of the revolutionary republic which, on 9 November 1918, had been proclaimed against his wishes. Five days earlier, he had entreated the Army to save the monarchy because he was convinced it was the only alternative to revolution, and he abhorred the very idea. "I want no part of it," he had said on the eve of the event, "I hate it as I hate sin." [148]

In a very real sense, there was no Revolution of 1918. To be sure, political change had taken place at the top—a president, after all, had replaced an emperor. But basic social, institutional and attitudinal patterns remained largely unaffected.* The forces that had dominated the Empire and had done so much to produce the "German condition" remained to plague the Republic: military ideals continued to pervade society; Junkers and Ruhr barons were untouched by revolution, as the same families controlled industry, banking, and agriculture; the imperial bureaucracy was left intact in central and local government, in the Foreign Office and in the judiciary; intellectuals still disdained politics and ridiculed parliament; authoritarian families and schools continued to inculcate attitudes inimical to democracy and favorable to fascism.

In short, from the outset of the revolution, prospects for democracy were not good. They did not improve when, after the regular army had been dissolved, President Ebert felt obliged to call on radically hostile soldiers—the Free Corps—to defend his precarious government from the leftist revolts which were sweeping Germany and establishing Soviet-style republics in major cities of the country.

THE FREE CORPS AS VANGUARD OF NAZISM

By the summer of 1919—when Hitler was still unknown—the Free Corps had become the most important political force in Germany and the greatest single source of future Nazi personnel and spirit. Some 500,000 strong, these self-styled Freebooters had smashed leftist movements with exultant brutality from the Ruhr to the Baltic, from Ham-

---

* Germans showed the depth of their desire to avoid change and to preserve the magic of a word when they refused to call the new government the "German Republic"; they chose instead "German Reich." Thus, constitutional purists can argue that the Third Reich actually began in 1919, when the new constitution was adopted, and not in 1933 with Hitler's "seizure" of power.

burg to Munich. Battle-tough veterans and radical youths too young to fight in the Great War, they had entered the service of the Republic not because they respected the government—they despised it—but because they needed money, food, and comradeship and an opportunity to fight and destroy. Listen to one of them:

> People told us that the War was over. That made us laugh. We ourselves are the War. . . . It envelops our whole being and fascinates us with the enticing urge to destroy. We. . . . marched onto the battlefields of the postwar world just as we had gone into battle on the Western Front: singing, reckless and filled with the joy of adventure as we marched to the attack; silent, deadly, remorseless in battle.[149]

The chief characteristics of the Free Corps were, without exception, those of Hitler's Storm Troopers. First, the *Führerprinzip,* which had been developing in the prewar youth movements, was now manifested at two levels. The commander of an individual corps was often called the Führer and idolized as the embodiment of all soldierly virtues. The leader was also an abstraction, a 20th-century version of the Barbarossa legend. Thus, in the black days after defeat in the Baltic in 1919, a *Freikorpskämpfer* wrote to his sister: "Someday a Man will come to lead us—a Man who unites German spirit and German power! Believe me . . . things will be a little better for us then!"[150]

Second, there was in these men a reckless desire to attack, to smash the whole philistine middle-class world. The acknowledged spokesman of the movement gave the clearest statement of this attitude:

> "What do we believe in?" you ask. Nothing besides action. . . . We were a band of fighters drunk with all the passions of the world; full of lust, exultant in action. What we wanted, we did not know. And what we knew, we did not want! War and adventure, excitement and destruction. An indefinable, surging force welled up from every part of our being and flayed us onward. . . .[151]

Third, like the Nazis, Free Corps members were racists who dedicated themselves to what they called the "*Volk* soul of the race." They were savagely anti-Semitic.

Fourth, like so many of their generation, Free Corps fighters dreamed of a new Germany, a Third Reich. They had no definite political program for this government. Indeed, they deliberately shunned one, for reasons suggested by an admirer:

> Nothing is more characteristic of the associative spirit of *Oberländer* than their Idea of the Third *Reich* . . . the men dreamed deep dreams of this Mystery—a mystery which would have been

debased into a concrete political program as soon as one attempted to define it precisely.

The mystery was partially penetrated by the same writer: "Two motifs are constantly repeated in the recitals of the *Oberländer:* the sacredness of the *Volksboden* and the heroic *Führerschicht,* which must be accepted by the *Gemeinschaft* as the force which will achieve the goal of the docile followship [*willige Gefolgheit*] of all." [152]

On a less abstract level, a Free Corps leader set forth his political program in words quoted here not for the delicacy of the language but because they are an honest reflection of the Freebooter mind addressing itself to problems of politics:

> We must . . . smash once and for all these damned revolutionary rats and choke them by sticking their heads in their own shit.[153]

The Freebooters made important contributions to the coming of Hitler's Germany. Negatively, they helped mightily to undermine and destroy Germany's first experiment in democracy. Positively, they contributed thousands of their members to positions of power in the Third Reich. Indeed, 48.6 percent of the Party leadership came from veterans who had taken an active part in the battles of the war and postwar years.[154] They also contributed a well-developed leadership principle, racism, the idea of labor camps and youth programs, and the concept of political shock troops.

But their main contribution lay in the realm of the spirit. Their contempt for humane values and their exaltation of power and brutality formed their chief legacy to Hitler's Reich.

A remarkably prophetic poem was written in 1919 by a man who had watched the Free Corps in action. Walther Mehring, who became one of Germany's most effective satirists, wrote the verse in bitter paraphrase of the Freebooter mentality which foretold atrocities to come:

> Come on, boys, let's all go . . .
> Off to the pogrom with a ho, ho, ho . . .
> Pull in your bellies and throw out the Jews
> With swastika and poison gas . . .
> Let's have a go at murder in the mass.[155]

THE ANTIDEMOCRATIC ESTABLISHMENT

Older established institutions also helped clear Hitler's path to power, either by refusing to support the democratic alternative or by contributing in more positive ways.

The Army supported Hitler because it saw in him a useful tool to militarize the masses. One of the more responsible military leaders later spoke quite candidly about the value they had seen in Hitler and suggested that the Nazi idea of militarism was not really very different from the army's:

> The Army . . . considered [Hitler] to be the right man to work up into a fury, passions . . . against Versailles. Actually, he trumpeted nothing different from their own call for power. . . .[156]

There was, of course, no doubt whatever in the mind of the High Command that it could order the former private first class to do its bidding.

At lower echelons of the Army, Hitler was supported with even greater enthusiasm. As noted, almost one-half of the leadership of the Nazi Party had been veterans of war or postwar fighting. A noncommissioned officer spoke for thousands of his comrades in giving his reasons for following Hitler:

> We . . . did not join the Storm Troopers for many rational considerations, or after much contemplation. It was our feelings that led us to Hitler. What . . . our hearts compelled us to think was this: Hitler, you're our man. You talk like [a man] who's been at the Front, who's been through the same mess we have . . . like us, an unknown soldier. . . .[157]

The Navy, if anything, was more adamant than the Army in its opposition to the Republic. One incident reflects its attitude. Immediately after the Ehrhardt Free Corps Brigade—with swastikas painted on their helmets—had marched into Berlin during the Kapp Putsch of 1920 to overthrow the republican government, the Navy incorporated whole units of the brigade.[158]

The civil service, which had proved so sedulous in supporting Prussian kings and German emperors, showed no such loyalty to the Republic. In every department of government, officials continued to foster nationalist, antidemocratic ideas. Continuity in both attitude and personnel from Second to Third Reich was striking. In the Foreign Office, for example, of the 15 most important German missions abroad in 1929, only one (London) was in the hands of a Weimar appointee —all the others had once sworn allegiance to the emperor. Hitler saw no need for changing the personnel in carrying out his aggressive policies. In 1939, of nine divisional chiefs of the diplomatic corps who endorsed Hitler's war, only one had been a Nazi appointee.[159] Nor was there any basic change in the judicial system. The Republic retained all the laws of the empire as well as its judges. As a leading authority on German law during the period has noted, "Between the new [republic] and the old Reich the judicial relationship is not one of succession, but one of identity." [160]

Documents of the Weimar period show clearly that while some

responsible officials recognized the danger of Hitler, their superiors refused to take any action against him. In 1924, for example, the Bavarian police recommended that Hitler be deported as a dangerous alien. Their report was prophetic:

> The moment he is set free, Hitler will . . . again become the driving force of the new, serious public riots and a continual menace to the security of the State.

As a result of this report, the Bavarian state attorney filed formal complaints protesting Hitler's parole, but the Bavarian minister of justice, Franz Guertner, intervened and ordered the withdrawal of all complaints. Hitler was released on parole and was not deported. Guertner was later made Reichminister of Justice in 1933 and served until his death in 1942.[161]

The bureaucracy that had helped Hitler into power proved indispensable in establishing his dictatorship. He could never have consolidated his control over Germany "without the technical help of tens of thousands of civil servants and the acquiescence of millions . . . complicity and silence, not refusal and dissent" characterized the German bureaucracy in the crucial early years of Hitler's dictatorship.[162]

Religious institutions were also helpful to Hitler. The Protestant hierarchy was generally hostile to the Republic, and its pastors thundered from a thousand pulpits against the "Treaty of Shame," which only the coming of a strong national leader could abolish. With the advent of Hitler, they continued their tradition of limiting religious statements to narrowly defined personal faith, with emphasis on the obligations of the "inner man," drawing their inspiration from Luther's famous, and fateful, pronouncement, "Politics are not the concern of the Church." Many Protestants came to accept without question Hitler's claim that his movement was the only alternative to Communism. Pastor Breuer spoke for many of his brethren in Christ when he said that he had joined the Nazi Party because the Church needed a powerful ally against "atheistic Communism and materialism," and that he "supported Nazism wholeheartedly" until 1943—that is, until the defeat at Stalingrad.[163] Lutherans generally found it difficult to take exception to Hitler's anti-Semitism, since it paralleled so closely Martin Luther's explicit statements about the Jews.

Like their Protestant counterparts, Catholic leaders were also basically conservative, largely monarchist, and distrustful of liberal democracy. And like the Protestants, they were unable to recognize the menace of Hitler and were ineffective in dealing with him. Let Father Falkan, a Catholic parish priest, speak for his colleagues:

> I must admit that I was glad to see the Nazis come into power, because at that time I felt that Hitler as a Catholic was a God-

fearing individual who could battle Communism for the Church.
. . . The anti-Semitism of the Nazis, as well as their anti-Marxism,
appealed to the Church . . . as a counterpoise to the paganism which
had developed after 1920.[164]

It must be emphasized that after Hitler's dictatorship was established many individual Christian clergymen—Protestant and Catholic alike—opposed Nazi barbarities and were martyred for their convictions. But the role played by the Christian churches in Hitler's advent and consolidation of power forms one of the most deplorable pages in the history of religion.

With a few notable exceptions, the news media opposed the Republic and welcomed Hitler. This was most strikingly true of the man who by all odds was the most powerful publicist in Weimar Germany, Alfred Hugenberg, who kept up a sustained, vitriolic, and effective attack on every position taken by the democratic government. Hugenberg had been Krupp's general manager and one of the founders of the Pan-German League. During the war he had endorsed Germany's most aggressive war plans; after the defeat he dedicated his fortune and organizational ability to the task of subverting democracy. He purchased a leading Berlin newspaper, newsreel rights, and a press service which sent out stories and set editorial policy for the provincial press. In one way or another, he gained control over some 1,600 newspapers with millions of readers. He also owned Germany's largest and most influential film corporation, UFA (*Universum Film Aktiengesellschaft*), which controlled distribution of films to scores of theaters. In 1928, when Hitler's fortunes were faltering, Hugenberg came to his assistance. In the crisis of 1933, he helped tip the scales in Hitler's favor. His promise to serve in a cabinet under Hitler made the idea of government by the "Bohemian corporal" more palatable to the establishment and a reluctant President Hindenburg.[165]

Other influential journalists were also helpful. The editor and publisher of the *Leipziger Neueste Nachrichten* were both enormously impressed with Hitler after long interviews with him. They were confident that any "rough edges" could easily be rubbed off, and that "men like Hindenburg, von Papen and Hugenberg will be able to bring him to reason." The *Deutsche Allgemeine Zeitung* agreed, endorsed Hitler as a foe of socialism, and urged that he be "brought into the team because of his energy and enthusiasm. . . ." All thought it was unwise to take his anti-Semitism too seriously, and all found in him a very healthy alternative to the Weimar Republic, which they called "the loathsome rule by party bosses." [166]

Germany's educational system remained authoritarian, nationalist, and unreconciled to democracy. The attitudes schoolteachers must have taken into the classrooms of the republic can be inferred from the alacrity with which they welcomed and supported Hitler. Of all the professions represented in the Nazi party, teachers—particularly in elementary schools—formed by far the largest group. About 97 percent of all schoolteachers became members of the Party or its affiliates, and many of them rose to positions of influence in the Third Reich, including Heinrich Himmler and Julius Streicher, along with some 3,000 local leaders of the Party. Altogether, more than 30 percent of the total leadership of the Party had been schoolteachers in the Weimar Republic.[167]

During the Republic, schoolchildren were reminded in many visible ways of past glories and present shame: pictures of the emperor, famous generals, and Bismarck still looked grimly down on classrooms where imperial flags hung and imperial stencils decorated the *Herr Lehrers* chair. As late as 1926 it was necessary for a member of the Reichstag to defend the motion that the republican colors of black, red, and gold be permitted to fly over the schools of Germany. There was no holiday associated with the Republic or the liberal tradition. Neither of the two most memorable days in the school year was designed to foster democratic attitudes. On Versailles Day, 28 June, schools and universities were draped in black. The Founding Day of Bismarck's Reich continued to be celebrated on 18 January with stirring displays of military pomp. The establishment of the Republic was not celebrated. Indeed, in one Founding Day address the director of the University of Freiburg used the occasion to accuse the "usurper" President Ebert of "high treason." [168] Meanwhile, undergraduate social life in the universities continued to be dominated by dueling societies. Students joined patriotic professors in ridiculing the Republic and cultivating a spirit of radical racial nationalism, often coupled with anti-Semitism.

On the eve of an important national election, during the Nazis' final bid for power, a declaration was signed by 300 professors from all the universities of Germany expressing confidence in Adolf Hitler and promising him their support. It is true that the signators were of no great academic distinction, but it is also true that respected names of German intellectual life set forth no counterdeclaration. They were silent, for they did not wish to become involved in anything so sordid as politics. As a common saying in university circles had it, "Whoever is concerned with politics, has no culture; whoever has culture, has no concern for politics." [169]

CONTRIBUTIONS OF WEIMAR INTELLECTUALS

Cultural life during the Weimar Republic produced a fascinating anomaly: dangerously destructive forces were at work at the very time that Germany was enjoying the most creative cultural flowering in its history. Creativity in all fields of human endeavor was simply astounding, as a few representative names attest: in architecture, Walter Gropius and the Bauhaus; in social studies, Max Weber, Karl Mannheim,

The Past As Prologue: Hitler and History

Friedrich Meinecke, and the Frankfurt School; in music, Richard Strauss, Paul Hindemith, and Kurt Weill; in theology and philosophy, Paul Tillich, Karl Barth, Ernst Cassirer, Edmund Husserl, and Martin Heidegger; in science, Max Planck and Albert Einstein; in the theatre, Max Reimann and Leopold Jessner; in the cinema, Fritz Lang and G. W. Papst; in literature, Thomas and Heinrich Mann, Bertolt Brecht, and Gottfried Benn, along with the Austrians Franz Werfel, Hugo von Hofmannsthal, and Rainer Maria Rilke.

Yet all these cultural attainments did little to advance political freedom or democratic institutions. Indeed, after the first fleeting enthusiasm for the Revolution passed, German intellectuals who might have been expected to support the Republic turned their backs upon it. Ernst Cassirer, the influential philosopher and publicist, saw in it "nothing but a great swindle." Others, like Germany's greatest living historian, Friedrich Meinecke, were at best lukewarm in their acquiescence, calling themselves "rational republicans" (*Vernunftrepublikaner*) who, without enthusiasm or commitment, agreed to tolerate the Republic as a rational necessity. Their position was well expressed in Meinecke's comment to a friend: "The German people are simply not ripe for parliamentary democracy, especially under the pressure of the Versailles peace. I said that to myself under my breath from the beginning." Disdain for the revolutionary change of 1918 was soon compressed into a single phrase. Intellectuals spoke of "the so-called Revolution." [170]

In the fall of 1971, a group of distinguished German émigrés who had participated in the cultural life of Weimar in their youth met in New York to reflect on their experiences. The occasion was not without melancholy. Hannah Arendt recalled that as a university student she had felt a "complete breakdown of values" and a general expectation that something new was in the offing, but the feeling did not produce optimism: "We knew that the Weimar Republic was doomed." She and her friends all shared "a contemptuous attitude to Weimar." She then added one of her many memorable aphorisms: "Contempt is a potent revolutionary force." Ivo Frenzel of the West German Radio agreed that "a feeling of apocalypse was in the air" and noted the morbid fascination of his generation with sickness in society, reflected in the popularity of Thomas Mann's *The Magic Mountain* and *Mario and the Magician*. Leo Loewenthal found that Weimar "never really jelled as a government or as a society. We had no models. Schoolchildren were torn away from outdated authoritarian models but unsure of what new ones to accept." Germany was ripe for a new system of symbols to give order and direction. "Nazism, as horrible as it was, seemed to be a model to follow." [171]

It has become a popular intellectual pastime for historians to seek "the roots of Nazism" in the intellectual soil of the Republic. Such roots certainly can be found. But at least as important in subverting parliamentary institutions and undermining the spirit of free society were the antidemocratic attitudes which continued to characterize and contribute to the "German condition." The irony and the tragedy consisted in the fact that Weimar intellectuals despised Hitler, yet—often unwittingly—they collaborated with him by helping to destroy the Republic.

Take, for example two influential journalists who saw themselves as enemies of Hitler, Ernst Niekisch and Kurt Tucholsky. Niekisch, a socialist who would suffer under the Gestapo for his courageous anti-Nazi pamphlets, hated Hitler; but like Hitler he wanted to destroy the Republic. He too talked of the necessity for a "new barbarism" to clear away the "hypocrisy of Weimar"; he too despised Western liberalism and put quotation marks around terms like "liberty" and "human values." [172] Tucholsky, the brilliant and biting satirist who was a founding editor of the important journal *Die Weltbühne* (The World Stage), sincerely believed in a Republic and in a free and humane society dedicated to equality and peace. But since he could find no political party he deemed worthy of support, he joined none and ridiculed them all; because Weimar political leaders were less than ideal, he tore them apart in clever caricature. Thus, in effect, though certainly not in intent, Tucholsky contributed to the success of the dictator he detested. As a few intellectuals struggled against Hitler, "Tucholsky stood aside and jeered at them. They could have used some help. All they got from him was scorn and laughter." [173]

Most Weimar intellectuals were not so much divided left from right as they were united in opposition to the middle. The two extremes had much in common, confessed Henry Pachter, a socialist in his youth: "We too were romantics about the state; we too agreed that the Republic had no *Geist*; we too lacked real contact with the masses; we too saw ourselves as members of the elite; we too ridiculed the Republic as an ugly thing. We agreed: The Republic had no style." [174]

The parallels between left and right are important and can be extended. Both groups were bitterly anti-West, in part because the Western powers were responsible for the hated Versailles Treaty, but also because the intellectuals felt themselves to be heirs of a long tradition which contrasted German *Kultur* with the degenerate civilization of the West. Many turned their gaze eastward: the left toward the new Russia, the right to plans for conquest and a renewed *Drang nach Osten*. Both left and right tended to deprecate intellect and extol *Lebensphilosophie*— a romantic urge which stressed emotions, instincts, and patriotic activism. Symptomatic of the attitude was a truly remarkable revival of interest in the early Romantic Heinrich von Kleist, who enjoyed the support of surprisingly diverse groups: the Nazis claimed him as a racial nationalist; the Communists called him a revolutionary; Thomas Mann enjoyed his humor; religious revivalists were attracted by his tormented Christianity. All agreed that "to stand by Kleist is to be German!" There may have been a morbid reason for the attraction which this early Romantic held for so many people over so long a period of time: "Kleist . . . gave a new respectability to the love affair with death that looms so large over the German mind . . . only three things were clear about the Kleist crusade: its intensity, its confusion, and its exaltation of irrationality—its blissful death wish." [175]

A romantic social vision beckoned both left and right, whether it was the socialist myth of a stateless, classless society or the nationalist myth of a Third Reich. This new Reich, it was fervently expected, would respond to three deeply felt desires: to establish a New Order of unspecified form but directed by a hero-leader; to solve all economic problems through some kind of authoritarian German socialism; and to respond to the spiritual crisis and weakening of traditional religion by a glowing Germanic faith. [176]

Both left and right rejected political individualism and endorsed, often with ecstatic intensity, the concept of community, or *Gemeinschaft*. It is a fact of very considerable historic importance that in Germany both conservative nationalists and radical revolutionaries supported socialism and *Gemeinschaft*, whether they saw this community as being achieved in the classless society of Marx or the racial community of Hitler. Both agreed that the individual should be sacrificed to the demands of the group. Hitler responded brilliantly to this spiritual longing of conservatives and revolutionaries for an all-embracing, cooperative German community. Fritz Stern is quite right in noting that this very important aspect of the rise of Hitler has been overlooked by both Marxist and psychoanalytical explanations for the success of his movement. [177]

Nazi emphasis on the primacy of community over the individual (as in Goebbels's slogan *"Gemeinnutz vor Eigennutz"*) also helps to explain how it was possible for so many German intellectuals to join the Nazi cult. Their support "would have been inconceivable," a German historian has written, "without the anti-democratic intellectual movement that preceded it, [which] in its contempt for everything liberal had blunted people's sensitivies to the inviolable rights of the individual and the preservation of human dignity." [178]

These general themes are seen most clearly in the thought of three of the period's most influential writers, Arthur Moeller van den Bruck (1876–1925), Oswald Spengler (1880–1936), and Martin Heidegger (1889–1976). All three illustrate what the noted German theologian and essayist Ernst Troeltsch had in mind when he concluded in 1922 that there was a "curious dualism" in the German mind. There was, he said, an abundance of Romanticism and lofty idealism; but there was also a form of realism pushed to the verge of cynicism and utter indifference to ideals and morality:

> But what you will see above all is an inclination to make an astonishing combination of the two elements—in a word, to brutalize Romance, and to romanticize cynicism. [179]

Like thousands of his generation, Moeller had participated in the prewar youth movement and had joyfully volunteered for the German

Army. In the midst of war and bombardments of the Western Front he had written his first book, *Der preussische Stil* (The Prussian Style). The original dust jacket bore a picture of Frederick the Great and the imperial (later Nazi) colors of black, white, and red. The book was dedicated "to the spirit of Hegel and Clausewitz." Its central theme was contained in the first chapter: *"Preussen ist ohne Mythos"* (Prussia Is Without Myth). Incomparably great as Prussia was, it still lacked something: it was much too practical, cold, rational. Germany needed a flaming Romantic urge, a soul-stirring dynamic. In short, Germany needed a *myth*, "a life-renewing force." One is reminded of Kohn's observation that Nazism resulted from the marriage of Prussianism and Romanticism.

After the armistice, which Moeller saw as a temporary truce in a holy crusade against the West, he was one of the cofounders of the *Juni Klub*, named after the month when the "Treaty of Shame" was signed. He dedicated his life and talents to the destruction of democracy and the establishment of a New Order. To this end, in 1923 he published his most important work which he entitled *Das dritte Reich* (The Third Reich). This book played a far greater role in German party politics in the Republic than any other single volume, not excluding *Mein Kampf*, and was widely read long before Hitler's. Moeller was admired by many different sorts of people. Niekisch, the National Bolshevist, said that Moeller's type of socialism "was a mood which gripped us"; Otto Strasser's splinter group of Nazis called Moeller "a great teacher" whose book was "the basic book of the Black Front"; and Goebbels, in his unpublished diary, noted in 1925 that he was deeply stirred by Moeller's writing.[180]

A brief review of the chapters of this book, published in 1923, will convey something of its spirit. Chapter 1, on revolution, indicts the Republic for treason and promises that Germany will arise triumphant from defeat and humiliation. Chapter 2 shows how much Moeller was attracted to socialism. But he cannot accept Marxism because of its materialism and internationalism. He calls for a socialism more in tune with the German tradition, an authoritarian national socialism must form the basis for the Third Reich. Chapters 3 and 4 are a sustained attack on liberal democracy which he calls, variously, "mental disease," "the seducer," and "the betrayer of youth." His hatred of the Republic is palpable:

> We can only speak with scorn of these intellectuals who lured the German *Volk* to its fate and who now stand with their stupid faces aghast at the result to which their ideology led them! . . . These intellectual blockheads have still not learned anything; they still mouth the eternal validity of their principles: world democracy, The League of Nations, international arbitration, the end of war, Peace on Earth. They will neither see nor hear nor con-

fess that through their guilt, men all around us are suffering under foreign domination. . . .

The concluding chapter, "The Third Reich," is full of magic and myth. "Remember," he pleads in 1923, "that the words themselves are a mystery, indeterminate . . . charged with feeling not of this world but of the next."

In 1925, when Germany seemed to be recovering economic and political stability and it looked as if the despised Republic might survive, Moeller committed suicide. His ideas were then promoted by the influential magazine *Die Tat* (The Deed), which proclaimed in 1929 the advent of a final crisis and the coming of a dictatorship which would bring about the kind of national socialist state that would fulfill Moeller's myth.[181]

Oswald Spengler had been an obscure high school teacher until the publication in 1918 of the first of two massive and murky volumes entitled *Der Untergang des Abendlandes*, well known in English as *The Decline of the West*. The work achieved surprising popularity throughout the world, but was read with something approaching morbid fascination in Germany, where it was "*the* most widely studied book" within a year of its publication.[182]

The atmosphere of gathering gloom with which Spengler's tomes begin deepened to something akin to a triumphant death wish as he announced the doom of Western civilization: "There is only one end of the eternal struggle, death: death of individuals, death of peoples, death of culture. . . ." There was, however, one glimmer of hope, at least for Germany. Though Western culture would inevitably die, a new breed of hard-hearted conquerors could arise in the Fatherland. Here, following the dictates of an ancient myth, a New Order would be established which, he wrote, would be called *Das dritte Reich*: "The Third Reich is the Germanic ideal, an eternal new dawn."

The last page of the book sounds a call to struggle and racial power that Hitler would re-echo in a hundred speeches:

> Ever in History it is life and life only—race quality, the triumph of the will-to-power—and not the victory of truths, discoveries, or money that signifies. *World-history is the world-court*, and it has ever decided in favor of the stronger. . . . Always it has sacrificed truth and justice to power and race. . . .[183]

In the summer of 1919, Spengler completed the manuscript of a work which was to become even more popular, particularly among German youth. Indeed, one historian of the Weimar youth movement has called this pamphlet, *Preussentum und Sozialismus* (Prussianism and Socialism), "one of the Holy Scriptures" of those young people reaching their maturity on or about the year 1933.[184] Spengler began with a savage indictment of the revolution of 1918 and the "November Criminals" of the Weimar Republic. He characterized the Revolution as "the most senseless act in German history. . . . In the heart of the German *Volk*, Weimar stands condemned. One can't even laugh at it . . . The future will most certainly look on this episode with profound contempt." The whole idea of erecting a parliamentary Republic in Germany was, he insisted, a laughable anachronism, repugnant to the whole of German history. "Parliamentarianism in Germany is either nonsense or treason [*Unsinn oder Verrat*]."

Spengler then launched his thesis: what Germany needed was not Western liberalism but socialism of a particular kind, namely, Prussian-German socialism. "Frederick William I and not Marx was the first conscious socialist." Indeed, Marx was not a socialist at all, he was a materialist with no conception of the German spirit; he was "exclusively an English thinker." Spengler gazed into a clouded crystal ball in 1919 to predict the imminent demise of Marxism: "Today Marxism is collapsing amid the clamorous orgy of its attempt to become reality . . . the *Communist Manifesto* has entered upon a career as a literary curiosity. . . ." The future belonged not to the Marxists but to the only genuine socialists in the world, the Germanic *Volk*: "I say *German* socialism for there is no other . . . we Germans are socialist. The others cannot possibly be socialist. . . . The only true socialism is German socialism. . . . Prussianism and socialism are one and the same."

Spengler, like Hitler after him, was much taken with the "power of blood" to form history, and he combined it with the world of ideas in a curiously aggressive way: "Ideas that have become blood demand blood. War is the eternal pattern of higher human existence, and countries exist for war's sake."

This little book of large consequence ends with a stirring challenge to the youth of Germany:

> I turn to youth. I call upon all those who have marrow in their bones and blood in their veins . . . to become men! We do not want any more ideologies, no more talk about culture and cosmopolitanism. . . .
>
> We need hardness, brave skepticism, we need a body of socialist supermen [*sozialistische Herrennaturen*]. Once again: socialism means power, power, and power over and over again [*Sozialismus bedeutet Macht, Macht, und immer wieder Macht*]. . . .[185]

Martin Heidegger, probably the most influential German philosopher of the 20th century, had nothing but scorn for democracy. Politically he sought a Hegelian synthesis between the apparently irreconcilable forces of Bismarckian Power and Nietzschean Spirit. Like many of his colleagues, he believed that a full reconciliation of political force and intellectual creativity could come only when it was imposed from above by a power state, a new Reich. "It would be a Reich," an admirer of Heidegger wrote in 1932, "which would vouchsafe the final order of the world. It would be the Reich in which Frederick of Prussia and Goethe of the Germans would become one. The impossible, long-impeded meeting between Bismarck and Nietzsche would be accomplished; against that, every attack of enemy powers would be shattered." [186]

The Führer of the Nazis was not really what these intellectuals had in mind. (Even Spengler was shocked and disillusioned.) Yet many of their most cherished ideas were embodied in his movement: the *Führerprinzip*, *Volksgemeinschaft*, Germanic socialism, the cult of power and the creed of force, heroic activism, the myth of a New Order, the promise of a Third Reich. Hitler, to be sure, was more uncouth than they would have liked, but the intellectuals "proved to be prisoners of their own dreams." [187] Thus it came about that many of the finest minds of Germany not only acquiesced in Hitler's ascension of power; they applauded it.

Heidegger was among the most enthusiastic. He used the occasion of his inaugural address as rector of the University of Freiburg in May 1933 to hail Hitler as the fulfillment of his fondest dream for Germany, the synthesis of idea and action. He disparaged rational inquiry, and he urged the academic community to dedicate itself to the mysterious, higher demands of race and heroic leadership. Having put academic freedom in quotation marks, he extolled something he vaguely but grandly called "the inexorability of that spiritual mandate which forces the destiny of the German *Volk* into the stamp of its history." He had no word of defense for his great teacher, Edmund Husserl, who was being defamed by the Nazis as a non-Aryan and a traitor. But he had no difficulty in bringing himself to a resounding endorsement of Adolf Hitler, whose power he said should extend beyond moral and human law: "Not theses and ideas are the laws of your being!" he told the academic world. "The Führer himself, and he alone, is Germany's reality and law today and in the future." In words that could have come directly from Hitler's propaganda mills, the philosopher proclaimed that the primary purpose of the university was to serve *Führer* and *Volk* by three kinds of service: "Labor service, military service, and knowledge service: they are equally necessary and of equal rank." The entire academic community, he concluded, must join with the rest of the *Volk* in a common struggle: "All powers of will and thought, all the forces of the heart and all the capacities of the body must be unfolded through struggle, elevated in struggle, and preserved as struggle." In that spirit he dedicated himself, his colleagues, and his students to join in one "battle community" (*Kampfgemeinschaft*).

The Nazis, of course, recognized at once the value of such an endorsement and had Heidegger's address printed up and distributed by the thousands. They also saw to it that his name and picture appeared in their official *Führer-Lexikon*. Heidegger raised no objections.[188]

The Prussian Academy also gave its support. One member of the academy called Hitler the long-awaited "charismatic leader"; another described him as "a Doric German" and "Frederician personality." Gerhart Hauptmann, Germany's leading playwright, displayed a swastika flag on his house; Gottfried Benn, Germany's finest living poet, urged his fellow intellectuals, in February 1933, to applaud this "victory of the national idea . . . this new version of the birth of man." He found in Hitler's totalitarian state "the complete identity of *Macht* and *Geist* . . . of freedom and necessity." [189]

The intellectuals had never given republican leaders similar praise or support.

CONSEQUENCES OF INFLATION AND DEPRESSION

Two economic crises helped precipitate the fall of the Republic and the rise of Hitler: the inflation of 1923 and the Great Depression of 1930–1933.

Although the value of German money had declined steadily since the end of the War, the French invasion of the Ruhr in January 1923 resulted in such a catastrophic plunge that by late summer the once stable mark quite literally was worth less than the paper it was printed upon. Statistics can never convey human despair, but they can give some indication of the economic distress suffered by the German people. In 1973, Americans came to think of inflation as a threefold increase in prices—ground beef that once cost 50¢ a pound rising to $1.50. In Germany in 1923 it rose to the equivalent of $10,000. A pound of potatoes that had cost 12 pfennig in 1918 cost 2 million marks by the summer of 1923. People quite literally could not afford food, clothes, medical care, or decent burial for their dead. A student who set out for the university with a check to cover room and board for the opening term might find, on arrival, that all his money would not buy one secondhand textbook.[190]

Those who relied upon fixed incomes, modest investments, and savings accounts experienced not only economic disaster but a deep crisis in values. For with the "death of money" there also died confidence in personal philosophies of life. Consider the experience, let us say, of Hans Schmidt, proud owner of a corner grocery store. His two sons and daughter have been scarred by early memories of childhood hunger in the terrible "turnip winter" of 1916–1917, and the blockade of 1918–1919; they have also been shaken by defeat, revolution, and the *Versailles-Diktat*. But through the turmoil of their lives they find stability and assurance in their father's authority. They trust his values and are reassured by his promises. He has told them that their future is secure. For as a result of his hard work, moderation, discipline, and thrift, he can pass on the business to Klaus. The 60,000 marks he has saved in the bank will mean that Fritz can attend the university and may perhaps become a *Herr Doktor*; Hilda is assured of owning her own beauty shop. Then, one day in the fall of 1923, Herr Schmidt receives a note from the local savings bank regretting that his life savings of 60,000 marks is no longer worth carrying on the books. A postage stamp is enclosed to cover the amount of the deposit. Money, the sign, symbol, and guarantee of security, has lost its value. All Herr Schmidt's preachments about moderation, sobriety, hard work, obedience, and thrift are so much *Quatsch*, and his children know it. They demand solutions—immediate solutions. Thus the slogan of German youth in the 1920s: "Radicalism is trumps." By the thousands, as we shall see, they joined Hitler's youth cohort.

Like other Germans, the Schmidt family demanded an explanation for the economic disaster that had engulfed them. The Republic was responsible; more specifically, "the speculators." But those were abstractions. A more tangible villain was needed and found: the Jews were to blame. Pearl Buck reports a conversation with a cultivated German friend who recalled her family's first experience with Hitler's persuasive propaganda. The inflation that had wiped out her father's business was caused by "speculators." But, it was asked,

> "Who speculates? The Jews. . . . Mother suddenly made such a clear distinction between the Jews, who knew how to do business, and the Germans, who were not so clever at it. Well, this was the first reflection in our family of this anti-Semitic National Socialist propaganda. It hammered into the heads of millions of people, a combination of words: 'Money—Exchange—Inflation—and the Jews.' . . . When inflation was over, the psychological preparation for Fascism was complete, the minds of the people were prepared for the Nazis." [191]

Not quite. Germans were to undergo an even greater shock, which increased their feelings of hopelessness and despair and produced a further radicalization of the once stable middle class—the Great Depression of 1930–1933. The Depression was of absolutely basic importance to Hitler's success. Without it, it is unlikely that any amount of demagoguery, however clever or compelling, would have brought him to power. But desperate times demanded desperate measures. To millions of Germans, Hitler's program of National Socialism and authoritarian leadership was far more appealing than either democracy or Marxism. Even those people who could not stomach anti-Semitism supported Hitler after convincing themselves that they need not take some of the "excesses" of his propaganda seriously. The important thing was that he would solve their economic distress.

The Depression in Germany had a particularly telling effect on young people. Partly because their generation had not been slaughtered in the war, there was a higher percentage of young adults in 1930 than at any time before or since in German history. "From a demographic viewpoint," a student of this period has observed, "the economic depression hit Germany at the worst possible time: employment was shrinking precisely at a time when the employable population reached its postwar peak." The German apprenticeship system contributed further to youthful frustration and fury. The number who could enter many trades was radically reduced. In metalworking, to take one example, there had been 132,000 openings for young apprentices in 1925; in 1932 there were a scant 1,900. University graduates were no better off. Indeed, the Depression produced "an underemployed intellectual proletariat that looked to National Socialism for relief and status." [192]

The effects of the Great Depression went far beyond economics. Indeed, its most important consequence was to accelerate the radicalization of the middle class, which must be considered one of the essential causes of Hitler's success. The Reichstag elections of September 1930 demonstrated unmistakably the connection between economic crisis and political radicalization. They showed, as Chancellor Philipp Scheidemann said in an unforgettable metaphor, that the Weimar Republic was "a candle burning at both ends." In the balloting, the moderate political parties, which relied on middle-class votes, lost more than half their support. By 1932 these parties altogether received only 11 percent of the total vote. The Communists gained on the left, but it was Hitler who registered one of the most dramatic advances in the history of electoral democracy. In 1928 his party had been a minor splinter group with 2.6 percent of the total vote; in 1932, it had won 37.4 percent and had become the largest party in the country.[193]

HITLER'S APPEAL TO THE LOWER MIDDLE CLASS

Nazism was not a class movement. It succeeded because it was "the first genuinely integrative movement in modern German history," the first political party to attract support from all levels of society.[194] Yet it depended particularly on the lower middle class both for votes and for leaders. Germans like Herr Schmidt and his children would comprise almost 60 percent of the total Party membership.

Why did so many average German citizens desert Weimar and turn to a political party which openly and clearly promised to kill democracy?* An important part of the answer lies in the psychological condition of the German middle class which has been well-described in one of Erich Fromm's most valuable books, whose thesis is contained in its title: *Escape from Freedom*. Fromm believes that historians have put too much stress on Western man's desire for freedom, in-

---

* Never had a political movement given so flat a promise. An editorial in Goebbels's newspaper *Der Angriff* (The Attack) of 30 May 1928 answered its own question "What do we want in the Reichstag?" with brutal frankness which left no doubt about Nazi intentions: "We are the enemies . . . of this democracy . . . so why do we want to get into the Reichstag? We are going there in order to destroy the arsenal of democracy with its own weapons. . . . We come not as friends and not as neutrals, we come as enemies! [*wir kommen als Feinde!*] As the wolf breaks into the sheepfold, so are we coming."

dividuality, and liberty. Confronted by the complexities of life in the modern world, people desire authority more than freedom. Indeed, when faced by staggering social and economic problems, they may long to escape from the burdens and responsibilities of freedom. Such was largely true of the German *Kleinbürgertum* in the postwar world. In Bismarck's Reich the rising middle class enjoyed security without the responsibility of making political decisions; its members proudly associated themselves with the power and glory of authoritarian institutions. With the collapse of the Empire they were suddenly given the freedom to run their own government, but freedom had brought only failure and humiliation: the democracy had been forced to sign a hated treaty; it had ruined itself through inflation; it was incapable of coping with the Depression.

The despair and bewilderment of the middle class was caught by two men of letters: in the title of Hans Fallada's 1932 best-seller, *Kleiner Mann—Was Nun?* (Little Man—What Now?), and in Gerhart Hauptmann's plaintive cry, "If only life would demand no more solutions from us!" There was one way the powerless could gain power: they could get it vicariously. Hitler's system fostered the heartening illusion that merely by accepting him as Führer, there was conferred "a kind of magical participation in the source of all power." [195]

The "little man" submitted because he wanted desperately to attain a posture of power denied to him as an individual. In Germany by the 1920s, Fromm believes, something akin to group sadomasochism developed: the "little man" wanted to be dominated, but he also wanted to dominate others, to hate and destroy. He could identify very closely with Adolf Hitler, whose own sadomasochistic impulses fit, in a remarkable way, the mood of the times.

Hitler also offered salvation based upon faith, not reason. The burden of individual opinion was thus lifted from the "little man," for he was joining a community of faith in which he could participate by shouting the mindless confession of faith, *"Ein Volk! Ein Reich! Ein Führer!"* which in the Third Reich replaced the slogan of the Second, *"Ein Volk! Ein Reich! Ein Gott!"*

By the thousands, the Schmidt families of Germany longed to escape from a burden of freedom that had become unbearable. They sought the security of authority—but authority of a particular kind. Traditional conservatism was dead; Communism offered little comfort, for it demanded that the lower middle class sink into the proletariat and that feelings of nationalism give way to international solidarity. Aggressive nationalism was appealing to postwar Germans because they found the idea of personal defeat so traumatic. They were happy to shift responsibility onto the nation. In effect, they assured themselves that their own failures and damaged self-esteem were not really their own fault but were part of a national disaster. Hence, their problems would be solved only when the nation was redeemed. Psychologically they needed nationalism, and since Hitler's system was nationalism incarnate, they responded to him with enthusiasm. It was also comforting to damaged egos to hear that the German people were not merely equal to other nations but were the master race.

Hitler's movement and its "dynamism of rancor" also promised something else: that deep-seated feelings of anxiety and fear could find an outlet in primitive hatred and aggression. As Fritz Stern has noted, "It is naive . . . to suppose that aggression must spring from lust of conquest. Fear too impels aggressive action."

The German middle class in 1930–1933 was gripped by what one writer has called *die grosse Angst*—an all-pervasive "great fear" of many things, including economic catastrophe, personal failure, social upheaval, moral decline, the Communist menace, the Jewish peril. Everywhere there was apprehension and alienation. Hitler understood. He personally felt their fears, for he too was a "little man" riven by alienation, self-doubt, and *Angst*. He played brilliantly upon the fears of others and convinced them that salvation lay through hatred and aggression.[196]

Albert Speer, looking back from his prison cell in Spandau and attempting to fathom the strange personality of the man who had captivated him for so long, finally reached the conclusion that at the core of Hitler lay nothing but "pathological hatred." As a person who was himself consumed by hatred, Hitler knew its power to move others. One reason for his political success in 1933 was the stunningly effective way he applied the axiom he had laid down a decade earlier in *Mein Kampf*, when he wrote that hatred is more powerful than love and noted scornfully that the leaders of the Republic had done nothing whatever to cultivate the most valuable of all political qualities: "wrathful hatred." He promised that under his leadership "hate would become a single fiery sea of flames." He kept that promise. His confidant Joseph Goebbels recorded in his early diaries what he considered to be one of his master's best epigrams: "For our struggle, God gave us His abundant blessing. His most beautiful gift was the *hate* of our enemies, whom we too *hate* with all our heart." Years later, a Swiss diplomat noted that "the main energy of Hitler is the energy of hatred" and showed how he used this energy to his political advantage. Thousands of Germans were drawn to him, the Swiss said, because they too needed to hate and this man supplied that need. "Never," he said, had he "met any human capable of generating so terrific a condensation of envy, vituperation, and malice." [197]

Hitler's general appeal to the lower middle class was well summarized by a thoughtful German observer:

Nazism contained an incomparable and unsurpassable combination of all those psychological elements which the masses needed . . . [Hitler] could not immediately give bread to the starving and wages to the unemployed but he absolved the weary, the desperate and the downtrodden from the heaviest burdens of their souls. He allowed them . . . to gather hope and to feel superior. He released them from the loads of reason, responsibility, and morality. He led them back into the regressive paradise of irresponsibility and implicit faith. He let them relax into a precivilized, presocial, infantile stage. He allowed them to hate and believe, to strike and obey, to march and feel as the masters of the world.

Hitler also offered concrete programs well calculated to catch the interests of the lower middle class. He was careful to stress in hundreds of electrifying speeches that he stood, point by point, for the exact opposite of everything that troubled the "little men" of Germany. Democracy was at fault, so he offered authoritarian government; class privilege and exploitation were resented, so he promised *Gemeinschaft*; in place of international cooperation and the League of Nations, associated with the *Versailles-Diktat*, he promised militant nationalism. Above all, he sensed the longing for a heroic leader, a longing as old as the Barbarossa legend, and as current as this memoir of 1934 written by a high school teacher:

> I reached the conclusion that no party, but a single man alone could save Germany. This opinion was shared by others, for when the cornerstone of a monument was laid in my home town, the following lines were inscribed on it: "Descendants who read these words, know ye that we eagerly await the coming of the Man whose strong hand may restore order." [198]

Hitler also knew the attraction that a particular kind of socialism could have in thousands of households where the inflation and the Depression had wiped out bourgeois aspirations. Hitler's socialism had great appeal, for it allowed the lower middle class to escape a desperate dilemma: economic disaster had prevented a rise to bourgeois status, but social traditions prevented them from sinking into the *Lumpenproletariat*. Hitler's socialism permitted the Hans Schmidts to become socialists in a national system without becoming proletarianized or internationalized. His system was one in which all racial Germans could be members of one *Volksgemeinschaft*, a racial community in which social distinctions were blurred and rendered unimportant.

With remarkable adroitness, Hitler adjusted socialist slogans to make them fit the needs of the lower middle class. He changed Marxist hatred for the bourgeois to hatred for the Republic and the Jews. He agreed that Germans were victims of exploitation—but by the Jews. Like the socialists he provided a vision of future utopia—not of a classless society but of a racially equal *Volksgemeinschaft*. The world would yet be conquered—not by the proletariat but by "Brown battalions marching." The revolution would be completed—not by the dictatorship of the proletariat but by the dictatorship of the Führer. Hitler also confiscated and modified socialist symbols: the red flag was preserved in his swastika; "comrade" became a Nazi salutation; his Party's name preserved the words "Socialist" and "Workers;" he organized mass demonstrations, approved marching songs, and encouraged the raised-arm salute; May Day was converted into a National Socialist holiday.[199]

One suspects that a key reason why Hitler was so successful with the lower middle class was that they recognized him as one of themselves. In the phrase of a German essayist, Hitler appealed because he was a "mirror of bourgeois boobery" (*Spiesserspiegel*). He was *Kleinbürger* incarnate, whose manners were banal and whose speeches were larded with hackneyed nationalist clichés, but whose very stylistic mediocrity had its appeal. He was "a man of the masses" who did not so much conquer the common man as identify with him.[200]

He looked the part. And his very nullity was a source of his strength. The anxious and ineffective "little man" of Germany who longed for power and greatness could identify with Hitler, for he was a kindred soul; he was one of them. They could "see greatness emerging from a creature who was smaller than you or I—that is what made Hitler an experience for millions." [201]

Dorothy Thompson, one of the very few foreign correspondents who was permitted a personal interview with Hitler, was surprised and disappointed by the "startling insignificance of this man who has set the world agog. . . . He is the very prototype of the 'Little Man,' " she wrote in the spring of 1932. And when she thought of him sitting in a seat of power, "involuntarily I smiled: Oh, Adolf! Adolf! You will be out of luck!" [202] Miss Thompson was mistaken. Like so many others, she underestimated this nondescript politician and failed to recognize the paradox that part of his power lay in his "startling insignificance."

But only part of his power. For while he was one of the masses, he was set apart from them by the touch of political genius. It is only a half-truth that he was a product of his time and place. True, he profited enormously from the economic, psychological and political chaos of 1930–1933—but he had prepared for his moment and knew how to use it. The tide of history had lifted him up, but he could succeed only because he was "a superbly prepared swimmer." [203]

Consider how he cast his own speeches and the meticulous care with which he organized the demogogic assaults of other Party orators. He set up special Party Speakers' Schools to train hundreds of orators who toured the entire country. Their style and forensic ability may not have been sophisticated, but throughout Germany they convinced thousands that they had answers to all pressing problems, that this Party cared for and understood the needs of the masses and would act to fulfill them. Hitler's own speeches reflected with studied spontaneity the longings of the people. None of his competitors showed a remotely comparable ability to combine ideology and propaganda or anything like his capacity to sense the psychic needs of his audiences. Hjalmar Schacht, Hitler's adroit finance minister, was right in saying that he played on the *Kleinbürgertum* like a skilled harpsichordist plucking the chords of middle-class sentiments. Two examples of hundreds of speeches must suffice to show how closely he identified with the masses. He too had been a common laborer, a soldier at the front; he too had known hunger and privation. He was proud to be one of his people:

> When I speak to you today and thus to millions of other German workers, I have more right to do this than anyone else. I have grown out of you yourselves; once I myself stood among you, I was among you in the war for four and a half years and now I speak to you to whom I belong, with whom I feel myself to be bound still today and for whom in the final analysis I carry on the struggle. . . .
>
> In my youth I was a worker like you, and then I worked my way up by industry, by study, and, I can say, by starving.

And again, his words flew like an arrow to their hearts:

> We are so happy to be able to live among this people and I am proud to be permitted to be your Leader! So proud that I cannot imagine anything in this world that I would rather be. I should a thousand times rather be the last *Volksgenosse* [fellow country-man] among you than to be a king anywhere else. . . . When I drove through the streets just now and saw those hundreds, thousands, and millions of *Volksgenossen* to the right and to the left of me, from all enterprises and workshops, from all factories and offices, my heart beat faster and I thought to myself; that is our Germany! That is our people, our glorious German people, our beloved German Reich.[204]

HITLER AND THE "GERMAN CHARACTER"

Hitler's appeal went far beyond the lower middle class to embrace millions of Germans in all walks of life. An explanation for this enormous popularity must consider both the personality of Hitler and the character of the German people. For what has been said of Martin Luther was at least as true of Adolf Hitler: "It is inconceivable that he should have evoked so great a popular response unless he had succeeded in expressing the underlying, unconscious sentiments of large numbers of people and providing them with an acceptable solution to their . . . problem." [205]

Social psychologists, psychoanalysts, and cultural anthropologists have said that by 1933 the German people *as a group* were suffering from psychological problems which made them particularly responsive to some sort of authoritarian leader. Erik Erikson has called them "charisma hungry"; Eric Fromm found them to be sadomasochistic; Else Frenkel-Brunswick characterized them as "authoritarian personalities"; Kecskemeti and Lietes have spoken of the Germans' "compulsive character." Of course, one should take any broad generalization about group character and national temperament both with a grain of salt and a dash of humor. Nevertheless, Hitler's personality was remarkably in tune with the group personality traits described by reputable social psychologists and psychoanalysts.

Dr. Frenkel-Brunswick, for example, in setting forth the behavior patterns of "authoritarian personalities," has accurately described the most characteristic traits of Adolf Hitler: great admiration for the strong and contempt for the weak; a tendency to demand total and unquestioning surrender to authority and to conform compulsively; glorification of an "ingroup" and rejection of "outgroups" as weak, impotent, immoral, hostile, or depraved; self-perception as a person with massive willpower and iron determination; conception of hardships "in the image of unmitigated brutality"; and an ego ideal of ruggedness, toughness, and hardness, with a rigid and exaggerated separation of masculinity and femininity. Such people run to extremes, with opposite personality tendencies constantly in conflict. Projection is very important to them; they feel weak, and resulting anxiety prompts them to project, that is, externalize what they consider to be evil. There is "a striving for compensatory feelings of superiority" by the condemnation of others, especially of outgroups; sympathy for the weak cannot develop, for there is ingrained fear of weakness which serves only as a target for aggression.[206]

During and after World War II, teams of trained psychologists interviewed a thousand German prisoners of war from all walks of life, from privates to colonels, from Ph.D.'s to illiterates. The investigators discovered similar personality traits and noted particularly among Nazi or "near-Nazi" soldiers certain common characteristics. All of them are familiar to the student of Hitler's personality. The German POW's showed fluctuations between feelings of omnipotence and impotence, between belief in the magical powers of their own will and fears that they were unable to struggle against "inscrutable or inexorable destiny." Every one of the people interviewed expressed a need for power and domination "precisely because the personal ego is experienced as weak, helpless, and the sport of inner or outer forces." The picture is one of deeply split personalities, with the emphasis on submissive/dominant conformity.[207]

Two other social psychologists who have studied the "German character" found it to be characterized by polarization: the people interviewed showed a tendency to think in terms of extremes—total victory or total defeat, rigid organization or complete anarchy. They did not wish to make decisions. Instead, they desired to escape from responsibility and often expressed the idea in a German proverb which suggests how painful decision-making can be: *Wer die Wahl hat/Hat die Qual* (Who makes a choice/Must suffer pain). Aggressive tendencies as compensations for feelings of anxiety and guilt were marked among those interviewed; they all expressed a fear of infection and poisoning; they tended to be obstinate and found it very difficult to depart from a set path once it was taken; they preferred the irrational and the abstract to the rational; they felt themselves to be unusually gifted and unique and had a belief in magic, myth, and destiny. They were particularly taken by the secret meanings of words. Finally, they thought in disjunctives, saying, for example, that the only alternative to total obedience was high treason.[208] It is not surprising that Adolf Hitler was able to appeal so successfully to such people. He was indeed, as he said, "one of them."

Apart from psychological affinity, Hitler was also successful because of his uncanny ability to attract political opposites and, in so doing, to offer history an intriguing paradox: his movement was both conservative and revolutionary; he promised both preservation and radical change. Thus he won favor both with conservatives who believed he would strengthen old traditions and with radicals who were convinced they were participating in a sweeping revolution. Further, he promised to defeat the enemies of both and, at the same time, to reconcile all antagonisms in one patriotic, united *Volksgemeinschaft*. As a political tactician, Adolf Hitler should not be underestimated.

FATHERS AND CHILDREN: THE NAZI YOUTH COHORT

Members of Hitler's own generation, born in the 1890s, gave him broad support whether they were shopkeepers or journalists, soldiers or peasants, priests or professors. But those who turned to him with particular fervor were the sons and daughters of this generation—those, born during and shortly after the Great War, who would become the radical youth of 1930–1933. These young people were of the utmost importance to Hitler, and he responded to their needs so effectively that one historian of the Weimar youth movement concluded, "National Socialism came to power as the party of youth." Statistics bear him out: of all Germans in the 18–30 age group who were members of political parties, over 42 percent had joined the Nazis by 1932, compared with less than 20 percent in the Social Democratic Party. In Hamburg, 66 percent of the Party members were younger than 30; in Halle the percentage was 86 percent. In the Reichstag, 60 percent of the National Socialists were under 40; among the Social Democrats only 10 percent were of that age group.

It was symptomatic of a rising trend that even before Hitler achieved sweeping success at the polls, the official German Students' Association (*Bund Deutscher Studenten*) in 1931 elected a fanatic Nazi as its president. Hitler's drawing power for youth was remarkable. One Sunday in 1932 more than 100,000 young people came to hear him speak in Berlin and marched past him for seven-and-a-half hours.[209]

The sheer numbers of youth were impressive. So was their aggressiveness. As one writer concluded, "It was evidently the good luck of the Nazi movement to become the chief beneficiary of an *enormous, destructive tidal wave* in the ebb and flow of the generations." [210] Why were these young people so peculiarly attracted to Hitler and his primitive program of calculated hatred and aggression? What forces made this the most violent generation in German history? Why precisely in the years 1930–1933 did so many students turn to Hitler? Peter Loewenberg, trained in both history and psychoanalysis, has suggested that answers may be found by combining our knowledge of the two disciplines: psychoanalysis, which supplies an understanding of personality function, and the "cohort theory" of generational change, developed by cultural anthropologists and social historians.

Surely *external* historical forces—an authoritarian tradition, an ethos that denigrated democracy, and the economic and social consequences of inflation and depression—are important to an understanding of the rise of Hitler. But so too is an understanding of individual personal experience and psychological development. In studying these young people who proclaimed Hitler their Führer and savior, Loewenberg has found a direct and important connection between anxieties and hatreds experienced during the Great Depression and infantile experiences associated with the Great War and its aftermath. The Great Depression served, in Freud's term, as an "external disturbance" which triggered reversion to a childhood trauma. In this instance, the trauma was World War I, a time when this generation, as infants, experienced fear, hunger, feelings of abandonment, and longing for the return of an idealized soldier-father. The renewed trauma of 1930–1933 evoked in this "Nazi Youth Cohort" the political response of welcoming Hitler because he fulfilled the psychological needs both of early childhood experience and the renewed crisis of adolescence.[211]

The term "cohort" is used rather than "generation" because a group attains identity and psychological cohesion not as a result of the date of their birth but because it has shared a significant psychological experience. As Robert Jay Lifton has shown in his studies of the survivors of Hiroshima, the entire group—regardless of age—suffered similar psychological reactions. Similarly, the concentration camp experience marked for life all those who survived. Although a major catastrophe has an effect on all ages, it will have the greatest influence on the very young because their personalities are the most malleable. World War I was such an event for those who later turned to Hitler. Broadly speaking, the war affected most deeply two age groups: the generation we have already considered, born in the period of 1890–1900, which participated in the prewar youth movement, the *Fronterlebnisse* of the war, and the Free Corps movement; and their children of the Nazi Youth Cohort. Much too young to have fought in the war, they were not too young to have been scarred by it. Most notably they remembered hunger. Dozens of memoirs of this generation recall prolonged and gnawing hunger as the first terrible memory of childhood. To take only one illustration, a German friend told Pearl Buck how vividly she remembered as a little girl that during 1916–1917 her family collected nettles to boil as a vegetable, and that once, when she was sick, she had the glorious—but guilty—experience of drinking, ever so slowly, a whole glass of milk all by herself.[212]

Hunger increased after the armistice, as the Allies continued the blockade until Germany accepted the Versailles Treaty. The birth-weights of babies went down alarmingly. Mothers were unable to nurse, and cow's milk—when available—was lacking in fats and vitamins. Schoolchildren of those years showed a marked increase in bed-wetting and "nervous disorders." A hardened British war correspondent reported from Cologne in 1919: "Although I have seen many horrible things in the world, I have seen nothing so pitiful as these rows of babies feverish from want of food, exhausted by privation to the point that their little limbs are like slender wands, their expression hopeless and their faces full of pain."[213] An American historian who was a student in Germany in 1921 recalls being asked over and over, "How could you, a civilized human being, withhold food from us after the fighting had stopped?" [214] Hunger, coupled with anxiety and fear, produced in these children—as it had in the infant Hitler—feelings of hostility, hatred, and aggression. Normally, society requires that children repress such feelings, but the war atmosphere actually encouraged destructive impulses.

Children tend to reflect the attitudes of the society in which they live. The sales of toy bombing planes and machine guns, for example, declined in America each Christmas between 1971 and 1973 while the United States was committing what parents increasingly came to believe were outrages against the people of Vietnam and Cambodia. On the other hand, in Northern Ireland sales of war games and guns increased during the same years. In Germany during World War I, children learned a kind of "primitive idealization": the world was either all good (German) or all bad (the Enemy). The Enemy was to be hated, feared, and killed. Thus, instead of repressing destructive impulses and turn-ing away from horror and hatred, children turned "toward them with primitive excitement." [215]

The Nazi Youth Cohort, during their wartime infancy, must have felt abandoned when their mothers, by the thousands, left their tradi-tional roles in nursery, kitchen, and church to work in armament fac-tories. One of the most remarkable social facts in German history is the statistic that in Prussia by 1917 there were 500 percent more women working in industry than in 1913, and 1,000 percent more serving as railway workers.

As children, members of the Cohort tended to have an ambivalent attitude toward their absent fathers. They were idolized as heroes who would certainly save the Fatherland and return in glory. But there must also have been resentment and hostility toward a father who had left his children alone for so long with their mother. Child psychologists have demonstrated that when fathers are absent for protracted periods, Oedipal desires increase, along with guilt feelings and hostility toward the absent father. Such feelings of guilt, mixed with separation anxiety, often result in rage and aggression, which may break out in later periods of life: witness the excesses of the Free Corps, which thousands of the older Cohort joined, and the violent aggressive tendencies many contemporaries observed among the young adults of the Great Depression.

It is true, of course, that in other belligerent countries mothers and fathers left home and children felt neglected. But two facts made a critical difference in the German experience and had a significant effect on the Nazi Youth Cohort in the days of their early childhood: first, they suffered persistent hunger not experienced in the countries of the Entente; second, the German father, if he returned home at all, came back in defeat and not as a hero. Further, in Germany the traditional authoritarian father-figure of the emperor had fled and abandoned his people. The Revolution provided no one to take his place.

The children of the Cohort had other experiences that seared their memories: defeat was followed by near starvation and revolution. The Versailles Treaty added to the syndrome, for it made all Germans—including the young—formally responsible for all the disasters of the war. The inflation of 1923 reinforced the conviction that fathers had failed to provide order and security. The frustrations and fears and hunger of the Great Depression reawakened infant memories of hunger in 1919 and 1916–1917—hunger that evoked aggressive and destructive impulses.

It is not nearly enough to make the general comment that German youth were attracted to Hitler because he was "an authoritarian figure who offered a radical program." Young Germans were drawn to Hitler for *very specific reasons.* He alone, among all the political leaders of the postwar world, responded to their particular, deeply felt psychological needs. He was the incarnation of the idealized father-Führer they had imagined during the disturbing years of their infancy; he was what they had always hoped their own fathers would be—"the unknown hero of the trenches" who returned in glory wearing the Iron Cross First Class. He was a soldier-leader who promised to establish a military state where children and adults would wear uniforms and march in purposeful, disciplined ranks. They could swear an oath of total fidelity to this deified and distant Führer and help him build a resurgent and powerful German nation. The very fact that Hitler looked so average and nondescript and that so little was known about his personal life helped to strengthen the image of the father substitute. For their own fathers were average Germans who had been absent so long as to become strangers to their children.

It is difficult to convey the depths of desire young Germans felt in the postwar years for a father-Führer they could believe in and follow. A lead article in a national student magazine for January 1924 sent forth "a call for the Führer" who would have "faith in himself, in us, and in his mission." Students at Göttingen University as early as July 1920 proclaimed, "We are *consumed* [*wir verzehren uns*] with *long-*

ing for a great Führer. . . ." The Protestant Association of University Students expressed the same hope: "*A cry from the heart* responds to an *urgent, pent-up demand* that lives within all of us . . . for the coming of the Führer of our people." [216]

Young women of the Cohort also found Adolf Hitler to be the father-image of their dreams. Two sisters born in 1913 and 1915 recalled that their earliest memory was of their mother wearing black and weeping over their missing father. They found it impossible to describe the excitement they felt on seeing Hitler in person in 1931. So emotionally stirred that they could not sleep, they stayed up all night talking about the wondrous Führer who was everything they had longed for. Together they prayed that nothing would harm him or remove him from them; together they asked forgiveness for ever doubting him as their Führer. They joined the Party and volunteered for service to help feed and care for Nazi Storm Troopers.[217]

In reflecting on the amazing success of Adolf Hitler, an American psychiatrist wondered why Germans followed this particular leader who was essentially so *childish*; what was it in them, he asked, that responded to this immature person who was in so many ways ridiculous? [218] It seems likely that the Youth Cohort felt drawn to Hitler precisely *because* he was childlike and exhibited traits so similar to their own. He too used the defense of regression; he too, they believed, had suffered hunger and deprivation; he too was filled with hatred and capable of furious temper tantrums. Like themselves, he was defensive and vulnerable, but he could also be brutal and dictatorial in his demands, a destroyer and creator who would repay the insult of Versailles and build a New Order. He, too, practiced "primitive idealization": the world was divided into the All Good and the All Evil—the good, creative Aryans, the evil, destructive Jews.

Above all, the Youth Cohort came to Hitler because his movement institutionalized hatred and sanctified aggression. It was exactly what the Cohort needed to cope with the rage and frustration that had been experienced during their infancy and reinforced in late adolescence, during the Depression. The sheer violence of Hitler's movement served to redirect feelings of hostility. For the father-Führer was not merely a replacement for the distant and idealized father. He also served as a psychological defense against the destructive resentment they still felt toward their fathers who had deserted them.[219] In short, the psychological problems of the Youth Cohort gave Hitler a unique opportunity to project upon the German masses the same unconscious conflicts that had shaped his own infancy. In this instance, as in many others, "his own pathology harmonized with that of Germany." [220]

Hitler's hatred of the Jews was another major attraction for the young people of Germany. For his racist ideology spoke directly to their own prejudices. Anti-Semitism was one of the striking features of the Weimar youth movement, as it was of the Free Corps and of university life. Almost all the dueling fraternities, for example, contained "Aryan clauses" in their charters, as did the largest Catholic association of university students.[221]

Martin Wangh, an American psychiatrist who has investigated the psychological origins of the genocide of the Jews, has found roots in the Nazi Youth Cohort's infantile experience during World War I. He believes that as young boys during the war, they discovered that their Oedipal longings increased during the father's long absence. Since strong incestuous desires for the mother could not be tolerated, they were projected and blamed on someone else. The psychological defense used was the same as the one employed by young Adolf Hitler: they, too, ascribed incest to the Jews, who sought the ruination of the German people. The Jews were the racial enemy who should be punished and removed as "incestuous criminals" and "defilers of the race." Thus, exactly as with Hitler, "self-contempt was displaced onto the Jews . . . thereby assuaging feelings of unworthiness and masochistic fantasies of rejection." According to Dr. Wangh, such fantasies of self-destruction led to a more ominous displacement when feelings of suicidal depression were transformed into a program of mass murder.[222]

It is probably true that anti-Semitism was less important in Hitler's accession to power than the economic crisis of 1930–1933. Nevertheless, the economic and social distress of those years served to reinforce already existent anti-Semitism, particularly among the Youth Cohort. For hatred of the Jews was a very effective way of bringing together primitive urges to hate, attack, and destroy. Hitler's anti-Semitism also appealed to the Cohort because it provided a way to lessen guilt feelings for having abandoned traditional Christian teachings. As Erikson has reminded us, young people seek some sort of faith and commitment. In this era of national humiliation, resentment, and the *Versailles-Diktat*, thousands of young Germans found Christianity irrelevant to their needs. They wanted hatred and revenge, not love and reconciliation. But they still felt uneasy about rejecting the religion of their childhood. To such people, as Maurice Samuel has suggested in *The Great Hatred*, anti-Semitism was a kind of displaced hatred of Christianity, a way of decreasing guilt feelings by attacking the traditional enemy of Christianity, the Jew. Thus the emphasis of the Oberammergau passion plays of the period: hate the Jews, for the Jews killed Jesus. Hitler's anti-Semitism provided "the official rehabilitation of hatred." [223]

There was a need to hate, and Hitler supplied it. But it is a mistake to see his appeal solely in negative terms. Rather, he was effective because he spoke *both* to the basest and to the most lofty impulses of man: to hatred, cruelty, aggression, and terror, but also to faith, hope, love, and sacrifice. One of the reasons why Hitler was such an effective leader was that he thoroughly understood a profound psychological truth: neither a man nor a political party lives by bread alone. Both need sustaining ideals. Political programs are never successful if they cast their appeals solely in terms of materialism, self-interest, and cupidity. Hitler's Youth Cohort wanted very much to believe that their leader could inspire them with ideals of service, sacrifice, and patriotism.

Hitler, an opportunist but also man of faith, found it easy to put on the armor of righteousness: he would save Germany from selfishness, materialism, factionalism, moral depravity, racial corruption. The effectiveness of his propaganda lay finally in this—he made it seem that his party's nihilism was idealism, its brutality strength, its vicious "ideology" altruism.[224] And his converts in the name of idealism were legion. Trevor-Roper is right in reminding us that not all adherents of Hitler were vicious anti-Semites, sadistic brutes, bullies, and neurotics. "Many young people," he has written, "bewildered by the confusion of their time, were inspired by the message of hope, the simple, crystal-clear, infectious insurance" that a nation defeated and bound could, by the exercise of faith and willpower, arise again to a position of pride and independence.[225]

The memoirs of hundreds of young people who gladly joined Hitler's movement speak eloquently of such hope and idealism. Young people were particularly attracted by the promise of a *Gemeinschaft* where common good would come before personal interest, where brotherly concern and support of an inspired leader would solve the problems of Germany and end the awful feelings of individual isolation and individual responsibility. Many who were incensed by national defeat and the dishonor of Versailles might normally have supported traditional nationalist parties. But such parties as the Conservatives and the German National People's Party had nothing to offer this Youth Cohort, who believed that the conservative groups merely talked about patriotism while seeking to restore caste privilege. The idealistic young people wanted a united cooperative community, not the old social order. They found what they sought in Hitler. A student wrote:

> How different from [traditional party politics] was the daring proposition that sprang from Hitler's warm, sympathetic heart! His idea was not to use the resources of the State to help industrialists and landowners, but to take advantage of them immediately to relieve the misery of millions of unemployed Germans!

A young laborer was attracted to Hitler because he believed that Hitler shared his desire for sacrifice and his faith in the Fatherland: "Faith was the one thing that always led us on, faith in Germany, faith in the purity of our nation and faith in our Leader." The memoir of a young soldier strikes the same note of faith and sacrifice: "It is superfluous to describe the sacrifices I made. . . . [They] were made in the spirit of *Gemeinsshaft*." [226]

Hitler, it should never be forgotten, was a master of mass psychology. As early as 1923 he showed that he knew the power of appeals to service and sacrifice, the longing for *Gemeinschaft*, the "hunger for wholeness," the call to national greatness. He confided the secret of his approach to an intimate: "When I appeal . . . for sacrifice, the first spark is struck. The humbler the people are, the greater the craving to identify themselves with a cause bigger than themselves . . . [to] become part of an irresistible movement embracing all classes." [227]

He worked out this formula in public speeches of the early 1930s when, over and over again, he sounded the call he knew his audience wanted most to hear:

> We are determined to create a new community out of the German peoples—a community formed of men of every status and profession and of every so-called class. . . . All classes must be welded together into a single German nation.

And again a few months later:

> You could look upon me as the man who belongs to no class, who belongs to no group, who is above all such considerations. . . . To me, everyone is entirely equal. . . . I am interested only in the German people. *I belong exclusively to the German people* and I struggle for the German people.

And again, after coming to power:

> Only when the entire German people becomes a single community of sacrifice [*Opfergemeinschaft*] can we hope and expect that Providence will stand by us in the future.[228]

By the millions, Germans heard him and believed.

HITLER AS MYTH FULFILLMENT

Political realists have said that Hitler's appeal was an appeal to illusions—the illusion of a nonexistent Jewish menace, the illusion of the infallible Führer. The realists are right. But they have failed to appreciate the power of illusion in human affairs especially when it acquires the force of myth. As Georges Sorel noticed many years ago, illusions are stronger than facts, and myths shape the lives of men and nations. "Guided by the myth," he wrote, a society "is ready for any act of heroic aggressiveness." The psychoanalyst Rollo May agrees; he stresses the power of myth to "give a person the ability to handle anxiety, to face death, to deal with guilt. . . . We don't understand the power of the thirst for myth." [229]

Effective political leaders who do understand either create myths or manipulate them for their own purposes. Charles de Gaulle, for example, in appealing to Frenchmen in 1940 created a myth. When he said, "I in London, you at home are united in resistance in a common cause," there was in fact at that time no such French resistance to the Nazis. But when Frenchmen came to believe that the factually false was symbolically true, the Resistance became a fact of historic force. Hitler too knew how desperately his people wanted to believe in heroic myths. He articulated them and made them his own. By the alchemy of his charisma and the force of his propaganda, the most cherished myths of German history became Nazified and irresistible to millions of Germans. He was the long-awaited Barbarossa, the Savior who would fulfill the yearnings of the centuries and create a new Reich of the German Nation.

And Hitler offered more than new forms for old legends. He provided a new system of values which justified a new morality. Psychologists would call it "an alternative superego system." It can also be seen as a secular religion, complete with Messiah, a holy book, a cross, the trappings of religious pageantry, a priesthood of black-robed and anointed elite, excommunication and death for heretics, and the millennial promise of the Thousand Year Reich.

Thus Hitler succeeded, in part, because he appeared to many Germans as a godlike Messiah. In the historic context of national humiliation and despair, his religion seemed a vast improvement over the old. Where Christianity called for love and reconciliation, Hitler sanctified hatred and revenge; where Christianity demanded that God be loved with mind as well as heart, Hitler dispensed with reason and required that the Führer be accepted by faith and faith alone; where Christ preached individual responsibility and freedom of will, Hitler provided an escape from freedom into authority. The essence of Hitler's appeal was set forth long ago by Dostoyevsky in the Inquisitor General's confrontation with the returning Christ: "We too have a right to preach a mystery, and to teach them that it's not the free judgment of their hearts, not love that matters, but a mystery which they must follow blindly. . . . So we have done. We have corrected Thy work and have founded it upon *miracle, mystery* and *authority*. And men rejoiced that they were again led like sheep." [230]

Hitler's "Seizure of Power"

> *Das war kein Sieg, denn die Gegner fehlten.*
> —Oswald Spengler (1933)

From reading this chapter, one might think that Hitler's attainment of power in 1933 was a foregone conclusion. Apparently all German history had been conspiring to aid him; the economic, social, and psychological crisis following 1930 was obviously pushing him along; the magic of his personality did the rest. And thus was Hitler hailed as savior and swept into power by a mesmerized and ecstatic people. But it did not happen that way. The strange career of Adolf Hitler provides many insights into the vagaries of history, and this is one of them: not even he was inevitable.

The combination of past history, present crisis, and charismatic personality helps explain why Hitler had become such a political force by the fall of 1932. But none of this explains *how* he actually became Führer of Germany. He was not voted into power by the German people, nor did he seize power, as Nazi legend later asserted, by a heroic *Machtergreifung*. Political power was handed to him in a sordid political deal.

He had tried three different ways to attain his goal. First, he had sought to seize power by coup d'état in 1923; he had failed in that memorable fiasco. Second, he had tried to win a mandate from the German people; but he had failed to win the simple majority he had promised President von Hindenburg. The best he could do in the summer of 1932 was to get 37.4 percent of the vote. And even after attaining the chancellorship, profiting from the Reichstag fire, and then utilizing all the wiles of Goebbels's propaganda machine, his own brilliant demagoguery, and the intimidating power of his Storm Troopers—even after all that, Hitler could get only 43.9 percent of the vote. A majority of the German people still withheld their confidence from him. True, they had given him more votes than anyone else. But not a majority.

After failing in these efforts, Hitler decided to get into power through intrigue and political deals. A. J. P. Taylor is correct: the answer to the question of *how* Hitler came to power lies less with Hitler and the Nazis than with other parties and politicians.[231] Every one of the political parties of the Republic made a contribution to the death of democracy and the victory of Hitler. There is considerable truth in Oswald Spengler's scathing comment about the much-trumpeted Nazi triumph: "That was no victory; there was no opposition." [232] The German Communist Party, for example, constituted by 1932 the strongest Communist movement in Europe. Yet it succumbed to Hitler without a struggle. By the summer of 1933 the KPD was dissolved, its leaders jailed, its funds confiscated. Among the reasons for this surprising failure was the strangely erratic policy emanating from Stalin's Kremlin. From 1924 to 1928, the orders were to cooperate with the moderate German Social Democrats; after 1928, orders went out to fight them as "Social Fascists." In this phase, Stalin actually cooperated with Hitler in order to undermine bourgeois democracy. The theory was that once fascism ("the last stage of monopoly capitalism") attained power, the time would be ripe for a final communist takeover. But after helping Hitler into power, the Communist Party took no action at all. "The Party which for fifteen years had talked of nothing but revolution failed when the crisis it had itself prescribed as the revolutionary moment came." [233]

The moderate Social Democrats, founders of the Republic and, until 1932, its largest party, were unable or unwilling to act effectively. Seized by apathy bordering on fatalism, they could not or would not act to stop

Hitler. "We were driven by the force of circumstance," one leader said pathetically in August 1933. "We were really only the passive object of developments." [234] The moderate socialists later protested that it was not their fault that Hitler came to power—their theoretical Marxist allies, the Communists, had cooperated with Hitler and attacked them instead of helping them. There is truth to the charge, but it overlooks the crucial fact that the Social Democrats themselves had done little to fulfill social promises and had done nothing when, in July 1932, Chancellor von Papen and his "Cabinet of the Barons" illegally seized the government of Prussia—two-thirds of Germany. At this time, as later, the moderates lacked the will to take effective action. Totally misjudging the nature of Hitler and his threat, they kept thinking that "the ultimate victory of the working class movement" was indeed inevitable, and that Hitler was merely a passing phenomenon. In accordance with that tradition, they put their faith in the "potential energy of a mass party" and kept reassuring themselves with that empty and amorphous slogan. A corollary of this belief was that Hitler, as the head of "reactionary forces," would of his own accord disintegrate along with his supporters, whereas the power of the working class was "indestructible." [235]

The conservative parties of the right, which had spent so much of their energies vilifying the Republic, showed that they had no political program of their own except to devise ways to make accommodations with Hitler. By 1932, German conservatism was intellectually sterile and politically bankrupt.

The chancellor of the republic during the critical years of 1930–1932 was Dr. Heinrich Brüning of the Catholic Center Party. He has often been portrayed as an able political leader who struggled manfully against the Nazi tide. His record does not support that reputation. He made the critical political mistake of dissolving the Reichstag in 1930 and attempting to rule by emergency presidential decree, thus making his government dependent upon the whim of old President Hindenburg, who was increasingly influenced by a clique of military reactionaries. Brüning's myopic and stubborn policy of deflation exacerbated the Depression, idling factories and throwing millions of workers out on the street. The "Hunger Chancellor" did little to help democracy. The position he had maneuvered himself into between left and right produced this devastating political joke: "Why is Brüning like a guitar? Answer: Because he's held by the left hand and played by the right."

But Brüning may not have been merely inept. Recent studies have raised very serious questions about his purported commitment to democracy and opposition to Hitler. It is now clear that his chief hope as chancellor was to win Hitler's secret support for a restoration of the monarchy; that Cardinal Pacelli, later Pope Pius XII, urged Brüning, a devout Catholic, to make special accommodations with Hitler; and that Brüning himself assisted Hitler in writing one of the Führer's key speeches. The Weimar chancellor's attitude toward Hitler at this time

—whatever his later protestations may have been—was well expressed by a statement that shows how totally he misjudged the Führer of the Nazis. On the very eve of the Third Reich, Brüning said: "If Hitler would become chancellor under normal conditions [sic], one could then regard the situation with a certain amount of calm." [236]

That was precisely the problem. The leaders of the democracy in its most desperate hour were not attempting to stop the menace of a Hitler dictatorship or to exclude him from office; rather, all their political energies were expended in efforts to bring him into a cabinet—with each political faction trying to win him over to its side. Each group hoped that Hitler would supply the votes and remain the "prisoner" of his "superiors." All were confident that they knew how to handle him. It was also assumed that once he was involved in the government, the responsibilities of political power would teach him humility and moderation.

It has been said that the story of Hitler's rise to power is the story of his underestimation. It must also be said that "there would have been no story of Hitler at all had not outstanding men and forces estimated him highly—for their own purposes." [237]

Never was vapid expectation more effectively exploited.

Thus was Germany delivered unto the Austrian. It was all perfectly legal. Late in the morning of 30 January 1933, Adolf Hitler took a great oath to preserve the Republic; he then placed his softly effeminate hands between the leathered palms of *Der alte Herr*, the senile Field Marshal–President, in an ancient German gesture of fealty and trust.

In the ecstatic city, a Catholic nun was heard to say, "What a blessing that friendly Herr Hitler has taken power! Praise be to God!" There was one act of protest. A little Jewish boy, driven half-mad by watching Storm Troopers whip his grandmother with lengths of garden hose, tried to beat off the Nazis with his fists. He was quickly silenced. Adolf Hitler, the failure of Linz and Vienna, could now fulfill his boyhood promise that he would become master of the Motherland, founder of a new Reich of the German nation.

That night he pushed back thoughts of death to stand, quivering with excitement, stiffly erect, on the balcony of the Chancellery. His eyes flashed and his face shone with the triumph of a man who had accomplished the impossible. He looked down on the Wilhelmstrasse, a sea of flames as wave after endless wave of torch-bearing followers, roaring the *Horst Wessel* song, surged below him.

The flames of that night were to become a symbol of his entire career. As an adolescent he had spoken reverently of the "Flame of Life"; as a street agitator he had demanded hatred so intense it would become "one single, fiery sea of flames"; a good speech, he said, was "a flaming javelin which sets the crowd afire." Later, fires that he lit would gut Warsaw, Rotterdam, Coventry, London, and Leningrad; on his orders, stinking black smoke would go up the chimneys of Auschwitz. Still later, in defeat, he would want all Germany to burn. At the end, amid the crash of Red Army artillery shells in Berlin, he would command that his own petrol-soaked body be set aflame. But on this overcast Monday night in 1933, the smell of burning oil rags was incense to the Psychopathic God.

CHAPTER 5

From Private Neurosis to Public Policy

> He who knows not how to rule his inner self
> would gladly rule his fellow men according to his
> own arrogant conceit.
> —Johann Wolfgang von Goethe
>
> In political leaders, private motives become pro-
> jected and rationalized as public policy.
> —Harold Lasswell

A COMPELLING REASON for studying the personalities of political leaders in any country was set forth decades ago by the American political scientist, Harold Lasswell. In a pioneering study of 1930, he showed that the private and public lives of political leaders are often intimately related and that successful statesmen make assets out of psychological difficulties by displacing and rationalizing them as national policy. Put in another way, emotionally disturbed leaders may find it both personally therapeutic and politically profitable to "externalize" their internal conflicts. When personal needs coincide with those of their countrymen, the externalization may be very profitable indeed.[1]

Hitler's private life and public career show this process at work. In this concluding chapter we shall suggest a diagnosis of his psychological condition and discuss the specific ways it contributed both to his success and failure—how his psychopathology actually helped him attain power and implement national policy and how, in the end, it led to his own destruction and to that of his Reich.

From Private Neurosis to Public Policy

WHAT KIND OF "NEUROSIS"?

> I suffer from tormenting self-deception.
> —Adolf Hitler

There are at least three reasons for hesitating to make a diagnosis of Hitler's mental illness. First, even a professional analyst would feel uneasy in reaching conclusions about the mental condition of a person with whom he has never spoken. Second, a diagnostic label may suggest to the unwary that all personality traits and behavior patterns fit the medical description and that, if they do not, they must be of marginal importance. Third, a diagnosis may also conjure up another mistaken notion, namely, that the person so labeled is like any other mental patient suffering under the same diagnosis. The fact, of course, is that each case is quite different.

Nevertheless, a medical diagnosis of Hitler's mental condition may be useful in our efforts to understand his particular kind of psychopathology and the ways it affected his political leadership. In making such a judgment, we would be greatly helped if we knew whether he had ever been examined by a competent specialist in mental disorders.

Several leads can be tracked down. In May, 1945 the *Basler Nachrichten* of Switzerland reported that "in the 1920's" Hitler was treated in a Heidelberg clinic for hysteria; in January, 1967 *The New York Times* carried a story from Frankfurt that a German psychiatrist, one Friedrich Panse, had testified that in 1918 Hitler had been treated for "blindness induced by hysteria." Dr. Panse has assured me in a personal letter, however, that he "never treated Hitler and only saw him once from a distance." He too, had heard that Hitler had been treated in Heidelberg by a Dr. Wilmanns.

The director of the Psychiatric and Neurological Clinic of Heidelberg, Dr. Ritter von Baeyer, reports, however, that Hitler had never been a patient there. It is true, Baeyer writes, that his predecessor and teacher, Dr. Karl Wilmanns, had called Hitler an "hysteric" during a lecture, but he had never actually examined him. As soon as Hitler came to power Dr. Wilmanns was examined by the Gestapo and relieved of his duties.

Other doctors at the Heidelberg clinic had heard that "in the twenties" Hitler was treated for mental disorders in a Linz hospital. But a letter from the director of mental health of the Upper Austrian Health Institute states that Hitler had never been a patient at the Institute or at any other mental facility in Linz.[2]

We can assume that Hitler was given medical examinations in connection with temporary blindness associated with gassing in 1918; again in 1923 when he was imprisoned in Landsberg am Lech after the Beer Hall Putsch; and during World War II on the occasion of the Bomb

Plot of June 1944. But there is, to my knowledge, no extant psychiatric report for any of these examinations. It is possible that he was seen briefly at the Pasewalk military hospital in 1918 by a psychiatrist named Edmund Forster. But the records of this examination, if it ever took place, were apparently destroyed, perhaps at Hitler's orders. Forster apparently committed suicide in 1933.*

There does exist a brief "Report of the Mental Condition of Prisoner Adolf Hitler" dated 8 January 1924 and signed by Dr. Brinsteiner, the prison doctor at Landsberg.[3] But this report was not the result of psychiatric examination. The doctor, who was obviously impressed with his famous prisoner, wrote very general comments stressing that he was a man of high intelligence, extraordinary range of knowledge and great oratorical ability. At the time of his arrest, Hitler was depressed, the doctor said, and suffering from "a very painful neurosis" (*sehr schmerzhaften Neurose*). No details are given. The report emphasized the ephemeral nature of the condition and that the prisoner was soon in excellent spirits. A few months later, on 2 April 1924, Brinsteiner filled out a standard medical form for the prisoner, "Hitler, Adolf":

Physical condition and general health:	healthy; condition moderately strong
Evidence of mental illness and psychopathic feelings of inferiority (*Minderwertigkeit*)	[no entry]
work capability	adequate
special remarks	[no entry]

In 1945, Hitler's doctors told American officials that to their knowledge the Führer had never received psychiatric care.[4] There seems no reason to change that opinion. Given the lack of evidence to the contrary, and given Hitler's dismissal of psychology as "Jewish medicine" and his strident insistence that there was absolutely nothing amiss with

* John Toland and Rudolph Binion both contend that Doctor Forster not only examined Hitler in 1918, he actually gave him psychiatric *treatment*. Toland, for example, calls Forster "the first psychiatrist to treat Hitler." There are no records to substantiate that claim. And one may well ask if it is credible that in the hectic days of November, 1918, a distinguished and over-worked director of a German university clinic would have taken the time to give special psychiatric treatment to an unknown common soldier who, like scores of his comrades, was suffering from "shell shock." To support their thesis, Binion and Toland rely on an inconsequential and factually innaccurate report on Hitler made for U.S. Naval Intelligence in 1943 by a Viennese "nerve specialist" named Karl Kronor. Kronor, it is claimed, was present during Hitler's examination at Pasewalk in 1918—Binion even says flatly that Kronor was Forster's "psychiatric assistant." But Kronor himself makes no such claim. If he had actually been in attendance, he certainly would have said so in his report which insists that Hitler's blindness in 1918 was due to hysteria. Instead, Kronor does not even claim that he had ever seen Hitler—much less served as a "psychiatric assistant" in treating him. (Dr. Karl Kronor, "Adolf Hitler's Blindness," OSS Document #31963, National Archives; Toland, *Adolf Hitler*, xviii–xix, picture facing 125, 925; Binion, *Childhood Quarterly* (Fall, 1973), 203–206, and *Hitler Among the Germans* (New York, 1976), 6–14, and *passim*)

his mind, it is highly unlikely that he was ever treated for mental disorder.*

Consequently, any diagnosis must come after the fact and without benefit of consultation with the patient. Two such attempts were made during and shortly after World War II. In 1943 the American psychoanalyst Walter C. Langer prepared a psychological report on Hitler for the Office of Strategic Services. Based on materials then available to him, Langer concluded generally that Hitler was a hysteric and a psychopath.[5] And the prison psychiatrist at Nuremberg, Dr. Douglas Kelley, after extensive interviews with 22 Nazis who had been in Hitler's immediate circle, concluded that the Führer could be classified as a "psychoneurotic of the obsessive and hysterical type . . . he also showed paranoid or persecution patterns. . . . In simple terms, Hitler was an abnormal and mentally ill individual. . . ." [6]

Before attempting a more specific diagnosis, we must first respond to the argument that there was never anything wrong psychologically with Hitler and that any peculiarities in his behavior can be traced to physical causes.

Neurological Explanations

Eyewitness accounts of Hitler's physical appearance, particularly during the last months of his life, have led some doctors to the conclusion that he suffered from a neurological disease which impaired his brain and central nervous system. Several people who observed him closely noticed how "his left hand and the entire left side of his body shook." A visiting general reported that "his gait became shuffling . . . his movements slow as in a slow-motion film." A Party leader was shocked to discover that his Führer was now "an old, stooped, disintegrated man . . . a trembling, broken man." Another recalled that "he was bathed in sweat, the saliva literally poured from his mouth. . . . I experienced the explosion of a hate-filled soul." Another remembered seeing "a frightful picture . . . he stared dully . . . his hands were pale and the fingertips bloodless. . . . He spoke clearly [but] he no longer concentrated well." [7]

---

* During the war a remarkable book appeared which purported to be the memoirs of an émigré psychiatrist who claimed to have had Hitler under analysis for a protracted period of time from August 1919 to July 1934. Relying on this account, reputable psychiatrists and psychologists have reached a general diagnosis of schizoid hysteria. The diagnosis suffers from the fact that "Dr. Krueger's" memoirs are a fraud (see Appendix, "A Note on Spurious Sources"). Hitler may actually have had one brief encounter with a genuine psychiatrist. One of his secretaries, usually a reliable witness, recalled that in 1943 "a well-known psychiatrist . . . whose name I have forgotten" was called to Hitler's headquarters. He concluded that Hitler needed a long period of complete rest in a special sanatorium. Instead, shortly after the consultation, the doctor was committed to Himmler's care. "Not a trace of him was ever found." See Albert Zoller, ed., *Hitler Privat: Erlebnisbericht seiner Geheimsekretärin* (Düsseldorf, 1949), p. 69.

Relying on descriptions such as these, some German specialists have concluded that Hitler's mental and physical condition was due entirely to Parkinson's disease (*paralysis agitans*), an illness of uncertain origins that attacks the nervous system and typically produces involuntary tremors, slowness of movement, insomnia, speech impairment, sweating, hypersalivation, and excitability. Delusional paranoid trends may also develop.[8] In the spring of 1945 a noted "nerve specialist," one Dr. Max de Crensis of Berlin, having heard reports of Hitler's behavior and having examined photographs of him, diagnosed brain damage associated with *paralysis agitans*.[9] After the war, the director of a psychiatric clinic in Hamburg, Professor Hans Berger-Prinz, agreed and stated confidently that Hitler was never ill "in a psychiatric sense." His trouble was simply that he suffered from Parkinson's disease.[10] Another German specialist concluded "not only with probability but with certainty" that Hitler suffered from Parkinsonism. This disease, the doctor insisted, resulted in remarkable changes in Hitler's personality and explains the atrocities and the political and military failures after 1942.[11]

Still another German doctor agrees that Hitler had the illness but believes that it was "late Parkinsonism," caused originally by epidemic encephalitis contracted in childhood. He suggests that young Hitler caught an infection from his brother Edmund, who died of measles in 1900 when Adolf was 11 years old. He thinks the disease lay dormant for many years. There was a remission from 1914 to 1918 and intermittant manifestations from 1919 to 1933; it broke out later as fully developed Parkinsonism.[12] Recently, an American authority on epidemic encephalitis has endorsed these findings, but has placed the onset of the disease later, probably in the epidemic of 1916. Like his German colleagues, the American doctor believes Hitler had a remission until the disease suddenly manifested itself as *paralysis agitans*, which caused "moral insanity" and "altered his personality in a way which led to the tragedies and horrors" of the Third Reich.[13]

It is true that Hitler showed some symptoms that might indicate Parkinson's disease, but he failed to show others. Most notably, the trembling and shaking observed by witnesses was not progressive; it was intermittent. In 1923 his left arm and left leg had trembled, but the condition went away. Again after Stalingrad in 1943 the same symptom was observed, and then it disappeared. It came on strong in June 1944, but was not apparent later that year when he planned the Ardennes offensive. In Parkinsonism the tremor is not intermittent; it is "relentlessly progressive." No motor disturbances were noted in the movements of Hitler's wrists, hands, fingers, and thumbs—and no evidence of the "pill-rolling" movement so characteristic of the illness.[14]

Others have offered a different explanation for Hitler's physical and mental condition: it was caused by the malpractice of his quack doctor, Theodor Morell. In a book entitled *Hitler: Die Zerstörung einer Persönlichkeit* (Hitler: The Destruction of a Personality), a physician insists that, apart from certain eccentricities indulged in by all great and gifted men, Adolf Hitler was perfectly normal until he fell into the clutches of the diabolical Morell, who slowly destroyed him through bizarre and irresponsible medication. And indeed, any responsible physician must be shocked by the drugs Morell prescribed. Over a stretch of years from 1935 to 1945 they included massive doses of vitamins and sex hormones; some 3,000 injections of simple syrup; huge daily dosages of stimulants and sedatives; thousands of "Dr. Köster's Anti-Gas Tablets" (prescribed for the Führer's chronic flatulence), containing a mixture of belladonna and strychnine; and a potency pill which Morell concocted out of "pulverized bull testicles," apparently designed to counteract the prescription of female hormones. Thus, the argument goes, Germany might well have won the war and held back the Communist menace to Europe had not Hitler been incapacitated by Morell.[15]

The author of a popular German biography of Hitler is also convinced that his subject underwent a sudden personality change during his mid-50s. He had been quite normal and sensible until on or about 1942, when "within a very short time, he [became] quite literally a different person." Dr. Morell's pernicious medications contributed to this miraculous metamorphosis, but the chief etiological factor, we are told, was "a bad head cold" (*eine schwere Kopfgrippe*). As a result of this monumental cold, Hitler and history were transformed: all at once the Führer became "suspicious and distrustful"; suddenly he "began to repeat himself"; he started to concoct "fantastic, unreal projects"; he now reacted "obstinately to situations that displeased him." This was also the time he gave orders for the massacre of the Jews, and "now, too, occurred the catastrophe of Stalingrad."[16]

It is quite possible that Morell's medications contributed to his patient's physical and emotional deterioration; it is unlikely that his troubles can all be traced back to a head cold—no matter how severe.

A diagnosis which must be taken seriously is suggested by Hitler's medical records and the affidavits of his physicians collected after the war by U.S. Military Intelligence and now in the National Archives. These reports, which include four electrocardiagrams dated 9 January 1940, 14 July 1941, 11 May 1943, and 24 September 1944, show clearly that Hitler suffered from "rapidly progressive coronary arteriosclerosis."[17] This medical evidence suggests another explanation for the descriptions of Hitler provided by eyewitnesses, for generalized arteriosclerosis can produce tremors, insomnia, slowness of motion, and confusion of thought. It can also produce personality changes. Hitherto psychologically stable persons may begin to exhibit delusions of grandeur, paranoid tendencies, and moral aberrations.[18]

Heinrich Himmler and others in the immediate entourage favored a different explanation. They suspected that their Führer's deteriorating condition was caused by the ravages of syphilis, which he had contracted either as a youth in Vienna or during World War I. According to Felix Kersten, Himmler's Swedish masseur and father-confessor, a distraught Himmler summoned him to his office one day in 1942. After demanding absolute secrecy, he asked Kersten to interpret a "blue manuscript of 26 pages" which Himmler had taken from a secret Gestapo file. Purportedly, it contained Adolf Hitler's medical record dating from his hospitalization at Pasewalk during World War I. The records convinced Kersten "beyond any shadow of doubt" that Hitler was suffering from progressive paralysis associated with neurosyphilis.[19] Support for the theory that Hitler had once contracted syphilis may be found in the rather curious fact that he chose as his personal physician a specialist in venereal disease, "Professor" Theodor Morell. Hitler's fascination with syphilis, manifested in page after page of his memoirs, is also pertinent. Then, too, rumors were rife in German medical circles that Hitler had been treated during 1932 in a Jena clinic by a Dr. Bodo Spiethoff for mental disorders associated with syphilis. Certainly the symptoms of advanced neurosyphilis correspond to some of the descriptions we have of Hitler in the last months of his life. Syphilis can produce tremors, insomnia, difficulties in walking, and personality changes. Patients may become irritable, their conscience dulled, memory weakened. They may be alternately depressed and exuberant with grandiose fantasies; paranoid tendencies are not uncommon.[20]

It is conceivable that Hitler, at one time or another, may have contracted syphilis. But it is unlikely. The mysterious blue pages which Kersten insists prove the case have never appeared, and Kersten was neither a medical doctor nor an unimpeachable witness. It is also possible that Hitler was treated for syphilis in a Jena clinic in 1932. But in correspondence, Jena medical authorities state emphatically that they can find no evidence that Hitler was ever treated there. Further, the fact that Hitler's medical records show a negative Wassermann test for 15 January 1940 does not argue in support of syphilis.[21]

Recent studies of the human brain have suggested yet another approach to Hitler's physical and emotional problems. Neurologists have now reached conclusions that raise disturbing questions about the personality of Hitler—and of everyone else. Until the last few years, we have taken it for granted that each individual has one brain, one consciousness, one personality. But the ancient and comforting assumption may be an illusion. We may all be two people. For split-brain research with patients who have had the connections severed between their cerebral hemispheres has demonstrated unequivocally that the two spheres of the human brain (unlike the brains of other animals) operate separately. Further, it has been shown that "each of the two halves is *independently conscious.* That is, there exist *two separate, conscious minds* in every individual." People can live quite effectively with either one or the other or both of these minds operating.

The two independent cerebral hemispheres exhibit two quite different modes of mental activity. The left half specializes in the specific. It is adept at manipulating separate, isolated elements and has little or no capacity to comprehend or recognize the whole. Patients with a badly impaired left hemisphere, for example, may be quite rational and intelligent but unable to recognize themselves in a mirror. Most notably, the forte of the left hemisphere is the memory of details and language. By contrast, the right half of the brain is ineffective in dealing with disparate data. Its specialty is synthesis and interpretation. It sees the whole, the pattern, the *Gestalt*. It thinks in images, emphasizes intuition; it is strong on visual and musical formations. While the specialization of each side is clearly established, neurologists "do not yet know exactly how the two hemispheres interact and get along with each other." [22]

In an article entitled "Hitler: A Neurohistorical Formulation," a team of university psychologists has attempted to use such neurological discoveries about the brain as the key to an explanation of Hitler's behavior. They argue that his right cerebral hemisphere was abnormally active because the left half was defective and underdeveloped. They point to evidence of a defective left side: a missing left testicle; weakness and trembling in the left arm and leg. They suggest that his family history of early deaths, malformation, and retardation supports the possibility of hereditary neurological damage. They believe that Hitler's mental activity supports their theory of right hemisphere domination: he was impatient with facts and logical argumentation; he trusted intuition and reveled in sweeping musical and architectural constructions. Further, his hyperactive right hemisphere had a profound effect on history, according to this theory, because two of Hitler's central policies derived from it: conquest of *Lebensraum* and distrust of the Jews. Both "can be seen as resulting from a neurological abnormality." For the dominant right side of his brain demanded that he command huge spaces and see Jews as diabolically scheming and logical people, characteristics rejected by his right cerebral hemisphere. He therefore sought to conquer Russia and destroy the Jews.[23]

The hypothesis that Hitler might have suffered brain damage to his left cerebral hemisphere is suggestive. But the evidence is indirect and inconclusive—and the patient and his brain quite beyond the reach of neurological confirmation. Moreover, some of the data point away from the theory of a damaged left hemisphere. We are reminded particularly of Hitler's effective command of language, his infatuation with detail, his astonishing memory file of factual data. Furthermore, weakness and trembling in Hitler's *left* arm and leg would indicate disabilities in his *right* cerebral hemisphere, not weakness of the left, which the theory requires.

The difficulty in making any specific neurological diagnosis is increased by the fact that many of the suggested diseases show similar symptoms. Involuntary tremors, insomnia, temper tantrums, lack of concentration, personality changes, hallucinations, and paranoid tendencies ascribed to Parkinsonism can also be found in both neurosyphilis and generalized arteriosclerosis. Many of these symptoms could also have been caused by nerve damage produced by Morell's irresponsible medications.

Most important, Hitler's psychological development from infancy rejects the main argument made by the proponents of a neurological explanation of his behavior—namely, that nerve and brain damage was responsible for sudden and dramatic changes in Hitler's personality during the last years of his life. I see no such sudden transformation. Indeed, the most striking thing about Hitler's behavior patterns is not change but continuity and the intensification of tendencies whose roots can be traced back to infancy.

Neurological difficulties of one form or another may well have exacerbated Hitler's mental condition, but they did not cause it.

Hitler As "Borderline Personality"

Since the death of Hitler in 1945, two developments have made it possible to propose a diagnosis of his mental illness. First, recovery of the Nazi archives, the work of research institutes, and the publication of dozens of monographs and special studies have provided an enormous amount of information about him which was unavailable to earlier writers. Second, important advances have been made in clinical psychology.

Let us suggest that the condition now called the "borderline personality" best describes Hitler's behavior patterns. But let us not try to fit all his behavior neatly into that description. Our primary purpose is to reach a better understanding of Hitler, not to reduce his career to a diagnosis.

Generally speaking, borderline personalities are those who, while mentally ill, can still function in some areas with great effectiveness. Their pathology differs from neurosis and is less severe than psychosis; they occupy an area on the borderline between the two. The professional literature about such patients is so technical and extensive,[24] and their psychological problems so complex, that a full discussion of this diagnosis as it applies to Hitler must await the study now being prepared by a noted psychiatrist who is a close student both of borderline personality and of Hitler's life.* Nevertheless, for present purposes, as an aid to understanding Hitler's personality as it influenced political decision-making, we can set forth the chief characteristics of the borderline personality. In so doing, we will note that the specific symptoms described by Otto Kernberg, Robert Knight, Norbert Bromberg, and Eric Pfeiffer fit to a remarkable degree with those we have found in Hitler.[25]

---

* Norbert Bromberg, M.D., professor of clinical psychiatry at the Albert Einstein College of Medicine, has conducted seminars devoted to borderline personalities for third-year residents in psychiatry. He is now working on a volume entitled *Adolf Hitler: A Psychoanalytic Study*. I am grateful to Dr. Bromberg for the critical reading he has given this chapter.

From Private Neurosis to Public Policy

Borderline patients characteristically show paranoid tendencies. They distrust and are highly suspicious of other people; they consider themselves "especially privileged persons"; they fantasize about their "magical omnipotence"; they believe that they have a right to exploit others for their own gratification.[26] All borderlines have unreconciled Oedipal problems—which, in Hitler's case, were intensified by monorchism and the "primal scene trauma." * An impulse to self-destruction—a problem we must deal with later—and some forms of mutilation have also been reported.

Patients tend to be infantile. They show "childlike, oral-aggressive demandingness." Selfish and narcissistic, they often display "a contradiction between an inflated concept of themselves and an inordinate need for tribute from others." Typically, while they express fantasies of omnipotence, their behavior may also reveal deep-seated uncertainty, self-doubt, and insecurity. Borderline patients also tend to have phobias about dirt, feces, and contamination. Significantly, they are prone to gross forms of sexual perversion involving filth: "Primitive replacement of genital aims by eliminatory ones (urination, defecation) are . . . indicative of an underlying borderline personality."[27] We are reminded of Hitler's reported perversion involving urine and feces.

Typical of borderline patients is a confused sense of self-identity. Since they are not able fully to integrate their ego, they have what Erikson calls "identity diffusion." One of their defenses against anxiety generated by such uncertainty is to act as if they were someone else, to "reenact partial identification." (The political consequences of Hitler's propensity for acting out various roles will be discussed below.)

The most basic characteristic of borderline personalities is a "splitting of the ego." Patients exhibit dramatically opposing personality traits: they are cruel and kind, sentimental and hard, creative and destructive; they swing violently between excessive protestations of love and wild outbursts of hate. It often appears, Dr. Kernberg has noted, as if there were in each patient "two distinct selves . . . equally strong, completely separated from each other." His description corresponds closely with Albert Speer's picture of Hitler as a person who was "cruel, unjust, cold, capricious, self-pitying and vulgar," but who was also "the exact opposite of almost all those things . . . a generous superior, amiable, self-controlled, capable of enthusiasm for beauty and greatness."[28]

When a therapist comments on contradictions in a borderline patient's behavior, his first reaction is to deny any contradiction or inconsistency. If the doctor persists, the patient becomes extremely anxious. Apparently, borderline personalities do not want to reconcile their two "equally strong" selves. Kernberg concluded in italics: "*Splitting, then, appears to be not only a defect of the ego, but also an*

---

* The symptoms associated with these experiences are consistent with those of the borderline and would serve to intensify them (see Chapter 3, pp. 150–168).

active and very powerful defense operation." [29] The main reason for this need to preserve a kind of dual identity is that the ego of a borderline is too weak to cope with the problem of reconciling violent extremes of love and hate; instead, it seeks to protect itself from the anxiety of choosing between the two by accepting both images. But the defense of splitting does not solve the problem, for it serves to weaken the ego further by reinforcing identity diffusion.

The feeling of being split apart, of suffering "tormenting self-deception," seems to have plagued Hitler throughout his life. A confused and contradictory sense of his own identity, coupled with doubts about his masculinity, produced gnawing questions about self-control and mastery. Thus it was very important to him to insist, over and over again, that he had no such problem, that he was always completely under control. Hence the endless assertions about his "iron will," his constant insistence that he was very cool under pressure. He also felt compelled to master and control others. Indeed, his whole political system was basically a system for dominating other people.

Borderline personalities characteristically reinforce splitting through introjection and projection: the good is introjected by the patient; the bad is projected onto others. Hitler introjected and claimed as his own all the attributes he considered good: Aryan toughness, iron will, masculinity, creativity. He projected all the bad onto others, especially the Jews: degeneracy, femininity, softness. Projection produced in Hitler—as it invariably does in borderline patients—a terrifying view of the world as irreconcilably split between good and bad, with the forces of evil constantly conspiring against the good. He felt compelled to fight and destroy the encircling and ubiquitous enemy before it destroyed him. While the split world created in his own image was dangerous and constantly threatening him, it served as an important defense, and hence as a kind of therapy. For it enabled him to externalize a conflict which, if left bottled up within, could have led to mental disintegration and collapse.

The diagnosis of Hitler as a borderline personality helps to explain why, though he may have experienced psychotic episodes, he never crossed over the border into full-blown psychosis. He was able to project and externalize his own "neuroses," rationalize them, and proclaim them officially as a "world view" and governmental policy.

The theory, noted above, that Hitler may have suffered neurological damage to one of his cerebral hemispheres does not invalidate the conclusion that he was a borderline personality with a deeply split ego. Indeed, it may complement and support that diagnosis. At some future time, neurology may be able to show the physiological basis for split personalities. But it cannot explain the specific behavior of such people. The problem is succinctly put by a physician, trained in both psychiatry and neurology, who specializes in split-brain research: "We have not gone nearly far enough to make any generalization about the connection between split brains and split psyches." Certainly a person's entire personality and life history cannot be "explained" by neurology.[30]

The theory that Adolf Hitler had a hyperactive right cerebral hemisphere does not explain why he hated the Jews with such incandescent fury; why he wanted to kill them all; why he needed aggressive war; why he was so fond of wolves, ravens, and lobsters or so infatuated with decapitation; why he was frightened by horses and terrified by the thought of sexual intercourse. Split-brain research cannot explain why the splitting of his ego took the specific forms and patterns which it did. Neurological findings, in short, may deepen and complement psychohistorical understanding; they cannot replace it.

PSYCHOLOGICAL ROOTS OF HITLER'S IDEOLOGY

> My beliefs are my Movement
> My faith is my Weapon
> —Hitler, notes for a speech, (c. 1928)

Hitler's fantastic view of the world, it has often been pointed out, bore very little relationship to external reality. But it did correspond very closely to his own psychic needs. In this respect his fantasies were not unlike those of thousands of other mentally disturbed people. What was different about Hitler was that he was not given psychological treatment; he was granted the political power which enabled him to transform his private fantasies into objective reality.

Hitler's distinctive political ideas cast him as the heroic leader called by destiny to save the Motherland from the Jewish menace. His political theory institutionalized distrust and hatred; it preached aggressive warfare as the rule of life; it exalted brutality and demanded total obedience to a racist dictator.

There were many reasons why Hitler adopted such an ideology. But a primary reason was that it helped him meet personal psychological needs deeply rooted in infantile and childhood experience: bitter memories of conflict with parents; a primal scene trauma; resentment over childhood beatings and desertion; inadequacy felt as a monorchid; the suspicion that his father might have been "tainted" with Jewish blood and had thus corrupted his children; and the searing memory of his beloved mother's last illness and death while under the care of a Jewish doctor.

Mother and Motherland

Basic to Hitler's ideology was the idea that Germany was a living organism. Of course, the concept of social *Organismus* was not new —it was at least as old as the Romantics. But Hitler's unusual metaphors and turns of phrase indicate something very personal: that he transferred his love for his own mother to Germany and saw himself as the savior of a Motherland menaced by the "Jewish peril." Thus he projected his infantile desire—greatly intensified by the primal scene experience—to rescue his mother from being debased by a lecherous father, and to possess her himself. Germania to him was living flesh which, like his mother's, had been lacerated and torn:

> Could anyone believe Germany alone was not subject to exactly the same laws as all other human organisms?
>
> An attempt to restore the border of 1914 would lead to a further bleeding of our national body.
>
> The Polish Corridor . . . is like a strip of flesh cut from our body.
>
> France was tearing piece after piece out of the flesh of our national body.[31]

He saw her ill and dying. Both in *Mein Kampf* and in later speeches he repeated the image of himself as a surgeon operating on his Motherland, who, like Klara Hitler, was dying of cancer. For a time, like his mother, she seemed to recover, but then she "obviously languished more and more." Only drastic measures by Surgeon Hitler could save her, for "brutal determination" was needed in "breaking down incurable tumors." No one else was capable of "combating . . . malignant cancers" or of "lancing the cancerous ulcer."

Other metaphors used by Hitler support the conjecture that Hitler, quite erroneously, may have believed that his mother's cancer had been treated by iodoform in an effort to burn out the disease (see Chapter 3, p. 189). In a speech at Stuttgart of 15 February 1933, Hitler set his task after coming to power by saying "we want to *burn out* the symptoms of decomposition . . . in our whole culture; we want to *burn out* this whole poison which has flowed into our lives." And in a wild harangue before the Reichstag on 13 July 1934, he sought to justify the Röhm Purge by saying:

> I further gave the order to *burn out down to the raw flesh the ulcer*s of this poisoning of the wells of our domestic life.[32]

Young Hitler's reaction to his mother's death was of direct importance to his ideology about the German nation. Just as he raged against her dying, so he raged against Germany's, insisting that both must live on or—if they had already died—that both must be resurrected. He was unable to save his mother's life, but when, in Koenigsberg's phrase, he "relocated his mother in Germany," his conviction had consequences. He would prevent the death of the Motherland by utterly destroying those who sought to injure, poison, and kill her—the Jews. He would root them out. Germany *must* be saved:

> Therefore let no one object, "But this is impossible." That no one can—no one dare—say to me! . . . It must be possible, for Germany must live!

He would perform great miracles to keep Germany alive—or to resurrect her. It is surprising how often it was necessary to repeat the resurrection after he had already saved her in 1933. Thus, two years later, in February 1935, he said:

> We celebrate the proud *resurrection* of Germany.

In September 1935:

> Through us and in us the nation has *risen again*.

In September 1937:

> Today Germany has in truth *risen again* and *risen again* as our work.

Again in October 1938:

> It is like a miracle that in so few years we should be able to experience a new German *resurrection*.

And yet again in November 1940:

> I am convinced that Providence has led me here and has preserved me from all dangers so that I could lead . . . *a new resurrection* of our people . . . We shall reestablish a Germany of power and strength and glory. Germany must *rise again*. One way or another! [33]

As we have seen, Hitler's racial theory seems to have been engendered, at least in part, by the primal scene trauma of infancy and later fantasies of his mother being attacked by a Jew or a part-Jew. Over and over again he used sexual images in speaking of his Motherland's being raped, or he attributed alleged female qualities of submissiveness and acquiescence to the nation or to the masses. "By what wiles," he asked, "was the soul of Germany *raped*?" Or he commented bitterly that "our German pacifists will pass over in silence the most bloody *rape* of the nation." The masses are always seen as weak; they are a woman who yields to a strong and audacious male. Like a woman—and more particularly like his mother—the masses "permit sexual substance to enter the body," and in so doing they become contaminated with poison and lose their purity.[34]

The association of his mother's body being poisoned by a Jew— whether through sexual union or through medical treatment—and the body of the Motherland's being exposed to racial poisoning is manifest through dozens of speeches and writings. Only a few examples can be cited here:

> The Jews eat like poisonous abscesses into the nation. . . . A continuous stream of poison is being driven into the outermost blood vessels of this once heroic body by a mysterious power.

> We will not pause until the last trace of this poison is removed from the body of our people.

> The Jewish poison was able to penetrate the bloodstream of our people unhindered to do its work.

> The Jew becomes a ferment of decomposition among people and races.[35]

In talking about his own relationships with the Motherland, Hitler used a peculiar phrase which seems to indicate an unconscious desire to possess his mother. Not only did he speak of "seizing power" in Germany, but he used a feminine form for the country, saying that he had conquered her. Thus, in his headquarters at the *Wolfsschanze* on the night of 16–17 January 1942, he retold for the hundredth time the saga of how the unknown hero had come to a nation in order "to conquer her" (*Um eine Nation zu erobern*).[36]

Years before he had confided to an intimate that he could not marry because "my only bride is my Motherland." [37]

Foundations of Hitler's Anti-Semitism

> The anti-Semite is a man who wishes to be a pitiless stone, a furious torrent, a devastating thunderbolt—anything except a man.
> —Jean-Paul Sartre

Apologists for the Third Reich simply misunderstand when they say that "Hitler was all right—he just went too far with the Jewish problem." Anti-Semitism was not peripheral to his system, and not one of its "excesses"; it was absolutely essential to it. It was *the* justification for the whole ideology. As President Theodor Heuss observed, anti-Semitism was as important to Hitler as economics was to Marx. Both claimed to have discovered "iron laws of history." For Marx, history was class conflict; for Hitler it was racial conflict. Marx considered the bourgeoisie as the enemy of the proletariat; Hitler called the Jew the enemy of the *Volk*. To Marx the final goal was a Communist society; for Hitler the goal was a racially pure community.[38]

In Hitler's mind, anti-Semitism was joined indissolubly with nationalism and socialism to form the mystical trinity of his ideology. As he put it in an early speech:

> Socialism can only be carried out in association with nationalism and anti-Semitism. The three concepts are inseparably bound together.[39]

Hitler was an opportunist and a cynic about many things. But not about anti-Semitism. The depth and intensity of his hatred was revealed in a conversation of 1922. In talking about Jews, Hitler was suddenly "seized by a sort of paroxysm" and promised that when he came to power he would see to it that every Jew in Germany would be killed. The method of the murders shows Hitler's continuing personal concern about filth, stench, putrefaction, and strangulation:

> As soon as I have the power, I shall have gallows after gallows erected, for example in Munich on the Marienplatz . . . Then the Jews will be hanged one after another, and they will stay hanging until they stink. They will stay hanging as long as hygienically possible. As soon as they are untied, then the next group will follow and that will continue until the last Jew in Munich is exterminated. Exactly the same procedure will be followed in other cities until Germany is cleansed of the last Jew! [40]

Anti-Semitism was an ideological conviction and an obsession. But it was even more than that. It was, as Hitler said, "a personal thing." He wanted personally to be involved in punishing the Jewish people: "I regret that I am Chancellor of the Reich. I would like to be a young SA or SS man and be able to meet the Jews with doubled-up fists or bludgeon." [41] As we have seen, the single word "Jew" was enough to trigger violent emotional reactions.

Hitler tried to externalize his hatred and fear of Jews, but he never managed to do so. Remarkably revealing phrases indicate that he felt Jewishness to be an evil within himself, a poison to be purged, a demon to be exorcised. Thus, in a speech of 17 April 1920, he said that it was imperative to get rid of the poison "within us" (*Wir müssen das Gift . . . in uns ausmerzen*). In a conversation during the 1930s he despaired of ever doing so. The Jew, he said, is "an invisible demon" who can never be eradicated because, Hitler concluded bitterly, "the Jew is *always within us [Der Jude sitzt immer in uns]*." [42]

German historians have recognized the importance of Hitler's personal anti-Semitism but have been unable to explain it. Certainly there were "practical" and "rational" reasons for Hitler's anti-Semitism: as a political opportunist he saw, quite rightly, that it was smart politics in postwar Germany to be a Jew-baiter. But the question of Hitler's personal anti-Semitism is more subtle than these answers suggest. Why, *as a personality*, was Hitler attracted to anti-Semitism? Why did he make it the very cornerstone of his life and work?

Since the question involves personal motivation, irrationality, and pathology, we must turn to the work of psychopathologists who have treated anti-Semitic patients and have concluded that anti-Semites display recognizable clinical syndromes. A fuller understanding of Hitler's personality and personal anti-Semitism may be gained by comparing him with hundreds of American patients who have been described as "anti-Semitic personalities."

Such people show symptoms which reinforce and intensify many of the characteristics of borderline personalities we have already met in Hitler. Anti-Semites, too, tend to be infantile personalities with immature ideas about social and political life. They, too, are troubled by "identity diffusion"; seeing themselves as both all-powerful and vulnerable, they swing between self-doubt and swaggering self-assurance. They exalt the powerful and despise the weak. Their defenses are many, but they rely chiefly on projection and introjection—they project onto the Jews the traits they most fear in themselves, and they insist that they possess the qualities of a pure and creative elite. Like borderline personalities, anti-Semites see the world split into all good and all bad, with the Jews mounting an evil conspiracy aimed directly at the anti-Semite and all other good and virtuous people.[43] Typically, anti-Semites have unsatisfactory interpersonal relations; male anti-Semites often have perverted relations with women.

Psychiatrists and clinical psychologists have contributed to our understanding of anti-Semitism. So too have philosophers. One of the clearest and most perceptive statements of the condition was made by Jean-Paul Sartre who, in effect, gave an incisive description of Adolf Hitler:

We are now in a position to understand the anti-Semite. He is a man who is afraid. Not of the Jews, to be sure, but of himself. . . . He is a coward who does not want to admit his cowardice to himself; a murderer who represses and censures his tendency to murder without being able to hold it back. . . . The existence of the Jew merely permits the anti-Semite to stifle his anxieties. . . . The anti-Semite is a man who wishes to be a pitiless stone, a furious torrent, a devastating thunderbolt—anything except a man.[44]

It seems clear, then, that Hitler displayed symptoms of an emotional disorder which uses hatred of Jews as its chief defense. But merely to identify Hitler as "an anti-Semitic personality" does not solve our problem. There are thousands of such prejudiced people in the world. The diagnosis—even if clinically acceptable—is much too broad to account for his particular pathology and its historical consequences.

From Private Neurosis to Public Policy

Hatred and fear of the Jews dominated his life and haunted him in his hour of death—to the last word of his last public statement. Never in history has there been such an anti-Semite. He established a government dedicated to anti-Semitism; he sought to kill every Jew in Europe. Is there any possible way for a biographer to explain these historic facts? Perhaps not. History is not a science, and there are many historical facts that defy explanation. This may well be one of them. But since it is not possible to explain Hitler's anti-Semitism by relying on traditional tools of historic analysis, let us, with due recognition of the difficulties, attempt to apply psychoanalytical techniques in a discussion of reasons for Hitler's personal hatred of Jews.

It seems likely that Hitler's hatred was precipitated by the traumatic events of his infancy and childhood. As we have seen, these included the primal scene trauma, the rumors of his Jewish ancestry, and the suffering and death of his mother while being treated by a Jew. The bitter memory of her suffering in 1907 was reinforced in 1918 when —according to his view—the Motherland was betrayed and defiled by Jewish traitors. His historic decision to become a politician was directly related to his desire to destroy the Jews and save the Motherland.

The mother was important, but so was the father. The role played by Alois Hitler in the development of his son's anti-Semitism may be seen from the perspective provided by an American psychoanalyst. In this view, Hitler's famous projection onto the Jews was a specific type derived from the ego-splitting characteristic of borderline personalities. Since he saw himself as Christ, the symbol of absolute purity and goodness, he required an opposite symbol of evil, the Devil incarnate. The Jew became for him such a symbol of total evil, a kind of negative absolute. In exalting the Jew as the one threat and persecutor, the one enemy both of himself and of the Motherland, Hitler's hatred reached the dimensions of a persecution mania. According to classical psychoanalysis, there is a peculiarity about this kind of mania, this manifestation of paranoia. Freud believed that whenever a paranoid raised anyone to the level of *sole* persecutor, "He is raising him to the rank of *father*; he is putting him into a position in which he can blame him for all his misfortunes."

Thus, in attempting to destroy all the Jews, Hitler was attempting to destroy his father. That he was never able to accomplish his objective was more than a problem of logistics; it was also a problem of internalization. As Harry Slochower has written, "No matter how many Jews Hitler sent into his hell-fires, the Jew—the father-figure—remained ineradicable. . . . Wherever Hitler went, along came his satanic shadow —the Jew." [45] And thus it was, as Hitler himself said, *"Der Jude sitzt immer in uns."*

It is commonly said that Hitler made the Jews a "scapegoat" for all the Motherland's problems. Psychologically, scapegoats are helpful in alleviating feelings of inadequacy, self-hatred, and guilt. If, for example, a person feels guilty about incest or sexual perversion, he can make his own feelings more bearable by shifting the finger of guilt away from himself and pointing it at the Jews. But this kind of projection does not really solve his problem. Indeed, it creates a kind of vicious circle: "The hated scapegoat is merely a disguise for persistent and unrecognized self-hatred. . . . The more the sufferer hates himself, the more he hates the scapegoat. But the more he hates the scapegoat, the less sure he is of his logic and his innocence; hence the more guilt he has to project." [46]

The greater the guilt feelings, the more the scapegoat must suffer. Since Hitler's hatred of the Jews was monumental, his feelings of guilt and self-loathing must have been very great indeed. The specific accusations he projected onto the Jews are particularly revealing. In public speech and private conversation, his chief charge against them was that they were guilty of dark and evil sexual practices. Hitler made Jews directly responsible for almost every crime known to man, but "never did he become so emotional, so arbitrary and so absurd" as when he fulminated against Jewish sexual perversions. Jews are the kind of people, for example, who have sex with their mothers.[47]

The question of Hitler's sexual relations with his own mother illustrates one way in which a historian's approach to a problem differs from that of the clinical psychologist. All the training and professional instincts of the historian focus on the question: Did it actually happen? Did this incest really take place? The psychologist is more interested in a different question: Did the patient actually have this fantasy—did he *believe* that it happened? It is doubtful that Hitler actually had sexual relations with his young mother, but psychological evidence indicates that he had fantasies about Oedipal fulfillment and that he felt guilty about them. By using the word "incest" so often, he showed that it was on his mind; he hung a portrait of his mother over his bed in all his bedrooms; a poem he wrote about her is redolent of sex and the death wish; his only bride, he said, was the Motherland, and he talked of "conquering" her. All the women with whom he had sexual relations, of one sort or another, were mother substitutes; all had attributes of age or physical qualities or family relationship or nicknames that reminded him of his mother and her relations with her husband. One can also surmise that Hitler had incestuous fantasies and felt uneasy about them because he found it so important to deny that he had them: it was not he, it was the Jews who practiced incest.

The Jews were also useful to Hitler in fulfilling his need to blame someone else for his own uneasiness about sexual perversion. One incident will serve as an illustration. In 1938 he professed absolute moral outrage when he discovered that General Blomberg, the minister of defense, had married a former prostitute. Hitler had the Gestapo collect incriminating evidence against Frau Blomberg. They supplied him with photographs showing her plying her profession by participating in various forms of deviant sexual activity. (A man who has seen the photographs has written that they were of the "most shocking depravity.") What concerns us is Hitler's immediate reaction upon first examining the pictures. He said at once that the male partner in the photos *must have been* of Jewish extraction." The writer who reported the incident believed that Hitler then became "absolutely convulsed by the wildest anti-Semitic fulminations." [48] A reaction as violent as this lends credence to the finding that Hitler himself had a perversion which produced feelings of guilt and self-loathing so intense as to require urgent projection.

As we have noted, the evidence is strong that Hitler believed he might have had a Jewish grandfather (see Chapter 3, pp. 126–131). Hitler talked incessantly about blood poisoning by Jews; he sought to get rid of his own blood; he destroyed the village he associated with his grandmother and his illegitimate father. In short, he was terrified by the thought that he himself might be "part Jewish." Such a suspicion was simply unbearable. Psychologically, he had based his very identity on the projection of his own feelings of guilt, inadequacy, and failure onto Jews. Politically, he had staked his entire career on the principle of the superiority of the Aryans, the inferiority of the "sub-human Jews," and the terrible threat of the "Jewish peril." He simply had to get rid of his awful suspicion. First, we recall, he ordered his personal lawyer and then his secret police to investigate his ancestry in order to prove positively that he could not possibly have any Jewish blood. But they could not prove it because they could not determine the identity of his paternal grandfather. And that is one reason why, we shall shortly suggest, he tried to establish his innocence in a different way—a way that would have ghastly historical consequences.

HISTORIC CONSEQUENCES OF HITLER'S ANTI-SEMITISM

> My enemy is Germany's enemy: always and only, the Jew!
> —Adolf Hitler

Political Value of a Private Scapegoat

Hitler's personal need for a scapegoat proved to be a distinct political asset in helping him come to power. For Hitler's phobia was soon shared by thousands of Germans who desperately wanted to find one simple explanation for all their manifold woes. True, other political parties also offered scapegoats; but they were not nearly so good as Hitler's. The Communists offered "the exploiting middle class," "feudal landlords," "Social Fascists," and "intellectual lackeys." But they were too various and too vague. Besides, they tended to divide and alienate Germans from each other. Hitler's scapegoat was monolithic, discernible, and defenseless. Through anti-Semitism, ethnic Germans of all classes and callings were brought together in a common hatred of a traditional enemy of German *Kultur*. "The Jew" was the single, simple answer to all problems. Who had stabbed Germany in the back during the war and caused the disastrous defeat? Who had signed the armistice? (The answer to that one was a little trickier. As given by Hitler, it was Erzberger, and he was not Jewish. But small matter. Hitler found for him a Jewish grandparent.) Who had accepted the "Treaty of Shame"? Who were the profiteers and exploiters who caused the inflation and the Great Depression? The answer was clear and compelling; "always and only the Jew!"

His personal enemy was also a political asset in helping him reconcile conflicting parts of Nazi ideology and enhance its appeal to very different social groups. He assured the propertied middle class that he was fighting only "Jewish capitalists"; to the workers he said he was opposed only to "Jewish socialism." In an adroit speech in Munich, 28 July 1922, he showed the political advantage of having it both ways by making the Jew serve as a common enemy of opposing interests:

> In all this we can see again and again how well they work together, the Jew from the stock exchange and the leader of the workers. . . . While the business agent Moses Cohn persuades his company to react most unfavorably to the demands of the workers, his brother Isaac Cohn, the labor leader, stands at the factory yard, arouses the masses and shouts: . . . "throw off your chains." And upstairs his brother sees to it that those chains are well forged.

In attacking the Jew as the enemy of all Germans, Hitler fulfilled a personal psychic need and at the same time greatly widened his political appeal.

His anti-Semitism had other political advantages. The Jew served as a safe outlet for hatred and aggression when war against an external enemy was not feasible. He could be presented as "an outsider" and thus provide Germans with an opportunity to defend their "Germandom" from "alien" forces by attacking the Jews within the country. It was also reassuring, at a time when national effectiveness was in doubt, to assert basic racial superiority. Further, the Jews were said to be intellectuals, and in denouncing them many Germans found a convenient way to deprecate the rationalism which they had so long found suspect. There was also a moral and religious problem that anti-Semitism helped assuage. The Weimar period was not only a time of economic, social, and political confusion; it was also a decade of crisis in traditional moral values. Many Germans were shocked by what they considered to be the depravity of cinema, stage, cabaret life, and literature. It was comforting to be told that such depravity was due entirely to "Jewish influences." In dozens of effective speeches, Hitler appeared as a "pious deacon" articulating the outrage and conscience of the petty bourgeoisie.[49]

During the postwar period, cherished beliefs, long accepted as eternal verities, were being challenged by three of history's most influential thinkers, all of whom were Jews. To many Germans, Marx, Freud, and Einstein were dangerous radicals bent on overthrowing whole systems of social, economic, ethical, and scientific order. All three found popularizers who spread their ideas with disturbing effectiveness. Emotional reaction against "subversive Jewish thinkers" increased the appeal of Hitler's demagoguery, which thundered against "Jewish Ideas" and exalted a simple "Germanic faith."

Anti-Semitism Institutionalized

After Hitler attained power, his personal rancor against the Jews was indeed "projected and rationalized as public policy." His anti-Semitism became the law of the land.

Hitler's first measures against the "Jewish peril" were designed to stop Jews from participating in the civic and cultural world to which they had contributed for many generations. An "Aryan paragraph" in the Law for the Restoration of the Civil Service of 7 April 1933 dismissed all Jewish civil servants. This paragraph was soon expanded to include lawyers and doctors, then writers, artists, and university and high school teachers and students. Subsequent legislation required that all Jews designate as their first name either "Sara" or "Israel." When war came in the summer of 1939, Jews were not permitted to drive motor vehicles or take part in German cultural events.

Two laws in particular document Hitler's personal obsession with racial purity, his fear of "bad blood" and tainted ancestry. The Law for the Prevention of Progeny Suffering from Hereditary Disease (*Gesetz zur Verhütung erkrankten Nachwuchses*) provided death or sterilization for "hereditary diseases" ranging from schizophrenia to congenital blindness and deafness. Women could also be sterilized for color blindness, since, as an SS official pointed out, "We must not have soldiers who are color-blind. It is transmitted only by women." Jews, by definition, were carriers of "hereditary disease." [50]

Hitler's concern about "Jewish blood" also produced the Nuremberg Racial Laws of September 1935, whose wording he personally supervised. Officially entitled *Gesetz zum Schutze des deutschen Blutes und der deutschen Ehre* (Law for the Protection of German Blood and German Honor), this legislation made it a criminal offense for a German to have sexual intercourse with a Jew, and specifically forbade German women from working as domestics in Jewish households. But no amount of restrictive civil legislation could solve the "Jewish problem." As Hitler saw it, the threat was biological; this racial enemy, he was desperately afraid, had poisoned his own blood and threatened that of his people. The "Final Solution" was inherent in the very statement of the problem: he and Germany could be safe only after all Jews had perished.

Mass Murder of the Jews

Another reason for the genocide grew out of the Führer's psychopathology. Since he never knew whether his own grandfather was Jewish, and no one could prove he was not, Hitler had to prove to himself beyond the shadow of a doubt that he could not possibly be "corrupted" by Jewish blood. In order to convince himself that such a direct threat to his personal identity and his life work was an utter impossibility, he became history's greatest scourge of the Jews. In effect he was saying: "See, I cannot possibly be Jewish. I'll *prove* it. I am the killer of Jews." And thus he screamed that he would "annihilate the Jews down to the *third* generation" that is, down to the degree of blood relationship he was trying so desperately to prove could not possibly be his own.

There were probably other reasons for the genocide. It seems, for example, to have been associated with Hitler's curious preoccupation with death (see Chapter 1, pp. 18–20). His thoughts of killing himself may have been displaced in the politics of genocide; perhaps he relieved personal anxieties about self-destruction by destroying others. Thus, when he spoke of spreading terror and said "The important thing is the *sudden shock of an overwhelming fear of death*," he was saying in effect: "People will recoil with fear of death (as I do); I can command them and I can command death by terrorizing or killing them." [51]

Genocide may also have been a by-product of the deep feelings of guilt we have found in Hitler. Robert Jay Lifton has observed that paranoid despots seek to externalize guilt feelings in the form of an unending number of enemies whose death they exult in surviving. Thus, Hitler externalized guilt feelings by displacing them upon others and then killing them—by the millions—thereby demonstrating his special dispensation from death and his power over it. [52]

The number of times Hitler used the word "exterminate" is psychologically interesting. The word in German, *ausrotten*, is much more "externalizing" than it is in English. Because it is a verb with a separable prefix, emphasis is placed strongly on the preposition, *aus* (out): *Ich rotte den Juden* AUS! or *Ich will den Juden* AUSrotten! Hitler promised publicly as early as 1920 that he would take the evil of Jewry by the roots and exterminate it: *mit Stumpf und Stiel ausrotten!*[53] And after he came to power he repeated the promise—and the same word—with a "monotonous insistence" that is "truly astounding." * Apparently he was afraid that people might not believe him when he promised that the Jews would be exterminated, and he did not want to be laughed at when he made this prophecy. In a speech of 30 January 1942, for example, he warned that "I am careful not to make hasty prophecies," and he told his audience that already on 1 September 1939,** when he had prophesied that the Jews would be annihilated, people *"laughed* about my prophecies." Eight months later, being laughed at was still on his mind: "People always *laughed* about me as a prophet. Of those who *laughed* then, innumerable numbers no longer *laugh* today, and those who still *laugh* now will perhaps no longer *laugh* a short time from now." [54] Hitler's concern about being laughed at seems to support our suggestion that he felt a serious personal need to externalize an internal fear and to exterminate it in the form of the Jewish people.

He probably chose gas as the means of extermination both for practical and personal reasons. Gas was an efficient way to kill 5 or 6 million people; but Hitler may also have ordered the gassing of the Jews to get revenge for the gassing he himself had suffered in 1918, which he blamed on the Jews. A passage in *Mein Kampf* shows his resentment and makes the suggestion in 1924 which he would later implement in the genocide:

> If at the beginning of the war and during the war twelve or fifteen thousand of these Hebrew defilers had been put under poison gas as hundreds of thousands of our very best workers from all walks of life had to endure at the front, then the sacrifice of millions at the front would not have been in vain. [55]

Hitler's annihilation of the Jews was also a consequence of military defeat. Admittedly, it is difficult to set any precise moment when Hitler realized that he could not win the war, and he kept proclaiming the inevitability of victory long after he stopped believing in it. But Percy Schramm is probably corect in saying that Hitler realized by the end of 1941, after the first defeats in Russia during the catastrophic winter, that the kind of victory he had hoped to win was no longer obtainable. [56] If so, it is no chronological accident that the final

---

* This characterization, which is Jäckel's, is borne out in the following speeches and conversations in which the word "extermination" appears: March 1941 to his military advisers; October 1941 to his entourage; 1 January 1942 in a New Year's message; the Berlin Sport Palace speech of 30 January 1942; speeches of 24 February 1942, 30 September 1942, 8 November 1942; and in a conversation of 13 February 1945.

** It is curious—and to me inexplicable—that he should give the wrong date for his prophecy. His Reichstag speech of 1 September made no mention of the Jews. He must have been referring to his Reichstag speech of 30 January 1939. It seems likely that this mistake was unintentional, since he was usually accurate about the contents and dates of speeches.

decision to kill the Jews of Europe was made at the Wannsee Conference, 20 January 1942. By thus "defeating" the Jews, Hitler may have been attempting to demonstrate his own victorious strength and to quiet his growing feelings that he was a weakling and a failure.

All his life he had been plagued by self-doubts about his masculinity and physical powers—doubts that were manifested every time he insisted that he really was not a weak and pitiful person at all. But after 1941 it was increasingly evident that the soft-muscled, slightly paunchy man with the trembling, effeminate hands and the shuffling gait did not at all fit his own picture of the indomitable, brutal, all-conquering, masculine Führer. Indeed, each military defeat unnerved him further and required more and more proof that he was the ice-cold, steel-hard, and ruthless victor of his fantasies. He could not play that role by conquering Russia or the Western allies; he therefore manufactured ruthless and brutal "victories" over the Jews and conquered his helpless enemy in the gas ovens of the greater Reich. Walter C. Langer recognized this sphere of weakness in Hitler's personality and foresaw the consequences. In 1943, long before he and his colleagues had knowledge of Hitler's death camps and massacre of the Jews, Dr. Langer predicted that Hitler would compensate for self-doubt and defeat by increasingly ruthless acts of destruction and brutality:

> Each defeat will shake his confidence still further and limit his opportunities for proving his own greatness to himself. . . . He will probably try to compensate for his vulnerability . . . by continually stressing his brutality and ruthlessness . . . for only in this way [can] he prove to himself that he is not a weakling . . . but made of the stuff becoming his conception of what a Victor should be.[57]

Finally, Hitler massacred the Jews because of one of his fantasies. He really did believe that Jews were the archenemy of all mankind and that in destroying them, as he had promised 20 years earlier, he was "doing the work of the Lord."

Thus did private fantasy become public policy.

Military Consequences of Genocide

Hitler's personal phobia about Jews contributed to Germany's military defeat. As Albert Speer has reported, a key reason why Germany never attempted to develop the atomic bomb was that the Führer distrusted what he called "Jewish physics." And his personal orders to kill all the Jews of Europe resulted in serious disruptions of the national war effort. The sheer logistics of collecting, transporting, and disposing of so many "units"—as Eichmann called human beings—were immense. And the project required other sacrifices. By 1944 the shortage of labor created by removing Jews from the work force ran to some

4 million men; the value in war production lost to the Reich amounted to billions of Reichsmarks.[58]

Viewed pragmatically, genocide was counterproductive. During the militarily disastrous years of 1942–1945, Germany simply could not afford to embark on the "Final Solution" to a problem which never in fact existed. It made no sense. But Hitler did not see it that way. His sense of priorities in a national crisis was as clear as it was horrendous: *nothing mattered more to him* than killing Jews.

Thus did the pathological fears and rages of one man send millions of innocent people to their death and decide the fate of a nation.

THE BENEFITS OF IDENTITY DIFFUSION

> The Führer could have become the greatest German actor.
>
> —General Jodl

> In retrospect, I am completely uncertain when and where he was ever really himself, his image not distorted by playacting.
>
> —Albert Speer

A man who had observed Hitler's face closely on many occasions concluded that no photograph could possibly capture the person hidden behind the image. The face, he said, "always amazed me because of the multiplicity of expressions it contained. It was as though it were composed of a whole series of individual elements without adding up to a single total. . . . A photographer, by selecting only a single moment out of context, could show only one aspect, thereby giving a false impression of the duplicity or multiplicity of being which lay behind it. . . ." [59]

Without knowing it, the observer was giving a good description of a salient characteristic of a borderline personality: one who does not quite "add up." Such people lack an integrated concept of self, and experience "identity diffusion." As a result, Dr. Kernberg has written, the borderline displays a "chameleon-like quality." He constantly plays different roles; he "acts as if he were someone else." [60]

Hitler was indeed a "multiplicity of being." Since he was besieged by doubts of his own identity and stability, it became terribly important to convince himself, over and over again, that he was a man of poise and power, one who could dominate any other person or group. One of the best means of such self-persuasion was for him to *act the part* and thus become—at least for the moment—the person he wanted so much to be. But he was not always sure who that person was. Such inner confusion helps to account for two facts about his early career that have puzzled historians: for years he refused to pose for pictures and he insisted on using a false name.

Normally, aspiring young politicians do not go to extraordinary lengths to conceal their identity or hide themselves from the public. But for several years after he had made his "momentous" decision in 1919 to enter politics, Hitler refused to have his picture taken. He did so, we are suggesting, because he was too unsure of his own image to have it "set" by photography. As late as 1922 a picture of Hitler was so rare that an American photographic agency offered a professional German photographer $100 for a picture of him. (The going rate at that time for a photograph of President Ebert was $5.) The American agency's surprise over the discrepancy was no doubt increased when it learned that the asking price in Germany for a good snapshot of Hitler was $30,000. Posed pictures were simply unavailable.[61] Also during these years Hitler preferred not to use his real name. He asked people to call him "Herr Wolf"; he repeatedly referred to himself as the "nameless fighter" of the Western Front. It was only after he gained control over the Party that the nameless and faceless period was over. He had established his identity at last as the Messiah and Leader of the Germans. He then became the most photographed political leader in the world—but he never got over the need of creating other images and playing at play-acting.

Hitler As an Actor

While he sometimes smiled sardonically at his own theatrics, there was an intensity about them that was little touched by humor. He never wanted people to find out who he really was. When he felt that they might be getting close, he would change his characterization and appear as somebody else, lying to his associates in order to conceal his own private thoughts. He worked at his acting and sometimes rehearsed the part he would play in meeting a stranger he wanted to impress or control:

> *Hitler:* What does he expect?
> *Hess:* Authority, of course. You can speak at length. Your will is unshakable. You give laws to the age.
> *Hitler:* Then I'll speak with a firm voice.

Hitler would try a few sentences. Hess would listen carefully and comment, "No, not like that. Quiet. No passion, commanding. It is Destiny that is speaking. . . ." Hitler would try again with a firmer voice. After six or seven minutes he would stop, already somewhat moved by his own acting. "Good, now I think we have it," he would say.[62]

Hitler's thundering temper tantrums were famous—and, upon occasion, carefully staged. For he knew the shattering effect his outbursts could have on certain types of people, particularly upon the quiet and introspective.[63] When dignified conduct would be more effective, Hitler could be appropriately discreet.

Hitler himself recognized his talent and once referred to himself as "the greatest actor in Europe." He illustrated his ability in a scene involving Hjalmer Horace Greeley Schacht, then minister of finance. Schacht had come into conflict with Göring over the economy and had threatened to resign. Hitler called him to his office, urged him to stay on and pleaded with him, tears welling up in his compelling blue eyes. Schacht was deeply moved and agreed once more to do his Führer's bidding. But the moment the door was closed behind the minister, Hitler turned to his associates and snarled viciously, "That fellow is always sabotaging everything!" [64]

On another occasion, on 23 August 1939, when he saw an advantage in intimidating the British ambassador, Sir Neville Henderson, Hitler staged another theatrical triumph. The German secretary for foreign affairs recalled that "only after Henderson had left the room did I realize that Hitler's performance was premeditated and acted. Hardly had the door closed on the Ambassador, when Hitler slapped his thigh, laughed and said to me, 'Chamberlain will never survive this conversation. His Cabinet will fall by tonight.' " [65]

Late in the war, in a situation report of 24 January 1945, Hitler commented, "I have an unpleasant task to perform today. I have to 'hypnotize' Quisling today." [66]

Throughout his career, Hitler's ability to play a variety of roles with intensity and conviction was a distinct political asset. He appeared as a very different person to an extraordinary range of people; he impressed almost all of them.*

To the sophisticated French ambassador, he appeared as "a well-balanced man, filled with experience and wisdom." An intellectual found him "charming," a person of " 'common sense' in the English sense." The British historian Arnold Toynbee came away from an interview thoroughly "convinced of his sincerity in desiring peace." The elegant and precise Anthony Eden was impressed by Hitler's "smart, almost elegant appearance" and found his command of diplomatic detail "masterful." [67]

The cynical Hermann Göring was never cynical about Hitler. He confided first to a colleague and then to the British ambassador, "Every time I face him my heart falls into my stomach. . . ." Even after Hitler had turned against him, called him a traitor, and drummed him out of the Party, Göring was close to despair when he heard of his

---

* There was one notable exception. Hitler's dramatic talents were wasted on Generalissimo Franco of Spain. Hitler later recognized his inability to impress Franco and said that rather than meet him again he would rather have a tooth pulled—and that, as we have noted, was a terrifying experience for him. To the Spaniard, Hitler was "an affected man with nothing sincere about him . . . an actor on a stage and one could see the mechanics of his acting!" See George Hills, *Franco: The Man and His Nation* (New York, 1967), 363.

leader's death. His wife recalled that he said, "He's dead, Emmy. Now I shall never be able to tell him that I was true to him to the end!" [68]

Admiral Dönitz, commander in chief of the German Navy, felt psychically drained by being in the presence of his Führer's commanding personality:

> I personally went very seldom to his headquarters, for I had the feeling that I would thus best preserve my own power of initiative, and also because . . . I always had the feeling that I had to disengage myself from his power of suggestion. [69]

The early diaries of Goebbels, which were never intended for publication, show the consummate artistry with which Hitler wooed and won this bright and brittle young man who was to become the "evil genius" of Hitler's Ministry of Propaganda and Enlightenment and one of the most influential leaders of the Third Reich. Hitler responded brilliantly to all his psychological needs. Goebbels needed, above all, someone who could dominate him; Hitler appeared as "my master . . . my father." He craved love and attention; Hitler embraced him and sent him flowers. He needed to hate; Hitler showed him "how to hate with passion." He needed flattery; Hitler deferred to his judgment. He longed for a savior; Hitler convinced him that "he is Christ." He wanted to feel paternal; Hitler appeared as "a child, kind, good, warm-hearted." He admired cunning; Hitler appeared as "a cat, sly, clever, shrewd." He admired masculine strength; Hitler seemed to him to be a lion, "roaring, immense . . . a great guy! A man!" [70]

Hitler played a very different role for Albert Speer, the cultivated young architect and engineer who became Hitler's minister of armament production and by 1944 the man largely responsible for Germany's war economy. Speer recalls how, as a student at Berlin University in 1931, he was captivated by Hitler. He remembers a controlled and modulated voice, quiet humor, South German charm. "Here it seemed to me was hope. Here were new ideals and new understanding. . . ." In looking back over this and a dozen other encounters with Hitler, Speer wonders in his memoirs why he was so attracted: "I find it incomprehensible that these tirades should have impressed me so profoundly. What had done it?" [71]

Speer is unable to answer his own question. It seems likely that he believed, in part, because of Hitler's remarkable ability to sense the psychic needs of others and to respond with a totally convincing performance. But Speer also believed because he, like Goebbels, wanted desperately to believe. Here again, desire was stronger than reason. Fascinated by Hitler, he came to view him with awe and fear. "They were all under his spell, blindly obedient to him and with no will of their own—whatever the medical term for this phenomenon may be. I noticed during my activities as architect that to be in his presence for any length of time made me tired, exhausted, and void. Capacity for independent [thought] was paralyzed." [72]

Toward the close of the war, Speer wanted to oppose Hitler's orders for the deliberate destruction of Germany, but he could not bring himself, even then, to stand up against the power of the man: "Face to face, his magnetic power over me was too great up to the very last day. . . . without reflection and without completely committing myself, my lips spoke the words '*Mein Führer*, I stand unreservedly behind you!' . . . I realized that I had lost all urge to continue my opposition. Once more Hitler had succeeded in paralyzing me psychically." [73]

Speer was not the only one who was "paralyzed psychically" by Hitler. It had happened to Goebbels, Göring, Himmler, Ribbentrop, Hess—and many, many others. It seems clear that a part of the explanation lies in this: his satraps felt a compelling attraction to Hitler because, like Hitler himself, they manifested sadomasochistic tendencies; they too needed both to dominate and to be dominated. All of them hungered for power over other men, and Hitler gave each the kind he longed for. To Goebbels, who had failed as writer and dramatist, Hitler gave authority to stage enormous political pageants, to control radio, press, and propaganda, and through his spoken and written word finally to command respect and to force men to do his will. The young and ambitious Speer was given power to allocate "labor units" of millions of men and to build colossal, brutal buildings that demeaned and intimidated human beings.

Hitler also satisfied another impulse in his followers: they felt a thrill at being dominated, at quivering in the Führer's presence. Little wonder that even at the end, when Speer knew rationally what a disaster Hitler was for Germany, he found that he still submitted to Hitler's overpowering will—he had wanted to submit all along. And two decades later, long after the death of the god he worshipped. Speer's memoirs revealed the power Hitler still exerted over him. In spite of his best efforts, Speer could not make himself the hero of his own book. The hero, in the end, was Adolf Hitler. True, throughout the 600 pages he is "a malignancy," but still one that captivated Speer and gave his life meaning by supplying his deepest needs both to exert power and to be "blindly obedient" to a master. [74]

Although Hitler was truly an actor, it must not be concluded that he was "merely putting on an act," that he was merely a person of deceit and deliberate cunning. He was that, but he was more than that. He was also a person of faith and conviction, a genuine fanatic.

It might be helpful to put the matter in a different way: when Hitler acted a role he did so with both calculation and conviction. While consciously he no doubt calculated his effect, there was at bottom a psychic need to *be* the character or myth-person he was portraying —to *be* the man of Decision, the Man of Destiny. He needed to convince himself that the role he was playing was true. More important for history, he compelled others to believe it was true. How else can one explain the statement of Professor Percy Schramm, who had watched Hitler for many years:

> It is almost impossible to convey to those who never experienced it the personal impact of Hitler. Such could be its strength that it sometimes seemed a kind of psychological force radiating from him like a magnetic field. It could be so intense as to be almost physically tangible.[75]

Hitler never actually possessed the personal strength, integrity, and purpose that he projected. But he gave the illusion of possessing them. And that was sufficient. He moved men because he was able—in Heiden's phrase—"to act out greatness," to change himself from a hesitant and unsure little man to a person of towering historic force who paralyzed opposition and commanded millions to do his will.

Thus the "acting out" which was for him a psychic necessity became one of his greatest political assets.

The Power of Delusion

> I go the way that Providence dictates . . .
> —Adolf Hitler

Hitler, it has often and rightly been said, was a man of delusions. Like other borderline personalities, he indulged in "omnipotent fantasies . . . of power, greatness and perfection."[76] In Hitler's case, delusions were an important source of his political effectiveness.

Ever since 1918, when he imagined he heard a strange voice calling to him in his hospital bed at Pasewalk, he had deluded himself into believing that destiny had chosen him as the German Messiah. This delusion would sustain him through the darkest days of his career and help him to convince millions that he really was their heaven-sent savior.

It seems likely that this hallucination was psychologically related to his role playing, which was so effective in winning followers. The incident also shows the splitting of his ego—another mark of the borderline. In his hospital bed, one part of himself had spoken to another part through the means of a disembodied "voice." He did not conclude that he was delirious; he firmly believed that he had established a profound relationship between himself and destiny, or God, or the Spirit of the Motherland—a relationship that held the absolute assurance of life-sustaining and life-saving properties. Years later he would say, "I go the way that Providence dictates, with all the assurance of a sleepwalker." Convinced that he had undergone the experience of being called by destiny, Hitler was able to inspire in others exactly the same reaction, only now it would be *his* miraculously compelling voice which became the "outer" voice of Germany's destiny. And when his followers had the choice between following the dictates of reason and independent thought or the call of irrational faith, they too, like Hitler before them, preferred delusion.

Albert Speer, a notably rational person, has shown with remarkable clarity how this process worked both in himself and in his compatriots —indeed, in all those who kept the faith long after reason had told them that all was lost. Speer wrote:

> Hitler's obsessive faith inevitably influenced his entourage. One part of my consciousness certainly acknowledged that now everything must be approaching the end. But despite that, I spoke all the more frequently of "restoration of the situation." Strangely, *this confidence existed apart from the recognition of inevitable defeat.*[77]

BRUTALITY AND OBSTINACY IN ACTION

> In the struggle between two conceptions of life, only the weapon of brute force used continuously and ruthlessly can bring about decision.
> —Adolf Hitler

It was very important for Hitler to avoid any suggestion of feminine softness and always to appear masculine and masterful. One way of doing so was by acting the part; another was through the repetition of adjectives which he considered descriptive of masculine virtues. A tribute to Field Marshal Göring revealed Hitler's own masculine ideals:

> The *Reichsmarschall* went through many a crisis with me and has proven himself to be *ice-cold*. There is no better adviser in times of need than the *Reichsmarschall*. The *Reichsmarschall* is in times of crisis *brutal* and *ice-cold*. . . . Bend or break, he proves himself to be without consideration an *ice-cold* man, and they could not get a better one than him. He was with me through all the difficult days, he was always *ice-cold*. Whenever it became really bad, he turned out to be *ice-cold*.[78]

A man who had survived dozens of "Table Conversations" with Hitler recalled that "never once have I heard from his lips words which would show that he had a warm or feeling heart in his breast." [79]

The cultivation of hardness and brutality ran through Hitler's political career. As early as his trial after the Beer Hall Putsch, he set forth his solution to the problem of French occupation of the Ruhr in 1923, saying, "Only fervent, *reckless, brutal fanaticism* could have saved the situation at that time." A witness at the trial recalled that throughout Hitler's long harangue he "concentrated on the word *brutality*." [80]

In a public speech many years later, on 8 November 1940, he proclaimed: "I am the *hardest man* Germany has had for many decades, perhaps for centuries." Hitler's secretaries have said that one of his speeches, given without notes and never published in the Third Reich, gave particular insight into Hitler's deepest personal thoughts. The Führer was addressing young Wehrmacht cadets on 20 May 1942. Within a few paragraphs—and in many Freudian slips—he demonstrated his personal concern about hardness and being hard:

> Struggle leads to the selection of the *hardest*. . . . It makes the stronger even *harder*. . . . We must fight a *hard* and bitter battle for existence. . . . It has been a much *harder* trial which many could not understand. . . . A bloody, *hard* battle . . . *hardness* must be applied in order to be able to create *hardness*. . . . Pressure was created . . . through *hardness* . . . we made the German nation even *harder* . . . [with] an inner *hardness*.[81]

Among all the words in his litany of masculinity, his favorite was "brutal." Hitler extolled the virtues of brutality on many occasions, saying, for example, that among the masses of people "*brutality* is respected, *brutality* and physical strength. The plain man on the street respects nothing but *brutal* strength and ruthlessness—women too for that matter, women and children. . . . Why babble about *brutality* and be indignant about tortures? The masses want that. They need something that will give them a thrill of terror." [82] The conflict between soft femininity and hard masculinity which was constantly being waged in Hitler's mind is compressed into one sentence of his memoirs, in which he says that his political faith "exchanges the slogan of a weak and cowardly defense with a battle cry of courageous and *brutal* attack." [83]

Psychologically it seems likely that one of the reasons the Führer found it necessary to create and constantly reaffirm the image of brutality, infallibility, and iron purpose was that he himself—like other borderlines—was a deeply divided person with a diffused and uncertain sense of identity. But the overtones of sexuality are so pronounced, and his protestations of masculinity (as he defined it) so strident, as to suggest that he was also defending against fears about his own masculinity. He was determined that no one would ever suspect him of sexual inadequacy, femininity, or homosexuality.

Hitler's personal infatuation with hardness and brutality became a normative value in the Third Reich. Brutality was not one of the "excesses" of the system, it was part of its essence. It was the distinguishing characteristic, for example, of all Nazi Führers from the idealized leader at the top down through all the echelons of his society. The district leaders of the Party, the leaders of youth, cultural, educational, athletic, literary, and medical societies—all cultivated the toughness, brutality, and compensatory masculinity of their master.

Brutality and humiliation of other people were, of course, the prevailing tone of Hitler's concentration camps. But brutality was also a virtue to be cultivated in the training of Hitler's elite SS, as shown in the following characteristic excerpts from the memoirs of a member of the Waffen SS:

> There was a special method of humiliating a man. If anyone, while filling cartridges into a charger, let a cartridge fall to the ground, he had to pick it up with his teeth. I made up my mind that I would not do that. They can do what they like with me, I said, but I will not pick up a cartridge with my teeth; I shall use my hand. Naturally I took care not to let the situation arise and determined to do everything I could not to let a cartridge fall to the ground. One day of course it happened. On these occasions no one gives an order; the N.C.O. simply turns down his thumb and the man concerned knows what he has to do. In my case of course he turned down his thumb—and I bent down and picked the cartridge up with my hand. He rushed at me like a wild animal, stuck his face close up to mine so that there was hardly an inch between his nose and mine and bellowed whatever came into his head. Of course I could not understand a word because he was bellowing so loud that he was choking. Eventually I gathered that he was yelling: "Have you forgotten what to do?" When he had finished bellowing he handed me over to the deputy section commander. . . .

> [The recruit was forced to do physical exercise to the point of exhaustion; he was then ordered to do 50 deep knee-bends while holding his rifle out at arm's length.]

> After twenty knee-bends I stopped counting. I just couldn't go on. I did one more knee-bend and then I lowered my rifle and stood up. I can't say that I thought this out; I just knew that I was all in. I heard him bellowing all over again but that left me cold because suddenly I could control myself no longer. I felt I had to weep although I knew that it was neither manly nor soldierly. I couldn't answer his questions because I was so shaken with sobbing that I couldn't speak. I was not in a rage and I was not in pain. I had just had enough. When he saw that he bellowed: "Look at this!" and then: "Mollycoddle! Mother's little darling! Cry baby! Who's ever heard of an SS man blubbering! All our dead will turn in their graves! Is this what we're trying to take to war—etc. etc." Then "assembly" was blown and the training period ended. He ordered me to clean out all the first floor latrines for a week and then report to him so that he could inspect them. And straightaway he ordered: "Chuck this cartridge away." I did so, and then without even waiting or looking to see whether he had turned his thumb down I picked it up with my teeth. . . .[84]

Hitler's need to dominate was also reflected in his judgment of nations. He defined the greatness of a people in terms of its capacity to humiliate and annihilate other nations, telling the Danish minister of foreign affairs, for example, "Should the German people ever fail to be sufficiently strong . . . it might just as well disappear and be annihilated by another, stronger people. It would have lost its right, the place that it has conquered at this moment." [85]

That he meant what he said was made clear on 22 August 1939 when he lectured his generals on the nature of the war he planned to conduct against Poland. The terse diary notes of a general who was present at the meeting convey the spirit:

> Goal is destruction of Poland—removal of its living strength. Means are immaterial. Victor will never be asked if his motives were just. Question is not whether we have justice on our side; only whether we are victorious . . . hard and ruthless. Steel ourselves against all considerations of pity.[86]

Yet aggression in a man or nation is no demonstration of poise, confidence, and power. On the contrary, it arises out of a feeling of inadequacy. As Hannah Arendt has observed, "Violence is an expression of impotence." The psychoanalyst, Rollo May, agrees and has given a memorable addendum to Lord Acton's famous aphorism that power corrupts: "Weakness tends to corrupt and impotence corrupts absolutely." [87]

Along with brutality, Hitler considered obstinacy to be an essential masculine trait and prided himself that he had it in abundance. A psychiatrist who has studied the matter disagrees with him and shows that roots of obstinacy lie not in masculinity and mastery but in anxiety; it is a defense against fears of inadequacy and impotence.[88]

There can be no doubt that Hitler's "iron will and stubbornness" sometimes stood him in good stead. He was probably right when he said that during the Rhineland crisis of 1936 he was saved by what he called "my unshakable obstinacy and amazing aplomb." And military historians generally agree that his rigidity and stubbornness in refusing to retreat during the first setbacks of the Russian campaign in the winter of 1941 helped bring him out of the immediate crisis. But, in the long run, the Führer's obstinacy meant military disaster and death for thousands of his men.

Hitler's personal psychological problems influenced military performance in another way. His conception of masculinity condemned him constantly to take the offensive because to assume a defensive posture was feminine. A military historian has shown the strategic consequences of this attitude:

Hitler recognized only the principle of the offensive. He could not bring himself to retreat for any reason, and thus the fateful errors he made in his war leadership.

The consequences of this were that repeatedly he wasted elite units in the wrong places and at the wrong time, so that on other fronts other objectives could not be obtained. . . .[89]

Even after victory had been won, he could not stop himself from further attack. "Wherever our success ends," he wrote, "it will always be only the point of departure for a new struggle." [90]

The very word capitulation (*Kapitulation*) threw him into a frenzy. In an interview after the war, German State Secretary Otto Meissner said he realized for the first time that Hitler was mentally unbalanced when it was suggested in March 1945 that Germany really ought to sue for peace. Hitler's reaction was violent:

He paced the room. His voice was out of control. He shouted and cried. He spoke without coherence. He exclaimed repeatedly; "*Ich kapituliere nie . . . Ich kapituliere nie!*" [91]

Hitler would "never surrender as a woman surrenders to a man"— for that would reveal feminine qualities. Nor could he ever yield again, as he had been forced to yield to his father to be humiliated by him:

One word I never recognized as a National Socialist in my battle for power: capitulation. That word I do not know and I will never know as Führer of the German people and as your Supreme Commander: that word is again capitulation, *that is the surrender of will to another person.* Never! Never! [92]

And so it continued to the end. Because he personally could not surrender, Germany must perish. It was less painful for him psychologically to have Germany destroyed than for him to capitulate.

TRUST AND MISTRUST IN HITLER'S REICH

> I can trust no one . . . they all betray me.
> —Adolf Hitler

Erik Erikson believes that one of the most formative periods of the human life cycle takes place in earliest childhood, when the infant develops an attitude of either basic trust or mistrust. If a child is unable to master trust, he will have great difficulty with the personality problems which Erikson finds characteristic of later stages of development: autonomy, identity and integrity.

Hitler's childhood, we have found, was plagued by feelings of suspicion, resentment, and mistrust. These attitudes—so typical of borderline personalities—remained throughout his life. They helped shape political decisions, and they contributed to the atmosphere of distrust that permeated his Reich.

The Führer could never open himself to another person. He had no friends. His closest associates, men who had been with him for years, never really knew him. He lied to them all, he said, and the closer they seemed to come to him, the more he lied.

Distrust of others entered into the routines of his life. "Always at his desk were three pencils," his valet recalled, "one red, one green, one blue." The colors were used to make notes or to mark documents or letters, not in accordance with their intrinsic importance but to remind himself whether he trusted or distrusted the person involved. He explained the system: "I use the red one when I write about or to an enemy; the green one when I make notes about friends; the blue when I have a feeling that I should be cautious [about someone]." [93]

Mistrust became the hallmark of his government and set the tone for the society. "The Third Reich," an anonymous official observed, "is a system wherein no one trusts anyone else." One of the consequences was governmental confusion. Western observers, impressed with gigantic displays of Nazi pomp and propaganda such as the Olympic Games of 1936, the great Party rallies at Nuremberg, and the Wehrmacht and Luftwaffe maneuvers, concluded that Hitler's Reich was operated with machine-like efficiency. They were mistaken. His government was shot through with corruption and inefficiency. It was a chaos of competing and overlapping jurisdictions jealously guarded by leaders who did not trust their colleagues.

When, after four years of war, Albert Speer became Reichsminister for munitions in 1942, there existed four separate "Supreme Reich Authorities," each with independent power over German war production: the Four-Year Plan, the Armed Forces Ministry of Economics, the Ministry of Labor, and Speer's own Munitions Ministry. "Only slightly lower in rank and essentially as independent were at least eight more: the Ordnances Offices of the Army, Navy and Air Force and five plenipotentiaries under the Four-Year Plan. (Iron and Steel, Construction, Chemical Industry, Machinery and Water Power.)" In addition, "Himmler had been building an economic empire of his own through the SS main office of Economics and Administration, which ran all its own business enterprises free of all outside control."

Hitler refused to adjudicate serious disputes over war production and allocation of resources which developed between Göring and Speer, or between the *Gauleiter* and Goebbels, or between Himmler and Bormann. He could not choose among them, for he could trust no man with too much power. True, Speer's influence over the economy became extensive, but it always remained limited. And his power derived from "a process of attrition, not through authority explicitly granted by Hitler." [94]

The same problem can be seen in the field of intelligence gathering, where Hitler also allowed conflicting agencies to develop. There were the military *Abwehr*, headed by Admiral Canaris, and *Nachrichtendienst* of the SS; Ribbentrop in the Foreign Office had a separate espionage system; Himmler developed his own private agency to spy on the enemy but also to spy on Ribbentrop and others; Goebbels in the Ministry of Propaganda had a special service to watch Göring and Himmler; Rosenberg in the *Ostministerium* developed an espionage organization to spy on Russia—and on his colleagues in the Nazi hierarchy. The Führer's mistrust filtered down through his satraps.

Nor was there any consistent policy in the occupied areas of the Greater Reich. In Czechoslovakia, for example, Hitler could not trust either the first "Protector," Konstantin von Neurath, or his deputy, Karl Frank—and they could not trust each other. Neurath was relatively humane; Frank was brutal; and Hitler's policy was split between the two. In the end he tried to support both irreconcible positions, just as he tried to live with both parts of his deeply split ego.[95]

Literally dozens of times, when conflicts and confusions produced important disputes crying out for decision, Hitler refused to make a judgment. The result was that his government, as Franz Neumann wrote with some exaggeration, was a "non-State, a chaos . . . disorder and anarchy." [96] The obvious question, once again, is why? In part, confusion and refusal to make decisions among subordinates was technique —the ancient method of the Roman emperors, "divide and conquer." But Hitler had already conquered. He continued to fear and mistrust his subordinates long after he had consolidated total political power and established the principle that he and he alone was the source of all authority in the Reich.

A monographic study dealing with Hitler's methods of government notes his refusal to define his subordinates' spheres of authority or to choose among them. The author wonders what Hitler was afraid of and concludes that "This view of Hitler—*the man who does not decide*— would help to explain the eternal confusion of the men working for him." [97]

A political leader who creates conflicting agencies, who sets forth irreconcilable policies, who thinks he conquers when he divides is a person who is externalizing profound splits and conflicts in his own psychological makeup.

These personal conflicts, rooted in his lifelong mistrust of others, had far-reaching consequences for the home front during the war. Because Hitler distrusted people, he believed the masses to be selfish and avaricious, incapable of sacrifice for the common good and prone to revolt. The masses, he kept saying, were like women, fickle and untrustworthy. That was one of the reasons why Hitler felt he could not demand heavy sacrifices from the German people for the war effort. One of the anomalies of World War II was that two Western democracies, England and America, had far more stringent controls over the economy than Hitler's dictatorship. Hitler apparently felt that he could not call on the German people for the kind of personal sacrifices accepted as a matter of course in Churchill's England. Indeed, the Nazi dictator was leery about interruptions in the flow of consumer and luxury goods. In 1942, after three years of war, production of consumer goods was only 3 percent below peacetime. For a time in 1942, Speer tried to raise that percentage, but the most he could manage was a 12 percent cutback. Even then, after only three months of relative austerity, Hitler changed his mind and decreed the resumption of production "for the general supply of the population." [98] Not even after Stalingrad and the opening of a second front in Normandy did Hitler dare cut luxury items. Hundreds of tons of wallpaper and cosmetics, hair-set lotions, hair dryers, and perfume continued to be manufactured.[99]

Hitler's mistrust of others was also reflected in his foreign policy. It was largely responsible for the serious misjudgment which turned his attack on Poland into a general war. He felt free to invade Poland on 1 September 1939 because he had used his own standards of suspicion and duplicity in evaluating England's intentions. He simply could not believe that Britain would honor her treaty with the Poles. A general's private diary for 14 August 1939 records Hitler's scornful dismissal of the argument that the invasion of Poland might precipitate a European war: "Why should England fight? *One does not die for an ally.*" [100]

Among the many reasons he attacked the Soviet Union in June 1941 was his conviction, against all evidence, that his ally Stalin was about to launch an attack on him. "My own personal nightmare," he said, "was that Stalin . . . sooner or later would abandon us and go over to the enemy. . . . It was absolutely certain that one day or other [he] would attack us." [101] His declaration of war on America was also prompted, in part, by the conviction that Roosevelt was about to declare war on him.

PSYCHOLOGICAL ROOTS OF AGGRESSIVE WAR

> I am totally convinced that this struggle does not differ one hair's breadth from the battle which *I once fought out within myself.*
> —Adolf Hitler

There are, regrettably, sound psychological reasons why, throughout history, there have been "wars and rumors of war." Warfare permits the individual to act out in socially approved ways what in peacetime he is required to repress: impulses of aggressive rage and violent destruction. Human capacity for both intense hatred and intense love is also given an outlet in war, when citizens are urged to show complete devotion to their country and to project total hatred against the enemy. Sadistic and masochistic impulses are also generally stimulated by war.[102]

Such emotions may be awakened in all people, but two things made them especially important to Adolf Hitler. First, his personal psychological need for aggression and war was particularly acute; second, he held a position of totalitarian power in a modern mechanized state. When he wanted war, a world became involved in his need. Moreover, as a deeply split borderline personality, he externalized his own inner conflict by projecting a view of the world that was dangerous and threatening: the Jews in particular had organized an international conspiracy against him; England and America, goaded by the Jews who controlled both societies, were about to attack; Stalin was plotting invasion. Like the borderline patients of Dr. Kernberg, Hitler felt "severe aggressive stirrings" because it was imperative that he "destroy potential enemies" before they destroyed him.[103] And it was not only he personally who was being attacked; the Jews and their allies in Russia and the West were attempting to destroy the Motherland. He must defend her.

Aggression was also made necessary by his private fears of personal inadequacy, weakness, and impotence. War against his foes could prove his strength. He would utterly crush anyone who opposed him or doubted his power. This need welling up within him prompted him to remark after unleashing World War II: *"The resolve to strike has always been a part of me."* [104] How closely he identified himself with war and found it a challenge to his personal masculinity and toughness was revealed in a speech of 1940:

> I know that this [war] must be the hardest challenge ever laid before the German people. I not only flatter myself that I am the hardest man that Germany has had for many decades, perhaps for centuries, but I also possess the greatest authority.
>
> But above all I believe in my success. Indeed I believe in it unconditionally!
>
> I am totally convinced that this struggle does not differ one hair's breath from the battle which *I once fought out within myself!* [*den ich einst im Inneren ausfochte!*]
>
> I am convinced that Providence has preserved me from all dangers in order to have me lead this battle of the German people. . . .[105]

To fulfill his personal need, he militarized a nation and led it into battle. The war was not, as A. J. P. Taylor prefers to think, somehow forced upon a reluctant Hitler. It was in his bones and viscera; it was the very *raison d'être* of his Reich. Hitler's Germany meant war; it had meant war from the very beginning for its Führer had proclaimed that war was the final goal of politics, the law of life, absolutely essential to man. (Chapter II.)

In a real sense, World War II began not in 1939 with Hitler's invasion of Poland but with his accession to power in 1933. Psychologically, however, it had begun long before that: perhaps in the conflicts and aggressive rages repressed in early childhood, but certainly in his plans of the 1920s. That war was essential to Hitler was brought home suddenly to Albert Speer while talking with his Führer in Paris in 1940, as they looked at the Arc de Triomphe. Hitler was totally unimpressed because he had created a design for a triumphal arch, to be erected in his new capital of "Germania," which would dwarf the one in Paris. But what astonished Speer was that Hitler's sketch was dated 1925. He comments: "Now I think you will see what I mean by the connection between his blueprints and his aggressions. For the historians must ask themselves, 'Where was Adolf Hitler, the unknown, in 1925?'" [106]

The answer is that Hitler, released from Landsberg prison, was somewhere in Bavaria, but with very little Party and very little support. That he drafted a plan for an enormous triumphal arch in that year indicates both belief in his destiny and the depth of his feeling that the resolve to strike was indeed "always within him."

Again in the 1920s, in a noteworthy passage in his second book, Hitler showed the inner aggression that drove him insatiably onward: "We shall attack and it is immaterial whether we go 10 or 1,000 kilometers beyond the present lines. For whatever we gain, it will always be only a starting point for new battles." [107] To live in peace with another country was simply not possible for him, for as he told his foreign minister, "You know, Ribbentrop, if I am an ally of Russia today, I could attack her tomorrow. *I just can't help myself.* [*Ich kann halt nicht anders*]." Indeed, Hitler talked so often of *battle* and *attack* and *enemy* that an intimate spoke of his master's "pathological need for battle." [108]

There was another psychological reason why Hitler required war: he saw it as a way to cleanse the body of the Motherland from impure and tainted blood. And total war, with its conditions of maximum state security and the movement of thousands of people, would provide the optimum circumstances in which he could launch a vast program of mass murder of the "unfit and unworthy." Furthermore, conquest of foreign land would permit him to set up extermination camps where polluted blood would not defile the sacred soil of his Reich. Both the wording and the dating of Hitler's decree for mass killings are important. He called it the "Order for the Destruction of Lives Which are Unworthy of Being Lived" (*Vernichtung lebensunwerten Lebens*), and he set the date of the order for 1 September 1939. That is, he would begin the war for his New Order on the same day that he would start the process of "internal cleansing" (*innere Reinigung*). As the German historian who noticed the connection between Hitler's idea of "cleansing" and genocide has commented: "If a biography of Hitler is undertaken from a psychoanalytical approach, his compulsions about hygiene and cleanliness would be its most important point of departure." [109]

Thus were private feelings projected into public policy: because the Führer felt unclean and unworthy, millions of people had to die.

Nazi foreign policy also illustrates the way personal fantasies and unconscious desires affected national decisions. The dizzy pace of crisis upon crisis—from the Rhineland to Austria to the Sudetenland to Prague to Poland—was related to Hitler's personal battle against time and his fantasies about the imminence of death. Against all medical evidence, he was convinced that, like his mother, he was suffering from terminal cancer. He must do his conquering *now* before death conquered him. [110]

His decision to seize Austria in the *Anschluss* (annexation) of 1938 provides a particularly vivid illustration of the connection between private feelings and foreign relations. Of course it is true there were other reasons for the *Anschluss*, but since they have been set forth in many books, they need no emphasis here.

We have seen that in Hitler's imagery his mother was identified with Germany. He loved her with the intense "primitive idealization" associated with borderline personalities. As he loved her as the racially pure Motherland, so he hated the bureaucratic, racially mixed Austria, which he associated with his bureaucratic and racially suspect father. Just as he spoke well of his father publicly in stilted, standard phrases, so he could also refer to Austria as his "beautiful, beloved homeland." But basically he despised them both. To his mind, the "debauched" Austrian dynasty—exactly like his father—had defiled and "betrayed" Germany again and again. [111]

Even as a boy, he said, he knew that Austria—like his cold and distant father—"did not and could not provide any love for us Germans." Austria, in ways reminiscent of his father's treatment of him, had also tried "to oppress and handicap every truly great German." Hitler's hatred for his father was intense; his hatred for Austria was, he said, "fanned into flaming indignation and contempt." [112]

Both his father and Austria evoked in him fears of blood contamination by the Jews. The Austrian capital (to which his father had gone before him) was a cesspool of racial pollution: "Czechs, Poles, Hungarians, Ruthenians, Serbs, Croats, etc.—but among them all the eternal fission-fungus [*Spaltpilz*] of humanity: Jews and more Jews. To me the city was the personification of incest [*Blutschande*]." [113]

The emotional young German patriot must have despised his father's rejection of Germany. The old man's grandson, Adolf's nephew William, testified that "He [Alois Hitler] considered it a grave insult to be classed [as a German] and stoutly maintained that he was an Austrian, and that was something entirely different." [114]

Hitler later recalled that a favorite childhood book was an illustrated history of the Franco-Prussian war, glorifying Bismarck and the victory of German arms. As a young boy he remembered asking himself why Austria had not fought for the cause of German unity. Why, specifically, had his father not joined the battle? A psychiatrist has suggested that the question may be put in a different way: "Why didn't my father die a heroic death?" It may also be suggested that years later, when Hitler talked about the annexation by announcing the death of Austria, he was also celebrating the death of his father: "There is no longer an Austria. The country that calls itself Austria is a *corpse*." [115]

He did not want an *alliance* with Austria, he thundered at the Austrian chancellor during their famous confrontation at the Obersalzberg; alliance was totally out of the question. He wanted complete *union* of Austria with the Motherland—the union he had longed for when he ran away from Vienna to Germany as a youth, "drawn by secret wishes and secret loves," when "the most ardent wish" of his heart was "to return to the bosom of the faithful Mother." [116] But that union could not be accomplished until old Austria was first destroyed. Was this not the Oedipal death wish of childhood that he would fulfill as Führer?

> From my earliest youth I came to the conviction which never deserted me . . . the protection of Germandom [the mother] presupposes the destruction of Austria [the father].[117]

Austria would not be completely destroyed, however. Hitler would see to it that it was mastered and disciplined—just as he had longed as a boy to turn the tables on his authoritarian father, who had so often disciplined him. Thus he told an intimate on the eve of the *Anschluss* that "he regarded it as his special task to train Austria to Germandom. He would be a harsh taskmaster in training them in German ways. He would make them sweat. He would drive out their indolence. . . . There had been enough softness. . . ." Childhood rage against the father who had never brooked contradiction found expression in the fury he directed against Dollfuss and other Austrian leaders. He screamed, "He dares to contradict me! But wait, gentlemen! You will see them before long crawling on their knees to me. But, with icy coldness, I shall have them put to death as traitors." [118] Only after Austria was racially purified, severely disciplined and thoroughly "trained" by Adolf Hitler would it be worthy of uniting with the Motherland.

We therefore suggest that Adolf Hitler unconsciously used foreign policy as his means of defeating his Austrian father and achieving the union with his young mother which he had fantasied as a child and had promised on the very first page of his memoirs: "German-Austria must return to the great German Motherland. [*Deutschösterreich muss wieder zurück zum grossen deutschen Mutterlande.*]" [119]

HITLER'S NEED TO DESTROY

> The only choice is between triumph and destruction.
>
> —Adolf Hitler

In his split way of viewing things, Hitler saw himself as both creative genius and ruthless destroyer. His need to destroy was manifested on two levels: consciously he punished and destroyed others, but unconsciously he turned punishment inward upon himself. We shall attempt to show in some detail that this masochistic, self-punitive urge—a characteristic of borderline personalities—was a part of the pattern of his life; that it directly influenced his political and military decisions, and that, in the end, the destructive impulse sealed his own fate.

Choices for Failure; Desires for Defeat

> Many of Hitler's actions are inexplicable unless we assume that he did not . . . always intend to succeed.
>
> —James McRandle

In reading Hitler's speeches, and soliloquies, one is surprised by the number of times this man who prided himself on his brutality talked about unworthiness, guilt, and conscience.* He showed his concern by mentioning it so often and by protesting so stridently that he himself was completely worthy—it was everyone else who was not. It seems clear that the Führer had feelings of guilt and unworthiness about something. But when we ask the question why he had those feelings, we are obliged, once more, to guess.

One possibility can be quickly eliminated. He did not feel guilty about the brutality of his government; he gloried in it. He felt no remorse whatever over the calculated murder of millions of "racially inferior" people, or the holocaust of war, or the squandered lives of young German soldiers, or the planned destruction of the country he professed to love. Atrocities did not disturb Hitler.

He may have felt unworthy of being Führer of a racially pure Germany because he suspected that he himself was "guilty of having Jewish blood." He may also have felt guilty about incestuous desires. And he may have developed acute feelings of unworthiness, guilt, and self-loathing as a consequence of a particularly loathsome sexual perversion.

Whatever the reasons for his feelings of guilt, he sought security through an elaborate system of psychological defenses. These included

---

* See Chapter 1, p. 16f. Such expressions are not common among borderline personalities, who are prone to "severe self-punishment" but usually do not display feelings of remorse. See Kernberg, "Borderline Personality Organization," 674–675.

"reaction formation," masking voyeurism and perverse sexual interests behind ostentatiously prudish behavior. His scrupulous personal cleanliness and compulsive handwashing indicates unconscious guilt feelings and the desire to wash away "dirtiness." He also sought to dull feelings of unworthiness by a kind of "introjection" in which he took unto himself the role of moral and religious leader. He could not possibly be guilt-ridden because he was the chosen instrument of God Almighty, the Messiah who spoke the words of Jesus, proclaimed himself as infallible as the Pope, and established his Reich upon patterns perverted from the Catholic Church.

His many references to other people as being "unworthy" indicate continuing concern about his own worth. One way he found to reassure himself was to put the onus of unworthiness onto others and then have them destroyed. In 1929, at the conclusion of an early Nuremberg rally, he declared that if a million children were born in a year and 800,000 of the weakest and most "unworthy" were killed, the end result would be a strengthening of the population. In his decree of September 1939 which called for the "Destruction of Lives which Are Unworthy of Being Lived," he said that as "the father of his people" he had the responsibility of making sure that unworthy members of his family were destroyed.[120] In the late stages of the war, as his difficulties and self-doubts increased, so did his list of those who were "unworthy" to live. By the spring of 1945 he had reached the conclusion that the entire German people had proved unworthy of him. They all must perish.[121]

In addition to punishing others, he may also have tried to lessen feelings of guilt by punishing himself. As a young man he stayed on for years in Vienna, a city he detested, when he could easily have moved to the Germany he loved; he suffered needlessly from hunger and privation; his reported perversion was monstrously masochistic; and he talked repeatedly of killing himself, the ultimate masochistic act. There is strong evidence to support a German psychiatrist's conclusion that as a personality Hitler was "massively self-destructive." One form of self-punishment can be seen in a curious pattern in Hitler's life. Time after time he seemed to cultivate difficulties for himself and to court disaster. "Many of Hitler's actions," an observer has written, "remain inexplicable unless we assume that he did not (either consciously or unconsciously) always intend to succeed . . . Hitler was . . . a man bent on doing injury to himself." [122]

This suggestion needs to be investigated, for if Hitler had an impulse for self-injury and an unconscious desire for defeat, it would help to explain some surprising facts about his career.

Of course, Hitler's life can be read as a remarkable success story. The unlikely hero is played by a neurotic dropout from Linz and Vienna who, though he had failed in all his previous undertakings and had been jailed at the start of his political career, became master of Germany and arbiter of Europe within a decade. Surely biographers are justified in dwelling on Hitler's remarkable successes: his skill in pulling the Party together after the disaster of the Beer Hall Putsch; his insight and perseverance during the political crisis of 1932; his brilliant diplomatic coups and smashing military victories at the start of the war.

And yet another, very different pattern of behavior also is characteristic of this complex and deeply divided personality: throughout his life Adolf Hitler flirted with failure, talked of defeat even in moments of triumph, and repeatedly involved himself unnecessarily in situations that were fraught with danger to himself and his movement. He liked to think of himself as a ruthless and ice-cold gambler, but he gambled at very bad odds. He once confessed that somehow he felt compelled to court disaster: "You know, I am like a wanderer who must cross an abyss on the edge of a knife. But I *must*, I just *must* cross." [123]

Declined Opportunities of Youth

Even though he had contrived to drop out of *Realschule*, young Adolf was still given a marvelous opportunity when he arrived in Vienna in 1908 to enter the artistic world he had set his heart on. A friend of his mother's had connections with Alfred Roller, a noted artist and director of scenery at the Imperial Opera. Adolf could have had a job painting backdrops for the Vienna Opera, thus combining two of his greatest loves, painting and Wagner. A friend wrote in Hitler's behalf, and Professor Roller offered to help the young man. But Adolf refused to take advantage of his opportunity.[124] Instead, quite on his own, he tried to get into the Viennese Academy of Art. He failed his first examination and then, when given a second chance, refused to apply himself. It may be true that he took a few art lessons from a man named Panholzer in Vienna. But there is no basis for the conclusion, reached by one biographer, that after failing his first examination he "now did what he had failed to do in school: worked industriously, effectively and purposefully." [125]

On the contrary, his roommate during these months reported that Hitler did no serious painting at all. He went to operas almost every night; he spent hours walking around the Ring; he designed grandiose buildings; he set forth schemes for traveling orchestras; he wrote sketches for dramas and operas; he chattered about life, sex, and politics by the hour. Indeed, he did almost everything but apply himself effectively and purposefully to his painting. The result was that he was not even admitted to the entrance examination when he reapplied in October 1908.[126]

The Fiasco of 1923

Hitler's first try for political power also illustrates the pattern of choosing alternatives least likely to succeed. In 1923 he had proclaimed that he planned not merely a *Putsch* in Bavaria, but a march on Berlin to overthrow the "Weimar traitors." Openly and explicitly promising either a new German national government or his death, he announced to cheering crowds that his purpose would be fulfilled "only when the black-white-red swastika banner floats over the Berliner Schloss." [127]

But he had made no effort to get the support of the two military leaders whose help for such an undertaking was absolutely essential: the commander of the national army, General von Seeckt, and the prestigious leader of patriotic causes, General Ludendorff. In the week preceding his attempted revolution, Hitler's newspaper, the *Völkischer Beobachter*, gratuitously insulted von Seeckt, calling him a tool of a "Masonic conspiracy," and libeled his Jewish wife. General Ludendorff later insisted that prior to the actual night of the coup he had not been consulted about Hitler's plans.

Nor had he won the confidence and support of local authorities who would be indispensable to the success of his revolution: General Otto von Lossow, the army commander for Bavaria; Colonel Hans Ritter von Seisser, the commander of the Bavarian State Police; Gustav von Kahr, the "strongman" of Bavaria. Indeed, both Lossow and Seisser had given Hitler unmistakable warning on 7 November that they would crush any attempt at a *Putsch*. The next night, Hitler did nothing to win the favor of this powerful triumvirate by embarrassing them publicly and holding them hostage at pistol point.[128]

If he had decided to rely solely on his own Brown Shirts rather than the regular army or police forces, he had done little to prepare them. Up to the very day of the event, many district leaders of the SA knew nothing about plans for a revolution. The arms hastily collected were in "terrible shape." There were a few artillery pieces, but almost no ammunition; 80 percent of the machine-guns were completely useless.[129]

Preparations for a national revolution were grossly inadequate in Munich; outside the city they were nonexistent. In the north, for example, SA Commander Peter Heydebreck, a former Free Corps leader who was itching to march on Berlin, tried to get an audience with Hitler in Munich and was rebuffed. He wrote, "I was not the only man of the North who received similar cool treatment," and went on to complain that the SA in Berlin were given no information about the impending national revolution.[130]

On the actual night of the *Putsch*, after arresting Lossow, Seisser, and Kahr and making an impassioned speech, Hitler sank into despondency and seemed incapable of taking any effective action. He sat and brooded, he paced ineffectively up and down, he talked excitedly about minutiae, he left the beer hall intermittently on impromptu missions of no importance. He was heard to mutter morosely, "If it comes out all right, well and good; if not, we'll hang ourselves." [131]

The author of a massive monograph on the event has reached a conclusion that is not supported by his own extensive evidence: "He [Hitler] ran everything himself." On the contrary, nobody ran anything that night. The first ten or 12 hours of any coup d'etat are of crucial importance to its success. During these hours, when it was imperative for Hitler to act quickly and decisively, *"no orders at all came from the Putschist high command. . . ."* [132]

No effort was made to do the obvious—seize such key buildings as the telephone exchange, transport facilities, telegraph stations, and police headquarters. Above all, Hitler did not even try to capture Kahr's headquarters, the official center of political power in Munich. Even after the government had abandoned it, Hitler inexplicably gave no orders to take it over. During the first 12 vitally important hours, the Führer had managed to occupy one beer hall.*

Astonishingly, he refused to concern himself with those areas in which he was an acknowledged expert. This specialist in propaganda, this master demagogue who had promised to lead a revolution did not even visit the propaganda headquarters that had been set up by two assistants. He chose not to deliver one of the great orations he had promised for the next day, relegating speech-making to the unpredictable Julius Streicher, fanatic Jew-baiter of Nuremberg—scarcely the man to be the spokesman for a national revolution. He actually scribbled on a piece of paper, "Streicher is responsible for the entire organization." [133]

As Hitler's influence waned and forces of the counterrevolution gathered in strength, it is indeed "interesting," as the leading authority on the event has written, that Hitler "did not even make any serious attempt to gather more troops" to reinforce his badly depleted ranks. There were many SA units in Southern Bavaria that would have come quickly to Hitler's help. He did not send for them. [134]

During the course of the night, he left the beer hall and permitted his hostages to escape, thus allowing them to rally the forces that would overthrow him on the morrow. "One can only wonder why, in an adventure of such high stakes," one historian has written, "Hitler could have committed such an elementary error of judgment." Others have called Hitler's conduct "inexplicable" and "unfathomable." [135]

The famous march the next morning was not Hitler's idea. He was apparently not even consulted. The order seems to have come from General Ludendorff, who was furiously impatient with Hitler's uncertain behavior. "No one knew where the march was going, and no one had known from the start." [136]

We would suggest that one explanation for his irrational and self-defeating behavior was that as a borderline personality with a deeply divided ego, he was torn by inner conflict and contrary impulses. One part of him wanted to succeed; another wanted to fail. Since he could not cope with the conflict, he sank into a depression, then ran

---

* Röhm, it is true, had taken the district army headquarters across the city, but had somehow failed to seize its telephone switchboard. He surrendered the building next morning upon orders from General Ludendorff.

away and hid. As we have seen, when confronted by total disaster, he summoned all his verbal skills to convert his trial into a triumph; after his release from prison, he worked effectively to reconstitute his Party.

Hitler's Preparations for War

Hitler's prewar diplomacy may be seen as a triumph of opportunism and cunning. It can also be seen as a series of invitations to disaster.

Three different interpretations may be considered. First, in the unlikely event that A. J. P. Taylor is correct in insisting that all Hitler really wanted was peace in his time and a negotiated revision of Versailles, then the methods he employed to attain those ends were "singularly inappropriate." [137] Second, if we are to suppose that Hitler wanted only a limited, localized war with Poland to gain Danzig and the Corridor, his belligerent speeches against Western powers, his atrocities against minority groups, and his broken promises to both British and French statesmen show him proceeding in ways that were unlikely to isolate Poland and most likely to prod his victim's strong allies to come to her defense. Finally, if he really plotted the great European war of conquest that he had promised in *Mein Kampf*, in his second book of 1928, and in dozens of public and private speeches, his preparations for fighting such a war were conspicuously inadequate. The scholarly Franz von Halder, chief of the Army General Staff in 1939, said in an interview that "unbelievable as it may sound, he [Hitler] did not even have a general plan for the war." [138]

Hitler also failed to give the orders to supply his army. Halder recorded in his diary that there were monthly shortages of 600,000 tons of steel, and that munitions in general were in such short supply that no large-scale combat was possible. "Supply was sufficient for only one-third of the available divisions for fourteen days. Current production was just enough to keep the same one-third active." [139]

It may be argued that Hitler was not concerned with building up massive reserves of arms, raw materials, and foodstuffs, or with converting to a full war economy, because he had not planned that kind of war. He had put his trust in piecemeal *Blitzkrieg* victories and in looting materials from countries as he conquered them. There is merit to this argument, except for the fact that even after it became obvious he could no longer carry on that kind of war, he still refused to take effective action on the economic front. Economic mobilization was not really ordered until the autumn of 1944—that is, well after his "Fortress Europe" had been entered from the West and Russia was moving in from the East. Only then, when it was much too late, did Hitler move haltingly in the direction of full economic mobilization. And even then he could never bring himself to give the orders for conversion to a complete war economy.

While the British and American war industries were working around the clock on three-shift schedules, German industry, with only minor exceptions, worked only one shift. Full use of plant and equipment was never achieved. Speer had finally been made minister of munitions, but he was never given full power. And even in 1944, when German armament production reached its height, Speer admits that it still lagged behind the accomplishments of World War I. Luxury goods were still being produced, and Hitler continued to use millions of man-hours and vitally needed rolling stock to transport Jews to their deaths and art objects into hiding.[140]

We suggest that his divided psyche felt compelled to give opposing orders: to destroy and to preserve; to demand victory, but to invite defeat.

Hitler's Military "Mistakes"

Almost any historian, serene in the knowledge of how the future turned out, can look back on a lost war and point out the strategic errors which led to defeat. It is also indubitably true that even the most brilliant military commander can make a mistake. But Hitler's blunders were so many, so costly, and so gratuitous as to suggest that these "mistakes" were the result of a strong, unconscious impulse for self-destruction. If so—as the blighted career of Richard Nixon was to prove —Adolf Hitler would not be the last national leader with a compulsion to arrange his own downfall.

Hitler's performance as the supreme commander of all German forces in World War II must be given a mixed review. It is certainly true that he sometimes showed an uncanny ability to judge his enemy aright, as when he concluded that France would not attack his undermanned Western Front while he was invading Poland or when he guessed correctly that the Red Army would counterattack at Stalingrad in the Fall of 1942 and not at Smolensk as his generals were insisting. Indeed, a British military historian has concluded that "no strategist in history has been more clever in playing on the minds of his opponents—which is the supreme art of strategy." [141] He also showed an impressive capacity for innovation in the use of armor and air power.

All this is true. Hitler, it bears repeating, could act with devastating effectiveness, and his military victories in Poland, Norway, the Low Countries, and France should not be disparaged. Yet during the war there were repeated hints of unconscious desires to punish himself in the very midst of success.

DUNKIRK

After his smashing breakthrough in France in May 1940, Hitler began flirting with failure. Suddenly and inexplicably, just as a clear path lay ahead of his armored divisions, he imposed a two-day halt and removed from command General Guderian, the brilliant tank commander who had led the victorious German drive. If the French had been able to take advantage of the breathing space Hitler had given them, the pause could have been fatal to his prospects of victory.

Something even stranger took place a few weeks later at Dunkirk, when Hitler refused the opportunity of smashing the entire British expeditionary force in Europe. Instead, on 15 May, he suddenly gave orders to halt all tank movements on the Dunkirk salient. The significance of this order has been well summarized by a British military historian:

> His action preserved the British forces when nothing else could have saved them. By making it possible for them to escape he enabled them to rally in England, continue the war, and man the coasts to defy the threat of invasion. Thereby he produced his own ultimate downfall, and Germany's five years later. Acutely aware of the narrowness of the escape, but ignorant of its cause, the British people spoke of "the miracle of Dunkirk." . . . It will never be possible to learn for certain why he came to his decision and what his motives were.[142]

Some explanations, of course, have been given. Robert Payne, for example, believes that Hitler took pity on the English because he had come to admire them as a youth during a visit to Liverpool and wanted to "spare Churchill a bitter humiliation." [143] The difficulty with that explanation is that Hitler had never visited England as a youth and had despised Churchill all his life. (See Appendix, "A Note on Spurious Sources.") It has also been suggested that Hitler stopped his armor before Dunkirk because the terrain was too soft; or that he believed the Luftwaffe alone could smash the British without risking the tanks he needed in the south. Hitler himself tried to explain his odd behavior by saying that on a mere whim he had decided to let the British go "in a sporting spirit," after the English manner.

But none of these explanations convinced German generals at the time; nor have they satisfied military historians. At headquarters, Generals Warlimont and Halder were simply "flabbergasted by Hitler's order," which they found "incomprehensible." Field commanders were equally appalled. General Guderian wrote increduously, "We were stopped within sight of Dunkirk!" Baffled members of General Rundstedt's staff concluded that the only possible solution to "the riddle of Dunkirk" was that Hitler for some inexplicable reason "wished to help the British." Certainly that is what he accomplished.[144]

It may well be true that no rational explanation can be given for Hitler's decision at Dunkirk. We therefore suggest that he was acting irrationally: unconsciously he did not really want a victory.

"HITLER'S GOLDEN OPPORTUNITY"

In an important study of World War II, two American historians argued convincingly that Hitler's "golden opportunity" came a year after his self-induced failure at Dunkirk. By the spring of 1941 his submarines were creating havoc with British shipping; his armies had crushed Norway, France, and the Low Countries during the preceding year and had just won decisive victories in the Balkans and Libya; there was a realistic chance that he could win control of the entire Mediterranean basin by taking Egypt, Suez, all North Africa, and Gibraltar, thus forcing Spain to align itself with the Axis. There was no force in the Mediterranean or the Middle East capable of stemming the tide of Nazi triumph. These historians therefore conclude: "History may well record that in May and June 1941, Adolf Hitler was closer to victory than at any time in the course of the epic struggle known as the Second World War." [145] And that is not mere hindsight. The German Naval High Command fully recognized the marvelous opportunity and implored Hitler to attack in the Mediterranean. He refused to do so. Again, one must ask why, and again the question invites speculation.

Göring suggested one possible explanation: he noted that the Führer was never comfortable about naval matters and could think only in "continental terms." It is true that Hitler had always been uneasy about the water, from pleasure-boat rides to major naval operations. That fact may help explain his halfhearted preparations for a cross-channel invasion of England, its final cancellation, and his neglect of the Mediterranean theater. He once confessed to an aide, "On land I am a hero; but at sea, I am a coward." [146]

Or was Hitler's failure to attack in the spring of 1941 a consequence of his infantilism? He might have been unable to decide among so many appealing strategic alternatives because, "like a child, he could not bear to disregard any attractive objectives; no more could he bring himself to give up ground once gained. . . ." And like a child he wanted everything quickly and cheaply: he wanted to defeat England without an amphibious invasion; he wanted to win the Mediterranean with the Luftwaffe and a few army corps; he wanted to conquer all of Russia right away.[147]

There was, of course, a totally different alternative for Hitler in the spring of 1941. He did not need to attack anyone, anyplace. He was already the master of Europe. He had smashed Poland and conquered France, and he controlled the western coastline from Norway to Spain. Secure from western attack and at peace with the Soviet Union, how could his Greater German Reich have been challenged? It is unlikely that beleaguered Britain, herself vulnerable to attack and still without allies in Russia or America, could have found either the material resources or the will to do anything but accept the fait accompli. It was Hitler who opened up alternatives for his enemies. It was he who decided that "enough was not enough," that the war must continue.[148]

And it was he alone who would make the decision which was to prove his downfall.

OPERATION BARBAROSSA: THE INVASION OF RUSSIA

For several weeks during the summer of 1940, after the fall of France, Hitler was unsure of what to do next. As so often in his life, when plagued by uncertainty and self-doubt, he turned to Wagner for inspiration and direction. Now, on 23 July 1940, he journeyed to the shrine at Bayreuth to attend a performance of *Die Götterdämmerung*. Once again Wagner worked his magic upon him. His portrayal of heroic catastrophe, the destruction of gods and men, somehow reassured Hitler and confirmed his conviction of heroic destiny. In the darkness of the loge he passionately kissed the hand of Frau Winifred Wagner. He left Bayreuth composed, his mind made up. Within the week he issued the orders that would lead to his own *Götterdämmerung*.[149]

Thus, in the spring of 1941, with the European continent in his grip, instead of consolidating his vast New Order, instead of concentrating his forces against his only remaining foe, an isolated and desperately wounded England, Hitler turned to court his nemesis: he sent his armies marching into Russia. He did so at a time when the Soviet Union was his most valued ally, shipping him thousands upon thousands of tons of vital war supplies, including huge stocks of oil which the Russians were purchasing from the United States and sending on to Germany through Vladivostok and across Siberia. One of the more memorable pictures in the annals of warfare shows Hitler's soldiers, as they marched eastward into Russia, looking at Soviet freight trains traveling westward loaded with supplies for Hitler's Wehrmacht.[150]

Both rational and irrational factors seem to have been at work in Hitler's momentous decision. He wanted the wheat of the Ukraine and oil of the Caucasus; * he had long planned to find *Lebensraum* for his Reich in Eastern Europe; he was getting old and wanted to win his race with death; he mistrusted the Russians and—against all evidence to the contrary—was convinced that they were about to attack him at any moment; and his racial theory demanded that the Slavs be enslaved. Furthermore, since no one else had conquered Russia, this was his chance to prove that he was "the greatest military commander of all time"—far greater than Charles XII or Napoleon. There was also Hitler's fascination with space. "In my youth I dreamed constantly of vast spaces," he mused one night in his "Wolf's Lair" headquarters, "now life has enabled me to give the dream reality. . . . Space lends wings to my imagination. . . ."[151]

All these reasons were probably operative. But in addition, he may, unconsciously, have gone to war with the Soviet Union because of a compulsion to punish himself and to fail. The reason Hitler himself gave was that he invaded Russia in order to defeat England—not, one would think, the most direct way to achieve that objective. The result was the opposite of the stated intent. England was greatly relieved and

---

* But the argument that Hitler invaded Russia because he needed war supplies is blunted by two facts: Stalin was already shipping him hundreds of thousands of tons of phosphates, iron ore, scrap iron, and chrome ore, as well as oil, platinum, rubber, and timber. Further, Hitler already had at his disposal great quantities of oil and wheat after his army had moved into Rumania in September 1940 to "protect" Rumanian oil and wheat fields. See Rich, *Hitler's War Aims*, 1:207, 190.

strengthened when Hitler abandoned "Operation Sea Lion" and involved himself in a two-front war.

It is a remarkable fact that in launching the invasion of Russia, Hitler did not ask Japan, his ally in the Tripartite Pact, to help him in any way. Indeed, he gave explicit orders that "no hint of the *Barbarossa Operation* must be given the Japanese." [152] A close student of Japanese foreign policy believes that Japan, whose options were still open in the spring of 1941, might well have been persuaded to attack the Russians at the time of Hitler's invasion. But Hitler's refusal to ask for aid or even to consult his ally needlessly offended the Japanese, who henceforth cited the incident as an example of Hitler's "perfidy." [153] Norman Rich has concluded that if Japan had attacked Russia in the Far East while the Wehrmacht was invading from the West, Hitler could have conquered Russia. The same writer can find no adequate reason to account for Hitler's "extraordinary attitude" in failing "to do anything to secure Japanese cooperation of any kind" before launching the invasion.[154]

Hitler's attitude continued to be extraordinary. As late as the winter of 1941–1942, when it was clear that he would need all the help he could get if he were to defeat Russia, when all reason demanded that he seek aid from Japan, he refused to do so. He did not even ask his ally to hinder American shipments of supplies to the Soviet Union via Vladivostok as a modest return for his own declaration of war on the United States. His conduct was indeed irrational. It suggests the possibility that unconsciously, once again, he was asking for punishment.

The struggle against the Soviet Union, everyone knew, was a vast undertaking requiring enormous amounts of supplies—the mobilization of the entire economic power of a great industrial nation. But Hitler never gave the order for such mobilization. In fact, on the very eve of the invasion, he actually gave orders *to reduce* the level of armaments production! [155]

This was no act of mere bravado. Hitler was not nearly so confident of an easy victory over Russia as has been alleged. It is noteworthy how often he repeated a metaphor which bespeaks a premonition of misfortune. At three o'clock on the morning after the invasion he told his press secretary, "I feel as if I've opened a door into a dark, unseen room—without knowing what's lurking behind the door." To his private secretaries he also talked about opening a door into a darkened room, and concluded apprehensively, "One never knows what is hidden there." He said the same thing to Bormann and repeated it to Ribbentrop. And again in a speech of October 1941 to his generals, in which he attempted to explain why it was necessary to attack the Soviet Union, he said, "At every such step a door opens behind which only a mystery [*Geheimnis*] is hidden, and lies in wait. . . ." [156]

When Hitler was a little boy, had he ever opened a door into a darkened room to be confronted by some terrifying secret?

There were other premonitions of disaster. A full month in advance of the event, Hitler set the date of invasion for 22 June, the precise anniversary, according to tradition, of Napoleon's ill-fated campaign. And why, of all the thousands upon thousands of alternatives, did he choose the code name of "Barbarossa" for the Russian campaign? His military planners had called the operational scheme "Fritz," after the victorious Prussian king. But on Hitler's direct personal order the name was changed to Barbarossa.[157]

Why that particular name? It may be true that Hitler saw himself, like Friedrich Barbarossa, as a crusader with a mission to destroy an infidel enemy to the East. But Barbarossa had failed. In fact, he was the most celebrated failure of medieval German history: he had failed in five campaigns against the Italian city-states; he had failed to unify the Holy Roman Empire of the German Nation; and he had failed during the Third Crusade, and had drowned while bathing in the Seleph River in 1190. Adolf Hitler knew these things about Barbarossa. Among the books he borrowed from a private library there was a biography of the Hohenstaufen ruler recording these facts which, indeed, were common knowledge to any patriotic schoolboy interested in German medieval history.[158]

Hitler was pathologically afraid of water and had nightmares about loss of breath, strangulation, and drowning. The words he used in announcing the invasion of Russia are therefore worth remembering. "The world," he had said, *will hold its breath.*" When Adolf Hitler held his breath and counted anxiously to ten while his valet tied his tie, he was, on one level, symbolically enacting suicide and self-destruction.[159]

At first the invasion went so well that Hitler's Ministry of Propaganda announced in triumph, "In seven short days, the Führer's offensive has smashed the Red Army to splinters . . . the eastern continent lies, like a limp virgin, in the mighty arms of the German Mars." It did indeed look as if the Soviet Union would have to capitulate, as Hitler's troops battled into the very suburbs of Moscow and as his soldiers, like Napoleon's, saw through their field glasses the gilded towers of the Kremlin against the darkening sky.

That Moscow never fell is to be credited to the heroism of Soviet defenders, but also to Hitler's self-defeating mistakes. Instead of concentrating his forces for the drive on the capital, Hitler suddenly insisted on weakening that drive disastrously by splitting his armies. Against the advice of his generals, he insisted upon swinging south with half his forces into the Ukraine. Then, when the Ukrainians, with their long history of independence and hatred of Stalin's police state, welcomed Hitler's troops with shouts of joy and offered alliance, Hitler ordered their leaders shot and their people enslaved. It was, one historian of the war has written, "one of the most colossal errors" of Hitler's career. Moscow was also saved by Russia's most historic field commander—General Winter. When the temperatures during the first week of December dropped below zero, German soldiers froze by the thousands because, thanks to Hitler's personal orders, no winter clothing had been issued. The boots of his soldiers were fitted so precisely that they permitted the wearing of only one pair of light socks.[160]

Throughout Operation Barbarossa, Hitler continued to make strange decisions. Incredibly, for example, he left an entire German army behind in the Crimea, saying that it could not possibly be withdrawn, for to do so might adversely affect the overall political situation in Turkey. Later in the war, an army group was left in the Baltic area because, Hitler explained, he wanted to show the Swedes that he was still a power in the Baltic.[161] Looking at these and other self-defeating decisions of the Russian campaign, a German authority on Hitler's military leadership asked, "What was going on in the head of this man. . . ?"[162]

The question must be broadened beyond Hitler's separate tactical and strategic blunders, for the entire enterprise was basically irrational. Consider the awful and unnecessary gamble he took in attacking so cooperative and powerful an ally. If he lost the military campaign, the whole war was lost; even if he "won" and defeated some of the Red armies in Western Russia, the war was far from over. For he would have been sucked ever further eastward, while England, aided by America, still pounded him from the air. The two-front war he had created would continue. Why take these risks at all? Was it not more rational to remain at peace with his ally and co-conspirator? Why did he not simply consolidate the vast land areas he had attained through the secret protocols of the Nazi-Soviet Pact and his own conquests, the European continent stretching from the English Channel to central Poland which he already held in thrall?

Reason, it seems, did not dictate Hitler's Eastern policy.

WAR ON THE UNITED STATES

In the midst of catastrophic failures on the Russian front, Hitler on 11 December 1941 took the initiative to declare war on the United States, the greatest industrial power on earth.

Immediately after the war, the State Department sent a delegation of specialists to Germany to interrogate Nazi leaders about Hitler and his conduct of the war. Neither members of the commission themselves nor top German officials of the army and Foreign Office could give an adequate explanation for Hitler's decision. The leader of the mission reported: "We found the most baffling question in the whole Nazi story to be the prompt German declaration of war on the United States."[163] Years later, an American historian writing an account of Nazi-American relations recognized the same problem and acknowledged that he too could give no satisfactory answer:

This declaration [of war on the United States] . . . has never been satisfactorily explained. It was indeed contrary to everything which Hitler had practiced and preached about German foreign policy in general and the United States in particular from the early days in

Munich to the final hours in Berlin. . . . His reasons for declaring war are not entirely clear.[164]

Another diplomatic historian agrees: "The underlying logic of the Führer's policy towards the United States defies analysis . . . it was an irrational act. . . . By the declaration of war, Germany lost finally and irrevocably all hope of winning the war against the Soviet Union." [165]

Since the rational mind recoils from mysteries, rational explanations have been provided. First, Hitler declared war on America, it is said, because he held the country in contempt and was convinced that it presented him with no military problem. There is some evidence to support this view. Hitler told Mussolini that American armament statistics were "lies pure and simple." To General Halder he said that American military power was "one big bluff," and concluded roundly that the United States was "incapable of conducting war." Hitler's racial theory also led him to the conclusion that America was "half-Judaized, half-Negrified . . . Americans have the brains of a hen." [166]

But Hitler also flatly contradicted his own denigration of America. His split way of viewing things permitted him to argue that because of its Nordic stock Americans were a superior people—they were "unbelievably clever." He concluded that "compared to the old Europe . . . America emerges as a young, racially select peple." He told Hanfstaengl that the key reason Germany lost World War I was because of the entry of the United States, and "that must never happen again." [167]

Whatever else Hitler said about America's decadence and incapacity to wage war, his orders to commanders of the German Navy and Luftwaffe showed respect and fear of U.S. power. The orders were clear: America was not to be antagonized. All naval and air incidents in the Atlantic must be avoided to keep America out of the war. When naval leaders protested that lend-lease supplies were hurting Germany, Hitler was adamant. As late as November 1941 he said that "under no circumstances should Germany risk American entry into the war." His orders were not to be changed even if the Neutrality Acts were repealed. He was particularly concerned lest Germany become involved in fighting the United States and the Soviet Union simultaneously. Again and again he repeated that there should be no war with America until the Soviet Union had surrendered. These were the standing orders until the very day of the Japanese attack on Pearl Harbor.[168] Hitler also gave the German press repeated instructions not to offend Americans. In particular, the press was to stop attacking its favorite targets, the American president and his wife. One such order reads, "Even statements of Mrs. Roosevelt are not to be mentioned." [169]

Second, it has been suggested that Hitler declared war on America out of loyalty to his Japanese ally and in fulfillment of his treaty obligations. But Hitler's concept of honor was not one of his more conspicuous virtues. Further, the Tripartite Pact with Japan and Italy of 1940 was purely defensive; there was no obligation whatever for Germany to go to war *unless America attacked Japan*. That is not what happened at Pearl Harbor. The Tripartite Pact remained, as one historian has described it, a "Hollow Alliance" torn by suspicion and mutual distrust. After Hitler had caused his ally to lose face by refusing to inform the Japanese about Barbarossa, Japan had attacked America without Hitler's knowledge and independent of his support. Hitler was completely surprised and unprepared for Pearl Harbor. He did not declare war on the United States because he felt bound by a treaty.[170]

It is true that during the first week of December (at precisely the time when his attack on Russia was in serious trouble) he made verbal promises to join Japan in war against the United States, and he drew up a draft treaty to that effect. It is said that he did so because he desperately wanted Japan to attack the Soviet Union from the rear. But this draft treaty of 5 December *makes no mention whatever* of Japanese help in fighting Russia.[171] Nor did the Japanese give any verbal promises of such help. As Rich has noted, "Once Japan had committed itself to war with the United States . . . Hitler might surely have found excuses to procrastinate about fulfilling his pledge to join Japan in that war. At the very least he might have demanded Japanese support against Russia in return for German support against America, if only a promise to stop American shipments to Russia via Vladivostok." [172] But Hitler did nothing of the kind. With absolutely no assurance of help from his ally, and fully aware that no treaty required him to do so, he personally decided to declare war on America.[173]

A third explanation has been given. It is said that Hitler declared war in December 1941 because he believed that sooner or later America would attack, and he wanted to fight at the most propitious time. It is true that he harbored suspicions of a Jewish plot, and believed that "Roosevelt, urged on by Jewry, [had] already quite resolved to go to war and annihilate National Socialism." [174] But the timing of Hitler's declaration of war on America was very peculiar indeed. The Russian problem was not only unsolved, it was becoming downright menacing. During the first week of December, a member of the German Operational Staff noted that "the Red Army almost overnight snatched the initiative all along the Front and thus administered to German Supreme Headquarters a series of shocks such as it had never known before." On 6 December 1941 the Red Army under Marshal Georgi Zhukov started a counteroffensive west of Moscow with 100 fresh divisions which Hitler had insisted did not exist. The Germans were hurled back amid enormous losses in men and material. "In Hitler's headquarters," Domarus reported, "there spread a feeling that the end of the world [*Weltuntergangsstimmung*] had come." An adjutant recorded, "Everything indicates that the goals of the campaign cannot be reached . . ."; Field Marshal Keitel, chief of the High Command, wanted to commit suicide; Hitler sat gloomily staring off into space.[175]

The news was not much better in North Africa, where the British were pushing Rommel back to his original starting point. During this first fortnight in December, headquarters was additionally depressed by a cold wave that swept the Eastern Front: "Temperatures of −30 [to] −35 degrees centigrade were paralyzing the troops and making weapons unusable and reports kept coming in that the danger of severe defeat was . . . limitless." [176]

The timing of the declaration thus took place amid clear and ominous signs of Hitler's military failure. After insisting for months that he would never provoke America, he suddenly declared war at a time when he could least afford so powerful an enemy. *Why had he done it?* It was a personal decision about which he had informed neither the Foreign Office, nor the Wehrmacht. "As a result," Deputy Operations Chief Warlimont wrote, "we were now faced with a war on two fronts in the most serious conceivable form."

It is now clear from the testimony of German Army and Navy and the chief of the Wehrmacht Operations Staff (General Jodl) that there were *no plans whatever for war against the United States.*

General Warlimont quotes a conversation with his superior which must be considered among the most remarkable in the annals of the Prussian-German Army on the eve of war:

Jodl: The Staff must now examine where the United States is most likely to employ the bulk of her forces initially, the Far East or Europe. We cannot take further decisions until that has been clarified.

Warlimont: Agreed. This examination is obviously necessary, but so far, we have never considered a war against the United States and so have no data on which to base this examination; we can therefore hardly undertake this job just like that.

Jodl: See what you can do. When we get back tomorrow we will talk about this in more detail.

As Warlimont commented laconically, "This and no more was the beginning for our headquarters of German strategy against America. . . ." [177] In an interview after the war, Field Marshal Göring, commander of the Luftwaffe, also confessed his ignorance of Hitler's declaration and concluded, quite rightly, that his Führer must have acted "impulsively." [178]

Certainly the Nazis welcomed the Japanese attack on America and were very pleased indeed to see the Arsenal of Democracy attacked from the rear. But that had already been achieved by Pearl Harbor, without any commitment on Hitler's part. As General Jodl commented after the war, "We should have preferred a new and powerful ally without a new and powerful enemy." [179]

Hitler's declaration of war was of very considerable political help to President Roosevelt. After the Japanese attack on Pearl Harbor, Roosevelt was afraid that the American people would demand a concentration of military forces in the Pacific and thus force a complete revamping of the priority that Roosevelt was giving to the European theater. James MacGregor Burns has emphasized Roosevelt's problem: "Was it possible, after all Washington's elaborate efforts to fight first in Europe, with only a holding action in the Pacific, that the United States would be left with only a war in the Far East? . . ." [180]

A formal German declaration of war on America would solve President Roosevelt's dilemma and clear the political air. Hitler, who had never declared war formally on any other country, obliged Roosevelt now. In doing so, he cut the ground from under the president's political opponents. For after Hitler had declared war on America, even the most vociferous "noninterventionist" could hardly object to sending all-out aid to our European comrades in arms. Proof of how much Hitler had helped Roosevelt came on the very day of Hitler's declaration. When, on 11 December, the president asked Congress to recognize that a state of war existed between the United States and Germany, not one member of Congress voted against a resolution which, had it been taken a few days earlier, almost surely would have failed. It is, of course, quite possible that the United States could have been drawn into war against Hitler at some future time anyway. We shall never know. We do know that "the Führer's initiative gave immeasurable aid and comfort to his opponents and victims." [181]

These, then, are the "rational" explanations that have been given for Hitler's self-defeating decision to declare war on America: he had a confused conception of the United States; he wanted to help his Japanese ally; he preferred to attack America before being attacked. But the reasons, somehow, do not add up. Both in retrospect and at the time, judged in either military or political terms, it was an unnecessary and irrational act which benefited his enemies far more than it helped him. "Hitler had not only blundered," one authority has concluded, "he had ruined his own cause." The Führer himself ruefully admitted that there was no logic for what he had done. "War with the United States," he said, "was a tragedy and illogical." [182]

We must agree with him. Why, then, had he done it?

It would be gratifying, at the end of this discussion, if we could now show how easily psychohistory can solve a problem that has baffled conventional historians. But it is not at all clear that it can. For again we encounter problems of human motivation which no historian can feel confident about solving. Psychology can help us here, but that is all it can do. For psychohistory cannot supplant traditional history; it can only supplement it by adding depth to our understanding of historical personalities. And even with its help, we may doubt that we shall ever be able to "explain satisfactorily," fully, and finally why it was that Hitler did what he did.

The question, ultimately, is unanswerable. But let us not despair.

We can respond to it the way all historians—and psychoanalysts—must respond when asked to explain the motivations of man: we can venture some cautious guesses.

Let us guess first that both Hitler and the historians are correct: his declaration of war on America (like many of his acts) cannot be understood by logic and common sense. It was indeed "an irrational act." But that assertion scarcely concludes the matter. Rather than terminating discussion, it leaves us with the problem of trying to find reasons for his irrational behaviour. It is my guess that Hitler's fateful decision was influenced by three things: his lifelong difficulty with personal identification; his unconscious desire for defeat; and his irrational belief that ultimate triumph lay in total destruction.

Personal pride and prestige, it has often been asserted, were reasons why Hitler declared war on America. Among all the Nazi leaders interviewed after the war, "the answer uniformly obtained was that Hitler had acted from motives of prestige." He wanted to declare war on Roosevelt before Roosevelt could get America to declare war on him.[183]

"Prestige" certainly was involved. But it went far deeper than a mere desire to upstage FDR. This decision cut to the very core of Hitler's being, for his identity as a person was being threatened on the Eastern Front by the "subhuman Slavs" and "Bolshevized Jews" who led the Red Army. This scum was actually defeating him! His self-image as an invincible, masculine, all-conquering Führer was dissolving before his eyes. That must never be allowed to happen. He would show *them* —that is, he would show himself. He would prove to himself that he still existed as the invincible myth-person he had created. Since he had condemned himself to military infallibility as the "Greatest Field Commander of All Time," he must strike a new and even more commanding image; he must conquer an even more unconquerable foe than Russia. He would destroy America.

This interpretation of Hitler's motivation, based partly on Erikson's formulation of identity crises, would stress that throughout his life Adolf Hitler was plagued by problems of identity diffusion. He worried continually about "finding" himself as a person (see Chapter 3, p. 173, Chapter 5, p. 357). Such people, Erikson has shown, have recurrent and intense feelings of anxiety about their very existence. When they act in ways which seem totally irrational, even dangerous to themselves, they do so because they are trying to resolve the question of who they really are; they are reaffirming that they really do exist as the person they want to be. Hence, when they are confronted by a crisis situation in which they feel their psychological existence threatened, they may provoke encounters that bring an even more acute crisis in order to reassure themselves. These self-imposed crises may actually be more self-destructive than self-affirming, but they are covertly intended to test and reaffirm precariously held feelings of personal identity which seem to be slipping away.

From Private Neurosis to Public Policy

Thus, when Hitler's existence as a person was threatened on the Eastern Front during the first weeks of December 1941, it was psychologically imperative for him at that time to take a prompt and even greater risk. "It would be exactly then," an Eriksonian psychiatrist has suggested, "that a character such as Hitler would be most stirred to provoke a crisis in order to reassert his very existence. He would try to do so by making *direct* contact with a very powerful counterforce, such as the United States. In fact, the stronger the counterforce the better, in order to heighten his sense of contact, of being in touch, and thus to counteract the terrifying feeling that his 'self' was being dissolved." [184]

Another psychological interpretation of Hitler's irrational action also seems possible: he declared war on America not so much to test and confirm his own identity as to respond to an unconscious urge for self-destruction. Hitler—like other borderlines—thought in totalities. He simply could not conceive, he often said, of any alternative between complete victory and absolute catastrophe. He would either be a conquering lion or a sacrificial lamb; if he could not be creator, he would be destroyer.

The moment that Hitler decided he could no longer be a conqueror for Germany and must therefore become its destroyer was a decisive moment in history. It was also a moment that is difficult to pinpoint. Certainly Hitler kept talking about "inevitable victory" long after his reason told him it was not possible. But it seems most likely that he realized, after the first major defeats in Russia in early December 1941, that he could not gain the kind of victory he required. He articulated that conclusion to others sometime later. General Jodl's war diary records that by the turn of the year 1941–1942, Hitler had made it clear to him that "victory could no longer be attained." An authority on Hitler's military strategy puts the date even earlier, saying that by mid-November Hitler realized that victory was "no longer attainable." Certainly he knew it by the time of the Red Army's sweeping winter offensive of 6–7 December 1941.[185] It was an ominous conclusion. For it was at this time that he decided to defeat a different kind of enemy and ordered the massacre of the Jews; it was at this time also, during the first defeats in Russia, that he declared war on America.

He did so, we are speculating, because his deeply split mind saw total defeat as the only alternative left to him. The question now became *how to achieve a catastrophic defeat worthy of his historic greatness.* This seems to have been the problem on his mind when he confided to an intimate, "I have to attain immortality even if the whole German nation perishes in the process." [186]

Hitler's thinking often went back to World War I, an experience that had burned deeply into his mind. As a front-line soldier and racist demagogue after the war, he believed that German defeat had been caused by two things: Jewish traitors and American intervention. Over and over again he told Hanfstaengl: "The only thing that brought our defeat in 1918 was that America entered the war—that and the Jews." [187]

But now—very late in 1941—the Jews were no longer available to provide this kind of explanation. They were, as the horrifying euphemism had it, about to "go up the chimney." Only America could guarantee the *total* destruction of Germany. And it worked out that way.

As America's power was asserted and the Second Front advanced, as the Soviet Union and the United States—the two powerful enemies he had created—closed in on him, his passion for destruction increased. He wanted everything destroyed: not only positions of military value but churches and art galleries, hospitals, nursery schools, farm animals and pets, statistical records, marriage certificates—everything he could think of. On 21 April 1945, for example, he yelled at the startled chief of staff of the Luftwaffe that "the entire leadership of the Luftwaffe is to be hanged immediately." He thought of announcing the shooting of all RAF war prisoners in order to ensure the retaliatory saturation air raids that would level German cities. He thought of giving orders—indeed, he apparently gave them—to kill German soldiers wounded in the war, for they were no longer "useful" to him. [188]

Again, when one asks the obvious question about this planned holocaust, namely *why*, the answers are either very difficult or too easy. "It was because he was evil," it is said, "completely evil." But he had been evil all along—though never completely so. Others have explained his conduct by saying, "He was seized by demons." One must ask, *what kind*? "Well, he was just crazy," it has been asserted by those who agree with the ancient Greeks that "whom the Gods would destroy they first make mad." But *what kind* of madness was his?

Evidence of Hitler's last days—as we shall see—does not indicate that he had become psychotic. He was a physical wreck by April 1945, but he talked coherently enough as he dispensed to his admirers cyanide capsules and autographed pictures of himself. He had not suddenly become "mad" or seized by demons. His behavior during the last months of his life was not an aberration; it was deeply rooted in his early life. It illustrates Erikson's observation that every basic conflict of childhood lives on, in some form, in the adult. The child, Adolf, was the father of this man.

Hitler's desire to punish and destroy was a part of a persistent pattern of his life. We should not try to make the pattern too clear, too neatly assembled. But into it fits, somewhere, the childhood conviction that evil had been done to him; he would do evil in return. Into it belongs the searing memory of being beaten and hurt and unable to get revenge; he would get it now. Very early in his life he had learned to mistrust; he would now destroy those who had abandoned him. He had been made to feel inadequate and guilty; he would show them all that he had power—if no longer to conquer and create, then to destroy. He was still omnipotent; he could order the death of a nation.

From Private Neurosis to Public Policy

There was, we have also been suggesting, another pattern in his life: the unconscious impulse to punish himself and to fail. Very often he had tried to direct that impulse away from himself by punishing others. The juxtaposition of two decisions he made within two days in December 1941 suggests a link connecting punishment of self with punishment of others. On 11 December he had assured himself of defeat by declaring war on the United States while Russia was attacking him; on the next day, 12 December, he set forth a decree designed to inflict upon others the most terrifying punishment he could imagine. He called it the *Nacht und Nebel* decree. Literally it meant "Night and Fog." And that meant that any person who was deemed guilty of less than total loyalty to him could be arrested without charge, that no relative would be informed of the prisoner's disappearance, that his whereabouts would never be learned—the person was to disappear into perpetual night and fog. But even that was not enough. He had to project in a different way: he would destroy *all* Germans. For all Germany was guilty and unworthy. Thus he cried out: "Germany is not worthy of me [*meiner nicht würdig*]; let her perish." [189]

But what did these words really mean? In destroying Germany he was, in a sense, destroying himself, for as he had so often said, "*Ich bin das deutsche Volk!*" But all his life he had also identified Germany with his mother. Is it possible that he was destroying the Motherland now because she was deserting him, just as his mother, Klara, had abandoned him when he was little and allowed his father to punish him? "Let her perish." Was this punishment for his mother? Or was it something else?

He had tried to blame the German people for his own failure and guilt. He had repeated over and over again that "they" were not worthy of him; he had killed them by the millions. But the haunting fear could not be exorcised. Perhaps, after all, he was not worthy of them—*let him perish*. Perhaps. At any rate, that is what he was about to do, thus fulfilling the promise he had made in a dozen moments of despair: he would kill himself.

TRIUMPH THROUGH SELF-DESTRUCTION

> Our Führer, Adolf Hitler, fighting to the last breath against Bolshevism, fell for Germany this afternoon. . . .
> —German radio announcement.
> 1 May 1945

During his last days, members of Hitler's entourage were shocked to discover that their once indomitable Führer had become a trembling, broken old man, his once immaculate uniform now flecked with sputum and stained by sweat, vegetable soup, and chocolate-covered cherries. Hitler was aware of his physical condition and even called attention to it in order to demonstrate once again how hard and cold he really was, and how much he resembled his hero, Frederick the Great. He delivered his last speech to his *Gauleiter* on 24 February 1945, while sitting at a table; his left hand shook so violently that he could not control it. After an hour and a half of turgid oratory, he concluded with these words:

> As you see, I am at the moment not in the best of physical condition. My left arm trembles. . . . I hope it doesn't go into my head so that I also waggle my head. Anyway, come what may, my heart remains *ice-cold*. . . . Now for the first time, I understand Frederick the Great so completely who, after the end of his military campaigns, came back home a sick and broken man. . . . Just as Frederick the Great lived out his last years with bowed upper body and plagued by palsy and all other possible sufferings, so this war has also left its deep marks on me.[190]

Although several writers have insisted that Hitler's physical decline was accompanied by a remarkable psychological transformation, the evidence shows no radical departure from previous patterns, but rather reinforcement and intensification of lifelong personality traits and habits. Even in the last months, when his physical condition deteriorated rapidly, we note an intensification rather than a change of behavior patterns. As an infant, he had learned to mistrust people; now he said that he could trust no one except his dog—and, perhaps, Eva Braun. Both as child and man he had liked to stay up very late at night; now, in the spring of 1945, he often did not go to bed before six or seven o'clock in the morning. As an adolescent he had wanted to tear down buildings and build them anew; destruction and reconstruction now became a mania with him. He had always liked to talk about the same things; now he "told the same stories at lunch, dinner, and supper and at nighttime tea." At least once a day, he would say, word-for-word: "That animal, Blondi, woke me up again this morning. . . . When I asked her 'Do you need to do a business?' she put her tail between her legs and crawled back to her corner. She is certainly a clever animal." Or he would repeat daily: "Look, my hand is getting better. The trembling is not so bad—I can hold it completely still." He had always been a bore in private conversation, but now his monologues grew longer and duller. Increased volubility was also shown in his military briefings (*Lagebesprechungen*). In 1942 the average length of the briefings recorded each day by stenographers was 89 pages of typescript. As defeats mounted, so did Hitler's oral aggression. By the spring of 1945 the average number of daily pages had grown to 150.[191]

He had always been inordinately fond of sweets and the childhood delights of candy and cakes, but now, after his *Lagebesprechungen*, at about 6:00 A.M. he would "lie back fully exhausted, apathetically filled only with the thought that soon would come his favorite meal of the day: chocolate and cakes. . . . Whereas in earlier days he ate at most three pieces, he now had his plate heaped high three times. . . . He said that he didn't eat much for supper, so that he could eat more cakes. While he greedily satisfied his craving . . . by way of apology he always observed that he simply couldn't understand anybody who did not like to eat sweets."

Throughout his life he had expressed affection for animals; now he took his greatest pleasures in one of Blondi's pups, whom he called "Wolf." After the two-hour morning tea, he would personally go to the kennel in the bunker and fetch the little dog that no one else was allowed to touch. "He stroked the animal interminably, all the while sweetly repeating his name, Wolf." [192]

Hitler had always been both cruel and kind, thoughtful and inconsiderate of others; now he heaped flattery on his secretaries and, upon a whim, ordered people to risk their lives flying into Berlin so that he could twaddle with them about trivia. He had often swung between euphoric expectation and deep despair. He continued to do so. When he heard that the U.S. and Soviet troops had met, historically, at the Elbe River on 26 April 1945, he seemed

> as if electrified. His eyes flashed again. He leaned back and cried "Gentlemen, that is another clear proof of the disunity of our enemies! Wouldn't the German people and history stamp me as a criminal if I signed peace today . . . and tomorrow . . . our enemy became disunited. . . . Cannot daily, yes hourly, the battle between the Bolsheviks and the Anglo-Saxons begin?" [193]

Psychologically, it is a revealing statement. All will yet be saved, he is saying, all will be back in its proper order and brought together, as soon as something *out there* splits apart.[194]

But the saving battle never took place. Instead, by 27 April, the Red Army under Marshals Zhukov and Koniev had completely surrounded Berlin with 2,500,000 well-equipped and battle-tough men, 42,000 artillery pieces, 6,250 tanks, 7,560 airplanes. To oppose them, Hitler had available 44,600 soldiers, 42,500 old men in home-guard units, and 3,500 boys of the *Hitlerjugend* ranging from 12 to 16 years of age. There was one rifle for every two defenders. On that day, Hitler leaned back from his military maps, smiled confidently, and contemplated glorious new conquests. "When I get this thing solved," he said, "we must see to it that we get back all those oil fields." [195]

Hitler's lust for killing reached its apogee just before his own death in 1945; but he had always enjoyed contemplating the death of others. During his abortive coup of 1923, he had promised that as leader of a new Germany he would hang on the highest gallows "all the November Criminals and arch-traitors" of the Weimar Republic. In a speech made at his Party rally in Nuremberg in 1929 he proclaimed that ideally 70 to 80 percent of the babies born in Germany every year should be killed off in order to strengthen the blood line.[196] He had promised in 1932 that when he came to power, "heads will roll in the sand." In 1934 he ordered the "Blood Purge" which killed hundreds of people he suspected of personal disloyalty. Prior to the war he told a British diplomat that the best way to deal with political opponents was to shoot them in groups of 12; if that was unsuccessful, they should be shot in groups of 200. In 1935 he had planned a sweeping "euthanasia" program to kill off the physically and mentally defective. His plan was implemented, in 1939, with instructions that action "should cover any category of 'unworthy' persons." Beginning with patients in mental institutions, the program was later extended to include senile and tubercular patients and those with birth defects. Within five years, some 100,000 people were killed.[197]

In 1945 he sought the destruction of Germany in the greatest planned *Götterdämmerung* of history. But had he not foretold even that? Was that the meaning of a curious and little-noted sentence of a speech he made in 1932, in the electoral district of Lippe, before he became chancellor? It was then that he uttered strange words which later events would make ominous. "We are the last people," he said, "who will make history in Germany. [*Die letzten, die in Deutschland Geschichte machen, sind wir.*]"   What do these words mean? Is it not conceivable that Hitler, from the very beginning—perhaps unconsciously—had been working for the total destruction of Germany? [198]

His mind, to the very end, was no more irrational—or rational—than it had ever been. Reports of his staff conferences from December 1944 through 27 April 1945 show a familiar pattern: an incredible memory for detail used both as a crutch and as a weapon against those who disagreed with him; long disquisitions on his career as a soldier in World War I and the "battle years" after the war; a compulsive need to dominate every conversation. On 28 December 1944, to take one example, in a conference with his generals, he delivered a monologue which went on for the equivalent of eight single-spaced, typewritten pages. The speech was as coherent as any of its predecessors.[199]

Prior to destroying himself, Hitler performed one of the genuinely kind acts of his life. He married Eva Braun, the woman who had loved him devotedly for years and who had risked death to be with him at the end. Hitler now granted her most cherished wish: to commit suicide with her bridegroom. There was a minor contretemps at the wedding, which was held between one and three o'clock on the morning of 29 April. The ceremony was performed by a hastily summoned city official who was so flustered by the honor that he misspelled his own name on the wedding certificate. The name was Wagner.[200]

After the wedding, Hitler withdrew with a secretary, Frau Junge, to dictate the personal will and political testament which would blame the war and all the evils of mankind upon "the universal poisoner of all peoples, international Jewry." The two documents are quintessential Hitler. The style, phraseology, content, and thought processes could have come from almost any one of his speeches or conversations of the preceding decade.[201]

Having signed these historic documents, Hitler returned to his bride, and together they planned their funeral.

The way Hitler died has become one of the most disputed questions about his life. For many years it was assumed that the problem had been solved by Hugh Trevor-Roper, an Oxford historian who, as an officer in British Intelligence, was charged in 1945 with the task of finding out exactly what had happened to the Führer. Trevor-Roper interviewed many of the survivors of Hitler's air raid bunker and wrote his report in 1946. Published the following year, Trevor-Roper's little book must still be considered a masterpiece of historical literature, combining all the excitement of a mystery thriller with the scholarship of a distinguished historian who is also a master of English prose.

In solving this mystery, however, the author was confronted by two formidable obstacles: the body of the victim had not been found, and key witnesses at the death scene were missing. Goebbels and his family were dead, as was Ludwig Stumpfegger, the SS physician who had pronounced his Führer dead and helped to burn him. Presumed dead and certainly missing was Martin Bormann, the immensely knowledgeable and influential private secretary to Hitler and head of the Party Chancellery. Also unavailable for interviews were Hitler's personal adjutant, Otto Günsche, and his valet, Heinz Linge, both of whom had been captured by the Soviets in May 1945.

Nevertheless, by careful use of hearsay testimony and circumstantial evidence, Trevor-Roper reconstructed a version of Hitler's death that was so persuasive it was accepted by most subsequent historians —including the writer of these lines. Trevor-Roper concluded that Hitler had entered his sitting room in the air raid shelter with his new bride at about 3:30 on the afternoon of 30 April 1945; that *he had killed himself by a shot through his mouth*; that Eva Braun-Hitler had died of self-administered cyanide poisoning; that Linge and others had wrapped the bodies in blankets, and carried them up to the Chancellery courtyard, where they were burned with 180 liters of petrol for some two-and-a-half hours; and that *"these bones have never been found."* [202]

If Trevor-Roper's eminently readable and persuasive account were all we had to go on, the mystery of Hitler's death would be solved. There would be, as Lord Tedder wrote in his foreword to the book, "no possibility of distortion in this case." Since its publication, however, new testimony has appeared to muddy the issue and to remind us anew that clarity—if not accuracy—in history is often achieved more by a paucity of evidence than by a plenitude.

In 1950, for example, Erich Kempka, Hitler's chauffeur, the man who was ordered to collect the petrol and to destroy Hitler's body, published his account of the event in a book graphically entitled *Ich habe Adolf Hitler verbrannt* (I Cremated Adolf Hitler). He reported that he had totally destroyed the bodies by burning them with "several hundred liters" of petrol from two o'clock in the afternoon until 7:30 in the evening. In a previous report to American journalists Kempka had said that "it was obvious Eva Braun had shot herself" with her 6.35 pistol, and that he and Günsche had rolled up the blood-soaked carpet "pistols and all and later in the day burned it." [203]

Others who helped burn the bodies agreed with the chauffeur. One aide testified that "I saw his body burn to ashes. . . ." Another is reported to have told a friend that the body was incinerated, and spoke of the "horrible charred remains of Hitler's head." [204]

But Hitler's personal pilot, Hans Baur, also present at the scene, was not at all sure that Hitler's wishes had actually been carried out. In an interview in 1971 he confessed, "If I had known that Kempka had only been able to collect 180 liters of petrol to burn both the Führer and his wife, I would have seen to it that he was cremated in one of our large coke ovens." Baur also said that he had been told directly by Goebbels that Hitler had been shot not through the mouth but through the temple.[205]

In an interview after the war, Frau Traudl Junge remembered that Hitler had distrusted the potency of the cyanide pills Heinrich Himmler had distributed in the bunker, and that he had asked apprehensively, "But who would give me the *coup de grâce* if I didn't kill myself?"

Frau Junge also said that Hitler had *not* been shot through the mouth: "Blood flowed onto his uniform from a small hole in his right temple." She claimed that his 7.65 Walther pistol lay at his feet with one shot fired; that Eva Braun had been killed by cyanide and that her smaller pistol (the Walther 6.35) lay on a table "still completely loaded" near a pink scarf; that the bodies had been placed in a shallow trench near a cement mixer and burned for about three hours.[206]

Other testimony showing similar conflicts has also surfaced. But three developments of major importance have taken place since Trevor-Roper wrote his account. First, in 1955 a star witness, Hitler's faithful valet Heinz Linge, returned after a decade spent in a Russian prisoner-of-war camp. Second, there was published the report of a woman who —as a kind of Russian counterpart to Trevor-Roper—had been a member of the Soviet commission charged with finding out what actually happened to Hitler. Third, the long-missing corpus delicti suddenly appeared—or at least the Soviets in 1968 permitted the publication of the autopsy report which Red Army pathologists had performed on Hitler's body on 8 May 1945 in a hospital in Buch near Berlin.

Upon his return to Germany in 1955, Heinz Linge, who was among the last to see Hitler alive and the first to see him dead, told the following story. The Führer, whom he had served night and day for more than a decade, had instructed him on 30 April 1945 to burn all his personal effects wih one exception: his portrait of Frederick the Great was to be smuggled out of the bunker and hidden in Bavaria. Hitler said he would kill himself, and it was up to Linge and others in the SS to make sure that his body was burned "without a trace." After saying farewell, Hitler and his bride entered the Führer's small living room in the air raid shelter. Linge had not heard a shot because, he admitted, he had been so overcome with emotion that he had temporarily panicked and had run up the steps. But he recovered himself and returned. Not wishing to enter the death room alone, he asked Martin Bormann to accompany him. When they entered, they saw Hitler sitting at the right side of a sofa (Linge's left as he entered). Hitler's hands were either resting on his knees or in his lap. His head had flopped over the right arm of the sofa. A hole "the size of a German silver mark" showed on his right temple, and a trickle of blood was still dripping onto the carpet. In the left temple was a hole from which no blood came.

Linge was not sure about some important details. In the near-trauma of seeing his Führer dead, he did not notice which of two pistols had been fired, and he has given two different accounts of their location at the death scene. In a newspaper story, he said that Hitler's 7.65 Walther lay on the floor, with the 6.35 "a meter or so away"; in an interview a decade later he thought that the larger pistol had been on the table in front of the sofa, and the smaller one under it. But he distinctly remembered smelling gunpowder in the room. He admitted that he was experiencing "mental confusion" at the time and could not be sure exactly what happened. He assumed, however, that Hitler had shot himself through the left temple with his own pistol. He remembered clearly that Eva Braun-Hitler had been found seated on the sofa at Hitler's left. She had definitely taken cyanide; there were no bullet wounds on her body.[207]

Linge spread a gray army blanket over Hitler's body, covering the bloody head; then he and three other SS men carried their Führer and his bride up to the courtyard for burning. They placed the corpses in a small crater in the ground, poured petrol on them, and tried to burn them amid the crash of Red Army artillery shells. Because the bodies could not be thoroughly destroyed, Bormann ordered them buried. They were thrown in a shallow hole and covered with sand, broken stone, and shattered bits of wood. "It was more rubbish than earth." [208] The next day Linge tried to escape from the bunker but was taken prisoner by the Red Army.

Meanwhile, during the first days of May 1945, a Soviet search party led by Lieutenant Ivan Klimenko was following orders to find the Fascist dictator, dead or alive. Attached to the group was a young woman, Mrs. Elena Rzhevskaia, who served as a German-language interpreter for the search party. In 1967 she recorded her experiences in a Russian-language publication, *Znamia* (The Banner).

On 4 May 1945, she recalled, a Soviet soldier by the name of Ivan Dmitrievich Churekov noticed a small crater to the left of the entrance to the Führer Bunker as he stood facing it. His attention was caught by something that looked like the edge of a gray blanket. He began digging and soon found the half-charred bodies of a man and a woman. He called an officer and together with two comrades they brought the stinking corpses to the surface. At first Klimenko did not pay much attention to the bodies, because he believed he had already found Hitler—he was the dead man with a mustache in a picture taken 3 May, which showed him lying amid the marble wreckage of the Reichs-chancellery with a picture propped against his chest. It was only when Hitler's cook, Wilhelm Lange, and the motor pool director, Karl Schnei-der, told him that the picture definitely was not that of Hitler that Kli-menko looked more carefully at the two bodies found on 4 May.*

Mrs. Rzhevskaia had heard that an autopsy had been performed, but she had not attended the operation; she understood the doctors had reported that Hitler had died by cyanide poisoning. She was directly involved in establishing the fact that the body found by the Red soldiers was indeed that of Adolf Hitler. On 9 May she and a Soviet colonel called on Hitler's dentist, Dr. Hugo Blaschke. But he had already fled to Berchtesgaden. Instead, they interviewed Fräulein Käthe Heuser-mann, Blaschke's assistant, who showed the Russians X rays of Hitler's teeth and several gold crowns ready to be placed in the Führer's mouth. The Russians asked her to describe Hitler's teeth from memory and provide a sketch. After studying the X rays and sketches which she provided, Red Army medical specialists later questioned her again, and only then showed her Hitler's teeth—which they had brought with them in a small, cheap jewel case. Fräulein Heusermann identi-fied them at once as Hitler's. The same procedure was followed with Fritz Echtmann, the dental technician who had actually made the bridges and crowns for Hitler's mouth. The result was the same. He recognized them as being Hitler's teeth. Mrs. Rzhevskaia concluded, "Investigation was completed. Hitler's teeth, the irrefutable proof of his death, and all of the documents were dispatched to Moscow." [209]

In 1968 the Soviet government authorized the publication, first in German and later in English, of the findings of the autopsy performed on the bodies of Adolf Hitler, Eva Braun, and others found hastily buried in the Reichschancellery courtyard. As we have noted, the au-topsy was performed on 8 May 1945 by leading pathologists of the Red Army.

The post-mortem examination states that Hitler's corpse was badly damaged by fire; that the skin was completely gone from the face and much of the body; that the top of the skull was missing and the brain

* In June 1965, *Der Spiegel* published the picture over the caption "False Body of Hitler." Robert Payne, in his biography published in 1973, accepted the photo as genuine and included it in his book to illustrate an inventive passage he wrote describing Hitler's death: "There was just time enough for someone to take a flashbulb photograph of the dead Hitler, holding his mother's picture against his chest. . . ." See Payne, *The Life and Death of Adolf Hitler* (New York, 1973), 568.

cavity visible; that the lower cheekbones and upper and lower jaws were preserved; that glass splinters from the wall and bottom of a thin-walled ampule were found in the mouth; that the scrotal sac was burned but intact and the left testicle missing (see Chapter 3, pp. 150–151). They determined that "no visible signs of severe lethal injuries or illnesses could be detected." There was a distinct smell of bitter almonds emanating from the body; forensic chemical tests of internal organs established the presence of cyanide. The commission of Soviet doctors concluded that death was caused by poisoning with cyanide compounds.

The Soviet journalist who published the official autopsy report asked the chief of the Medical Commission specifically about the presence or absence of a pistol wound. Dr. Shkaravski replied:

> The fact of the poisoning is incontrovertibly established. No matter what is asserted today, our Commission could not detect any trace of a gunshot on May 8, 1945. Hitler poisoned himself.

The Soviet author was greatly relieved by this statement, for it supported his conviction that the fascist dictator had sought a coward's death through poisoning rather than shooting himself "like a man." [210]

Since the facts of Hitler's death are so confusing, how are we to tell what happened in his Berlin bunker on the afternoon of 30 April 1945?

It is a truism of history—as it is of traffic accidents, divorce courts, and judgments about pass interference on football fields—that eyewitnesses give conflicting testimony. But the reconstruction of this historical event is further complicated by unusual circumstances. Everyone who cowered in the air raid shelter that day was frightened to the point of hysteria by the Red Army. One thought spread trauma: the Russians are coming! Soviet artillery had already zeroed in on the Chancellery and was shaking the bunker; advance platoons of the Red Army were within a few blocks of the shelter. Hitler's entourage was confronted by an awful choice: to stay and be captured and, they believed, tortured or raped and killed; or try to "escape" to the blazing hell of a city that was now a battlefield, there, in all probability, to suffer the same fate.

Furthermore, the man who had just died was no ordinary mortal. Children had prayed to him, women had swooned upon hearing him, soldiers had died whispering his name. To the people in the bunker he was the Messiah. And now this god had killed himself. Small wonder the minds of these witnesses to history were confused and contradictory.

There is another reason why the testimony is conflicting. Witnesses like to believe those facts that support their personal convictions. Thus the Nazis, who had been ordered to carry out their Führer's last command, wanted very much to believe that his body really had been reduced to ashes. Hence the chauffeur—consciously or unconsciously—moved up the time when he said he started to burn the bodies to 2:00 P.M., whereas every other witness sets the time at about 4:00 P.M. The Russians, who wanted Hitler to die by poison, have consistently played down the possibility of a pistol shot, or, like Mrs. Rzhevskaia, have conjectured that the bullet entered Mrs. Hitler's body, not her husband's.

Historians are not immune from the inclination to accept that testimony which supports their own point of view. Hugh Trevor-Roper understandably wants Hitler to have died the way he did in his admirable little book. He therefore scoffs at the Soviet autopsy report and those who take it seriously.[211] Werner Maser has persuaded himself that the body found by the Russians was not Hitler's because he prefers to believe that Hitler was sexually normal. Therefore the cadaver with one missing testicle found by the Russians could not belong to his Hitler.[212] And what about Waite? He is not without his own prejudices. He prefers to think that the Russian autopsy proved Hitler to be a monorchid. He would also like to believe that Hitler was discovered in the death room with his hands folded in his lap. That, however, is a conjecture. Eyewitnesses are not quite sure where Hitler's hands were placed; they may have been resting on his knees. But given Hitler's continual concern about his scrotum and his lifelong habit in moments of tension of covering it protectively with folded hands, it seems likely that *in extremis*, while awaiting death, he would have folded his hands over his crotch. Let us assume that he did. And until new discoveries appear to prove us wrong—as they may very well do—let us accept the evidence of the autopsy and suggest a solution to the problem of how Hitler died: he took poison and then was shot, but not through the mouth.

We are assuming that in planning their deaths, Hitler and his bride agreed to take cyanide together. Capsules had been prepared for them, and cyanide was said to be virtually instantaneous and very sure. That they both swallowed cyanide is attested by the autopsy.

How then justify and explain the pistol shot? One of the few points of agreement among many witnesses is that a shot was fired in the death room. Everyone except Linge heard a shot, and gunpowder was smelled by everyone entering the room. But why a pistol shot at all when Hitler and his bride already had available lethal doses of cyanide? The answer must lie in Hitler's psyche. *He could not trust people* —he never could.

In particular, he could no longer trust Heinrich Himmler, the man who had supplied the cyanide capsules, for this man, "*Der treue Heinrich*" as Hitler had called him in a better day, was now a traitor treating with the enemy behind his back. What if Himmler in his perfidy had adulterated the capsules so that they would only render the Führer unconscious—to be handed over by Himmler to the Anglo-Saxons? Hitler was suspicious. He tested one of the vials of poison on his dog. It worked beautifully—but it might not work on him.

It was absolutely crucial that he should die, and that his body be totally consumed—that nothing, absolutely *nothing,* be left to the enemy. It must never happen to him and Eva what the wireless had reported had happened to Mussolini and his mistress: shot, then hanged upside down in a public square to be pelted with filth and invective by a hate-filled crowd. Nor could he stand the thought of his body's being suspended from a meathook, as he himself had exhibited the bodies of German generals in June 1944. Never, *never,* he had screamed, would he go on display as a freak in a Russian circus. He must be very sure indeed that he was dead and his body consumed "without a trace." He could not trust the poison. But who, he had asked, would perform the *coup de grâce?* Who indeed?

Linge, his valet of many years, or Günsche, his personal adjutant, or Bormann were obvious candidates. But there was one thing wrong with all of them: they were members of the SS. And Himmler's SS— which Hitler had once called his Society of Jesus, sworn to absolute fealty to him alone—was now honeycombed with treason. The motto of their belt buckles had become a mockery: "My Honor is My Loyalty." There was, Hitler was now convinced, no honor left in the world, no perfidy he had not suffered.

In the whirling world of his paranoid suspicion, there was only one person he could rely upon to perform this act of cosmic importance, and that was Eva Braun-Hitler. She was a woman of courage who had flown into a doomed city to be with him; she had demonstrated her obedience by fulfilling his every wish and his most unusual sexual demands; she was a sportswoman who knew how to handle pistols. Indeed, she wrote to a close friend on 19 April 1945 that constant pistol practice made her "so good at it that none of the men dared to compete." [213] And she had been found seated at Hitler's left side.

But Linge thought Hitler himself had fired the shot which entered his left temple and exited from his right.[214] He must have been mistaken, for Hitler was not left-handed, and we know that his left hand shook so badly he could not control it. That the larger bullet hole was in the right temple would indicate entrance from the left only if the shot were made an inch or two away from Hitler's skull—as would probably have been the case if Eva Braun-Hitler had shot him. A shot fired with the muzzle pushed tightly against the skull would have produced a gaseous recoil, leaving a large hole at the point of entry and probably pulling portions of the brain out with it.[215]

Cyanide acts quickly but not instantaneously. Hitler probably could have had time to bite the ampule, swallow its contents, put the pistol tightly against his right temple and pull the trigger. But it was said that he was found with his hands resting quietly on his knees—or, more likely, folded characteristically over his crotch. If so, it is unlikely that he had shot himself.

The shot could have been fired through the mouth, except that the same problem of timing arises, and the Russians found no evidence of a wound in the oral cavity, a part of the skull that was preserved. It also seems likely that an explosion in the mouth would have precluded finding glass shards from the ampule. The top of the cranium was missing —the part that, presumably, would have shown bullet wounds. It had probably been blown off by the steam generated from a brain that had been bubbling in the heat of petrol fire.[216]

Thus, we conjecture, that at about 3:30 on the afternoon of 30 April 1945, Adolf Hitler swallowed a lethal dose of cyanide, clasped his hands over his crotch, and waited for his dutiful bride who, following his orders, shot him through the left temple either with her own 6.35 Walther pistol or with his 7.65. She then tucked her feet beneath her as she liked to do when listening to phonograph records, took poison herself, and died seated beside the man she loved.

Hitler's body was badly burned but not completely consumed. Apart from the evidence of the Russian autopsy, there is another reason for believing that the bodies were not totally destroyed. Linge stresses the lack of effective planning and the confusion surrounding the whole incident. He and his helpers had collected enough petrol, they thought, to do the job; but they had not planned on where they would burn the bodies. Hence, with Russian artillery bursting about them, they hurriedly placed the corpses in a shallow indentation in the sandy soil of the courtyard. That, of course, was a mistake, for the soil rapidly absorbed much of the petrol. Both Linge and the chauffeur, Kempka, recalled that it was a windy day. The men had trouble relighting the bodies with petrol when the flames died down. Thus the bodies burned, off and on, for perhaps two or three hours. It was not enough. Having failed to fulfill their promise to Hitler that his body would be utterly destroyed, they tried to bury it. Again the job was botched, for no shovels were available; and with the Russians coming closer by the minute, there was little desire to risk lives for a now thoroughly dead Führer. He was covered as well and as quickly as possible with loose earth and rubble. A few days later the charred body was found by the Russians. An autopsy was performed after identification had been made by a careful examination of his rotting teeth.

The finale had not been as Wagnerian as Hitler might have wished, but it was not an inappropriate ending to his career.[217]

Having attempted to answer the traditional historical question of "what actually happened," let us call upon psychology to help us with the more difficult question of *why* Hitler killed himself.

One might quickly conclude that suicide, given the external conditions, was the obvious way to end his life. But deliberate self-destruction, we are told by those who have studied the matter, is never a completely logical act. Indeed, suicide defies the basic drive of the ego for survival—a drive that is not easily thwarted, as the low number of suicides in the concentration camps, on terminal cancer beds, and in survival rafts at sea testifies. Once again, we are confronted by the interplay of the rational and irrational in the life of man.

On the rational level, Hitler may have decided that by 30 April 1945 the military situation really was impossible and his personal anguish unbearable. Certainly he had told his entourage, time after time, that he planned to put a bullet in his head—it was the only sensible thing to do. But he may also have chosen self-destruction for less apparent yet equally compelling reasons.

The act of suicide has fascinated psychoanalysts for years; some of their findings may help us gain a better understanding of Hitler's life and death.*

Freud thought he had mastered the problem of self-inflicted death by deriving its dynamics from melancholia. But as a recent study of the problem has shown, a great number of suicidal patients do not show clinical symptoms of depression; and a far larger number of people who are deeply depressed are not suicidal.[218]

It is popularly supposed that most suicides are forms of escape from reality. And indeed, there may be external circumstances so desperate that "normal" people apparently decide to kill themselves. That does not preclude the possibility, however, that under these very special conditions psychological mechanisms come into play which in more usual circumstances would only be found in "abnormal" people.[219]

There is something else inadequate about the notion that suicide is a rational decision, a logical consequence of circumstances such as humiliation, ill health, discouragement, defeat, or the loss of either job or loved one. The idea assumes that the forces which compel suicide are wholly external. In the workings of the human mind, however, the push from within is often more powerful than the pull from without.[220]

Suicide may be seen as a masochistic act, the ultimate resolution of an unconscious desire for self-punishment. This was an impulse, we

---

* The clinical literature on suicide is extensive. Reference is made here, specifically, to the following studies: Sigmund Freud, "Mourning and Melancholia" (1917), in *Collected Papers*, (London, 1949), vol. 4; Kate Friedlander, "On the 'Longing to Die,'" *International Journal of Psychoanalysis* 21 (1940); Herbert Hendin, "Suicide," *Psychiatric Quarterly* 30 (1956); Ives Hendrick, "Suicide as Wish-Fulfillment," *Psychiatric Quarterly* 14 (1940); Donald D. Jackson, "Theories of Suicide" in *Clues to Suicide*, ed. Edwin S. Schneidman, (New York, 1957); Lewis Siegal and Jacob Friedman, "The Threat of Suicide," in *Diseases of the Nervous System* 16 (February 1955); Charles W. Wahl, "Suicide as a Magical Act," *Bulletin of the Menninger Clinic* (May 1957); Karl Menninger, "Psychoanalytic Aspects of Suicide," *International Journal of Psycho-Analysis* 14 (1933), and *Man Against Himself* (New York, 1961); Gregory Zilboorg, "Considerations on Suicide," *American Journal of Orthopsychiatry* 3 (1937). I am indebted to James McRandle for first suggesting this line of approach to Hitler's death; see his *Track of the Wolf*, 226–227.

have found, that Hitler had displayed throughout his life: he had often threatened to kill himself. It should be emphasized that to the masochist, suicide is not seen as defeat; rather, it is a twisted sort of triumph. Indeed, after years of clinical experience with masochism, Theodor Reik concluded that the essence of the masochist's attitude toward life can be summarized in three words: *"Victory through Defeat."* Others may view the suicide of such a person as an obvious admission of failure, but he himself feels vindicated and triumphant.[221]

Suicide may also gratify feelings of hostility and aggression. One way to externalize masochism is to inflict punishment on others. The suicide punishes his survivors—parents or spouse and anyone else who has abandoned the sufferer.[222] Certainly Hitler felt that he had been deserted by everyone. As his country lay in rubble, the Führer's thoughts turned inward. "Nothing is spared me," he lamented on 26 April 1945, "no allegiances are kept, no honor lived up to . . . no betrayals I have not experienced. . . . Nothing remains. Every wrong has already been done me." [223]

Karl Menninger has shown a different facet of the problem which reflects an important aspect of Hitler's personality. Menninger has found in suicide a connection between fear of examination and feelings of omnipotence. People who consider themselves unique, who refuse to be examined physically or to have their beliefs questioned, may find in suicide a confirmation of their omnipotence. "To kill oneself instead of being executed or slain by fate," Menninger has written, "is to retain for oneself the illusion of being omnipotent since one is, even by and in the act of suicide, master of life and death." Thus, paradoxically, the instinct for life may be fulfilled through death.[224]

Another psychiatrist agrees: "Through the primitive act of suicide, man achieves a fantasied immortality . . . it is another method of restating and reasserting one's own immortality." Such fantasy, according to most observers, is a reversion to infancy.[225]

It will be remembered that all his life Hitler—like other borderline personalities—was given to infantile fantasizing. In his boyhood he delivered impassioned orations to the trees on lonely hills near Leonding; in his teens, he saw himself winning lottery sweepstakes, rebuilding entire cities, and establishing a new Reich; as an adult, he was convinced that he was the German Messiah to whom it was proper that the prayers of children be addressed. Sometimes he thought of himself as Christ; at other times, he said, he was one of the immortals who would live forever among his fellow Olympian gods.

But at the end, he saw himself as a different kind of deity. He was really like neither Jesus nor one of the serene and radiant company on the azure heights of Olympus. Rather, he was a darkly brooding Teutonic god enthroned in Valhalla, the shadowed hall of the dead. Especially as he hid in his Berlin bunker, he may have reverted to a childhood fantasy that he was Wotan, dread ruler of the universe. The two had much in common. Wotan appears in German mythology as a deeply split deity, the god both of creation and of destruction. A magic worker who—like Hitler—appeared in different forms to different people, he was the all-knowing god, source of inspiration, inventer of the runes. But he was also the god of desolation and death, insatiable in demanding human sacrifices.

Wotan was also the Wild Huntsman who rode forth to lead the ravaging horde of the Furious Host (*wütendes Heer*). Hitler, we have said, saw himself in precisely that role as depicted in the painting *Die wilde Jagd*, by his favorite artist, von Stuck. Indeed, he may have identified so completely with this Wotan figure, and found the resemblance to himself so striking, that it does not seem too fanciful to suggest that he would see in this painting of 1889 a miraculous portrait of himself: "Hitler as Wotan, the Wild Huntsman." He was also convinced that the "Hand of Wotan" had miraculously appeared at his own Eagle's Nest in the Obersalzberg. He preserved it as his personal talisman.

Hitler and Wotan also shared similar tastes in animals. The reader will recall the curious fact of Hitler's special fondness for ravens and wolves, but these were the emblems of Wotan. Two ravens, Hugin and Munin, perched on his shoulders; the great grey wolf, Fenrin, symbol of chaos and destruction, crouched fettered at his feet, eating food from his hand alone. (In his last days, Hitler permitted no one but himself to touch or feed Blondi's pup "Wolf.") When Wotan orders the time of *Ragnarok*, the end of the world, there will be cataclysmic battle and "appalling deeds of murder and incest . . . The wolf Fenrin advances, his great gaping jaws filled the gap between earth and sky" . . . relentlessly, hideously, he devours gods and men.[226]

In ordering the *Götterdämmerung* for his world, we are suggesting, Hitler envisaged himself as Teutonic god fulfilling ancient myth. We know that one of his most precious boyhood possessions, a treasure "with which he never parted," was a book of German mythology.[227] We know, also, of his lifelong infatuation with the ancient legends as recast by Richard Wagner. These myths foretold the inevitable destruction of the world in a tremendous holocaust, with gods and men consumed by flames. Hitler was familiar with Wagner's conception of Wotan as "rising to the tragic height of willing his own destruction." * It seems likely that in the end he was drawn once again to Wagner, his ever-present refuge and strength in time of trouble, the fellow artist and creative genius who had inspired his Reich. He had said that "it all began" with Wagner. And thus it would end.

Fantasy was often confused with reality in the mind of "the greatest actor in Europe." For his own death scene he may have created a role of Wotan-Siegfried, a commanding Wagnerian hero who would

---

* He may have reinforced this image by recalling another boyhood hero of Nordic legend who, though vanquished, yet triumphed over his foes by laughing in splendid defiance as they cut his heart from the living flesh. See Edith Hamilton, *Mythology* (New York, 1942), 444.

rise above death by defying it. At his side was his beloved Brünnhilde-Eva, soaring into her final aria, *Lachend lass' uns verderben, lachend zu Grunde geh'n!* (Laughing, let us perish; 'mid laughter face our doom!) Hero and heroine embrace to confront death. Together their bodies are consumed by flames.

Such fantasies would be consistent with both Hitler's personality and recent studies of the psychology of self-destruction which describe suicide as a *"magical* act, actuated to achieve irrational, illusional ends." [228] For a person given to grandiose fantasies, death through suicide is not defeat, nor is it merely an escape from intolerable reality. It is "an act whereby one acquires power, qualities, and advantages" never possessed in life. Confronted by terrifying feelings of failure and impotence, the suicide brings up his most powerful defensive artillery: repression and magic. By *choosing* to destroy his own life, he believes that he has become master of life itself; through not-being, he advances to a superior order of being. Thus he "achieves, as does the infant, a kind of cosmic identification." That is, he equates the world with himself; he shares the delusion of medieval mystics who said, with St. Eustace, "Nothing outside my own mind is real; the world and all persons in it are, in reality, me." In killing himself, such a person destroys not one individual but many: "He commits not only suicide but vicarious matricide, patricide . . . even genocide." [229] For he feels, finally, that no one—no one in an entire nation—"is worthy of me. Let them perish."

So it may have been with Hitler. Hemmed in by a host of enemies and scoffers who dared to doubt his power and who boasted that they would destroy him, he would show them that he was still infallible and omnipotent. Little did they know that he could rise far above time and space and the travail of mortal life.

He would prove his dominion over them all by a miraculous leap into a whole new dimension of power. He who had created the Reich would destroy a world and gain immortality. Let there be darkness. In one single, crashing act of oblivion, the Psychopathic God would proclaim that his was the power and the glory forever.

APPENDIX

A Note on
Spurious Sources

KNOWLEDGE of Hitler's life during the Vienna period comes from the authentic and valuable memoirs of his closest boyhood friend, August Kubizek; from court, police, and Party records; and from the affidavits and memoirs of men who lived with him in the Home for Men (*Männerheim*) in the Meldemannstrasse. These people include one Reinhold Hanisch, alias Fritz Walter, a petty thief, forger, and confidence man who, for a time, sold Hitler's paintings. Before hanging himself prior to yet another conviction for embezzlement, Hanisch left an affidavit for the Party archives and wrote several exposé articles, including one for the *New Republic*, "I Was Hitler's Buddy." There is also a straightforward and useful affidavit given to the Party Archives by a Karl Honisch who knew and admired Hitler during the late Vienna years. Honisch distrusted Hanisch thoroughly: "Please do not confuse me with Hanisch, an untruthful man" (Hauptarchiv der Partei, folder 17a, reel 1).

Many writers have relied on the memoirs of one Josef Greiner, *Das Ende des Hitler-Mythos* (Zurich, 1947). Historians who have accepted Greiner with varying degrees of confidence include Bullock, Fest, Daim, Görlitz, Lüthy, Maser, Bradford Smith, Toland, Trevor-Roper, and, alas, Waite. Greiner claimed to have been a close friend of Hitler during the period from 1907–1908 in Vienna and again in 1913 in Munich. It is unlikely, however, that Greiner ever knew Hitler personally.

Both in his book and in private conversation, Greiner insisted that he befriended Hitler in the *Männerheim* during the year 1907–1908. When it was pointed out to him that at that time Hitler was living across the city in the Stumpergasse with Kubizek, and that consequently

Greiner must have been mistaken and had perhaps meant that he met Hitler sometime later, say, from 1909 to 1913, Greiner was adamant. No, he said, the time he knew Hitler was certainly from 1907 to 1908; it could not have been during the post-1909 period because he himself was not in Vienna at that time, he was studying for his engineering diploma in Berlin.*

In his "memoirs," Greiner describes Hitler in 1907–1908 as a "really poor devil," so filthy and impoverished that he could not wear his underclothing because it was tattered and full of lice (p. 13). In fact, during this time Hitler was living quite comfortably on his father's inheritance and his orphan's pension while, in carefully groomed clothing, he attended the opera or theater almost nightly.

Greiner says that Hitler's "favorite sister Paula" lived in Vienna at that time and that "since the fall of 1907, with only short interruptions," Adolf lived with her. He says he recalls how Adolf faked antique pictures by roasting his oil paintings in the kitchen oven at his sister's home. In point of fact, Hitler's sister Paula—whom he heartily disliked —was 11 years old at this time and living with her mother in Linz. The apocryphal story of the oven-baked oils was not invented by Greiner. Like so many of the alleged incidents in his "memoirs," he took it from someone else and added his own embellishments. The source for this story was an early, often inaccurate biography written by a German journalist who had heard the story, apparently, from Hanisch; see Rudolf Olden, *Hitler* (New York, 1936).

Greiner says that on one occasion, while he accompanied Hitler as he tried to sell his postcards in a restaurant, an old acquaintance of Hitler's from the Braunau days came up and greeted him with, "Well, for Heaven's sake, Hitler!" Adolf beat an embarrassed retreat (p. 19). Since Adolf had left Braunau at the age of three, it is unlikely that he would have been recognized by a person who had not seen him for 17 or 18 years.

Greiner talks about the great love which Adolf bore for Geli Raubal, who was, he says, a Czech beauty. On page 32 of his book there appears a picture of a Slavic face above the name "Gelly Raubal." The picture is patently not of Geli. Moreover, this young woman for whom Hitler allegedly felt great passion was at this time a one-year-old infant. She was born shortly after Christmas 1907, not in Vienna, as Greiner has it, but in Linz, where she lived continuously until she finished secondary school.

Greiner makes the same mistakes in chronology that Konrad Heiden made in his generally valuable books on Hitler. Thus when Hitler's father Alois changed his name, his purported grandfather, Johann

---

* The account given here is based on Greiner's book, conversations with Franz Jetzinger of 12 and 14 April 1960, and an unpublished memoir which Jetzinger kindly gave me shortly before his death: "Eine erlogene Hitler-Biographie" (typescript, 1959). Dr. Jetzinger had talked with Greiner on several occasions. All citations, unless otherwise noted, are to Greiner's book.

Georg Hiedler, is said to be 84 years old. Actually, he had died at the age of 65.

In an obvious effort to appeal to sensationalism, Greiner attributes all manner of hetero- and homosexual exploits to Hitler (pp. 59–60). Such activity is totally inconsistent with what we know of Hitler's sexual life. According to Greiner, Hitler spent a great deal of time poring over his horoscope (p. 91). According to those who knew him, he had no confidence in astrology.

In an early manuscript of his book, Greiner wrote that in July 1913, Hitler invited him to his rooming house in Munich where he lived with "a dear old woman who was the very model of a student-mother." Here Hitler allegedly got breakfast free in return for doing various household chores. When he ran out of money he "made little loans from the little old mother" (Greiner quoted in Jetzinger manuscript, p. 22). In fact, during the entire period from 26 May 1913 to August 1914, as the Munich police records show, Hitler lived in the Schleissheimer- strasse 32, above the tailor shop of Josef Popp.

In commenting on the disappearance of Hitler from the Home for Men, Greiner says that it was easy for him to disappear because no registration certificate or departure certificate was needed (p. 127). On the contrary, every resident of the Home for Men was required to fill out registration certificates exactly as in any Viennese hotel or pension. Further, Hitler's registration and departure cards still exist (HAP folder 1741, reel 86).

Greiner asserts that while he lived in the Home for Men he received a pathetic letter from Klara Hitler written in a trembling, dying hand, urging him to be friendly to her dear son. He attributes her death to a "lung disease" (pp. 134–135). Since—as his mother very well knew— Adolf was living in the Stumpergasse, on the other side of the city from the *Männerheim*, it is doubtful if such a letter could have been delivered in the improbable case that it was ever written. Klara, it will be re- called, died of cancer.

Greiner is simply not telling the truth when he writes, "In the year 1922, when we were exchanging reminiscences about the war, Hitler told me that because of illness he had not gone up to the front until two years after the outbreak of war" (p. 131). Regimental records and the memoirs of wartime companions make it clear that immediately after his basic training in Lechfeld, Hitler entrained with his regiment for the front on 21 October 1914. He fought in the brutal and critical first battle of Ypres (19 October–22 November). As early as December 1914 he was awarded the Iron Cross, Second Class. Hitler would not have told Greiner a lie that reflected unfavorably on himself. He was proud of his war record and justifiably so.

In his last dramatic chapter, Greiner assures us that Hitler escaped from the Berlin bunker. "A man whom he had known well for many years" had told him in confidence that on 30 April 1945 at the Templehof airfield in Berlin "at 15 minutes past 4 o'clock," he had seen a specially equipped new Messerschmidt turbine jet, Type 332, made ready to take off and ". . . no doubt about it, there was the Supreme War Commander himself, Adolf Hitler!" He was clearly visible in "the bright light of the setting sun" (pp. 340–342). One would think that even the inventiveness of a Greiner would be hard put to have the sun set in Berlin in April at four in the afternoon.

Greiner's stories of how the mighty of the world confided in him and sought his counsel show the fecundity of his imagination. When Hitler came to power, Greiner says that he was immediately offered a "high post" in the government. In his memoirs he does not divulge its nature, but he told Jetzinger privately that he was slated to become Reichsminister of finance. (Jetzinger's conversation with Waite, 12 April 1960.) Greiner was also invited, he says, to make a special trip to see Mussolini, for the Italian dictator valued his opinion on political and religious matters (pp. 261, 264). Reinhard Heydrich, we are told, confided in Greiner the Nazi plans for war against the Soviet Union (p. 272); and in intimate conversations, Himmler revealed to him his plans for eradicating the Jews (p. 282) and General Udett consulted with him about the war against Poland (p. 324). Ulrich von Hassel, a leader of the Resistance, trusted him so completely that he told him all about the conspiracy against Hitler and gave him a list of those who would succeed to office in the new German government (pp. 324–325). The German Navy invited Greiner to serve as "Special Consultant for Technological Development" (p. 331); leaders of the Luftwaffe asked him to design a special compass which would enable a plane to fly over the North Pole to Japan and thus let leading Nazis escape (p. 334). At the very end of the war, Himmler pleaded with Greiner to use his inventive genius to develop a special death ray that would disintegrate the enemy (p. 335).

Prior to all this, according to Greiner, the Nazi minister of propaganda, Dr. Goebbels, had sent special envoys to him urging that he write a biography of Hitler showing that the Führer was "God incarnate sent to the German people." But Goebbels demanded too much of Greiner: namely, that he distort the truth. He asked Greiner to give an incorrect date for Klara Hitler's death—to predate it in order to give the impression that Hitler had been orphaned at a younger age than in fact he was (pp. 267–270). Greiner did write a biography in 1938 but was not allowed to publish it, he says, because he refused to be as laudatory as Goebbels demanded and could not bring himself to falsify facts. This biography was prepared with the help of a certain Professor D.

There is one grain of truth in this story. Greiner had indeed written a manuscript with the help of a Professor D. But this gentleman, who has asked that his name not be divulged, gives a very different and more believable reason why the manuscript was unacceptable to the Nazis. In a private letter, Professor D. wrote that Greiner's manuscript was so patently inaccurate it was manifestly unbelievable. Moreover, it "deified the Führer to such a crass degree that it was not even usable as propa-

ganda material, for it would have made the Führer appear ridiculous."
(Letter to Jetzinger, quoted in Jetzinger Ms., 35.) Quite apart from
that, Goebbels could not conceivably have demanded falsification of
the dates of Klara's death, since the correct date was inscribed in marble
on her tombstone in Leonding and accurately given in the so-called
Ahnentafel des Führers, which had already been published in 1937.

In his book, Greiner describes himself as a selfless patriot and
courageous opponent of Hitler: "When, by the end of 1938, I recognized
the danger which Hitler had brought to Germany and Austria, I placed
myself on the side of the patriots who considered the only solution
lay in getting rid of Hitler" (p. 7). He then describes alleged efforts to
develop plans for Hitler's assassination. Actually, during the Nazi
period Greiner tried to join the Party but was rejected. He then sought
to ingratiate himself—and make a profit—by writing a fawning memoir
of Hitler. But it was so crass that not even the Nazis would accept it.
Failing to publish this first version of his "memoirs," he saw another
opportunity after Hitler's defeat. Hoping to capitalize on the general
aversion to the dead dictator, Greiner wrote a very different version of
his life with Hitler, maligning and misrepresenting him in falsified
testimony.

It may be concluded that Greiner could not have known Hitler in
the Home for Men in 1907–1908 because Hitler was not there; that he
did not know him in 1910–1913 because Greiner, by his own testimony,
was not there; and that the factual errors in his account are so many
and so serious as to render his book worthless.

One of the reasons historians have believed Greiner is that Reinhold Hanisch mentions him in his account and vouches for him—as
Greiner vouched for Hanisch. But to accept this reciprocal endorsement
is not unlike accepting mutual character testimonials from Uriah Heep
and Seth Pecksniff. It is important to note that Karl Honisch, who,
indisputably, had lived in the Home for Men during the period after
1910 and had known both Hitler and Hanisch, makes no mention whatever of Greiner.

If Greiner's book is a fraud, why has it been so generally accepted? Perhaps because the name Greiner is indeed mentioned by
Konrad Heiden, an early and valued authority on Hitler. Heiden asserted that among the people Hitler knew in Vienna were "Hanisch,
Neumann, and a third man by the name of Greiner"; see Heiden, *Adolf
Hitler: Das Zeitalter der Verantwortungslosigkeit. Eine Biographie*, 2
vols., (Zurich, 1936–1937) 1: 38. Since Greiner's first name was not
given, our Josef Greiner apparently saw a chance of turning this statement to his own advantage. He exploited the information (and misinformation) he found in Heiden and Olden; he used an early, inaccurate
Hanisch article and added rumors of the time to patch together out of
whole cloth his own purported "memoirs" of Hitler. At that time it
seemed perfectly safe to write so expansively, because little was then
known about this period of Hitler's life. No one, Greiner must have

thought, would ever be able to dispute his stories. He could not have imagined that Kubizek and Honisch would later write bona fide accounts of the Vienna years, that the indefatigable Jetzinger would check up on him, and that the Nazi Party Archives would be recovered and made available to scholars.

Another unreliable "memoir" has caused further misconceptions about Hitler's life. John Toland used this spurious source for his biography; *Adolf Hitler* (New York, 1976), 365, 917, 964; and Robert Payne relied on it for a chapter entitled "A Journey to England" in which he has Adolf leave Vienna in 1912 to spend several months visiting relatives in Liverpool. It was during this visit, according to Payne, that Hitler learned to respect the English people and fear the British Navy— hence his refusal to smash the English at Dunkirk and his desire for a separate peace with England during World War II. See Robert Payne, *The Life and Death of Adolf Hitler* (New York, 1973), 384, 394, and *passim*.

There is only one source for this story: a 250 page undated typescript (now in the New York Public Library Manuscripts Division) entitled "My Brother-in-Law Adolf" and written about 1940 by Brigid Dowling Hitler. She was the Irish wife of Adolf's half-brother, Alois Jr., a wandering waiter and razor-blade salesman. Their son, William Patrick Hitler, purportedly tried to blackmail his famous uncle in the early 1930s.

It seems likely that Brigid Hitler, like Josef Greiner, had noted that early biographies of Hitler spoke of a "lost year" during the Vienna period in which virtually nothing was known about him. Brigid therefore must have felt safe in filling the gap by having Adolf go to England to visit her family for the entire period from November 1912 until April 1913 (p. 13). There are several reasons for believing that this trip was an invention of Brigid's—as was most of her "memoir" of Adolf Hitler.

(1) Vienna police records show that during the months in which Brigid—and Robert Payne—put Hitler in England, he was actually living in the Home for Men in the Meldemannstrasse, Vienna. Official records for this period are supported by reliable testimony of Karl Honisch, a resident of the Home who knew Hitler during these months. (HAP, folder 17a, roll 1).

(2) In any case, it is highly unlikely that the Germanophile Hitler would have left Austria and gone, not to Germany, but to a foreign land whose language he did not know in order to visit a half-brother he despised.

(3) There is something very wrong with the picture Brigid (and Payne) paint of the arrival scene at the Liverpool station: "He looked as though he had always been famished . . . he was badly dressed and obviously had not changed his shirt for many weeks" (Payne, *Life and Death*, p. 95). Hitler was compulsively clean; in 1912 he was enjoying a financial windfall from his aunt and living comfortably in Vienna.

A Note on Spurious Sources

(4) Brigid's imagination is unable to cope with her brother-in-law's turbulent personality. "I cannot imagine," she writes, "a less interesting or prepossessed guest . . . I found him weak and spineless" (p. 13). Young Hitler was many things, but placid, uninteresting, and spineless he was not.

(5) Her guest, she insists, was so ignorant of music that when he heard Liverpudlians singing *God Save the King* he thought it was *Deutschland über Alles* (p. 17). Hitler, the avid German patriot and music lover, would not have made that mistake.

(6) Her imagination also fails her—as do her facts—in writing about other people and events. She has the wrong year for Klara Hitler's death, and she thinks that after Klara's funeral Adolf and Paula moved to Vienna to live with their half-sister Angela (p. 21). Neither Paula nor Angela lived in Vienna at that time; Hitler never lived alone with his sisters; she has the wrong color for Geli Raubal's hair; and she gives the wrong name for Hitler's housekeeper in the flat at Prinzregentenplatz.

(7) Brigid describes Paula as "the only person who might exert any influence on Adolf" (p. 129). Adolf had little respect for his rather pleasant and mentally limited sister; she exerted no discernible influence upon him.

(8) Brigid is mistaken in thinking that Hitler once registered in the "Vienna Municipal Lodging House" under the name of his dead brother, Edmund (p. 11). Police files show that Hitler always registered under his correct name; the lodging house she describes did not exist.

(9) Brigid's adventures in the Third Reich as she sought to rescue her beloved son Patrick from the clutches of the Gestapo read like the script for a very bad television spy story; the long, verbatim conversations she says she recalls with Rudolf Hess, Baldur von Schirach, Heinrich Himmler, and other Nazi leaders are inventions.

(10) There is no mention of a visit to England in any of Hitler's speeches, books, or lengthy "Table Conversations," nor is it mentioned in any authentic memoir written by people who knew him well. Indeed, his valet of ten years' service, Heinz Linge, says flatly that with the exception of brief trips to Italy and Paris, the Führer "had visited no other country" (*News of the World*, 13 November 1955).

(11) The British Home Office has reported that "a careful search" through all the files of the Immigration Service for the period of November 1912 to April 1913 shows no record of Adolf Hitler having visited England. (H. G. Pearson, Departmental Record Officer, British Home Office, letter of 30 May 1975. Used with permission of Professor Peter Loewenberg, University of California at Los Angeles.)

A book entitled *Inside Adolf Hitler*, purportedly written by "Hitler's psychiatrist Kurt Krueger," appeared in New York in 1941. It was endorsed by Upton Sinclair and an officer in the U.S. Medical Corps, both of whom wrote laudatory prefaces. A reputable American publishing house considered republishing the book in 1973; it has been taken seriously in several articles dealing with Hitler's psychopathology, and cited as evidence in a popular biography.*

"Dr. Krueger" claims to have had Hitler under analysis from August 1919 to August 1934. But it is obvious that the writer had no training in psychology and could not have known Hitler. He misuses the terminology of psychoanalysis; while his patient is still alive, he reveals his most intimate confidences; he admits that he took no notes of any conversations he had with Hitler but says that "it all comes back now" and reprints verbatim, page after page, of invented conversations. Time after time, this "psychiatrist" displays his ignorance of his alleged patient. A few examples must suffice:

(1) *Hitler became an anti-Semite at the age of ten after watching a Jew, who was the village grocer, rape his mother.* There was no Jewish grocer in Leonding; the alleged incident is mentioned neither by anyone living in the village nor in any record or memoir of Hitler's boyhood. Hitler did not become an anti-Semite until many years later.

(2) *Up to the age of ten, little Adolf slept in a big bed between his father and mother.* Anyone who knows anything about Alois Hitler would be amused by the idea of his sharing his conjugal bed with Adolf.

(3) *All the children in the neighborhood called Adolf a Jew and refused to play with him.* There is widespread and reliable testimony that Adolf was a popular leader of boyhood games.

(4) *When "Dr. Krueger" knew him, Adolf wore a goatee and gave his name as Adolf Schickelgruber.* Hitler never wore a goatee and never used the name, which was never his own.

(5) *All during this time Hitler lived in "an obscure part of Munich . . . in a filthy room painted green."* Hitler actually lived in comfortable, clean rooms in Munich's famous Schwabing quarter and later in a spacious apartment in the fashionable Bogenhausen District.

(6) *All the Nazi leaders knew Krueger as Hitler's psychiatrist, and many sought him out to be their doctor.* "Dr. Krueger" is not mentioned in any of the memoirs or testimonials of the Nazi hierarchy. Hitler despised psychiatry as "Jewish medicine." There is no reliable testimony that he was the patient of a psychiatrist.

(7) *Max [sic] Weber was a leading Nazi orator; Captain Heinrich [sic] Goerring [sic] organized the Beer Hall Putsch.*

Another spurious document, purporting to be the intimate diaries of Eva Braun, was edited by a certain Paul Tabori and published in London in 1949. The publishers wrote that they had received the manuscript from Luis Trenker, "a well-known Austrian writer, film director, and

---

* See, for example, Wolfram Kurth, "Hitler," in *Genie, Irrsinn und Ruhm: Eine Pathographie des Genies*, ed. Wilhelm Lange-Eichbaum (Munich, 1956); and W. H. D. Vernon, "Hitler, the Man—Notes for a Case History," *Journal of Abnormal Social Psychology* 37 (July 1942):295–308. The popular biography is Glenn B. Infield, *Eva and Adolf* (New York, 1974), 350, 356.

film star." Trenker allegedly knew Eva Braun and had met her again near the end of the war in the winter of 1944–1945 at Kitzbühel, the Austrian ski resort. There, he said, she handed him a sealed package, asking him to keep it for her. It was marked only "E.B." After Trenker learned of her suicide, he took the package to a notary. They opened it and found pages of typescript. We are assured that the published version contains the whole diary in literal translation, omitting only passages which "because of obscenity" could not be reproduced. There can be no question about the value of this book: it is a worthless forgery. That the author could have known neither Hitler nor Fräulein Braun is manifest on virtually every page. A few examples may be noted here:

(1) *Adolf contracted syphilis in Vienna when he visited a brothel on his 17th birthday.* There is no persuasive evidence that Hitler ever had syphilis. On the stated birthday, 20 April 1906, Adolf was living with his mother in the comfortable flat in Linz at Humboldtstrasse, 31.

(2) *Hitler was a filthy person who seldom bathed, taking only footbaths while otherwise fully clothed.* Actually, he was habitually a clean person who took a full bath at least once a day.

(3) *Adolf had his first erotic experience at the age of 12 with his sister, who was then 13.* Hitler's sister Paula was seven years younger than he, thus five years old when he was 12; he was furious whenever she tried to give him a sisterly hug.

(4) The author has Hitler doing what reliable testimony shows he never in fact did: consult astrologers, participate in group sex, drive an automobile.

These fraudulent "diaries" of Eva Braun should not be confused with the authentic diary entries and letters which have been reprinted in a book written by a confidant of the Braun family; see Nerin E. Gun, *Eva Braun-Hitler: Leben und Schicksal* (New York and Bruchsal/Baden, 1968). See also her early, authentic diary for the period from 6 February to 28 May 1935 which exists, both in German script and in English typescript translation, in the National Archives, Washington, D.C. (Record Group Number 242).

NOTES

PREFACE

1. Helm Stierlin, *Adolf Hitler: Familienperspektiven* (Frankfurt am Main, 1975), 11.
2. Alan Bullock, foreword to the English translation of Franz Jetzinger's *Hitler's Youth* (London, 1958), 10.
3. William E. Gladstone's characterization of the government of the Two Sicilies under the notorious King Bomba. *Gleanings of the Past Years*, 7 vols (New York, 1879), IV, 7.
4. Carl L. Becker, "Mr. Wells and the New History," in *Everyman His Own Historian: Essays on History and Politics* (New York, 1935), 169.
5. For a warning against the indiscriminate use of "the same Oedipal key" see Cushing Strout's review article in *History and Theory*, 13 (1974): 322.
6. Erik Erikson, *Young Man Luther* (New York, 1958), 35–36; italics are mine.
7. A. J. P. Taylor, *The Origins of the Second World War* (New York, 1961); personal communication, 19 March 1973. For an excellent anthology of commentary on Taylor's view of Hitler, see Wm. Roger Louis, ed. *The Origins of the Second World War: A. J. P. Taylor and His Critics* (New York, 1972); italics are mine.
8. Barbara Tuchman, Comment in symposium, "The Independence of Psychohistory," *History of Childhood Quarterly: The Journal of Psychohistory*, 3 (Fall, 1975), 184. I am indebted to Frederick L. Schuman for this reference.
9. *New York Review of Books*, 18 April 1974.
10. For Hitler as "neurotic character" and "Unperson," see Joachim Fest, *Hitler: Eine Biographie* (Frankfurt am Main, 1973); Fest expressed a similar view in seminar discussion, Harvard University, 17 October 1975. For Hitler as "mad," see Robert Payne, *The Life and Death of Adolf Hitler* (New York, 1973). Hans Gatzke, who quotes these passages with apparent approval and calls Hitler a "madman" does not call for a more precise diagnosis; see his book review in *American Historical Review*, 79, (February, 1974), 179. Hitler as "violent megalomaniac," A. L. Rowse, *Appeasement* (New York, 1963); Hitler as a "pathological egoist" and megalomaniac, Norman Rich, *Hitler's War Aims* (New York, 1973); Hitler as "crazy neurotic," A. J. P. Taylor, review article in *Times Literary Supplement*, 23 March 1973; John Toland quotes with apparent approval a diagnosis of Hitler as a "psychopath with hysterical symptoms." But he pursues the matter no further. (*Adolf Hitler*, New York, 1976, xix, 925)
11. Edward Crankshaw, *Gestapo: Instrument of Tyranny* (London, 1956), 21.
12. George M. Trevelyan, *Clio, A Muse and Other Essays Literary and Pedestrian* (London, 1913), 9.
13. The quotation from St. Paul is from his First Letter to the Corinthians as it appears in the *New English Bible*.
14. Quoted in Leon Edel's perceptive essay "The Biographer and Psychoanalysis," *International Journal of Psycho-Analysis*, 42 (July-October 1961): 458–466.

Notes

CHAPTER 1

1. William L. Shirer, *Berlin Diary: The Journal of a Foreign Correspondent, 1934–1941* (New York, 1941), 16–18.
2. Lloyd George's article in *Daily Express* (London), 17 November 1930, quoted in Joachim Remak, ed., *The Nazi Years: A Documentary History* (Englewood Cliffs, N.J., 1969), 82.
3. Winston S. Churchill, *Great Contemporaries* (New York, 1937), 226.
4. Helmut Heiber, *Adolf Hitler: Eine Biographie* (Berlin, 1960), 116.
5. Frederick Oechsner, *This Is the Enemy* (New York, 1942), 77. For a physical description of Hitler, in addition to published memoirs, see "Hitler as Seen by His Doctors," Military Intelligence, Consolidated Interrogation Report, 29 May 1945, National Archives (hereafter cited as "Hitler's Doctors," MIR).
6. René Juvet, *Ich war dabei: 20 Jahre Nationalsozialismus, 1923–1943: Ein Tatsachenbericht* (Zurich, 1944), 13; Robert Coulondre, *Von Moskau nach Berlin, 1936–1939: Erinnerungen des französischen Botschafters* (Bonn, 1950), 307; Hermann Rauschning, *The Voice of Destruction* (New York, 1940), 258; Martha Dodd in "Hitler Source Book," edited by Walter C. Langer from documents collected by the OSS in 1942–1943, National Archives, 58 (hereafter cited as OSS Source Book).
7. Ernst Hanfstaengl, personal interview, Munich, April 1967; Stefan Lorant, "The Hitler I Knew," *Saturday Review* (May 2, 1970): 21; Friedlinde Wagner, *The Royal Family of Bayreuth* (London, 1948), 30; Albert Speer, *Inside the Third Reich; Memoirs*, trans. Richard and Clara Winston (New York, 1970), 100.
8. August Kubizek, *The Young Hitler I Knew*, trans. E. V. Anderson (Boston, 1955), 17–18.
9. Quoted by Werner Maser in *Der Spiegel*, (7 May 1973), 134; Gerhard Boldt, *Hitler: The Last Ten Days: An Eyewitness Account* (New York, 1973), 15.
10. Testimony of Christa Schroeder, one of Hitler's secretaries, in Albert Zoller, ed., *Hitler Privat: Erlebnisbericht seiner Geheimsekretärin* (Düsseldorf, 1949), 69; Oechsner, *The Enemy*, 113–114.
11. OSS Source Book, 935; Heinz Linge, "Kronzeuge Linge," *Revue* (Munich), 26 December 1955; Ernst Hanfstaengl, *The Missing Years* (London, 1957), 238; Baldur von Schirach, *Ich glaubte an Hitler* (Hamburg, 1967), 268.
12. Richard M. Hunt, "Joseph Goebbels: A Study of the Formation of His National-Socialist Consciousness (1897–1929)," Ph.D. dissertation, Harvard University (1960).
13. Hanfstaengl interview; Weidemann Papers (microfilm), Berlin Document Center, group 7, reel 32.
14. Zoller, *Privat*, 23; Willie Schneider, "Aus nächster Nähe," *Die 7 Tage: Wochenschrift aus dem Zeitgeschehen* (Baden-Baden), 17 October 1952 (hereafter cited as 7 *Tage*), 32; Linge, *Revue*, 3 March 1956.
15. Speer, *Inside*, 97; Zoller, *Privat*, 23.
16. Heinrich Hoffmann, *Hitler Was My Friend*, trans. R. H. Stevens, (London, 1955), 83–84, 102; Schneider, 7 *Tage*.
17. Sir Ivone Kirkpatrick, *The Inner Circle* (London, 1959), 96; Karl Wahl ". . . es ist das deutsche Herz": Erlebnisse und Erkenntnisse eines ehemaligen Gauleiters* (Augsburg, 1954), 204, 340; Gerhard Herrgesell, interviewed in *Time*, 21 May 1945.
18. Birger Dahlerus, *Der letzte Versuch: London-Berlin, Sommer 1939* (Munich, 1948), 65–67.
19. Douglas M. Kelley, M.D., *22 Cells in Nuremberg* (New York, 1947), 227.
20. Richard Hanser, *Putsch! How Hitler Made Revolution* (New York, 1970), 17–18; *Hitler's Secret Conversations, 1941–1944*, trans. Norman Cameron and R. H. Stevens (New York, 1953), 257 (hereafter cited as *Conversations*); Linge, *Revue* (December 1955); Oechsner, *Enemy*, 97.
21. OSS Source Book, 791.

22. Oechsner, *Enemy*, 92.

23. Nerin E. Gun, *Eva Braun-Hitler: Leben und Schicksal* (Brucksal/Baden), 14.

24. Quoted in Kirkpatrick, *Circle*, 97.

25. Kubizek, *Young Hitler*, 26; Ernst von Weizsäcker, *Erinnerungen* (Munich, 1950), 200; Zoller, *Privat*, 84; Schneider in 7 *Tage*; Speer, *Inside*, 123; Hoffmann, *Hitler*, 198. *Hitlers Tischgespräche im Führerhauptquartier*, ed., Percy Ernst Schramm, 2nd ed. (Stuttgart, 1965), 216 (hereafter cited as *Tischgespräche*).

26. Speech of 14 September 1936, reprinted in *Hitler: Reden und Proklamationen, 1932–1945*, ed., Max Domarus (Munich, 1965), 646 (hereafter cited as Domarus, *Reden*).

27. Adolf Hitler, *Mein Kampf* (New York, Reynal and Hitchcock, 1939), 30, 84, 161–162 (unless otherwise noted, this is the edition that will be cited here); *Conversations*, 211; italics are mine.

28. Kubizek, *Young Hitler*, 35; Hans Karl von Hasselbach, M.D., "Hitler's Doctors," MIR; Carl J. Burckhardt, *Meine Danziger Mission, 1937–1939* (Munich, 1960), 108; Speer as cited in George L. Mosse, *The Nationalization of the Masses* (New York, 1975), 190.

29. Percy Ernst Schramm, "Erläuterung" to *Tischgespräche*, 31; Nathan Eck, "Were Hitler's Political Actions Planned or Merely Improvised?" *Yad Vasham* 5 (1963):368–369; Norman H. Baynes, ed., *The Speeches of Adolf Hitler, 1922–1939*, 2 vols. (London and New York, 1942), 1-17 (hereafter cited as *Speeches*).

30. Werner Maser, *Hitlers Mein Kampf: Entstehung, Aufbau, Stil, Aenderungen, Quellen, Quellenwert* (Munich, 1966), 94; Herman Hammer, "Die deutschen Ausgaben von Hitlers Mein Kampf," *Vierteljahrshefte für Zeitgeschichte* 4 (1956):178 and passim (hereafter this periodical will be cited as VfZ).

31. Otto Dietrich, *Hitler*, trans. Richard and Clara Winston (Chicago, 1955), 216. See also the memoirs of Weidemann, Krause, Kubizek, Linge, Schroeder, and the affidavit of Dr. Hans Karl Hasselbach in Budesarchiv, *Bestand*, 441–3b.

32. Gordon W. Prange, ed., *Hitler's Words* (Washington, D.C., 1944), 87, 90; Domarus, *Reden*, 2076, 2186; italics are mine.

33. Walter C. Langer, *The Mind of Adolf Hitler: The Secret Wartime Report* (New York, 1972), 190; italics are mine. The *schlechtes Gewissen* of dogs appears in *Tischgespräche*, 165.

34. Hitler, *Mein Kampf*, 40, 700, 992; italics are mine.

35. Ibid., 309. Italics are mine.

36. Domarus, *Reden*, 2186; see also 336, 670, 804; italics are mine.

37. Zoller, *Privat*, 21.

38. *Hitlers Lagebesprechungen: Die Protokollfragmente seiner Militärkonferenzen, 1942–45*, ed. Helmut Heiber (Stuttgart, 1962), 18; Karl Wilhelm Krause, *Zehn Jahre Kammerdiener bei Hitler* (Hamburg, n.d.), 41; Zoller, *Privat*, 44, 74.

39. Domarus, *Reden*, 2291; Zoller, *Privat*, 73; Linge, *Revue*, 3 March 1956.

40. *Testament politique de Hitler*, quoted in Joachim Fest, *Hitler: Eine Biographie* (Frankfurt am Main, 1973), 1012.

41. Ibid., 541, 1842; *Conversations*, 553.

42. S. Lane Faison, Jr., "Linz: Hitler's Museum and Library," Consolidated Interrogation Report no. 40 (15 December 1945), War Department, Art Looting Investigation Unit (hereafter cited as Faison Report); Zoller, *Privat*, 52; Rauschning, *Voice*, 252; Friedrich Heer, *Der Glaube des Adolf Hitler: Anatomie einer politischen Religiosität* (Munich, 1968), 293; italics are mine.

43. Erich Czech-Jochberg, *Hitler: Reichskanzler* (Oldenburg, n.d.), 160.

44. Günter Peis, "Die unbekannte Geliebte," *Stern* no. 24 (1959); Speer memoirs as quoted in *Life Magazine*, April 24, 1970.

45. Domarus, *Reden*, 2194; Hanfstaengl, *Missing Years*, 137; Schirach, *Ich glaubte*, 114; *Tischgespräche*, 216, 222.

46. See Fest, *Hitler*, 704–706.

47. Dietrich Orlow, *The History of the Nazi Party*, 2 vols. (Pittsburgh, 1969–1973), 1:272; OSS Source Book, 936; Rauschning, *Voice*, 203; Hans Frank, *Im*

Notes

Angesicht des Galgens: Deutung Hitlers und seiner Zeit auf Grund eigener Erlebnisse und Erkenntnisse (Munich, 1953).

48. *Documents in German Foreign Policy* Series D., (Washington D.C., 1956), vol. 7, 201–202; Baldur von Schirach, quoted in *Stern*, 3 September 1967.

49. Reginald Phelps, "Dokumentation: Hitler als Parteiredner im Jahre 1920," *VfZ* 11 (1963): 309; Rauschning, *Voice*, 252.

50. OSS Source Book, 410; "Hitler's Doctors," MIR.

51. Kubizek, *Young Hitler*, 64; Werner Maser, *Die Frühgeschichte der NSDAP: Hitlers Weg bis 1924* (Frankfurt am Main, 1965), 446, 448; Hans Otto Meissner, quoted in *Wiener Bulletin* 12 (1958); Zoller, *Privat*, 108; OSS Source Book, 630.

52. Walter Warlimont, *Inside Hitler's Headquarters*, trans. R. H. Barry (New York, 1964), 305–306; Hitler Staff Conferences, National Archives, folder 2; Zoller, *Privat*, 95, 98.

53. Linge, *Revue*, 26 November 1955.

54. Joseph Goebbels, *The Early Goebbels Diaries, 1925–1926*, ed. Helmut Heiber, trans. Oliver Watson (New York, 1962), 100.

55. A photostat of this note may be seen in the Library of Congress, Prints and Photographs Division, folder 4589.

56. Hanfstaengl, *Missing Years*, 141.

57. Hanfstaengl, *Unheard Witness*, 69; "Adolf Hitler," General Services Administration, National Archives and Records Services, December 1942. This report is based largely on the testimony of a "Dr. Sedgewick" who was actually Hanfstaengl, as he told me in a personal interview. The report may be found in the Franklin D. Roosevelt Library (hereafter cited as "AH" in FDR).

58. Personal letter from Jan Stepan, director, Harvard Law School Library, 4 December 1974; Albert Speer as interviewed in *Playboy*, June 1971, 193.

59. Hanfstaengl interview, Munich, June 1967. A picture of the desk may be seen in *Die Kunst im Dritten Reich* 3 (1939):413; see also Frank, *Galgens*, 179.

60. Sigmund Freud, "Medusa's Head," *International Journal of Psychoanalysis* (London) 21 (1941); Coulondre, *Erinnerungen*, 422; Burckhardt, *Danziger Mission*, 345; italics are mine.

61. Ernst Nolte, *Three Faces of Fascism*, trans. Leila Vennewitz (New York, 1965), 420; Hitler, *Mein Kampf*, 251; italics are mine.

61a. Zoller, *Privat*, 232.

62. "Hitler über Justiz," *VfZ*, 11 (1964):95; Nolte, *Three Faces*, 416.

63. Kubizek letter in *Oberösterreichisches Landesarchiv* (Linz), folder no. 64 (hereafter cited as *OLA*).

64. Adolf Hitler, *Hitler's Secret Book*, trans. Salvator Attanasio (New York, 1961), 186.

65. Hitler, *Mein Kampf*, 38, 39, 43–44, 65, 75, 116–118, 416; italics are mine.

66. Kubizek, *Young Hitler*, 160–161; Schramm affidavit in Bundesarchiv, Bestand 441-b; "AH" in FDR; Dr. Karl Brandt testimony, "Hitler's Doctors," MIR.

67. Dr. Hugo Blaschke, "Hitler's Doctors," MIR.

68. Schirach, *Ich glaubte*, 115, 130; Dr. Erwin Giesing, "Hitler's Doctors," MIR; Zoller, *Privat*, 91; *Tischgespräche*, 451; Rauschning, *Voice*, 229.

69. Hanfstaengl Interview, Munich, June 1967; *Der Hitler Prozess vor dem Volksgericht in München* (Munich, 1924), 26.

70. Hitler, *Mein Kampf*, 748; memoirs of Linge, Reiter, Hoffmann, Schirach, and Fräulein Schroeder; the "wolf has been born" is quoted in Reginald H. Phelps, "Hitler and the *Deutsche Arbeiterpartei*," *American Historical Review*, 68 (July 1963):983; information about Wolfhardt from Professor Lane Faison; interview with Frau Wolf cited in Kempner, *Im Kreuzverhör*, 33, 43; Nicholas Sombart, "Zum dokumentation über Winifred Wagner," *Merkur* (Munich) 331 (December 1975).

71. "AH" in FDR; Georg Schott, *Das Volksbuch vom Hitler* (Munich, 1924), 74; Rudolf Augstein, in *Der Spiegel*, no. 38 (17 September 1973), 68; Domarus, *Reden*, 208, 214, 1421.

72. OSS Source Book, 901; Domarus, *Reden*, 18, 1421, 446, 214, 421; italics are mine.

73. Interrogation of Baron Steengracht van Moyland, De Witt Poole Mission, National Archives, microfilm, roll 3.

74. Domarus, *Reden*, 541, 1842, Prange, *Hitler's Words*, 93.

75. Heinz Assmann, "Some Personal Recollections of Adolf Hitler" *United States Naval Institute Proceedings* 79 (July 1953): 1290; Linge, *Revue*, 24 March 1956; Robert M. W. Kempner, *Das dritte Reich im Kreuzverhör* (Munich, 1969), 198.

76. Hans Müller, "Der pseudoreligiöse Charakter der nationalsozialistischen Weltanschauung," *Geschichte in Wissenschaft und Unterricht*, Heft 6 (1961): 339, 349; Heer, *Glaube*, 449.

77. *Mein Kampf*, 7; Albert Krebs, *Tendenzen und Gestalten der NSDAP: Erinnerungen an die Frühzeit der Partei* (Stuttgart, 1959), 123; *Conversations*, 167.

78. Heer, *Glaube*, 118; Müller, "Weltanschauung," 344–346.

79. *New York Times*, 7 April 1969.

80. Heer, *Glaube*, 302; personal communication from former SS officer.

81. Quoted in J. S. Conway, *The Nazi Persecution of the Churches, 1933–45* (New York, 1968), 146–147.

82. Heer, *Glaube*, 316.

83. Müller, "Weltanschauung," 345.

84. Müller, "Weltanschauung," 341.

85. Hans-Jochen Gamm, *Der braune Kult* (Hamburg, 1962), 213–214.

86. Conway, *Persecution*, 155.

87. Heer, *Glaube*, 266, 262; "AH" in FDR.

88. Nazi film, *Der Triumph des Willens*; Domarus, ed., *Reden*, 61.

89. Schott, *Volksbuch*; Prange, *Hitler's Words*, 11; Bracher, *Dictatorship*, 151.

90. André François-Poncet, *The Fateful Years: Memoirs of a French Ambassador in Berlin, 1931–1938*, trans. Jacques LeClercq (New York, 1949), 286.

91. Burckhardt, *Danziger*, 344; *Tischgespräche*, 168.

92. Thomas P. O'Donnell, "The Devil's Architect," *New York Times Magazine*, 26 October 1969, 48.

93. Frank, *Angesicht*, 312; Bracher, *Dictatorship*, 347.

94. Zoller, *Privat*, 174; Speer, *Inside*, 403 and passim.

95. "Winnie und der Gute Wolf," *Der Spiegel*, no. 10 (1 May 1976), 146; *Conversations*, 257; Hoffmann, *Hitler*, 189; Speer, *Inside*, 227, 284.

96. Domarus, *Reden*, 226, 1423; see also interviews by DeWitt Poole Mission, microfilm, roll 3.

97. Dahlerus, *Letzer Versuch*, 71.

98. See the text of the following speeches: Ludwigshaven, 25 March, 1934; Nuremberg, 16 September 1935; Koenigsberg, 18 March 1936; Berlin, 7 March 1936; Breslau, 22 March 1936; Berlin, 21 May 1935; Berlin, 26 September 1938.

99. Domarus, *Reden*, 2035. Italics are mine.

100. Zoller, *Privat*, 48; "AH" in FDR.

101. *Conversations*, 292.

102. Domarus, *Reden*, 214; *Documents on British Foreign Policy*, Third Series, 2:499.

103. H. D. Röhrs, *Hitler: Die Zerstörung einer Persönlichkeit* (Neckargemünd, 1965), 106–111.

104. Hitler, *Mein Kampf*, 514.

105. Reginald Phelps, *American Historical Review* (July 1963): 974–986.

106. Schramm affidavit in Bundesarchiv, Bestand 441.

107. *Kriegstagebuch des Oberkommandos der Wehrmacht, 1940–1945*, 4 (2): 1703; Karl Koller, *Der letzte Monat: die Tagebuchaufzeichnungen des ehemaligen Chefs des Generalstabes der deutschen Luftwaffe vom 14 April bis 27 Mai 1945* (Mannheim, 1949), 25; Joseph Goebbels, *The Goebbels Diaries, 1942–1943*, trans. Louis P. Lochner (New York, 1948), 383.

108. Nolte, *Three Faces*, 401–405, 420.

109. "Hitler's Doctors," MIR.

110. Schneider, 7 *Tage*. On the other hand, Hoffmann reports that Hitler did not object to women using lipstick.

Notes

111. Kelly, 22 *Cells*, 213.

112. Speer, quoted in *New York Times Magazine*, October 26, 1969; Oran J. Hale, "Adolf Hitler: Taxpayer," *American Historical Review*, 60 (July 1955):830–842.

113. Rauschning, *Voice*, 80; Hitler's table conversations as recorded in *Tischgespräche* and *Secret Conversations*.

114. Hans Baur, *Hitler's Pilot*, trans. Edward Gerald (London, 1958), 78; Maser, *Hitlers Mein Kampf*, 112; Kubizek, *Young Hitler*, 24; Schirach, *Glaubte*, 122; OSS Report, 31; Franz von Halder, *Tagebuch* (photocopy of typescript), Institut für Zeitgeschichte, Archives, Munich; testimony of Lutz Graf Schwerin von Krosigk, in "Hitler: A Composite Picture," Military Intelligence, Special Report no. 36, National Archives (hereafter cited as "Hitler: Composite," MIR); Fritz Weidemann, *Der Mann der Feldherr werden wollte: Erlebnisse und Erfahrungen des Vorgesetzten Hitler im 1. Weltkrieg* . . . (Haan, 1964), 92; conversations with Hanfstaengl, Munich, June 1967.

115. Kubizek to Franz Jetzinger, 6 May 1949, in OLA Folder no. 64; *Reichsgesetzblatt* nos. 39 (21 April 1933) and 132 (25 November 1933); *Deutsches Tierschutzrecht*, 179–181; for Hitler's fondness for ravens see affidavit of Schramm on Hitler in Bundesarchiv, Bestand 441.

116. Hermann Rauschning, *Gespräche mit Hitler* (Zurich, 1940), 81.

117. Schirach in *Stern*, 11 June 1967; Speer, *Inside*, 127, 94, 165.

118. Joachim C. Fest, *The Face of the Third Reich: Portraits of the Nazi Leadership*, trans. Michael Ballock (New York, 1970), 35.

119. "AH" in FDR; Hoffmann, *Hitler*, 88, 197.

120. Zoller, *Privat*, 69, 73; Peter Hoffmann, *Widerstand, Staatsstreich, Attentat: Der Kampf der Opposition gegen Hitler* (Munich, 1969), 476.

121. *Conversations*, 260.

122. Speer, *Inside*, 99–100.

123. Krebs, *Tendenzen*, 137.

124. Max Planck, radio script for RIAS, Berlin, 24 November 1966; Friedrich Hossbach, *Zwischen Wehrmacht und Hitler: 1934–1938* (Wolfenbüttel, 1949), 23.

125. Domarus, *Reden*, 1629; italics are mine.

126. Zoller, *Privat*, 56; Dietrich, *Hitler*, 16; Paul Schmidt, *Hitler's Interpreter: The Secret History of German Diplomacy, 1935–1945* (London, 1951), 266.

127. Kubizek, *Young Hitler*, 176.

128. Koller, *Letzter Monat*, 31; Domarus, *Reden*, 2186.

129. Wiedemann, *Feldherr*, 220–221.

130. Brandt affidavit in Bundesarchiv, Bestand 442 and interrogation, "Hitler's Doctors," MIR; interview with Hanfstaengl; memoirs of Mimi Reiter, Linge, Ludecke, Speer; interviews in DeWitt Poole Mission, microfilm; OSS Source Book; "Hitler: Composite," MIR.

131. Dr. Forster, former Chargé d'Affairès, German Embassy in Paris, Letter to the editor, *Wiener Bulletin*, 10, nos. 5–6 (1956), 46.

132. Quoted in Schneider, 7 *Tage*.

133. Linge, *Revue*, 3 March 1956 and 28 January 1956; Kurt von Schuschnigg, *Austrian Requiem*, trans. Franz von Hildebrand (New York, 1946), 15; Miscellaneous OSS File, National Archives; for Hitler's "Monumental History," see Chapter 2, p. 56.

134. Domarus, *Reden*, 1424, 1842.

135. Ibid., 1842; Gun, *Eva Braun-Hitler*, 202; *Conversations*, 278.

136. Hitler, *Mein Kampf*, 65, 511; Rauschning quoted in Fest, *Face*, 51; Speer, *Inside*, 101; italics are mine.

137. Wilhelm Treue, "Dokumentation: Rede Hitlers vor der deutschen Presse, 10 November 1938," *VfZ* 6 (1958):175ff; italics are mine.

138. Domarus, *Reden*, 1312ff.

139. Goebbels, *Diary*, 193.

140. Hanfstaengl interview, Munich, June 1967; see also Hanfstaengl, *Missing Years*, 52; Richard Grunberger, *The Twelve-Year Reich: A Social History of Nazi*

Germany, 1933–1945 (New York, 1971), 369; Martha Dodd and Princess Olga as quoted in OSS Source Book, 58–60.

141. OSS Source Book, 627.

142. Personal letter from Karl Menninger, 10 October 1966.

143. I am indebted to Erik Erikson for calling my attention to Hitler's ambivalent treatment of the feminine goddess and for providing several of the examples given here. See also Hitler, *Mein Kampf*, 3, 28, 29, 32, 54, 76, 136, 205, 212, 213, 514, 753. The letter of 1914 is reprinted in Franz Jetzinger, *Hitlers Jugend: Phantasien, Lügen und die Wahrheit* (Vienna, 1956), 262–264; Munich speech in Phelps, *VfZ*, 68; Berlin speech in Prange, *Hitler's Words*, 19–20.

144. Grunberger, *Reich*, 236.

145. Kubizek, *Young Hitler*, 233; *Conversations*, 385.

146. Heer, *Glaube*, 273; Grunberger, *Reich*, 260.

147. Quoted in *Quick* (Munich), 3 May 1964, 104.

148. Kelley, 22 *Cells*, 211.

149. Hoffmann, *Hitler*, 145; Paula Hitler, interview *New York Times* 5 March 1959.

150. *Conversations*, 37.

151. Wagner, *Royal Family*, 91.

152. Goebbels, *Diary*, 367.

153. *Tischgespräche*, 188; Speer, *Inside*, 92; *Conversations*, 206; "AH" in FDR.

154. *Das Neue Tagebuch*, 28 September 1935, 921–922.

155. Hitler, *Mein Kampf*, 56.

156. *Conversations*, 391; OSS Source Book, 902–903.

157. "AH" in FDR.

158. Hitler, *Mein Kampf*, 137; German ed., 116–117; italics are mine.

159. Eva G. Reichmann, *Hostages of Civilization: The Social Sources of National Socialist Anti-Semitism* (London, 1950), 264; italics are mine.

160. "AH" in FDR; Schirach, *Ich glaubte*, 67.

CHAPTER 2

1. Among memoirs, see especially: Albert Zoller, ed., *Hitler Privat: Erlebnisbericht seiner Geheimsekretärin* (Düsseldorf, 1949); Otto Dietrich, *12 Jahre mit Hitler* (Munich, 1955); Heinrich Hoffmann, *Hitler Was My Friend*, (London, 1955); Albert Speer, *Inside the Third Reich: Memoirs*, trans. Richard and Clara Winston (New York, 1970); conversations with Ernst Hanfstaengl, April, May, June 1967, Munich; depositions of Percy Schramm, Karl Brandt, and Hans Karl Hasselbach in Bundesarchiv (Coblenz), Bestand 441; Military Intelligence Consolidated Interrogation Reports (National Archives): "Hitler as Seen by His Doctors" (hereafter cited as "Hitler's Doctors," MIR and as "Hitler: Composite," MIR); and the testimony given to OSS officials in 1942–1943 and edited by Walter C. Langer, "Hitler Source Book," National Archives (hereafter cited as OSS Source Book).

2. Heinz Assmann, "Some Personal Recollections of Adolf Hitler," *United States Naval Institute Proceedings* 79 (July 1953):1293.

3. Hasselbach in Bundesarchiv; Brandt in "Hitler's Doctors," MIR.

4. Erich von Manstein, *Verlorene Siege* (Frankfurt am Main, 1963), 305, 315, and passim.

5. Percy Ernst Schramm, ed., introduction to *Hitlers Tischgespräche im Führerhauptquartier, 1941–1942* (Stuttgart, 1965), 70, 73 (hereafter cited as *Tischgespräche*).

6. Bundesarchiv, Coblenz, nos 26–49. For extensive reprintings of these notes, see Werner Maser, *Hitlers Briefe und Notizen: Sein Weltbild in handschriftlichen Dokumenten* (Vienna, 1973), 290–353.

Notes

7. Hajo Holborn, "Origins and Political Character of Nazi Ideology," *Germany and Europe: Historical Essays* (New York, 1971), 214.

8. Hans Kaltenborn, "An Interview with Hitler: August 17, 1932," *Wisconsin Magazine of History* (Summer 1967):287.

9. John Kenneth Galbraith in *New York Times Book Review*, 22 April 1973; John Heyl, "Hitler's Economic Thought: A Reappraisal," *Central European History* 6 (March 1973):85.

10. Dorothy Thompson, *New York Post*, 3 January 1944.

11. *Tischgespräche*; Adolf Hitler, *Hitler's Secret Conversations, 1941–1944*, trans. Norman Cameron and R. H. Stevens (New York, 1953) (hereafter cited as *Conversations*); *The Testament of Adolf Hitler*, trans. R. H. Stevens (London, 1961); Library of Congress, Manuscript Division, "Hitler Papers."

12. Zoller, *Privat*, 50.

13. August Kubizek, *The Young Hitler I Knew*, trans. E. V. Anderson (Boston, 1955), 184.

14. Willie Schneider, "Aus nächster Nähe," *Die 7 Tage: Illustrierte Wochenschrift aus dem Zeitgeschehen* (Baden-Baden), October 1952 (hereafter cited as *7 Tage*); Karl Wilhelm Krause, *7 Tage*; Heinz Linge, "Kronzeuge Linge," *Revue* (Munich), November-December 1955.

15. Hans Frank memorandum quoted in G. M. Gilbert, *The Psychology of Dictatorship: Based on An Examination of the Leaders of Nazi Germany* (New York, 1950), 48.

16. *Oberösterreichisches Landesarchiv: Politische Akten #64* (hereafter cited as OLA).

17. Hans Frank as quoted by Gilbert, *Dictatorship*, 47–48.

18. Institut für Zeitgeschichte Archiv, 789.

19. Hoffmann, *Hitler*, xiv.

20. Reginald H. Phelps, "Die Hitler-Bibliothek," *Deutsche Rundschau* 80 (1954):929. My investigation of the Hitler library leads me to the same conclusion. See also Arnold Jacobus, Staff Librarian, Library of Congress, "The Books Hitler Owned." (Unpublished manuscript.)

21. Alfred Rosenberg, *Letzte Aufzeichnungen* (Göttingen, 1955), 320, 342.

22. Karl Menninger, *Man Against Himself* (New York, 1961), 386.

23. Kubizek, *Young Hitler*, 191–192.

24. Ibid., 205; Friedrich Heer, *Der Glaube des Adolf Hitler: Anatomie einer politischen Religiosität* (Munich, 1968), 37; "Adolf Hitler," Franklin D. Roosevelt Library, Hyde Park, N.Y., 1942 (hereafter cited as "AH" in FDR).

25. Kubizek, *Young Hitler*, 191.

26. *Tischgespräche*, 323.

27. OLA, Hitler Akten, folder no. 56; Baldur von Schirach, "Ich Glaubte an Hitler," *Stern*, 23 July 1967; Library of Congress Ms Division, A. Hitler Collection, folder 472F.

28. Speer, *Inside*, 74, 532; "Playboy Interview: Albert Speer," *Playboy* (June 1971), 80.

29. Armand Dehlinger, "Architektur der Superlativ: Eine kritische Betrachtung der N. S. Bauprogramme von München und Nürnberg," Institut für Zeitgeschichte, Munich.

30. Frederick Oechsner, *This Is the Enemy* (New York, 1942), 84; testimony of Percy E. Schramm, Bundesarchiv, Bestand 441.

31. Werner Maser, in *Der Spiegel*, 28 May 1973, 124; Speer, *Inside*, 159; italics are mine.

32. S. Lane Faison, Jr., "Linz: Hitler's Museum and Library," Consolidated Interrogation Report no. 4, 15 December 1945, Office of Strategic Services War Department (hereafter cited as Faison Report).

33. Ibid., 36, 73, and passim.

34. Kurt von Schuschnigg, *Austrian Requiem*, trans. Franz von Hildebrand (New York, 1946), 20; Hitler, *Conversations*, 559.

35. Speer, *Inside*, 44; Zoller, *Privat*, 52.

36. Hanfstaengl, conversation, April 1967.

37. Personal letters from Dr. Reke Wankmuller, 27 July 1970, and from Dr. Ruhmer, curator, Bavarian State Painting Galleries, July 1970; Hoffmann, *Hitler*, 175.

38. For the legend, see R. Lowe Thompson, *The History of the Devil* (London, 1929), 129–133.

39. Kubizek, *Young Hitler*, 154.

40. See letters reprinted in Franz Jetzinger, *Hitler's Youth*, trans. Lawrence Wilson (London, 1958), and in Maser, *Briefe und Notizen*.

41. Franz Jetzinger, *Hitlers Jugend, Phantasien, Luegen-Und Die Wahrheit* (Vienna, 1956), 201, 204, 262; compare the English translation, *Hitler's Youth*, 125, 128, 153.

42. Hermann Hammer, "Die deutschen Ausgaben von Hitlers *Mein Kampf*," *Vierteljahrshefte für Zeitgeschichte*, 4. Jahrgang (1956):163; *Wiener Bulletin*, 6, nos. 5, 6 (1952).

43. Adolf Hitler, *Mein Kampf* (New York, 1939), 501. I have followed here the English translation of the American edition except to keep the original German, *völkisch*, rather than to translate it as "folkish"; see Leuchtwanger cited in Richard Grunberger, *The Twelve-Year Reich: A Social History of Nazi Germany, 1933–1945* (New York, 1971), 361.

44. Rudolf Olden, *Hitler*, trans. Walter Ettinghausen (New York, 1936), 144–146.

45. *Conversations*, 205.

46. *Mein Kampf*, 704.

47. Eberhard Jäckel, *Hitler's Weltanschauung: A Blueprint for Power*, trans. Herbert Arnold (Middletown, Conn., 1972), 43.

48. Alan Bullock, "The Political Ideas of Adolf Hitler," in Maurice Baumont, John H. E. Fried, et al., eds., *The Third Reich* (New York, 1955), 351.

49. Karl Dietrich Bracher, *The German Dictatorship: The Origins, Structure and Effects of National Socialism*, trans. Jean Steinberg (New York, 1970), 199.

50. Otto Klineberg, "Racialism in Nazi Germany," in *The Third Reich*, 859; Ernst Nolte, *Three Faces of Fascism*, trans. Leila Vennewitz (New York, 1966), 23.

51. Svend Ranulf, *Hitlers Kampf gegen die Objektivität* (Copenhagen, 1946), 24.

52. *Tischgespräche*, 218, 425; Hitler, *Conversations*, 147, 442, 299.

53. Solomon F. Bloom, "The Peasant Caesar: Hitler's Union of German Imperialism and Eastern Reaction," *Commentary* 23 (May 1957):406–418.

54. Gordon W. Prange, ed., *Hitler's Words* (Washington, D.C., 1944), 8.

55. Hitler, *Mein Kampf*, 397, 601.

56. Max Domarus, ed., *Hitler: Reden und Proklamationen, 1932–1945* (Munich, 1965), 1423 (hereafter cited as Domarus, *Reden*). The speeches can be found conveniently in English in *The Speeches of Adolf Hitler, 1922–1939*, ed. Norman H. Baynes, 2 vols. (London, 1942) (hereafter cited as Baynes, *Speeches*), and in *Hitler's Words*, ed. Prange; see also Nolte, *Three Faces*, 240, 409–410, 420.

57. Alfred Rosenberg as quoted in Bracher, *Dictatorship*, 252.

58. Domarus, *Reden*, 1423.

59. Hitler, *Mein Kampf*, 947, 950–951; italics in original.

60. Speeches taken from *Völkischer Beobachter* as recorded in Prange, *Hitler's Words*; see also Adolf Hitler, *Hitler's Secret Book*, trans. Salvatore Attanasio (New York, 1961), 50, 74.

61. See especially conversations of 5–6 July 1941; 8–10 August; 13–17 October, and 11 April 1942 as recorded in *Tischgespräche* and *Conversations*.

62. Helmut Heiber, quoted in Jäckel, *Weltanschauung*, 19.

63. Speeches of 7 March 1936 and 8 November 1938, quoted in Fritz Nova, *The National Socialist Fuehrerprinzip and Its Background in German Thought* (Philadelphia, 1943), 4; *Conversations*, 143.

Notes

64. Hans Buchheim, "The SS: Instrument of Domination," in *Anatomy of the SS State*, ed. Helmut Krausnick (New York, 1968), 133.

65. Norman H. Baynes and Dr. Hans Frank, as quoted in Bullock, *Third Reich*, 368.

66. Gregor Ziemer, *Education for Death* (New York, 1941), 48, 59, 121.

67. William L. Shirer, *The Rise and Fall of the Third Reich* (New York, 1959), 249, 227.

68. Speech at Nuremberg Party rally, September 1935, in Prange, *Hitler's Words*, 126–127.

69. See Joseph Nyomarky's valuable monograph, *Charisma and Factionalism in the Nazi Party* (Minneapolis, 1967).

70. Dietrich Orlow, *The History of the Nazi Party: 1919–1933* (Pittsburgh, 1969), 1:9–10.

71. Grunberger, *12-Year Reich*, 350–351.

72. Birthday issues of *Völkischer Beobachter* as cited in Gertrud M. Kurth, "The Image of the Fuehrer: A Contribution to the Role of Imagery in Hero-Worship," (New School for Social Research Library), 53, 68–69, 74, 97, 100.

73. Hitler, *Mein Kampf*, 470, 406, 594.

74. Otto Strasser, *Aufbau des deutschen Sozialismus—Als Anlage das historische Gespräch mit Dr. Strasser* (Prague, 1936), 124, 118.

75. Baynes, *Speeches*, I, 662–664; Domarus, *Reden*, 449.

76. Hitler, *Mein Kampf*, 397–398; Prange, *Hitler's Words*, 5.

77. Ernst Deuerlein, "Dokumentation: Hitlers Eintritt in die Politik und die Reichswehr," in *Vierteljahrshefte für Zeitgeschichte*, Jahrgang 7 (1959).

78. Domarus, *Reden*, 2239.

79. Hitler, *Mein Kampf*, 413–414, 416–418, 421.

80. Dietrich Eckart, *Der Bolschewismus von Moses bis Lenin: Zwiegespräch zwischen Adolf Hitler und Mir* (Munich, 1924), 49; for a discussion of the authorship of the pamphlet, see below, 117; Dr. Hans Frank, *Im Angesicht des Galgens: Deutung Hitlers und seiner Zeit auf Grunde eigener Erlebnisse und Erkenntnisse* (Munich, 1953), 403. Fritz Wiedemann, *Der Mann der Feldherr werden wollte: Erlebnisse und Erfahrungen des Vorgesetzten Hitlers im ersten Weltkrieg und seines späteren persönlichen Adjutaten* (Haan, 1964), 205.

81. For a perceptive essay on terror, see Alex Inkeles in Carl J. Friedrich, ed., *Totalitarianism: A Symposium by the Leading Historians, Psychologists, Social Psychologists* (Cambridge, Mass., 1954).

82. *Völkischer Beobachter*, 15 September 1936, quoted in Aryeh L. Unger, *The Totalitarian Party: Party and People in Nazi Germany and Soviet Russia* (Cambridge, 1974), 34; Franz Neuman, *Behemoth: The Structure and Practice of National Socialism* (New York, 1944), 436.

83. Hitler, *Mein Kampf*, 313.

84. Ziemer, *Education for Death*, 80–81.

85. *New York Herald Tribune*, 15 July 1940.

86. Shirer, *Rise and Fall*, 90.

87. Hitler, *Mein Kampf*, 71, 125–129; William A. Jenks, *Vienna and the Young Hitler* (New York, 1960), 95–97; H. G. Adler, *Die Juden in Deutschland* (Munich, 1960), 128.

88. *Deutsches Volksblatt*, issues of May and June 1908.

89. Hitler, *Mein Kampf*, 73.

90. See nos. 32, 37, and 40 of his pamphlet *Ostara*.

91. See his pamphlet *Die Ostara und das Reich des Blonden*.

92. Daim, *Der Mann*, 20–22.

93. *Schädelform* (*Ostara* pamphlet).

94. Rauschning, *Voice*, 229–230; Herbert Luthy, "Der Führer persönlich," *Der Monat* 6 Jahrgang (October 1953):157. Italics are mine.

95. Guido von List, *Die Armanenschaft der Ario-Germanen*, pt. 2 (Vienna, 1911), 24–26, 108.

96. Lanz von Liebenfels, quoted in List, *Armanenschaft*, 2:54.

97. Ibid., 2:67, 86–87, 97–98.

98. Preface to Guido von List, *Die Rita der Ario-Germanen* (Vienna, 1920).

99. Reginald Phelps, "Theodor Fritsch und der Antisemitismus," *Deutsche Rundschau* 87 (1961):443. See also Peter G. J. Pulzer, *The Rise of Political Anti-Semitism in Germany and Austria* (London, 1964), 53.

100. Phelps, "Fritsch," 442.

101. Dedication to Theodor Fritsch, *Handbuch Der Judenfrage: die wichtigsten tatsachen zur Beurteilung des Jüdischen Volkes,* 36th ed. (Leipzig, 1934). This is the edition cited here.

102. Fritsch, *Handbuch*, 416. For the "allies" of the Jews see 229, 245, 265–269.

103. Ibid., 310ff., 295, 85, 400–402, and passim.

104. Phelps in *Rundschau*, 449.

105. Peter Viereck, *Metapolitics: From the Romantics to Hitler* (New York, 1941), 132.

106. Hitler, *Mein Kampf*, 23; Kubizek, *Young Hitler*, 188, 192.

107. Oechsner, *The Enemy*, 87.

108. See especially Bryan Magee's brilliant study, *Aspects of Wagner* (New York, 1969).

109. Kubizek, *Young Hitler*, 188; "AH" in FDR.

110. Hoffmann, *Hitler*, 171.

111. Kubizek, *Young Hitler*, 182.

112. *Conversations*, 205.

113. See Kubizek, *Young Hitler*, 193–202.

114. Magee, *Aspects*, 100, 93–97.

115. Hermann Rauschning, *The Voice of Destruction* (New York, 1940), 230.

116. William Ashton Ellis, ed., *Richard Wagner's Prose Works*, 8 vols. (London, 1900–1909), vol. 6, 283.

117. Deems Taylor, *Of Men and Music* (New York, 1937), 3–4.

118. Robert W. Gutman, *Richard Wagner: The Man, His Mind, and His Music* (New York, 1968), 242; see also *Works*, vol. 4, 160.

119. Wilhelm Altmann, ed., *Letters of Richard Wagner*, trans. M. N. Bozman (New York, 1927) 2:35, 243, and passim.

120. Louis L. Snyder, *German Nationalism: The Tragedy of a People* (Harrisburg, 1952), 156–157.

121. Wagner, *Letters* 2:230.

122. Thomas Lask, *New York Times Book Review*, 2 July 1968; Wagner, *Letters*, vol. 2, 406; Gutman, *Wagner*, 262.

123. Viereck, *Metapolitics*, 107; Richard Wagner, *Gesammelte Schriften und Dichtungen* (Leipzig), 6:202–203.

124. Quoted in Magee, *Aspects*, 72–73.

125. Wagner, *Schriften*, 10:242.

126. Gutman, *Wagner*, 332, 400, and passim.

127. Wagner to his mother, Karlsbad, 25 July 1835, in *Letters*, 1:28.

128. Richard Wagner, *My Life*, 2 vols. (New York, 1911), I, preface and 3.

129. See Ernst Newman, *The Life of Richard Wagner* (New York, 1941), 3: 558–559.

130. Gutman, *Wagner*, 5.

131. Wagner, *Letters*, 1:205; see also *Letters*, 1:23, 279–280; 2:35 passim.

132. Wagner, *Schriften*, 5:67–69; *Works*, 3:80–83. Unless otherwise noted, all quotations are from the German edition.

133. Magee, *Aspects*, 41–42.

134. Wagner, "Erkenne dich selbst," reprinted in *Schriften* 10.

135. Wagner, "Religion und Kunst," in *Schriften* 10:280, 232.

136. Wagner, *Works* 3:86–87; *Schriften* 10:271; *Works* 4:158.

137. Wagner, *Schriften* 10:274; *Works* 3:82, 121.

138. Wagner, *Schriften* 5:85; italics in original, my translation. For Ellis's bowdlerized version, see *Works* 3:100.

Notes

139. Wagner, "German Art and German Policy," in *Works* 4:40.

140. Wagner, *Schriften* 10:284.

141. Gutman, *Wagner*, 432.

142. George G. Windell, "Hitler, National Socialism and Richard Wagner," *Journal of Central European Affairs* 22 (January 1963):46.

143. See also Gutman, *Wagner*, 428.

144. Wagner, *Works* 6:309.

145. Rauschning, *Voice*, 230.

146. Wagner, *Works* 4:166–167.

147. Wagner, *Schriften* 10:130.

148. Quoted in Konrad Heiden, *Der Fuehrer: Hitler's Rise to Power*, trans. Ralph Manheim (Boston, 1944), 227.

149. Wagner, *Works* 4:13n.

150. Ibid., 4:16.

151. Fritz Fischer, *War of Illusions*, trans. Marian Jackson (New York, 1975), 29–30; Heiden, *Der Fuehrer*, 233, 237.

152. Joseph O. Baylen and Ralph F. Munster, "Adolf Hitler as seen by Houston Stewart Chamberlain: A Forgotten Letter," *Duquesne Review* (Fall 1967):83; Heiden, *Der Fuehrer*, 245–246; memoirs of Friedelind Wagner, *The Royal Family of Bayreuth* (London, 1948).

153. Hitler, *Mein Kampf*, 30.

154. Ibid., 296.

155. Joachim Besser, "New Light on the Pre-History of National Socialism," *Die Pforte*, nos. 21–22 (November 1950):779.

156. Bracher, *Dictatorship*, 81.

157. Georg Franz, "Entstehungs- und Frühgeschichte der Nationalsozialistischen Deutschen Arbeiterpartei Münchens, 1919–1923," Institut für Zeitgeschichte (Munich), 78.

158. Ibid., 81–82.

159. Zoller, *Privat*, 119; *Conversations*, 178.

160. As translated by the editors of the American edition of *Mein Kampf*, 993.

161. Hitler and Eckart, *Bolschewismus*, 28 and passim.

162. Ibid., 49.

163. Norman Cohn, *Warrant for Genocide: The Myths of the Jewish World Conspiracy and the Protocols of the Elders of Zion* (London, 1967), 181; Hitler, *Mein Kampf*, 423–424.

164. Rauschning, *Voice*, 238–241.

165. John Gwyer, *Portraits of Mean Men: A Short History of the Protocols of the Elders of Zion* (London, 1938), 96.

166. Cohn, *Warrant*, 153ff.

167. Ibid., 159.

168. Walter Laqueur, *Russia and Germany: A Century of Conflict* (London, 1965), 68.

169. Ibid., 69.

170. Heer, *Glaube*, 39–41.

171. Gustave Le Bon, *The Crowd: A Study of the Popular Mind* (London, 1913), passim.

172. Robert G. L. Waite, *Vanguard of Nazism: The Free Corps Movement in Postwar Germany, 1911–1923* (Cambridge, Mass.), 140–141.

173. Nolte, *Three Faces*, 256–258, 262–266, and passim.

CHAPTER 3

1. Letter of Father Ledl in Oberösterreichisches Landesarchiv (Linz) folder 2 (hereafter cited as OLA). The most reliable factual account of Hitler's family is given in Bradley Smith, *Adolf Hitler: His Family, Childhood and Youth* (Palo Alto, Calif., 1967).

2. Original file marked "Geheime Reichssache" is presently in the Prints and Photographs Division, Library of Congress; see also Photostat Documents Gestapo File, in Institut für Zeitgeschichte Archiv, Munich (hereafter cited as IfZ).

3. Letter in OLA folder 3.

4. Dr. Hans Frank, *Im Angesicht des Galgens: Deutung Hitlers und seiner Zeit auf Grund eigener Erlebnisse und Erkentnisse* (Munich, 1953), 320–321.

5. One biographer believes that the grandfather almost certainly was Jewish; another insists that he could not have been; a third reaches the surprising conclusion that Hitler would not have cared one way or another. Germany's leading newsmagazine, *Der Spiegel*, has devoted at least two detailed articles to the problem. In his careful book on Hitler's early years, Bradley Smith provided a special appendix in which he argued that Hitler's grandfather was not a Jew. See Franz Jetzinger, *Hitlers Jugend: Phantasien, Lügen und die Wahrheit* (Vienna, 1956), translated into English as *Hitler's Youth* (London, 1958); Hans Bernd Gisevius, *Adolf Hitler: Versuch einer Deutung* (Munich, 1963); Werner Maser, *Adolf Hitler: Legende, Mythos, Wirklichkeit* (Munich, 1971).

6. Walter C. Langer, "Psychological Analysis of Adolph [sic] Hitler: His Life and Legend," Office of Strategic Services Report, National Archives, (1943), 226. Hereafter cited as OSS Report. A printed version of this document was published as *The Mind of Adolf Hitler*, foreword by William L. Langer, afterword by Robert G. L. Waite (New York, 1972); Hitler, *Mein Kampf*, 610; Herman Rauschning, *The Voice of Destruction* (New York, 1940), 230; Hans Frank as quoted in Friedrich Heer, *Der Glaube des Adolf Hitler: Anatomie einer politischen Religiosität* (Munich, 1968), 350; Nerin E. Gun, *Eva Braun-Hitler: Leben und Schicksal* (New York and Bruchsal/Baden, 1968), 169.

7. Bernhard Lösener, "Das Reichsministerium des Innern und die Judengesetzgebung," *Vierteljahrshefte für Zeitgeschichte* 9 (1961):273 (hereafter cited as VfZ). During the Third Reich, Lösener had been the expert on "racial law." The full text of the law is given in *Völkischer Beobachter*, 16 September 1935.

8. Gerhart L. Weinberg, ed., *Hitlers Zweites Buch* (Stuttgart, 1961), 104; italics are mine.

9. Otto Dietrich, *Hitler*, trans. Richard and Clara Winston (Chicago, 1955), 156.

10. Adolf Hitler, *Hitler's Secret Conversations, 1941–1944* (New York, 1953), 269 (hereafter cited as *Conversations*).

11. Albert Speer, *Inside the Third Reich: Memoirs*, trans. Richard and Clara Winston (New York, 1970), 98.

12. General Knittersched's statement is in OLA folder 161.

13. Joachim Fest, *Hitler: Eine Biographie* (Frankfurt am Main, 1973), 30–31.

14. OSS Source Book, 73. Gordon W. Prange, ed., *Hitler's Words* (Washington, D.C., 1944), 79; italics are mine.

15. *The Testament of Adolf Hitler*, trans. R. H. Stevens (London, 1961), 56; italics are mine.

16. Testimony of Frau Rosalia Hörl, née Schichtl, who had worked as a cook and maid in the Alois Hitler ménage in Braunau, Hauptarchiv der Partei (Microfilm, National Archives, Washington, D.C.), folder 17A, reel 1 (hereafter cited as HAP).

17. *Linzer Tageblatt,* 8 January 1903, quoted in Jetzinger, *Hitler's Youth,* 53.

18. HAP folder 17A, reel 1.

19. August Kubizek, *The Young Hitler I Knew*, trans E. V. Anderson (Boston, 1955), 37; interview conducted 21 June 1940 by the Gestapo with Herr Hebenstreit, former customs office secretary in Braunau. HAP, folder 17A, reel 1.

20. Jetzinger's interview with Mayrhofer in OLA folder 159.

21. Erikson's Godkin Lecture, "Spheres of Play and Vision," quoted in *Harvard Today*, May 1972, 13.

22. See interviews in OSS Source Book, 924; Ernst Müller-Meinigen, *Die Parteigenossen* (Munich, 1948), 32.

23. Kubizek, *Young Hitler,* 38; Hitler, *Mein Kampf,* 6.

Notes

24. Compare the translations in *Conversations* with Lothar Gruchman, "Dokumentation: Hitler über Justiz," *VfZ*, 12 (1964):86–101; HAP folder 17A.

25. Hitler, *Mein Kampf*, 7, 10–14.

26. Conversation of 18 January 1942, Library of Congress, Ms. Division, "Adolf Hitler," Baldur von Schirach, as quoted in *Stern*, no. 31, July 30, 1967.

27. Frank, *Galgens*, 322.

28. Albert Zoller, ed., *Hitler Privat: Erlebnisbericht seiner Geheimsekretärin* (Düsseldorf, 1949), 46.

29. Quoted in Thomas A. Harris, M.D., *I'm O.K.—You're O.K.* (New York, 1973), 73.

30. Erik H. Erikson, *Young Man Luther: A Study in Psychoanalysis and History* (New York, 1962), 64; Theodor Reik, *Masochism in Sex and Society*, trans. Margaret H. Beigel and Gertrud M. Kurth (New York, 1962), 22–23.

31. Smith, *Hitler's Childhood*, 33.

32. Josef Mayrhofer, interviewed in *Revue* (Munich), 27 September 1952.

33. Dr. Eduard Bloch, "My Patient, Hitler," *Collier's Magazine*, 15 March 1941, 36.

33a. Helm Stierlin, "Hitler as his Mother's Delegate," *History of Childhood Quarterly*, 3: (Spring, 1976), 484.

34. Bloch, "My Patient," 36.

35. Interview with Friedlinde Wagner, OSS Source Book, 940; Karl Wilhelm Krause, *Zehn Jahre Kammerdiener bei Hitler* (Hamburg, early 1950s), 52; conversation with Hanfstaengl, Munich, May 1967.

36. Hitler, *Mein Kampf*, 267.

37. Testimony of the postmaster's widow and of Dr. Bloch, HAP, folder 17A, reel 1.

38. Karl and Jeanetta Lyle Menninger, *Love Against Hate* (New York, 1942), 57; italics in original.

39. Erik Erikson conversation, April 1968; Menninger, *Love Against Hate*, 118–119.

40. Jetzinger, *Hitler's Youth*, 78–93; Smith, *Hitler's Childhood*, 90–94.

41. Walter Langer, *OSS Report*, 150; conversations with Erik Erikson, Norbert Bromberg, and Lawrence Climo.

42. Ernst Deuerlein, "Adolf Hitler," *Politiker des 20. Jahrhunderts*, ed. Rolf K. Holcevar et al. (Munich, 1970), 181–182; Maser, *Hitler*, 53.

43. Erik Erikson, "The Problem of Ego Identity," *Journal of the American Psychoanalytical Association* 4 (1956):121 (hereafter cited as *Journal of APA*).

44. Phyllis Greenacre, M.D., "Influence of Infantile Trauma," in *Psychic Trauma*, ed. Sidney S. Furst (New York, 1967), 108–153.

45. Gertrud Kurth's comment on Rudolf Binion, "Hitler's Concept of *Lebensraum*: The Psychological Basis," *History of Childhood Quarterly* (Fall 1973):237. Binion has suggested that Adolf was nursed for a much longer time than Klara's other children.

46. HAP folder 17A, reel 1.

47. Kubizek, *Young Hitler*, 13–14, 18–19; Dietrich, *Hitler* (German ed.), 224–225.

48. Quoted in Reginald H. Phelps, "Dokumentation: Hitler als Parteiredner im Jahre 1920," *VfZ* 11 (1963):311; italics are mine.

49. Karl Abraham, *Selected Papers of Karl Abraham* (New York, 1968), 401.

50. Melanie Klein, *The Psychoanalysis of Children* (London, 1959), 343.

51. Erik Erikson, *Childhood and Society* (New York, 1963), 251–254.

52. Otto Fenichel, M.D., *The Psychoanalytic Theory of Neurosis* (New York, 1945), 278.

53. His word was *Scheisskerl*. See *Hitlers Tischgespräche im Führerhauptquartier*, ed. Percy Schramm, 2nd ed. (Stuttgart, 1965), 171 (hereafter cited as *Tischgespräche*); see also Albert Speer, *Spandau, The Secret Diaries* (New York, 1976), 346.

54. Bormann Papers, "Hitler Privat Gespräche," Berlin Document Center, microfilm group 7, reel 2; *Conversations*, 160; Smith, *Hitler's Childhood*, 99.

55. "Hitler as Seen by His Doctors," *Military Intelligence Report* (mimeographed), National Archives (hereafter cited as "Hitler's Doctors," MIR).

56. Quoted in Fenichel, *Psychoanalytic Theory*, 282.

57. See Maser's letters to the editor of *Die Zeit*, 21 December 1971, 29 February 1972, and his biography, *Hitler*, 346–350; Trevor-Roper, *Sunday Times* (London), 18 February 1973.

58. Detailed discussion, pictures of the evidence, testimony, letters to the editor, rejoinders, and rebuttals are given in *Die Zeit*, 7 December 1971, 21 December 1971, 29 February 1972.

59. Ellsworth K. Kelly, D.D.S., in *Journal of California Dental Association* 41 (1965):424–425.

60. Reidar F. Sognnaes and Ferdinand Ström, "The Odontological Identification of Adolf Hitler: Definitive Documentation by X rays, Interrogations and Autopsy Findings," *Acta Odontologica Scandinavica* 31 (1973):43–69.

61. See especially Werner Maser, 437–438, passim; also John Toland, *Adolf Hitler* (New York, 1976), 827.

62. Morell testimony of 29 November 1945, "Hitler's Doctors," MIR.

63. See his testimony of 15 October 1945, "Hitler's Doctors," MIR.

64. Maser, *Hitler*, 346; Toland, *Adolf Hitler*, 827.

65. Letter to *Die Zeit*, 21 December 1971.

66. Peter Blos, "Comments on the Psychological Consequences of Cryptorchism," *Psychoanalytic Study of the Child* 15 (1960):408–420.

67. Ibid.

68. Anita I. Bell, "The Significance of Scrotal Sac and Testicles for the Prepuberty Male," *Psychoanalytic Quarterly* 34 (1966):192.

69. Anita I. Bell, "Observations on the Role of the Scrotal Sac and Testes," *Journal of APA* 9 (1966):261–286.

70. Frederic V. Grunfeld, "Sunday Afternoon with the Monster," *Saturday Review of the Arts*, March 1973, 46.

71. Jetzinger, *Hitler's Youth*, 59–60; see also Maser, *Hitler*, 6.

72. Jetzinger, *Hitler's Youth*, 74–75.

73. HAP folder 14, reel 1.

74. Quoted in G. M. Gilbert, *The Psychology of Dictatorship: Based on an Examination of the Leaders of Nazi Germany* (New York, 1950), 18.

75. Kubizek, *Young Hitler*, 15–16.

76. The report card appears in Jetzinger, *Hitler's Youth*, 67.

77. Hugo Rabitsch, *Aus Hitlers Jugendzeit: Erinnerungen eines zeitgenössichen Linzer Realschulers* (Munich, 1938), quoted in Jetzinger, *Hitler's Youth*, 69; Rudolf Olden, *Hitler*, trans. Walter Ettinghausen (New York, 1936), 19.

78. See Werner Maser, *Hitlers Briefe und Notizen: Sein Weltbild in handschriftlichen Dokumenten* (Vienna, 1973), 38.

79. William G. Niederland, "Narcissistic Ego Impairment in Patients with Early Physical Malformations," *Psychoanalytic Study of the Child* 20 (1965):525.

80. Kubizek, *Young Hitler*, 83–92 and passim; italics are mine.

81. HAP folder 36, reel 2; italics are mine.

82. Albert Speer interview in *Playboy*, June 1971, 86.

83. Fritz Percy Reck-Malleczwen, *Diary of a Man in Despair*, trans. Paul Rubens (New York, 1970), 176; and see Chapter 2.

84. Douglas M. Kelley, 22 *Cells in Nuremberg* (New York, 1947), 22, 215.

85. Pictures in the *Neue Reichskanzlei*, 31; Frederick C. Oechsner, *This Is the Enemy* (Boston, 1942), 82, 96.

86. "Hitler's Doctors," MIR; see also Speer, *Inside*, 105.

87. Erich Kuby interview with Heinz Linge in Kuby, *Die Russen in Berlin, 1945* (Vienna, 1965), 204.

88. *Testament*, 64; italics are mine.

Notes

89. Hitler, *Mein Kampf*, English ed. 42–44; German ed., 32–34; Langer, *Mind of Adolf Hitler*, 142–145.

90. Hitler, *Mein Kampf*, English ed., 38; German ed., 28; italics are mine.

91. Peter Loewenberg, review article, *Central European History* (September 1974):265.

92. Sigmund Freud, "Medusa's Head," in *Works*, Standard ed., 18:273–274.

93. See letter to Gemlich, 17 September 1919, quoted in Joachim C. Fest, *The Face of the Third Reich: Portraits of the Nazi Leadership*, trans. Michael Bullock (New York, 1970), 16.

94. *Mein Kampf*, German ed., 135.

95. Conference of 13 February 1945, *Testament*, 51; *OSS Source Book*; Ernest Jones, *On the Nightmare* (New York, 1951), 44; italics in original.

96. Conversation with Norbert Bromberg, M.D., July 1973.

97. Günter Peis, "Die unbekannte Geliebte," *Stern* Nov. 24 (1959):59.

98. Freud, "From the History of an Infantile Neurosis," in *Works*, Standard ed., 17:78–79, 82ff.

99. Conversation with Bromberg.

100. See Phyllis Greenacre, *Trauma Growth and Personality* (New York, 1952), 132–148, 204–223, 224–238, 293–302; see also Greenacre, "Infantile Trauma," 108–153.

101. Hitler, *Mein Kampf*, 73; italics are mine.

102. Loewenberg, in *Central European History*, 267–268.

103. Conversation with Bromberg.

104. Zoller, *Privat*, 46.

105. Freud, "A Child Is Being Beaten," in *Collected Papers* 2:334.

106. Hitler, *Mein Kampf*, 44; italics are mine.

107. For interviews with the villagers of Leonding, see Thomas Orr, "Das war Hitler, das Ende eines Mythos," *Revue* (Munich), 4 October 1952.

108. Menninger, *Love Against Hate*, 35.

109. Ibid., 57.

110. Otto Kernberg, "Borderline Personality Organization," *Journal of APA* 15 (July 1967):641–683.

111. Statement of Dr. Edward Kriechbaum, 26 July 1952, OLA folder, 143.

112. Rudolf Olden, *Hitler*, trans. Walter Ettinghausen (New York, 1936), 15; OSS Report.

113. Robert Jay Lifton, *History and Human Survival: Essays on the Young and Old, Survivors and the Dead, Peace and War, and on Contemporary Psycho-History* (New York, 1970), 169–171; also "On Death and Death Symbolism" and "The Hiroshima Bomb," reprinted in *History and Human Survival*.

114. Ibid., 172.

115. Albert C. Cain, Irene Fast, and Mary E. Erickson, "Children's Disturbed Reactions to the Death of a Sibling," *American Journal of Orthopsychiatry* 34 (Summer 1974), 741–751.

116. H. R. Trevor-Roper, *The Last Days of Hitler* (New York, 1947), 72.

117. Kubizek, letter of 28 June 1949, in OLA folder 64.

118. Erik Erikson, "The Problem of Ego Identity," *Psychological Issues* 1 (1959):132–133; Lawrence Climo, letter of 12 April 1974.

119. Hitler, *Mein Kampf*, 14, 24.

120. OLA folder 64; Gertrud M. Kurth, "The Jew and Adolf Hitler," *The Psychoanalytic Quarterly* 16 (1947):25; *Collier's*, March 15, 1941.

121. HAP folder 17A, reel 1.

122. Jetzinger, *Hitler's Youth*, 90; Smith, *Hitler's Childhood*, 96–98.

123. Kubizek, *Young Hitler*, 83–86, 88, 92, and passim.

124. Ibid., 9–10.

125. "Meine Erinnerungen an meinen Klavierschüler Adolf Hitler," HAP folder 65, reel 13a; Jetzinger, *Hitler's Youth*, 95; Konrad Heiden, *Der Fuehrer: Hitler's Rise to Power*, trans. Ralph Manheim (Boston, 1944), 51.

126. Jetzinger, *Hitler's Youth,* 90–93; Kubizek reprints the cards, *Young Hitler,* 104–106.

127. Jetzinger, *Hitlers Jugend,* 169.

128. Kubizek, *Young Hitler,* 96.

129. Ibid., 74–75.

130. Ibid., 99–101.

131. Ibid., 62–63.

132. Ibid., 63–64; 59–60.

133. Jetzinger, *Hitler's Youth,* 106–107; Orr, in *Revue,* 25 October 1953.

134. Kubizek, *Young Hitler,* 68.

135. Hospital records, HAP folder 65, reel 13a.

136. Hitler, *Mein Kampf,* 25.

137. Klara Hitler's medical bills are given in HAP folder 65, reel 13a; see also Jetzinger, *Hitler's Youth,* 100.

138. Bloch interview, OSS Source Book, 22.

139. Kubizek, letter of 28 June 1949, OLA folder 64.

140. Kubizek, *Young Hitler,* 124 and passim.

141. Jetzinger, *Hitler's Youth,* 103–104; *Hitlers Jugend,* 176.

142. Hitler, *Mein Kampf,* 26; italics are mine.

143. "Erinnerungen an den Führer und dessen verewigte Mutter!" typescript affidavit, HAP folder 17a, reel 1. Handwritten versions of this statement and a letter to the Party archivist, Bleibtreu, dated 16 November 1938 may be found in HAP folder 65, reel 13a.

144. See his *Collier's* article, 15 March 1941, and interviews with OSS officials on 5 March 1943 in OSS Source Book.

145. HAP folder 17a, reel 1; italics are mine.

146. Interrogation of Paula Hitler, Berchtesgaden, 26 May 1945, Berlin Document Center (microfilm), group 7, reel 1.

147. Maser, *Hitler,* 79.

148. In an interview after the war, Frau Braun remembered asking her daughter, Eva, why she never spent Christmas with Hitler. Eva said that it was because he had had such a horrible Christmas in his youth that "he never wants to celebrate Christmas again. He must be alone at Christmas time" (interview with Herr and Frau Braun, Ropoldingen, 4 September 1948, Musmanno Archives).

149. Karl-Heinz Janssen, "Volksweihenacht," *Die Zeit,* 26 December 1975.

150. HAP folder 17a, reel 1.

151. *Der Spiegel,* 24 July 1967. Maser disputes this point and says that Hitler visited the grave on two other occasions; see *Hitler,* 24.

152. Erikson, "The Problem of Ego Identity," *Psychological Issues* 1 (1959): 113–116.

153. Erikson, Daedelus Leadership Conference, 20 October 1967.

154. Erikson, "Ego Identity," *Psychological Issues,* 131.

155. Erikson, *Luther,* 100.

156. Ibid., 42, 103.

157. Erikson, "Ego Identity," *Journal of APA* (1956):158.

158. Heiden, *Der Fuehrer,* 52; Ludwig Wagner, *Hitler, Man of Strife* (New York, 1942), 43.

159. Hitler, *Mein Kampf,* 83.

160. HAP folder 17a; conversation with Chamberlain at the Berghof, 15 September 1938, *Documents of German Foreign Policy,* Series D, 2:787.

161. Werner Maser, *Die Frühgeschichte der NSDAP: Hitlers Weg bis 1924* (Bonn, 1965), 96–99.

162. George L. Mosse, *The Crisis of German Ideology: Intellectual Origins of the Third Reich* (New York, 1964), 295–297. For a revised position, see his comments on Rudolph Binion's article "Hitler's Concept of *Lebensraum*: The Psychological Base," *History of Childhood Quarterly* 1 (Fall 1973), 230.

163. Hitler, *Mein Kampf,* 296.

Notes

164. August Kubizek, "Erinnerungen an die mit dem Führer gemeinsam verlebten Jünglingsjahre 1904–1908 in Linz und Wien," OLA folder 63.

165. Conversation with Norbert Bromberg, July 1973.

166. Hitler, *Mein Kampf*, 80–82; italics are mine.

167. Kubizek, as quoted in Bromberg, "Hitler's Character and Its Development: Observations," *American Imago* 28 (Winter 1971):297–298.

168. Michael A. Musmanno, *Ten Days to Die* (New York, 1950), 100.

169. See *Whitaker's Almanac* (London, 1972), which confirms Bromberg, "Hitler's Character," 299.

170. Hitler, *Mein Kampf*, 84; italics in original.

171. Hitler, *Mein Kampf* as quoted in Robert Payne, *Life and Death of Adolf Hitler* (New York, 1973), 78; italics are mine.

172. Kubizek, *Young Hitler*, 107.

173. Hitler, *Mein Kampf*, 28, 25.

174. HAP folder 17a, reel 1.

175. Jetzinger, *Hitler's Youth*, 123–124; Smith, *Hitler's Childhood*, 123; Maser, *Hitler*, 81.

176. Unpublished Kubizek letter, quoted in Jetzinger, *Hitler's Youth*, 119.

177. "Adolf Hitler," General Services Administration, National Archives and Records Service, December 1942, in Franklin D. Roosevelt Library (hereafter cited as "AH" in FDR).

178. Jetzinger, *Hitler's Youth*, 121; supported by Kubizek letter in OLA folder 63.

179. Kubizek, *Young Hitler*, 207, 211–213.

180. Kubizek to Jetzinger, letter dated 25 April 1949, in OLA folder 64.

181. Kubizek, *Young Hitler*, 252.

182. William A. Jenks, *Vienna and the Young Hitler* (New York, 1960), 31–33.

183. HAP folder 1741, reel 86.

184. HAP folder 19, reel 1. Folders 19 through 43 contain pictures of Hitler's paintings and correspondence about them.

185. Statement by Jacob Altenberg, HAP folder 1741, reel 86. See also folder 64, reel 3; folder 19, reel 2; folder 22, reel 2; and Maser, *Hitler*, 88.

186. For discussions of the orphan's pension and its forced renunciation, see Jetzinger, *Hitler's Youth*, 138ff; *Hitlers Jugend*, 226–228; and Smith, *Hitler's Childhood*, 111–112. A different and unconvincing point of view is given in Maser, *Frühgeschichte*, 482–483.

187. Hitler, *Mein Kampf*, German ed., 135–136; English ed., 161.

188. HAP folder 17a.

189. Jetzinger, *Hitler's Youth*, 138ff.

190. Hitler, *Mein Kampf*, German ed., 138.

191. HAP folder 26, quoted in Maser, *Frühgeschichte*, 116.

192. For interviews and information on the Popps, see Maser, *Hitler*, 122 and passim.

193. Interview recorded in *Münchener Revue*, no. 46, 15 November 1952.

194. HAP folder 30, reel 2; folder 31, reel 2.

195. Baedeker, *Southern Germany*, 1914 ed.; see H. P. Pfensing, a son-in-law of Herr Popp, "Mit Adolf Hitler unter einem Dach," *Arbeitertum*, 1 May 1935, in Rehse Archiv, Library of Congress, Manuscript Division, box 791.

196. Hitler, *Mein Kampf*, German ed., 177–178.

197. Gilbert, *Psychology of Dictatorship*, 35.

198. B. Brandmayer, *Mit Hitler Meldegänger, 1914–1918* (Uberlingen, 1940), 52.

199. Interviewed in *Revue*, 22 November 1952. Maser shows, however, that Hitler got more mail than he admitted to; see *Briefe und Notizen* and *Der Spiegel*, 9 April 1973.

200. One of Popp's letters is in German script in the HAP and is reprinted in Maser, *Hitler*.

201. See Georges Schaltenbrand, "War Hitler geisteskrank?" Institut für Zeitgeschichte, 333; Heiden, *Der Fuehrer*, 84.

202. Maser, *Briefe und Notizen*, passim.

203. Hans Mend, *Adolf Hitler im Felde, 1914–1918* (Diessen, 1931), 55, 60, 123–125, 172. See also Richard Hanser, *Putsch! How Hitler Made Revolution* (New York, 1970), 89–91; Walter Görlitz and Herbert A. Quint, *Adolf Hitler: Eine Biographie* (Stuttgart, 1952), 84–86.

204. Mend, *Im Felde*, 134, 156; Brandmayer, *Meldegänger*, 52.

205. The postcard is in the Berlin Document Center, Hitler Personal folder.

206. HAP folder 17a; Berlin Document Center (microfilm), group 7, reel 2.

207. Alan Bullock, *Hitler: A Study in Tyranny*, rev. ed. (New York, 1962), 52.

208. HAP folder 12, reel 1a. See also Ernst Deuerlein, "Dokumentation: Hitler's Eintritt in die Politik und die Reichswehr," VfZ 7 (1959):192.

209. Fritz Wiedemann, *Der Mann der Feldherr werden wollte: Erlebnisse und Erfahrungen des Vorgesetzten Hitlers im erste Weltkrieg und seines späteren persönlichen Adjutaten* (Haan, 1964), 25–26.

210. Photocopies of his disability record are given in Central Information Office for War Casualties, HAP folder 12, reel 1a. See also Deuerlein, in VfZ 7 (1959): 182.

211. Hitler, *Mein Kampf*, German ed., 223.

212. Hanser, *Putsch!*, 141.

213. Hitler, *Mein Kampf*, German ed., 225. Statement about "voices" made in preliminary inquiries at his trial following the Beer Hall Putsch; see Olden, *Hitler*, 69. The central position of anti-Semitism is noted by Eberhard Jäckel, *Hitler's Weltanschauung: A Blueprint for Power*, trans. Herbert Arnold (Middleton, Conn., 1972), 53.

214. The account which follows is drawn from Robert G. L. Waite, *Vanguard of Nazism: The Free Corps Movement in Postwar Germany, 1918–1923* (Cambridge, Mass., 1952), 79–93. Documentation may be found in footnotes 60–102. Used with permission of the president and fellows of Harvard College.

215. The most readable brief discussion of this period is found in Hanser, *Putsch!*; see also Maser, *Frühgeschichte*, and Deuerlein, in VfZ 7 (1959); the most detailed is Harold J. Gorden, Jr., *Hitler and the Beer Hall Putsch* (Princeton, 1972).

216. Quoted in Hanser, *Putsch!*, 194.

217. Hitler, *Mein Kampf*, German ed., 235.

218. Maser, *Hitler*, 173.

219. Hanser, *Putsch!*, 195–200.

220. Heiden, *Der Fuehrer*, 377.

221. Otto Strasser, *Hitler and I*, trans. Gwenda David and Eric Mosbacher (Boston, 1940), 64–65.

222. This discussion is based on the pamphlet as published in the *Münchener Post*; on issues of the *Völkischer Beobachter* for July and August 1921; and on an unpublished manuscript by Georg Franz, "Entstehungs und Frühgeschichte der Nationalsozialistischen Deutschen Arbeiterpartei Münchens, 1919–1923," Institut für Zeitgeschichte (Munich).

223. See articles by Dietrich Eckart and Rudolf Hess in the *Völkischer Beobachter*, 4 August, 11 August 1921.

224. Franz, "Entstehungs," 178.

225. Quoted in Konrad Heiden, *Geschichte des Nationalsozialismus: Die Karriere einer Idee* (Berlin, 1932), 143; Gordon, *Beer Hall Putsch*, 243.

226. Heiden, *Der Fuehrer*, 155.

227. *Armes, Kellnerlein!*, quoted in Kurt G. W. Ludecke, *I Knew Hitler: The Story of a Nazi Who Escaped the Blood Purge* (New York, 1938), 185.

228. Müller as interviewed by Heiden, *Der Fuehrer*, 190; see also Müller's memoirs, *Im Wandel einer Welt: Erinnerungen* (Munich, 1966), 162–164.

229. Müller, *Im Wandel*, 163.

230. Heiden, *Der Fuehrer*, 198.

231. Johann von Leers, *Reichskanzler Adolf Hitler* (Leipzig, 1932), 53.

Notes

232. OSS Source Book, 19–20.

233. Interview with Ernst Hanfstaengl, Munich, July 1967.

234. Truman Smith, "Hitler and the National Socialists," typescript now in Yale University Library, Manuscript Division.

235. *Der Hitler-Prozess vor dem Volksgericht in München* (Munich, 1924), 224 and passim.

236. Ibid.; Hanser, *Putsch!*, 393; Görlitz-Quint, *Hitler*, 225.

237. Maser, in *Der Spiegel*, 23 April 1973; H. Kallenbach, *Mit Adolf Hitler auf Festung Landsberg* (Munich, 1933), 113–114.

238. Ernst Hanfstaengl, *Unheard Witness* (New York, 1957), 119–120; Otto Lurker, *Hitler hinter Festungsmauren* (Berlin, 1933), 52–56.

239. Conversation with Hanfstaengl, June 1967.

240. *Auf gut Deutsch*, 5 March 1920; ibid., 31 January 1921; Fest, *Hitler*, 196–197.

241. Hitler, *Mein Kampf*, 993.

242. Zoller, *Privat*, 119.

243. Quoted in Harold C. Deutsch, *The Conspiracy Against Hitler in the Twilight War* (Minneapolis, 1968), 32; italics are mine.

244. Joseph Nyomarky, *Charisma and Factionalism in the Nazi Party* (Minneapolis, 1967), 80–81.

245. Ibid., 145–150; Dietrich Orlow, *The History of the Nazi Party: 1919–1933* (Pittsburgh, 1969), 290–293 and passim.

246. *Hitler's Secret Conversations*, 16–17 January 1942, quoted in Bullock, *Hitler*, 134.

247. Görlitz-Quint, *Hitler*, 293–294.

248. Maser, *Frühgeschichte*, 408–409; Fest, *Hitler*, 199; and Hanfstaengl interviews.

249. See Oron James Hale, "Adolf Hitler; Taxpayer," *American Historical Review* 60 (July 1955):308–402.

250. Dietrich, *Hitler*, 146–147; see also memoirs of Krause and Linge.

251. Baldur von Schirach, *Ich glaubte an Hitler* (Hamburg, 1967), 53–54.

252. Spengler quoted in Oswald Bunke, *Erinnerungen und Betrachtungen: der Weg eines deutschen Psychiaters* (Munich, 1952), 170.

253. Oron James Hale, "Gottfried Feder Calls Hitler to Order: An Unpublished Letter on Nazi Party Affairs," *Journal of Modern History* 30 (December 1958): 308–402.

254. Speer, *Inside*, 128–131.

255. This account of Maria Reiter is taken from the taped interview she gave to Günther Peis, a German journalist. The story was subsequently printed in *Stern*, no. 24, 1959. A German writer, Eugen Kogon, has verified the story and checked names, dates, places, and the handwritten letters from Adolf Hitler. See also Max Domarus, ed., *Hitler: Reden und Proklamationen, 1932–1945* (Munich, 1965), 2220; *Time*, 29 January 1959.

256. Schirach, *Glaubte*, 105; Henrietta von Schirach, *Price of Glory*, trans. Willi Frischauer (London, 1960), 178; Heinrich Hoffmann, *Hitler Was My Friend*, trans. Lt. Col. R. H. Stevens (London, 1955), 149.

257. Hanfstaengl, *Witness*, 169; personal conversation, July 1967.

258. Zoller, *Privat*, 87; see also Nerin E. Gun, *Eva Braun-Hitler: Leben und Schicksal* (New York and Bruchsal/Baden), 23.

259. Schirach, *Glaubte*, 192; Otto Strasser, *The Gangsters Around Hitler* (London, 1942[?]), 4.

260. See the editor's note to Frank's account of her death in his memoirs, *Galgens*.

261. The clipping may be found in the Rehse Collection, HAP folder 13, reel 1.

262. Hanfstaengl, *Witness*, 175–176; Hanfstaengl repeated the story to me in April 1967. See also Ludecke, *I Knew Hitler*, 477.

263. Unpublished Greiner ms., quoted in Jetzinger typescript (see Appendix). For the Himmler story and its refutation, see Gisevius, *Hitler*, 125.

264. Hoffmann, *Hitler*, 157–159.

265. Ibid., 155; Albertstein, "Hitler Composite" in *MIR*; interview with Speer cited in Fest, *Hitler*, 445–446; interview with Hanfstaengl; Willie Schneider, "Aus nächster Nähe," in *Die 7 Tage: Illustrierte Wochenschrift aus dem Zeitgeschehen* (Baden-Baden), 17 October 1952 (hereafter cited as *7 Tage*); Domarus, *Reden*, 2220; Carl Haensel, *Das Gericht vertagt sich* (Hamburg, 1950), 63.

266. Hoffmann, *Hitler*, 163; Hasselbach interrogation, "Hitler Composite," *MIR*.

267. *Der Spiegel*, 27 November 1967.

268. Speer interview with James P. O'Donnell, *New York Times Magazine*, 26 October 1969, 100–102.

269. Interview with Frau Traudl Junge, Munich, 7 February 1948, Musmanno Archives, quoted in Glenn B. Infield, *Eva and Adolf* (New York, 1974), 315.

270. Gun, *Braun-Hitler*, 68, 164–165; Hoffmann, *Hitler*, 163–164.

271. OSS Source Book, 921–922.

272. Count Galeazzo Ciano, *The Ciano Diaries, 1939–1943* (New York, 1945), 85.

273. Albertstein, "Hitler Composite," *MIR*.

274. Hanfstaengl, *Witness*, 143; confirmed in personal conversation.

275. Domarus, *Reden*, 2221; for Fräulein Mueller's experience, see below.

276. Albert Krebs, *Tendenzen und Gestalten der NSDAP: Erinnerungen an die Frühzeit der Partei* (Stuttgart, 1959), 128.

277. Sir Neville Henderson, *Failure of a Mission: Berlin, 1937–1939* (New York, 1940), 41.

278. Hoffmann gives the best account; see *Hitler*, 164–165.

279. Theodor Reik, *Masochism in Sex and Society*, trans. Margaret Biegel and Gertrud M. Kurth (New York, 1962), 298.

280. Hanfstaengl, quoted in "AH" in FDR, and personal conversation.

281. OSS Source Book, 793, 921–922.

282. Domarus, *Reden*, 2240.

283. Harold Nicolson, *Diaries and Letters. Vol. 2: The War Years, 1939–1945* (New York, 1967), 39.

284. "AH" in FDR; William L. Shirer, *Berlin Diary* (New York, 1941), 137; Maser, *Hitler*, 309.

285. Kubizek in OLA folder 63 (original typescript).

286. Kubizek, *Young Hitler*, 237.

287. Hanfstaengl, OSS Source Book, 894.

288. Schneider, *7 Tage*, 28 November 1952; Krause, *10 Jahre*, 47.

289. Wolfgang Harthauser, *Die Verfolgung der Homosexualen im Dritten Reich*, quoted in Richard Grunberger, *The Twelve-Year Reich: A Social History of Nazi Germany, 1933–1945* (New York, 1971), 121.

290. See Hans Buchheim, "The SS, Instrument of Tyranny," in *Anatomy of the SS State*, ed. Helmut Krausnick (New York, 1968); Karl Dietrich Bracher, *The German Dictatorship: The Origins, Structure and Effects of National Socialism*, trans. Jean Steinberg (New York, 1970), 353.

291. Domarus, *Reden*, 1843.

292. Peter Loewenberg, "The Unsuccessful Adolescence of Heinrich Himmler," (typescript, University of California at Los Angeles), 26.

293. Sigmund Freud, *A General Introduction to Psychoanalysis* (New York, 1952), 317; and for a detailed discussion: "Psycho-Analytic Notes on an Autobiographical Account of a Case of Paranoia," (1911), *Collected Papers*, standard ed., Vol. 12, 3. (London, 1974), 1–80.

294. Robert Knight, "The Relationship of Latent Homosexuality to the Mechanism of Paranoid Delusions," *Menninger Clinic: Bulletin*, 4 (1940):149.

295. Ibid., 149.

296. Robert G. L. Waite, "Adolf Hitler's Anti-Semitism: A Study in History and Psychoanalysis," in *The Psychoanalytic Interpretation of History*, ed. Benjamin B. Wolman (New York, 1971), 225.

Notes

297. Walter G. Langer, *Mind,* 134.

298. H. R. Trevor-Roper, in *Book World,* 10 September 1972.

299. OSS Source Book, 919.

300. Langer, *Mind,* 134.

301. See Heiden, *Der Fuehrer,* 385–389.

302. See *Sexual Variants,* ed. Georg W. Henry, (New York, 1948); George W. Henry, L. S. London, and F. S. Caprio, *Sexual Deviations* (Washington, D.C., 1950); Harold Greenweld, *The Elegant Prostitute: A Social and Psychoanalytic Study* (New York, 1973); Richard von Krafft-Ebing, *Psychopathia Sexualis,* trans. F. J. Rebinan, rev. ed. (New York, 1937); Havelock Ellis, *Studies in the Psychology of Sex,* 3 vols. (New York, 1936); and testimony of Raymond de Saussure, OSS Source Book, 932.

303. Phyllis Greenacre, "Perversions: General Considerations Regarding Their Genetic and Dynamic Background," *Psychoanalytic Study of the Child* 23 (1968): 58; italics are mine.

304. Kubizek as quoted in Bromberg, "Hitler's Character," 297.

305. Langer, OSS Report, 222; italics are mine.

306. Conversation with Margaret Brenman, M.D., April 1968, Riggs Clinic, Stockbridge, Mass.

307. H. L. P. Resnik and Robert E. Litman, "Eroticized Repetitive Hangings: A Form of Self-Destructive Behavior," unpublished paper.

308. Henrietta von Schirach, *Price of Glory,* 73.

309. "AH" in FDR.

310. Hans Baur, *Hitler's Pilot,* trans. Edward Gerald (London, 1958), 64; Heinz Linge, "The Private Life of Adolf Hitler," *News of the World,* 20 November 1955.

311. Testimony of the cinema director A. Zeissler, in OSS Source Book, 22.

312. Loewenberg, in *Central European History,* 271.

313. Fenichel, *Psychoanalytic Theory,* 68.

314. Zoller, *Privat,* 231.

315. Kubizek to Jetzinger, 6 May 1949, OLA folder 64.

316. Hitler, *Mein Kampf,* trans. Manheim, 58; italics are mine.

317. *Conversations,* 409.

318. Freud, *General Introduction,* 320.

319. Greenacre, "Perversions," 57–58.

320. Fenichel, *Psychoanalytic Theory,* 332.

321. Ibid., 326; italics are mine.

322. See Bromberg, "Hitler's Childhood," *International Review of Psycho-Analysis* 1 (1974), p. 239.

CHAPTER 4

1. William L. Shirer, *The Rise and Fall of the Third Reich: A History of Nazi Germany* (New York, 1960), 90.

2. Geoffrey Barraclough, in *New York Review of Books* 19 (November 2, 1972): 34.

3. W. C. Sellar and R. J. Yeatman, *1066 and All That: A Memorable History of England Comprising All the Parts You Can Remember, Including One Hundred and Three Good Things, Five Bad Kings, and Two Genuine Dates* (London and New York, 1931), vii; italics in original.

4. Jean F. Neurohr, *Der Mythos vom dritten Reich: zur Geistesgeschichte des Nationalsozialismus* (Stuttgart, 1957), 20–22.

5. Daniel, *Lehrbuch für Geographie,* cited in Jonathan F. Scott, *Patriots in the Making: What America Can Learn from France and Germany* (New York, 1916), 177–179.

6. Heinrich Heine, *Sämtliche Werke* (Leipzig, n.d.), 4:190.

7. Martin Luther, "Treatise on Good Works," in *Luther's Works*, 54 vols., ed. Jaraslav Pelikan (St. Louis, 1955–1975), 44, 92, 96, 105, 113. See also George Sabine, *A History of Political Theory* (New York, 1937), 361.

8. Luther, "On the Jews and Their Lies," in *Works*, 47:135, 258, 266–267, 268–292. See also Walter Kaufmann, *Nietzsche: Philosopher, Psychologist, Antichrist* (Princeton, 1950), 139.

9. Birger Forell, "National Socialism and the Protestant Churches," in *The Third Reich*, ed. Maurice Baumont et al. (New York, 1955), 825.

10. Wilhelm Röpke, *The Solution to the German Problem*, trans. E. W. Dickes (New York, 1946), 117.

11. Hans Jakob Christoffel von Grimmelshausen, *Der abenteurliche Simplicissimus* (Zurich, 1967), 1:196–199. English version: *Simplicius Simplicissimus*, trans. from the original German edition of 1669 by Hellmuth Weissenborn and Lesley MacDonald (London, 1961), 178–183.

12. Kenneth C. Haynes, *Grimmelshausen* (London, 1932), 152.

13. Marc Raeff, "The Well-Ordered Police State," *American Historical Review* 80 (December 1975):1226–1229 (hereafter this periodical is cited as *AHR*).

14. Walter L. Dorn, "The Prussian Bureaucracy in the Eighteenth Century," *Political Science Quarterly* 46 (1931):408; 47 (1932), 75–94; See also Carl Heinrichs, *Friedrich Wilhelm I. König in Preussen: Eine Biographie* (Darmstadt, 1968); R. A. Dorwart, *The Prussian Welfare State Before 1740* (Cambridge, Mass., 1971).

15. Otto Hintze, *Die Hohenzollern und Ihr Werk: Fünfhundert Jahre vaterländischer Geschichte* (Berlin, 1915), 319–320; Oswald Spengler, "Preussentum und Sozialismus," in *Politische Schriften* (Munich, 1933, first published 1919), 31; Robert Ergang, *The Potsdam Führer: Frederick William I, Father of Prussian Militarism* (New York, 1941) 8–10.

16. George P. Gooch, *Frederick the Great: The Ruler, the Writer, the Man* (New York, 1947), 343; Neubauer's *Lehrbuch* quoted in Scott, *Patriots*, 169.

17. Frederick the Great, in *Oeuvres*, 17:83–84, quoted in Ergang, *Potsdam Führer*, 251.

18. Heinz Linge, "Kronzeuge Linge," *Revue* (Munich), 26 December 1955.

19. Quotations are from *Hitlers Tischgespräche im Führerhauptquartier*, 2nd ed., Percy Schramm (Stuttgart, 1965), 335, 186, 195, 148, 171 (hereinafter cited as *Tischgespräche*).

20. Gooch, *Frederick the Great*, 45.

21. Gordon A. Craig, "Johannes von Müller: The Historian in Search of a Hero," *AHR* 75 (June 1969):1498–1499.

22. *Treitschke's History of Germany in the Nineteenth Century*, 7 vols. trans. Eden and Cedar Paul (London, 1915), 1:508–511, 566.

23. Hans Kohn, "Arndt and the Character of German Nationalism," *AHR* 54 (1949):790, 796, 800–803.

24. *Lesebuch*, as quoted by Scott, *Patriots*, 186–187.

25. Rohan D. O. Butler, *The Roots of National Socialism, 1783–1933* (London, 1941), 52.

26. Peter Gay, *Weimar Culture: The Outsider as Insider* (New York: 1968), 61.

27. Quoted in Peter Viereck, *Metapolitics: From the Romantics to Hitler* (New York, 1941), 301.

28. Johann Gottlieb Fichte, *Addresses to the German Nation*, trans. R. F. Jones and G. H. Turnbull (Chicago and London, 1922), 208 and passim; Viereck, *Metapolitics*, 6–7, 192–194, 45; Neurohr, *Mythos*, 142–143.

29. Joseph Campbell, "Folkloristic Commentary," in *The Complete Grimm's Fairy Tales* (New York, 1944); see also the perceptive chapter on the Grimms in Louis L. Snyder, *German Nationalism: The Tragedy of a People* (Harrisburg, Pa., 1952).

Notes

30. *Grimm's Fairy Tales*, 534–535.

31. Ibid., passim.

32. Quoted in Viereck, *Metapolitics*, 73.

33. Carl Schurz, *Reminiscences* 3 vols. (New York, 1907), 1:112–114, 116–117.

34. Veit Valentin, *Geschichte der deutschen Revolution von 1848–49*, 2 vols. (Berlin, 1930–1931), preface; see also a collection of his lectures, *1848: Chapters of German History*, trans. Ethel Talbot Scheffauer (London, 1940), 426–470; 447–452 and passim.

35. Geoffrey Bruun, *Nineteenth Century European Civilization* (New York, 1960), 85.

36. Quoted by Louis L. Snyder in book review, *Journal of Modern History* 26 (December 1954):393.

37. Quoted in Roy Pascal, *The Growth of Modern Germany* (London, 1946), 42.

38. Henry A. Kissinger, "The White Revolutionary: Reflections on Bismarck," *Daedalus: Journal of the American Academy of Arts and Sciences* 97 (1969): 906, 907.

39. In addition to Bismarck's memoirs and letters and the standard biographies, see especially Otto Pflanze, "Towards a Psychoanalytic Interpretation of Bismarck," *AHR* 77 (April 1972):419–444.

40. Adolf Hitler, *Mein Kampf* (New York, 1939), 147, 191, 223–224, 317–318; *Tischgespräche*, 346.

41. Hans Delbrück, *Regierung und Volkswille: Eine akademische Vorlesung* (Berlin, 1914), 186.

42. Max Weber, *Politische Schriften* (Munich, 1921), and Marianne Weber, *Max Weber: Ein Lebensbild*, quoted in H. H. Gerth and C. Wright Mills, *From Max Weber: Essays in Sociology* (New York, 1958), 33; Mommsen as quoted by Fritz Stern, *The Failure of Illiberalism: Essays on the Political Culture of Modern Germany* (New York, 1972), 198.

43. The quotations are from Karl Dietrich Bracher, *The German Dictatorship: The Origins, Structure and Effects of National Socialism*, trans. Jean Steinberg (New York, 1970), 247. See also Ralf Dahrendorf, *Society and Democracy in Germany* (New York, 1967), 4. For a brilliant discussion of the problems of continuity and change in German history, see Stern, *Illiberalism*.

44. Hans Kohn, *The Mind of Germany: The Education of a Nation* (New York, 1960), 63–64.

45. Snyder, *Nationalism*, 132.

46. Dahrendorf, *Society*, 199–201.

47. G. W. F. Hegel, "Philosophy of Right and Law," in *The Philosophy of Hegel*, ed. Carl Friedrich (New York, 1963), 283, 293, 309, 323–324; italics in original.

48. Hegel, "Philosophy of Right," 318.

49. Heinrich von Treitschke, *Politics*, 2 vols. (London, 1916), 1:34, 35, 63; 2:389, 399. See also Andreas Dorpalen, *Heinrich von Treitschke* (New Haven, Conn., 1957), 227.

50. Treitschke, *Politics*, 2:123; Dorpalen, *Treitschke*, 229; Fritz Nova, *The National Socialist Fuehrerprinzip and Its Background in German Thought* (Philadelphia, 1943), 19–23, 46–47.

51. Friedrich List, *National System of Political Economy* (1855; reprint ed., New York, 1966), 177, 191, 414.

52. List as quoted in Snyder, *Nationalism*, 75.

53. H. Gollwitzer, "Der Cäsarismus Napoleons III. im Widerhall der öffentlichen Meinung Deutschlands," *Historische Zeitschrift* 173 (1952):58.

54. Hajo Holborn, *A History of Modern Germany, 1840–1945*, 3 vols., (New York, 1969), 2:281; Helmut Krausnick, "The Persecution of the Jews," in *Anatomy of the SS State*, trans. Richard Barry, Marian Jackson, and Dorothy Long (New

York, 1968), 7; Bracher, *Dictatorship*, 38–39; Peter G. J. Pulzer, *The Rise of Political Anti-Semitism in Germany and Austria* (London and New York, 1964), 50–51; Massing, *Rehearsal*, 7–8.

55. Paul de Lagarde, *Deutsche Schriften*, 5th ed. (Göttingen, 1920), 23, 33, 38–39, 348. See also Fritz Stern, *The Politics of Cultural Despair: A Study in the Rise of Germanic Ideology* (Berkeley and Los Angeles, 1961), 35, 49, 58, 72, 87; Jean-Jacques Anstett, "Paul de Lagarde," in *The Third Reich*, ed. Baumont et al., 161.

56. Julius Langbehn, *Rembrandt als Erzieher* (Leipzig, 1890), 219–223, 258–259, 309. See also Stern, *Despair*, 117, 137–138, 153–173; George L. Mosse, *Germans and Jews: The Right, The Left and the Search for a "Third Force" in Pre-Nazi Germany* (New York, 1970), 121–122.

57. Unless otherwise noted, quotations from Nietzsche are taken from the following: (1) *Gesammelte Werke*, 23 vols. (Musarion Verlag, Munich, 1923), hereafter cited as MusA; (2) the great new edition now in process; *Kritische Gesamtausgabe*, ed. Giogio Colli and Mazzino Montinari (Berlin and New York, 1972), cited here as KGW; and (3) Walter Kaufmann, ed., *Portable Nietzsche* (New York, 1968), cited as PN.

58. Albert Camus, *The Rebel*, trans. Anthony Bower (New York, 1954), 75.

59. See *The Antichrist*, conveniently available in PN; also Kaufmann, ed., *Will to Power* (New York, 1967), 117.

60. Nietzsche, *Twilight of the Idols*, PN, 541–542.

61. See for example, MusA, 16: 369, 370, and passim; and Fritz Nova, *The National Socialist Fuehrerprinzip and its Background in German Thought* (Philadelphia, 1943), 22.

62. Georg Lukács, *Die Zerstörung der Vernunft* (Berlin-Spandau, 1962), 312–313; Nietzsche, MusA, 13:268.

63. Nietzsche, MusA, 15:149; MusA, 16:366; see also KGA 8 (3):459.

64. Nietzsche, MusA, 15:132.

65. Nietzsche, MusA, 16:374; KGA, 8 (3):386.

66. Nietzsche, PN, 457.

67. Nietzsche, KGA, 7 (3):215, 458.

68. Karl Jaspers, *Nietzsche: An Introduction to the Understanding of his Philosophic Activity*, trans. Charles F. Wallraff and Frederick J. Schmitz (Tucson, 1965), 458.

69. Nietzsche, *Also sprach Zarathustra* (Kriegsausgabe, Leipzig, [1914]), 67, 359, 420, 476.

70. Nietzsche, MusA, 19:374; italics in original.

71. Nietzsche, PN, 326; italics in original.

72. Arthur G. Danto, *Nietzsche as Philosopher* (New York, 1965), 158–159, 177.

73. Nietzsche, KGA, 8 (3):452; italics in original.

74. Alfred Rosenberg, "Friedrich Nietzsche: Commemorative Speech of 15 October 1944 on the 100th Anniversary of Nietzsche's Birth," (Zentral Verlag, NSDAP, Munich, 1944), p. 14.

75. Thomas Mann, "Nietzsche's Philosophy in the Light of Recent History," in *Last Essays*, trans. by Richard and Clara Winston (New York, 1959), 175.

76. Quoted in Neurohr, *Mythos*, 272.

77. Thomas Mann, *Betrachtungen eines Unpolitischen* (Berlin, 1919). See also Ernst Keller, *Der Unpolitische Deutsche: Eine Studie zu den "Betrachtungen eines Unpolitischen" von Thomas Mann* (Munich, 1965), 46–49; the quotation as given here appears in Bracher, *Dictatorship*, 498.

78. S. D. Stirk, *German Universities: Through English Eyes* (London, 1946), 42–43.

79. J. Thomas Leamon, sermon, First Congregational Church, Williamstown, Mass., 12 November 1972.

80. Paul W. Massing, *Rehearsal for Destruction: A Study of Political Anti-Semitism in Imperial Germany* (New York, 1949), xvi.

Notes

81. Ibid., 306. For Fritsch's influence on Hitler, see Chapter 2, p. 97-98
82. For the popularity of Langbehn and Lagarde, see Holborn, *Germany*, 3: 411.
83. Eugen Dühring, *Die Judenfrage als Frage des Rassencharakters und seiner Schädlichkeiten für Existenz und Kultur der Völker*, 6th ed. (Leipzig, 1930), 281; Massing, *Rehearsal*, 7-8. Pulzer, *Anti-Semitism*, 49-51.
84. Stern, *Despair*, 60–63; Pulzer, *Anti-Semitism*, 62, 82, 84.
85. Ibid., 242; Stern, *Despair*, 138, 141, 168.
86. Gustav Freytag, *Soll und Haben*, 70th ed. (Leipzig, 1908), passim.; Mosse, *Germans and Jews*, 70.
87. Treitschke, *Politics*, 1: 299–302; Dorpalen, *Treitschke*, 243–245.
88. Fritz Fischer, *War of Illusions: German Policies from 1911–1914*, trans. Marian Jackson (New York, 1975), 283–284.
89. Pulzer, *Anti-Semitism*, 255–256.
90. Ibid., 273–274.
91. Walter Rathenau, *Briefe*, quoted in Martin Kitchen, *The German Officer Corps, 1890–1914* (London, 1968), 43.
92. Bracher, *Dictatorship*, 24–25.
93. Quoted in Ricard M. Brickner, *Is Germany Incurable?* (New York, 1943), 169.
94. Lagarde, *Deutsche Schriften*, 33–37; Stern, *Despair*, 56, 69.
95. Quoted in Kohn, *Mind of Germany*, 283.
96. Bracher, *Dictatorship*, 29.
97. Neurohr, *Mythos*, 93; Artur Moeller van den Bruck, *Das dritte Reich*, 3rd. ed. (Hamburg, 1931); S. D. Stirk, "Myths, Types and Propaganda," in *The German Mind and Outlook*, G. P. Gooch et al., eds. (London, 1945), 131.
98. Hegel, "Philosophy of Right and Law," 322.
99. See H. W. C. Davis, *The Political Thought of Heinrich von Treitschke* (New York, 1915), 150–153; Treitschke, *Politics*, 1:29–50, 67–68; 2:599, 390.
100. Spengler, "Preussentum und Sozialismus," quoted in Ergang, *Potsdam Führer*, 5.
101. Quoted in Gerhard Ritter, *Staatskunst und Kriegshandwerk: Das Problem des "Militarismus" in Deutschland*, 4 vols. (Munich, 1965), 1:246, 271.
102. Friedrich von Bernhardi, *Germany and the Next War* (New York, 1912), 31.
103. Instructions to German soldiers in 1900, quoted in Ludwig Reiners, *The Lamps Went Out in Europe*, trans. Richard and Clara Winston (New York, 1955), 30; conversation with Chancellor von Bülow, quoted in Fritz Fischer, *World Power or Decline: The Controversy Over Germany's Aims in the First World War*, trans. Lancelot L. Farrar, Robert Kimber, and Rita Kimber (New York, 1974), 8.
104. Fischer, *Illusions*, 92.
105. Alfred Kruck, *Geschichte des Alldeutschen Verbandes, 1890–1939* (Wiesbaden, 1954), 13–17.
106. Ibid., 63–64, 183; Fritz Fischer, *Germany's Aims in the First World War* (New York, 1967), 156–172.
107. Stern, *Illiberalism*, 154–156.
108. Ritter, *Staatskunst*, 2:159; Ergang, *Potsdam Führer*, 2.
109. Carl Schorske, *German Social Democracy, 1905–1919: The Development of the Great Schism* (Cambridge, Mass., 1955), 168.
110. Kitchen, *Officers Corps*, 132, 142.
111. W. F. Bruck, *Social and Economic History of Germany from William II to Hitler: 1888–1938* (London, 1938), 39; Kitchen, *Officers Corps*, 125.
112. Quoted in Gordon Craig, *The Politics of the Prussian Army, 1640–1945* (Oxford, 1955), 237.
113. Karl Demeter, *The German Officer Corps in Society and State, 1650–1945*, trans. Angus Malcolm (New York, 1965), 247.
114. Craig, *Prussian Army*, 298.

115. Hans W. Gatzke, book review in *Central European History* 5 (September 1972):279.

116. Bertram H. Schaffner, *Fatherland: A Study of Authoritarianism in the German Family* (New York, 1949), 13. The account given here is indebted to Schaffner's valuable study.

117. Rudolf Hoess, *Commandant of Auschwitz* (New York, 1959), introduction and 31–32.

118. Schaffner, *Fatherland*, 51.

119. Ibid., 76.

120. Quoted in Stern, *Illiberalism*, xix.

121. Holborn, *History*, 3:813.

122. Scott, *Patriots*, 135–140.

123. Schenk-Koch's *Lehrbuch*, as quoted in ibid., 183.

124. Robert G. L. Waite, *Vanguard of Nazism: The Free Corps Movement in Postwar Germany, 1918–1923* (Cambridge, Mass., 1952), 17–21.

125. Mario Damandi, "The German Youth Movement," Ph.D. thesis, Columbia University (1960), 365–366.

126. Mosse, *Jews*, 127–130; Pulzer, *Anti-Semitism*, 309.

127. Domandi, "Youth Movement," 288.

128. Friedrich Wilhelm Foerster, *Jugendseele, Jugendbewegung, Jugendziel* (Munich and Leipzig), as quoted in Waite, *Vanguard of Nazism*, 21.

129. Hermann Rauschning, *Revolution of Nihilism: Warning to the West*, trans. E. W. Dickes (New York, 1939), 63–64. I am indebted to Fritz Stern for this reference.

130. Friedrich Meinecke, *Die deutsche Katastrophe* (Wiesbaden, 1949). Preface i.

131. Jack J. Roth, ed., *World War I: A Turning Point in Modern History* (New York, 1967), 109.

132. Hitler, *Mein Kampf*, 227.

133. See Aryeh L. Unger, *The Totalitarian Party: Party and People in Nazi Germany and Soviet Russia* (Cambridge, England, 1974), 263–264.

134. Koppel S. Pinson, *Modern Germany: Its History and Civilization* (New York, 1954), 322–323; Gustav Stolper, Karl Häuser, and Knut Borchardt, *The German Economy: 1870 to the Present*, trans. Toni Stolper (New York, 1967), 110.

135. Neurohr, *Mythos*, 79, 121.

136. Ibid., 246.

137. See their life sketches in the "who's who" of the Party, *Das deutsche Führer-Lexikon* (Berlin, 1934).

138. Professor Doktor Witkop, ed., *Kriegsbriefe gefallener Studenten* (Munich, 1928), 7–8.

139. Ernst Toller, *Eine Jugend in Deutschland* (Amsterdam, 1936), 53.

140. Ernst Jünger, *In Stahlgewittern: ein Kriegstagebuch*, 16th ed. (Berlin, 1926), 152, 257, 265. See also his *Der Kampf als inneres Erlebnis*, 5th ed. (Berlin, 1933).

141. See Neurohr, *Mythos*, 76–77.

142. Waite, *Vanguard*, 31.

143. Pinson, *Modern Germany*, 335; Fischer, *German War Aims*, 247ff.

144. Henry Cord Meyer, ed., *The Long Generation* (New York, 1973), 105ff.

145. This discussion is based on Richard M. Hunt's perceptive article "Myths, Guilt and Shame in Pre-Nazi Germany," *Virginia Quarterly Review* 34 (Summer 1958):355–371.

146. Quoted in Ludwig F. Gengler, *Kampfflieger Berthold* (Berlin, 1934), 123–125.

147. Friedrich Wilhelm Heinz, *Sprengstoff* (Berlin, 1930), 26, 29; italics in original.

148. Conversation with Prince Max of Baden, as recorded in Prince Max's

Notes

memoirs, *Erinnerungen und Dokumente* (Stuttgart, 1927), 592, 600. See also Herzogin Viktoria Louise, *Im Strom der Zeit* (Göttingen, 1974), 93.

149. Heinz, *Sprengstoff*, 7.

150. Waite, *Vanguard*, 51.

151. Ernst von Salomon, *Die Geächteten* (Berlin, 1930), 72–73, 294, 307; *Nahe Geschichte: Ein Ueberblick* (Berlin, 1936), 30; "Der Verlorene Haufe," in *Krieg und Krieger*, ed. Ernst Jünger (Berlin, 1930), 116.

152. Ernst H. Posse, *Die politischen Kampfbünde Deutschlands*, 2nd ed. (Berlin, 1931), 46–47.

153. Quoted in Waite, *Vanguard*, 267.

154. Hans Gerth, "The Nazi Party: Its Leadership and Composition," *American Journal of Sociology* 55 (January 1940):530–531.

155. The verse was first published in 1919 in George Grosz and Karl Einstein, eds., *Der blutige Ernst*, quoted in Richard Hanser, *Putsch! How Hitler Made Revolution* (New York, 1970), 238–239.

156. Peter Bor, *Gespräche mit Halder* (Wiesbaden, 1950), 101.

157. Theodore Abel, *Why Hitler Came into Power: An Answer Based on the Original Life Stories of Six Hundred of His Followers* (New York, 1938), 69–70; Joachim Remak, ed., *The Nazi Years: A Documentary History* (Englewood Cliffs, N.J., 1969), 26, quoting manuscripts in the Abel Collection, of the Hoover Institution, Stanford, California.

158. Waite, *Vanguard*, 140–141; Holborn, *History*, 3:589.

159. Paul Seabury, *The Wilhelmstrasse: A Study of German Diplomats Under the Nazi Regime* (Berkeley, 1954).

160. Gerhard F. Kramer, "The Influence of National Socialism on the Courts of Justice and Police," in *The Third Reich*, 599.

161. See Robert M. W. Kempner, "Blueprint of the Nazi Underground—Past and Future Subversive Activities," *Research Studies of the State College of Washington* 13 (June 1945):130–133.

162. Stern, *Illiberalism*, 203.

163. David Rodnick, *Postwar Germans: An Anthropologist's Account* (New Haven, 1948), 189.

164. Quoted in ibid., 189; see also Guenther Lewy, *Catholic Church and Nazi Germany* (New York, 1964), 12–16.

165. Erich Eyck, *A History of the Weimar Republic*, 2 vols., trans by Harlan P. Hanson and Robert G. L. Waite (Cambridge, Mass., 1963), 2:219, 476.

166. See Edouard Calic, ed., *Secret Conversations with Hitler: The Newly Discovered 1931 Interviews*, trans Richard Barry, foreword by Galo Mann (New York, 1971).

167. See "Erzieherschaft und Partei," *Berliner Tageblatt*, no. 210 (May 1937); also *Der Schulungsbrief*, nos. 8 and 9 (1938), quoted in Gerth, *Journal of Sociology* (January 1940) 55:525.

168. Fritz K. Ringer, *The Decline of the German Mandarins: The German Academic Community, 1890–1933* (Cambridge, Mass., 1969), 216.

169. Carl J. Friedrich, comment at conference, "Weimar Germany 1919–1932: Intellectuals, Culture and Politics," New School for Social Research, New York, 29–30 October 1971, my notes (hereafter cited as New School Conference, 1971).

170. Gay, *Weimar Culture*, 10, 23.

171. New School Conference, 1971, my notes.

172. Kurt Sontheimer, "Anti-Democratic Thought in the Weimar Republic," in *The Path to Dictatorship: Ten Essays*, trans. John Conway, introduction by Fritz Stern (New York, 1966), 36–39; Klemens von Klemperer, *Germany's New Conservatism: Its History and Dilemma in the Twentieth Century* (Princeton, 1957), 150.

173. Paul Sethe, quoted in Gordon Craig, "Engagement and Neutrality in Weimar Germany," *Journal of Contemporary History* 2 (1967):59. On Tucholsky,

see especially Harold Poor, *Kurt Tucholsky and the Ordeal of Germany* (New York, 1968). For a sympathetic view of the *Weltbühne*, see Istvan Deak, *Weimar Germany's Left-Wing Intellectuals: A Political History of the Weltbühne and Its Circle* (Berkeley, 1968).

174. New School Conference, 1971, my notes.

175. Gay, *Weimar Culture*, 62–63.

176. Neurohr, *Mythos*, 25, 243–246.

177. Stern, *Despair*, 293.

178. Sontheimer, "Anti-Democratic Thought," 47.

179. Quoted in Kohn, *Mind of Germany*, 321.

180. Stirk, *German Universities*, 138; Stern, *Despair*, 265–266.

181. Ibid., 263–265.

182. Holborn, *History*, 3, 657. Italics are mine.

183. Oswald Spengler, *The Decline of the West: Form and Actuality*, 2 vols., trans. Charles Francis Atkinson (New York, 1926), 2:507; italics in original. See also Stirk, "Myths," in *German Mind and Outlook*, 138.

184. Domandi, "Youth Movement," 285; see also Holborn, *History*, 3:658.

185. Spengler, *Preussentum und Sozialismus*, 104–105.

186. Franz Schauwecker, quoted in Lukács, *Zerstörung*, 297.

187. The phrase is Carl Schorske's; see "The Weimar Intellectuals," *New York Review of Books* 14 (21 May 1970):20–25.

188. Martin Heidegger, *Die Selbstbehauptung der deutschen Universität* (Breslau, 1933); *Das deutsche Führer-Lexikon* (Berlin, 1934).

189. Gordon Craig, "Engagement and Neutrality in Weimar Germany," *Journal of Contemporary History* 2 (1967):49–63; Harry Pross, "On Thomas Mann's Political Career," ibid., 75.

190. See Kritz K. Ringer, ed., *The German Inflation of 1923* (Oxford, 1969); Hanser, *Putsch!*, 305–307.

191. Pearl S. Buck, *How It Happens: Talk About the German People, 1914–1933* (New York, 1947), 124.

192. Peter Loewenberg, "Psychohistorical Origins of the Nazi Youth Cohort," *AHR* 76 (December 1971):1468, 1472.

193. Dieter Petzina, "Germany and the Great Depression," *Journal of Contemporary History* 4 (October 1969):67–68.

194. Michael Steinberg, *Sabres and Brown Shirts: The German Students' Path to National Socialism, 1918–1935* (in press).

195. Else Frenkel-Brunswick, "The Role of Psychology in the Study of Totalitarianism," in *Totalitarianism*, ed. Carl J. Friedrich (Cambridge, Mass., 1954), 173.

196. The connection between mass fear and Hitler's appeal was first noted in a 1954 essay by Franz Neumann entitled "Angst und Politik," cited by Stern, *Illiberalism*, 96, xxviii, Joachim C. Fest discussed "die Grosse Angst" in *Hitler: Eine Biographie* (Vienna, 1973) and during a seminar at Harvard University, 17 October 1975.

197. Conversation with Harold Nicolson, in *Diaries and Letters: The War Years, 1939–1945* 3 vols. (New York, 1967), 2:39; Hitler, *Mein Kampf*, 468, 920; Joseph Goebbels, *The Early Goebbels Diaries: 1925–1926*, ed., Helmut Heiber, trans. Oliver Watson (New York, 1963), 91; italics are mine.

198. Eva G. Reichmann, *Hostages of Civilization: The Social Sources of National Socialist Anti-Semitism* (London, 1950), 193; Theodore Abel, *Why Hitler Came into Power: An Answer Based on the Original Life Stories of 600 of His Followers* (New York, 1938), 149–150.

199. See John Snell, ed., *Nazi Revolution: German's Guilt or Germany's Fate?* (Boston, 1959), introduction, xiii.

200. Hermann Glaser, "Adolf Hitlers *Mein Kampf* als Spiesserspiegel," *Aus Politik und Zeitgeschichte* 9 Jahrgang (24 July 1963), 13–22; Hans Kohn, "The Mass-Man: Hitler," *Atlantic Monthly* 173 (April 1944), 100–104.

Notes

201. Konrad Heiden, *Der Fuehrer: Hitler's Rise to Power*, trans. Ralph Manheim (Boston, 1944), 377–378.

202. Dorothy Thompson, *I Saw Hitler!* (New York, 1932); Miss Thompson misspelled his first name.

203. The metaphor is from Ernst Nolte, *Three Faces of Fascism*, trans. by Leila Vennewitz (New York, 1966), 373.

204. Gordon W. Prange, ed., *Hitler's Words* (Washington, D.C., 1944), 105, 109.

205. William L. Langer, "The Next Assignment," *AHR* 63 (January 1958): 302.

206. Frenkel-Brunswick, "Role of Psychology," 178–184.

207. Henry Dicks, "Personality Traits and National Socialist Ideology: A Wartime Study of German Prisoners of War," *Human Relations* 3 (1950): 111–153.

208. Powell Kecskemeti and Nathan Leites, "Some Psychological Hypotheses on Nazi Germany," *Journal of Social Psychology* 26–28 (1947–1948).

209. Gerth, "Nazi Party," 528–530; Richard Grunberger, *The Twelve-Year Reich: A Social History of Nazi Germany, 1933–1945* (New York, 1971), 234, 306; Fest, *Hitler*, 386; Mosse, *Germans and Jews*, 23; Baldur von Schirach, *Ich glaubte an Hitler* (Hamburg, 1967), 160; Steinberg, *Sabres and Brown Shirts*.

210. Peter Merkl, unpublished paper quoted by Loewenberg, "Nazi Youth Cohort," 1473; italics are mine.

211. See especially Loewenberg's important article, cited above. I have also profited greatly from personal discussion with Mr. Loewenberg.

212. Buck, *How It Happens*, 51, 66.

213. Quoted in Loewenberg, "Nazi Youth Cohort," 1477.

214. William L. Langer, comment at American Psychoanalytic Association Colloquium, Washington, D.C., May 1971 (hereafter cited as APA Colloquium, 1971).

215. Loewenberg, "Nazi Youth Cohort," 1484.

216. Hans Peter Bleuel and Ernst Klinnert, *Deutsche Studenten auf dem Weg ins dritte Reich: Ideologien, Programme, Aktionen, 1918–1935* (Gütersloh, 1967), 119–120; italics are mine.

217. Loewenberg, "Nazi Youth Cohort," 1499.

218. Martin Wangh, M.D., in APA Colloquium, 1971.

219. Loewenberg in APA Colloquium, 1971.

220. Andreas Dorpalen, "Commentary," *Childhood* (Fall 1973): 241.

221. Bleuel and Klinnert, *Deutsche Studenten*, 145.

222. Martin Wangh, "National Socialism and the Genocide of the Jews: A Psycho-Analytic Study of an Historical Event," *International Journal of Psycho-Analysis* 45 (1964): 386–395; see also Loewenberg, "Nazi Youth Cohort."

223. The phrase is from Reichmann, *Hostages*, 201.

224. See Fritz Stern, *Illiberalism*, 23.

225. H. R. Trevor-Roper, in *The Listener* (25 January 1973): 103.

226. Abel, *Why Hitler Came*, 128–129, 146, 218, 261.

227. Ernst Hanfstaengl, *Unheard Witness* (New York, 1957), 283–284.

228. Speeches in Norman H. Baynes, ed., *The Speeches of Adolf Hitler, 1922–1939*, 2 vols. (London and New York, 1942), 1:261–263; Prange, *Hitler's Words*, 106, 108; *Hitler: Reden und Proklamationen, 1923–1945*, ed. Max Domarus (Munich, 1965), 1767.

229. Georges Sorel, *Reflections on Violence* (New York, 1961), 17; Rollo May, in *New York Times*, 25 November 1968.

230. Fyodor Dostoyevsky, *The Brothers Karamazov*, trans. Constance Garnett (London, 1912), 305; italics in original.

231. A. J. P. Taylor, "The Seizure of Power," in *The Third Reich*, 523ff.

232. Oswald Spengler, *Jahre der Entscheidung* (Munich, 1933), viii.

233. Alan Bullock, "The German Communists and the Rise of Hitler," in *Third Reich*, 515.

234. Quoted by Erich Matthias, "The Social Democratic Party and Government Power," in *Path to Dictatorship*, 51.

235. Erich Matthias, "The Downfall of the Old Social Democratic Party in 1933," in *Republic to Reich: The Making of the Nazi Revolution*, ed. Hajo Holborn, trans. Ralph Manheim (New York, 1972), 72–73, 96.

236. Heinrich Brüning, *Memoiren: 1918–1934* (Stuttgart, 1970); see also E. W. Bennett's review in *Central European History*, 4: (June 1971), 180–187; and Holborn, *History* 3:673.

237. Nolte, *Three Faces*, 323.

CHAPTER 5

1. Harold D. Lasswell, *Psychopathology and Politics*, rev. ed. (New York, 1960), 261–262.

2. Personal letters from Drs. Friedrich Panse, 25 February 1967, Ritter von Baeyer, 3 March 1967, and G. Weiser, 12 May 1967.

3. "Gutachten über den Geisteszustand des Untersuchungsgefangenen Adolf Hitler," signed by Obermedizinalrat Dr. Brinsteiner, Landsberg a. L., 8 Januar 1924, reprinted in OSS Source Book, 19–20; Otto Lurker, *Hitler Hinter Festungsmauren* (Berlin, 1933), p. 35.

4. "Hitler as Seen by His Doctors," Military Intelligence, Consolidated Interrogation Report, 29 May 1945, National Archives (hereafter cited as "Hitler's Doctors," MIR).

5. Walter C. Langer, "Psychological Analysis of Adolph [sic] Hitler: His Life and Legend," Office of Strategic Services Report, National Archives (1943), 247 (hereafter cited as OSS Report). A printed version of this report was published as *The Mind of Adolf Hitler*, foreword by William L. Langer, afterword by Robert G. L. Waite (New York, 1972), 212.

6. Douglas M. Kelley, *Twenty-Two Cells in Nuremberg: A Psychiatrist Examines the Nazi Criminals* (New York, 1947), 235–236.

7. Heinz Guderian, *Erinnerungen eines Soldaten* (Heidelberg, 1957), 402–403; Dietrich von Choltitz, *Soldat unter Soldaten* (Zurich, 1951), 222; Percy Ernst Schramm, *Hitler: The Man and the Military Leader*, trans. Donald S. Detwiler (Chicago, 1971), 119; Gerhard Boldt, *Hitler: The Last Ten Days: An Eyewitness Account* (New York, 1973), 15, 63–64; Karl Wahl, ". . . es ist das deutsche Herz," in *Erlebnisse und Erkentnisse eines ehemaligen Gauleiters* (Augsburg, 1954), 391; Military Intelligence Service Center, U.S. Army, O.I. Special Report 36 (April 1947) "Adolf Hitler: A Composite Picture," National Archives (hereafter cited as "Hitler Composite," MIR).

8. See Israel Wechsler, *A Textbook of Clinical Neurology* (London, 1943), 597–600.

9. Heinz Guderian, *Panzer Leader*, trans. Constantine Fitzgibbon, foreword by B. H. Liddell Hart (London, 1952), 443; Willi Frischhauer, *Himmler: The Evil Genius of the Third Reich* (London, 1953), 242–243.

10. Dr. Hans Berger-Prinz, interviewed in the *New York Times*, 21 November 1968.

11. Anton Braunmühl, "War Hitler Krank?" *Stimmen der Zeit* 79 (May 1954): 98–99.

12. Johann Recktenwald, *Woran hat Adolf Hitler gelitten? Eine neuropsychiatrische Deutung* (Munich, 1963), 24, 42–64, and passim.

13. John H. Walters, "Hitler's Encephalitis: A Footnote to History," *Journal of Operational Psychiatry* 6 (1975):99–111.

14. Wechsler, *Textbook*, 600.

15. Dr. H. D. Röhrs, *Hitler: Die Zerstörung einer Persönlichkeit* (Neckargemünd, 1965), 49–51, 71–72, 118, and passim. Morell's prescriptions are given in "Hitler's Doctors," MIR; Röhrs, *Zerstörung*, 93–96; *Der Spiegel*, no. 18 (1969);

and Werner Maser, *Adolf Hitler: Legende, Mythos Wirklichkeit* (Munich, 1971), 326–328.

16. Maser as cited in Robert G. L. Waite, in *Central European History* 2 (March 1974):92–93. Geoffrey Barraclough tends to agree with Maser; see *New York Review of Books*, 3 April 1975, 16.

17. The EKG results were first interpreted in 1944 by Karl Weber, director of Bad Nauheim Heart Institute. An American heart specialist, Collier Wright, M.D., confirmed the diagnosis on 28 November 1968.

18. Wechsler, *Textbook*, 364–365.

19. Felix Kersten, *The Kersten Memoirs, 1940–1945*, trans. Constantine Fitzgibbon and James Oliver (New York, 1957), 165–166.

20. Wechsler, *Textbook*, 445–447.

21. Letter from Dr. Dieter Fricke, Chairman of School of Medicine, Jena University, 10 November 1969; Military Intelligence Annex 13; conversation with Robert K. Davis, M.D., 28 April 1975.

22. David Galin, M.D., seminar at Austen Riggs Center, Stockbridge, Mass., 9 October 1974, and his unpublished article, "Implications for Psychiatry of Left and Right Cerebral Specialization: A Neurophysiological Context for Unconscious Processes."

23. Colin Martindale, Nancy Hasenfus, and Dwight Hines, "Hitler: A Neurohistorical Formulation," unpublished paper, University of Maine.

24. See the bibliography in Otto Kernberg's important article "Borderline Personality Organization," *Journal of the American Psychoanalytic Association* 15 (July 1967):641–685.

25. See especially Kernberg, ibid., and "Structural Derivatives of Object Relationships," *International Journal of Psycho-Analysis* 47 (1966):236–253; Robert P. Knight, "Borderline States," and "Management and Psychotherapy of the Borderline Schizophrenic," in *Psychoanalytic Psychiatry and Psychology* (New York, 1954):97–109; and Eric Pfeiffer, "Borderline States," *Diseases of the Nervous System* (May 1974):216.

26. Kernberg, "Borderline Personality Organization," 652, 671–674.

27. Ibid., 649.

28. Albert Speer, *Spandau: The Secret Diaries*, as quoted in *New York Times Book Review*, 22 February 1976. For examples of conflicts and contrasts in Hitler's personality, see Chapter 1, pp. 33-48.

29. Kernberg, "Structural Derivatives," 238.

30. Conversation with David Galin, M.D., Austen Riggs Center, 9 October 1974; correspondence with Lawrence Climo, M.D., 5 September 1974.

31. Adolf Hitler, *Mein Kampf*, passim.; Hitler's speeches as quoted in Richard A. Koenigsberg, *Hitler's Ideology: A Study in Psychoanalytic Sociology* (New York, 1975), Table 1.

32. Hitler, *Mein Kampf*, passim.; Hitler's speeches as quoted by Koenigsberg, Table 6; Norman H. Baynes, ed., *The Speeches of Adolf Hitler, 1922–1939*, 2 vols. (London and New York, 1942), 1:240, 322; italics are mine.

33. Speeches as quoted in Koenigsberg, *Hitler's Ideology*, Table 8; and in *Hitler: Reden und Proklamationen, 1932–1945*, ed. Max Domarus (Munich, 1965), 1603, 1608; italics are mine.

34. OSS Report, 169; Koenigsberg, *Hitler's Ideology*, Tables 9, 10, 11.

35. Hitler, *Mein Kampf*, passim.; Hitler's speeches as quoted in Koenigsberg, *Hitler's Ideology*, Table 9.

36. Library of Congress, Manuscripts Division, Hitler file.

37. OSS Source Book, quoting Ernst Hanfstaengl, 903.

38. Theodor Heuss, *Hitlers Weg: Eine historisch-politische Studie über den Nationalsozialismus* (Berlin, 1932), 31.

39. Speech of 13 August 1920, quoted in Reginald H. Phelps, "Hitler's 'Grundlegende' Rede über den Antisemitismus," *Vierteljahrshefte für Zeitgeschichte*, 4 (1968):417 (hereafter cited as VfZ).

40. Affidavit of Joseph Hall, Institut für Zeitgeschichte, document ZS 640, Folio 6, as quoted by Toland, *Adolf Hitler*, 116.

41. Frederick Oechsner, *This Is the Enemy* (New York, 1942), 128.

42. Speech of 1920, quoted in Margarete Plewnia, *Auf dem Weg zu Hitler: Der "völkische" Publizist Dietrich Eckart* (Bremen, 1970), 96; conversation with Hermann Rauschning, *Gespräche mit Hitler* (Zurich and New York, 1940), 223; italics are mine.

43. See Nathan W. Ackerman and Marie Jahoda, *Anti-Semitism and Emotional Disorder: A Psychoanalytic Interpretation* (New York, 1950); Martin Wangh, "National Socialism and the Genocide of the Jews: A Psychoanalytic Study of a Historical Event," *International Journal of Psycho-Analysis* 45 (1964):386–395; and the essays in Ernst Simmel, ed., *Anti-Semitism: A Social Disease* (New York, 1946).

44. Jean-Paul Sartre, *Anti-Semite and Jew*, trans. by George J. Becker (New York, 1948), 26–27, 54–55.

45. Harry Slochower, "Hitler's 'Elevation' of the Jew: Ego-splitting and Ego-function," *American Imago* 28 (Winter 1971):305–309.

46. Gordon W. Allport, *The Nature of Prejudice* (Boston, 1954), 389.

47. Gertrud M. Kurth, "The Jew and Adolf Hitler," *Psychoanalytic Quarterly* 16 (1947):11–32.

48. Hans Bernd Gisevius, *Adolf Hitler: Versuch einer Deutung* (Munich, 1963), 383.

49. Gordon W. Prange, ed., *Hitler's Words* (Washington, D.C., 1944), 74; Harold D. Lasswell, "The Psychology of Hitlerism," *Political Quarterly* 4 (1933): 378.

50. Ernst Nolte, *Three Faces of Fascism*, trans. Leila Vennewitz (New York, 1965), 377–378; Gregor Ziemer, *Education for Death: The Making of the Nazi* (New York, 1941), 28.

51. Hitler as quoted in Langer, *The Mind of Hitler*, 190.

52. Robert Jay Lifton, *Death in Life: Survivors of Hiroshima* (New York, 1967), 521, 532–533.

53. Reginald H. Phelps, "Hitler als Parteiredner im Jahre 1920," *VfZ* 7 (1963), 278.

54. Speeches of 30 January, 30 September, and 8 November 1942 in Domarus, *Reden*; italics are mine.

55. Hitler, *Mein Kampf*, quoted in Karl Dietrich Bracher, *The German Dictatorship: The Origins, Structure and Effects of National Socialism* (New York, 1970), 424–425.

56. Percy Ernst Schramm, introduction to *Hitlers Tischgespräche im Führerhauptquartier*, 2nd ed. (Stuttgart, 1965), 35–37 (hereafter cited as *Tischgespräche*).

57. OSS Report, 248.

58. Albert Speer, *Inside the Third Reich: Memoirs*, trans. Richard and Clara Winston (New York, 1970), 228; Raul Hilberg, *The Destruction of the European Jews* (Chicago, 1961), 645–646.

59. Peter Kleist, *Die Europäische Tragödie*, quoted in Schramm, *Hitler*, 30–31.

60. Kernberg, "Borderline Personality Organization," 677.

61. Heinrich Hoffmann, *Hitler Was My Friend*, trans. R. H. Stevens (London, 1955), 41–42.

62. Konrad Heiden, *Der Fuehrer: Hitler's Rise to Power*, trans Ralph Manheim (Boston, 1944), 360.

63. Harold C. Deutsch, *The Conspiracy Against Hitler in the Twilight War* (Minneapolis, 1968), 229.

64. Lutz Graf Schwerin von Krosigk, *Es geschah in Deutschland: Menschenbilder unseres Jahrhunderts* (Stuttgart, 1951), 220.

65. Ernst von Weizsäcker, *Erinnerungen* (Munich, 1950), 252.

66. Staff Conferences, Folder 16; Adolf Hitler, *Hitlers Lagebesprechungen:*

Notes

Die Protokollfragmente seiner militärischen Konferenzen, 1942–1945 (Stuttgart, 1962), 24.

67. André François-Poncet, *The Fateful Years: Memoirs of a French Ambassador in Berlin, 1931–1938*, trans. Jacques LeClercq (New York, 1949), 286; Douglas Hamilton, *Motive for a Mission: The Story Behind Hess's Flight to Britain* (London, 1971), 63; Hermann Rauschning, *The Voice of Destruction* (New York, 1940), 258–259; *Wiener Bulletin* 10 (1956); Joachim C. Fest, *Hitler: Eine Biographie* (Vienna, 1973), 609.

68. Joachim C. Fest, *The Face of the Third Reich: Portraits of the Nazi Leadership*, trans. Michael Bullock (New York, 1970), 75, 76, 81.

69. Nuremberg documents quoted in Alan Bullock, *Hitler: A Study in Tyranny*, rev. ed. (New York, 1962), 409.

70. Joseph Goebbels, *The Early Goebbels Diaries, 1925–1926*, ed. Helmut Heiber, trans. Oliver Watson (New York, 1962).

71. Speer, *Inside*, 16, 60.

72. Quoted in Bullock, *Hitler*, 731.

73. Speer, *Inside*, 431, 455, 480, 487.

74. See O'Donnell's perceptive article on Speer in *New York Times Magazine*, 26 October 1969.

75. Schramm, *Hitler*, 35.

76. Kernberg, "Borderline Personality Organization," 671–674.

77. Speer, *Inside*, 358; italics are mine.

78. Staff Conference, folder 4; italics are mine.

79. Helmuth Greiner, *Die Oberste Wehrmachtführung, 1939–1943* (Wiesbaden, 1951), 26.

80. *Der Hitler-Prozess: Auszüge aus den Verhandlungsberichten* (Munich, 1924), 20, 114; italics are mine.

81. Domarus, *Reden*, 1603; italics in original; *Hitlers Tischgespräche im Führerhauptquartier*, ed. Percy Ernst Schramm, 2nd ed. (Stuttgart, 1965), 494ff; italics are mine.

82. Rauschning, *Gespräche*, 81; italics are mine.

83. Hitler, *Mein Kampf*, 570; italics are mine.

84. Hans Buchheim, "The SS: Instrument of Domination," in *Anatomy of the SS State*, ed. Helmut Krausnick et al. (New York, 1968), 340–341.

85. Lev Bezymenski, *The Death of Adolf Hitler: Unknown Documents from Soviet Archives* (New York, 1968), 26.

86. Franz von Halder, *Tagebuch* (photocopy of typescript), Institut für Zeitgeschichte Archives, Munich, 24.

87. Rollo May, as quoted in *New York Times Book Review*, 10 December 1972.

88. Christine Olden, "The Psychology of Obstinacy," *Psychoanalytic Quarterly* 12 (1943):240, 250.

89. Hans Buchheim, "Hitler als Soldat," in *Führer ins Nichts: Eine Diagnose Adolf Hitlers*, ed. Gert Buchheit (Cologne, 1960), 63.

90. Adolf Hitler, *Hitler's Secret Book*, trans. Salvatore Attanasio (New York, 1961), 43.

91. De Witt G. Poole Mission, National Archives, microfilm roll no. 2.

92. Domarus, *Reden*, 1695; italics are mine.

93. Heinz Linge, "Kronzeuge Linge," *Revue* (Munich), 3 March 1956.

94. Berenice A. Carroll, *Design for Total War: Arms and Economics in the Third Reich* (The Hague, 1968), 232, 249.

95. Vojtech Mastny, *The Czechs Under Nazi Rule: The Failure of National Resistance, 1939–1942* (New York, 1971), 128.

96. Franz Neumann, quoted in Carroll, *Design*, 180.

97. Edward N. Peterson, *The Limits of Hitler's Power* (Princeton, 1969), 15, 432; italics are mine.

98. Speer, *Inside*, 222.

99. See Chapter 1, p. 52. See also Alan S. Milward, *The German Economy at War* (London, 1965), 106.
100. Halder, *Tagebuch*, 11; italics are mine.
101. *The Testament of Adolf Hitler*, trans. by R. H. Stevens (London, 1961), 64–65.
102. See Peter Loewenberg, "Arno Mayers' 'Internal Causes and Purposes of the War in Europe, 1870–1956'—An Inadequate Model of Human Behavior, National Conflict and Historical Change," *Journal of Modern History* 42: (December 1970), 628–636.
103. Kernberg, "Borderline Personality Organization," 671.
104. Krosigk, *Es geschah*, quoted in Fest, *Face of Third Reich*, 321; italics are mine.
105. Domarus, *Reden*, 1603; italics in original.
106. Speer, interview with O'Donnell.
107. *Hitlers Zweites Buch: Ein Dokument aus dem Jahr 1928*, ed. Gerhard L. Weinberg (Stuttgart, 1961), 77.
108. Ribbentrop, quoted in Fest, *Hitler*, 949; Otto Dietrich, *Zwölf Jahre mit Hitler* (Munich, 1955), 156.
109. Klaus Dörner, "Nationalsozialismus und Lebensvernichtung," *VfZ* 15 (1967):149.
110. Hans Buchheim, "Hitler als Politiker," in *Führer ins Nichts*, 17; Speer, *Inside*, 31, 106.
111. Hitler, *Mein Kampf*, German ed. (Munich, 1941), 13.
112. Ibid., 14.
113. Ibid., 135.
114. Interview with William Patrick Hitler, September 1943, OSS Source Book, 928.
115. Jakob Steil, "Die Krankheit Hitlers," typescript, Institut für Zeitgeschichte, Munich, 45; Rauschning, *Voice*, 87; italics are mine.
116. Hitler, *Mein Kampf*, German ed., 136; Kurt von Schuschnigg, *Austrian Requiem*, trans. Franz von Hildebrand (New York, 1946), 13.
117. Hitler, *Mein Kampf*, German ed., 14.
118. Rauschning, *Voice*, 87–88.
119. Hitler, *Mein Kampf*, German ed., 1.
120. Dörner, "Lebensvernichtung," 148–151; italics are mine.
121. See Robert G. L. Waite, "Adolf Hitler's Guilt Feelings," *Journal of Interdisciplinary History* 1 (Winter 1971):231–232.
122. James H. McRandle, *Track of the Wolf: Essays on National Socialism and Its Leader, Adolf Hitler* (Evanston, Ill., 1965), 225. This study first called my attention to this aspect of Hitler's personality.
123. Quoted in Andreas Dorpalen, "Hitler—Twelve Years After," *Review of Politics* 19 (1957):501; italics are mine.
124. Bradley F. Smith, *Adolf Hitler: His Family, Childhood and Youth* (Stanford, Calif., 1967), 113–114; Fest, *Hitler*, 51; Maser, *Adolf Hitler*, 82.
125. Maser, *Hitler*, 84.
126. See Chapter 3, p. 192-194; Smith, *Hitler*, 122; August Kubizek, *The Young Hitler I Knew*, trans. E. V. Anderson (Boston, 1955), 143–225.
127. Harold J. Gordon, Jr., *Hitler and the Beer Hall Putsch* (Princeton, 1972), 264.
128. Ibid., 256–257, 286.
129. Ibid., 278.
130. Peter Heydebreck, *Wehrwölfe*, quoted in Gordon, *Putsch*, 385–386; see also Albert Krebs, *Tendenzen und Gestalten der NSDAP: Erinnerungen* (Stuttgart, 1959), 124.
131. Richard Hanser, *Putsch! How Hitler Made Revolution* (New York, 1970), 327, 342, 359, 365; Ernst Hanfstaengl, *Unheard Witness* (New York, 1957), 98, 108.
132. Gordon, *Putsch*, 401, 332; italics are mine.

Notes

133. International Military Tribunal (Nuremberg, 1949), 12:313.

134. Gordon, *Putsch*, 332.

135. McRandle, *Track*, 178; Bracher, *Dictatorship*, 116; Gordon, *Putsch*, 270ff; Helmut Krausnick, ed., *"Es Spricht der Führer": 7 Exemplarische Hitler Reden* (Gütersloh, 1960), 224. Werner Maser dismisses the problem of Hitler's behavior with the surprising comment that "it is idle to ask" why he failed to act during this important moment of his political career; see Maser, *Die Frühgeschichte der NSDAP: Hitlers Weg bis 1924* (Bonn, 1965), 453.

136. Hanser, *Putsch!*, 379; see also Gordon, *Putsch*, 352.

137. McRandle, *Track*, 200.

138. Peter Bor, *Gespräche mit Halder* (Wiesbaden, 1950), 23.

139. Halder, *Tagebuch*, cited in Deutsch, *Conspiracy*, 190.

140. Milward, *Economy*, 43–46, 88–89; Speer, *Inside*, 213; Carroll, *Design*, 232, 239, 249; Hajo Holborn, *A History of Modern Germany*, 3 vols. (New York, 1969), 3:756.

141. Manfred Kehrig, *Stalingrad* (Stuttgart, 1976), as reported in *Der Spiegel*, 9 February 1976; Sir Basil Liddell-Hart, "Hitler as War Lord," *Encounter*, 30–31 (1968); 70.

142. Sir Basil Liddell-Hart, *History of the Second World War*, 2 vols. (New York, 1972), 1:65, 74–75.

143. Robert Payne, *The Life and Death of Adolf Hitler* (New York, 1973), 384.

144. *The Testament of Hitler*, 96; Halder, *Tagebuch*, 302; Walter Warlimont, *Inside Hitler's Headquarters, 1939–1945*, trans. R. H. Barry (New York, 1964), 97–99; Bor, *Gespräche*, 170; Guderian, *Erinnerungen*, 105–106; Guenther Blumentritt, *Von Rundstedt: The Soldier and the Man* (London, 1952), 77; Hans-Adolf Jacobsen, *Dunkirchen: Ein Beitrag zur Geschichte des Westfeldzuges 1940* (Neckargemünd, 1958), 96–98; and Hans Meier-Welcker, "Der Entschluss zum Anhalten der deutschen Panzer-Truppen in Flandern, 1940," *VfZ* 2 (1954):274–290.

145. William L. Langer and S. Everett Gleason, *The Undeclared War, 1940–1941: The World Crisis and American Foreign Policy* (New York, 1953), 494.

146. Andreas Dorpalen, "Hitler, the Party and the Wehrmacht," in *Total War and Cold War*, ed. Harry L. Coles (Columbia, Ohio, 1962), 73; see also DeWitt C. Poole, "Light on Nazi Foreign Policy," *Foreign Affairs* 25 (October 1946):131–132.

147. Telford Taylor, *The March of Conquest: The German Victories in Western Europe, 1940* (New York, 1958), 368.

148. Alan Bullock, "Hitler and the Origins of the Second World War," Proceedings of the British Academy 53 (1967); reprinted in Wm. Roger Louis, *The Origin of the Second World War: A. J. P. Tayor and His Critics* (New York, 1972), 142.

149. For the connection between Hitler's decision to invade the Soviet Union and his attendance at the Bayreuth Festival, see Walter Ansel, *Hitler Confronts England* (Durham, N.C., 1960), 178, and Speer interview with Fest, *Hitler*, 712.

150. Gerhard L. Weinberg, *Germany and the Soviet Union* (Leiden, 1954), 162–163; Norman Rich, *Hitler's War Aims. Vol. 1: Ideology, the Nazi State and the Course of Expansion* (New York, 1973), 207; Albert Seaton, *The Russo-German War, 1941–1945* (New York, 1971), 215; Wilhelm Meier-Dörnberg, *Die Oelversorgung der Kriegsmarine 1935 bis 1945* (Freiburg, 1973).

151. *Hitler's Secret Conversations, 1941–1944*, trans. Norman Cameron and R. H. Stevens (New York, 1953), 276 (hereafter cited as *Conversations*).

152. Documents on German Foreign Policy, D., 12:220 (hereafter cited as DGFP); italics in original.

153. Johanna Menzel Meskill, *Hitler and Japan: The Hollow Alliance* (New York, 1966), 30–31.

154. Rich, *Hitler's War Aims*, 1:228–229.

155. Buchheit, "Hitler als Soldat," in *Führer ins Nichts*, 53–55; Milward, *German Economy*, 43.

156. Otto Dietrich, *Hitler*, trans. Richard and Clara Winston (Chicago, 1955), 67; Albert Zoller, ed., *Hitler Privat: Erlebnisbericht seiner Geheimsekretärin* (Düs-

seldorf, 1949), 160; Andreas Hillgruber, *Hitlers Strategie; Politik und Kriegsführung, 1940–1941* (Frankfurt am Main, 1965), 511; Bor, *Gespräche*, 203.

157. Barton Whaley, *Codeword Barbarossa* (Cambridge, Mass., 1973), 18.
158. Document 7 s89, Institut für Zeitgeschichte, Munich.
159. Nuremberg documents, 872-PS, *Trial of Major War Criminals*, 26:396; italics are mine.
160. Louis L. Snyder, *The War: A Concise History* (New York, 1960), 218–226; Friedrich Paulus, *Ich stehe hier auf Befehl*, cited in Fest, *Hitler*, 891.
161. Holborn, *Modern Germany*, 3:804.
162. Schramm, in *Tischgespräche*, 105.
163. Poole, "Nazi Foreign Policy," 147. Interviews with the German officials may be found on microfilm in the Department of State, General Records of the Department of State, Record Group 59, Special Interrogation Mission to Germany, 1945–1956.
164. James B. Compton, *The Swastika and the Eagle: Hitler, the United States, and the Origins of World War II* (Boston, 1967), xiii, 236.
165. Seaton, *Russo-German War*, 214.
166. Quoted in Compton, *Swastika and Eagle*, 31, 60, 17.
167. Hanfstaengl interview, Munich, June 1967.
168. "Führer Conference on Matters Dealing with the German Navy," 2 vols. (Washington, D.C., 1947); see especially conference of 13 November 1941; Compton, *Swastika and Eagle*, 169, 172–173; Langer and Gleason, *Undeclared War*, 749, 760; Paul Friedländer, *Prelude to Downfall: Hitler and the United States, 1939–1941*, trans. Alice and Alexander Werth (New York, 1967), 294–295.
169. Press conference, 18 September 1939; Instruction A 1068, Bundesarchiv Coblenz, quoted in Friedländer, *Prelude*, 50.
170. Meskill, *Hitler and Japan*, 30–31, 51; see also Paul Schroeder, *The Axis Alliance and Japanese-American Relations, 1941* (Ithaca, N.Y., 1958); Hans Trefouse, "Germany and Pearl Harbor," *Far Eastern Quarterly* 2 (1951):50.
171. DGFP, Series D, 13:958–959.
172. Rich, *Hitler's War Aims*, 1:230–235, 237.
173. See the testimony given at Nuremberg, IMT, 10:297–298; and *Nazi Conspiracy and Aggression*, Supplement B, 1199–1201.
174. *Testament of Adolf Hitler*, 76.
175. Domarus, *Reden*, 1790–1791; Gerhard Engel, *Heeresadjutant bei Hitler, 1938–1943* (Stuttgart, 1974), 116–118.
176. Warlimont, *Inside Headquarters*, 203.
177. Ibid., 208. See also Hillgruber, *Strategie*, 553.
178. Poole Mission, interview with Göring, 24 October 1945, microfilm.
179. IMT, 15:398.
180. James MacGregor Burns, *Roosevelt: The Soldier of Freedom, 1940–1945* (New York, 1970), 171.
181. Langer and Gleason, *Undeclared War*, 758, 941; see also Burns, *Soldier of Freedom*, 175.
182. Trefouse, "Germany and Pearl Harbor," 50; *Testament of Hitler*, 87.
183. Poole, "Nazi Foreign Policy," 147; for a similar explanation see Langer and Gleason, *Undeclared War*, 940; Friedländer, *Prelude*, 308–309; Rich, *Hitler's War Aims*, 1:245–246.
184. Lawrence H. Climo, M.D., Austen Riggs Center, conversations of 23 November and 30 December 1973.
185. Jodl papers, as cited by Maser, in *Der Spiegel*, 4 June 1973; *Kriegstagebuch des Oberkommandos der Wehrmacht, 1940–1945*, quoted in Schramm, *Hitler*, 36; Hillgruber, *Strategie*, 551–556.
186. Morell testimony, in "Hitler Composite," MIR.
187. Hanfstaengl conversation, June 1967.
188. Karl Koller, *Der letzte Monat: die Tagebuchaufzeichnungen des ehema-*

Notes

ligen Chefs des Generalstabes der deutschen Luftwaffe vom 14 April bis 27 Mai 1945 (Mannheim, 1949), 21; interview with Maser, *New York Times Magazine*, 28 October 1973.

189. There are several versions of this statement made on 18 April 1945; see Schramm, *Hitler*, 176. The *Nacht und Nebel* decree had been personally drawn up by Hitler on 7 December, the day after Zhukov's counteroffensive began; it was issued by Keitel at Hitler's order on 12 December 1941. Domarus, *Reden*, 1790.

190. Wahl, *Erkentnisse eines Gauleiters*, 390–391.

191. Zoller, *Privat*, 231; the last briefings for 23, 25, 27 April 1945 were published for the first time in *Der Spiegel*, 10 January 1966.

192. Zoller, *Privat*, 150–151.

193. Gerhard Boldt, *Die letzten Tage der Reichskanzlei* (Hamburg, 1947), 66.

194. Conversation with Lawrence H. Climo, M.D., 30 December 1973.

195. *Der Spiegel*, 10 January 1966.

196. Ibid., 17 September 1973.

197. J. S. Conway, *The Nazi Persecution of the Churches, 1933–45* (New York, 1968), 267–268.

198. The question was raised by Augstein in *Der Spiegel*, 17 September 1973.

199. Hitler Staff Conferences, folders 14–19; see also *Der Spiegel*, 17 September 1973.

200. Werner Maser, *Hitlers Briefe und Notizen: Sein Weltbild in handschriftlichen Dokumenten* (Vienna, 1973), 205.

201. A photostatic copy of these documents may be found in the Library of Congress, Manuscript Division, box 791, AC 10 076.

202. H. R. Trevor-Roper, *The Last Days of Hitler* (New York, 1947), 201–205.

203. Erich Kempka, *Ich habe Adolf Hitler verbrannt* (Munich, 1950), 116–118, and as interviewed in *Hearst's Cosmopolitan*, August 1946. He gave conflicting testimony at Nuremberg; see NCA, 6:575, 584.

204. Herman Karnau, as quoted in Michael A. Musmanno, *Ten Days to Die* (New York, 1950), 241; Günsche quoted by a friend, as quoted in Maser, *Hitler*, 432.

205. Kempka interview, 10 June 1971; Maser, *Hitler*, 433; Hans Baur, *Hitler's Pilot*, trans. Edward Gerald (London, 1958), 191.

206. Interview in Nerin E. Gun, *Eva Braun-Hitler: Leben und Schicksal* (New York and Bruchsal/Baden, 1968), 205–206.

207. Linge as interviewed by Erich Kuby, "Die Russen in Berlin, 1945" a series of five articles appearing in *Der Spiegel*, 12 May–2 June 1965; Linge in *Revue*, 26 November 1955, and in *News of the World*, 1 January 1956. For minor discrepancies in Linge's testimony, see Kuby's *Die Russen in Berlin, 1945* (Vienna, 1965), 188–193.

208. Linge, quoted in *Der Spiegel*, 26 May 1965.

209. Elena Rzhevskaia, "Berlinskie Stransitsy" in *Znamia* (The Banner), Moscow, 1967, no. 5 (May 1965), 154–198. I am grateful to my colleague, Romuald Misiunas, for his translation.

210. Bezymenski, *Death*, 74–75.

211. *Sunday Times* (London), 18 February 1973.

212. Maser, *Hitler*, 436–438.

213. Photostated letter reprinted in Gun, *Braun*.

214. *Der Spiegel*, 26 May 1965.

215. Interview with Russell Fisher, M.D., Maryland State Medical Examiner, 24 September 1973.

216. Ibid.

217. The suggestion that Eva Braun-Hitler performed the *coup de grâce* was first made by Kuby in *Der Spiegel*, 26 May 1965.

218. Hendin, "Suicide," 227–282.

219. Friedlander, " 'Longing to Die,' " 416.

220. Menninger, "Psychoanalytic Aspects," 377.

221. Theodor Reik, *Masochism in Sex and Society,* trans. Margaret H. Beigel and Gertrud M. Kurth (New York, 1962), 429; italics in original.

222. Siegel and Friedman, "Threat of Suicide," 38.

223. Interrogation of Hanna Reitsch, 8 October 1945, Nuremberg Document 3734-PS, NCA, 6:554–555.

224. Menninger, *Man Against Himself,* 63.

225. Gregory Zilboorg, "Suicide Among Civilized and Primitive Races," *American Journal of Psychiatry* 92 (1936):1638.

226. Hilda Roderick Davidson, *Gods and Myths of Northern Europe* (Baltimore, 1964), 31, 37, 205; Wolfgang Golther, *Handbuch der Germanischen Mythologie* (Leipzig, 1895), 284, 303, 313, 327.

227. Kubizek, *Young Hitler,* 55.

228. Wahl, "Suicide as a Magical Art," reprinted in *Clues to Suicide,* 23; italics are mine.

229. Ibid., 30.

INDEX

Index

Index

Index

Index